THE Calvin and Hobbes
PORTABLE COMPENDIUM
BOOK 5

BILL WATTERSON

Andrews McMeel
PUBLISHING®

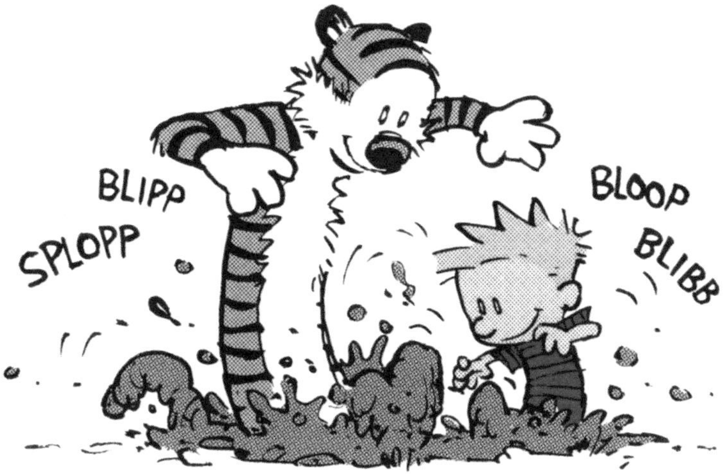
BLIPP
SPLOPP
BLOOP
BLIBB

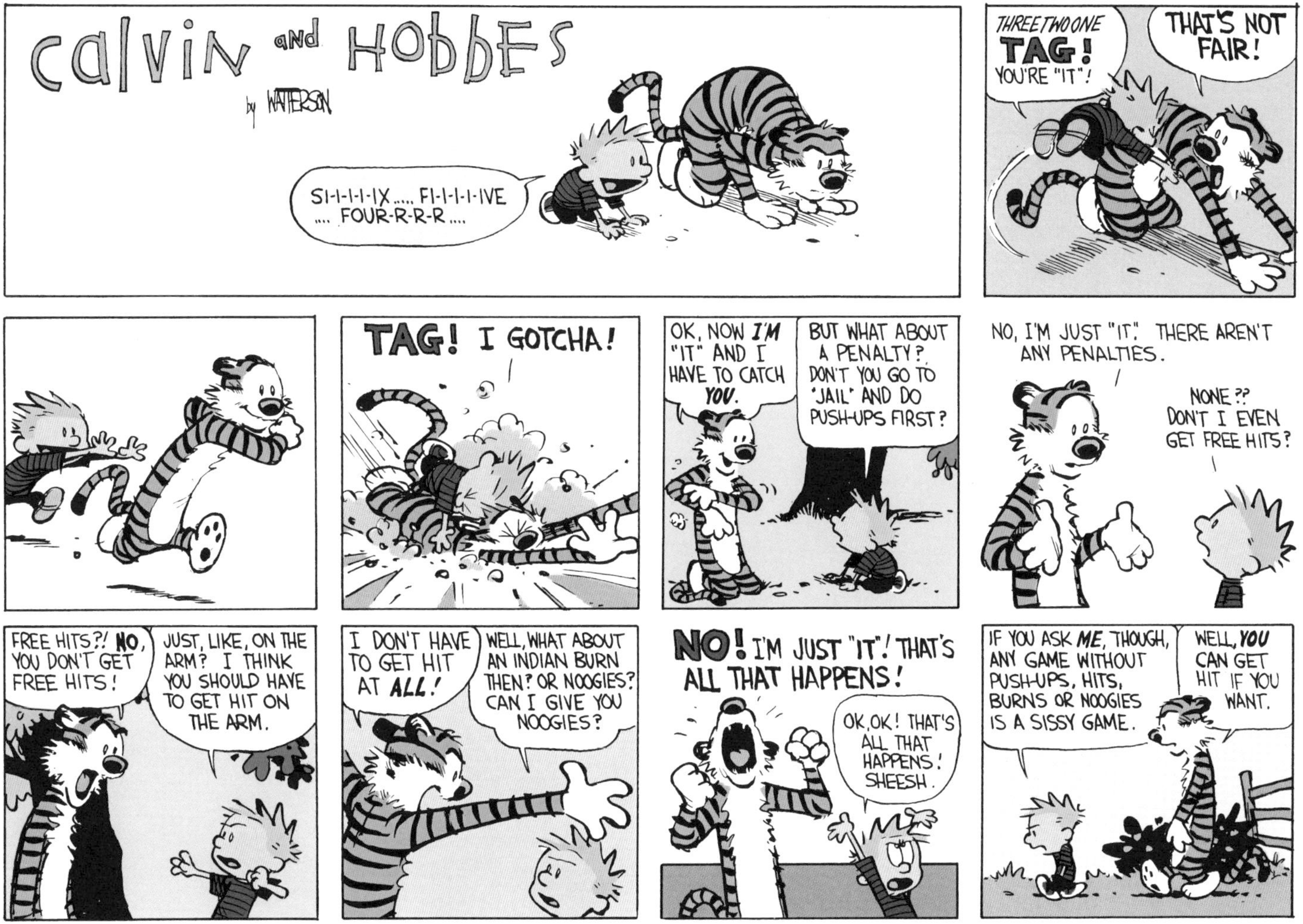
Calvin and Hobbes
by WATTERSON
SI-I-I-I-IX..... FI-I-I-I-IVE .... FOUR-R-R-R....
THREETWOONE TAG! YOU'RE "IT"!
THAT'S NOT FAIR!
TAG! I GOTCHA!
OK, NOW I'M "IT" AND I HAVE TO CATCH YOU.
BUT WHAT ABOUT A PENALTY? DON'T YOU GO TO "JAIL" AND DO PUSH-UPS FIRST?
NO, I'M JUST "IT". THERE AREN'T ANY PENALTIES.
NONE?? DON'T I EVEN GET FREE HITS?
FREE HITS?! NO, YOU DON'T GET FREE HITS!
JUST, LIKE, ON THE ARM? I THINK YOU SHOULD HAVE TO GET HIT ON THE ARM.
I DON'T HAVE TO GET HIT AT ALL!
WELL, WHAT ABOUT AN INDIAN BURN THEN? OR NOOGIES? CAN I GIVE YOU NOOGIES?
NO! I'M JUST "IT"! THAT'S ALL THAT HAPPENS!
OK, OK! THAT'S ALL THAT HAPPENS! SHEESH.
IF YOU ASK ME, THOUGH, ANY GAME WITHOUT PUSH-UPS, HITS, BURNS OR NOOGIES IS A SISSY GAME.
WELL, YOU CAN GET HIT IF YOU WANT.

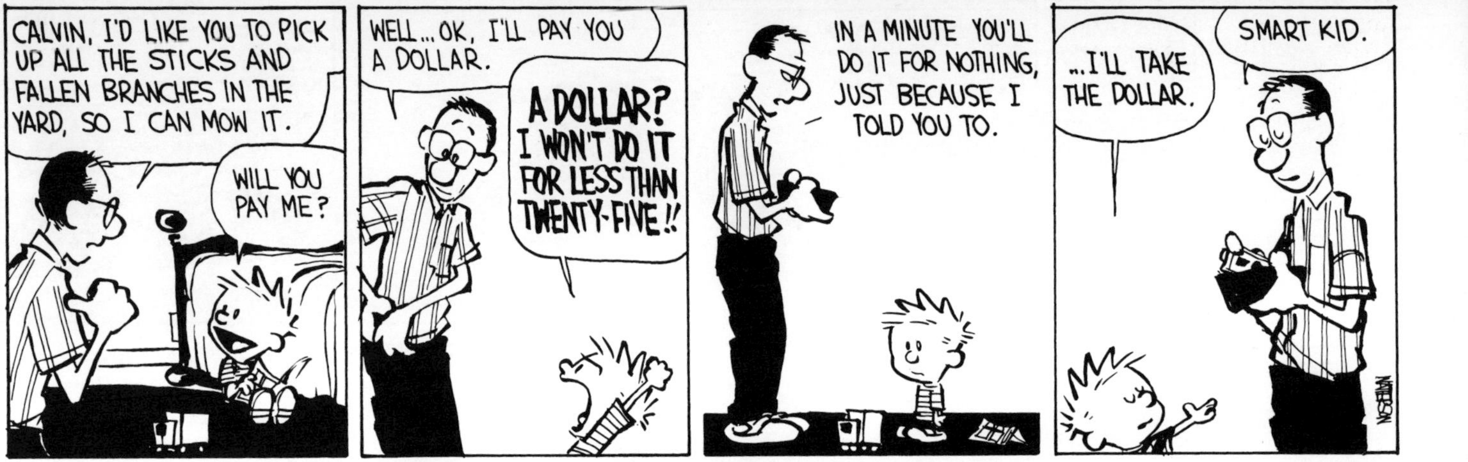
CALVIN, I'D LIKE YOU TO PICK UP ALL THE STICKS AND FALLEN BRANCHES IN THE YARD, SO I CAN MOW IT.
WILL YOU PAY ME?
WELL... OK, I'LL PAY YOU A DOLLAR.
A DOLLAR? I WON'T DO IT FOR LESS THAN TWENTY-FIVE!!
IN A MINUTE YOU'LL DO IT FOR NOTHING, JUST BECAUSE I TOLD YOU TO.
...I'LL TAKE THE DOLLAR.
SMART KID.

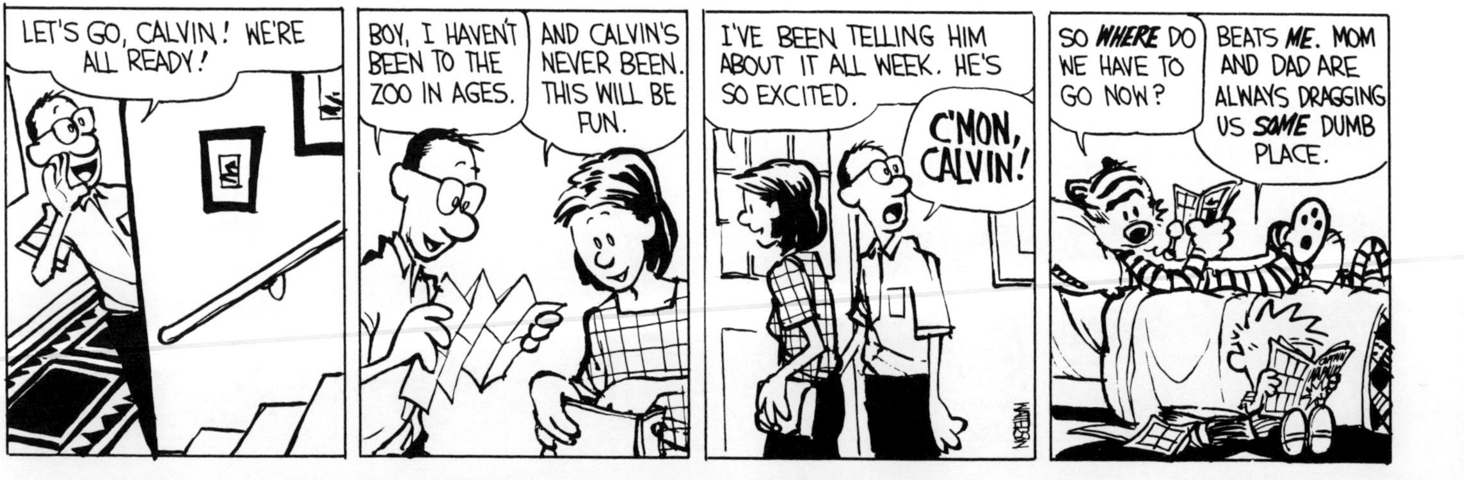
LET'S GO, CALVIN! WE'RE ALL READY!
BOY, I HAVEN'T BEEN TO THE ZOO IN AGES.
AND CALVIN'S NEVER BEEN. THIS WILL BE FUN.
I'VE BEEN TELLING HIM ABOUT IT ALL WEEK. HE'S SO EXCITED.
C'MON, CALVIN!
SO **WHERE** DO WE HAVE TO GO NOW?
BEATS **ME**. MOM AND DAD ARE ALWAYS DRAGGING US **SOME** DUMB PLACE.

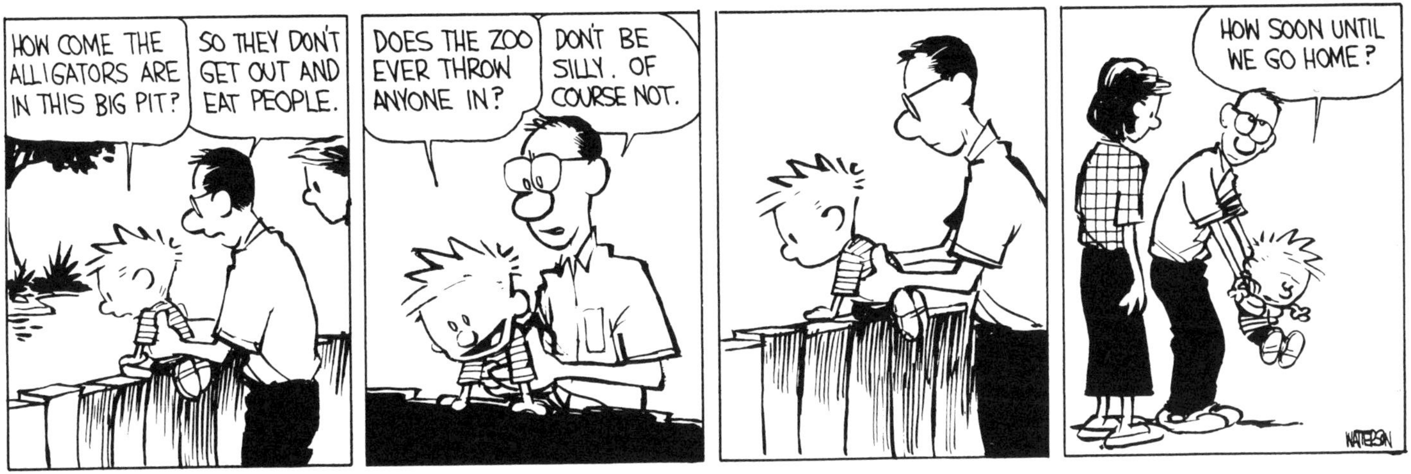
HOW COME THE ALLIGATORS ARE IN THIS BIG PIT?
SO THEY DON'T GET OUT AND EAT PEOPLE.
DOES THE ZOO EVER THROW ANYONE IN?
DON'T BE SILLY. OF COURSE NOT.
HOW SOON UNTIL WE GO HOME?
WATTERSON

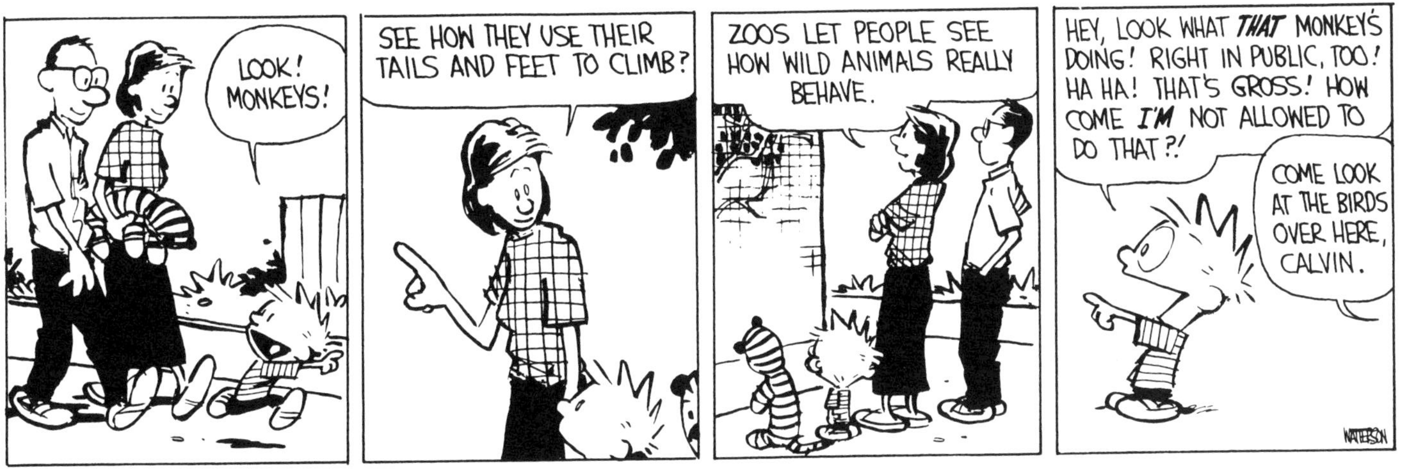
LOOK! MONKEYS!
SEE HOW THEY USE THEIR TAILS AND FEET TO CLIMB?
ZOOS LET PEOPLE SEE HOW WILD ANIMALS REALLY BEHAVE.
HEY, LOOK WHAT THAT MONKEY'S DOING! RIGHT IN PUBLIC, TOO! HA HA! THAT'S GROSS! HOW COME I'M NOT ALLOWED TO DO THAT?!
COME LOOK AT THE BIRDS OVER HERE, CALVIN.
WATTERSON

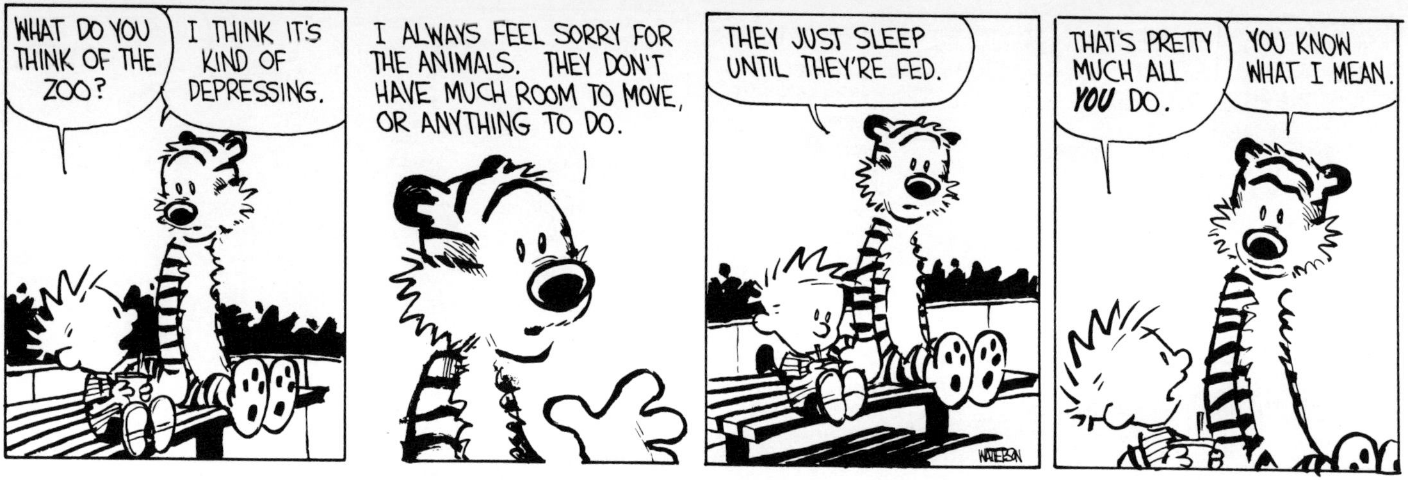
WHAT DO YOU THINK OF THE ZOO?
I THINK IT'S KIND OF DEPRESSING.
I ALWAYS FEEL SORRY FOR THE ANIMALS. THEY DON'T HAVE MUCH ROOM TO MOVE, OR ANYTHING TO DO.
THEY JUST SLEEP UNTIL THEY'RE FED.
THAT'S PRETTY MUCH ALL **YOU** DO.
YOU KNOW WHAT I MEAN.
WATTERSON

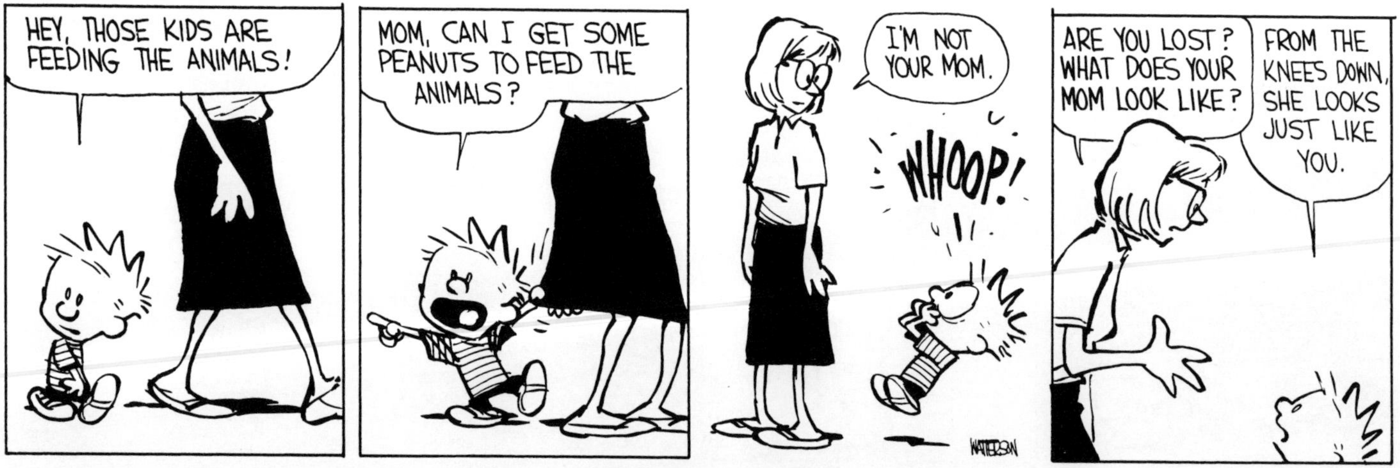
HEY, THOSE KIDS ARE FEEDING THE ANIMALS!
MOM, CAN I GET SOME PEANUTS TO FEED THE ANIMALS?
I'M NOT YOUR MOM.
WHOOP!
WATTERSON
ARE YOU LOST? WHAT DOES YOUR MOM LOOK LIKE?
FROM THE KNEES DOWN, SHE LOOKS JUST LIKE YOU.

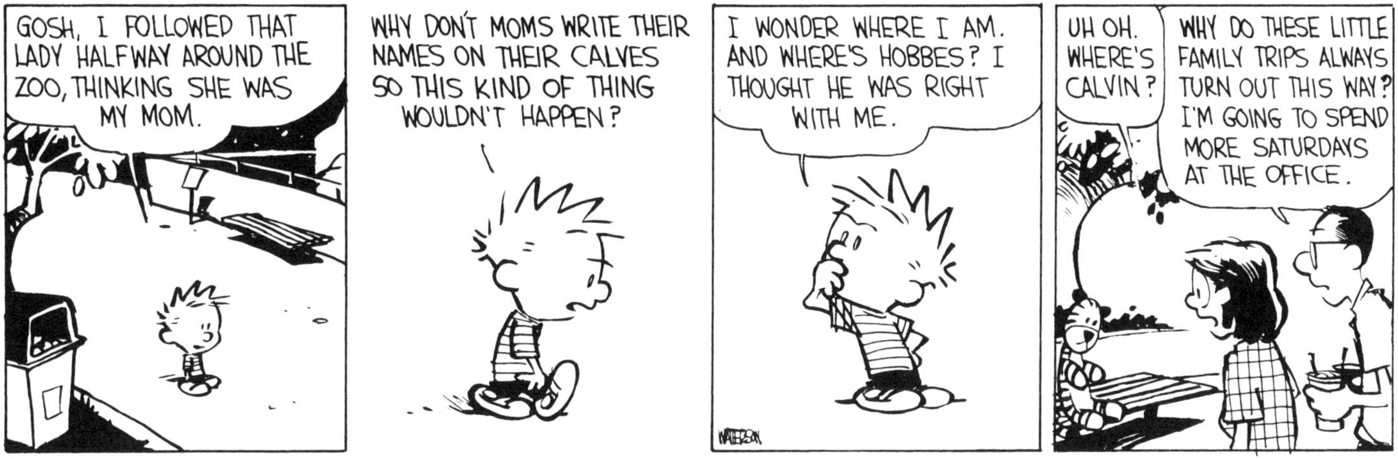
GOSH, I FOLLOWED THAT LADY HALFWAY AROUND THE ZOO, THINKING SHE WAS MY MOM.
WHY DON'T MOMS WRITE THEIR NAMES ON THEIR CALVES SO THIS KIND OF THING WOULDN'T HAPPEN?
I WONDER WHERE I AM. AND WHERE'S HOBBES? I THOUGHT HE WAS RIGHT WITH ME.
WATTERSON
UH OH. WHERE'S CALVIN?
WHY DO THESE LITTLE FAMILY TRIPS ALWAYS TURN OUT THIS WAY? I'M GOING TO SPEND MORE SATURDAYS AT THE OFFICE.

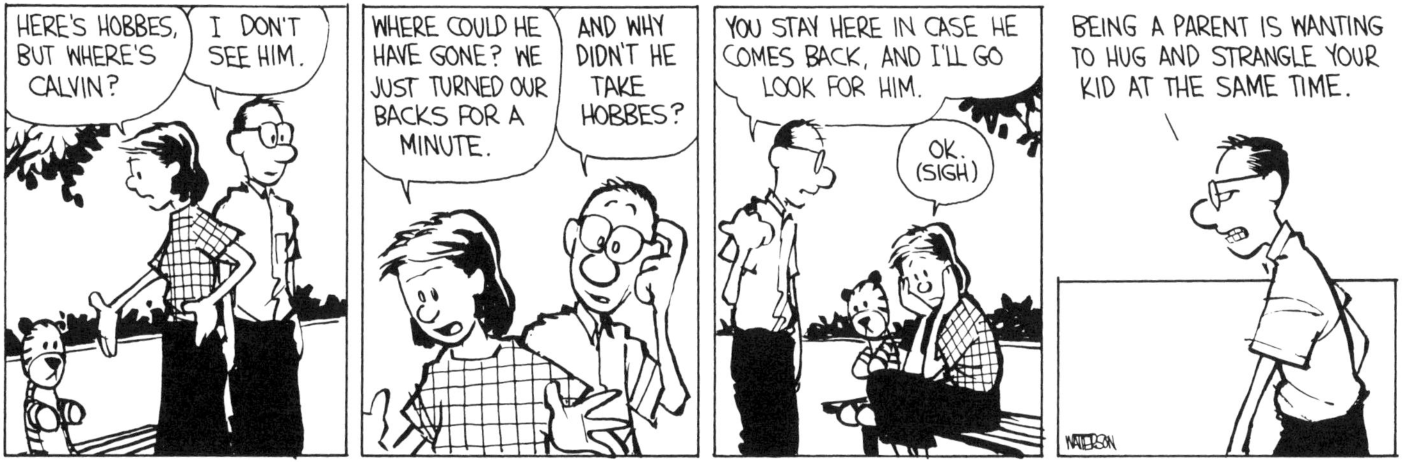
HERE'S HOBBES, BUT WHERE'S CALVIN?
I DON'T SEE HIM.
WHERE COULD HE HAVE GONE? WE JUST TURNED OUR BACKS FOR A MINUTE.
AND WHY DIDN'T HE TAKE HOBBES?
YOU STAY HERE IN CASE HE COMES BACK, AND I'LL GO LOOK FOR HIM.
OK. (SIGH)
BEING A PARENT IS WANTING TO HUG AND STRANGLE YOUR KID AT THE SAME TIME.
WATTERSON

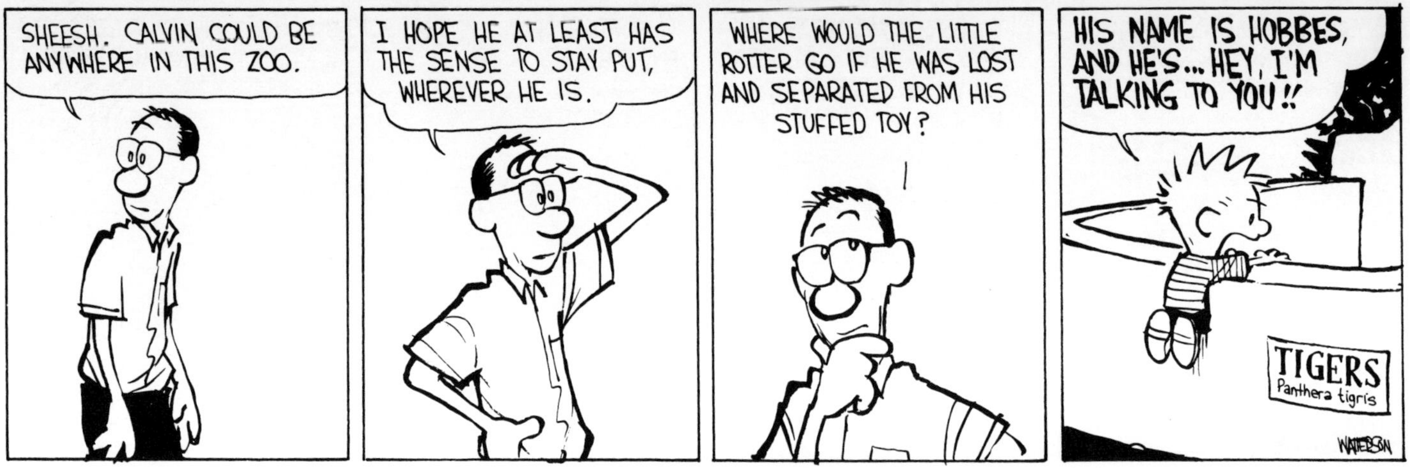
SHEESH. CALVIN COULD BE ANYWHERE IN THIS ZOO.
I HOPE HE AT LEAST HAS THE SENSE TO STAY PUT, WHEREVER HE IS.
WHERE WOULD THE LITTLE ROTTER GO IF HE WAS LOST AND SEPARATED FROM HIS STUFFED TOY?
HIS NAME IS HOBBES, AND HE'S... HEY, I'M TALKING TO YOU!!
TIGERS
Panthera tigris
WATTERSON

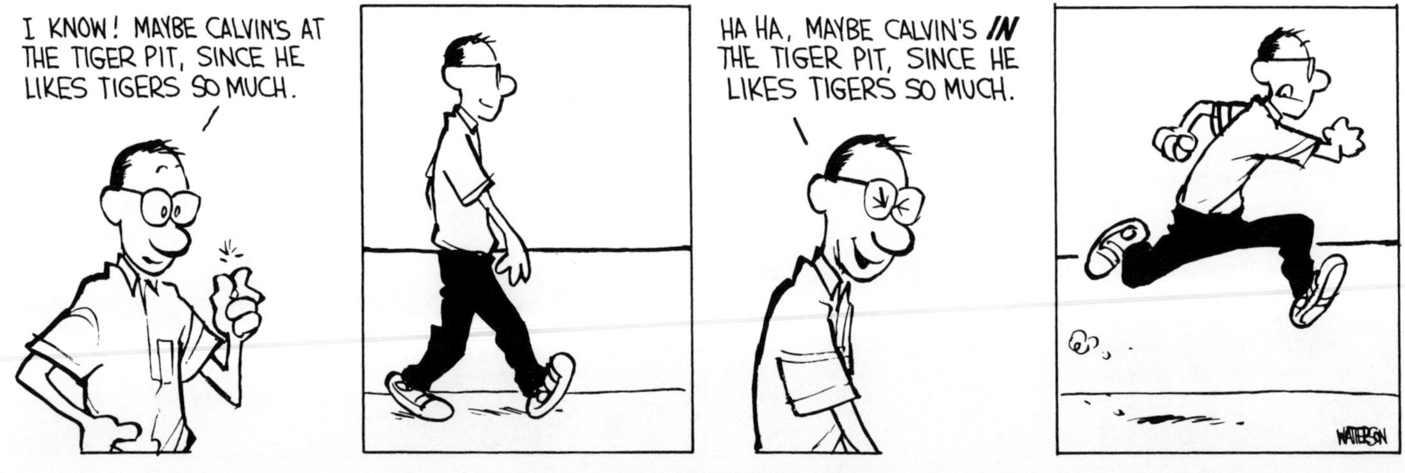
I KNOW! MAYBE CALVIN'S AT THE TIGER PIT, SINCE HE LIKES TIGERS SO MUCH.
HA HA, MAYBE CALVIN'S *IN* THE TIGER PIT, SINCE HE LIKES TIGERS SO MUCH.
WATTERSON

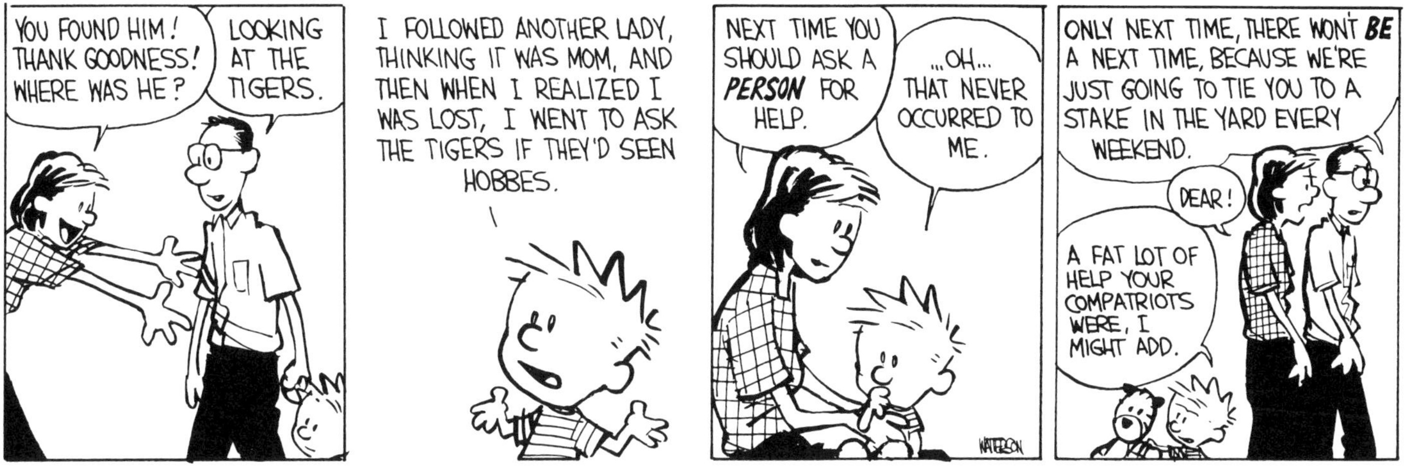
YOU FOUND HIM! THANK GOODNESS! WHERE WAS HE?
LOOKING AT THE TIGERS.
I FOLLOWED ANOTHER LADY, THINKING IT WAS MOM, AND THEN WHEN I REALIZED I WAS LOST, I WENT TO ASK THE TIGERS IF THEY'D SEEN HOBBES.
NEXT TIME YOU SHOULD ASK A *PERSON* FOR HELP.
...OH... THAT NEVER OCCURRED TO ME.
ONLY NEXT TIME, THERE WON'T *BE* A NEXT TIME, BECAUSE WE'RE JUST GOING TO TIE YOU TO A STAKE IN THE YARD EVERY WEEKEND.
DEAR!
A FAT LOT OF HELP YOUR COMPATRIOTS WERE, I MIGHT ADD.

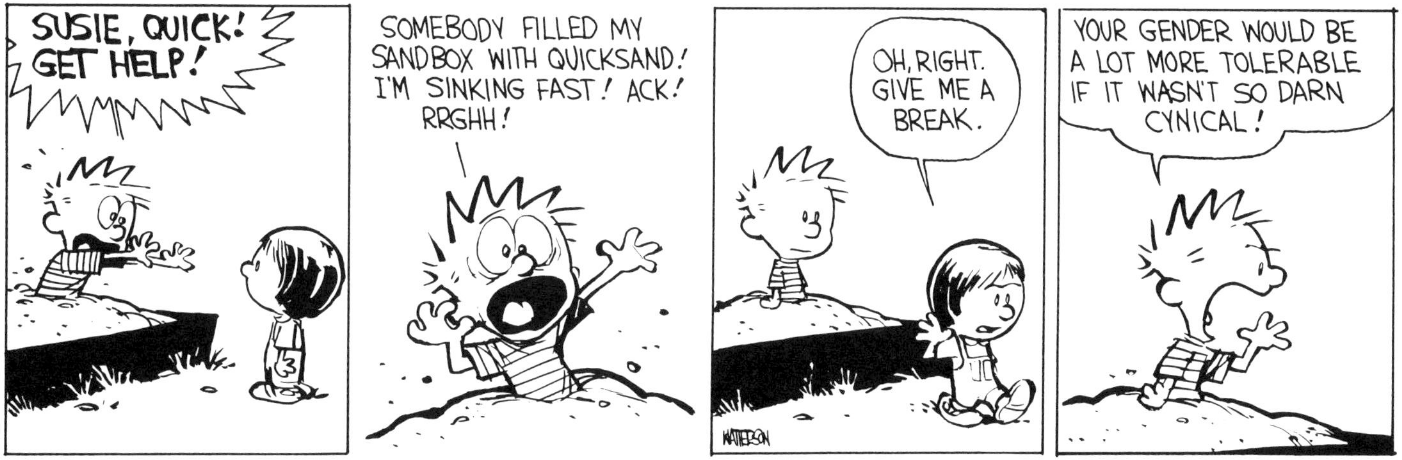
SUSIE, QUICK! GET HELP!
SOMEBODY FILLED MY SANDBOX WITH QUICKSAND! I'M SINKING FAST! ACK! RRGHH!
OH, RIGHT. GIVE ME A BREAK.
YOUR GENDER WOULD BE A LOT MORE TOLERABLE IF IT WASN'T SO DARN CYNICAL!

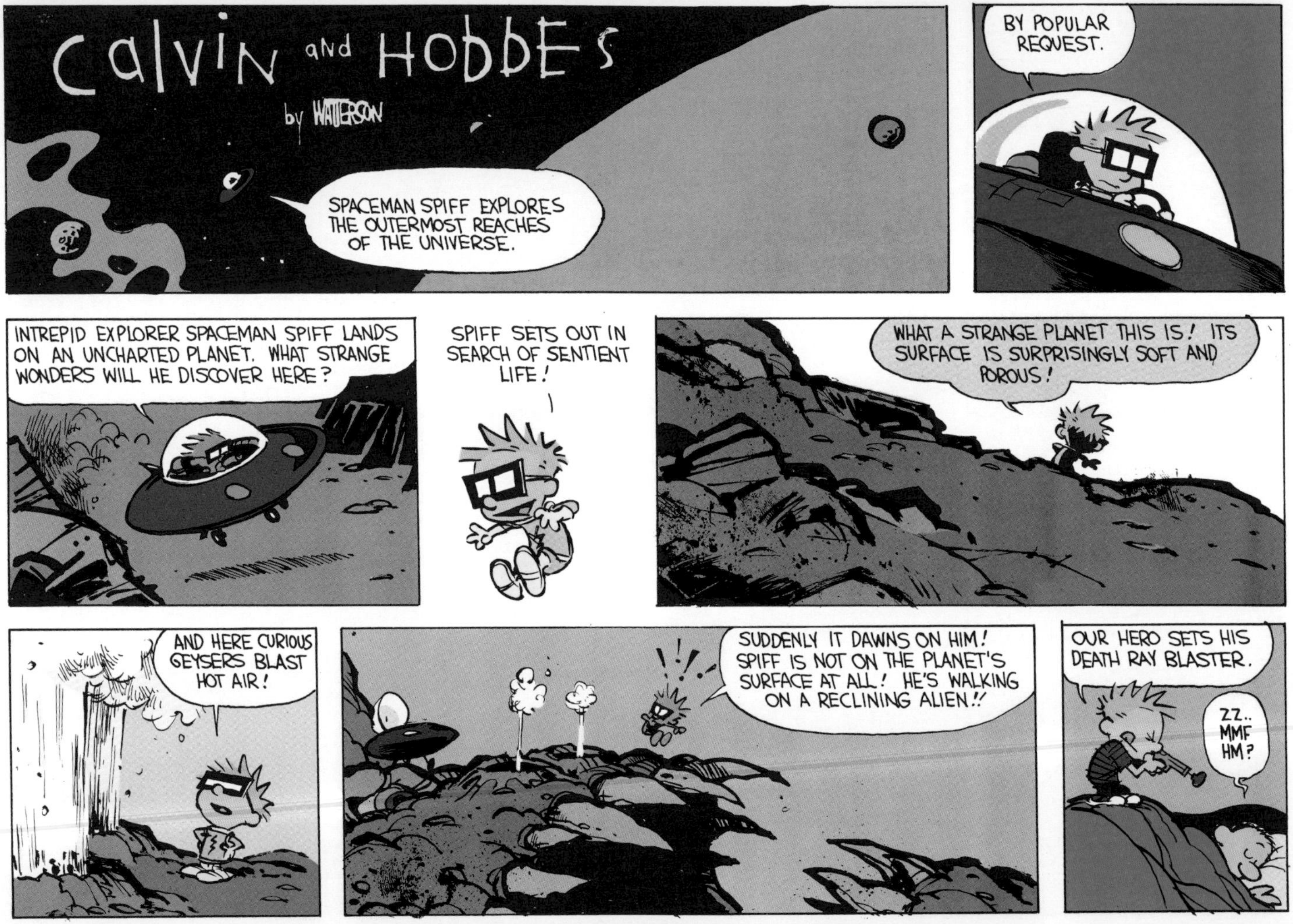
Calvin and HOBBES
by WATTERSON
SPACEMAN SPIFF EXPLORES THE OUTERMOST REACHES OF THE UNIVERSE.
BY POPULAR REQUEST.
INTREPID EXPLORER SPACEMAN SPIFF LANDS ON AN UNCHARTED PLANET. WHAT STRANGE WONDERS WILL HE DISCOVER HERE?
SPIFF SETS OUT IN SEARCH OF SENTIENT LIFE!
WHAT A STRANGE PLANET THIS IS! ITS SURFACE IS SURPRISINGLY SOFT AND POROUS!
AND HERE CURIOUS GEYSERS BLAST HOT AIR!
SUDDENLY IT DAWNS ON HIM! SPIFF IS NOT ON THE PLANET'S SURFACE AT ALL! HE'S WALKING ON A RECLINING ALIEN!!
OUR HERO SETS HIS DEATH RAY BLASTER.
ZZ.. MMF HM?

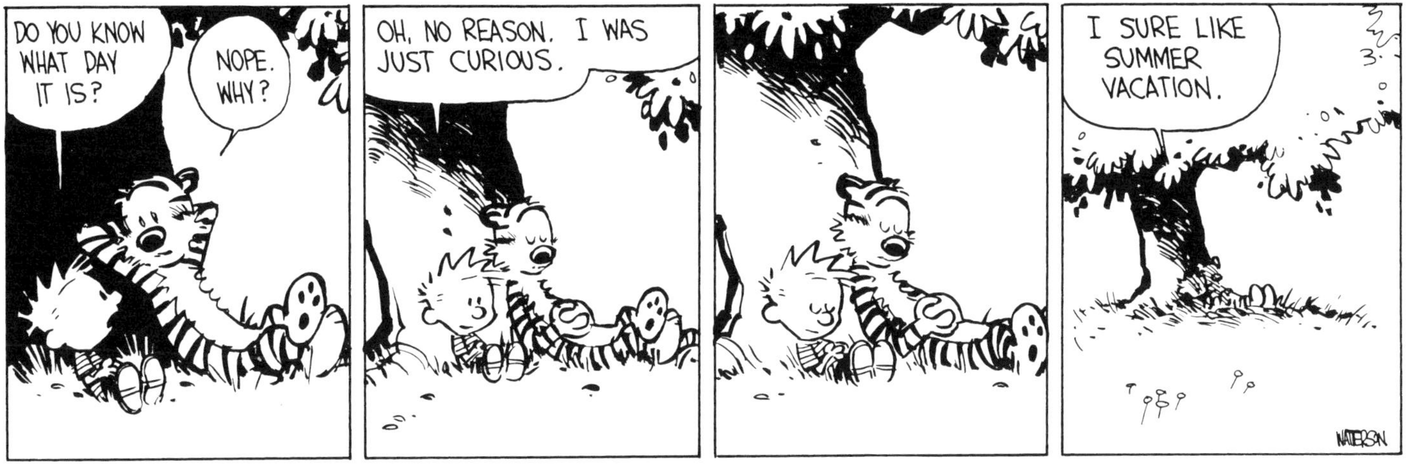
DO YOU KNOW WHAT DAY IT IS?
NOPE. WHY?
OH, NO REASON. I WAS JUST CURIOUS.
I SURE LIKE SUMMER VACATION.

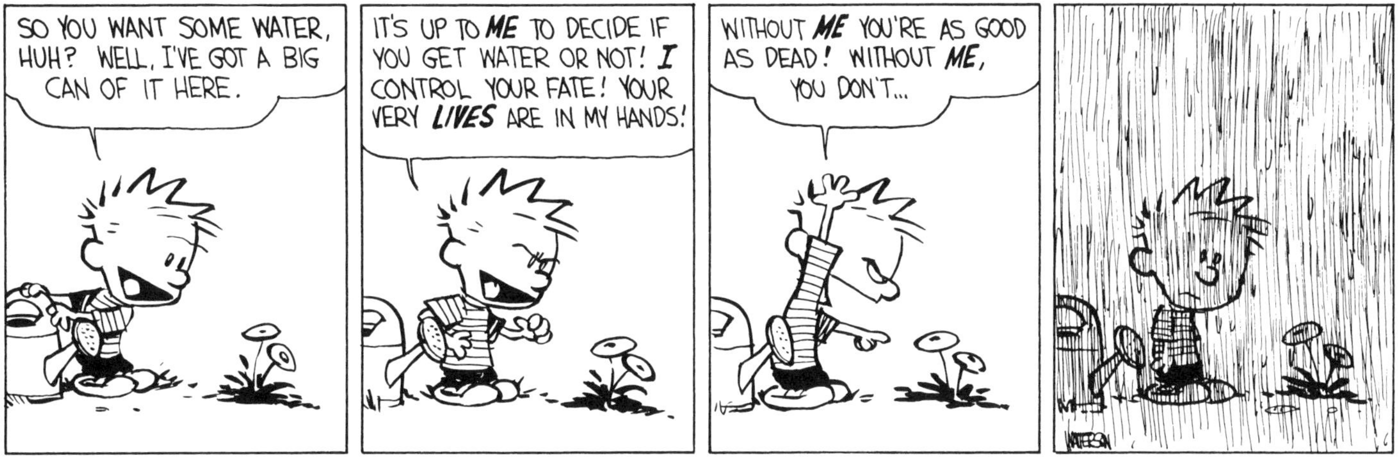
SO YOU WANT SOME WATER, HUH? WELL, I'VE GOT A BIG CAN OF IT HERE.
IT'S UP TO ME TO DECIDE IF YOU GET WATER OR NOT! I CONTROL YOUR FATE! YOUR VERY LIVES ARE IN MY HANDS!
WITHOUT ME YOU'RE AS GOOD AS DEAD! WITHOUT ME, YOU DON'T...

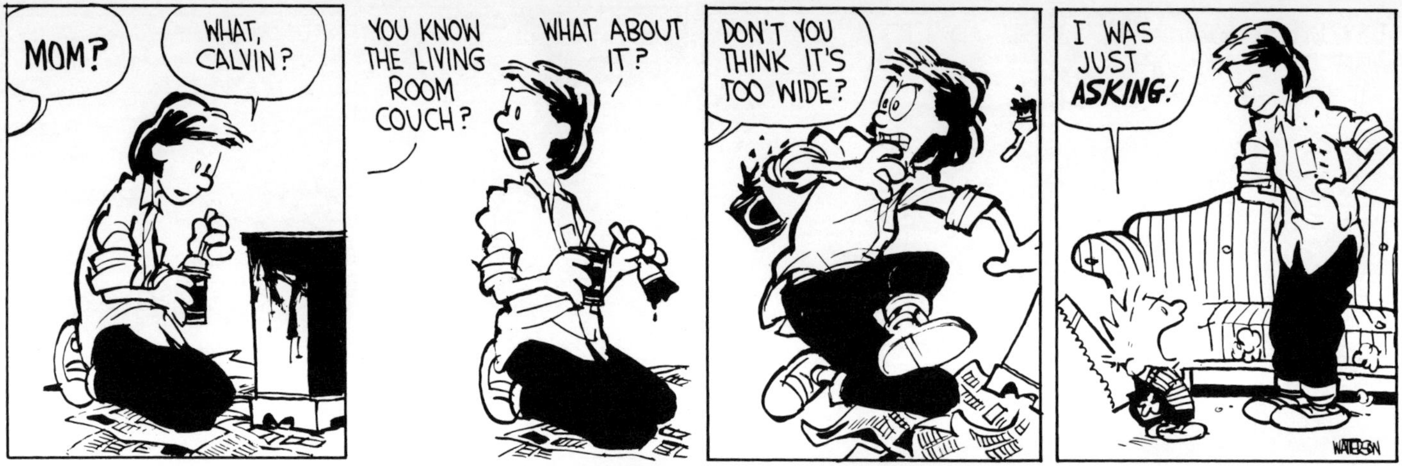
MOM?
WHAT, CALVIN?
YOU KNOW THE LIVING ROOM COUCH?
WHAT ABOUT IT?
DON'T YOU THINK IT'S TOO WIDE?
I WAS JUST ASKING!
WATTERSON

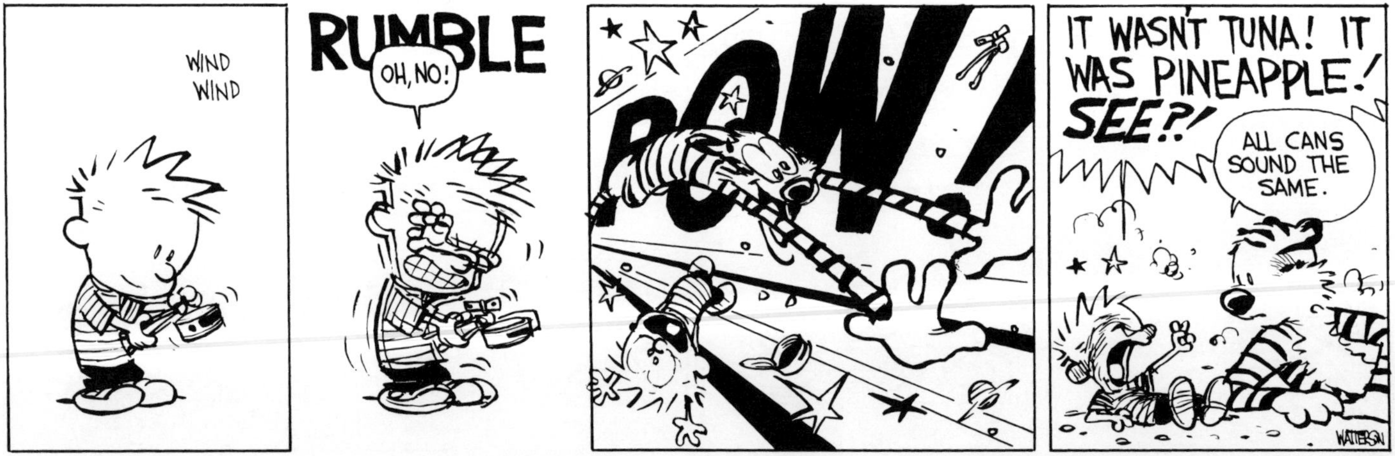
WIND WIND
RUMBLE
OH, NO!
POW!
IT WASN'T TUNA! IT WAS PINEAPPLE! SEE?!
ALL CANS SOUND THE SAME.
WATTERSON

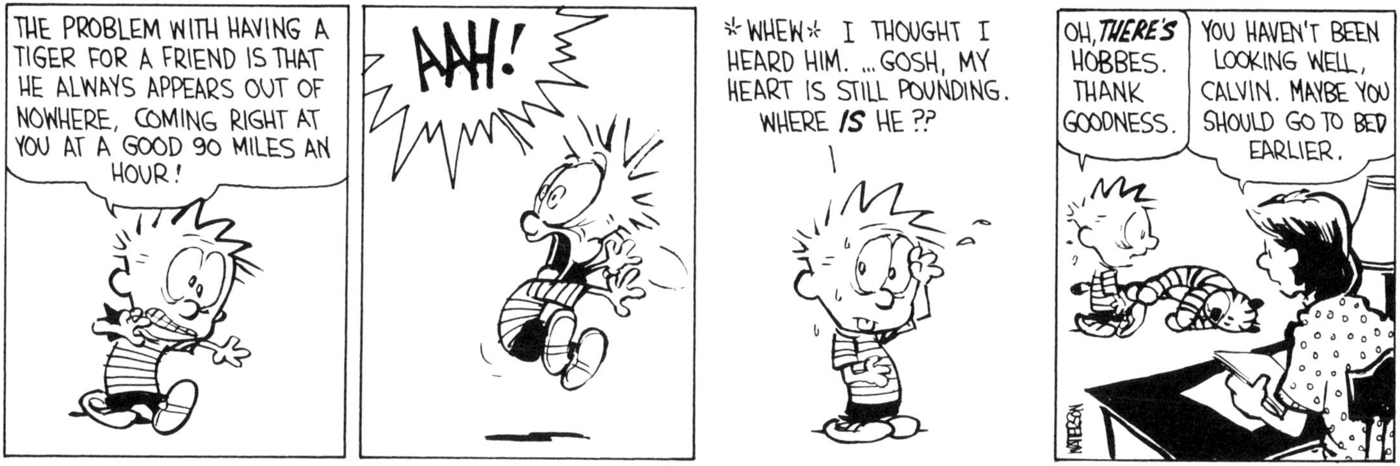
THE PROBLEM WITH HAVING A TIGER FOR A FRIEND IS THAT HE ALWAYS APPEARS OUT OF NOWHERE, COMING RIGHT AT YOU AT A GOOD 90 MILES AN HOUR!
AAH!
WHEW I THOUGHT I HEARD HIM. ...GOSH, MY HEART IS STILL POUNDING. WHERE **IS** HE??
OH, **THERE'S** HOBBES. THANK GOODNESS.
YOU HAVEN'T BEEN LOOKING WELL, CALVIN. MAYBE YOU SHOULD GO TO BED EARLIER.

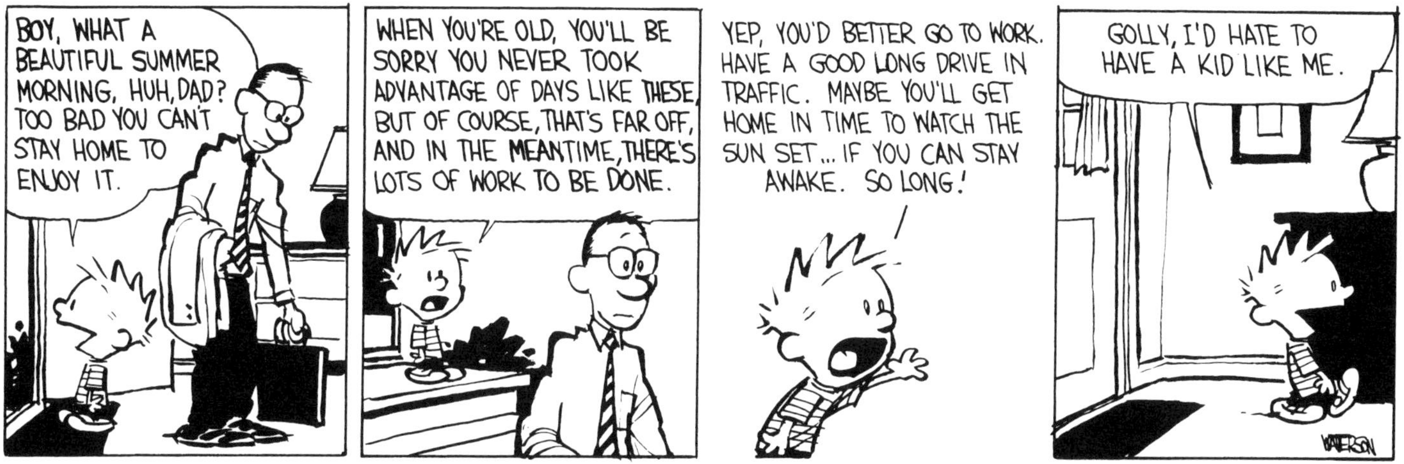
BOY, WHAT A BEAUTIFUL SUMMER MORNING, HUH, DAD? TOO BAD YOU CAN'T STAY HOME TO ENJOY IT.
WHEN YOU'RE OLD, YOU'LL BE SORRY YOU NEVER TOOK ADVANTAGE OF DAYS LIKE THESE. BUT OF COURSE, THAT'S FAR OFF, AND IN THE MEANTIME, THERE'S LOTS OF WORK TO BE DONE.
YEP, YOU'D BETTER GO TO WORK. HAVE A GOOD LONG DRIVE IN TRAFFIC. MAYBE YOU'LL GET HOME IN TIME TO WATCH THE SUN SET... IF YOU CAN STAY AWAKE. SO LONG!
GOLLY, I'D HATE TO HAVE A KID LIKE ME.

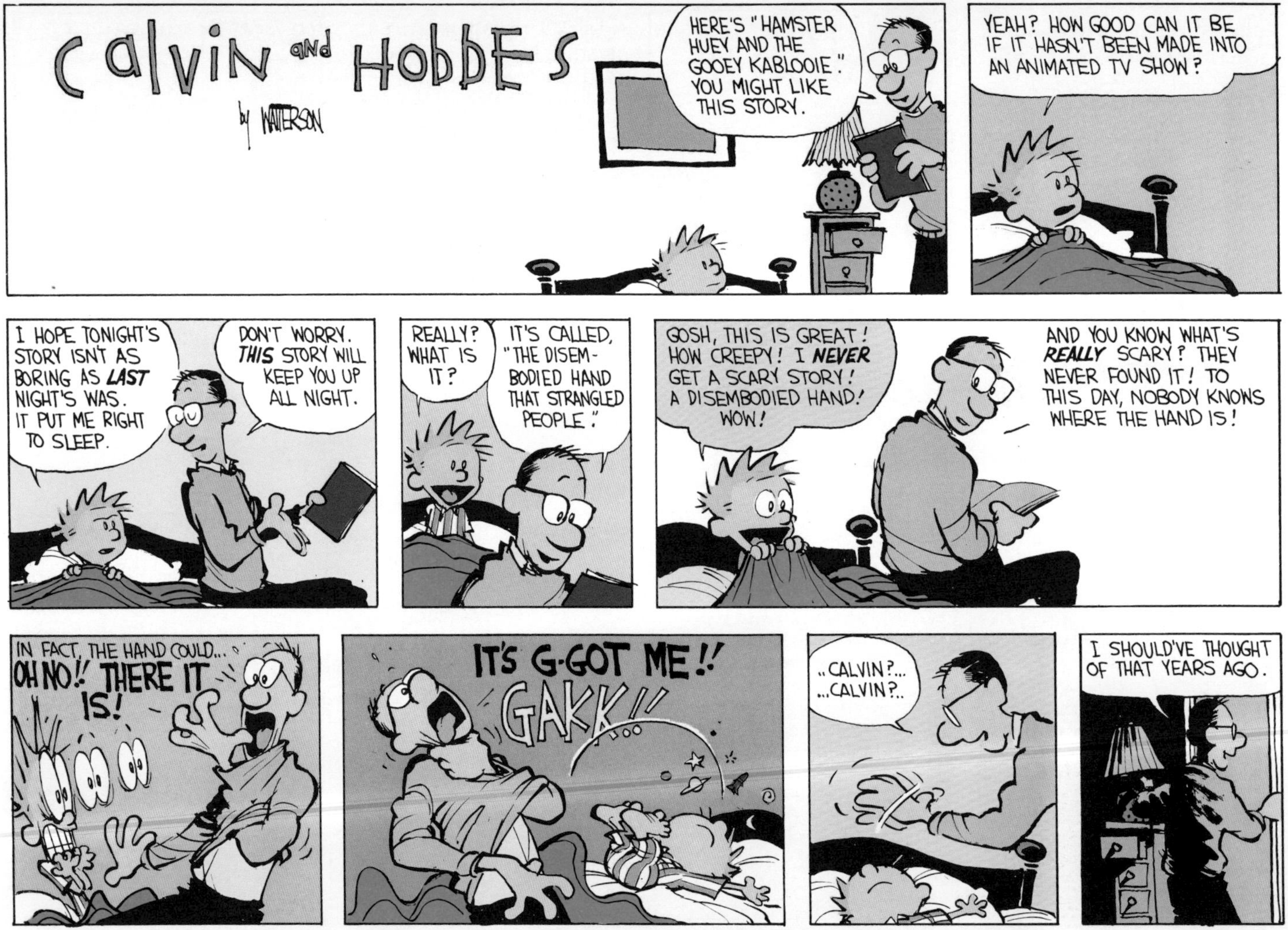
Calvin and HobbEs
by WATTERSON
HERE'S "HAMSTER HUEY AND THE GOOEY KABLOOIE." YOU MIGHT LIKE THIS STORY.
YEAH? HOW GOOD CAN IT BE IF IT HASN'T BEEN MADE INTO AN ANIMATED TV SHOW?
I HOPE TONIGHT'S STORY ISN'T AS BORING AS LAST NIGHT'S WAS. IT PUT ME RIGHT TO SLEEP.
DON'T WORRY. THIS STORY WILL KEEP YOU UP ALL NIGHT.
REALLY? WHAT IS IT?
IT'S CALLED, "THE DISEMBODIED HAND THAT STRANGLED PEOPLE."
GOSH, THIS IS GREAT! HOW CREEPY! I NEVER GET A SCARY STORY! A DISEMBODIED HAND! WOW!
AND YOU KNOW WHAT'S REALLY SCARY? THEY NEVER FOUND IT! TO THIS DAY, NOBODY KNOWS WHERE THE HAND IS!
IN FACT, THE HAND COULD...
OH NO!! THERE IT IS!
IT'S G-GOT ME!!
GAKK!!
..CALVIN?... ...CALVIN?..
I SHOULD'VE THOUGHT OF THAT YEARS AGO.

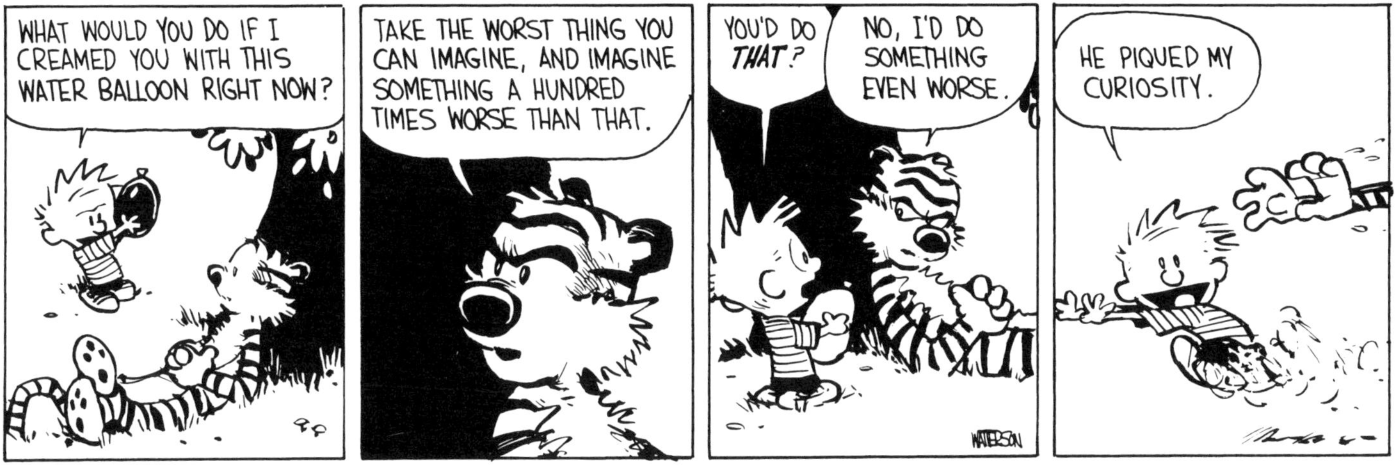
WHAT WOULD YOU DO IF I CREAMED YOU WITH THIS WATER BALLOON RIGHT NOW?
TAKE THE WORST THING YOU CAN IMAGINE, AND IMAGINE SOMETHING A HUNDRED TIMES WORSE THAN THAT.
YOU'D DO *THAT*?
NO, I'D DO SOMETHING EVEN WORSE.
HE PIQUED MY CURIOSITY.

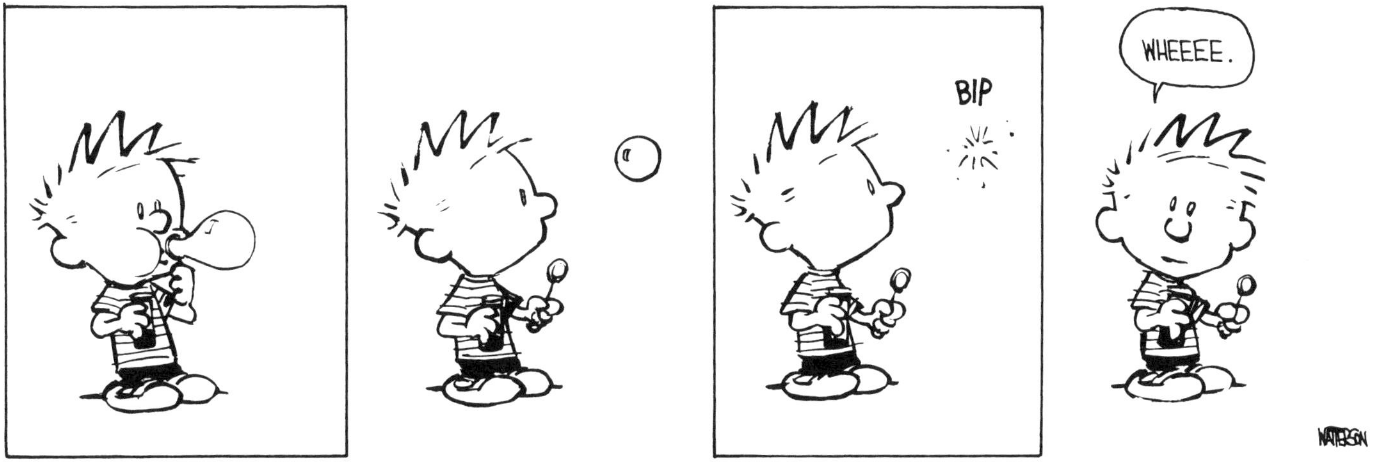
BIP
WHEEEE.

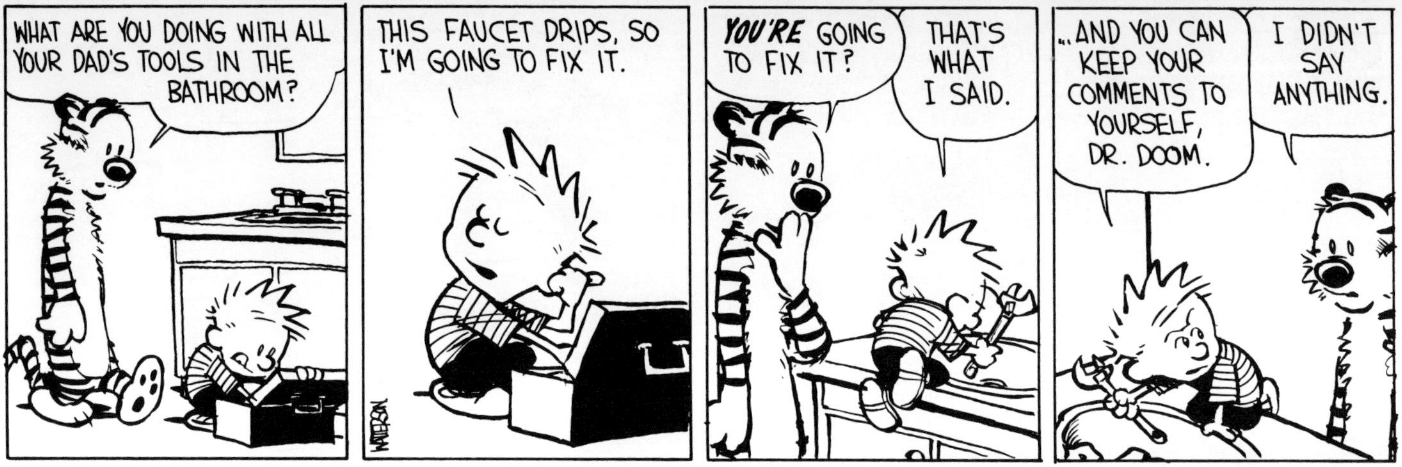
WHAT ARE YOU DOING WITH ALL YOUR DAD'S TOOLS IN THE BATHROOM?
THIS FAUCET DRIPS, SO I'M GOING TO FIX IT.
WATTERSON
YOU'RE GOING TO FIX IT?
THAT'S WHAT I SAID.
...AND YOU CAN KEEP YOUR COMMENTS TO YOURSELF, DR. DOOM.
I DIDN'T SAY ANYTHING.

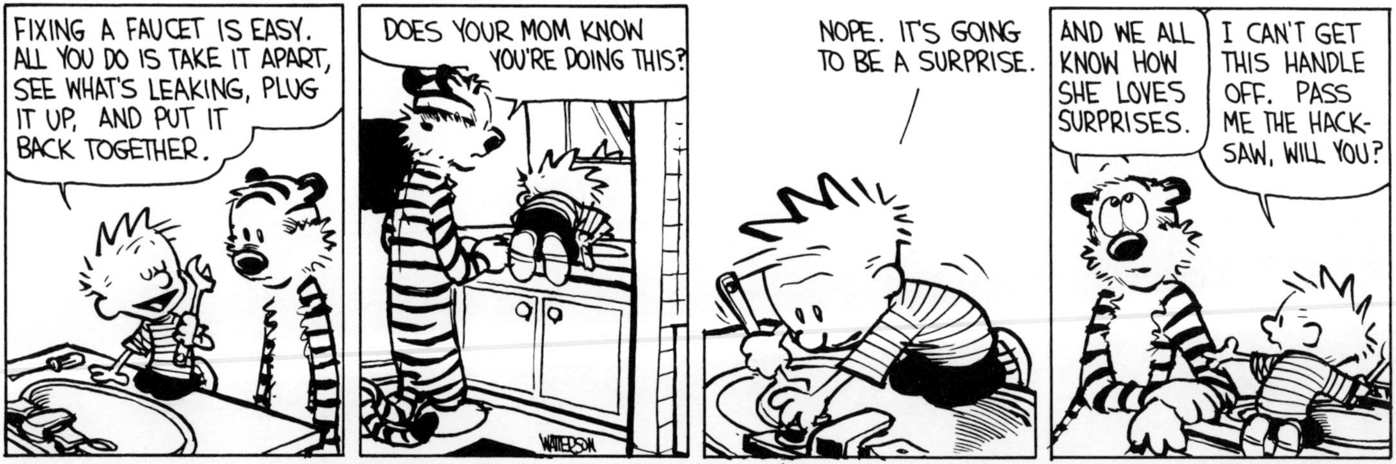
FIXING A FAUCET IS EASY. ALL YOU DO IS TAKE IT APART, SEE WHAT'S LEAKING, PLUG IT UP, AND PUT IT BACK TOGETHER.
DOES YOUR MOM KNOW YOU'RE DOING THIS?
WATTERSON
NOPE. IT'S GOING TO BE A SURPRISE.
AND WE ALL KNOW HOW SHE LOVES SURPRISES.
I CAN'T GET THIS HANDLE OFF. PASS ME THE HACK-SAW, WILL YOU?

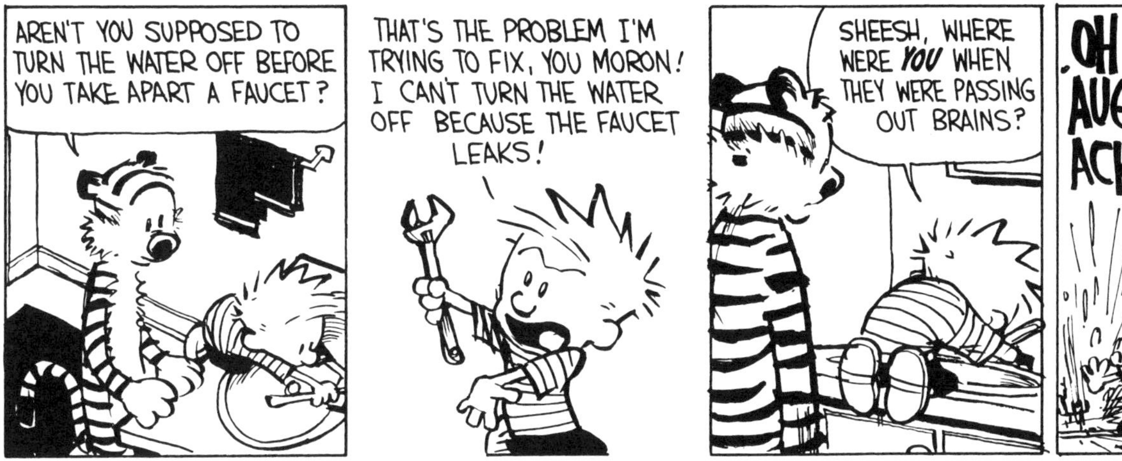
AREN'T YOU SUPPOSED TO TURN THE WATER OFF BEFORE YOU TAKE APART A FAUCET?
THAT'S THE PROBLEM I'M TRYING TO FIX, YOU MORON! I CAN'T TURN THE WATER OFF BECAUSE THE FAUCET LEAKS!
SHEESH, WHERE WERE *YOU* WHEN THEY WERE PASSING OUT BRAINS?
OH NO! AUGHH! ACKK!
I'LL GET YOU SOME PAPER AND CARBONS FOR YOUR WRITTEN APOLOGY.

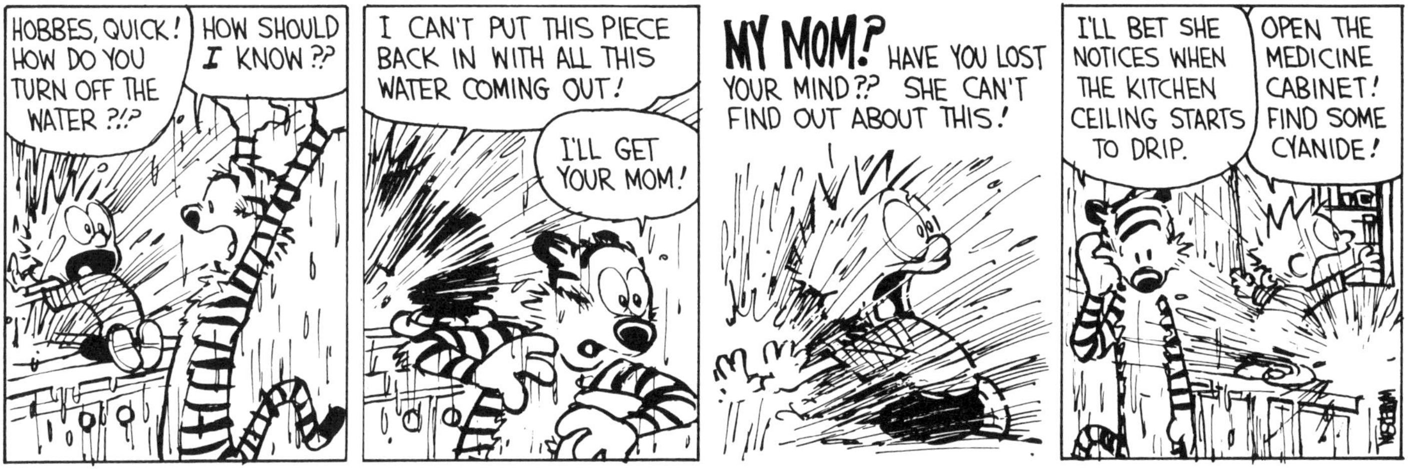
HOBBES, QUICK! HOW DO YOU TURN OFF THE WATER ?!?
HOW SHOULD *I* KNOW ??
I CAN'T PUT THIS PIECE BACK IN WITH ALL THIS WATER COMING OUT!
I'LL GET YOUR MOM!
MY MOM? HAVE YOU LOST YOUR MIND?? SHE CAN'T FIND OUT ABOUT THIS!
I'LL BET SHE NOTICES WHEN THE KITCHEN CEILING STARTS TO DRIP.
OPEN THE MEDICINE CABINET! FIND SOME CYANIDE!

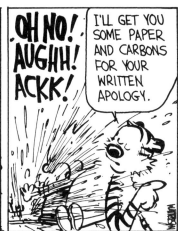

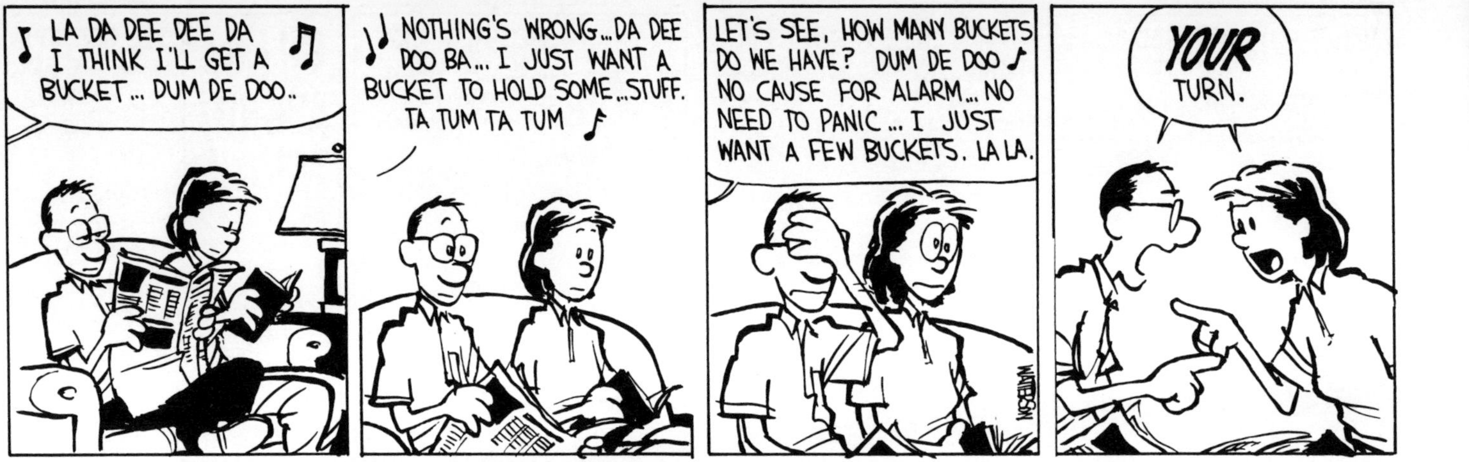
LA DA DEE DEE DA I THINK I'LL GET A BUCKET... DUM DE DOO..
NOTHING'S WRONG...DA DEE DOO BA... I JUST WANT A BUCKET TO HOLD SOME...STUFF. TA TUM TA TUM
LET'S SEE, HOW MANY BUCKETS DO WE HAVE? DUM DE DOO NO CAUSE FOR ALARM... NO NEED TO PANIC... I JUST WANT A FEW BUCKETS. LA LA.
YOUR TURN.

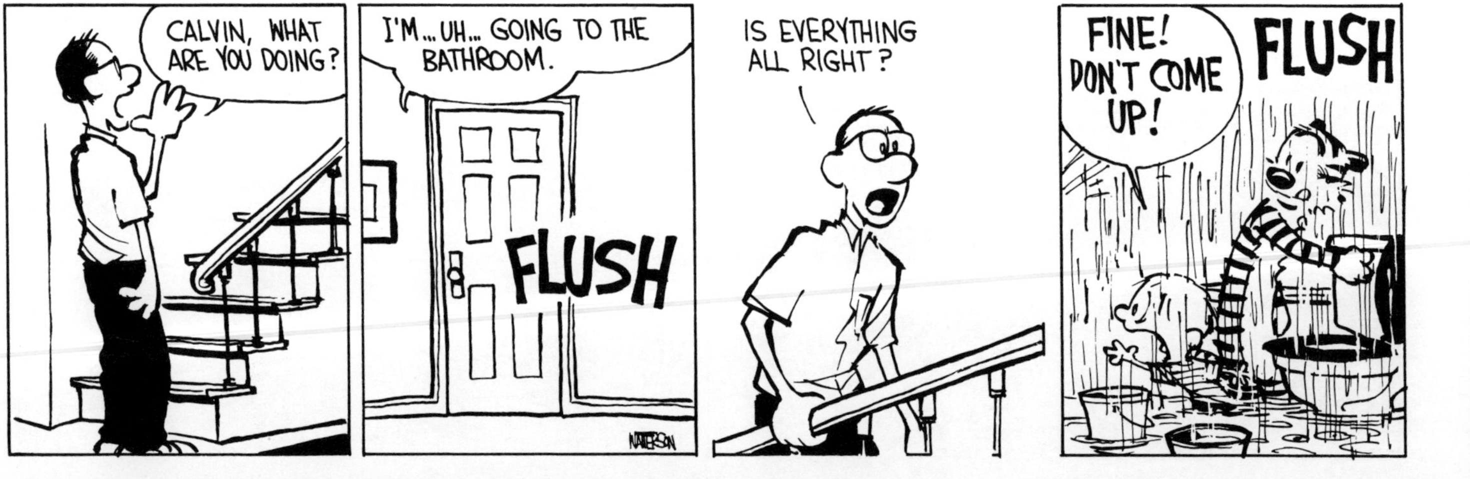
CALVIN, WHAT ARE YOU DOING?
I'M... UH... GOING TO THE BATHROOM.
FLUSH
IS EVERYTHING ALL RIGHT?
FINE! DON'T COME UP!
FLUSH

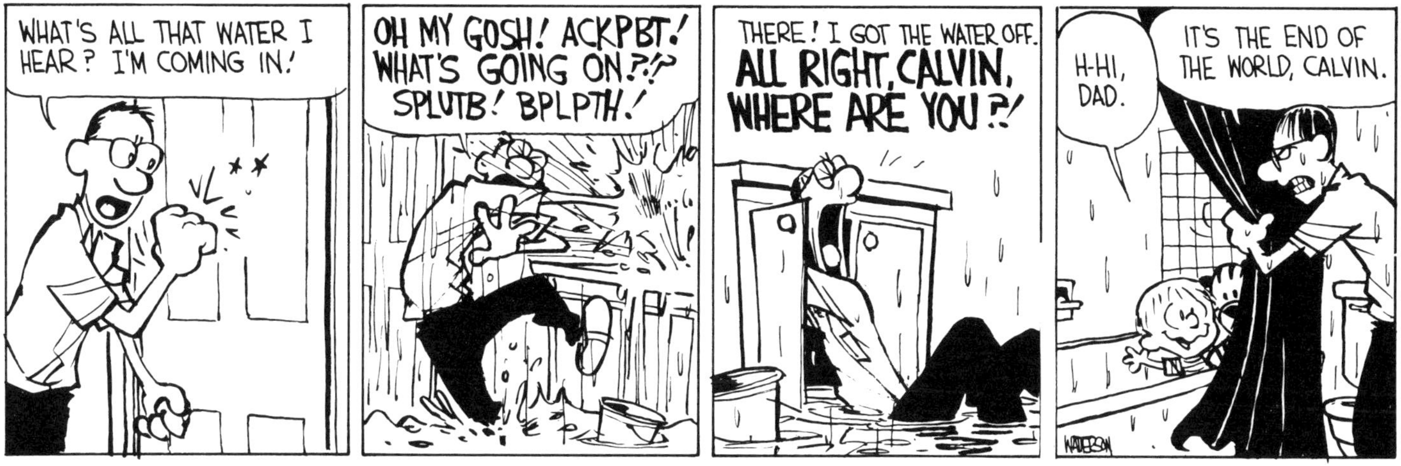
WHAT'S ALL THAT WATER I HEAR? I'M COMING IN!
OH MY GOSH! ACKPBT! WHAT'S GOING ON?!? SPLUTB! BPLPTH!
THERE! I GOT THE WATER OFF. ALL RIGHT, CALVIN, WHERE ARE YOU?!
H-HI, DAD.
IT'S THE END OF THE WORLD, CALVIN.
WATTERSON

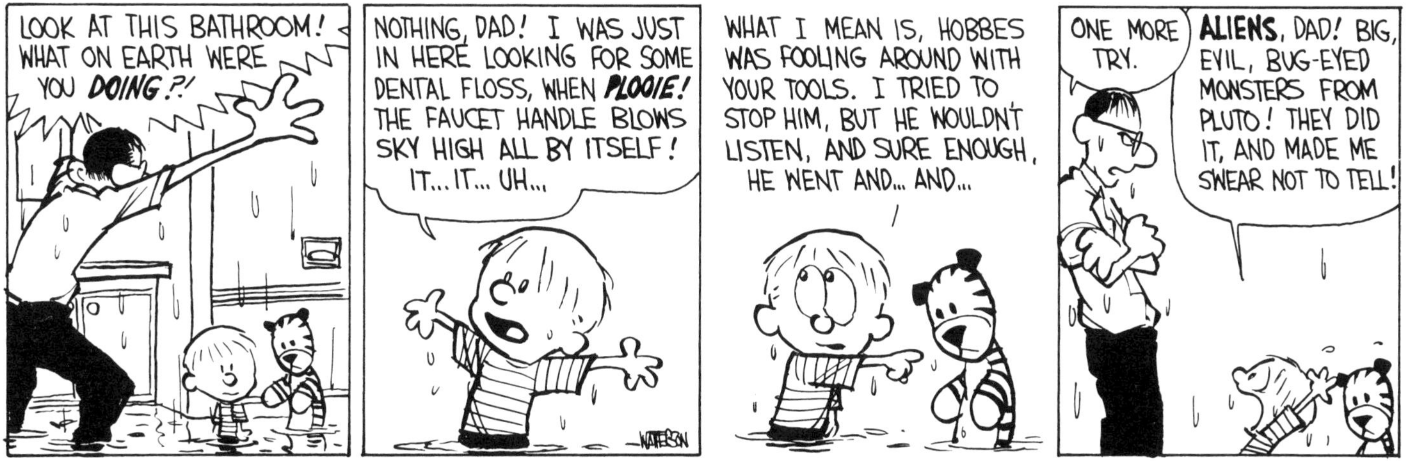
LOOK AT THIS BATHROOM! WHAT ON EARTH WERE YOU DOING?!
NOTHING, DAD! I WAS JUST IN HERE LOOKING FOR SOME DENTAL FLOSS, WHEN PLOOIE! THE FAUCET HANDLE BLOWS SKY HIGH ALL BY ITSELF! IT... IT... UH...
WATTERSON
WHAT I MEAN IS, HOBBES WAS FOOLING AROUND WITH YOUR TOOLS. I TRIED TO STOP HIM, BUT HE WOULDN'T LISTEN, AND SURE ENOUGH, HE WENT AND... AND...
ONE MORE TRY.
ALIENS, DAD! BIG, EVIL, BUG-EYED MONSTERS FROM PLUTO! THEY DID IT, AND MADE ME SWEAR NOT TO TELL!

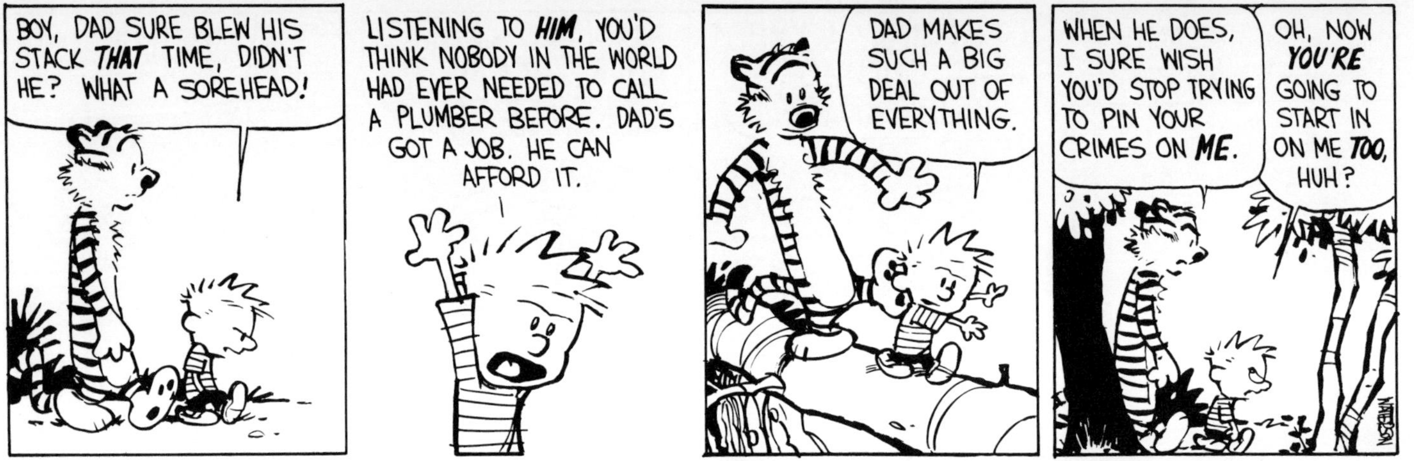
BOY, DAD SURE BLEW HIS STACK THAT TIME, DIDN'T HE? WHAT A SOREHEAD!
LISTENING TO HIM, YOU'D THINK NOBODY IN THE WORLD HAD EVER NEEDED TO CALL A PLUMBER BEFORE. DAD'S GOT A JOB. HE CAN AFFORD IT.
DAD MAKES SUCH A BIG DEAL OUT OF EVERYTHING.
WHEN HE DOES, I SURE WISH YOU'D STOP TRYING TO PIN YOUR CRIMES ON ME.
OH, NOW YOU'RE GOING TO START IN ON ME TOO, HUH?
WATTERSON

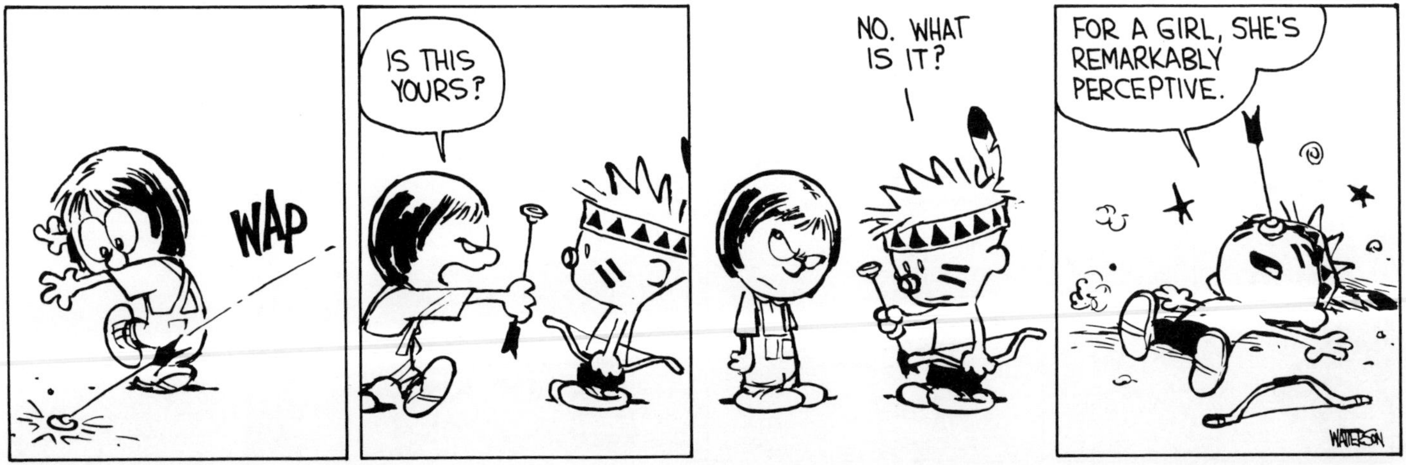
WAP
IS THIS YOURS?
NO. WHAT IS IT?
FOR A GIRL, SHE'S REMARKABLY PERCEPTIVE.
WATTERSON

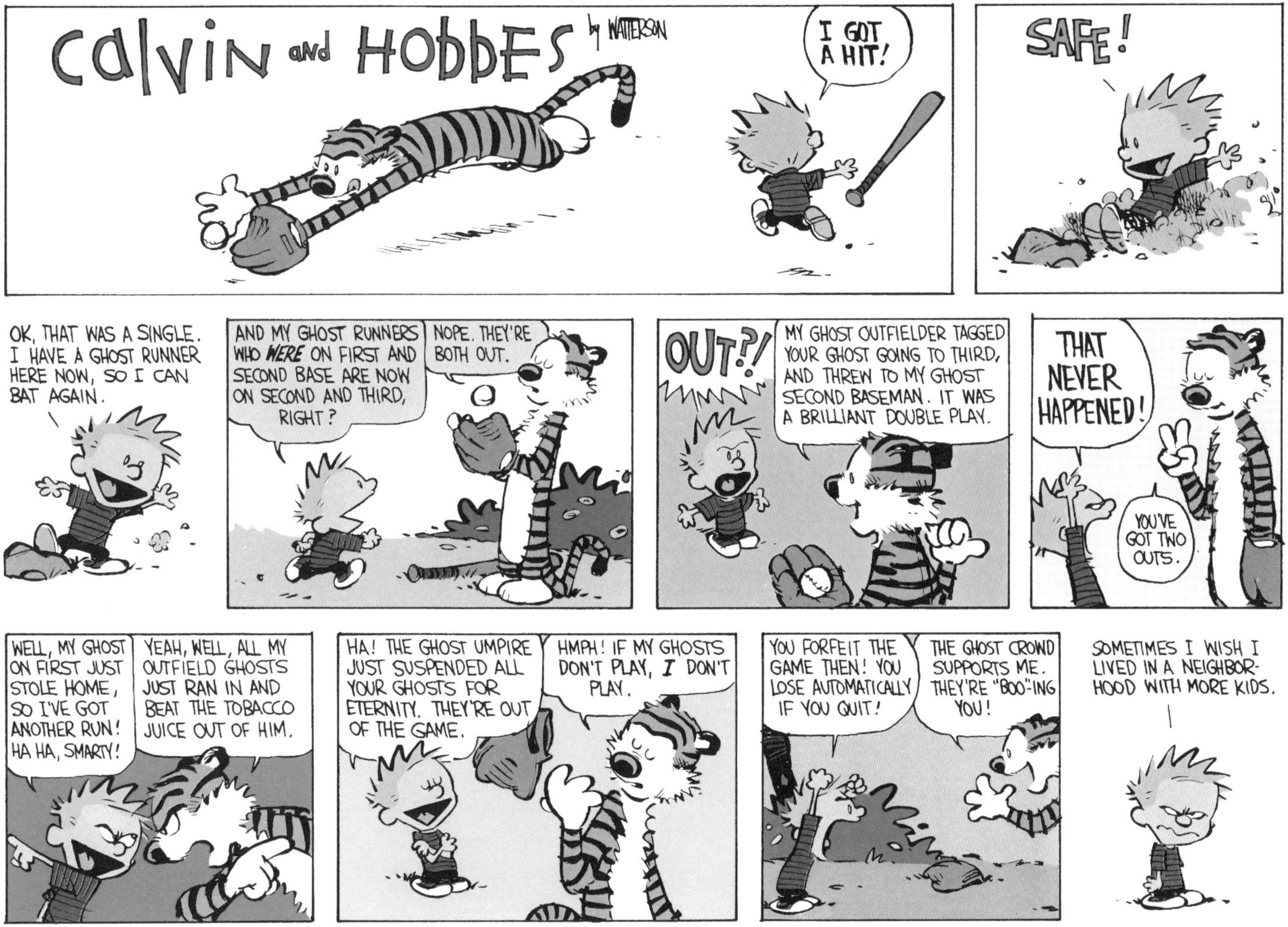
Calvin and HOBBES by WATTERSON
I GOT A HIT!
SAFE!
OK, THAT WAS A SINGLE. I HAVE A GHOST RUNNER HERE NOW, SO I CAN BAT AGAIN.
AND MY GHOST RUNNERS WHO *WERE* ON FIRST AND SECOND BASE ARE NOW ON SECOND AND THIRD, RIGHT?
NOPE. THEY'RE BOTH OUT.
OUT?!
MY GHOST OUTFIELDER TAGGED YOUR GHOST GOING TO THIRD, AND THREW TO MY GHOST SECOND BASEMAN. IT WAS A BRILLIANT DOUBLE PLAY.
THAT NEVER HAPPENED!
YOU'VE GOT TWO OUTS.
WELL, MY GHOST ON FIRST JUST STOLE HOME, SO I'VE GOT ANOTHER RUN! HA HA, SMARTY!
YEAH, WELL, ALL MY OUTFIELD GHOSTS JUST RAN IN AND BEAT THE TOBACCO JUICE OUT OF HIM.
HA! THE GHOST UMPIRE JUST SUSPENDED ALL YOUR GHOSTS FOR ETERNITY. THEY'RE OUT OF THE GAME.
HMPH! IF MY GHOSTS DON'T PLAY, *I* DON'T PLAY.
YOU FORFEIT THE GAME THEN! YOU LOSE AUTOMATICALLY IF YOU QUIT!
THE GHOST CROWD SUPPORTS ME. THEY'RE "BOO"-ING YOU!
SOMETIMES I WISH I LIVED IN A NEIGHBOR-HOOD WITH MORE KIDS.

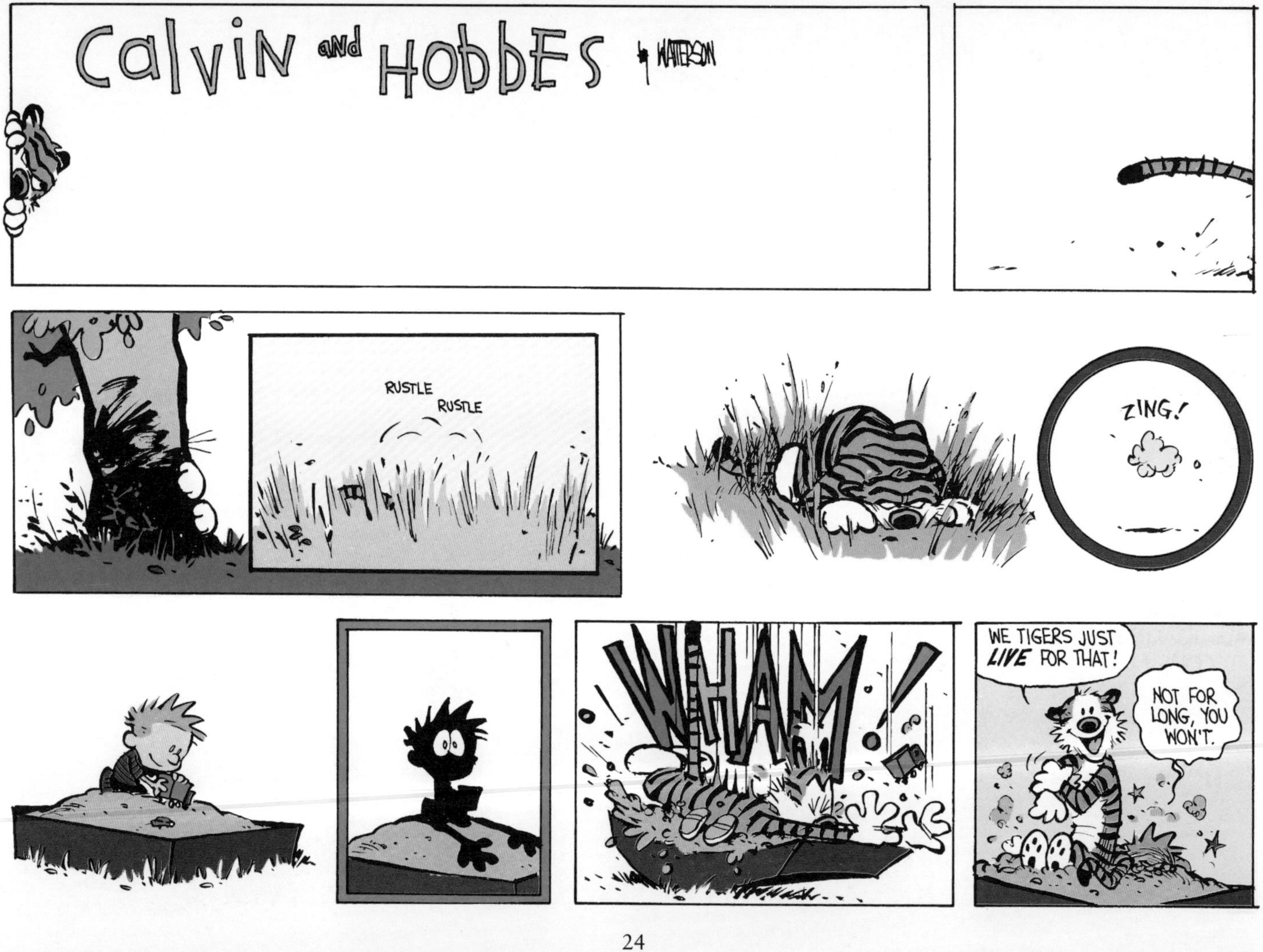
Calvin and HOBBES
by WATTERSON
RUSTLE
RUSTLE
ZING!
WHAM!
WE TIGERS JUST LIVE FOR THAT!
NOT FOR LONG, YOU WON'T.

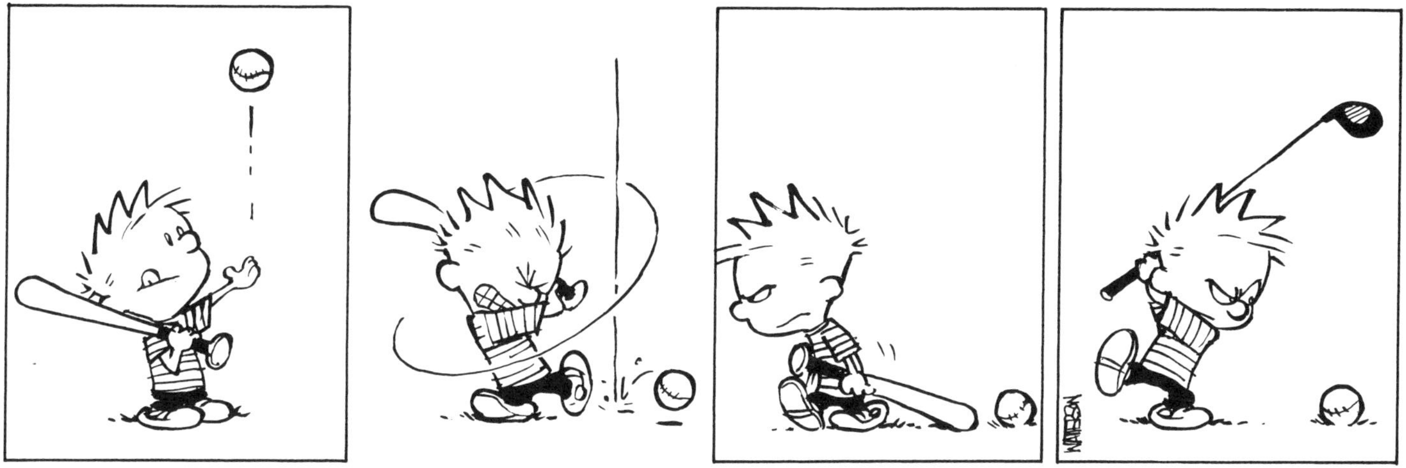

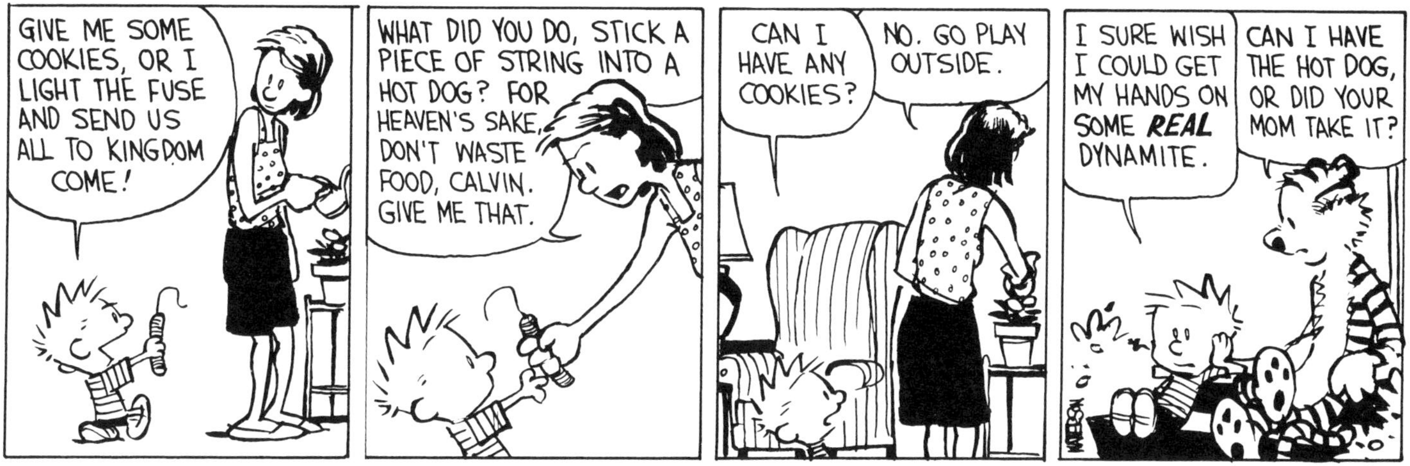
GIVE ME SOME COOKIES, OR I LIGHT THE FUSE AND SEND US ALL TO KINGDOM COME!
WHAT DID YOU DO, STICK A PIECE OF STRING INTO A HOT DOG? FOR HEAVEN'S SAKE, DON'T WASTE FOOD, CALVIN. GIVE ME THAT.
CAN I HAVE ANY COOKIES?
NO. GO PLAY OUTSIDE.
I SURE WISH I COULD GET MY HANDS ON SOME REAL DYNAMITE.
CAN I HAVE THE HOT DOG, OR DID YOUR MOM TAKE IT?

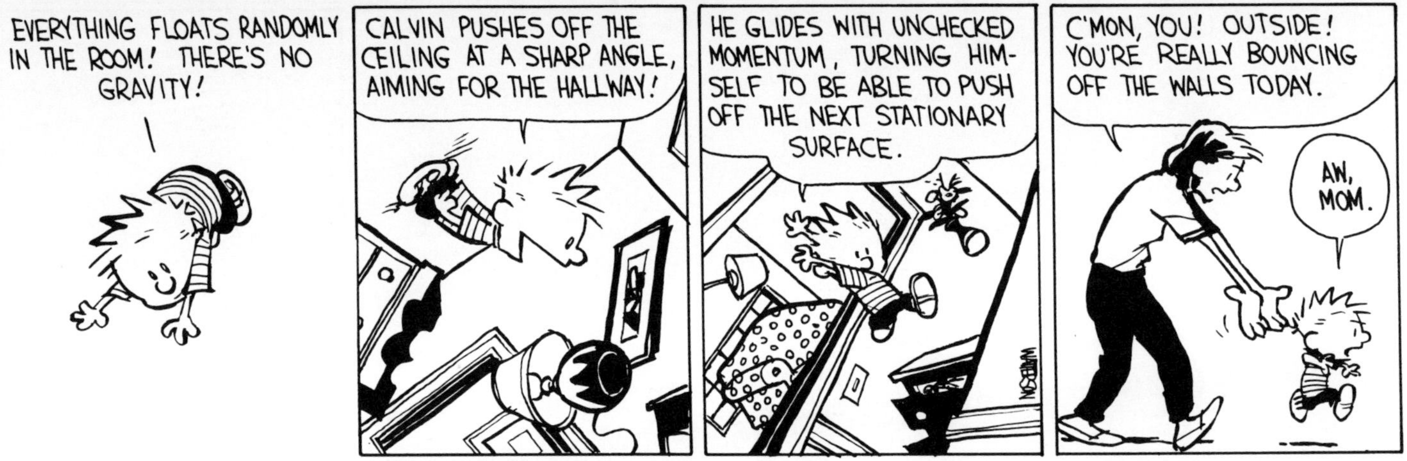
EVERYTHING FLOATS RANDOMLY IN THE ROOM! THERE'S NO GRAVITY!
CALVIN PUSHES OFF THE CEILING AT A SHARP ANGLE, AIMING FOR THE HALLWAY!
HE GLIDES WITH UNCHECKED MOMENTUM, TURNING HIMSELF TO BE ABLE TO PUSH OFF THE NEXT STATIONARY SURFACE.
WATTERSON
C'MON, YOU! OUTSIDE! YOU'RE REALLY BOUNCING OFF THE WALLS TODAY.
AW, MOM.

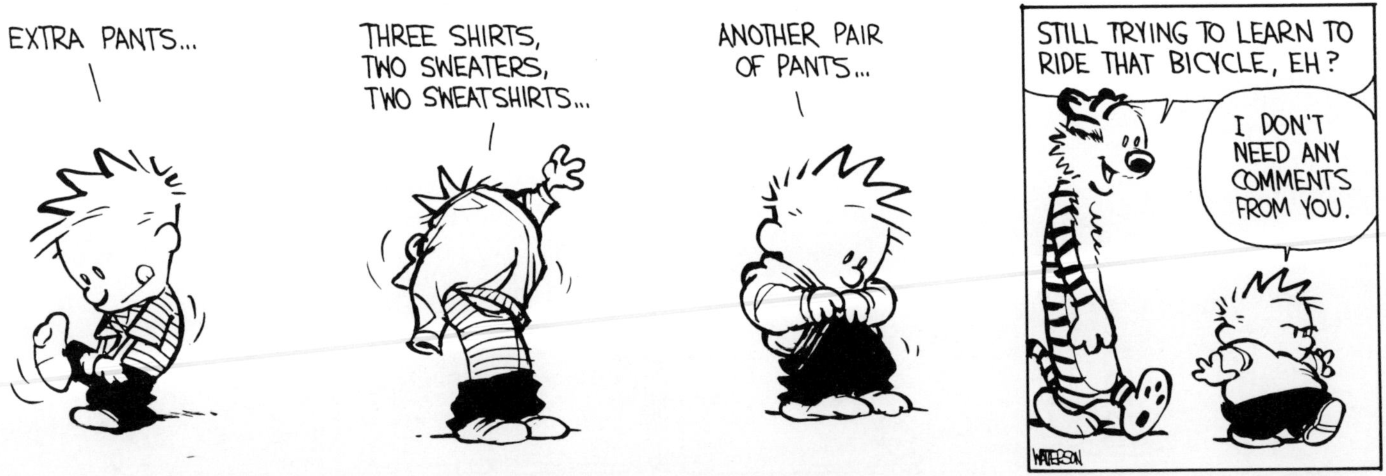
EXTRA PANTS...
THREE SHIRTS, TWO SWEATERS, TWO SWEATSHIRTS...
ANOTHER PAIR OF PANTS...
STILL TRYING TO LEARN TO RIDE THAT BICYCLE, EH?
I DON'T NEED ANY COMMENTS FROM YOU.
WATTERSON

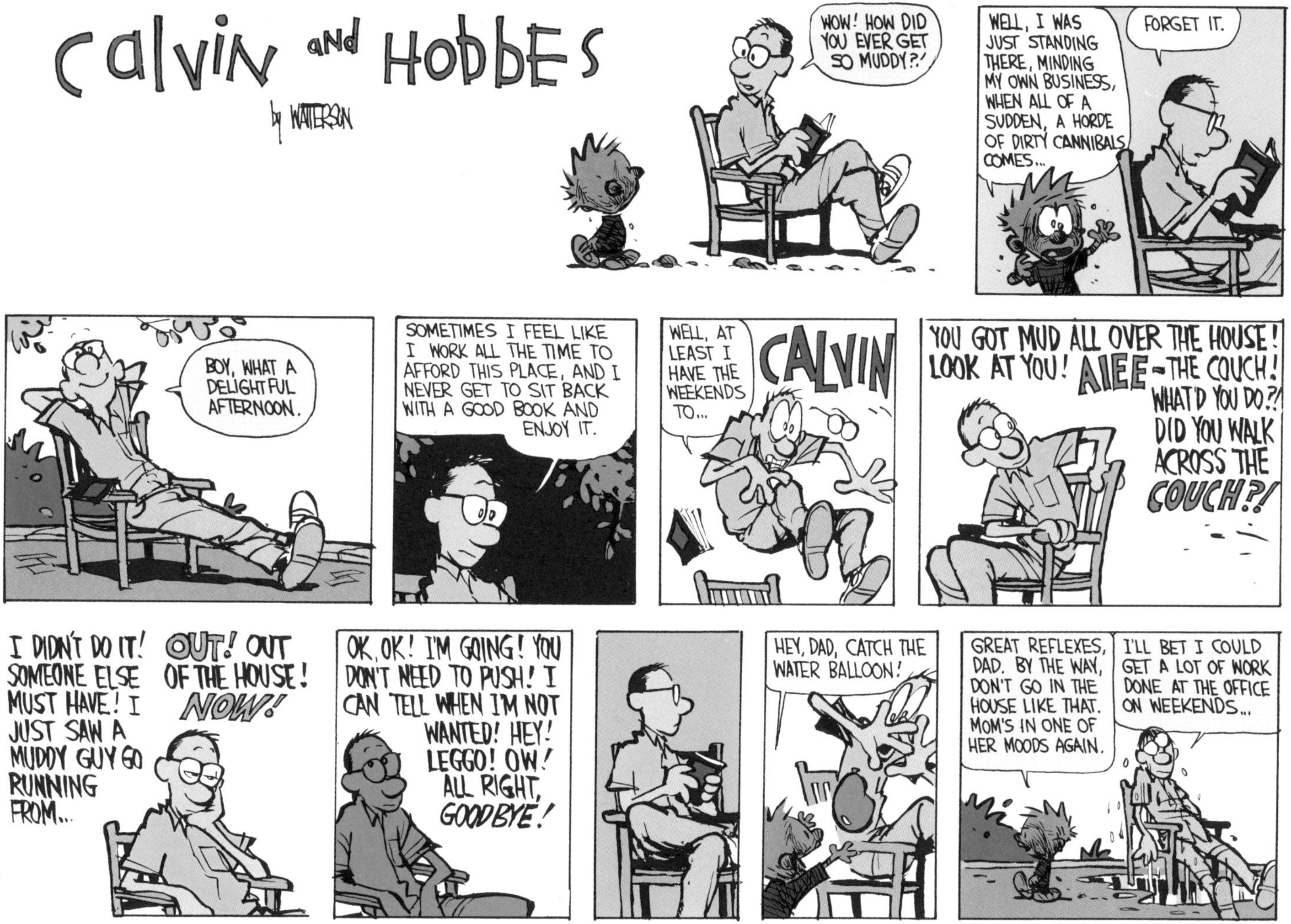
Calvin and Hobbes
by WATTERSON
WOW! HOW DID YOU EVER GET SO MUDDY?!
WELL, I WAS JUST STANDING THERE, MINDING MY OWN BUSINESS, WHEN ALL OF A SUDDEN, A HORDE OF DIRTY CANNIBALS COMES...
FORGET IT.
BOY, WHAT A DELIGHTFUL AFTERNOON.
SOMETIMES I FEEL LIKE I WORK ALL THE TIME TO AFFORD THIS PLACE, AND I NEVER GET TO SIT BACK WITH A GOOD BOOK AND ENJOY IT.
WELL, AT LEAST I HAVE THE WEEKENDS TO...
CALVIN
YOU GOT MUD ALL OVER THE HOUSE! LOOK AT YOU! AIEE-THE COUCH! WHAT'D YOU DO?! DID YOU WALK ACROSS THE COUCH?!
I DIDN'T DO IT! SOMEONE ELSE MUST HAVE! I JUST SAW A MUDDY GUY GO RUNNING FROM...
OUT! OUT OF THE HOUSE! NOW!
OK, OK! I'M GOING! YOU DON'T NEED TO PUSH! I CAN TELL WHEN I'M NOT WANTED! HEY! LEGGO! OW! ALL RIGHT, GOODBYE!
HEY, DAD, CATCH THE WATER BALLOON!
GREAT REFLEXES, DAD. BY THE WAY, DON'T GO IN THE HOUSE LIKE THAT. MOM'S IN ONE OF HER MOODS AGAIN.
I'LL BET I COULD GET A LOT OF WORK DONE AT THE OFFICE ON WEEKENDS...

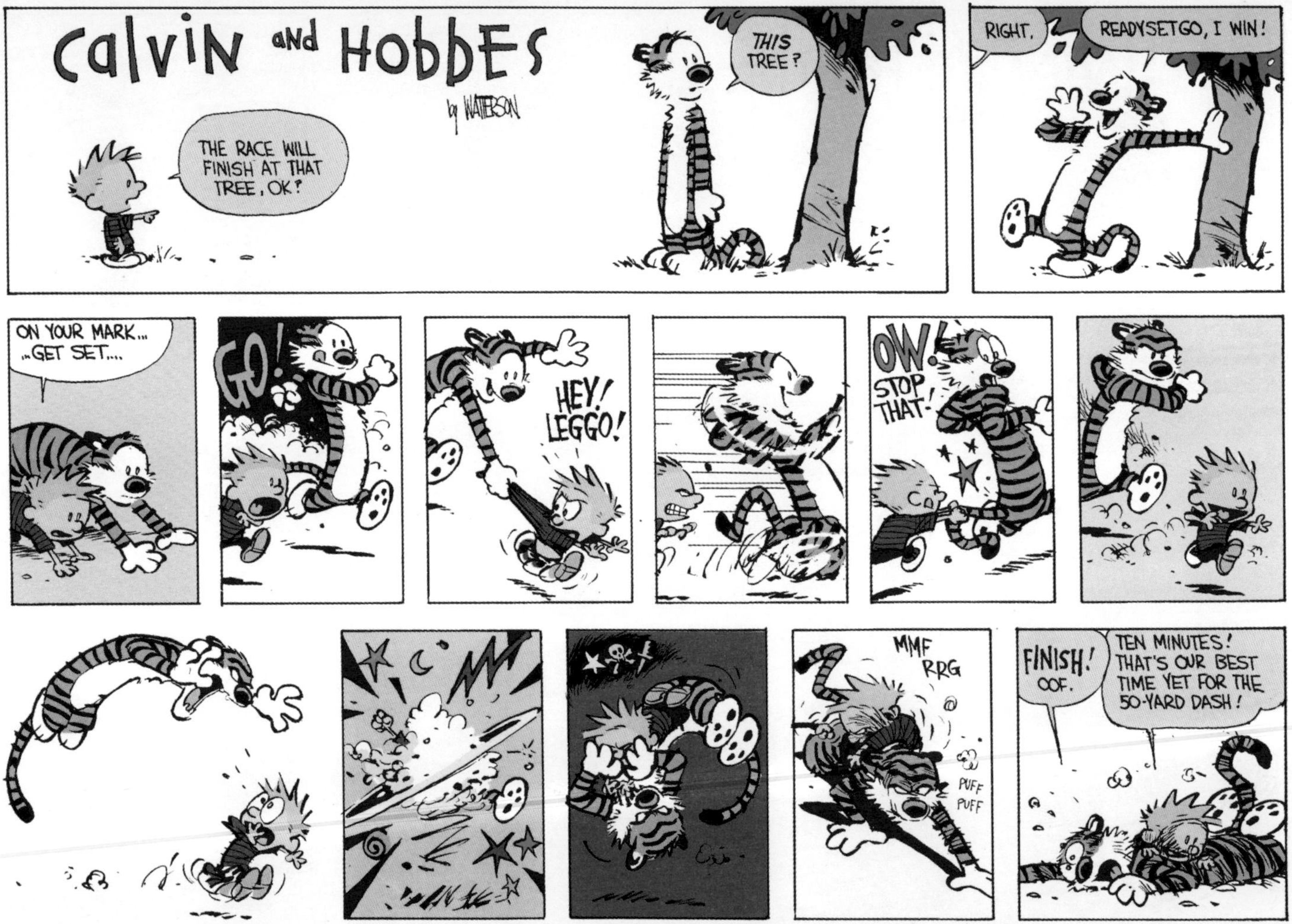
CALVIN AND HOBBES
by WATTERSON
THE RACE WILL FINISH AT THAT TREE, OK?
THIS TREE?
RIGHT.
READYSETGO, I WIN!
ON YOUR MARK... ...GET SET....
GO!
HEY! LEGGO!
OW! STOP THAT!
MMF
RRG
PUFF PUFF
FINISH! OOF.
TEN MINUTES! THAT'S OUR BEST TIME YET FOR THE 50-YARD DASH!

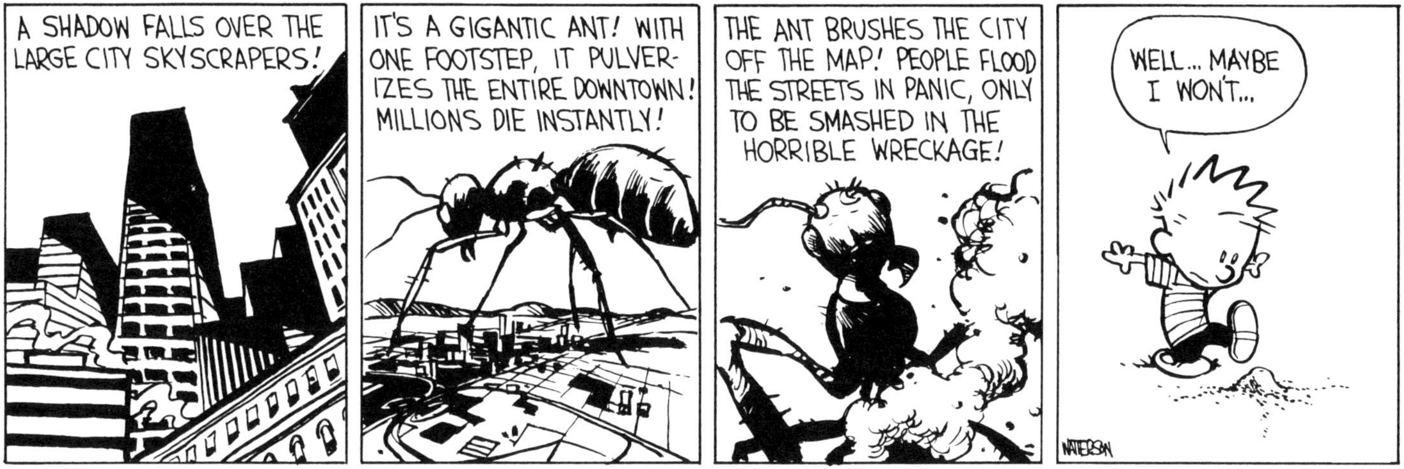
A SHADOW FALLS OVER THE LARGE CITY SKYSCRAPERS!
IT'S A GIGANTIC ANT! WITH ONE FOOTSTEP, IT PULVERIZES THE ENTIRE DOWNTOWN! MILLIONS DIE INSTANTLY!
THE ANT BRUSHES THE CITY OFF THE MAP! PEOPLE FLOOD THE STREETS IN PANIC, ONLY TO BE SMASHED IN THE HORRIBLE WRECKAGE!
WELL... MAYBE I WON'T...
WATTERSON

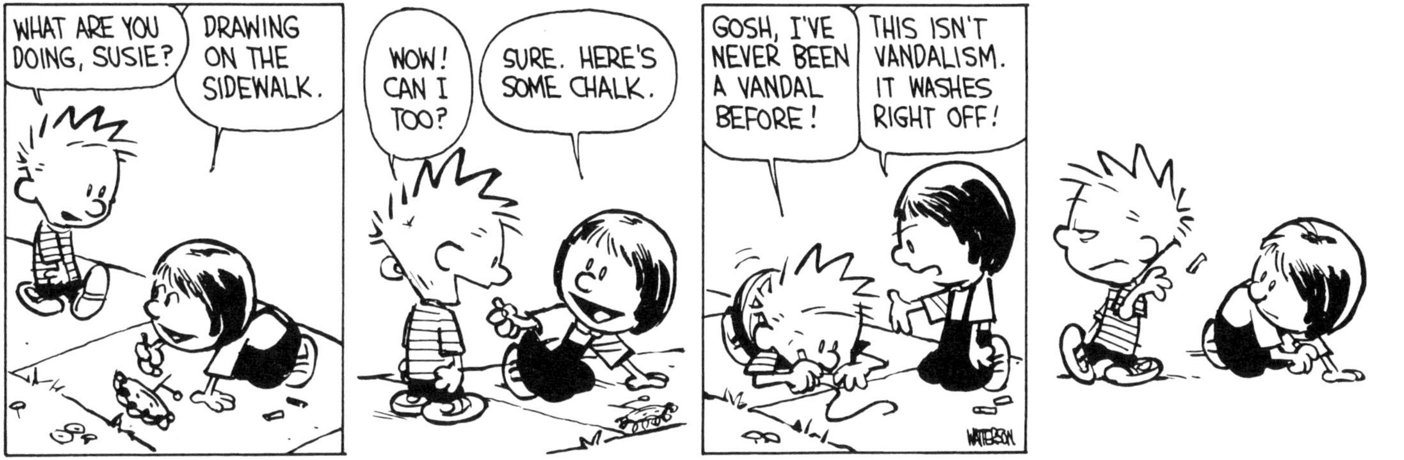
WHAT ARE YOU DOING, SUSIE?
DRAWING ON THE SIDEWALK.
WOW! CAN I TOO?
SURE. HERE'S SOME CHALK.
GOSH, I'VE NEVER BEEN A VANDAL BEFORE!
THIS ISN'T VANDALISM. IT WASHES RIGHT OFF!
WATTERSON

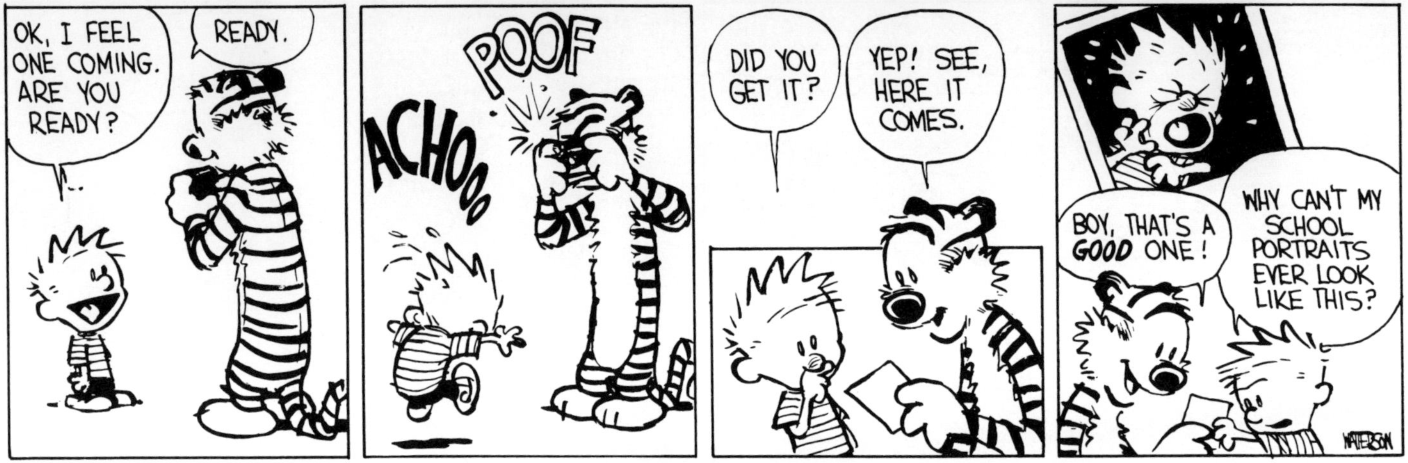
OK, I FEEL ONE COMING. ARE YOU READY?
READY.
ACHOOOO
POOF
DID YOU GET IT?
YEP! SEE, HERE IT COMES.
BOY, THAT'S A **GOOD** ONE!
WHY CAN'T MY SCHOOL PORTRAITS EVER LOOK LIKE THIS?
WATTERSON

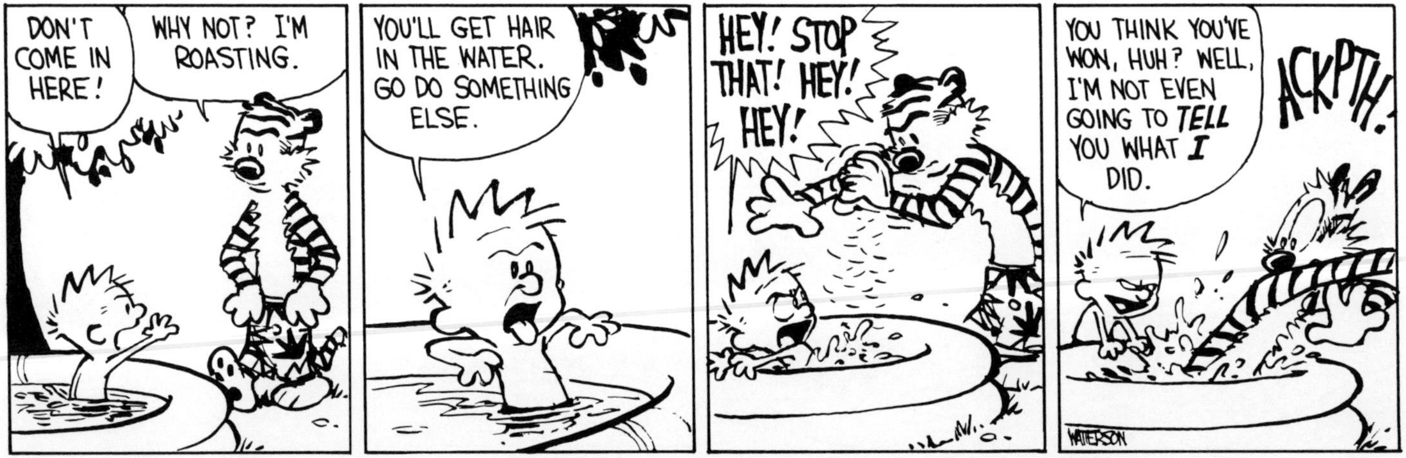
DON'T COME IN HERE!
WHY NOT? I'M ROASTING.
YOU'LL GET HAIR IN THE WATER. GO DO SOMETHING ELSE.
HEY! STOP THAT! HEY! HEY!
YOU THINK YOU'VE WON, HUH? WELL, I'M NOT EVEN GOING TO ***TELL*** YOU WHAT ***I*** DID.
ACKPTH!
WATTERSON

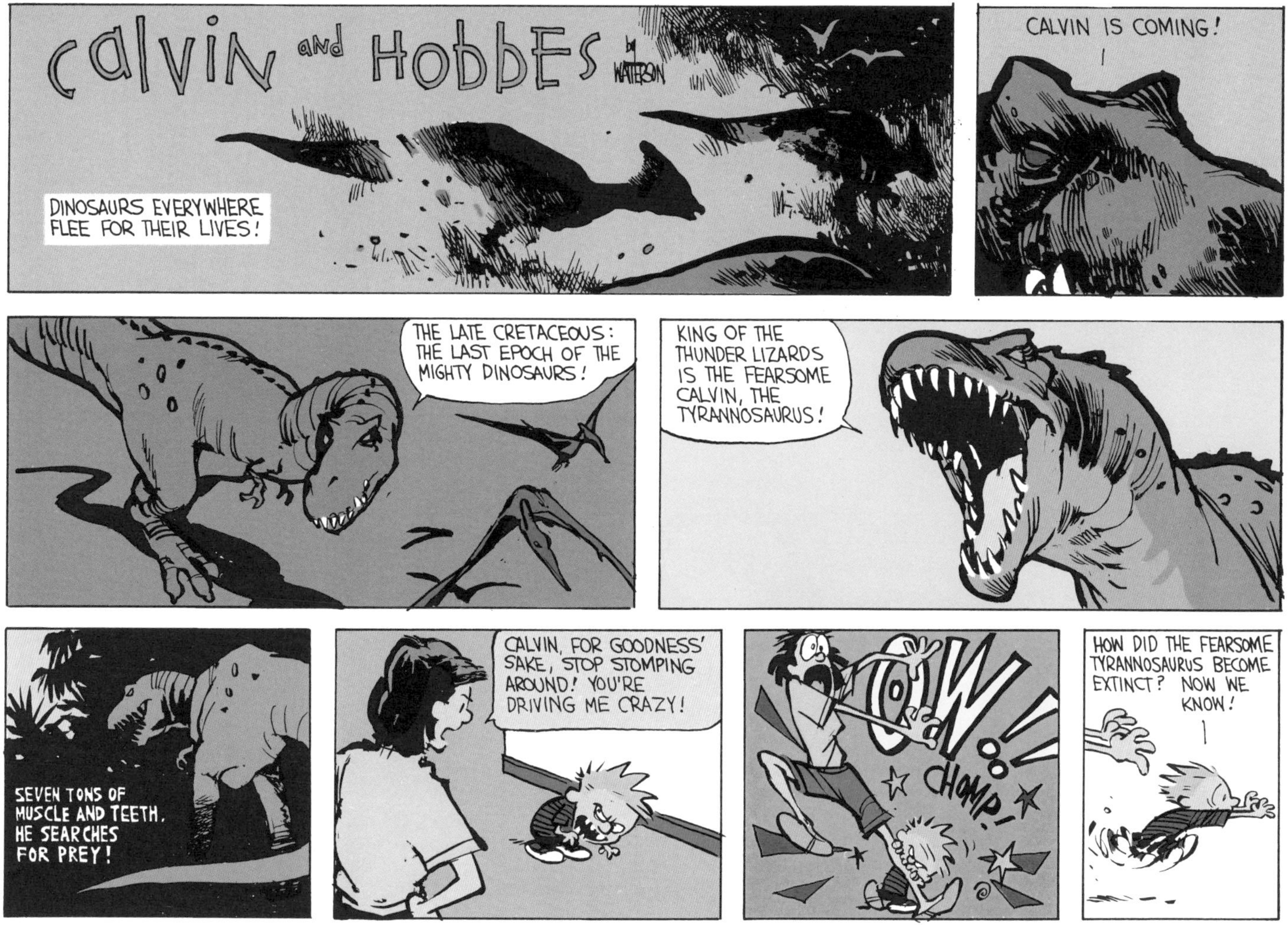
CALVIN and HOBBES by WATTERSON
DINOSAURS EVERYWHERE FLEE FOR THEIR LIVES!
CALVIN IS COMING!
THE LATE CRETACEOUS: THE LAST EPOCH OF THE MIGHTY DINOSAURS!
KING OF THE THUNDER LIZARDS IS THE FEARSOME CALVIN, THE TYRANNOSAURUS!
SEVEN TONS OF MUSCLE AND TEETH. HE SEARCHES FOR PREY!
CALVIN, FOR GOODNESS' SAKE, STOP STOMPING AROUND! YOU'RE DRIVING ME CRAZY!
OOW!!
CHOMP!
HOW DID THE FEARSOME TYRANNOSAURUS BECOME EXTINCT? NOW WE KNOW!

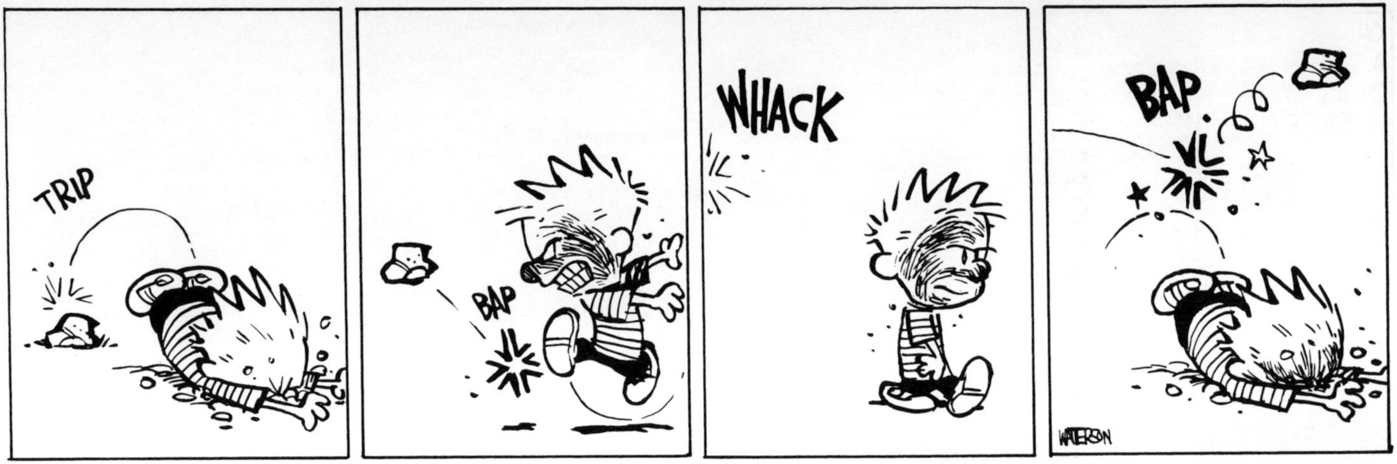
TRIP
BAP
WHACK
BAP

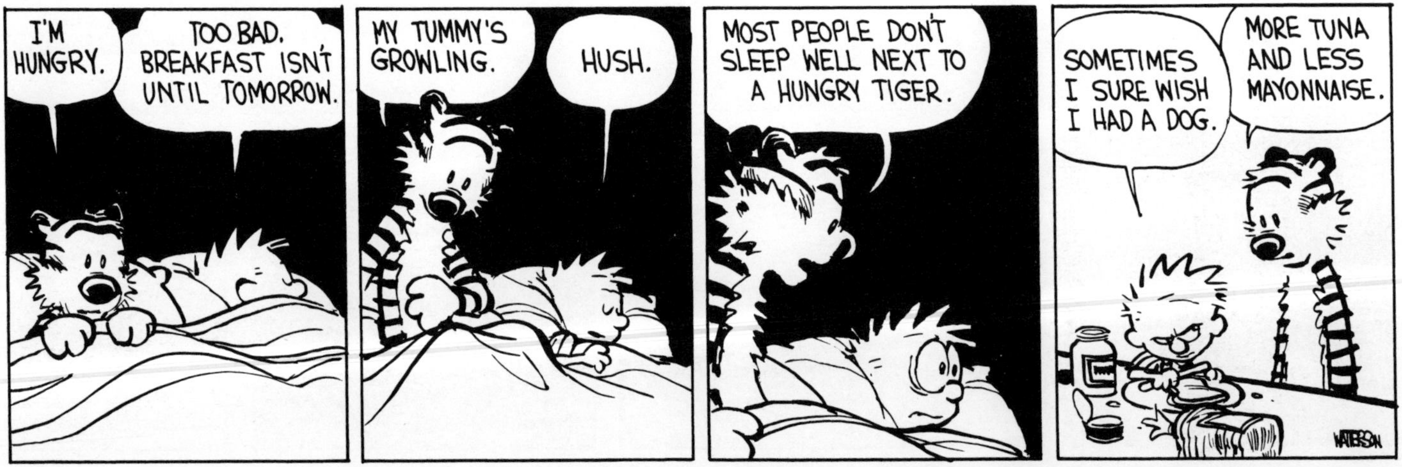
I'M HUNGRY.
TOO BAD. BREAKFAST ISN'T UNTIL TOMORROW.
MY TUMMY'S GROWLING.
HUSH.
MOST PEOPLE DON'T SLEEP WELL NEXT TO A HUNGRY TIGER.
SOMETIMES I SURE WISH I HAD A DOG.
MORE TUNA AND LESS MAYONNAISE.

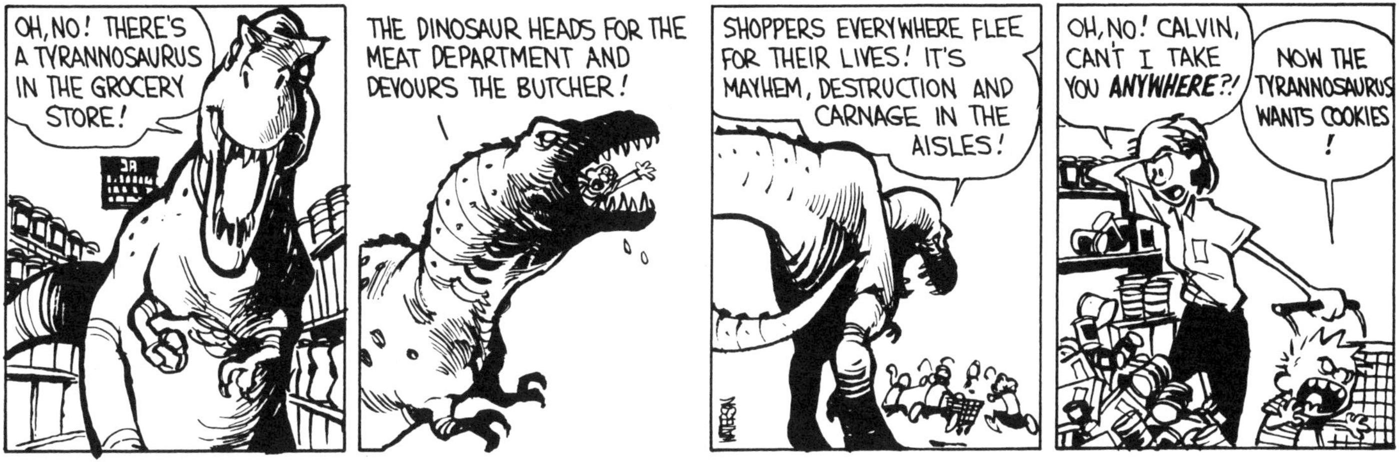
OH, NO! THERE'S A TYRANNOSAURUS IN THE GROCERY STORE!
THE DINOSAUR HEADS FOR THE MEAT DEPARTMENT AND DEVOURS THE BUTCHER!
SHOPPERS EVERYWHERE FLEE FOR THEIR LIVES! IT'S MAYHEM, DESTRUCTION AND CARNAGE IN THE AISLES!
OH, NO! CALVIN, CAN'T I TAKE YOU ANYWHERE?!
NOW THE TYRANNOSAURUS WANTS COOKIES!

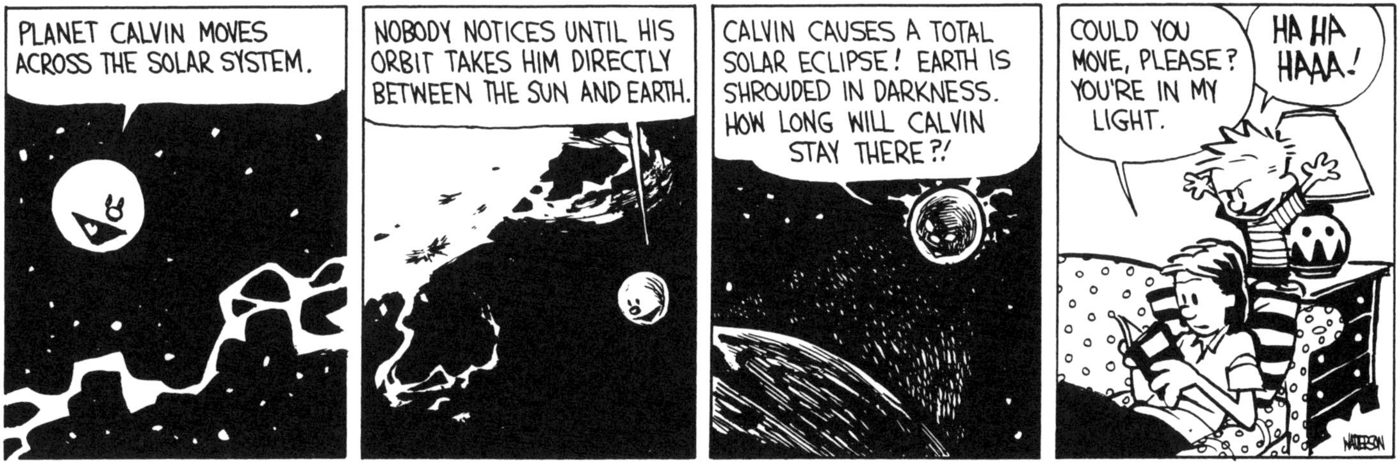
PLANET CALVIN MOVES ACROSS THE SOLAR SYSTEM.
NOBODY NOTICES UNTIL HIS ORBIT TAKES HIM DIRECTLY BETWEEN THE SUN AND EARTH.
CALVIN CAUSES A TOTAL SOLAR ECLIPSE! EARTH IS SHROUDED IN DARKNESS. HOW LONG WILL CALVIN STAY THERE?!
COULD YOU MOVE, PLEASE? YOU'RE IN MY LIGHT.
HA HA HAAA!

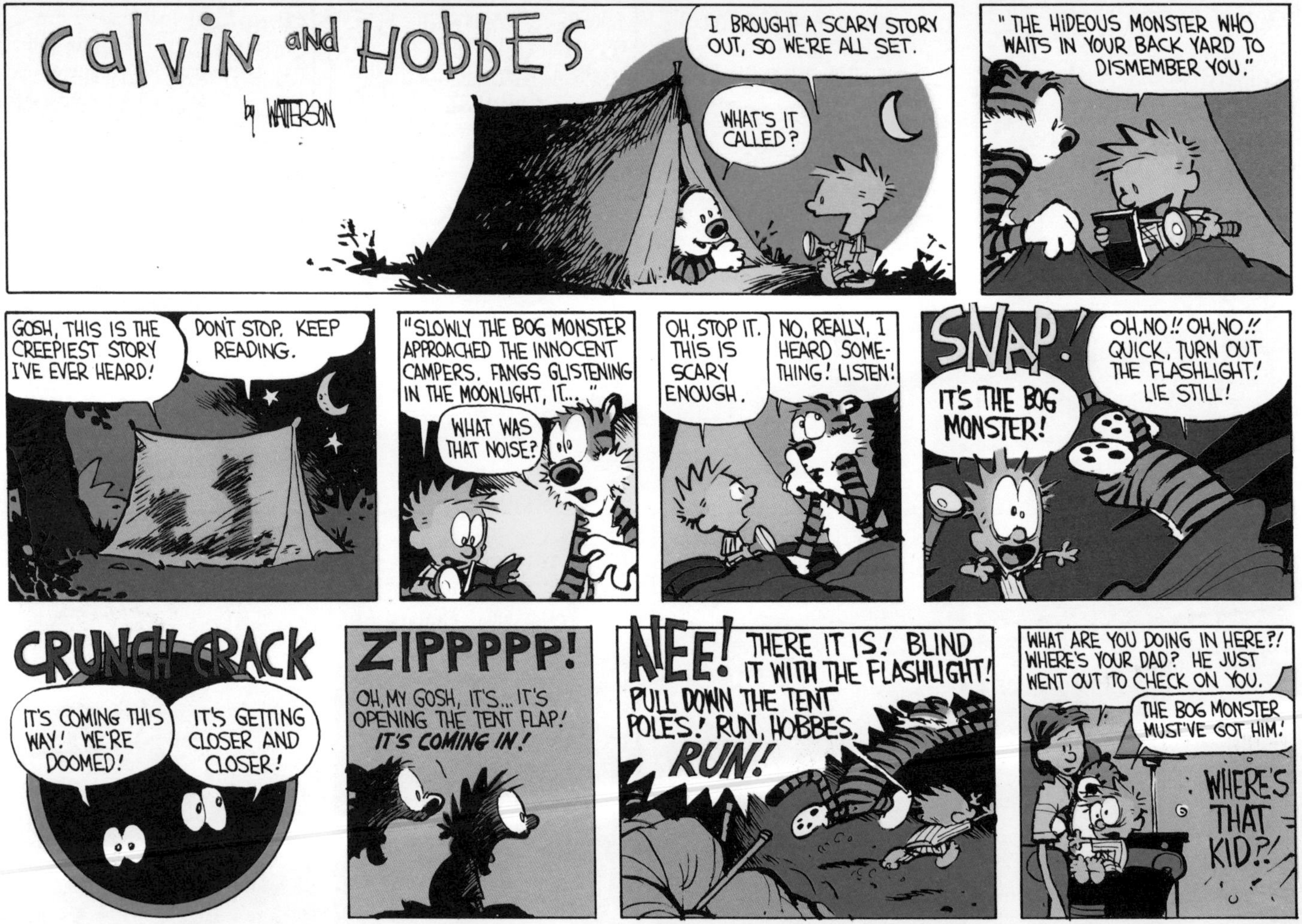
Calvin and HObbES
by WATTERSON
I BROUGHT A SCARY STORY OUT, SO WE'RE ALL SET.
WHAT'S IT CALLED?
"THE HIDEOUS MONSTER WHO WAITS IN YOUR BACK YARD TO DISMEMBER YOU."
GOSH, THIS IS THE CREEPIEST STORY I'VE EVER HEARD!
DON'T STOP. KEEP READING.
"SLOWLY THE BOG MONSTER APPROACHED THE INNOCENT CAMPERS. FANGS GLISTENING IN THE MOONLIGHT, IT..."
WHAT WAS THAT NOISE?
OH, STOP IT. THIS IS SCARY ENOUGH.
NO, REALLY, I HEARD SOMETHING! LISTEN!
SNAP!
IT'S THE BOG MONSTER!
OH, NO!! OH, NO!! QUICK, TURN OUT THE FLASHLIGHT! LIE STILL!
CRUNCH CRACK
IT'S COMING THIS WAY! WE'RE DOOMED!
IT'S GETTING CLOSER AND CLOSER!
ZIPPPPPP!
OH, MY GOSH, IT'S... IT'S OPENING THE TENT FLAP! IT'S COMING IN!
AIEE!
THERE IT IS! BLIND IT WITH THE FLASHLIGHT!
PULL DOWN THE TENT POLES! RUN, HOBBES, RUN!
WHAT ARE YOU DOING IN HERE?! WHERE'S YOUR DAD? HE JUST WENT OUT TO CHECK ON YOU.
THE BOG MONSTER MUST'VE GOT HIM!
WHERE'S THAT KID?!

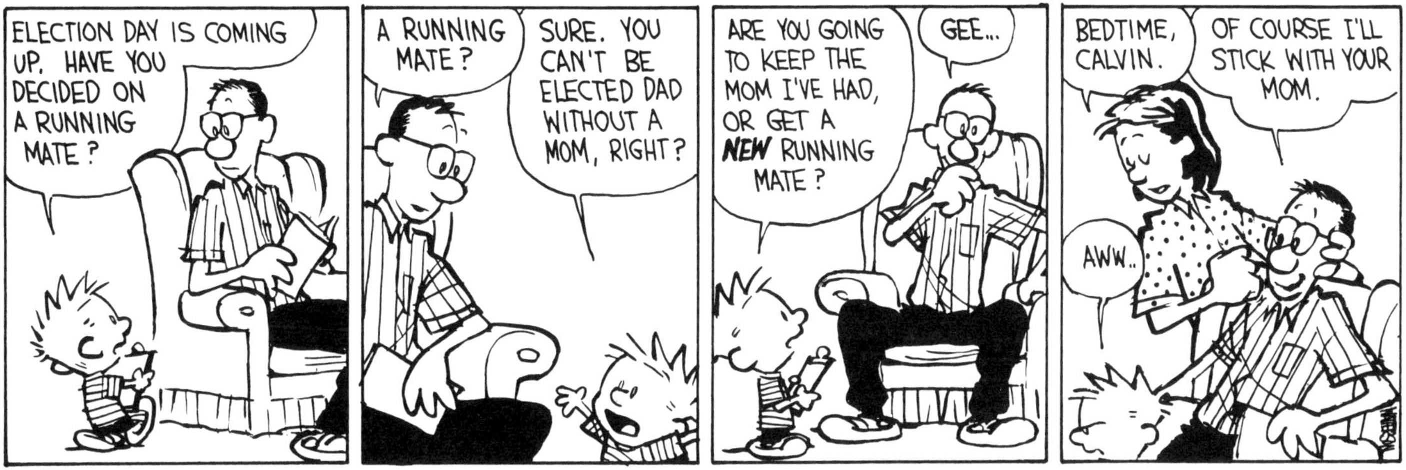
ELECTION DAY IS COMING UP. HAVE YOU DECIDED ON A RUNNING MATE?
A RUNNING MATE?
SURE. YOU CAN'T BE ELECTED DAD WITHOUT A MOM, RIGHT?
ARE YOU GOING TO KEEP THE MOM I'VE HAD, OR GET A NEW RUNNING MATE?
GEE...
BEDTIME, CALVIN.
OF COURSE I'LL STICK WITH YOUR MOM.
AWW..

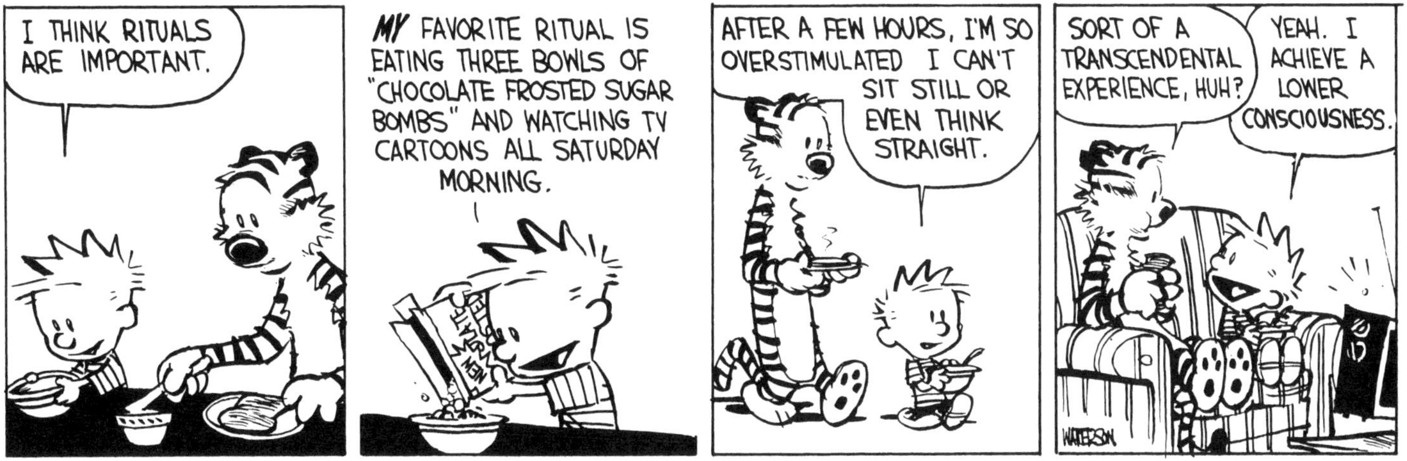
I THINK RITUALS ARE IMPORTANT.
MY FAVORITE RITUAL IS EATING THREE BOWLS OF "CHOCOLATE FROSTED SUGAR BOMBS" AND WATCHING TV CARTOONS ALL SATURDAY MORNING.
AFTER A FEW HOURS, I'M SO OVERSTIMULATED I CAN'T SIT STILL OR EVEN THINK STRAIGHT.
SORT OF A TRANSCENDENTAL EXPERIENCE, HUH?
YEAH. I ACHIEVE A LOWER CONSCIOUSNESS.

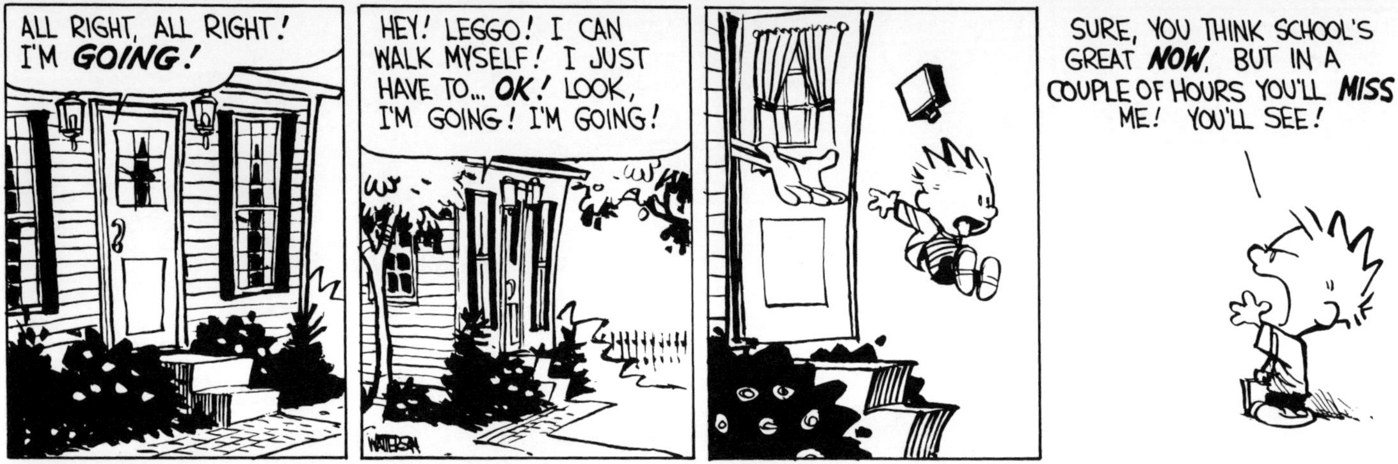
ALL RIGHT, ALL RIGHT! I'M **GOING!**
HEY! LEGGO! I CAN WALK MYSELF! I JUST HAVE TO... **OK!** LOOK, I'M GOING! I'M GOING!
SURE, YOU THINK SCHOOL'S GREAT **NOW**, BUT IN A COUPLE OF HOURS YOU'LL **MISS** ME! YOU'LL SEE!

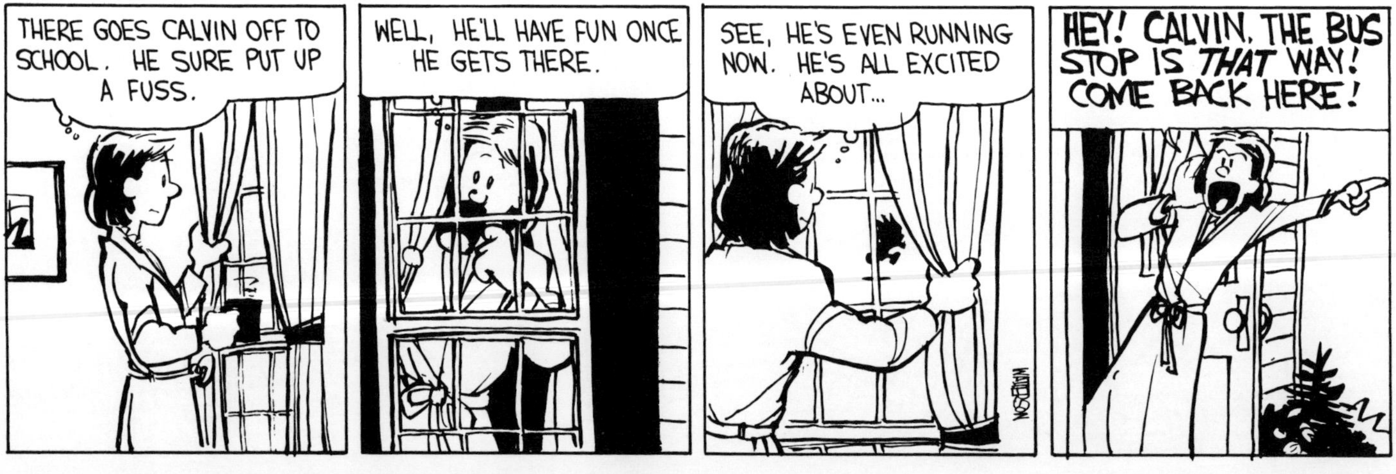
THERE GOES CALVIN OFF TO SCHOOL. HE SURE PUT UP A FUSS.
WELL, HE'LL HAVE FUN ONCE HE GETS THERE.
SEE, HE'S EVEN RUNNING NOW. HE'S ALL EXCITED ABOUT...
HEY! CALVIN, THE BUS STOP IS *THAT* WAY! COME BACK HERE!

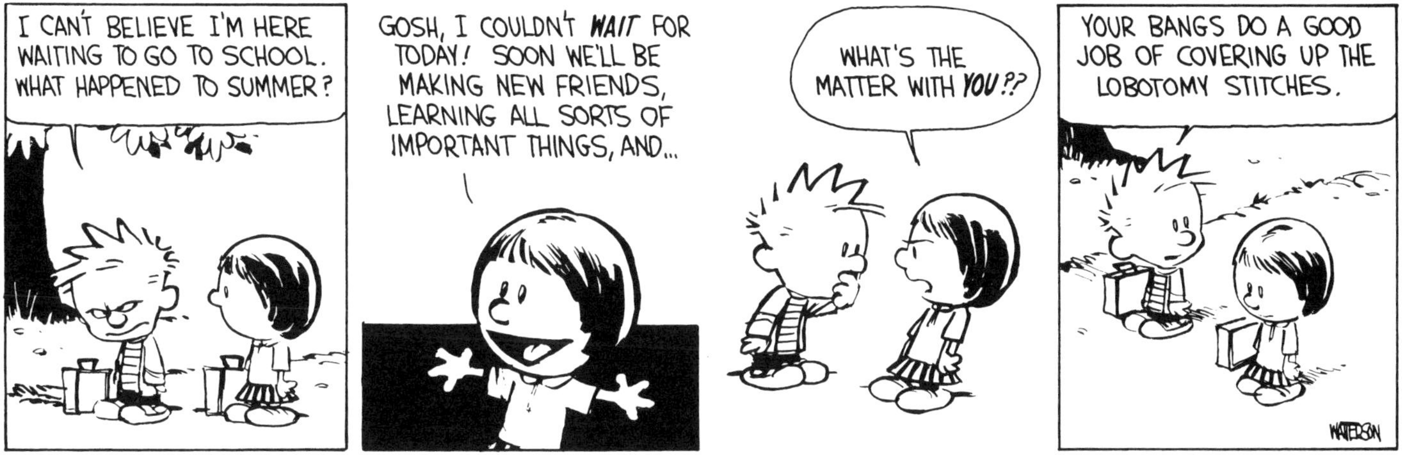
I CAN'T BELIEVE I'M HERE WAITING TO GO TO SCHOOL. WHAT HAPPENED TO SUMMER?
GOSH, I COULDN'T **WAIT** FOR TODAY! SOON WE'LL BE MAKING NEW FRIENDS, LEARNING ALL SORTS OF IMPORTANT THINGS, AND...
WHAT'S THE MATTER WITH **YOU**??
YOUR BANGS DO A GOOD JOB OF COVERING UP THE LOBOTOMY STITCHES.

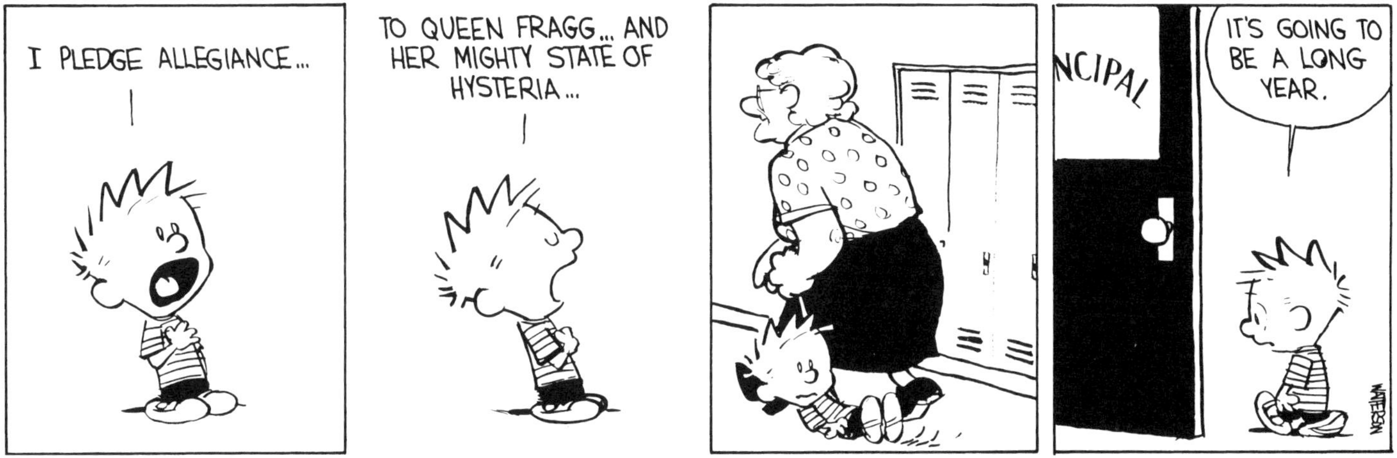
I PLEDGE ALLEGIANCE...
TO QUEEN FRAGG... AND HER MIGHTY STATE OF HYSTERIA...
NCIPAL
IT'S GOING TO BE A LONG YEAR.

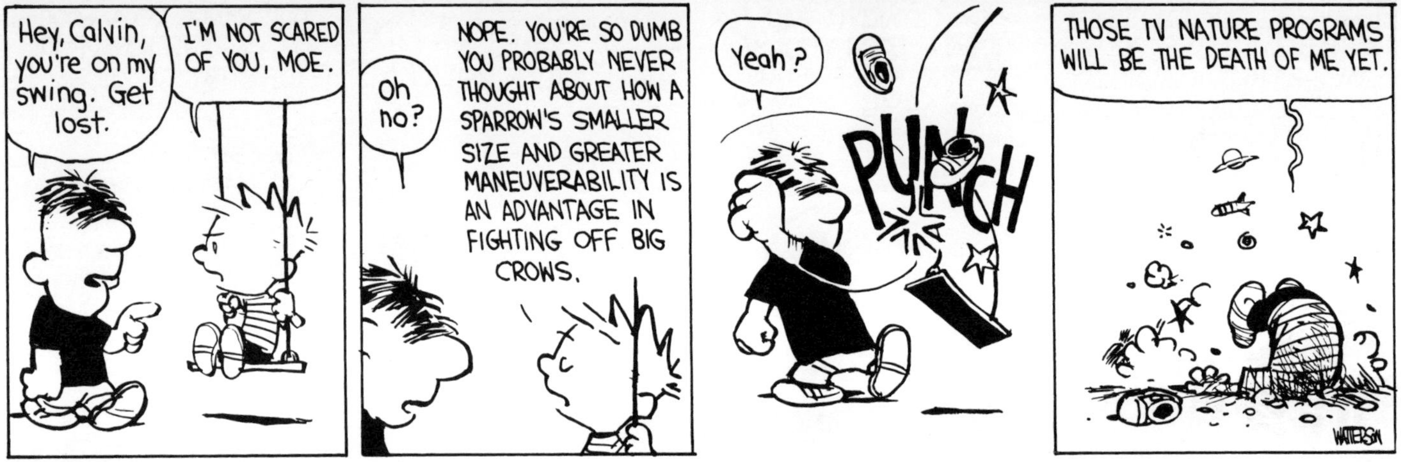
Hey, Calvin, you're on my swing. Get lost.
I'M NOT SCARED OF YOU, MOE.
Oh no?
NOPE. YOU'RE SO DUMB YOU PROBABLY NEVER THOUGHT ABOUT HOW A SPARROW'S SMALLER SIZE AND GREATER MANEUVERABILITY IS AN ADVANTAGE IN FIGHTING OFF BIG CROWS.
Yeah?
PUNCH
THOSE TV NATURE PROGRAMS WILL BE THE DEATH OF ME YET.
WATTERSON

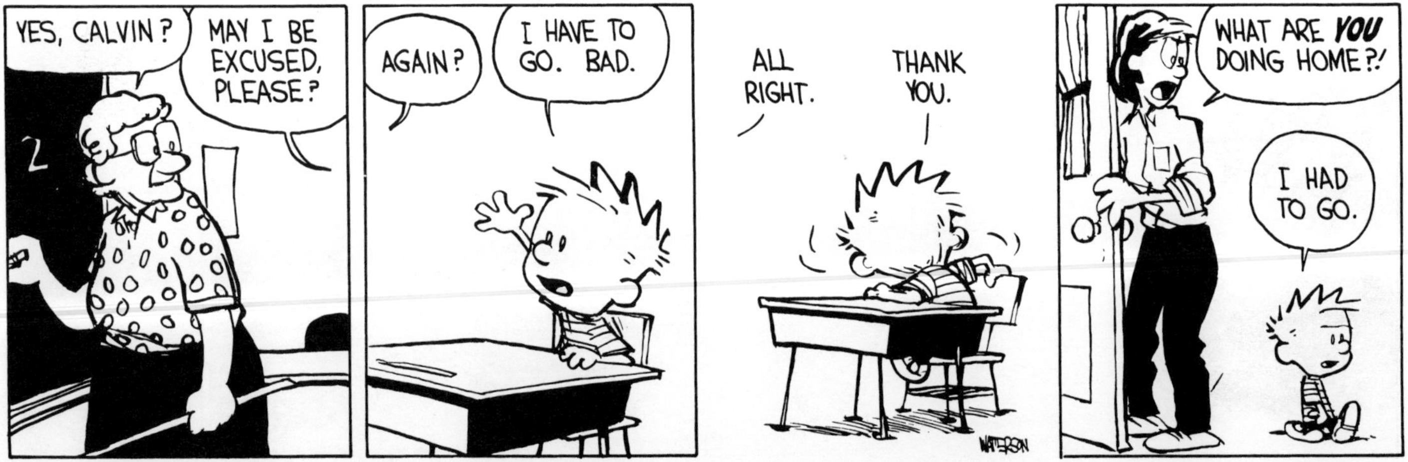
YES, CALVIN?
MAY I BE EXCUSED, PLEASE?
AGAIN?
I HAVE TO GO. BAD.
ALL RIGHT.
THANK YOU.
WATTERSON
WHAT ARE *YOU* DOING HOME?!
I HAD TO GO.

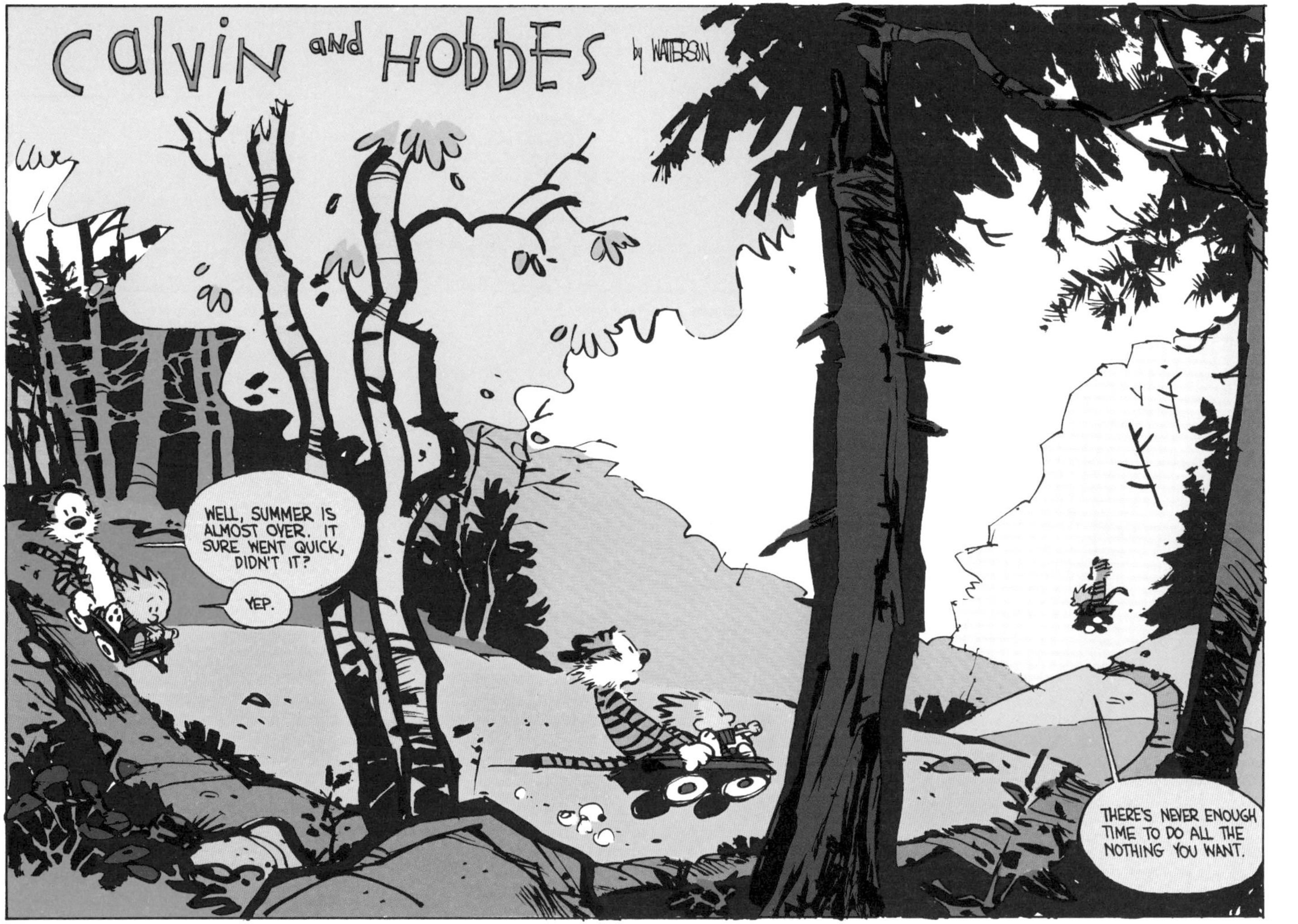
Calvin and HOBBES
by WATTERSON
WELL, SUMMER IS ALMOST OVER. IT SURE WENT QUICK, DIDN'T IT?
YEP.
THERE'S NEVER ENOUGH TIME TO DO ALL THE NOTHING YOU WANT.

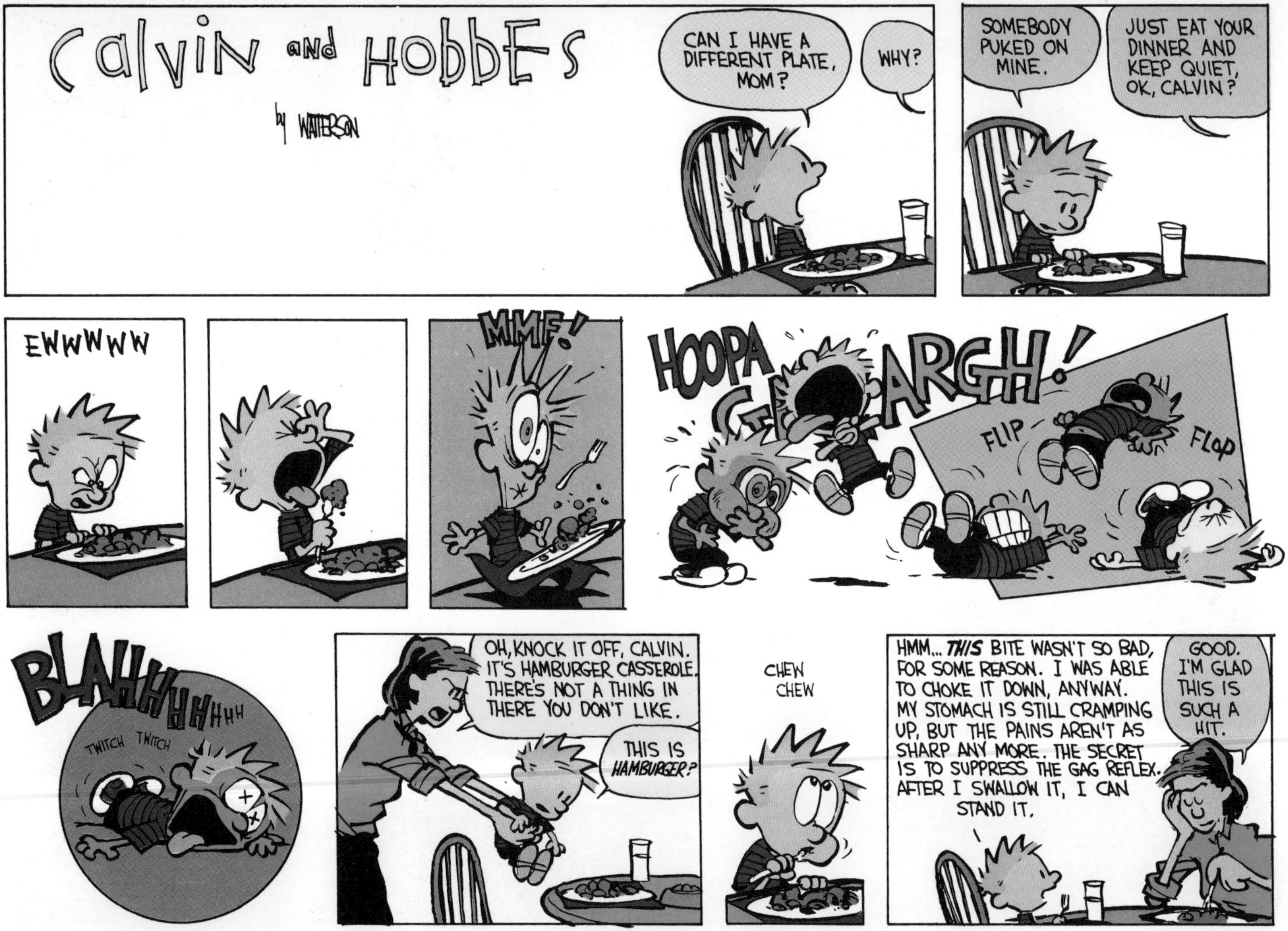
Calvin and HOBBES
by WATTERSON
CAN I HAVE A DIFFERENT PLATE, MOM?
WHY?
SOMEBODY PUKED ON MINE.
JUST EAT YOUR DINNER AND KEEP QUIET, OK, CALVIN?
EWWWWW
MIMF!
HOOPA
ARGH!
FLIP
FLOP
BLAHHHHHHHH
TWITCH TWITCH
OH, KNOCK IT OFF, CALVIN. IT'S HAMBURGER CASSEROLE. THERE'S NOT A THING IN THERE YOU DON'T LIKE.
THIS IS HAMBURGER?
CHEW
CHEW
HMM... THIS BITE WASN'T SO BAD, FOR SOME REASON. I WAS ABLE TO CHOKE IT DOWN, ANYWAY. MY STOMACH IS STILL CRAMPING UP, BUT THE PAINS AREN'T AS SHARP ANY MORE. THE SECRET IS TO SUPPRESS THE GAG REFLEX. AFTER I SWALLOW IT, I CAN STAND IT.
GOOD. I'M GLAD THIS IS SUCH A HIT.

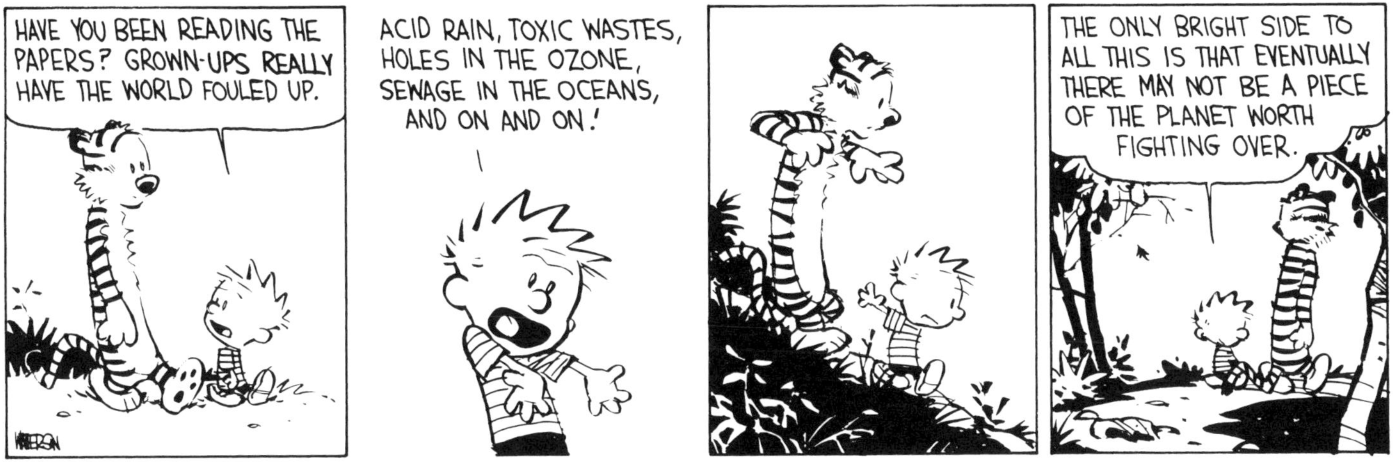
HAVE YOU BEEN READING THE PAPERS? GROWN-UPS REALLY HAVE THE WORLD FOULED UP.
ACID RAIN, TOXIC WASTES, HOLES IN THE OZONE, SEWAGE IN THE OCEANS, AND ON AND ON!
THE ONLY BRIGHT SIDE TO ALL THIS IS THAT EVENTUALLY THERE MAY NOT BE A PIECE OF THE PLANET WORTH FIGHTING OVER.
WATTERSON

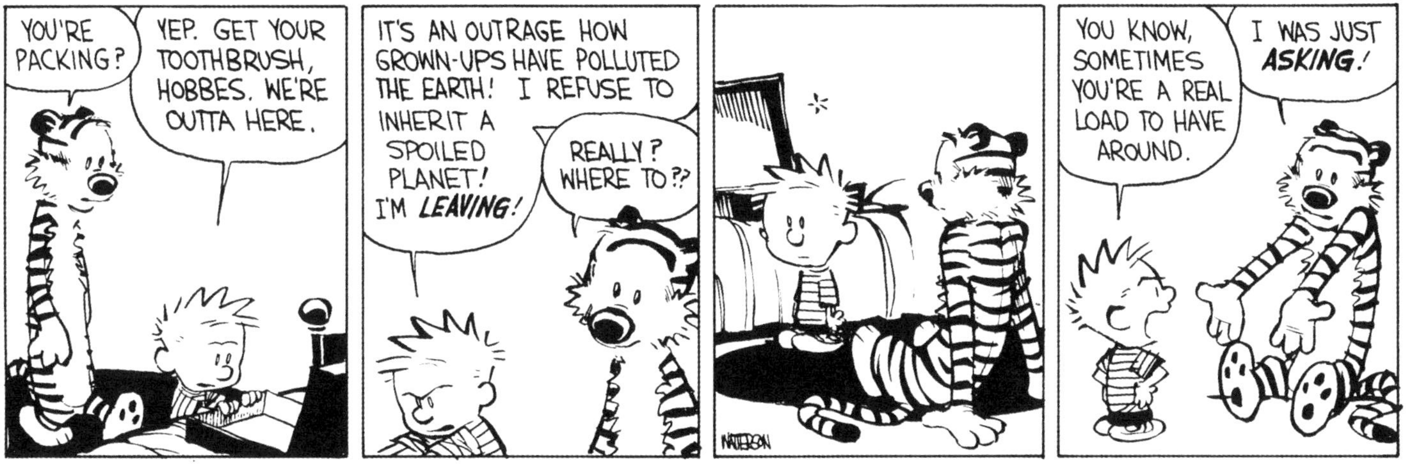
IT'S AN OUTRAGE HOW GROWN-UPS HAVE POLLUTED THE EARTH! I REFUSE TO INHERIT A SPOILED PLANET! I'M LEAVING!
REALLY? WHERE TO??
YOU'RE PACKING?
YEP. GET YOUR TOOTHBRUSH, HOBBES. WE'RE OUTTA HERE.
WATTERSON
YOU KNOW, SOMETIMES YOU'RE A REAL LOAD TO HAVE AROUND.
I WAS JUST ASKING!

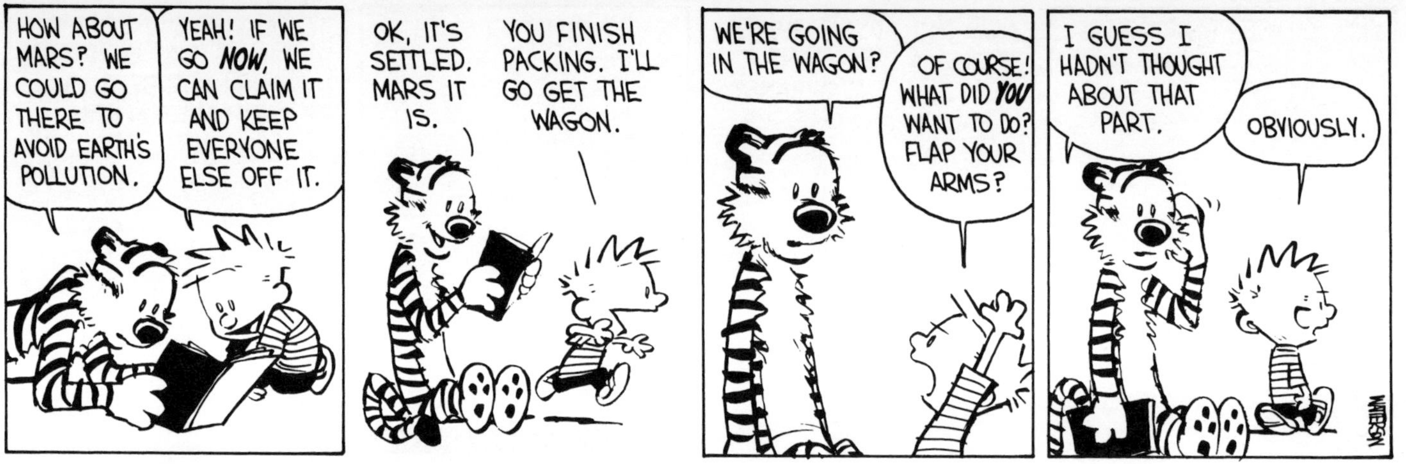
HOW ABOUT MARS? WE COULD GO THERE TO AVOID EARTH'S POLLUTION.
YEAH! IF WE GO *NOW*, WE CAN CLAIM IT AND KEEP EVERYONE ELSE OFF IT.
OK, IT'S SETTLED. MARS IT IS.
YOU FINISH PACKING. I'LL GO GET THE WAGON.
WE'RE GOING IN THE WAGON?
OF COURSE! WHAT DID *YOU* WANT TO DO? FLAP YOUR ARMS?
I GUESS I HADN'T THOUGHT ABOUT THAT PART.
OBVIOUSLY.
WATTERSON

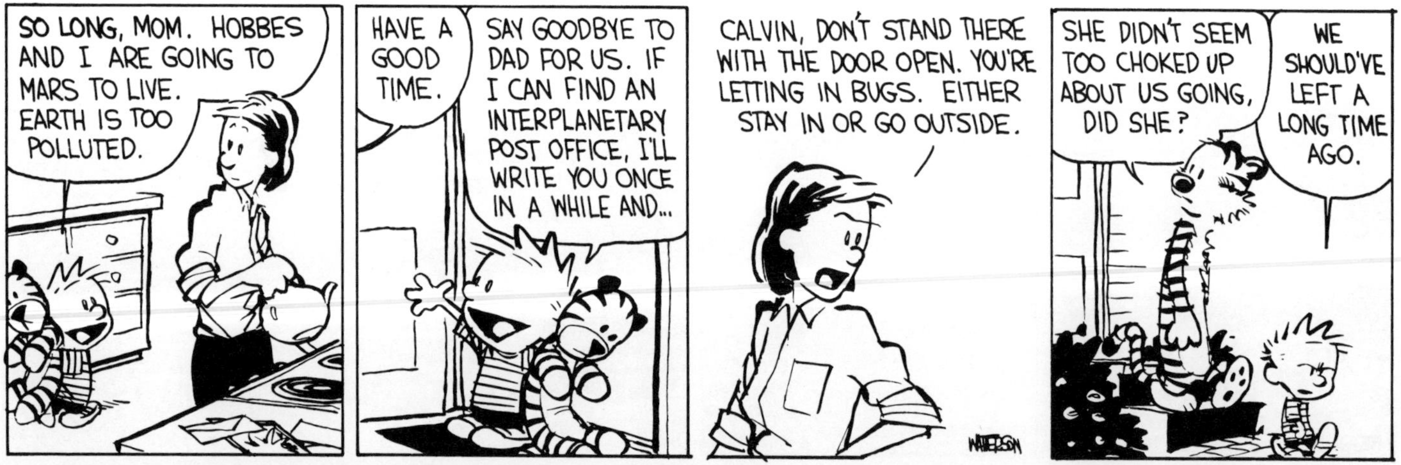
SO LONG, MOM. HOBBES AND I ARE GOING TO MARS TO LIVE. EARTH IS TOO POLLUTED.
HAVE A GOOD TIME.
SAY GOODBYE TO DAD FOR US. IF I CAN FIND AN INTERPLANETARY POST OFFICE, I'LL WRITE YOU ONCE IN A WHILE AND...
CALVIN, DON'T STAND THERE WITH THE DOOR OPEN. YOU'RE LETTING IN BUGS. EITHER STAY IN OR GO OUTSIDE.
WATTERSON
SHE DIDN'T SEEM TOO CHOKED UP ABOUT US GOING, DID SHE?
WE SHOULD'VE LEFT A LONG TIME AGO.

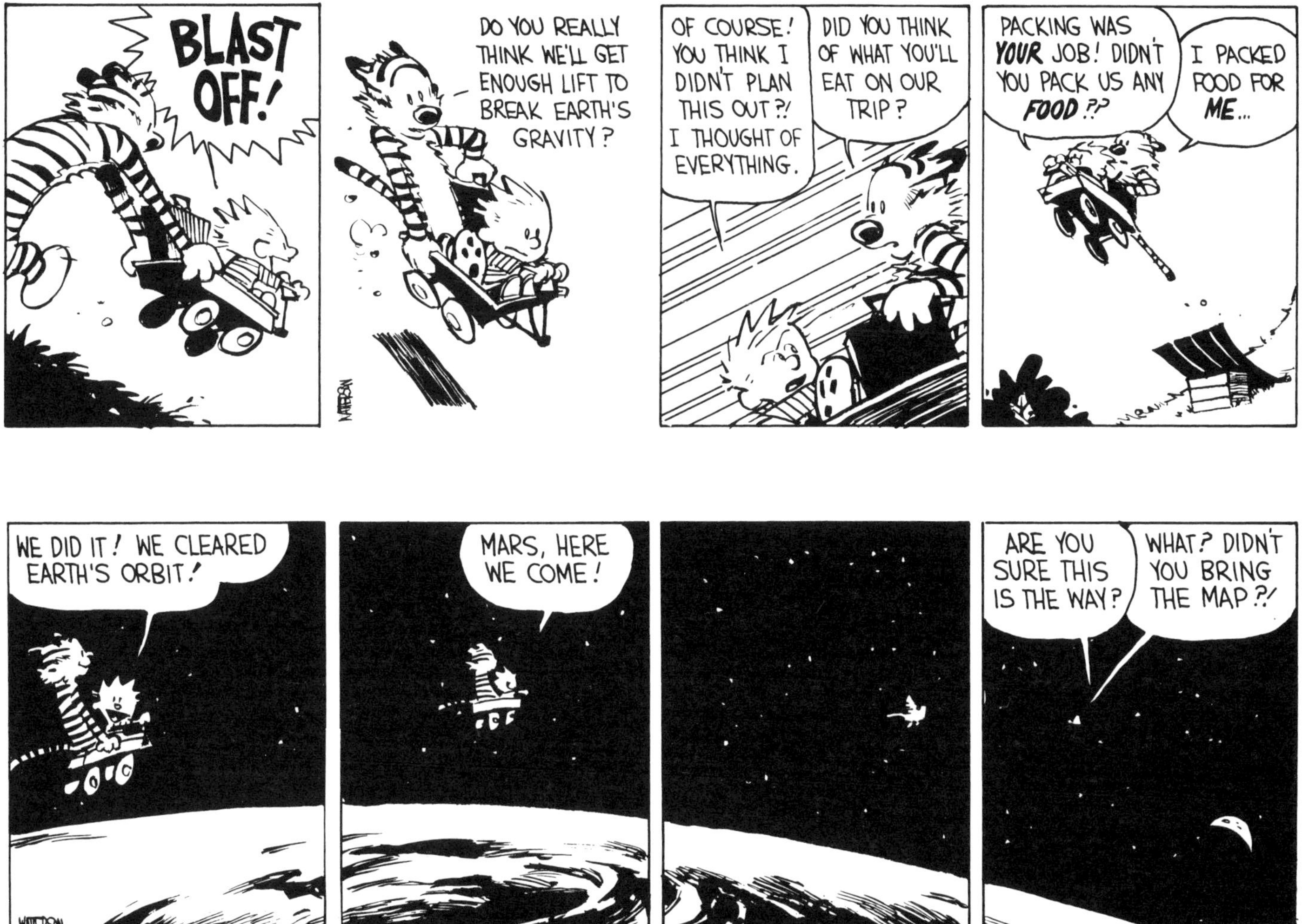
BLAST OFF!
DO YOU REALLY THINK WE'LL GET ENOUGH LIFT TO BREAK EARTH'S GRAVITY?
WATTERSON
OF COURSE! YOU THINK I DIDN'T PLAN THIS OUT?! I THOUGHT OF EVERYTHING.
DID YOU THINK OF WHAT YOU'LL EAT ON OUR TRIP?
PACKING WAS YOUR JOB! DIDN'T YOU PACK US ANY FOOD??
I PACKED FOOD FOR ME...
WE DID IT! WE CLEARED EARTH'S ORBIT!
WATTERSON
MARS, HERE WE COME!
ARE YOU SURE THIS IS THE WAY?
WHAT? DIDN'T YOU BRING THE MAP?!

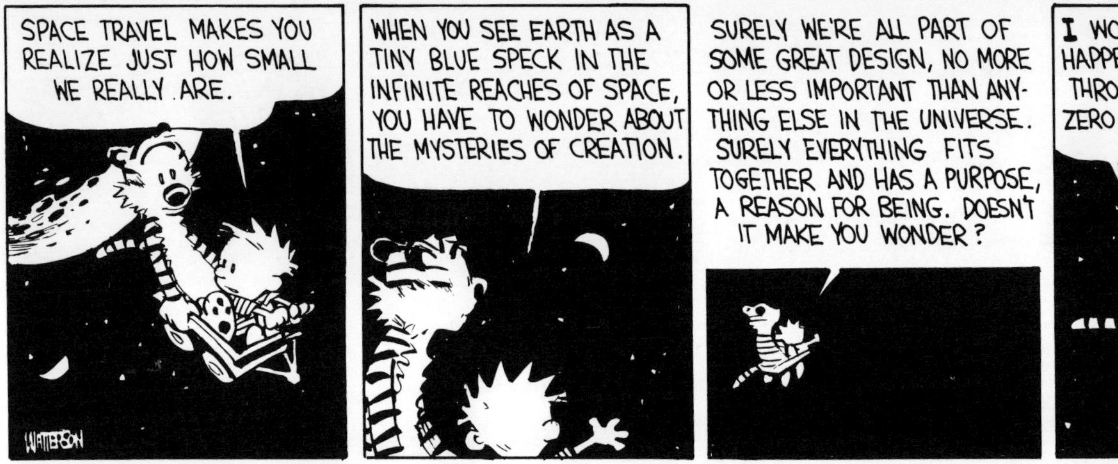
SPACE TRAVEL MAKES YOU REALIZE JUST HOW SMALL WE REALLY ARE.
WATTERSON
WHEN YOU SEE EARTH AS A TINY BLUE SPECK IN THE INFINITE REACHES OF SPACE, YOU HAVE TO WONDER ABOUT THE MYSTERIES OF CREATION.
SURELY WE'RE ALL PART OF SOME GREAT DESIGN, NO MORE OR LESS IMPORTANT THAN ANYTHING ELSE IN THE UNIVERSE. SURELY EVERYTHING FITS TOGETHER AND HAS A PURPOSE, A REASON FOR BEING. DOESN'T IT MAKE YOU WONDER?
I WONDER WHAT HAPPENS IF YOU THROW UP IN ZERO GRAVITY.
MAYBE YOU SHOULD WONDER WHAT IT'S LIKE TO WALK HOME.
9-19

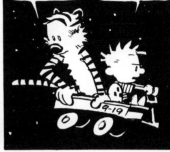

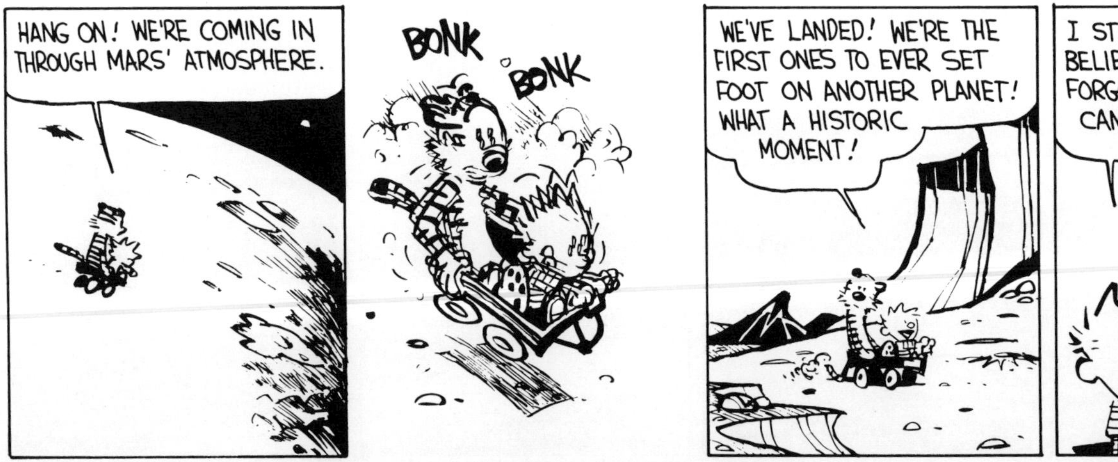
HANG ON! WE'RE COMING IN THROUGH MARS' ATMOSPHERE.
BONK
BONK
WE'VE LANDED! WE'RE THE FIRST ONES TO EVER SET FOOT ON ANOTHER PLANET! WHAT A HISTORIC MOMENT!
I STILL CAN'T BELIEVE YOU FORGOT THE CAMERA.
I REMEMBERED IT. YOU JUST DIDN'T WANT TO TURN AROUND.
WATTERSON

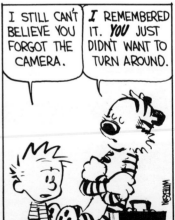

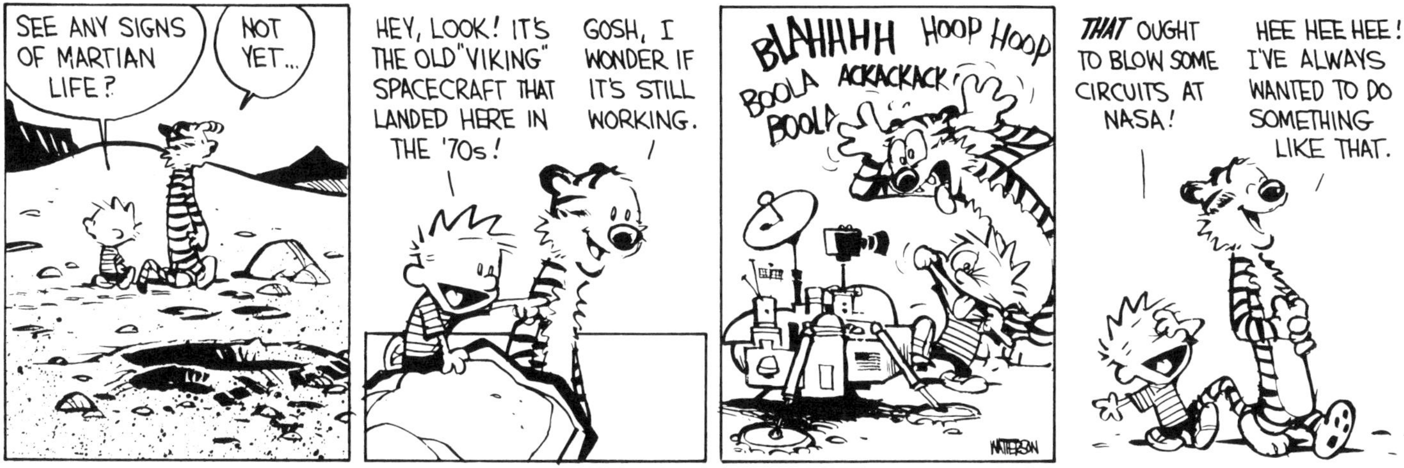
SEE ANY SIGNS OF MARTIAN LIFE?
NOT YET...
HEY, LOOK! IT'S THE OLD "VIKING" SPACECRAFT THAT LANDED HERE IN THE '70s!
GOSH, I WONDER IF IT'S STILL WORKING.
BLAHHHH HOOP HOOP BOOLA ACKACKACK BOOLA
THAT OUGHT TO BLOW SOME CIRCUITS AT NASA!
HEE HEE HEE! I'VE ALWAYS WANTED TO DO SOMETHING LIKE THAT.

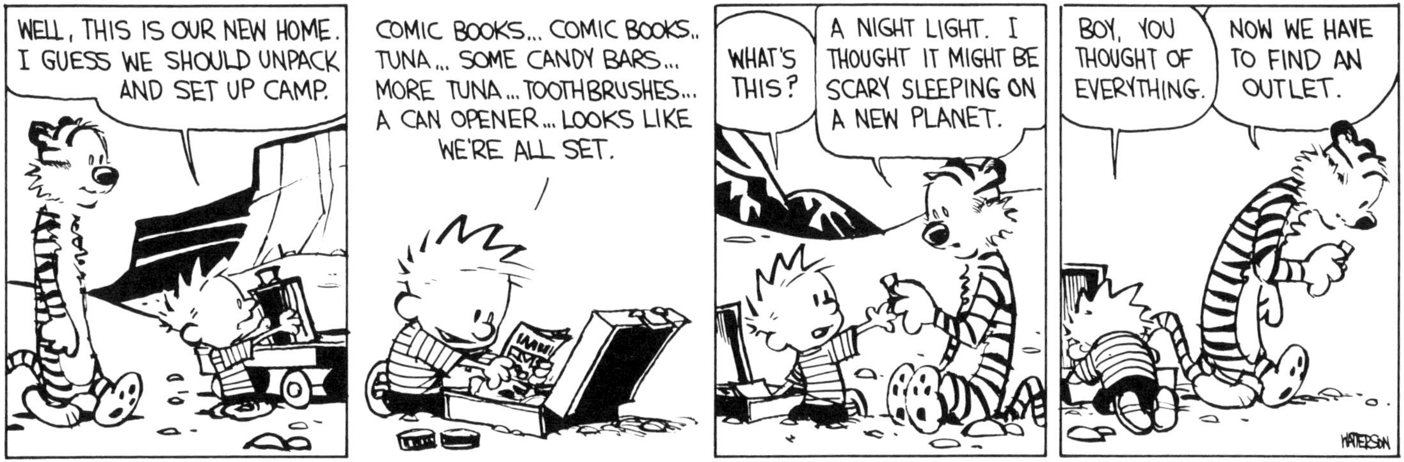
WELL, THIS IS OUR NEW HOME. I GUESS WE SHOULD UNPACK AND SET UP CAMP.
COMIC BOOKS... COMIC BOOKS.. TUNA... SOME CANDY BARS... MORE TUNA... TOOTHBRUSHES... A CAN OPENER... LOOKS LIKE WE'RE ALL SET.
WHAT'S THIS?
A NIGHT LIGHT. I THOUGHT IT MIGHT BE SCARY SLEEPING ON A NEW PLANET.
BOY, YOU THOUGHT OF EVERYTHING.
NOW WE HAVE TO FIND AN OUTLET.

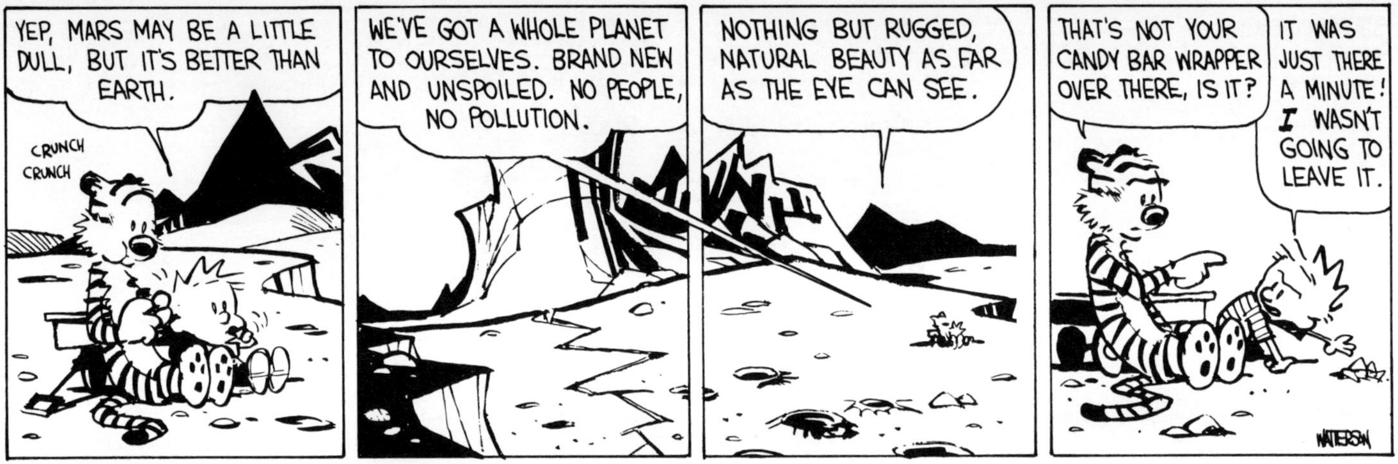
YEP, MARS MAY BE A LITTLE DULL, BUT IT'S BETTER THAN EARTH.
CRUNCH CRUNCH
WE'VE GOT A WHOLE PLANET TO OURSELVES. BRAND NEW AND UNSPOILED. NO PEOPLE, NO POLLUTION.
NOTHING BUT RUGGED, NATURAL BEAUTY AS FAR AS THE EYE CAN SEE.
THAT'S NOT YOUR CANDY BAR WRAPPER OVER THERE, IS IT?
IT WAS JUST THERE A MINUTE! *I* WASN'T GOING TO LEAVE IT.
WATTERSON

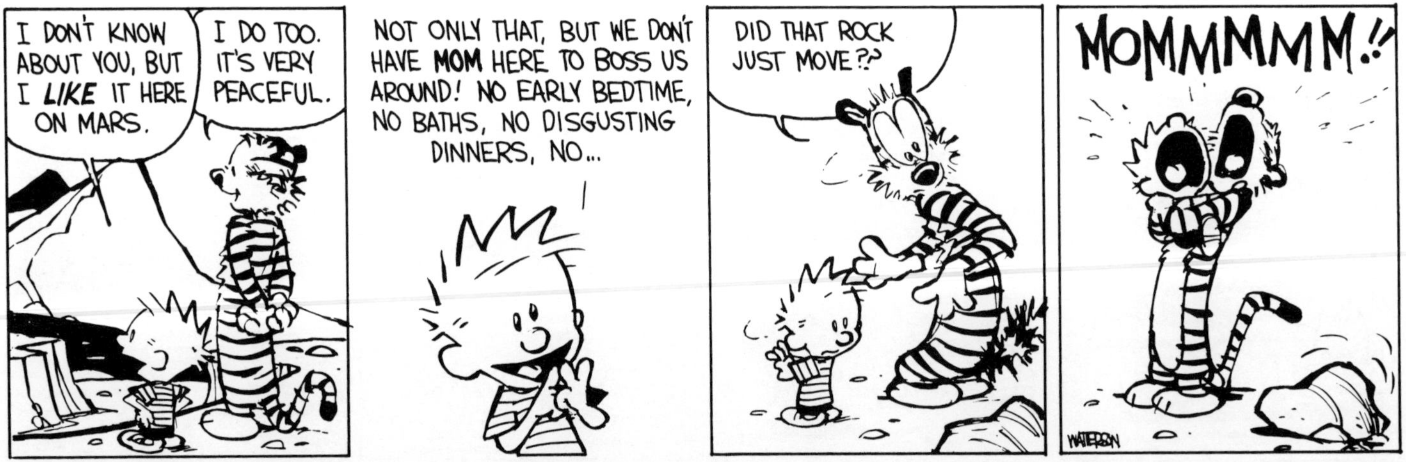
I DON'T KNOW ABOUT YOU, BUT I ***LIKE*** IT HERE ON MARS.
I DO TOO. IT'S VERY PEACEFUL.
NOT ONLY THAT, BUT WE DON'T HAVE **MOM** HERE TO BOSS US AROUND! NO EARLY BEDTIME, NO BATHS, NO DISGUSTING DINNERS, NO...
DID THAT ROCK JUST MOVE?!?
MOMMMMM!!
WATTERSON

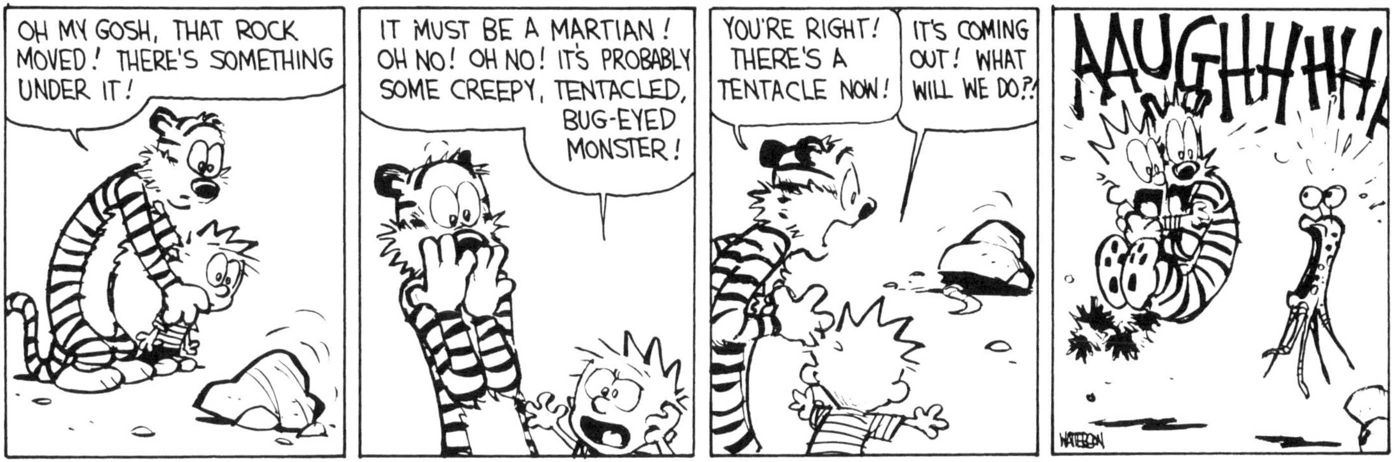
OH MY GOSH, THAT ROCK MOVED! THERE'S SOMETHING UNDER IT!
IT MUST BE A MARTIAN! OH NO! OH NO! IT'S PROBABLY SOME CREEPY, TENTACLED, BUG-EYED MONSTER!
YOU'RE RIGHT! THERE'S A TENTACLE NOW!
IT'S COMING OUT! WHAT WILL WE DO?!
AAUGHHHHH
WATTERSON

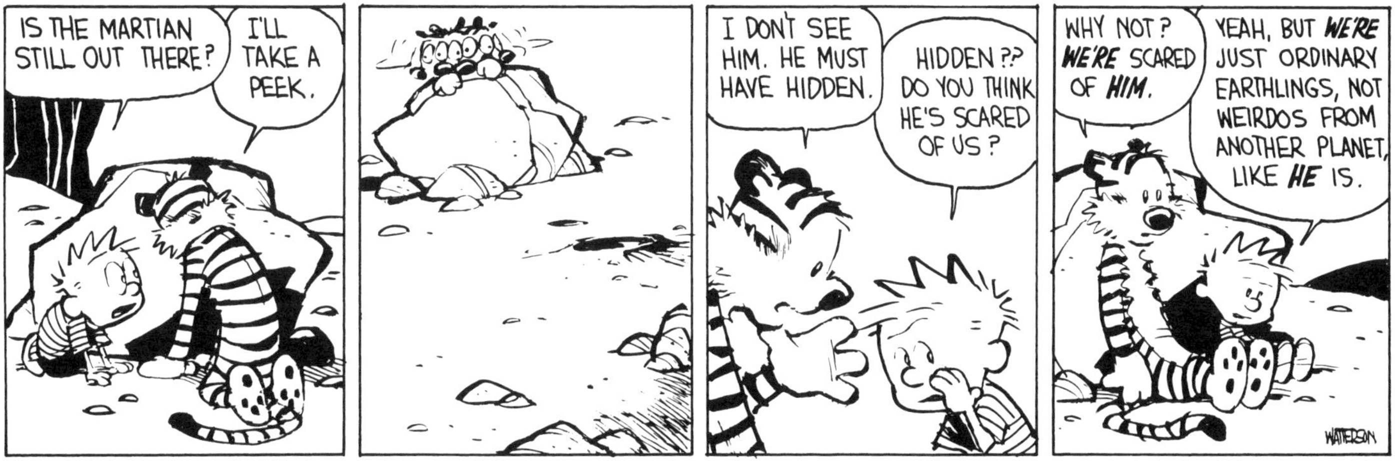
IS THE MARTIAN STILL OUT THERE?
I'LL TAKE A PEEK.
I DON'T SEE HIM. HE MUST HAVE HIDDEN.
HIDDEN?? DO YOU THINK HE'S SCARED OF US?
WHY NOT? WE'RE SCARED OF HIM.
YEAH, BUT WE'RE JUST ORDINARY EARTHLINGS, NOT WEIRDOS FROM ANOTHER PLANET, LIKE HE IS.
WATTERSON

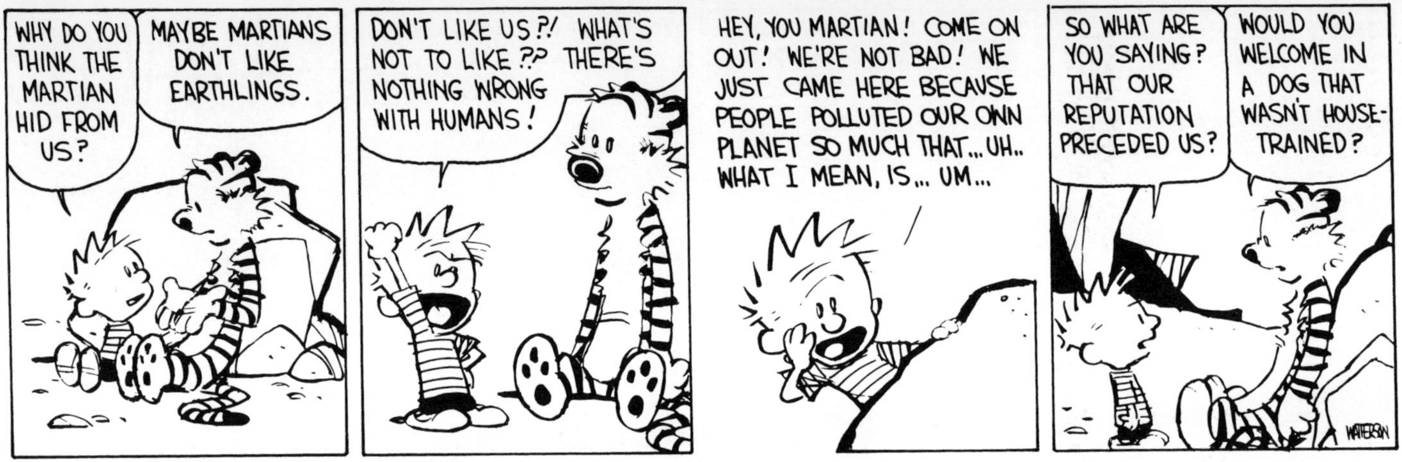
WHY DO YOU THINK THE MARTIAN HID FROM US?
MAYBE MARTIANS DON'T LIKE EARTHLINGS.
DON'T LIKE US?! WHAT'S NOT TO LIKE?? THERE'S NOTHING WRONG WITH HUMANS!
HEY, YOU MARTIAN! COME ON OUT! WE'RE NOT BAD! WE JUST CAME HERE BECAUSE PEOPLE POLLUTED OUR OWN PLANET SO MUCH THAT... UH.. WHAT I MEAN, IS... UM...
SO WHAT ARE YOU SAYING? THAT OUR REPUTATION PRECEDED US?
WOULD YOU WELCOME IN A DOG THAT WASN'T HOUSE-TRAINED?
WATTERSON

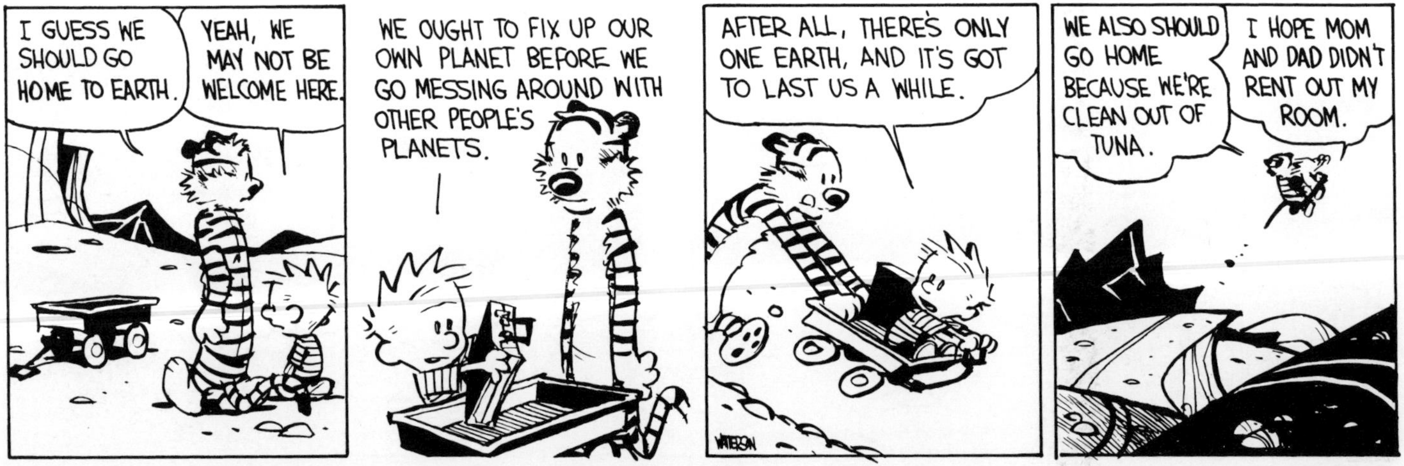
I GUESS WE SHOULD GO HOME TO EARTH.
YEAH, WE MAY NOT BE WELCOME HERE.
WE OUGHT TO FIX UP OUR OWN PLANET BEFORE WE GO MESSING AROUND WITH OTHER PEOPLE'S PLANETS.
AFTER ALL, THERE'S ONLY ONE EARTH, AND IT'S GOT TO LAST US A WHILE.
WATTERSON
WE ALSO SHOULD GO HOME BECAUSE WE'RE CLEAN OUT OF TUNA.
I HOPE MOM AND DAD DIDN'T RENT OUT MY ROOM.

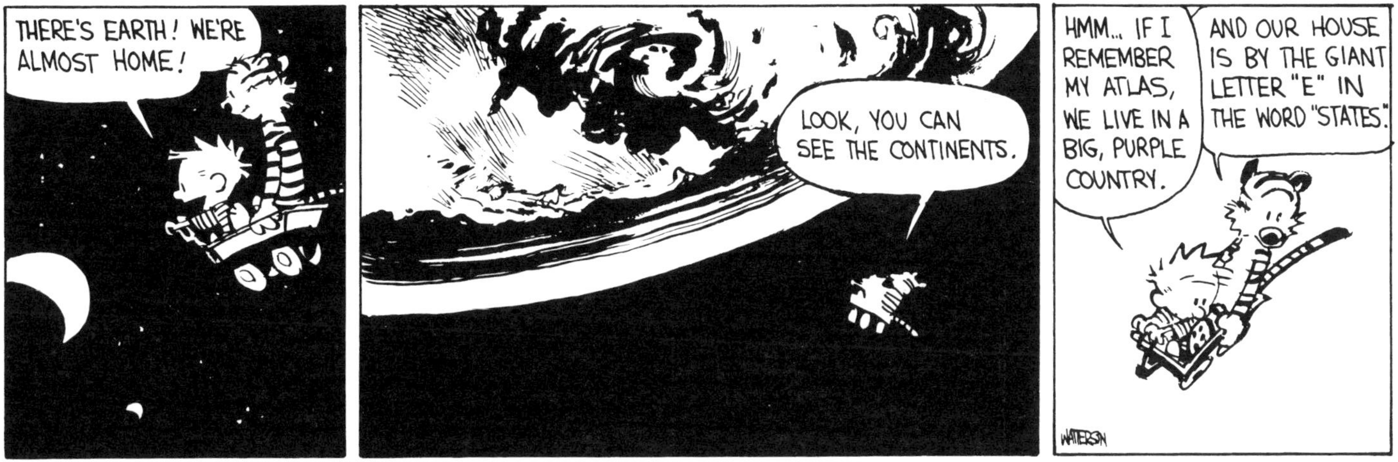
THERE'S EARTH! WE'RE ALMOST HOME!
LOOK, YOU CAN SEE THE CONTINENTS.
HMM... IF I REMEMBER MY ATLAS, WE LIVE IN A BIG, PURPLE COUNTRY.
AND OUR HOUSE IS BY THE GIANT LETTER "E" IN THE WORD "STATES."
WATTERSON

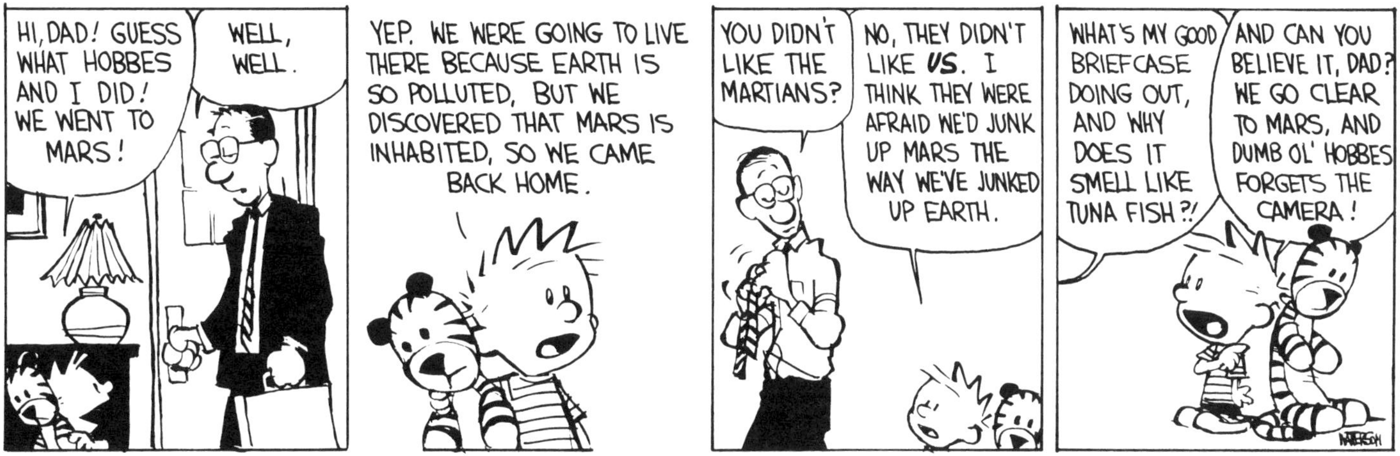
HI, DAD! GUESS WHAT HOBBES AND I DID! WE WENT TO MARS!
WELL, WELL.
YEP. WE WERE GOING TO LIVE THERE BECAUSE EARTH IS SO POLLUTED, BUT WE DISCOVERED THAT MARS IS INHABITED, SO WE CAME BACK HOME.
YOU DIDN'T LIKE THE MARTIANS?
NO, THEY DIDN'T LIKE US. I THINK THEY WERE AFRAID WE'D JUNK UP MARS THE WAY WE'VE JUNKED UP EARTH.
WHAT'S MY GOOD BRIEFCASE DOING OUT, AND WHY DOES IT SMELL LIKE TUNA FISH?!
AND CAN YOU BELIEVE IT, DAD? WE GO CLEAR TO MARS, AND DUMB OL' HOBBES FORGETS THE CAMERA!
WATTERSON

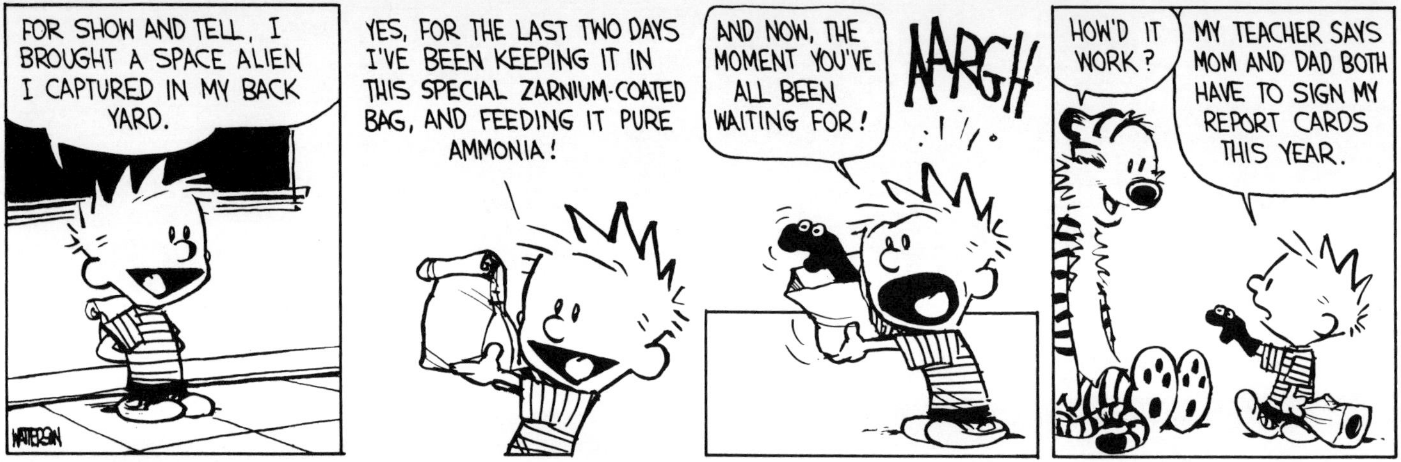
FOR SHOW AND TELL, I BROUGHT A SPACE ALIEN I CAPTURED IN MY BACK YARD.
YES, FOR THE LAST TWO DAYS I'VE BEEN KEEPING IT IN THIS SPECIAL ZARNIUM-COATED BAG, AND FEEDING IT PURE AMMONIA!
AND NOW, THE MOMENT YOU'VE ALL BEEN WAITING FOR!
AARGH
HOW'D IT WORK?
MY TEACHER SAYS MOM AND DAD BOTH HAVE TO SIGN MY REPORT CARDS THIS YEAR.

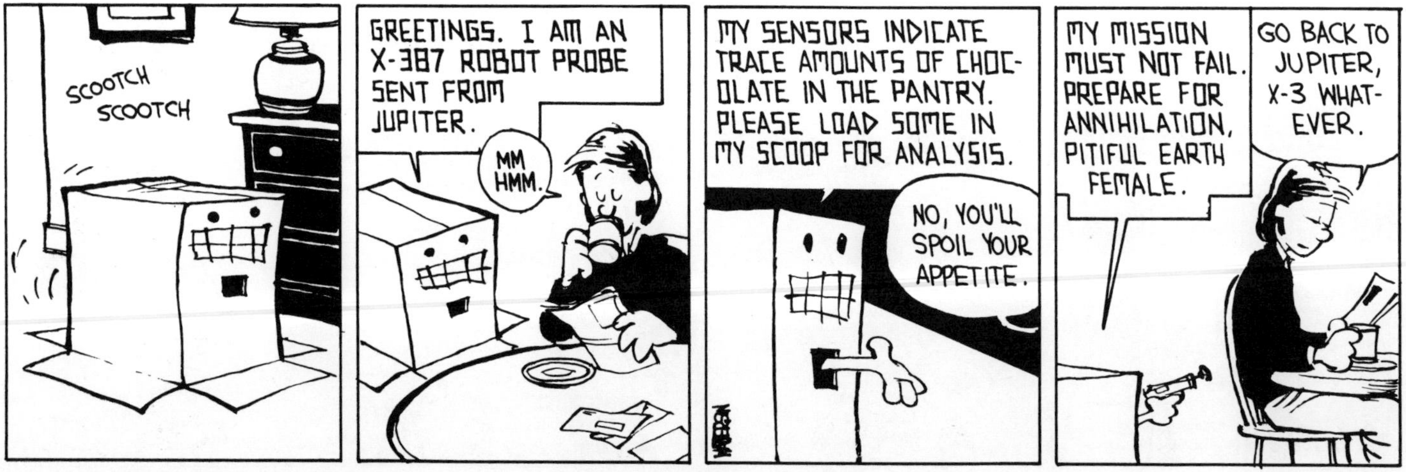
SCOOTCH
SCOOTCH
GREETINGS. I AM AN X-387 ROBOT PROBE SENT FROM JUPITER.
MM HMM.
MY SENSORS INDICATE TRACE AMOUNTS OF CHOC-OLATE IN THE PANTRY. PLEASE LOAD SOME IN MY SCOOP FOR ANALYSIS.
NO, YOU'LL SPOIL YOUR APPETITE.
MY MISSION MUST NOT FAIL. PREPARE FOR ANNIHILATION, PITIFUL EARTH FEMALE.
GO BACK TO JUPITER, X-3 WHAT-EVER.

Calvin and HOBBES
by WATTERSON
SCHOOL'S OUT! FREE AT LAST!
AND JUST SIX PRECIOUS HOURS BEFORE BED TO FORGET EVERYTHING I LEARNED TODAY.
I HATE COMING HOME FROM SCHOOL. I NEVER KNOW IF HOBBES IS WAITING TO POUNCE ON ME.
MAYBE I CAN STAND OFF TO THE SIDE HERE, AND PUSH THE DOOR OPEN WITH A STICK.
I'M HOME!
KAPOW!
WHAT DO YOU DO, WAIT UNTIL YOU SEE THE WHITES OF MY EYES?!?
BOY, YOU SHOULD'VE **SEEN** THEM! THEY WERE AS BIG AS DINNER PLATES! HOO HOO HOO!

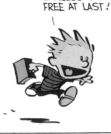

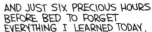

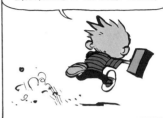

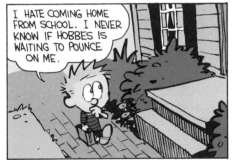

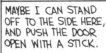

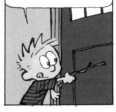

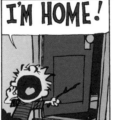

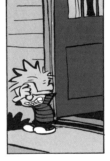

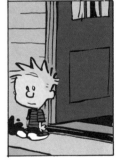

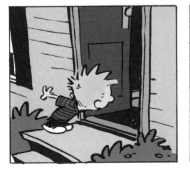

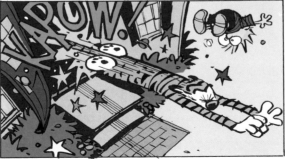

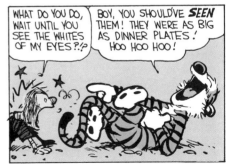

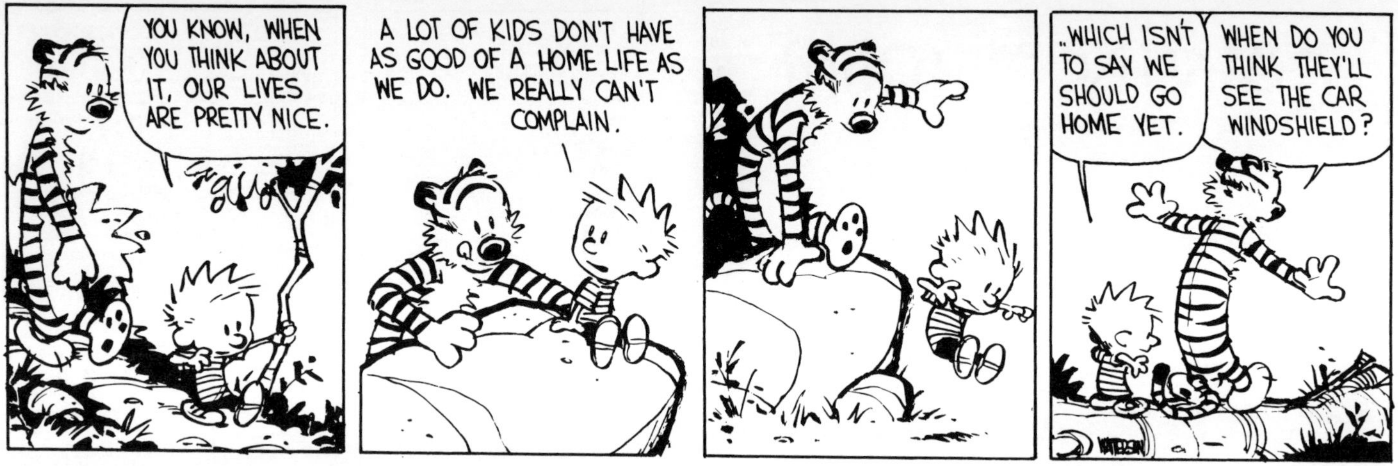

YOU KNOW, WHEN YOU THINK ABOUT IT, OUR LIVES ARE PRETTY NICE.
A LOT OF KIDS DON'T HAVE AS GOOD OF A HOME LIFE AS WE DO. WE REALLY CAN'T COMPLAIN.
..WHICH ISN'T TO SAY WE SHOULD GO HOME YET.
WHEN DO YOU THINK THEY'LL SEE THE CAR WINDSHIELD?
WATERSON

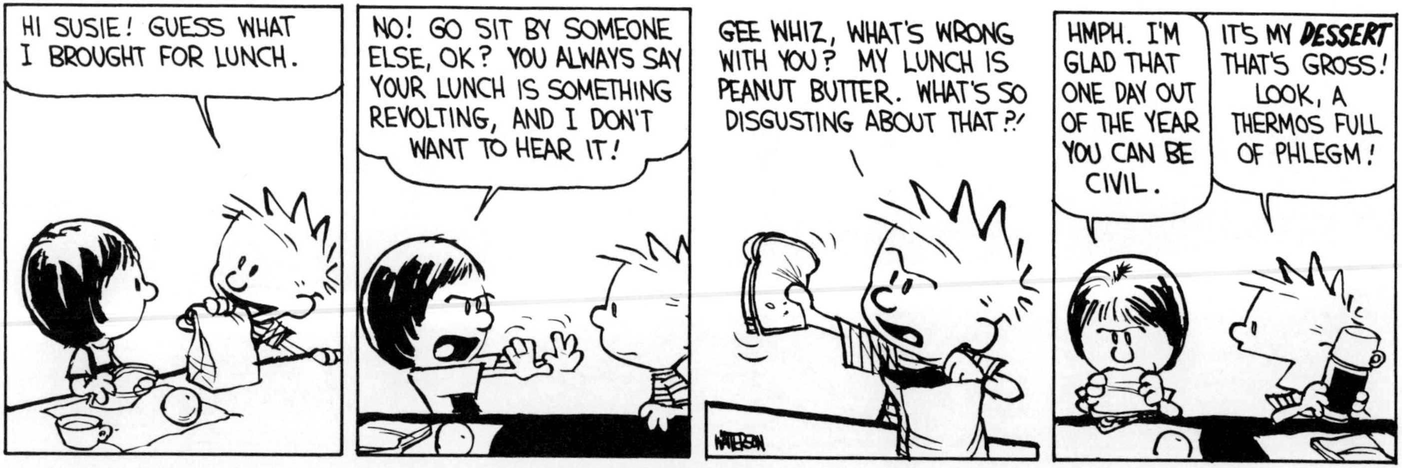

HI SUSIE! GUESS WHAT I BROUGHT FOR LUNCH.
NO! GO SIT BY SOMEONE ELSE, OK? YOU ALWAYS SAY YOUR LUNCH IS SOMETHING REVOLTING, AND I DON'T WANT TO HEAR IT!
GEE WHIZ, WHAT'S WRONG WITH YOU? MY LUNCH IS PEANUT BUTTER. WHAT'S SO DISGUSTING ABOUT THAT?!
WATERSON
HMPH. I'M GLAD THAT ONE DAY OUT OF THE YEAR YOU CAN BE CIVIL.
IT'S MY **DESSERT** THAT'S GROSS! LOOK, A THERMOS FULL OF PHLEGM!

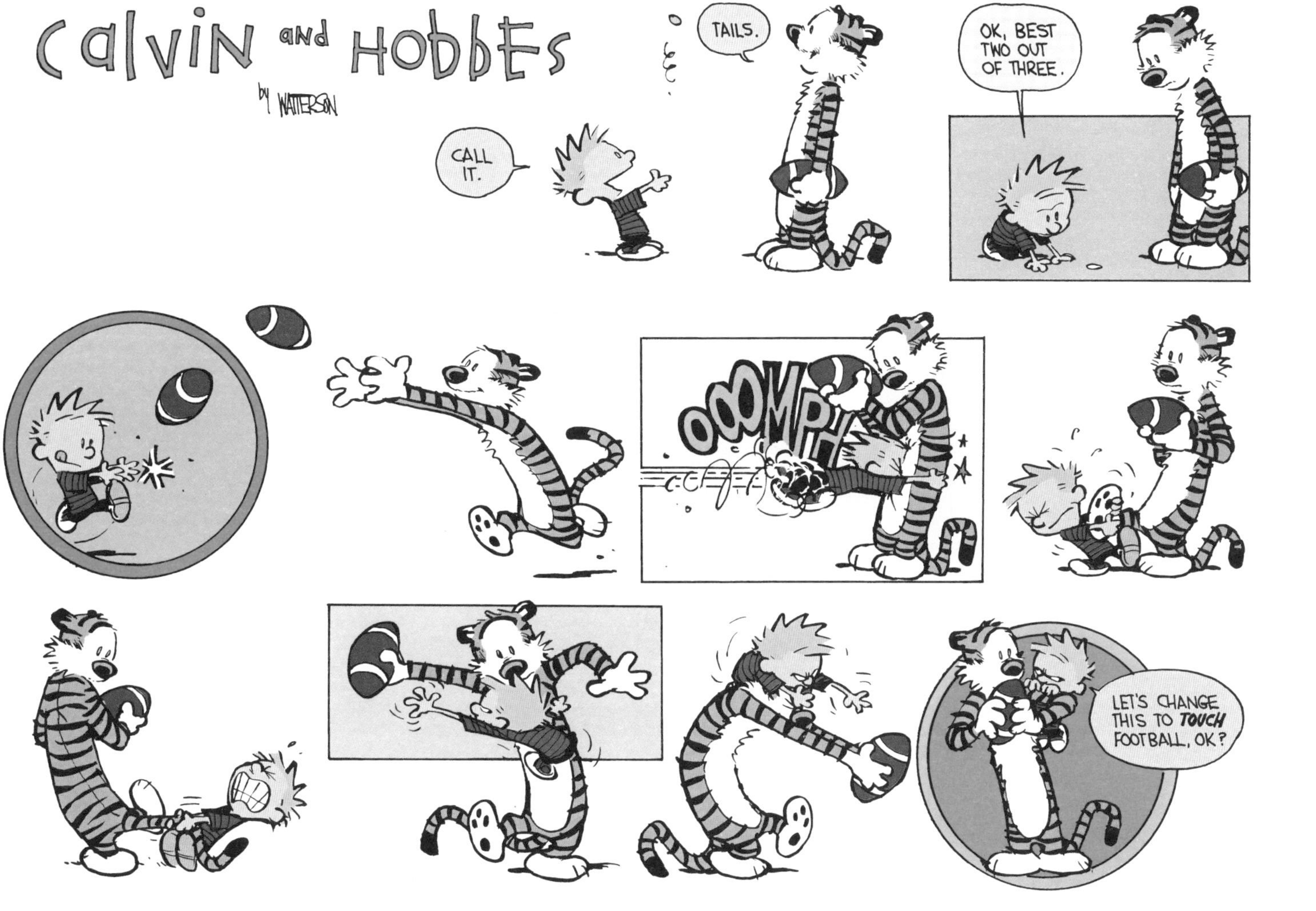
Calvin and HOBBES
by WATTERSON
CALL IT.
TAILS.
OK, BEST TWO OUT OF THREE.
OOOMPH
LET'S CHANGE THIS TO TOUCH FOOTBALL, OK?

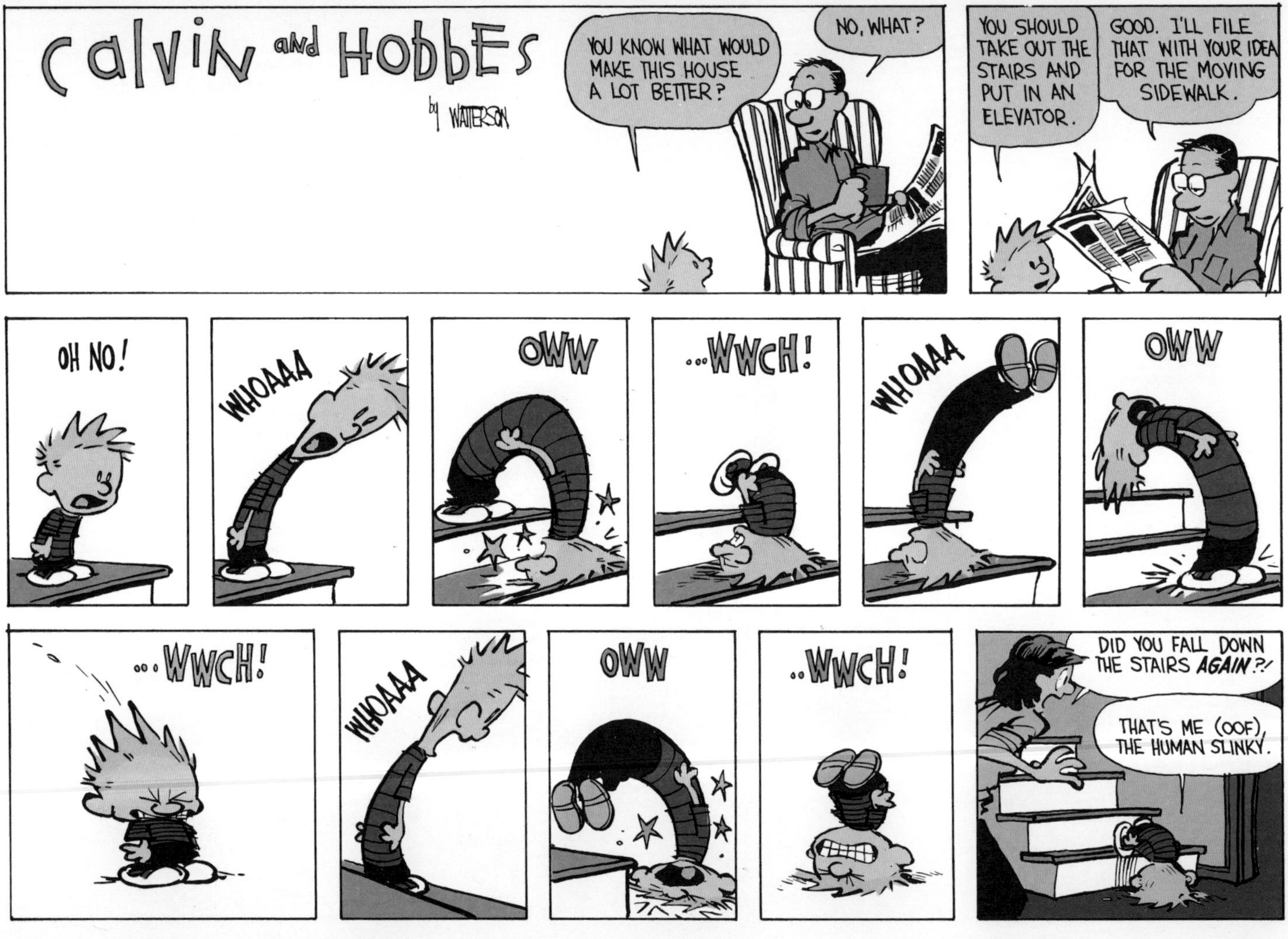
Calvin and HOBBES
by WATTERSON
YOU KNOW WHAT WOULD MAKE THIS HOUSE A LOT BETTER?
NO, WHAT?
YOU SHOULD TAKE OUT THE STAIRS AND PUT IN AN ELEVATOR.
GOOD. I'LL FILE THAT WITH YOUR IDEA FOR THE MOVING SIDEWALK.
OH NO!
WHOAAA
OWW
...WWCH!
WHOAAA
OWW
...WWCH!
WHOAAA
OWW
..WWCH!
DID YOU FALL DOWN THE STAIRS AGAIN?!
THAT'S ME (OOF), THE HUMAN SLINKY.

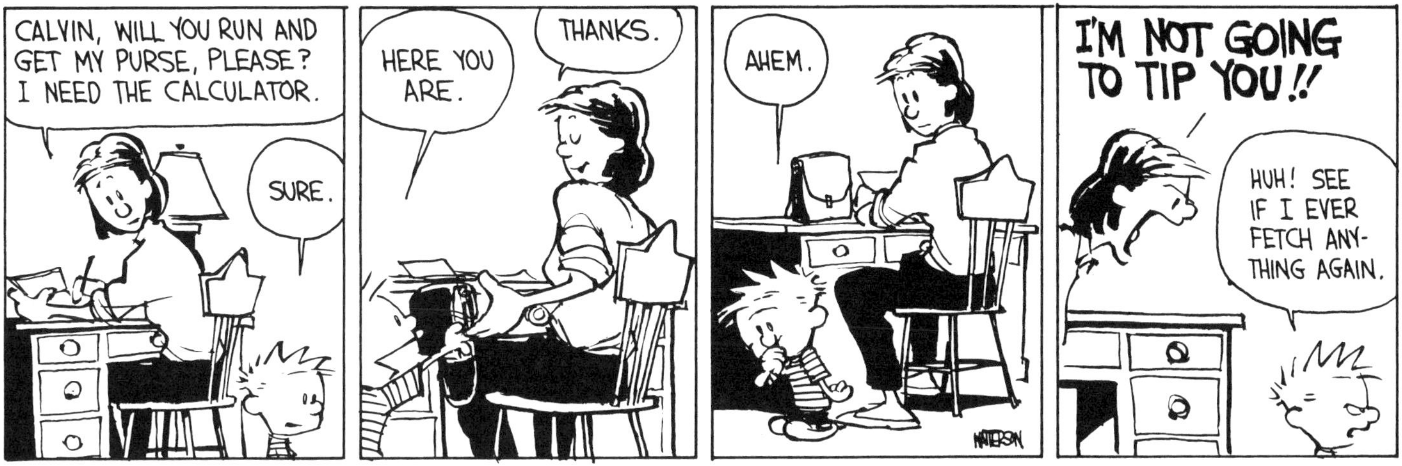
CALVIN, WILL YOU RUN AND GET MY PURSE, PLEASE? I NEED THE CALCULATOR.
SURE.
HERE YOU ARE.
THANKS.
AHEM.
WATTERSON
I'M NOT GOING TO TIP YOU!!
HUH! SEE IF I EVER FETCH ANYTHING AGAIN.

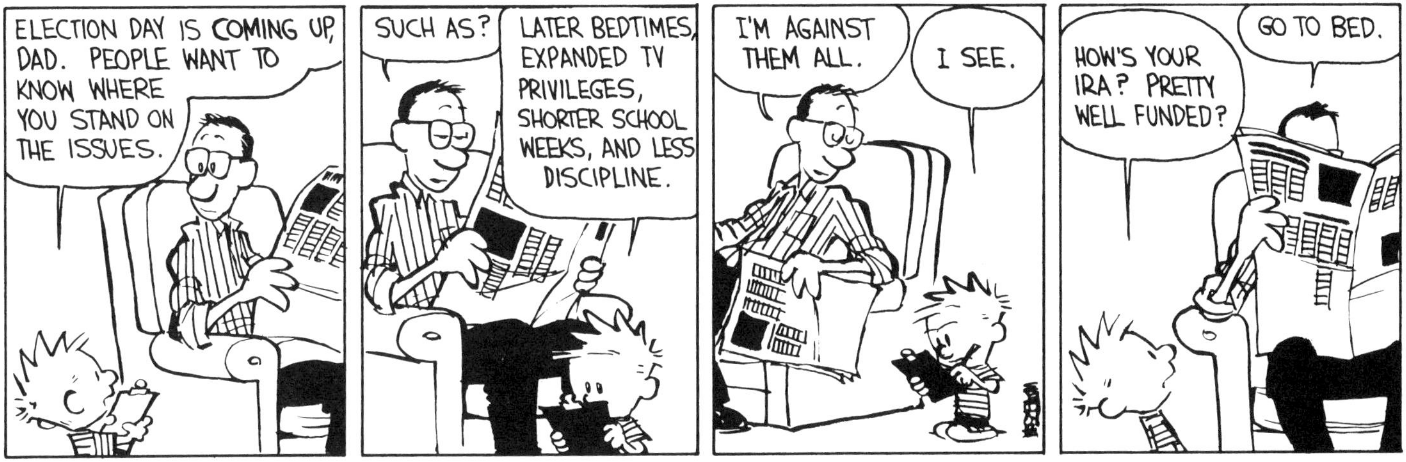
ELECTION DAY IS COMING UP, DAD. PEOPLE WANT TO KNOW WHERE YOU STAND ON THE ISSUES.
SUCH AS?
LATER BEDTIMES, EXPANDED TV PRIVILEGES, SHORTER SCHOOL WEEKS, AND LESS DISCIPLINE.
I'M AGAINST THEM ALL.
I SEE.
HOW'S YOUR IRA? PRETTY WELL FUNDED?
GO TO BED.

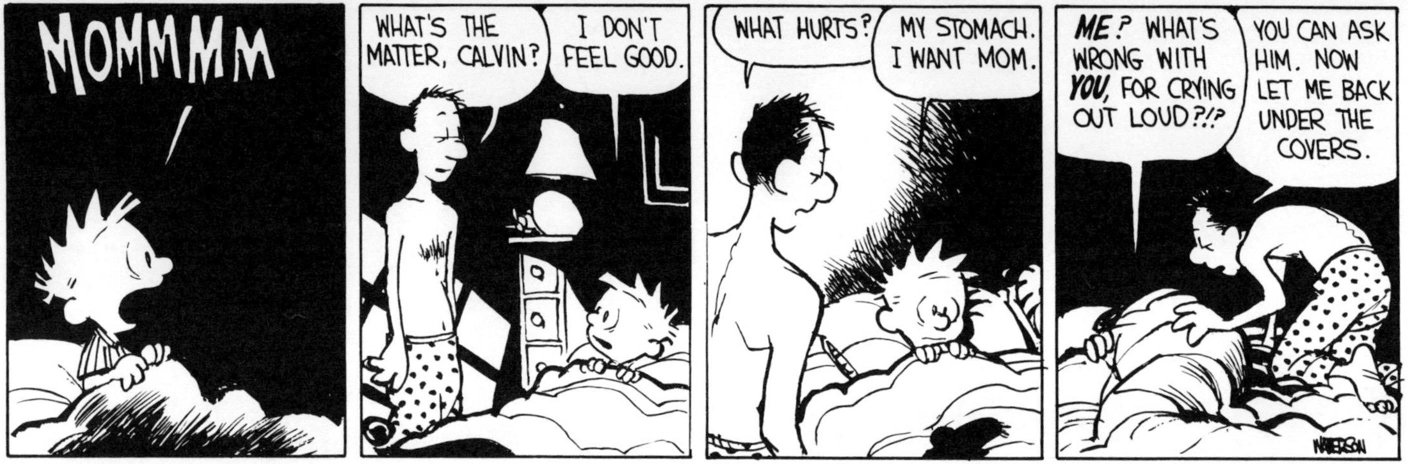
MOMMMM
WHAT'S THE MATTER, CALVIN?
I DON'T FEEL GOOD.
WHAT HURTS?
MY STOMACH. I WANT MOM.
ME? WHAT'S WRONG WITH YOU, FOR CRYING OUT LOUD?!?
YOU CAN ASK HIM. NOW LET ME BACK UNDER THE COVERS.
WATTERSON

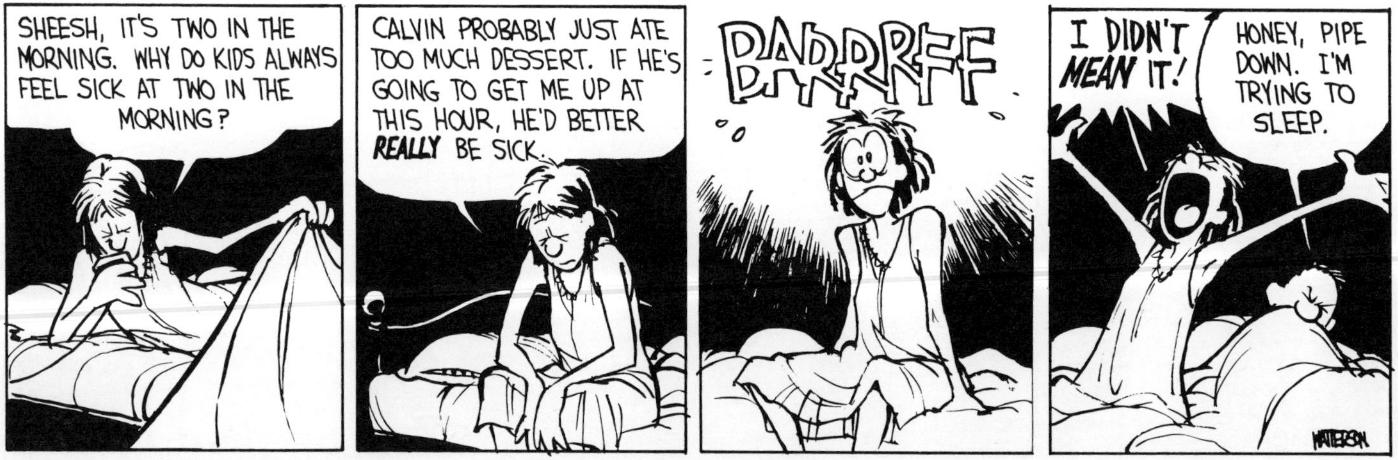
SHEESH, IT'S TWO IN THE MORNING. WHY DO KIDS ALWAYS FEEL SICK AT TWO IN THE MORNING?
CALVIN PROBABLY JUST ATE TOO MUCH DESSERT. IF HE'S GOING TO GET ME UP AT THIS HOUR, HE'D BETTER REALLY BE SICK.
BARRRFF
I DIDN'T MEAN IT!
HONEY, PIPE DOWN. I'M TRYING TO SLEEP.
WATTERSON

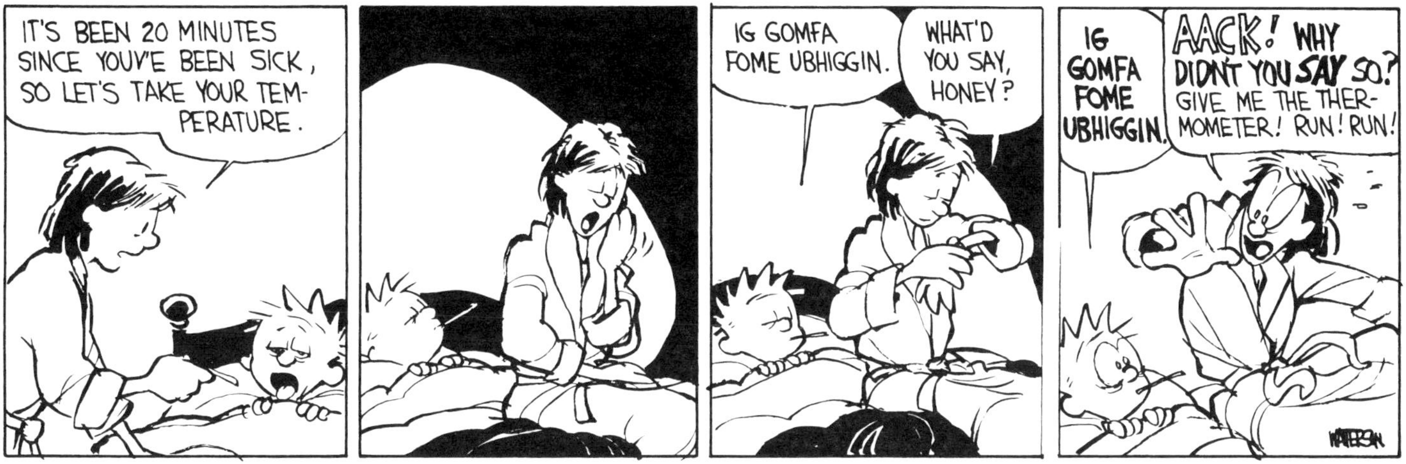
IT'S BEEN 20 MINUTES SINCE YOU'VE BEEN SICK, SO LET'S TAKE YOUR TEMPERATURE.
IG GOMFA FOME UBHIGGIN.
WHAT'D YOU SAY, HONEY?
IG GOMFA FOME UBHIGGIN.
AACK! WHY DIDN'T YOU SAY SO? GIVE ME THE THERMOMETER! RUN! RUN!
WATTERSON

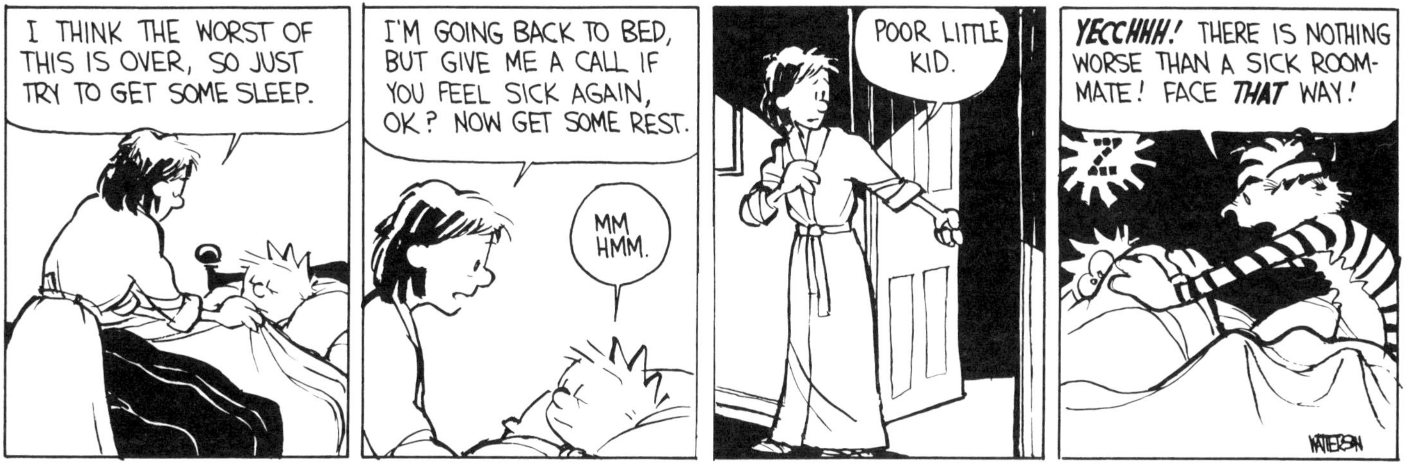
I THINK THE WORST OF THIS IS OVER, SO JUST TRY TO GET SOME SLEEP.
I'M GOING BACK TO BED, BUT GIVE ME A CALL IF YOU FEEL SICK AGAIN, OK? NOW GET SOME REST.
MM HMM.
POOR LITTLE KID.
YECCHHH! THERE IS NOTHING WORSE THAN A SICK ROOMMATE! FACE THAT WAY!
WATTERSON

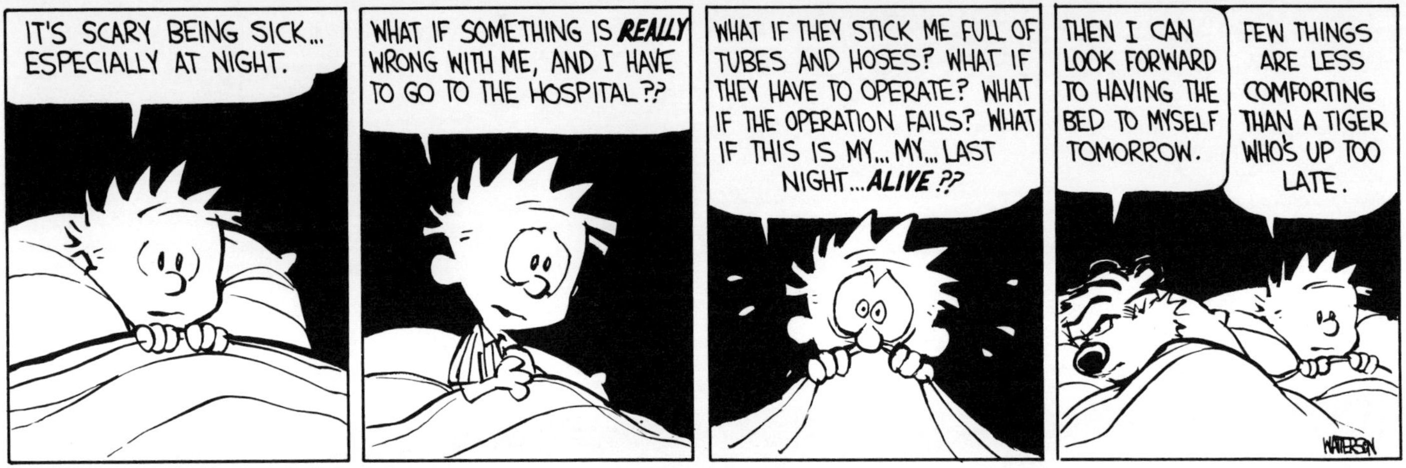
IT'S SCARY BEING SICK... ESPECIALLY AT NIGHT.
WHAT IF SOMETHING IS REALLY WRONG WITH ME, AND I HAVE TO GO TO THE HOSPITAL??
WHAT IF THEY STICK ME FULL OF TUBES AND HOSES? WHAT IF THEY HAVE TO OPERATE? WHAT IF THE OPERATION FAILS? WHAT IF THIS IS MY... MY... LAST NIGHT... ALIVE??
THEN I CAN LOOK FORWARD TO HAVING THE BED TO MYSELF TOMORROW.
FEW THINGS ARE LESS COMFORTING THAN A TIGER WHO'S UP TOO LATE.
WATTERSON

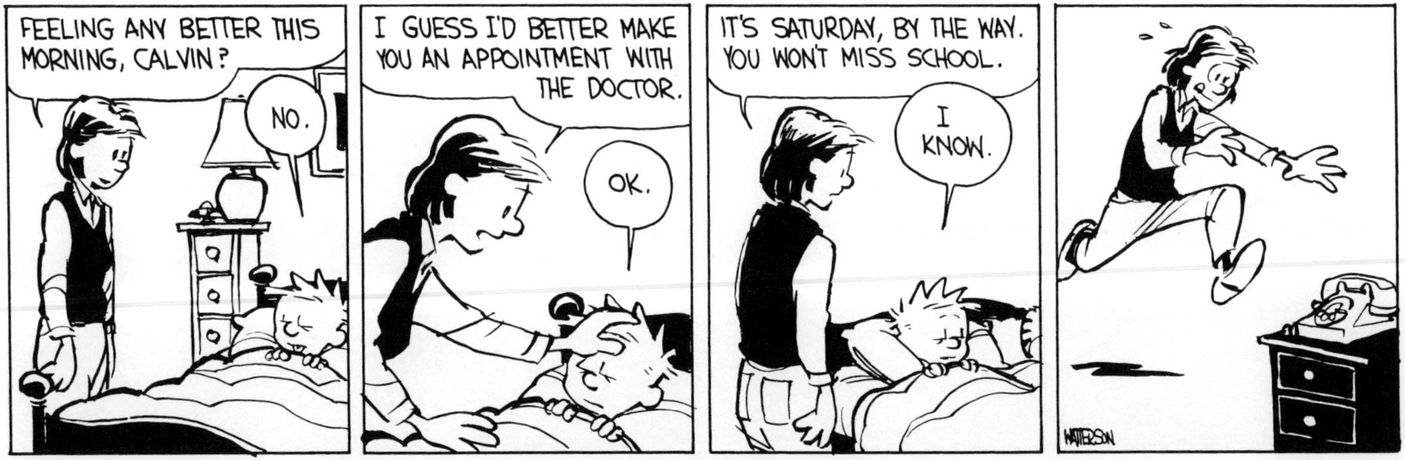
FEELING ANY BETTER THIS MORNING, CALVIN?
NO.
I GUESS I'D BETTER MAKE YOU AN APPOINTMENT WITH THE DOCTOR.
OK.
IT'S SATURDAY, BY THE WAY. YOU WON'T MISS SCHOOL.
I KNOW.
WATTERSON

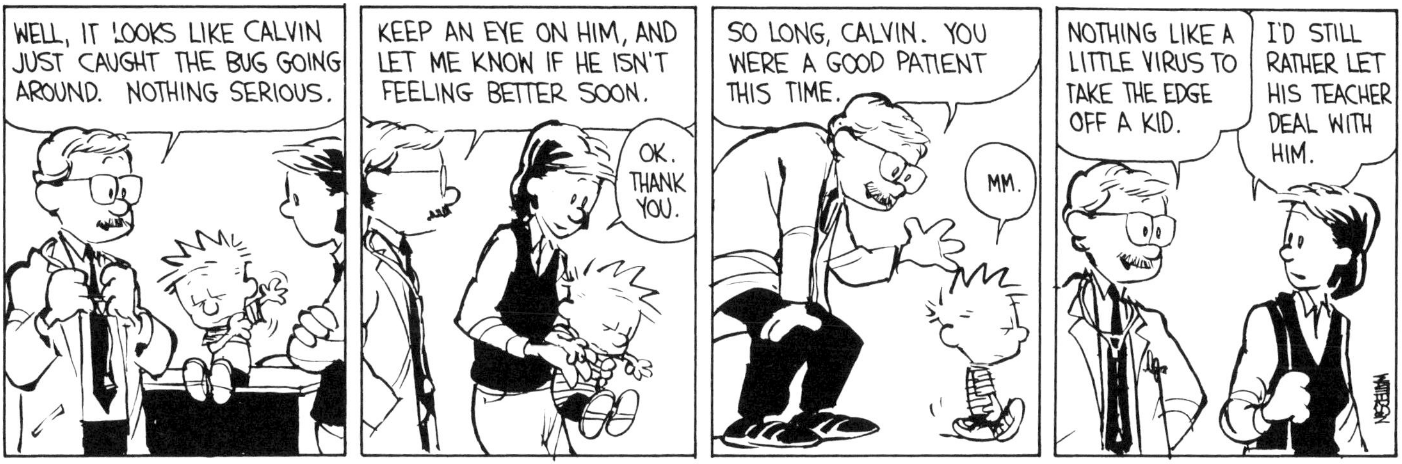
WELL, IT LOOKS LIKE CALVIN JUST CAUGHT THE BUG GOING AROUND. NOTHING SERIOUS.
KEEP AN EYE ON HIM, AND LET ME KNOW IF HE ISN'T FEELING BETTER SOON.
OK. THANK YOU.
SO LONG, CALVIN. YOU WERE A GOOD PATIENT THIS TIME.
MM.
NOTHING LIKE A LITTLE VIRUS TO TAKE THE EDGE OFF A KID.
I'D STILL RATHER LET HIS TEACHER DEAL WITH HIM.
WATTERSON

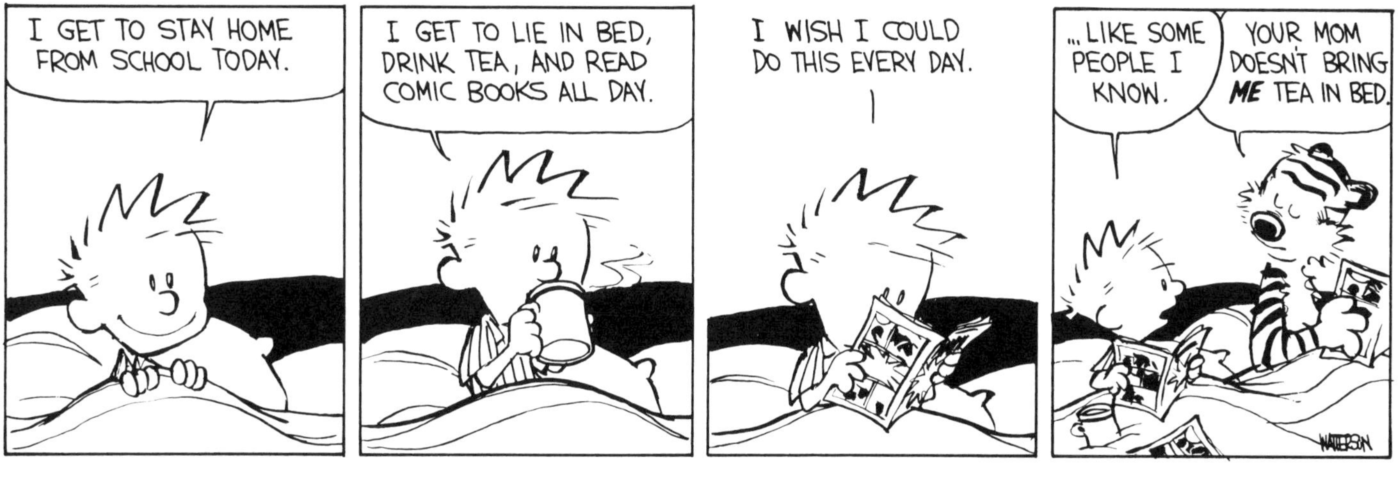
I GET TO STAY HOME FROM SCHOOL TODAY.
I GET TO LIE IN BED, DRINK TEA, AND READ COMIC BOOKS ALL DAY.
I WISH I COULD DO THIS EVERY DAY.
...LIKE SOME PEOPLE I KNOW.
YOUR MOM DOESN'T BRING **ME** TEA IN BED.
WATTERSON

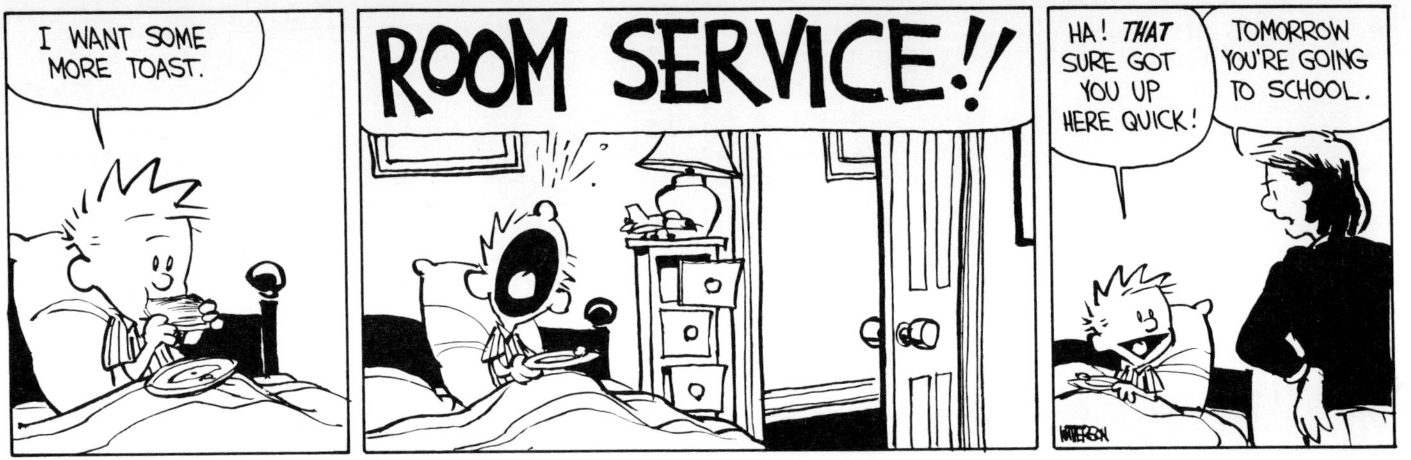
I WANT SOME MORE TOAST.
ROOM SERVICE!!
HA! *THAT* SURE GOT YOU UP HERE QUICK!
TOMORROW YOU'RE GOING TO SCHOOL.

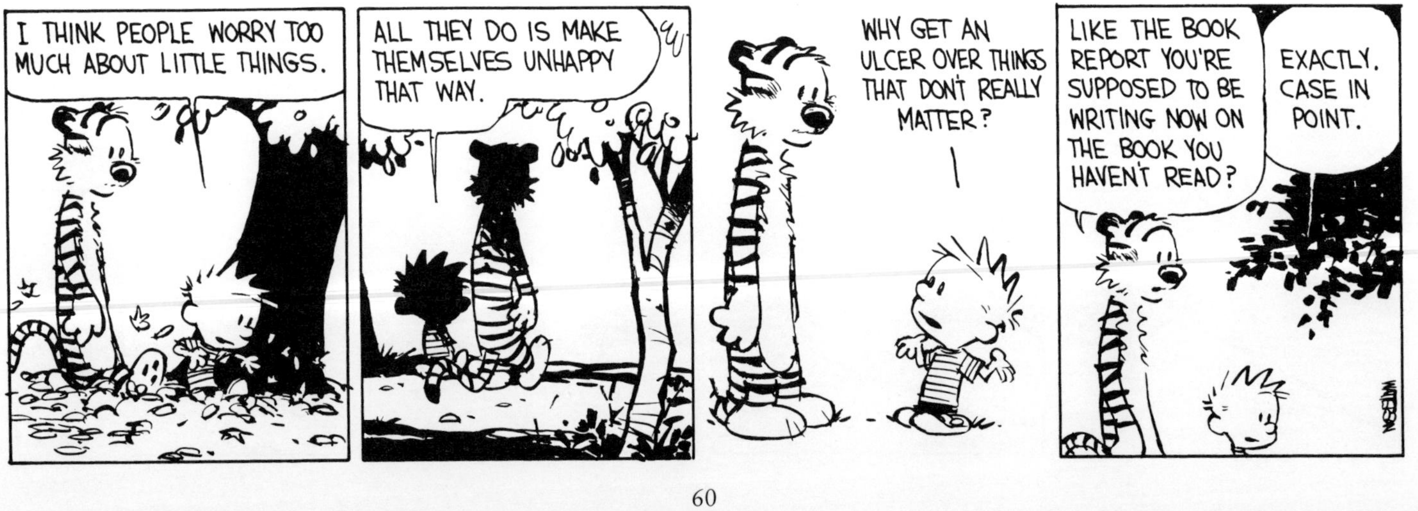
I THINK PEOPLE WORRY TOO MUCH ABOUT LITTLE THINGS.
ALL THEY DO IS MAKE THEMSELVES UNHAPPY THAT WAY.
WHY GET AN ULCER OVER THINGS THAT DON'T REALLY MATTER?
LIKE THE BOOK REPORT YOU'RE SUPPOSED TO BE WRITING NOW ON THE BOOK YOU HAVEN'T READ?
EXACTLY. CASE IN POINT.

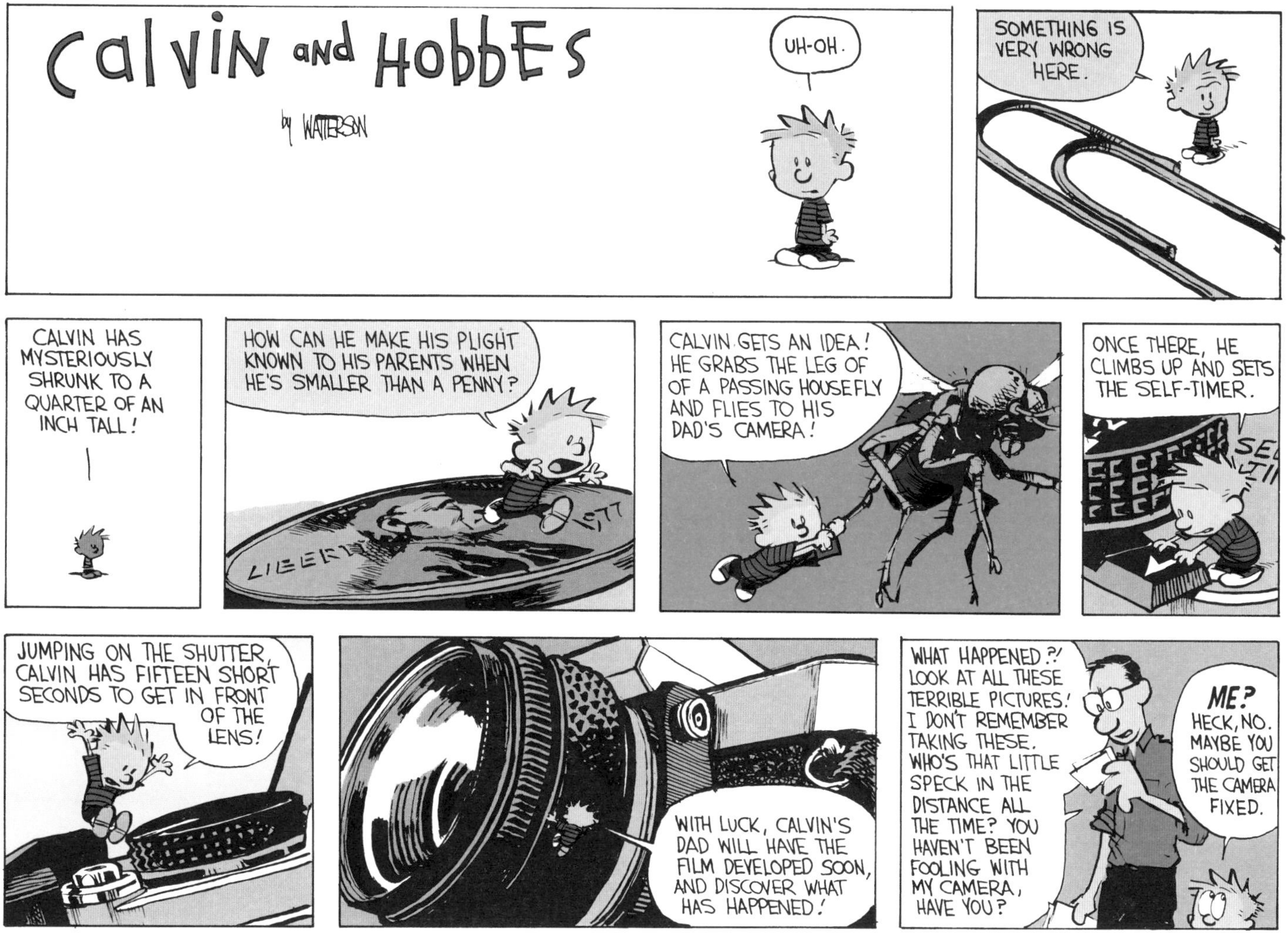

Calvin and Hobbes
by WATTERSON
UH-OH.
SOMETHING IS VERY WRONG HERE.
CALVIN HAS MYSTERIOUSLY SHRUNK TO A QUARTER OF AN INCH TALL!
HOW CAN HE MAKE HIS PLIGHT KNOWN TO HIS PARENTS WHEN HE'S SMALLER THAN A PENNY?
LIBERTY
1977
CALVIN GETS AN IDEA! HE GRABS THE LEG OF OF A PASSING HOUSEFLY AND FLIES TO HIS DAD'S CAMERA!
ONCE THERE, HE CLIMBS UP AND SETS THE SELF-TIMER.
JUMPING ON THE SHUTTER, CALVIN HAS FIFTEEN SHORT SECONDS TO GET IN FRONT OF THE LENS!
WITH LUCK, CALVIN'S DAD WILL HAVE THE FILM DEVELOPED SOON, AND DISCOVER WHAT HAS HAPPENED!
WHAT HAPPENED?! LOOK AT ALL THESE TERRIBLE PICTURES! I DON'T REMEMBER TAKING THESE. WHO'S THAT LITTLE SPECK IN THE DISTANCE ALL THE TIME? YOU HAVEN'T BEEN FOOLING WITH MY CAMERA, HAVE YOU?
ME? HECK, NO. MAYBE YOU SHOULD GET THE CAMERA FIXED.

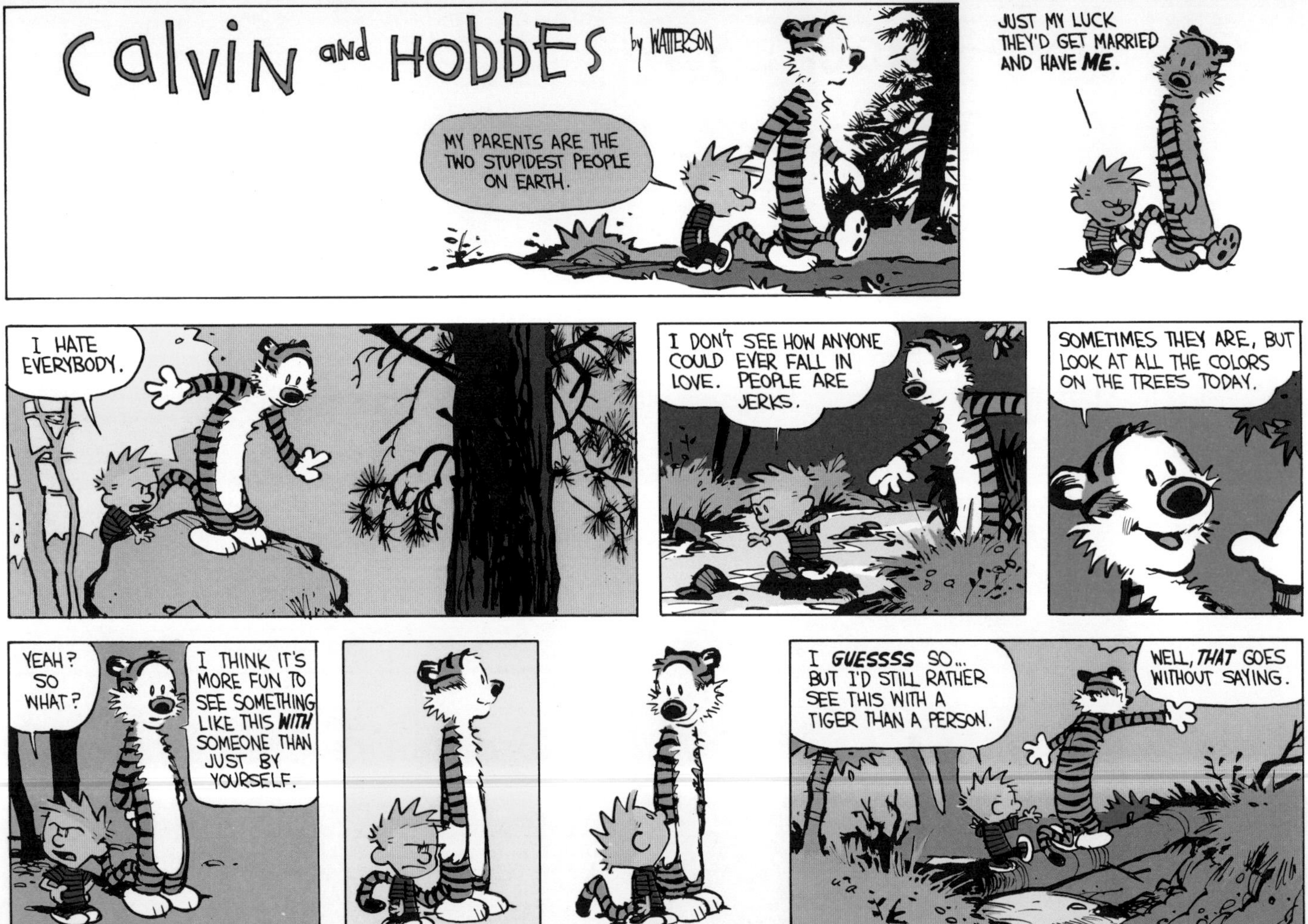
Calvin and HOBBES by WATTERSON
MY PARENTS ARE THE TWO STUPIDEST PEOPLE ON EARTH.
JUST MY LUCK THEY'D GET MARRIED AND HAVE ME.
I HATE EVERYBODY.
I DON'T SEE HOW ANYONE COULD EVER FALL IN LOVE. PEOPLE ARE JERKS.
SOMETIMES THEY ARE, BUT LOOK AT ALL THE COLORS ON THE TREES TODAY.
YEAH? SO WHAT?
I THINK IT'S MORE FUN TO SEE SOMETHING LIKE THIS WITH SOMEONE THAN JUST BY YOURSELF.
I GUESSSS SO... BUT I'D STILL RATHER SEE THIS WITH A TIGER THAN A PERSON.
WELL, THAT GOES WITHOUT SAYING.

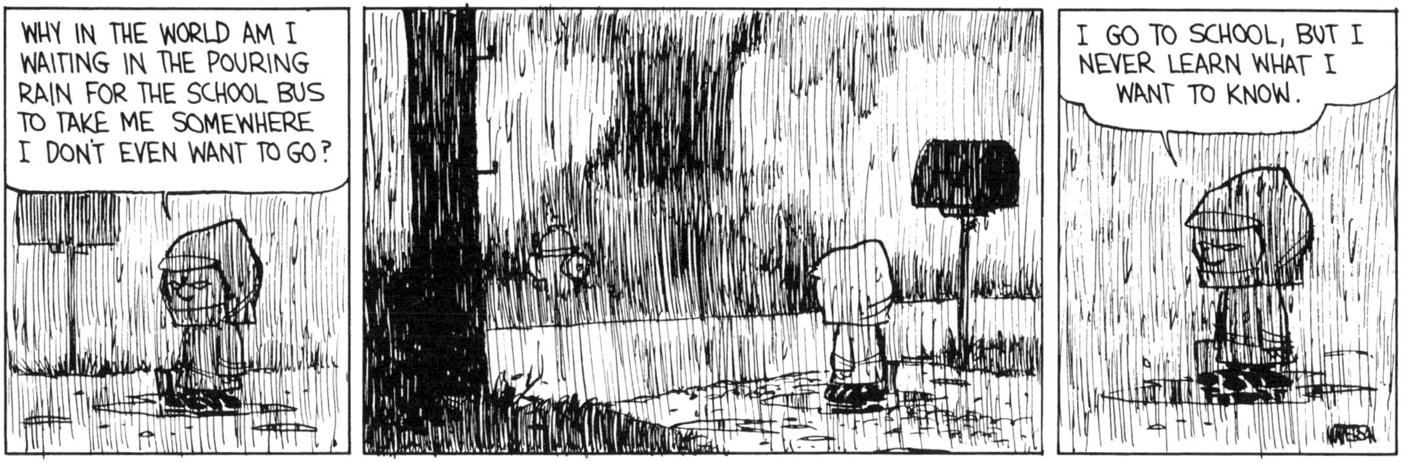
WHY IN THE WORLD AM I WAITING IN THE POURING RAIN FOR THE SCHOOL BUS TO TAKE ME SOMEWHERE I DON'T EVEN WANT TO GO?
I GO TO SCHOOL, BUT I NEVER LEARN WHAT I WANT TO KNOW.
WATTERSON

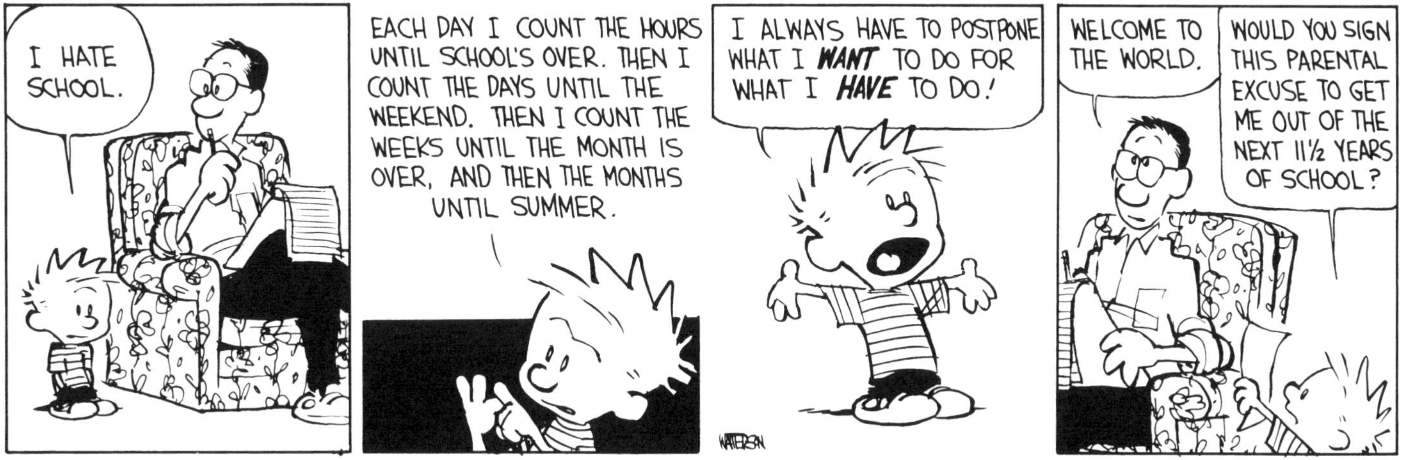
I HATE SCHOOL.
EACH DAY I COUNT THE HOURS UNTIL SCHOOL'S OVER. THEN I COUNT THE DAYS UNTIL THE WEEKEND. THEN I COUNT THE WEEKS UNTIL THE MONTH IS OVER, AND THEN THE MONTHS UNTIL SUMMER.
I ALWAYS HAVE TO POSTPONE WHAT I **WANT** TO DO FOR WHAT I **HAVE** TO DO!
WELCOME TO THE WORLD.
WOULD YOU SIGN THIS PARENTAL EXCUSE TO GET ME OUT OF THE NEXT 11½ YEARS OF SCHOOL?
WATTERSON

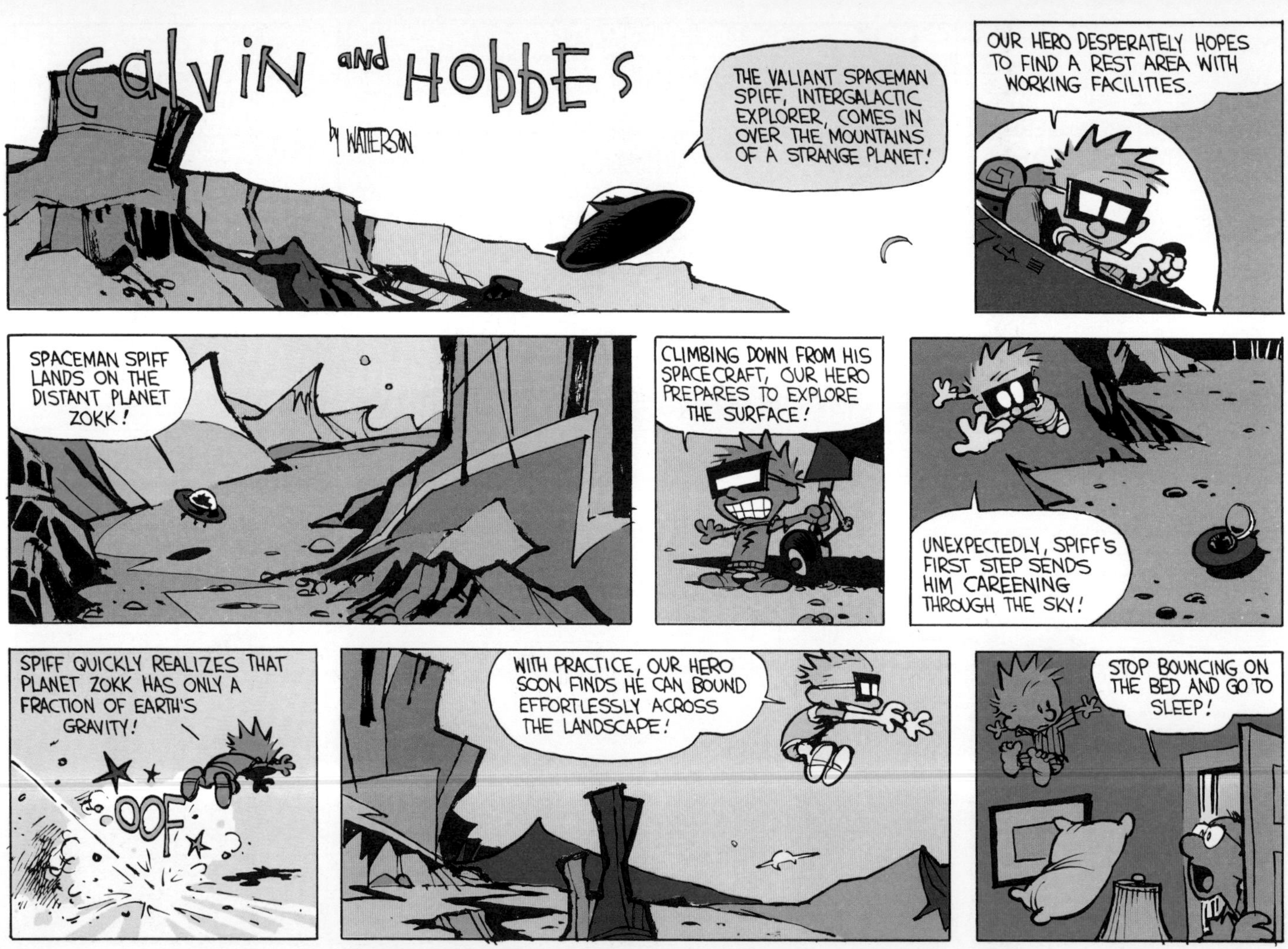
Calvin and HOBBES
by WATTERSON
THE VALIANT SPACEMAN SPIFF, INTERGALACTIC EXPLORER, COMES IN OVER THE MOUNTAINS OF A STRANGE PLANET!
OUR HERO DESPERATELY HOPES TO FIND A REST AREA WITH WORKING FACILITIES.
SPACEMAN SPIFF LANDS ON THE DISTANT PLANET ZOKK!
CLIMBING DOWN FROM HIS SPACECRAFT, OUR HERO PREPARES TO EXPLORE THE SURFACE!
UNEXPECTEDLY, SPIFF'S FIRST STEP SENDS HIM CAREENING THROUGH THE SKY!
SPIFF QUICKLY REALIZES THAT PLANET ZOKK HAS ONLY A FRACTION OF EARTH'S GRAVITY!
OOF
WITH PRACTICE, OUR HERO SOON FINDS HE CAN BOUND EFFORTLESSLY ACROSS THE LANDSCAPE!
STOP BOUNCING ON THE BED AND GO TO SLEEP!

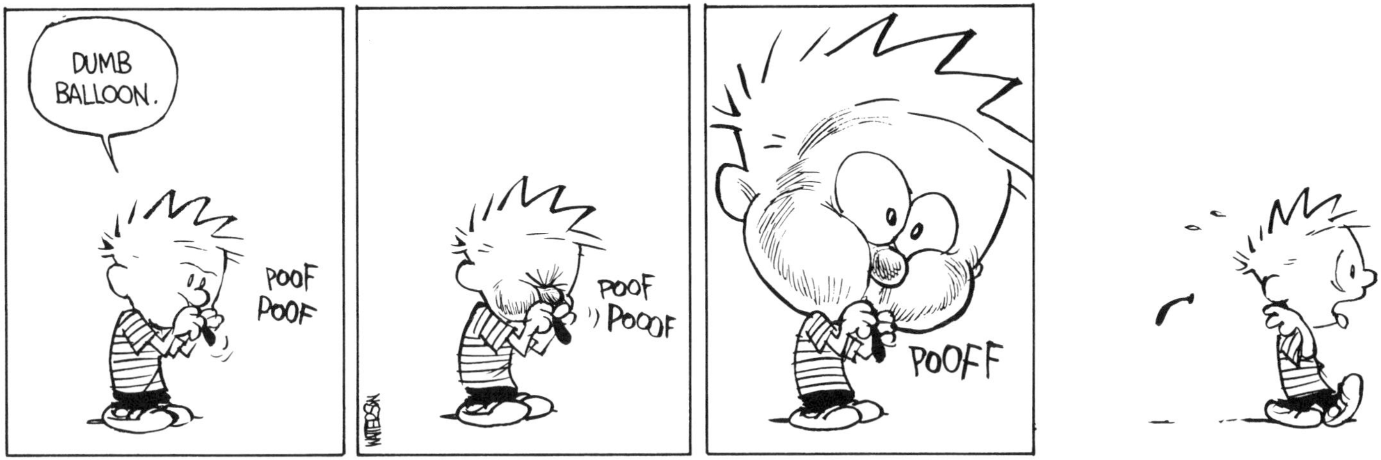
DUMB BALLOON.
POOF POOF
POOF POOOF
POOFF

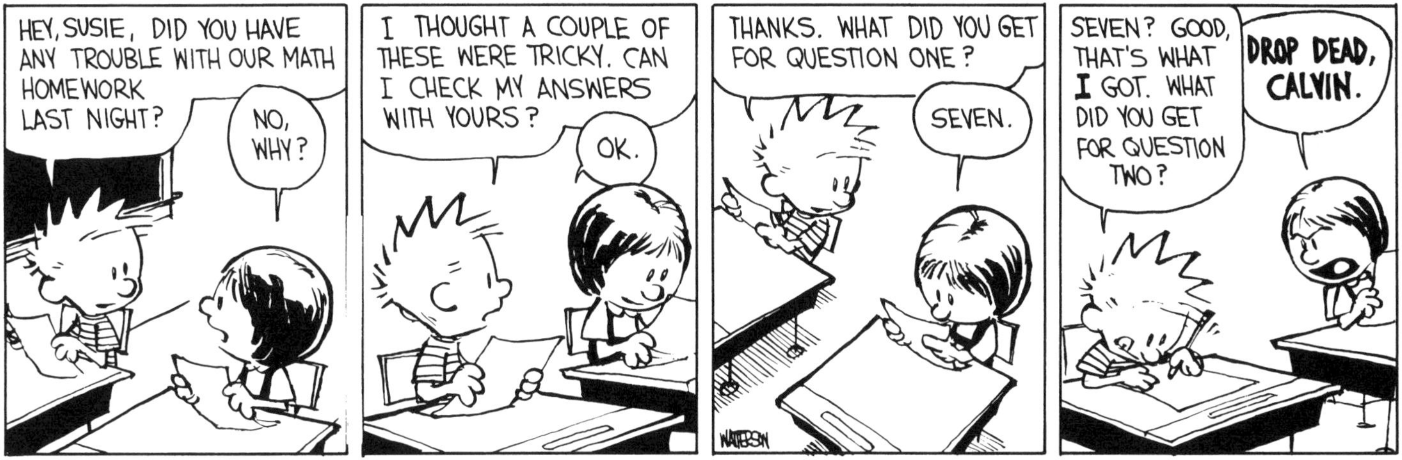
HEY, SUSIE, DID YOU HAVE ANY TROUBLE WITH OUR MATH HOMEWORK LAST NIGHT?
NO, WHY?
I THOUGHT A COUPLE OF THESE WERE TRICKY. CAN I CHECK MY ANSWERS WITH YOURS?
OK.
THANKS. WHAT DID YOU GET FOR QUESTION ONE?
SEVEN.
SEVEN? GOOD, THAT'S WHAT I GOT. WHAT DID YOU GET FOR QUESTION TWO?
DROP DEAD, CALVIN.

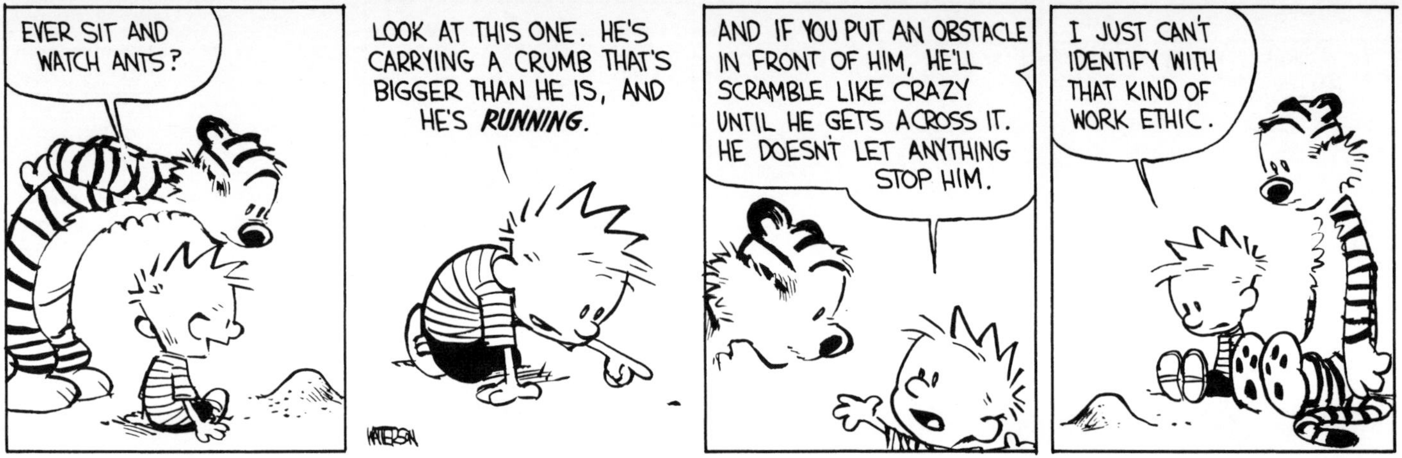
EVER SIT AND WATCH ANTS?
LOOK AT THIS ONE. HE'S CARRYING A CRUMB THAT'S BIGGER THAN HE IS, AND HE'S **RUNNING**.
AND IF YOU PUT AN OBSTACLE IN FRONT OF HIM, HE'LL SCRAMBLE LIKE CRAZY UNTIL HE GETS ACROSS IT. HE DOESN'T LET ANYTHING STOP HIM.
I JUST CAN'T IDENTIFY WITH THAT KIND OF WORK ETHIC.

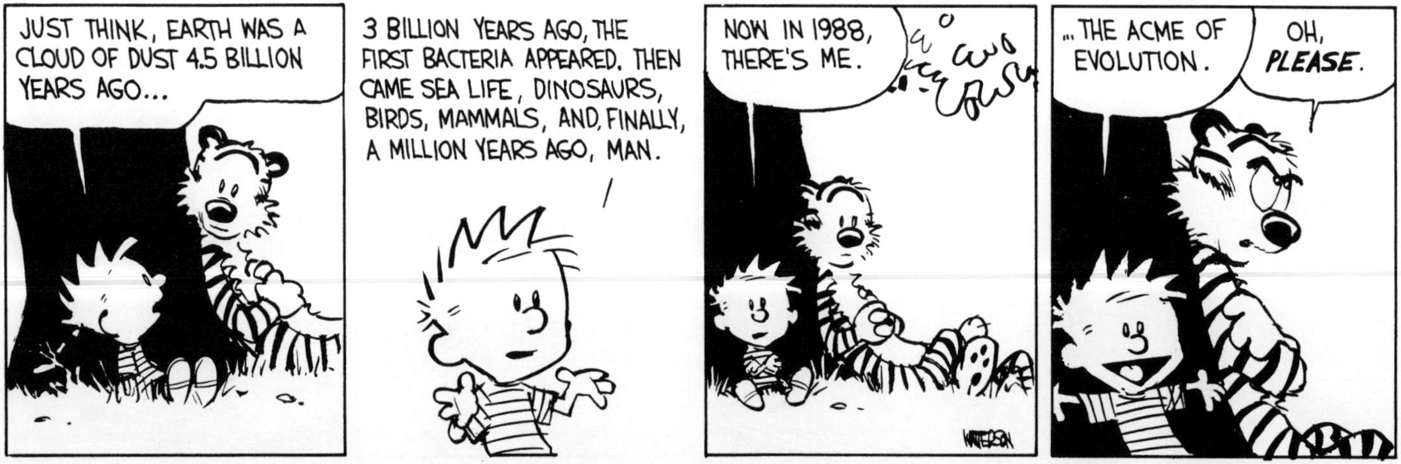
JUST THINK, EARTH WAS A CLOUD OF DUST 4.5 BILLION YEARS AGO...
3 BILLION YEARS AGO, THE FIRST BACTERIA APPEARED. THEN CAME SEA LIFE, DINOSAURS, BIRDS, MAMMALS, AND, FINALLY, A MILLION YEARS AGO, MAN.
NOW IN 1988, THERE'S ME.
...THE ACME OF EVOLUTION.
OH, **PLEASE**.

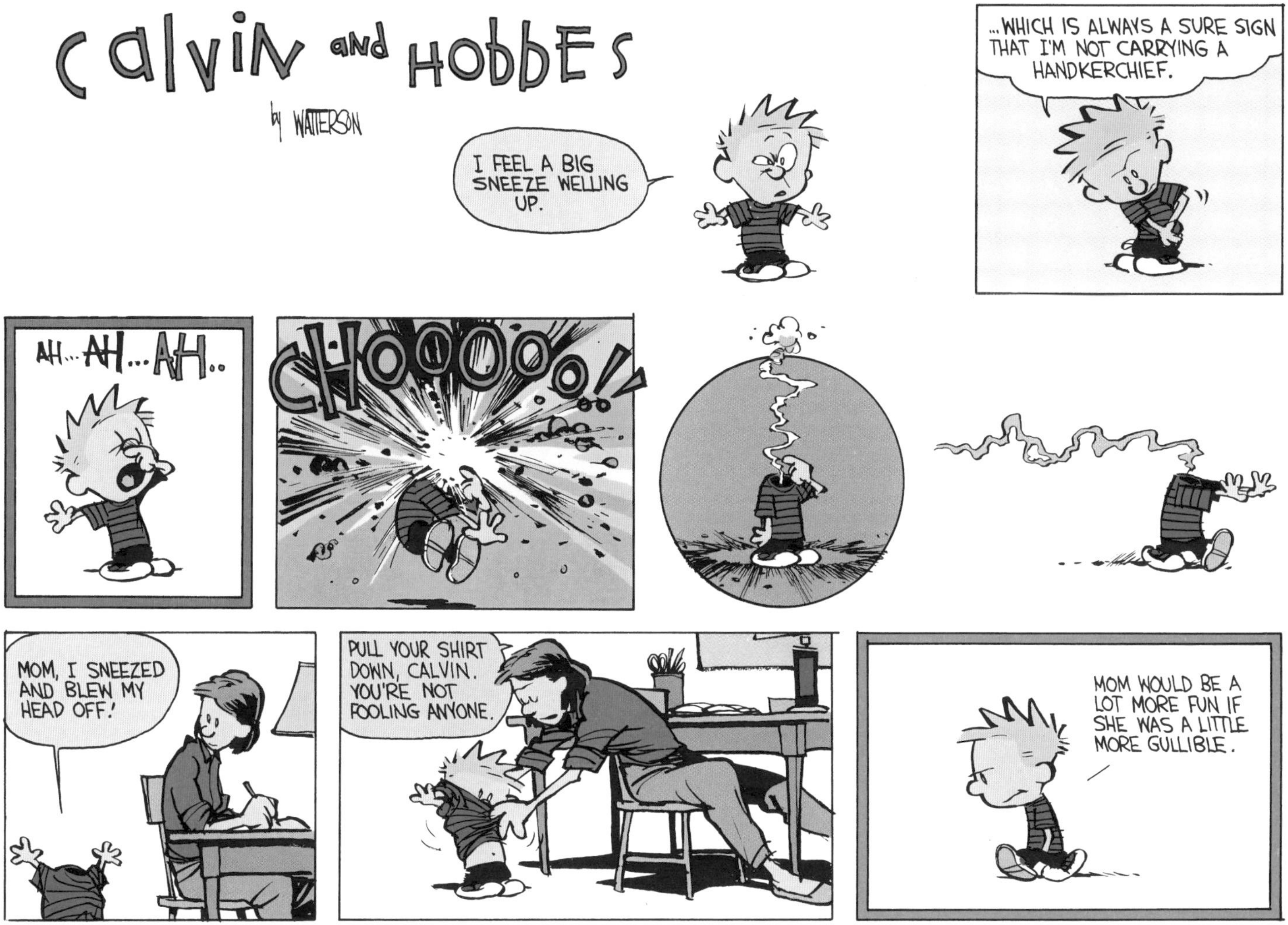
Calvin and HOBBES
by WATTERSON
I FEEL A BIG SNEEZE WELLING UP.
...WHICH IS ALWAYS A SURE SIGN THAT I'M NOT CARRYING A HANDKERCHIEF.
AH...AH...AH..
CHOOOOO!!
MOM, I SNEEZED AND BLEW MY HEAD OFF!
PULL YOUR SHIRT DOWN, CALVIN. YOU'RE NOT FOOLING ANYONE.
MOM WOULD BE A LOT MORE FUN IF SHE WAS A LITTLE MORE GULLIBLE.

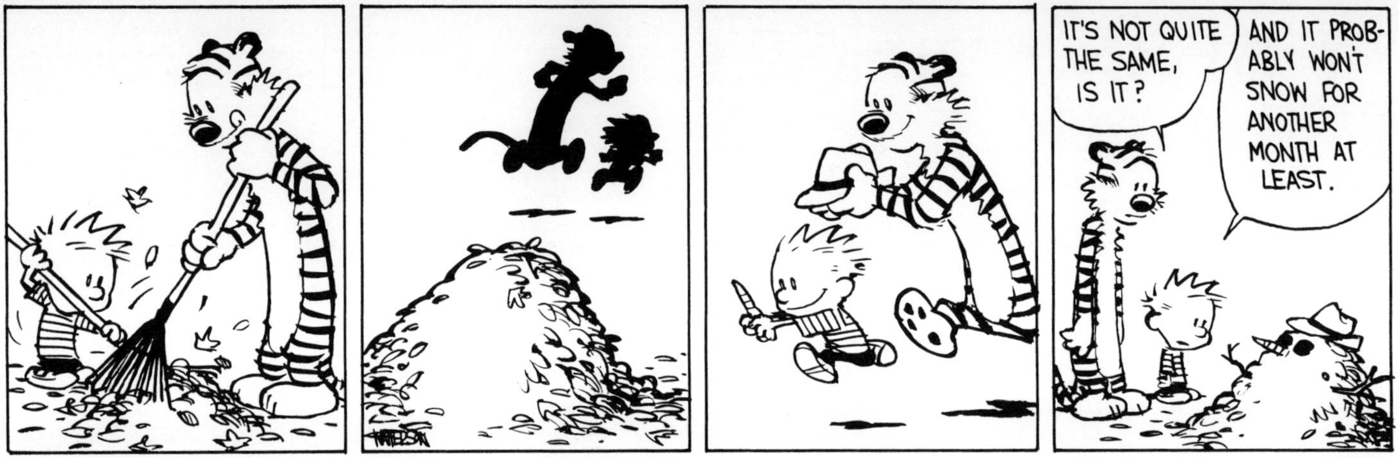
IT'S NOT QUITE THE SAME, IS IT?
AND IT PROB-ABLY WON'T SNOW FOR ANOTHER MONTH AT LEAST.

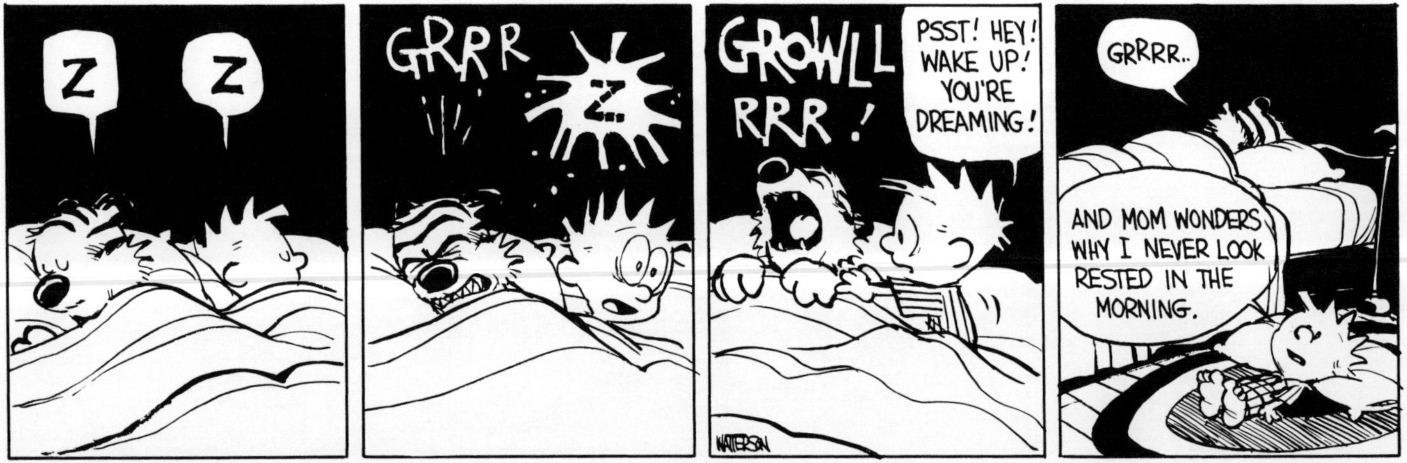
Z
Z
GRRR
Z
GROWLL RRR!
PSST! HEY! WAKE UP! YOU'RE DREAMING!
GRRRR..
AND MOM WONDERS WHY I NEVER LOOK RESTED IN THE MORNING.

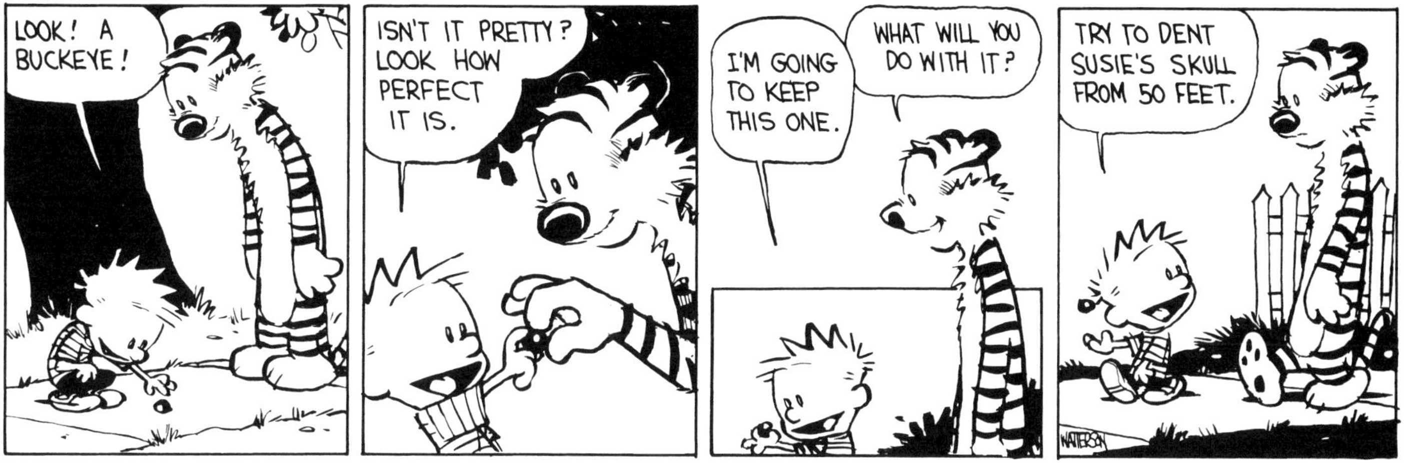
LOOK! A BUCKEYE!
ISN'T IT PRETTY? LOOK HOW PERFECT IT IS.
I'M GOING TO KEEP THIS ONE.
WHAT WILL YOU DO WITH IT?
TRY TO DENT SUSIE'S SKULL FROM 50 FEET.
WATTERSON

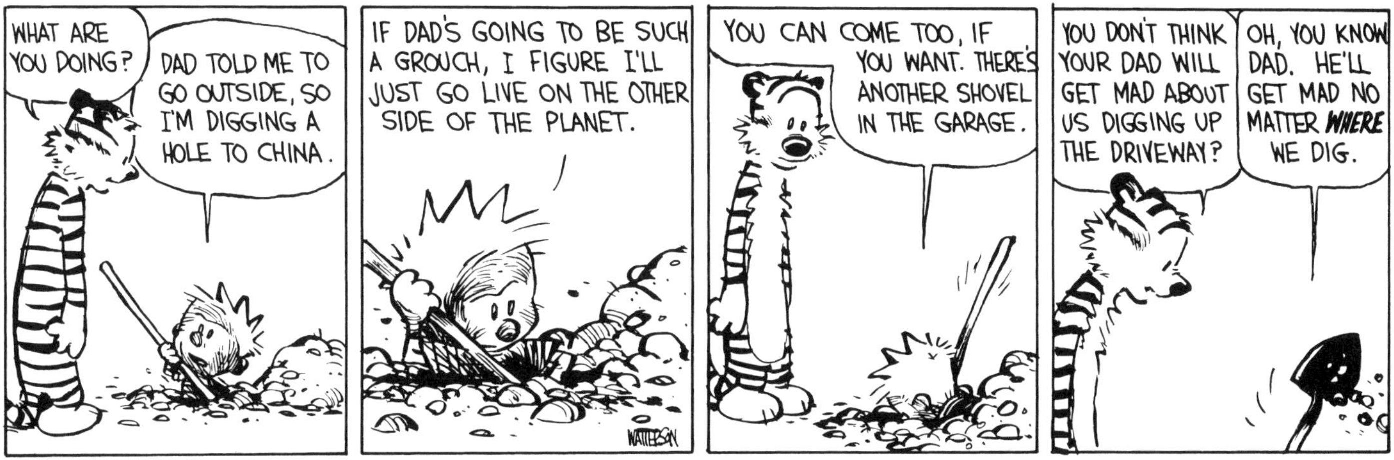
WHAT ARE YOU DOING?
DAD TOLD ME TO GO OUTSIDE, SO I'M DIGGING A HOLE TO CHINA.
IF DAD'S GOING TO BE SUCH A GROUCH, I FIGURE I'LL JUST GO LIVE ON THE OTHER SIDE OF THE PLANET.
WATTERSON
YOU CAN COME TOO, IF YOU WANT. THERE'S ANOTHER SHOVEL IN THE GARAGE.
YOU DON'T THINK YOUR DAD WILL GET MAD ABOUT US DIGGING UP THE DRIVEWAY?
OH, YOU KNOW DAD. HE'LL GET MAD NO MATTER ***WHERE*** WE DIG.

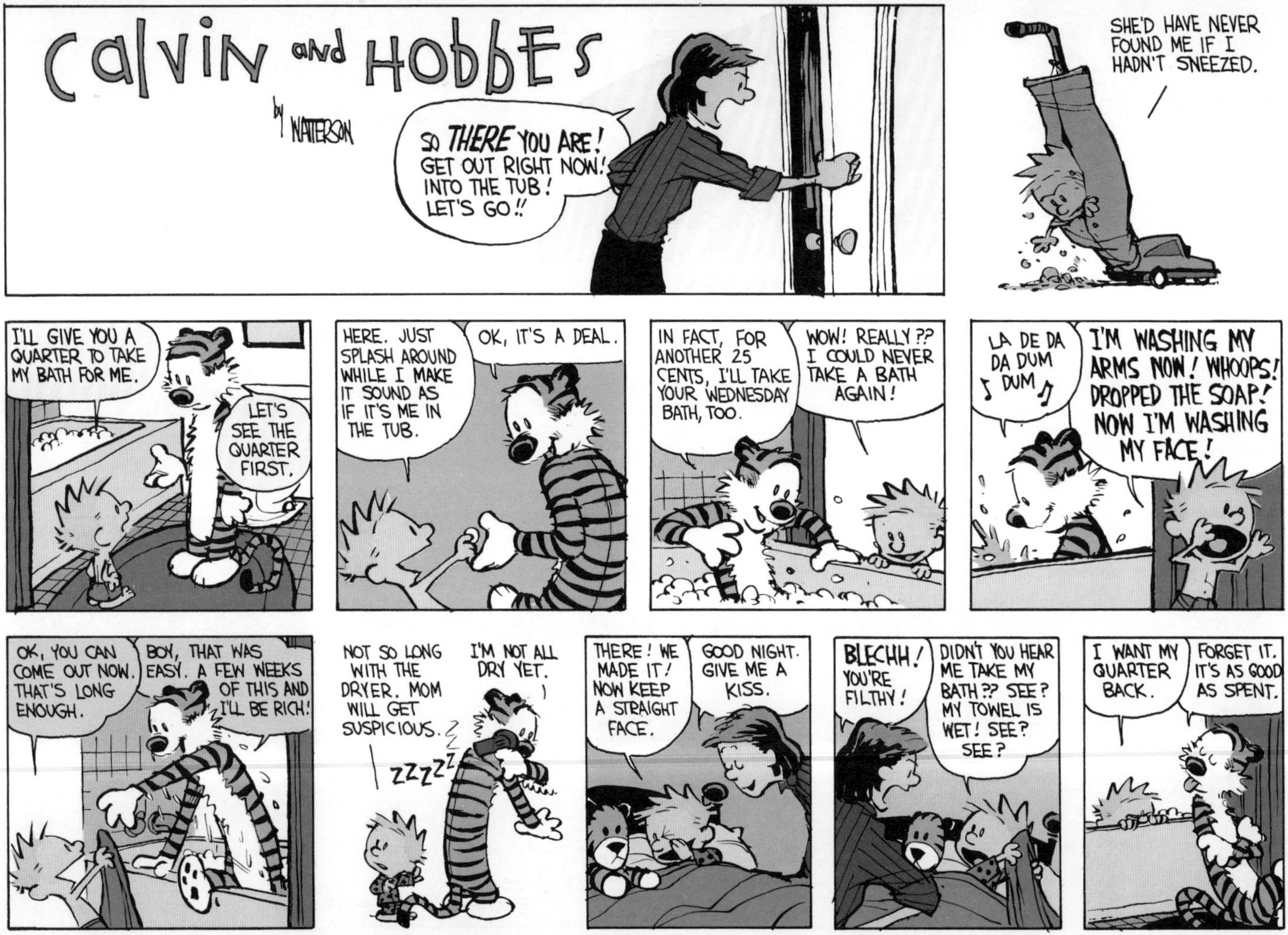
Calvin and HOBBES
by WATTERSON
SO THERE YOU ARE! GET OUT RIGHT NOW! INTO THE TUB! LET'S GO!!
SHE'D HAVE NEVER FOUND ME IF I HADN'T SNEEZED.
I'LL GIVE YOU A QUARTER TO TAKE MY BATH FOR ME.
LET'S SEE THE QUARTER FIRST.
HERE. JUST SPLASH AROUND WHILE I MAKE IT SOUND AS IF IT'S ME IN THE TUB.
OK, IT'S A DEAL.
IN FACT, FOR ANOTHER 25 CENTS, I'LL TAKE YOUR WEDNESDAY BATH, TOO.
WOW! REALLY?? I COULD NEVER TAKE A BATH AGAIN!
LA DE DA DA DUM DUM
I'M WASHING MY ARMS NOW! WHOOPS! DROPPED THE SOAP! NOW I'M WASHING MY FACE!
OK, YOU CAN COME OUT NOW. THAT'S LONG ENOUGH.
BOY, THAT WAS EASY. A FEW WEEKS OF THIS AND I'LL BE RICH!
NOT SO LONG WITH THE DRYER. MOM WILL GET SUSPICIOUS.
I'M NOT ALL DRY YET.
ZZZZZ
THERE! WE MADE IT! NOW KEEP A STRAIGHT FACE.
GOOD NIGHT. GIVE ME A KISS.
BLECHH! YOU'RE FILTHY!
DIDN'T YOU HEAR ME TAKE MY BATH?? SEE? MY TOWEL IS WET! SEE? SEE?
I WANT MY QUARTER BACK.
FORGET IT. IT'S AS GOOD AS SPENT.

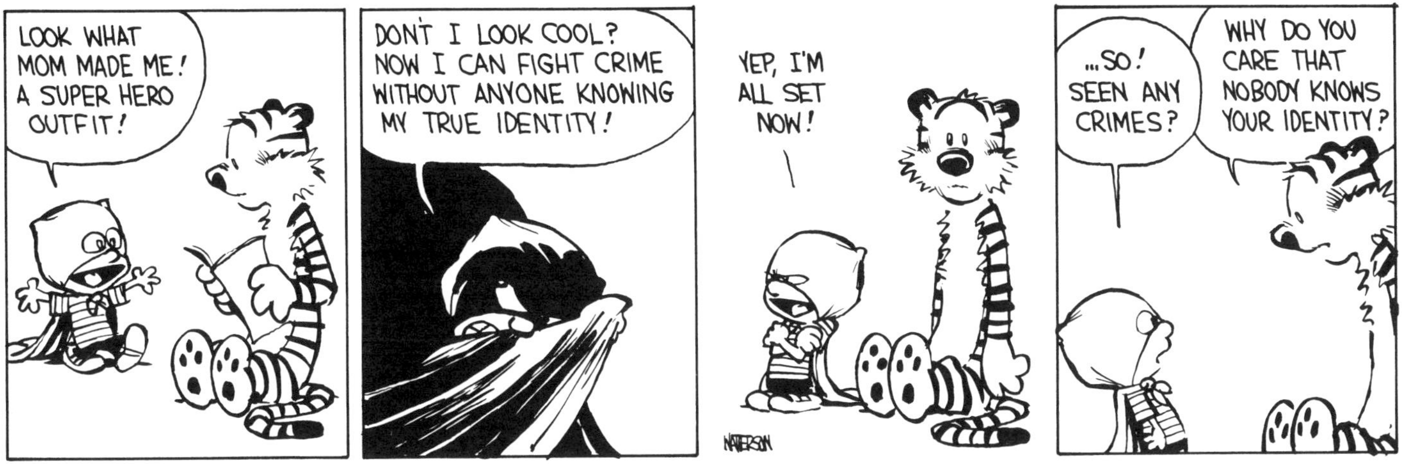
LOOK WHAT MOM MADE ME! A SUPER HERO OUTFIT!
DON'T I LOOK COOL? NOW I CAN FIGHT CRIME WITHOUT ANYONE KNOWING MY TRUE IDENTITY!
YEP, I'M ALL SET NOW!
...SO! SEEN ANY CRIMES?
WHY DO YOU CARE THAT NOBODY KNOWS YOUR IDENTITY?

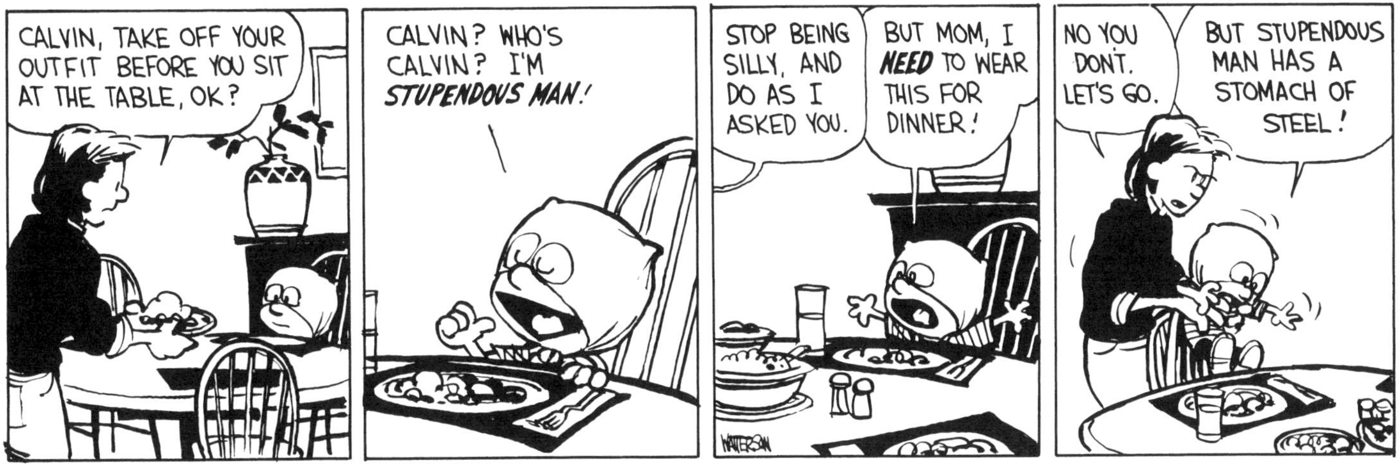
CALVIN, TAKE OFF YOUR OUTFIT BEFORE YOU SIT AT THE TABLE, OK?
CALVIN? WHO'S CALVIN? I'M ***STUPENDOUS MAN***!
STOP BEING SILLY, AND DO AS I ASKED YOU.
BUT MOM, I ***NEED*** TO WEAR THIS FOR DINNER!
NO YOU DON'T. LET'S GO.
BUT STUPENDOUS MAN HAS A STOMACH OF STEEL!

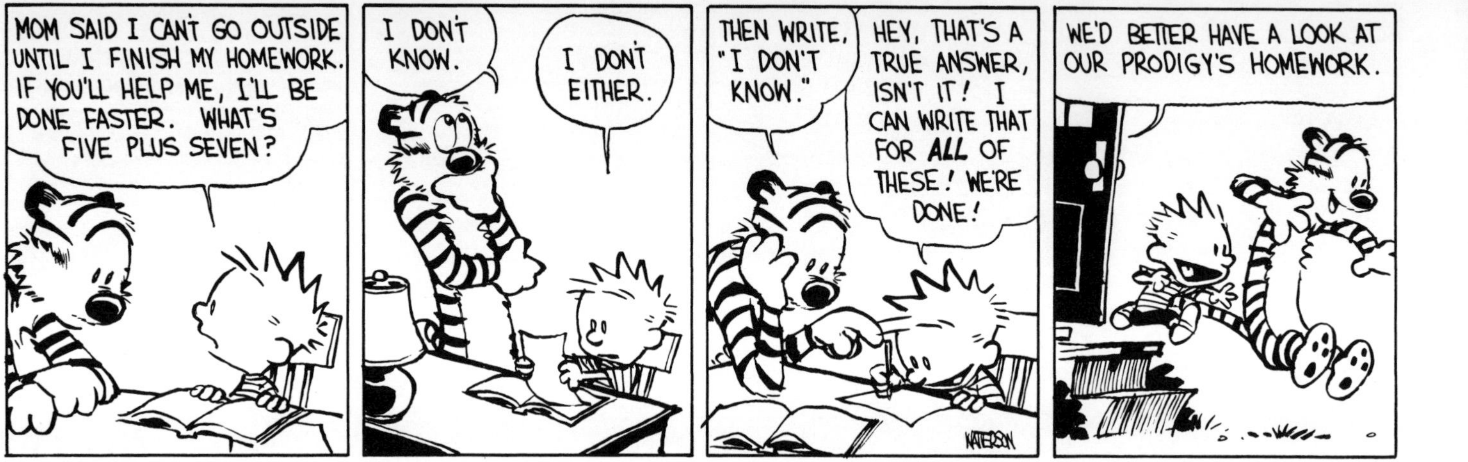
MOM SAID I CAN'T GO OUTSIDE UNTIL I FINISH MY HOMEWORK. IF YOU'LL HELP ME, I'LL BE DONE FASTER. WHAT'S FIVE PLUS SEVEN?
I DON'T KNOW.
I DON'T EITHER.
THEN WRITE, "I DON'T KNOW."
HEY, THAT'S A TRUE ANSWER, ISN'T IT! I CAN WRITE THAT FOR **ALL** OF THESE! WE'RE DONE!
WE'D BETTER HAVE A LOOK AT OUR PRODIGY'S HOMEWORK.
WATERSON

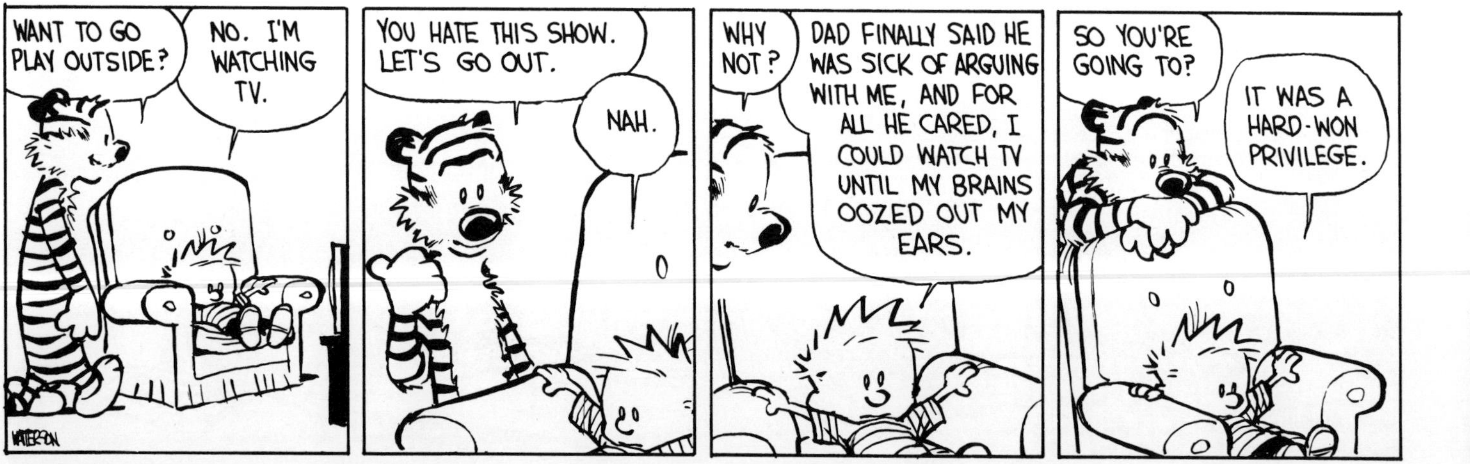
WANT TO GO PLAY OUTSIDE?
NO. I'M WATCHING TV.
YOU HATE THIS SHOW. LET'S GO OUT.
NAH.
WHY NOT?
DAD FINALLY SAID HE WAS SICK OF ARGUING WITH ME, AND FOR ALL HE CARED, I COULD WATCH TV UNTIL MY BRAINS OOZED OUT MY EARS.
SO YOU'RE GOING TO?
IT WAS A HARD-WON PRIVILEGE.
WATERSON

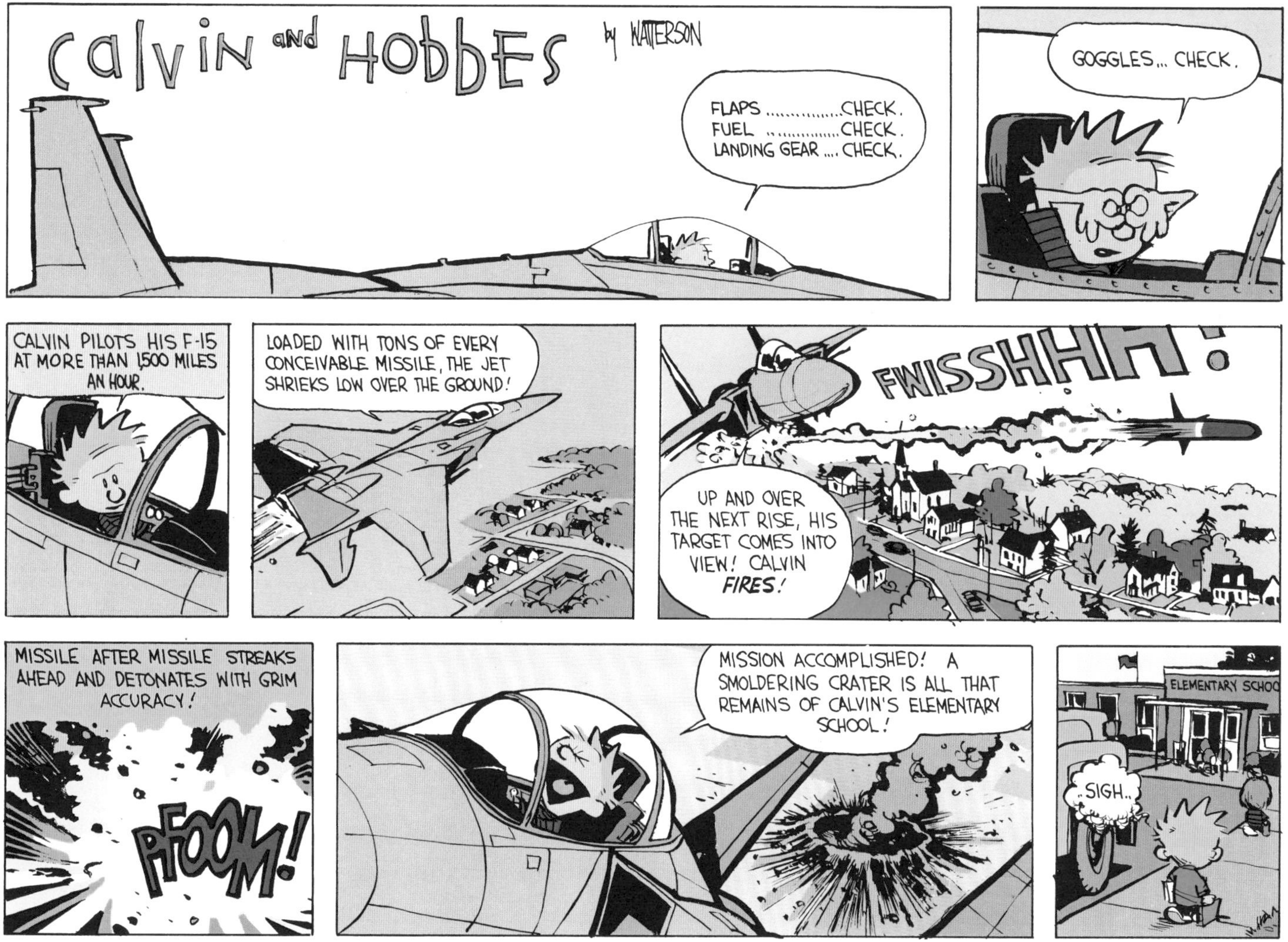
Calvin and HOBBES
by WATTERSON
FLAPS ....CHECK.
FUEL ....CHECK.
LANDING GEAR .... CHECK.
GOGGLES... CHECK.
CALVIN PILOTS HIS F-15 AT MORE THAN 1,500 MILES AN HOUR.
LOADED WITH TONS OF EVERY CONCEIVABLE MISSILE, THE JET SHRIEKS LOW OVER THE GROUND!
FWISSHHH!
UP AND OVER THE NEXT RISE, HIS TARGET COMES INTO VIEW! CALVIN FIRES!
MISSILE AFTER MISSILE STREAKS AHEAD AND DETONATES WITH GRIM ACCURACY!
PFOOM!
MISSION ACCOMPLISHED! A SMOLDERING CRATER IS ALL THAT REMAINS OF CALVIN'S ELEMENTARY SCHOOL!
ELEMENTARY SCHOO
..SIGH..

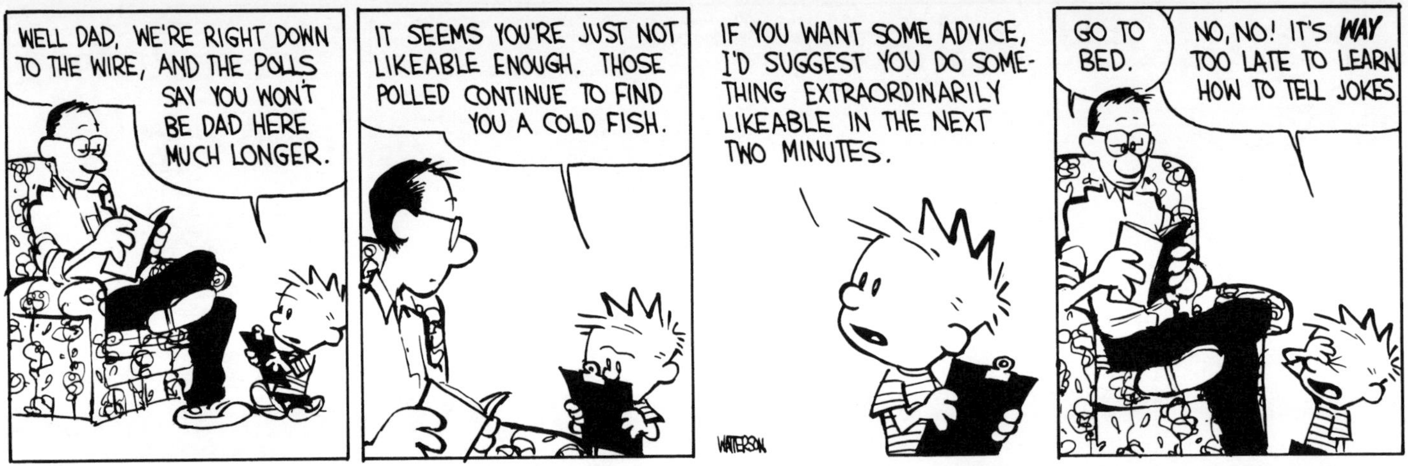
WELL DAD, WE'RE RIGHT DOWN TO THE WIRE, AND THE POLLS SAY YOU WON'T BE DAD HERE MUCH LONGER.
IT SEEMS YOU'RE JUST NOT LIKEABLE ENOUGH. THOSE POLLED CONTINUE TO FIND YOU A COLD FISH.
IF YOU WANT SOME ADVICE, I'D SUGGEST YOU DO SOMETHING EXTRAORDINARILY LIKEABLE IN THE NEXT TWO MINUTES.
WATTERSON
GO TO BED.
NO, NO! IT'S **WAY** TOO LATE TO LEARN HOW TO TELL JOKES.

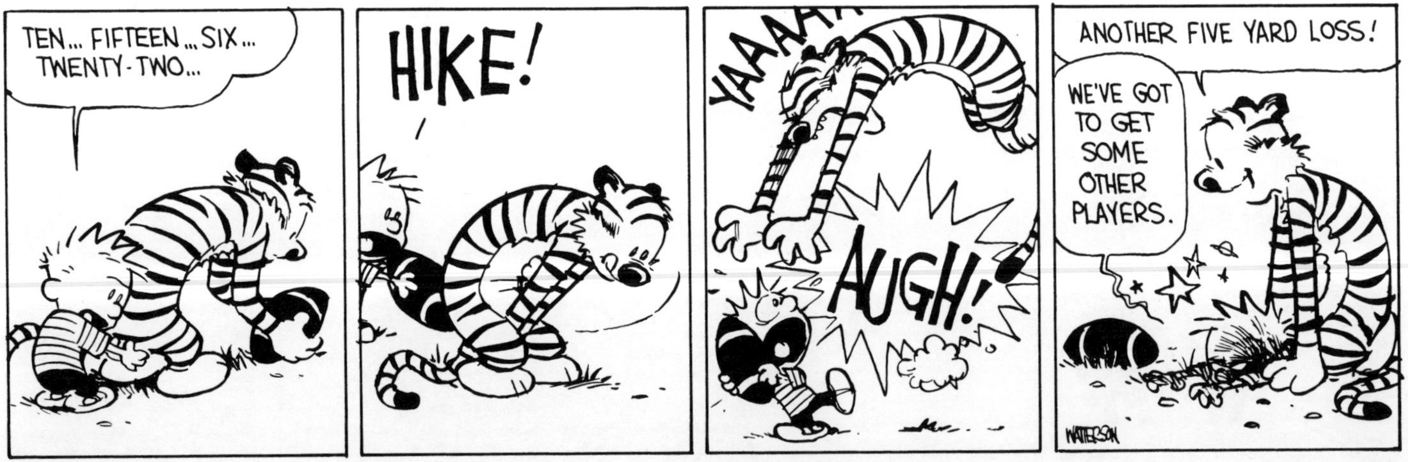
TEN... FIFTEEN... SIX... TWENTY-TWO...
HIKE!
YAAAA
AUGH!
ANOTHER FIVE YARD LOSS!
WE'VE GOT TO GET SOME OTHER PLAYERS.
WATTERSON

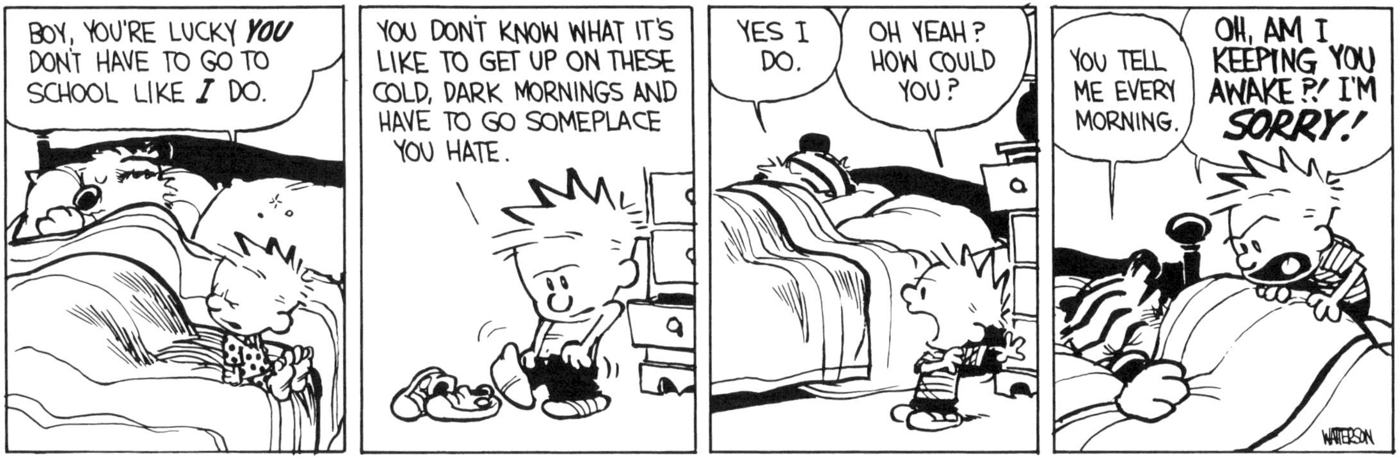
BOY, YOU'RE LUCKY ***YOU*** DON'T HAVE TO GO TO SCHOOL LIKE ***I*** DO.
YOU DON'T KNOW WHAT IT'S LIKE TO GET UP ON THESE COLD, DARK MORNINGS AND HAVE TO GO SOMEPLACE YOU HATE.
YES I DO.
OH YEAH? HOW COULD YOU?
YOU TELL ME EVERY MORNING.
OH, AM I KEEPING YOU AWAKE?! I'M ***SORRY!***
WATTERSON

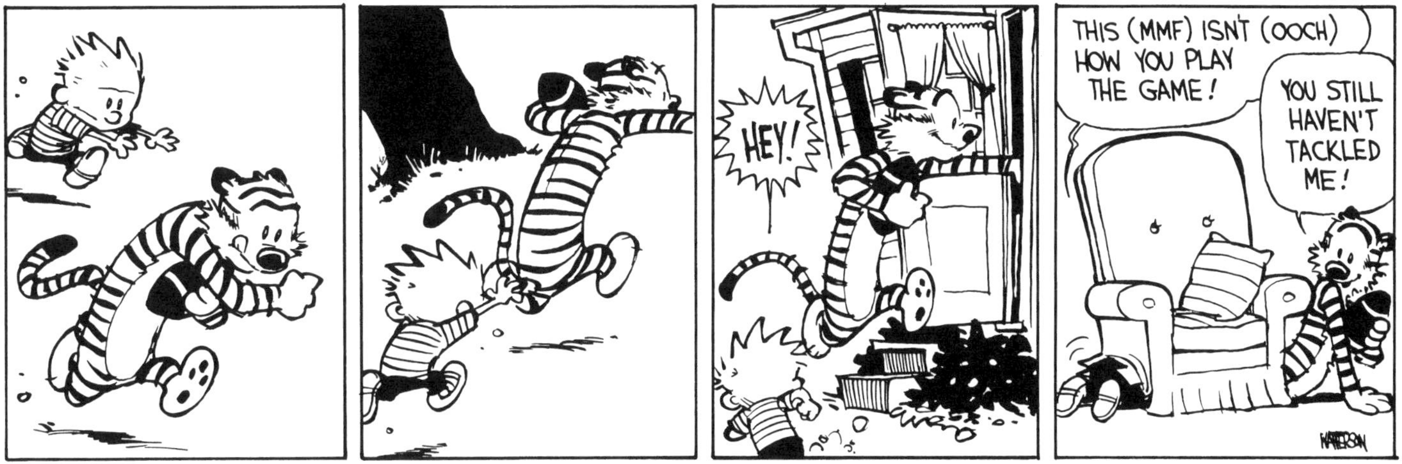
HEY!
THIS (MMF) ISN'T (OOCH) HOW YOU PLAY THE GAME!
YOU STILL HAVEN'T TACKLED ME!
WATTERSON

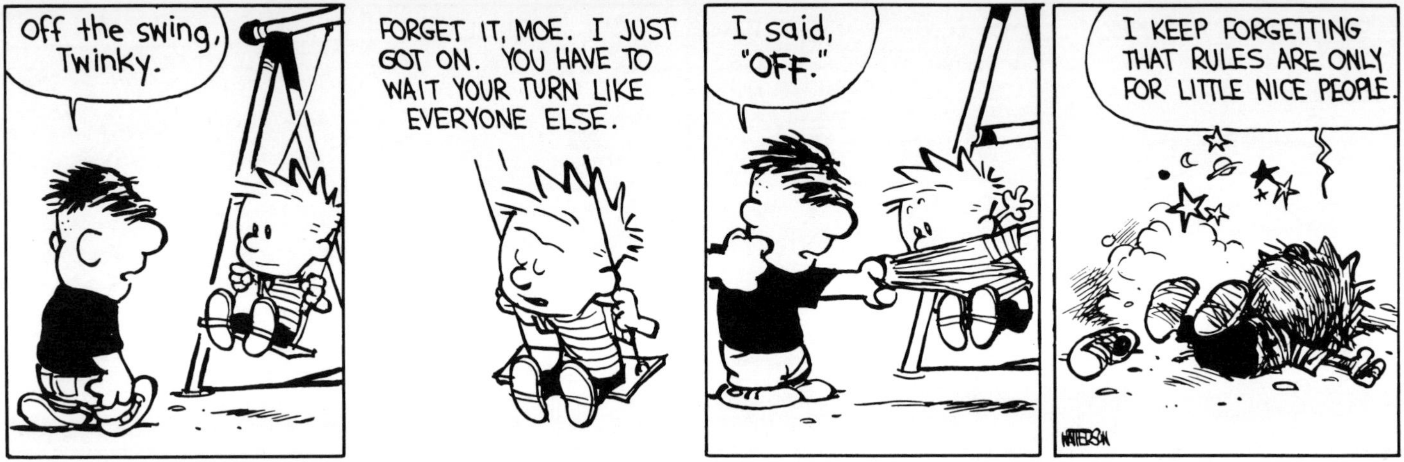
Off the swing, Twinky.
FORGET IT, MOE. I JUST GOT ON. YOU HAVE TO WAIT YOUR TURN LIKE EVERYONE ELSE.
I said, "OFF."
I KEEP FORGETTING THAT RULES ARE ONLY FOR LITTLE NICE PEOPLE.
WATTERSON

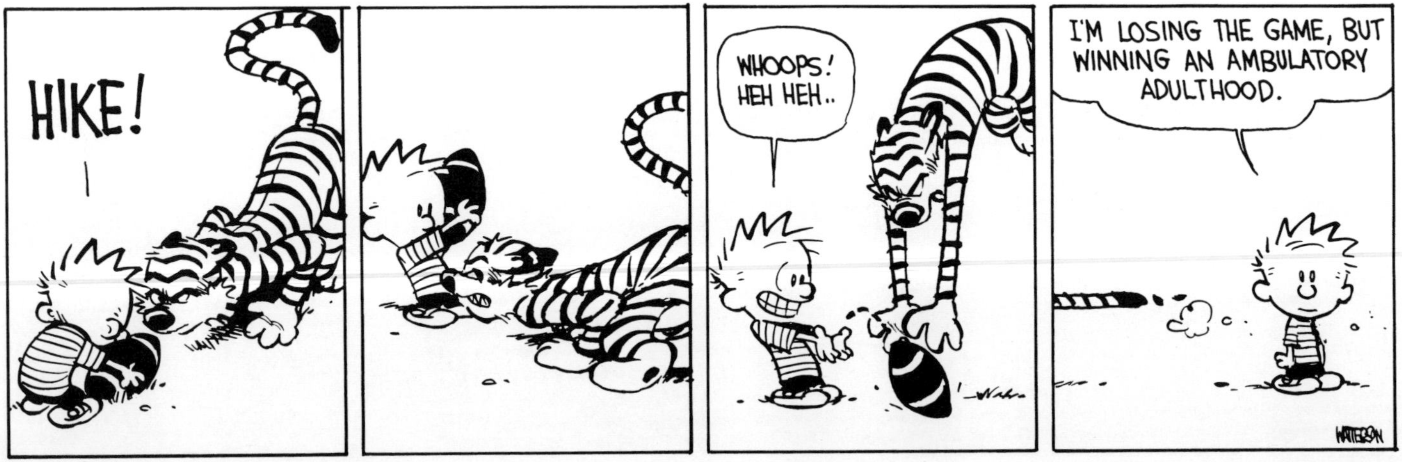
HIKE!
WHOOPS! HEH HEH..
I'M LOSING THE GAME, BUT WINNING AN AMBULATORY ADULTHOOD.
WATTERSON

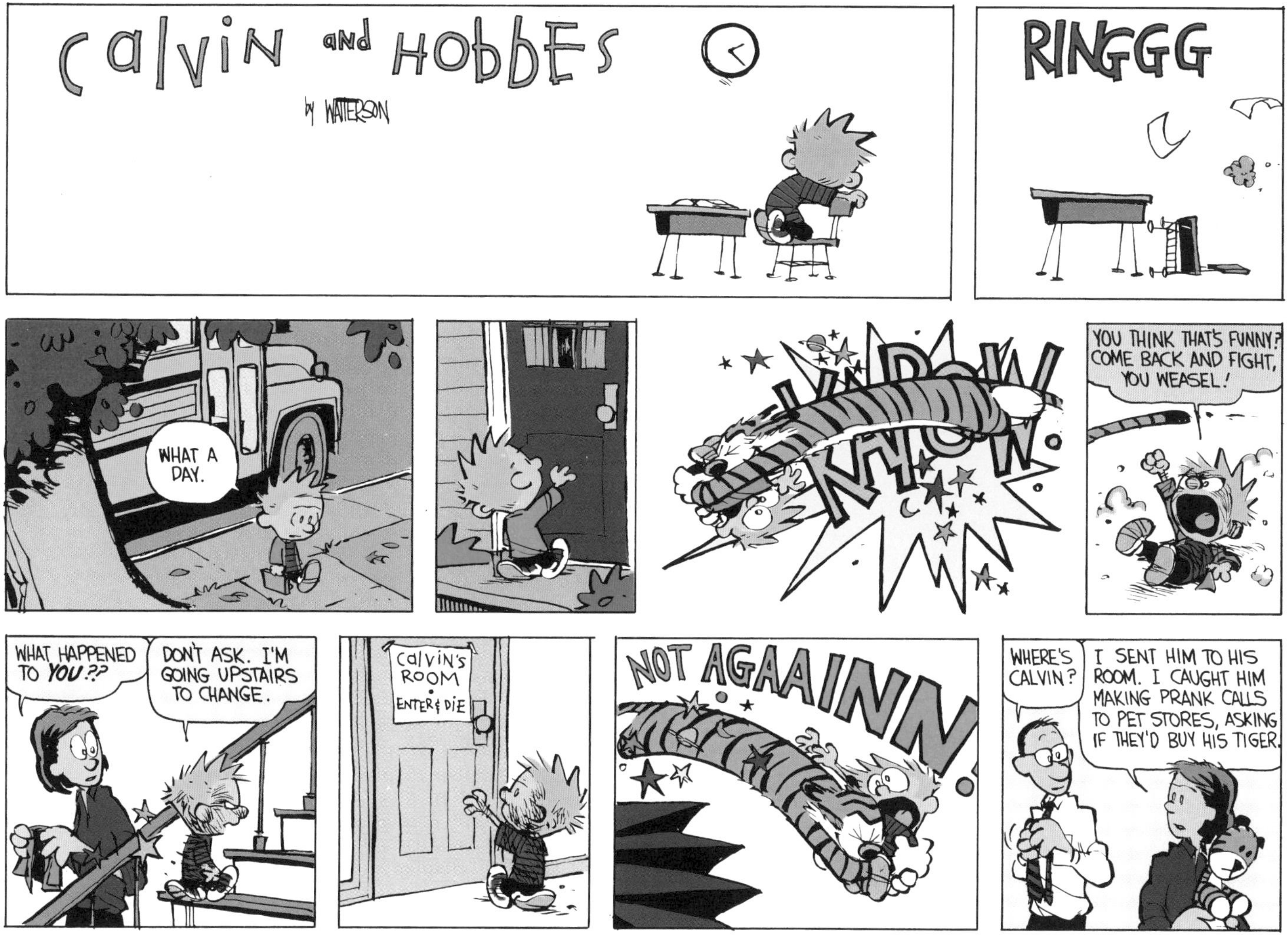
Calvin and HOBBES
by WATTERSON
RINGGG
WHAT A DAY.
KAPOW
YOU THINK THAT'S FUNNY? COME BACK AND FIGHT, YOU WEASEL!
WHAT HAPPENED TO ***YOU***??
DON'T ASK. I'M GOING UPSTAIRS TO CHANGE.
Calvin's ROOM • ENTER & DIE
NOT AGAAINN!
WHERE'S CALVIN?
I SENT HIM TO HIS ROOM. I CAUGHT HIM MAKING PRANK CALLS TO PET STORES, ASKING IF THEY'D BUY HIS TIGER.

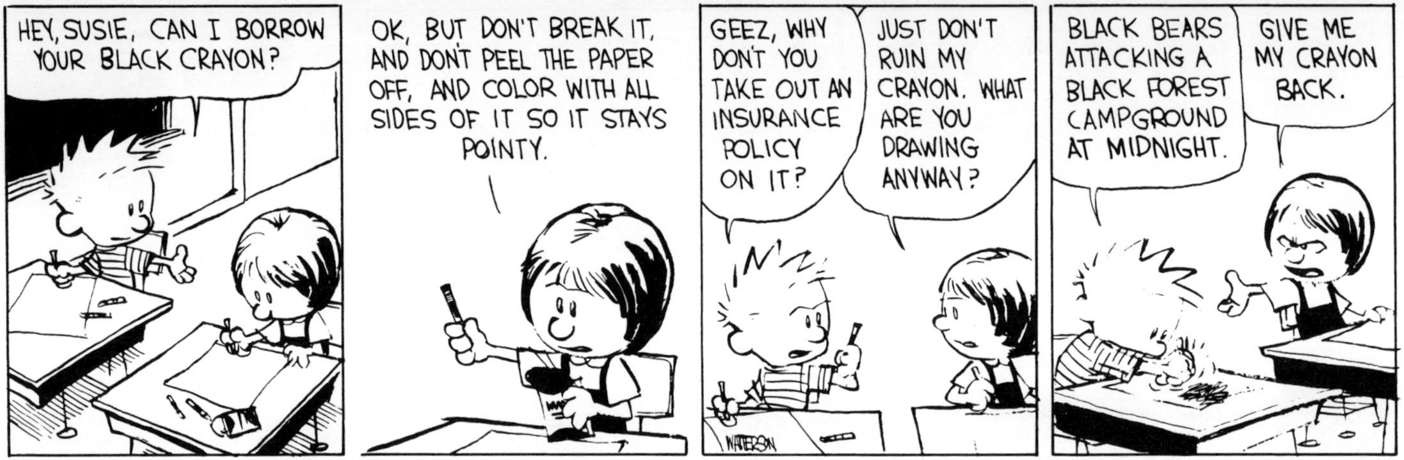
HEY, SUSIE, CAN I BORROW YOUR BLACK CRAYON?
OK, BUT DON'T BREAK IT, AND DON'T PEEL THE PAPER OFF, AND COLOR WITH ALL SIDES OF IT SO IT STAYS POINTY.
GEEZ, WHY DON'T YOU TAKE OUT AN INSURANCE POLICY ON IT?
JUST DON'T RUIN MY CRAYON. WHAT ARE YOU DRAWING ANYWAY?
BLACK BEARS ATTACKING A BLACK FOREST CAMPGROUND AT MIDNIGHT.
GIVE ME MY CRAYON BACK.

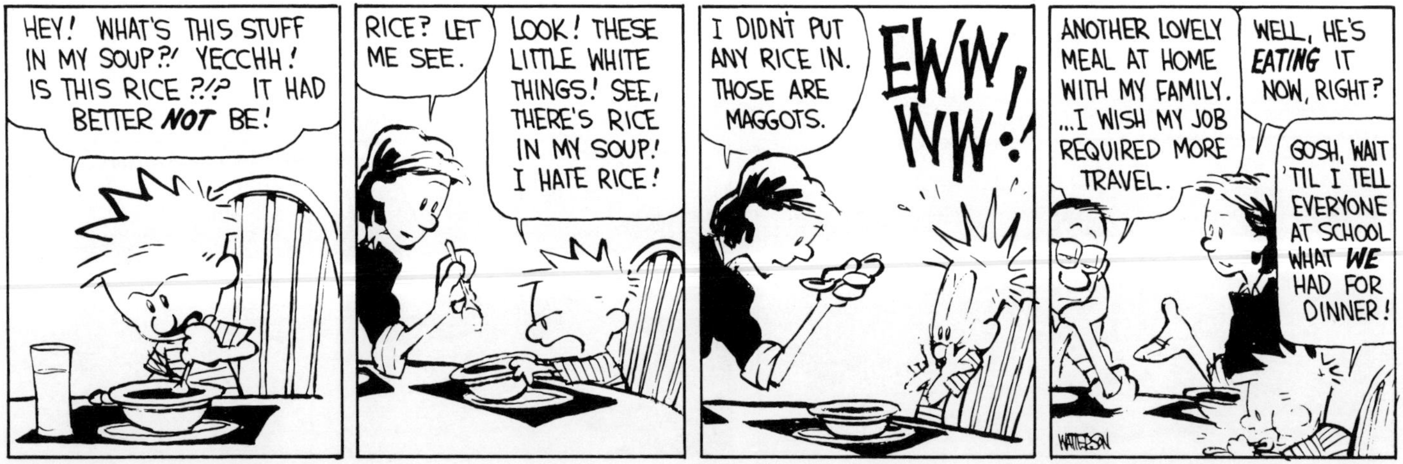
HEY! WHAT'S THIS STUFF IN MY SOUP?! YECCHH! IS THIS RICE ?!? IT HAD BETTER **NOT** BE!
RICE? LET ME SEE.
LOOK! THESE LITTLE WHITE THINGS! SEE, THERE'S RICE IN MY SOUP! I HATE RICE!
I DIDN'T PUT ANY RICE IN. THOSE ARE MAGGOTS.
EWWWW!!
ANOTHER LOVELY MEAL AT HOME WITH MY FAMILY. ...I WISH MY JOB REQUIRED MORE TRAVEL.
WELL, HE'S ***EATING*** IT NOW, RIGHT?
GOSH, WAIT 'TIL I TELL EVERYONE AT SCHOOL WHAT ***WE*** HAD FOR DINNER!

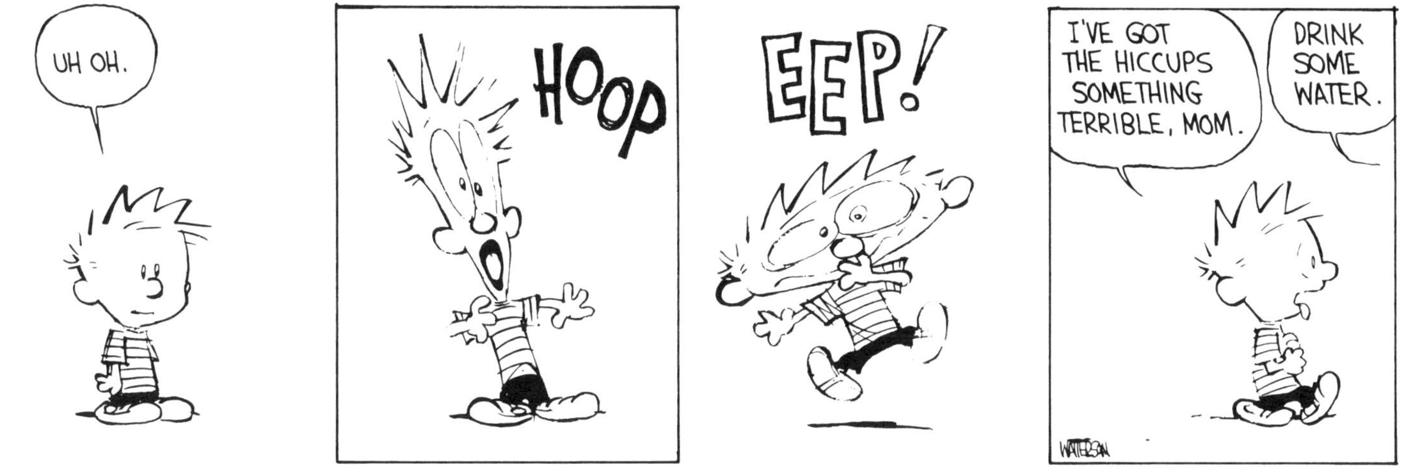
UH OH.
HOOP
EEP!
I'VE GOT THE HICCUPS SOMETHING TERRIBLE, MOM.
DRINK SOME WATER.
WATTERSON

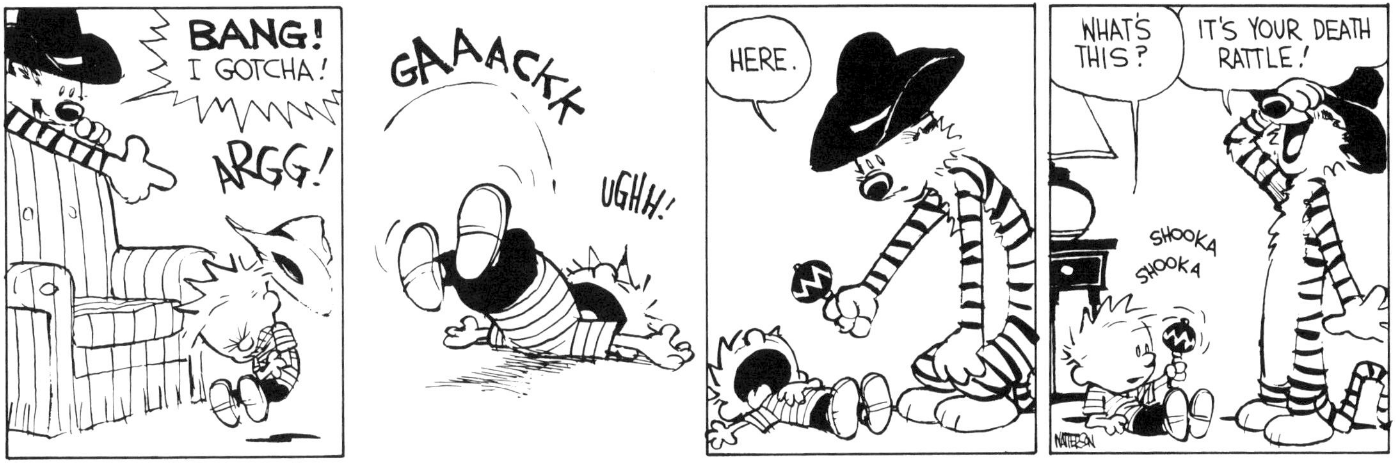
BANG! I GOTCHA!
ARGG!
GAAACKK
UGHH!
HERE.
WHAT'S THIS?
IT'S YOUR DEATH RATTLE!
SHOOKA
SHOOKA
WATTERSON

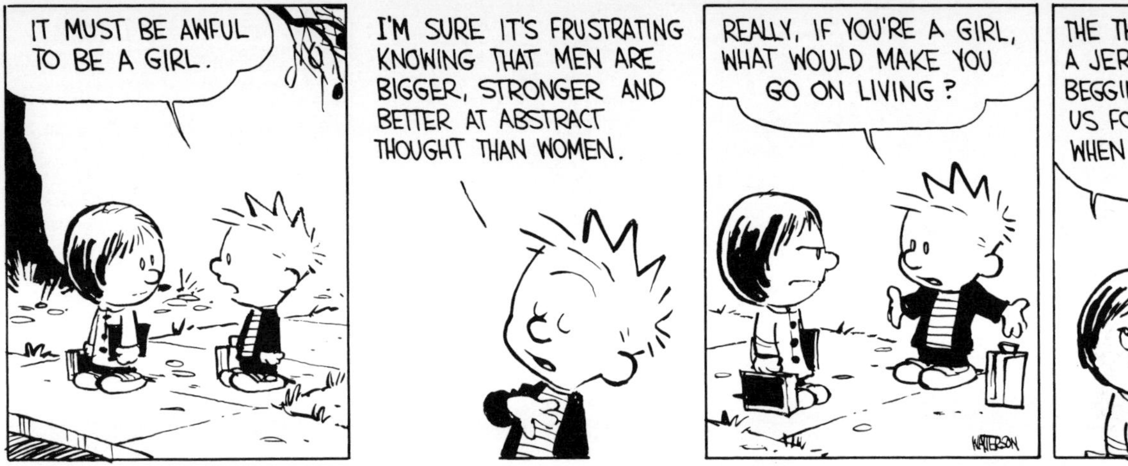
IT MUST BE AWFUL TO BE A GIRL.
I'M SURE IT'S FRUSTRATING KNOWING THAT MEN ARE BIGGER, STRONGER AND BETTER AT ABSTRACT THOUGHT THAN WOMEN.
REALLY, IF YOU'RE A GIRL, WHAT WOULD MAKE YOU GO ON LIVING?
THE THOUGHT OF A JERK LIKE YOU BEGGING ONE OF US FOR A DATE WHEN YOU'RE 17.
HA! NOT ME! GROSS!
WATTERSON

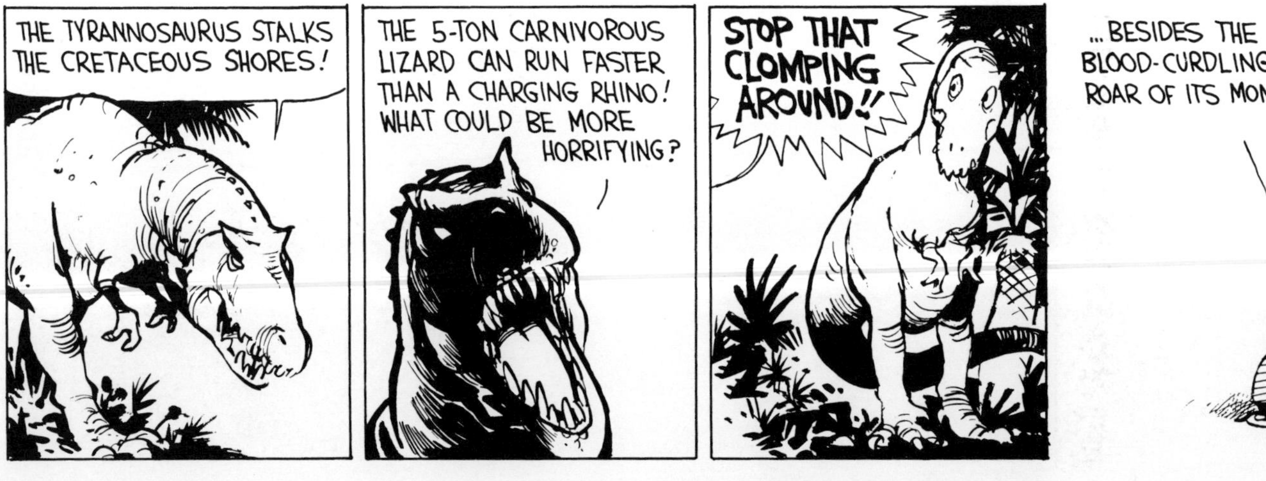
THE TYRANNOSAURUS STALKS THE CRETACEOUS SHORES!
THE 5-TON CARNIVOROUS LIZARD CAN RUN FASTER THAN A CHARGING RHINO! WHAT COULD BE MORE HORRIFYING?
STOP THAT CLOMPING AROUND!!
...BESIDES THE BLOOD-CURDLING ROAR OF ITS MOM...
WATTERSON

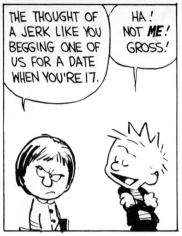

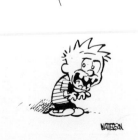

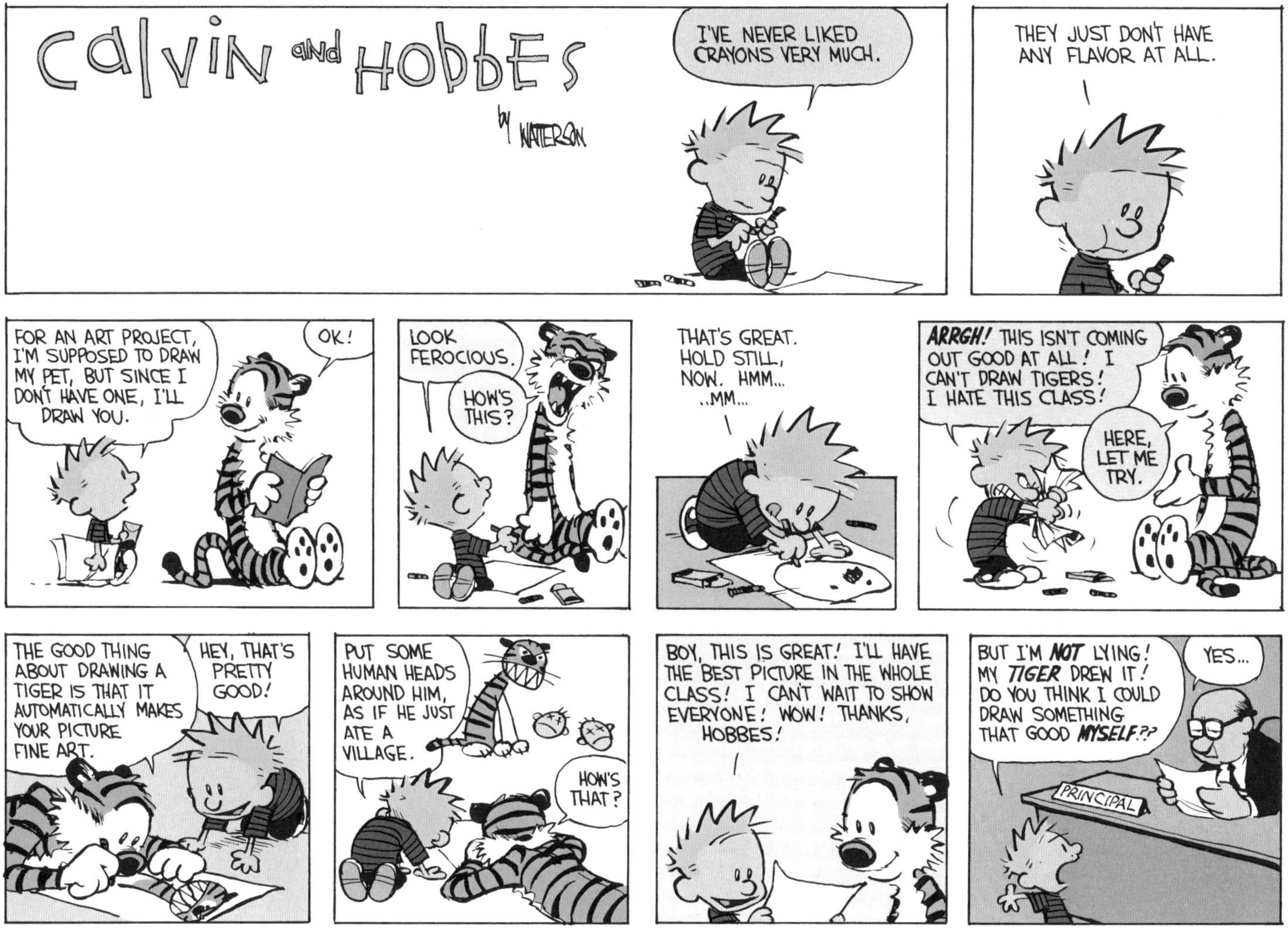
Calvin and HOBBES
by WATTERSON
I'VE NEVER LIKED CRAYONS VERY MUCH.
THEY JUST DON'T HAVE ANY FLAVOR AT ALL.
FOR AN ART PROJECT, I'M SUPPOSED TO DRAW MY PET, BUT SINCE I DON'T HAVE ONE, I'LL DRAW YOU.
OK!
LOOK FEROCIOUS.
HOW'S THIS?
THAT'S GREAT. HOLD STILL, NOW. HMM... ..MM...
ARRGH! THIS ISN'T COMING OUT GOOD AT ALL! I CAN'T DRAW TIGERS! I HATE THIS CLASS!
HERE, LET ME TRY.
THE GOOD THING ABOUT DRAWING A TIGER IS THAT IT AUTOMATICALLY MAKES YOUR PICTURE FINE ART.
HEY, THAT'S PRETTY GOOD!
PUT SOME HUMAN HEADS AROUND HIM, AS IF HE JUST ATE A VILLAGE.
HOW'S THAT?
BOY, THIS IS GREAT! I'LL HAVE THE BEST PICTURE IN THE WHOLE CLASS! I CAN'T WAIT TO SHOW EVERYONE! WOW! THANKS, HOBBES!
BUT I'M NOT LYING! MY TIGER DREW IT! DO YOU THINK I COULD DRAW SOMETHING THAT GOOD MYSELF?!?
YES...
PRINCIPAL

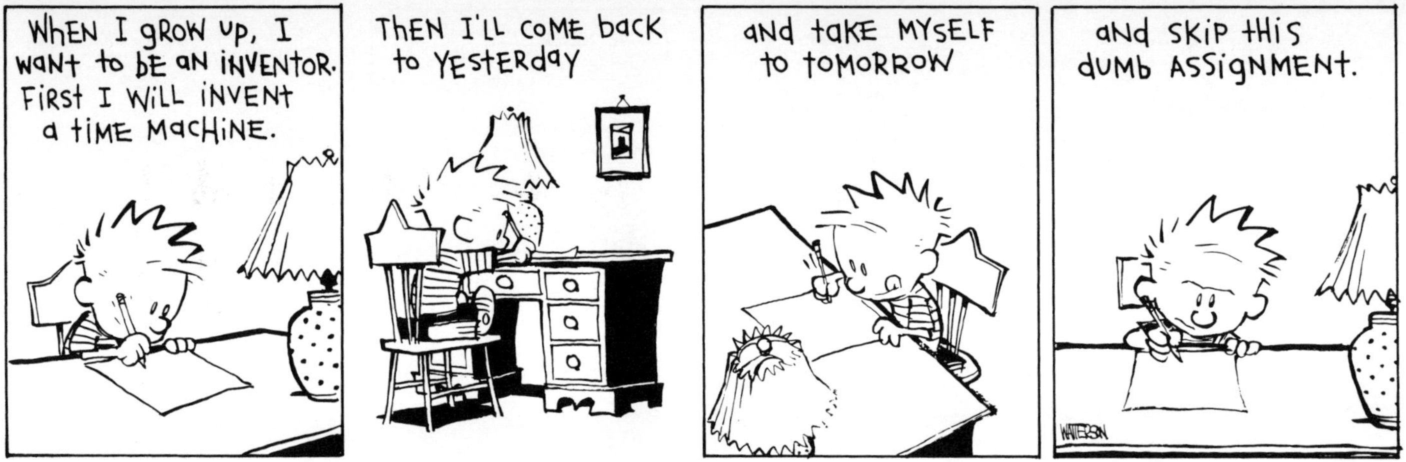
WHEN I GROW UP, I WANT TO BE AN INVENTOR. FIRST I WILL INVENT A TIME MACHINE.
THEN I'LL COME BACK TO YESTERDAY
AND TAKE MYSELF TO TOMORROW
AND SKIP THIS DUMB ASSIGNMENT.
WATTERSON

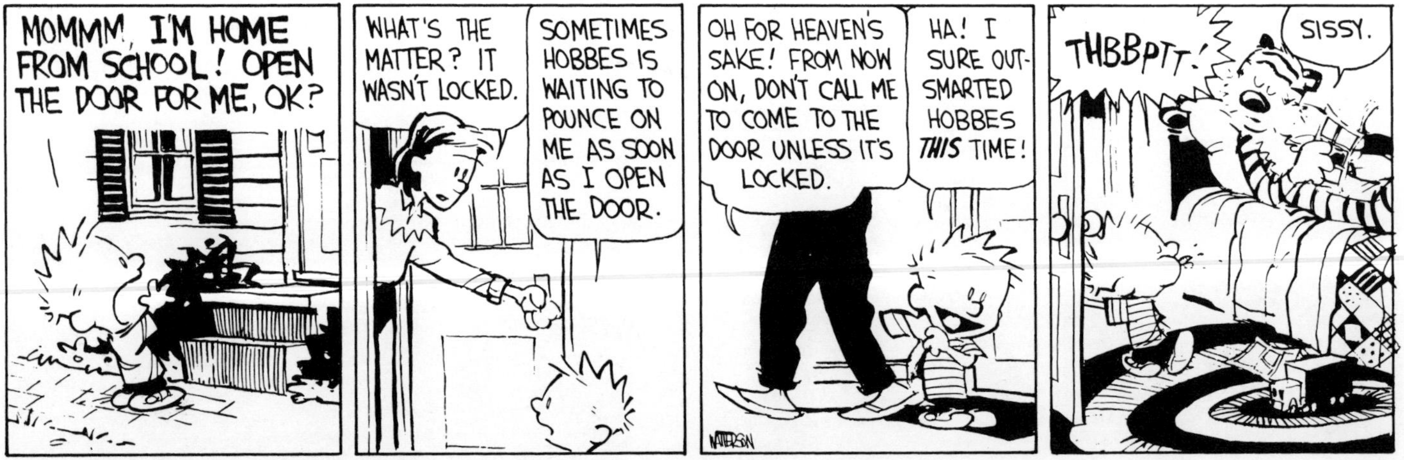
MOMMM, I'M HOME FROM SCHOOL! OPEN THE DOOR FOR ME, OK?
WHAT'S THE MATTER? IT WASN'T LOCKED.
SOMETIMES HOBBES IS WAITING TO POUNCE ON ME AS SOON AS I OPEN THE DOOR.
OH FOR HEAVEN'S SAKE! FROM NOW ON, DON'T CALL ME TO COME TO THE DOOR UNLESS IT'S LOCKED.
HA! I SURE OUT-SMARTED HOBBES *THIS* TIME!
WATTERSON
THBBPTT!
SISSY.

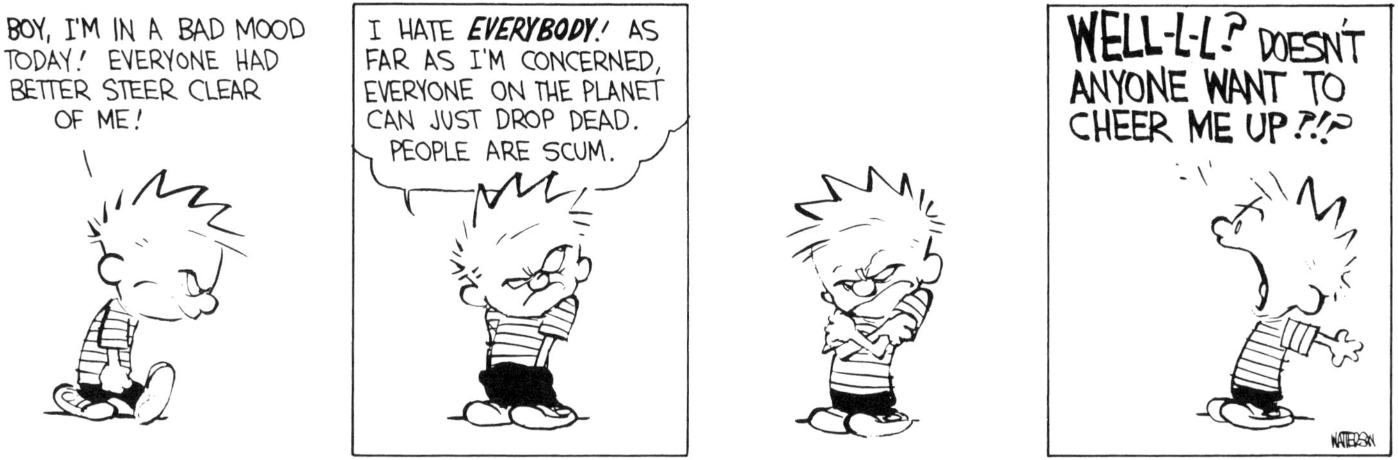
BOY, I'M IN A BAD MOOD TODAY! EVERYONE HAD BETTER STEER CLEAR OF ME!
I HATE ***EVERYBODY***! AS FAR AS I'M CONCERNED, EVERYONE ON THE PLANET CAN JUST DROP DEAD. PEOPLE ARE SCUM.
WELL-L-L? DOESN'T ANYONE WANT TO CHEER ME UP?!?
WATTERSON

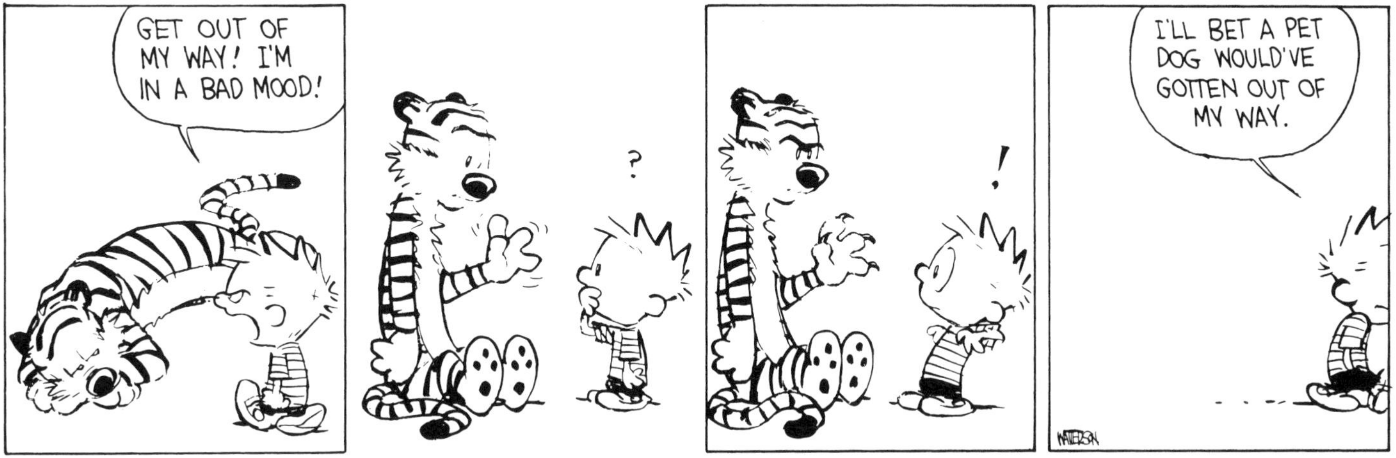
GET OUT OF MY WAY! I'M IN A BAD MOOD!
?
!
I'LL BET A PET DOG WOULD'VE GOTTEN OUT OF MY WAY.
WATTERSON

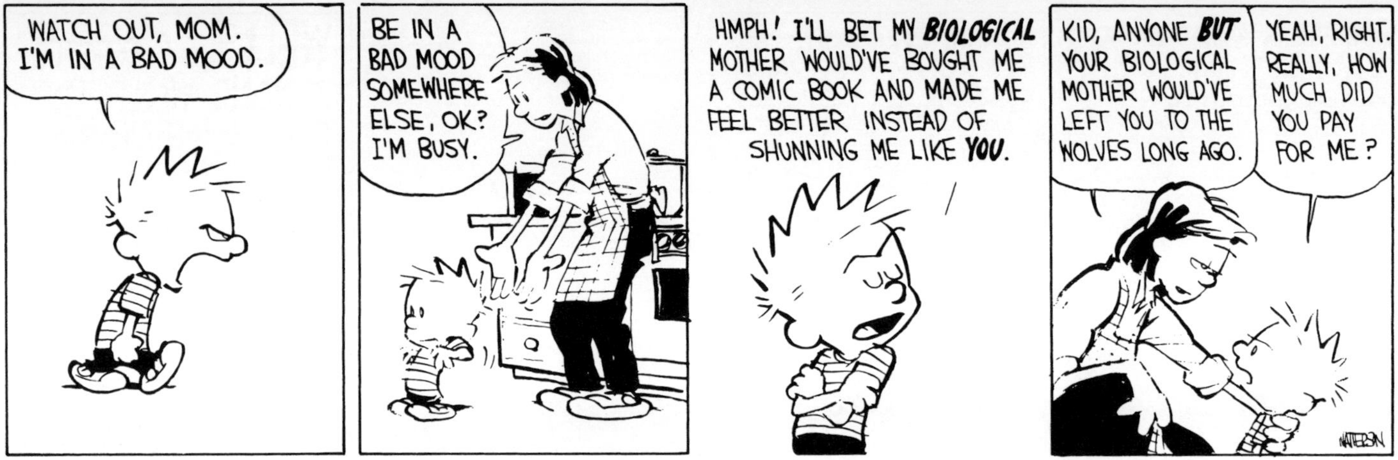
WATCH OUT, MOM. I'M IN A BAD MOOD.
BE IN A BAD MOOD SOMEWHERE ELSE, OK? I'M BUSY.
HMPH! I'LL BET MY BIOLOGICAL MOTHER WOULD'VE BOUGHT ME A COMIC BOOK AND MADE ME FEEL BETTER INSTEAD OF SHUNNING ME LIKE YOU.
KID, ANYONE BUT YOUR BIOLOGICAL MOTHER WOULD'VE LEFT YOU TO THE WOLVES LONG AGO.
YEAH, RIGHT. REALLY, HOW MUCH DID YOU PAY FOR ME?
WATTERSON

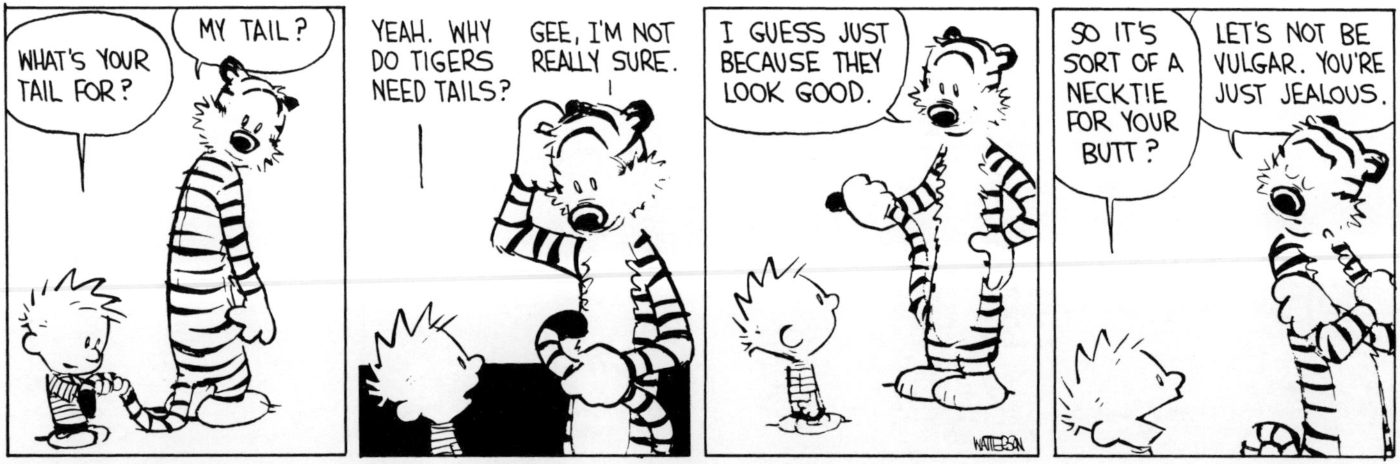
WHAT'S YOUR TAIL FOR?
MY TAIL?
YEAH. WHY DO TIGERS NEED TAILS?
GEE, I'M NOT REALLY SURE.
I GUESS JUST BECAUSE THEY LOOK GOOD.
WATTERSON
SO IT'S SORT OF A NECKTIE FOR YOUR BUTT?
LET'S NOT BE VULGAR. YOU'RE JUST JEALOUS.

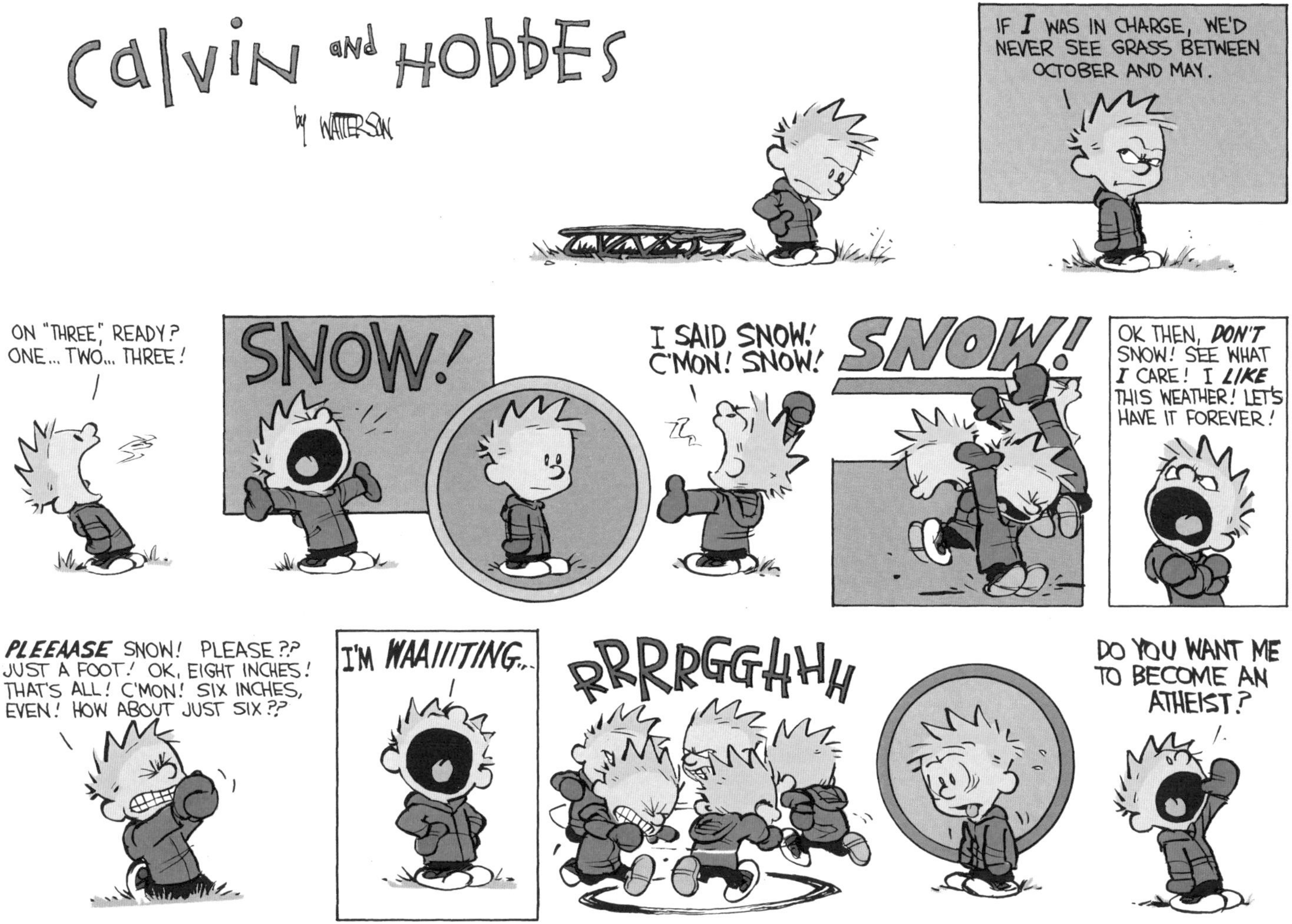
Calvin and HOBBES
by WATTERSON
IF I WAS IN CHARGE, WE'D NEVER SEE GRASS BETWEEN OCTOBER AND MAY.
ON "THREE," READY? ONE... TWO... THREE!
SNOW!
I SAID SNOW! C'MON! SNOW!
SNOW!
OK THEN, DON'T SNOW! SEE WHAT I CARE! I LIKE THIS WEATHER! LET'S HAVE IT FOREVER!
PLEEAASE SNOW! PLEASE?? JUST A FOOT! OK, EIGHT INCHES! THAT'S ALL! C'MON! SIX INCHES, EVEN! HOW ABOUT JUST SIX??
I'M WAAIIIITING...
RRRRGGHHH
DO YOU WANT ME TO BECOME AN ATHEIST?

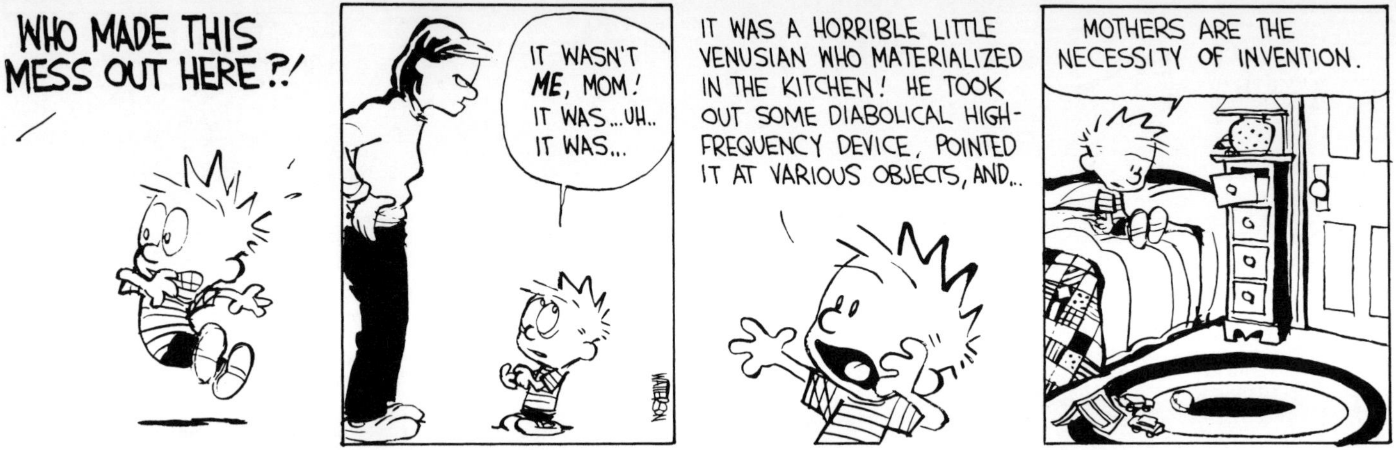
WHO MADE THIS MESS OUT HERE ?!
IT WASN'T ME, MOM! IT WAS...UH.. IT WAS...
IT WAS A HORRIBLE LITTLE VENUSIAN WHO MATERIALIZED IN THE KITCHEN! HE TOOK OUT SOME DIABOLICAL HIGH-FREQUENCY DEVICE, POINTED IT AT VARIOUS OBJECTS, AND...
MOTHERS ARE THE NECESSITY OF INVENTION.

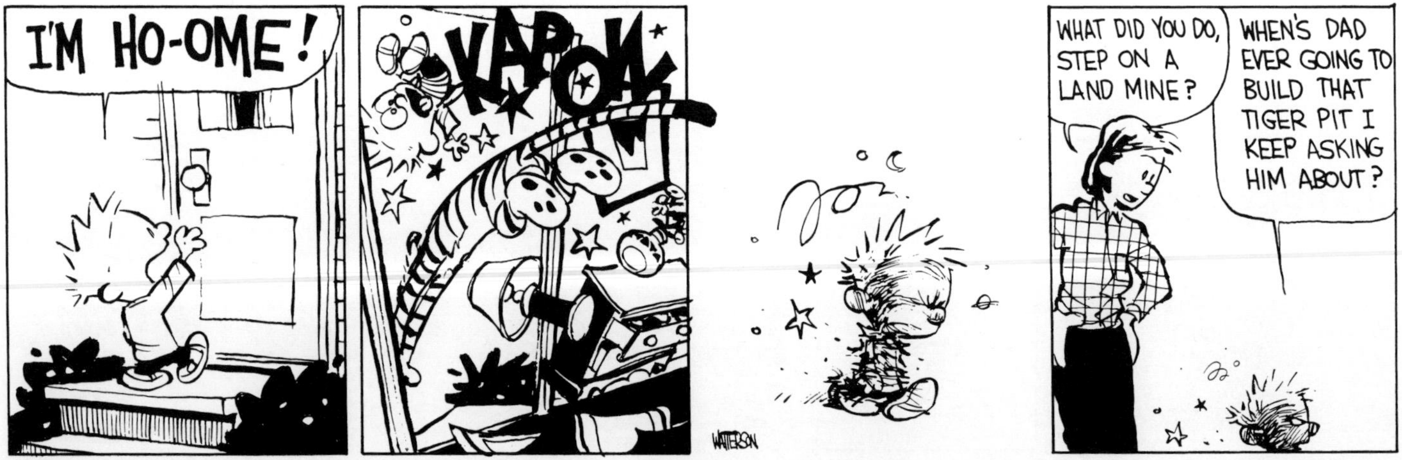
I'M HO-OME!
KAPOW
WHAT DID YOU DO, STEP ON A LAND MINE?
WHEN'S DAD EVER GOING TO BUILD THAT TIGER PIT I KEEP ASKING HIM ABOUT?

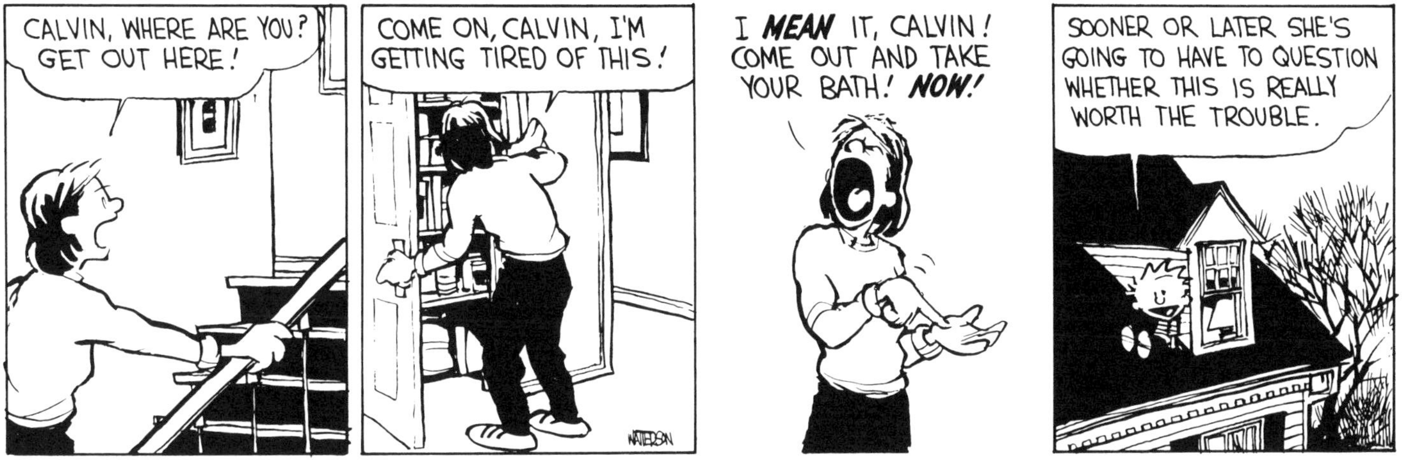
CALVIN, WHERE ARE YOU? GET OUT HERE!
COME ON, CALVIN, I'M GETTING TIRED OF THIS!
WATTERSON
I MEAN IT, CALVIN! COME OUT AND TAKE YOUR BATH! NOW!
SOONER OR LATER SHE'S GOING TO HAVE TO QUESTION WHETHER THIS IS REALLY WORTH THE TROUBLE.

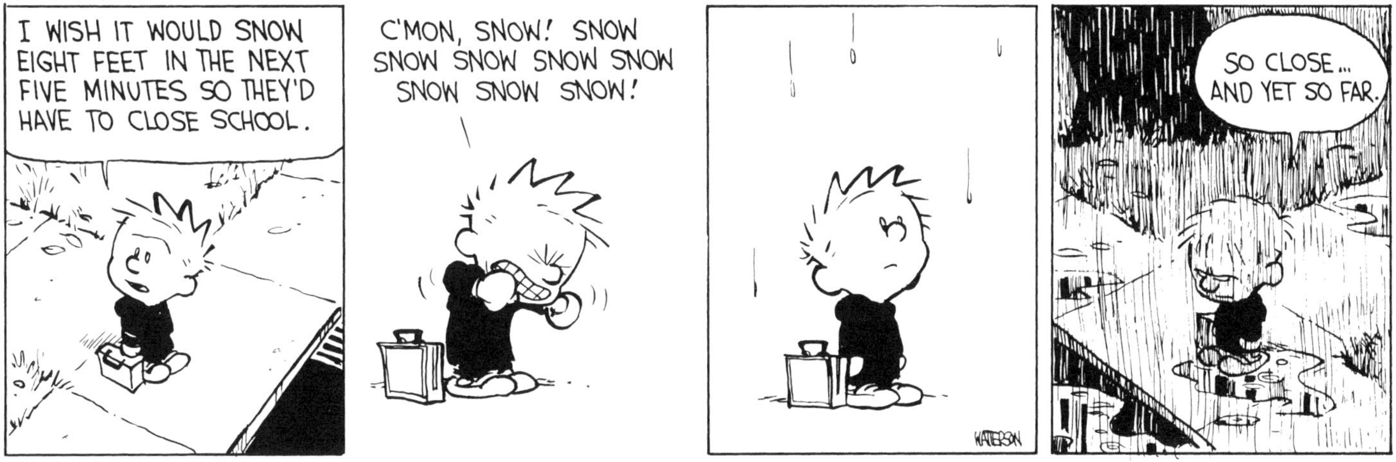
I WISH IT WOULD SNOW EIGHT FEET IN THE NEXT FIVE MINUTES SO THEY'D HAVE TO CLOSE SCHOOL.
C'MON, SNOW! SNOW SNOW SNOW SNOW SNOW SNOW SNOW SNOW!
WATTERSON
SO CLOSE... AND YET SO FAR.

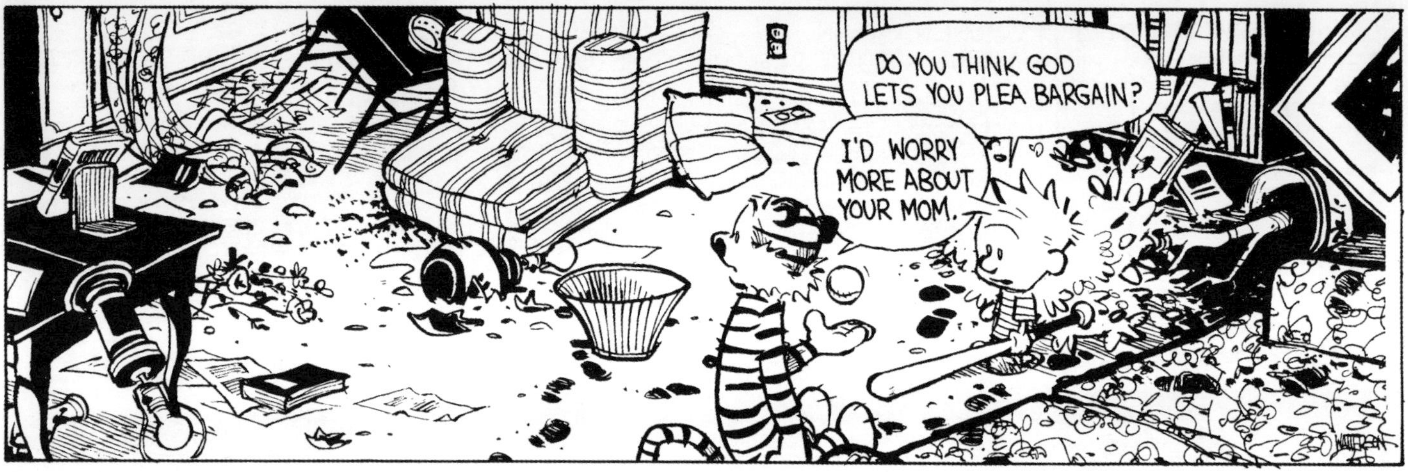
DO YOU THINK GOD LETS YOU PLEA BARGAIN?
I'D WORRY MORE ABOUT YOUR MOM.

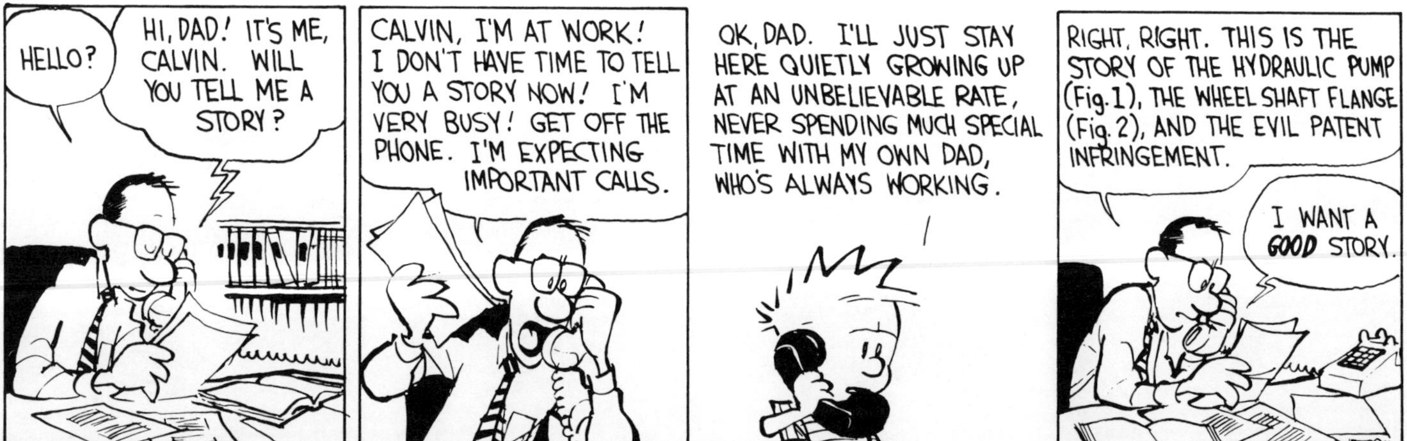
HELLO?
HI, DAD! IT'S ME, CALVIN. WILL YOU TELL ME A STORY?
CALVIN, I'M AT WORK! I DON'T HAVE TIME TO TELL YOU A STORY NOW! I'M VERY BUSY! GET OFF THE PHONE. I'M EXPECTING IMPORTANT CALLS.
OK, DAD. I'LL JUST STAY HERE QUIETLY GROWING UP AT AN UNBELIEVABLE RATE, NEVER SPENDING MUCH SPECIAL TIME WITH MY OWN DAD, WHO'S ALWAYS WORKING.
RIGHT, RIGHT. THIS IS THE STORY OF THE HYDRAULIC PUMP (Fig. 1), THE WHEEL SHAFT FLANGE (Fig. 2), AND THE EVIL PATENT INFRINGEMENT.
I WANT A GOOD STORY.

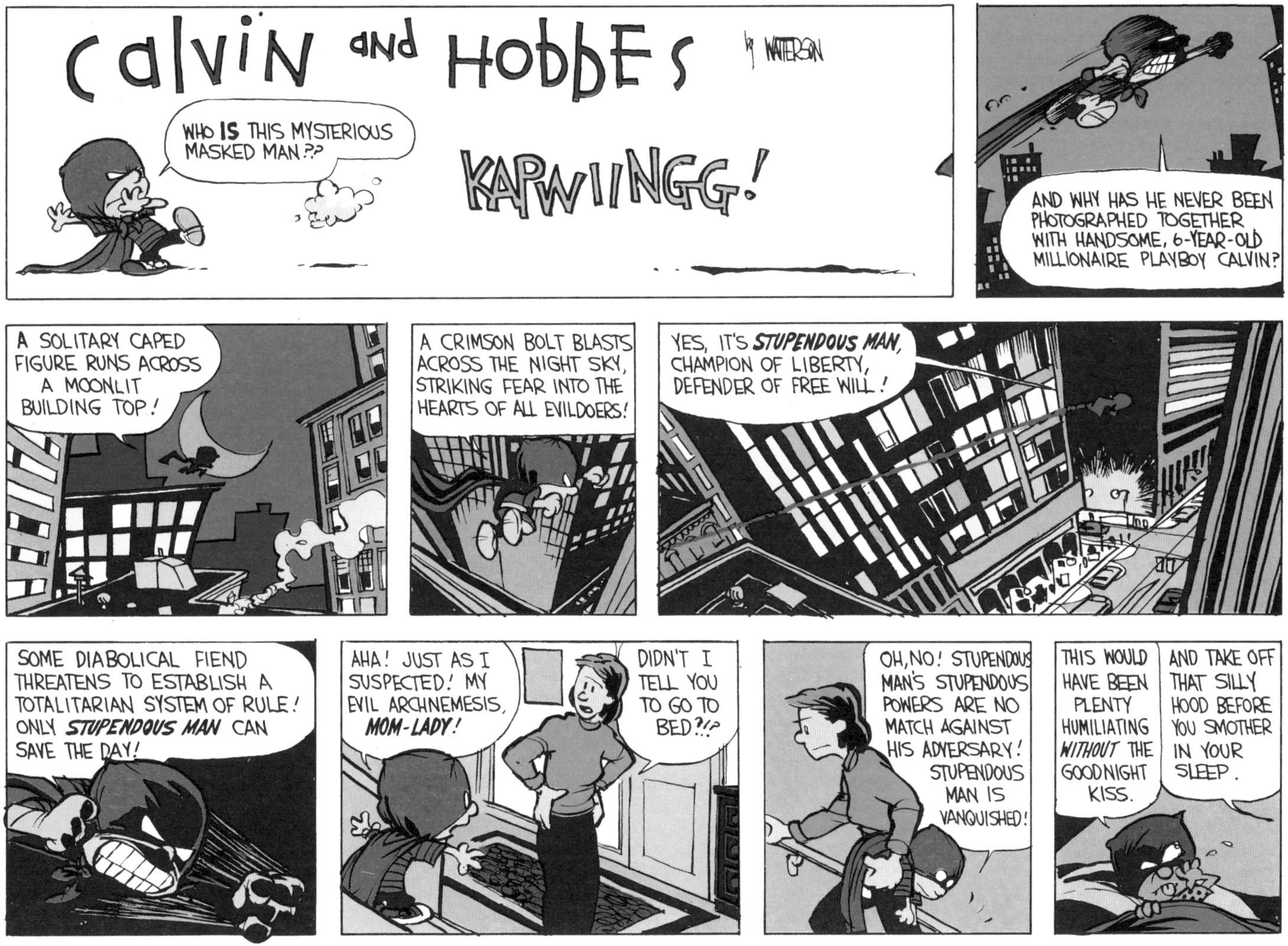
Calvin and Hobbes
by WATTERSON
WHO IS THIS MYSTERIOUS MASKED MAN?!?
KAPWIINGG!
AND WHY HAS HE NEVER BEEN PHOTOGRAPHED TOGETHER WITH HANDSOME, 6-YEAR-OLD MILLIONAIRE PLAYBOY CALVIN?
A SOLITARY CAPED FIGURE RUNS ACROSS A MOONLIT BUILDING TOP!
A CRIMSON BOLT BLASTS ACROSS THE NIGHT SKY, STRIKING FEAR INTO THE HEARTS OF ALL EVILDOERS!
YES, IT'S STUPENDOUS MAN, CHAMPION OF LIBERTY, DEFENDER OF FREE WILL!
SOME DIABOLICAL FIEND THREATENS TO ESTABLISH A TOTALITARIAN SYSTEM OF RULE! ONLY STUPENDOUS MAN CAN SAVE THE DAY!
AHA! JUST AS I SUSPECTED! MY EVIL ARCHNEMESIS, MOM-LADY!
DIDN'T I TELL YOU TO GO TO BED?!?
OH, NO! STUPENDOUS MAN'S STUPENDOUS POWERS ARE NO MATCH AGAINST HIS ADVERSARY! STUPENDOUS MAN IS VANQUISHED!
THIS WOULD HAVE BEEN PLENTY HUMILIATING WITHOUT THE GOODNIGHT KISS.
AND TAKE OFF THAT SILLY HOOD BEFORE YOU SMOTHER IN YOUR SLEEP.

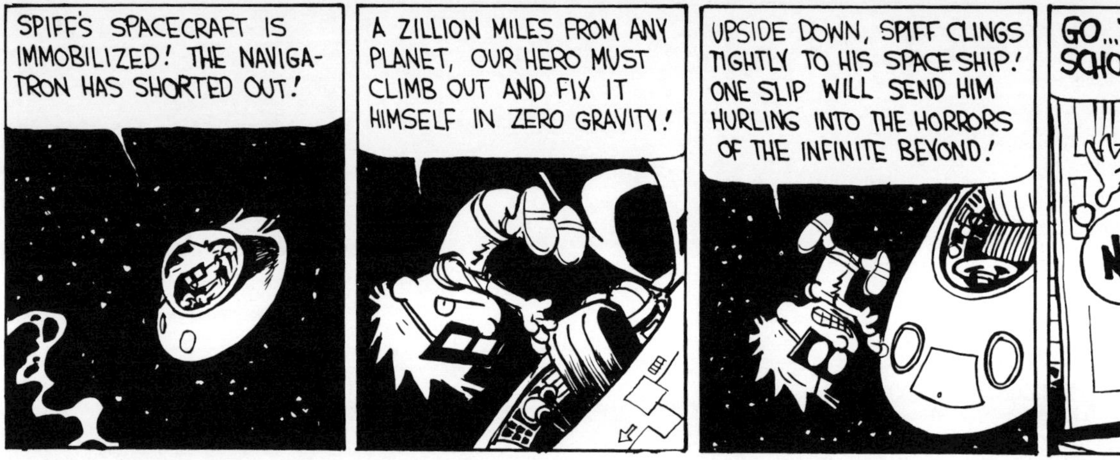
SPIFF'S SPACECRAFT IS IMMOBILIZED! THE NAVIGA-TRON HAS SHORTED OUT!
A ZILLION MILES FROM ANY PLANET, OUR HERO MUST CLIMB OUT AND FIX IT HIMSELF IN ZERO GRAVITY!
UPSIDE DOWN, SPIFF CLINGS TIGHTLY TO HIS SPACE SHIP! ONE SLIP WILL SEND HIM HURLING INTO THE HORRORS OF THE INFINITE BEYOND!
GO... TO... SCHOOL!
NO!

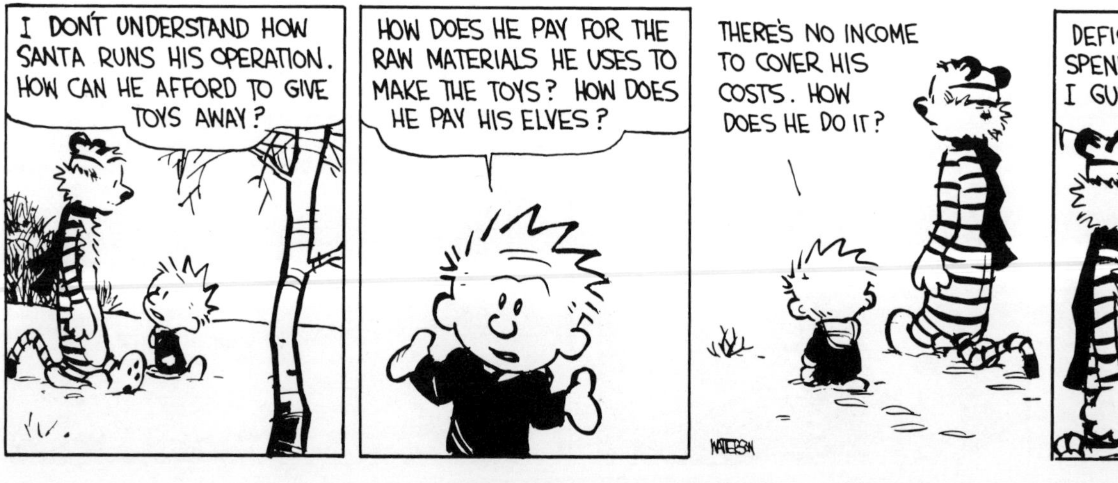
I DON'T UNDERSTAND HOW SANTA RUNS HIS OPERATION. HOW CAN HE AFFORD TO GIVE TOYS AWAY?
HOW DOES HE PAY FOR THE RAW MATERIALS HE USES TO MAKE THE TOYS? HOW DOES HE PAY HIS ELVES?
THERE'S NO INCOME TO COVER HIS COSTS. HOW DOES HE DO IT?
DEFICIT SPENDING, I GUESS.
SURE, BUT SOONER OR LATER IT'S GOING TO CATCH UP TO HIM, AND THEN WHERE WILL I BE?!

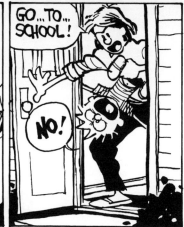

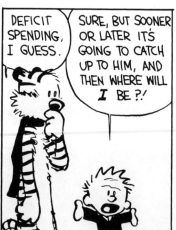

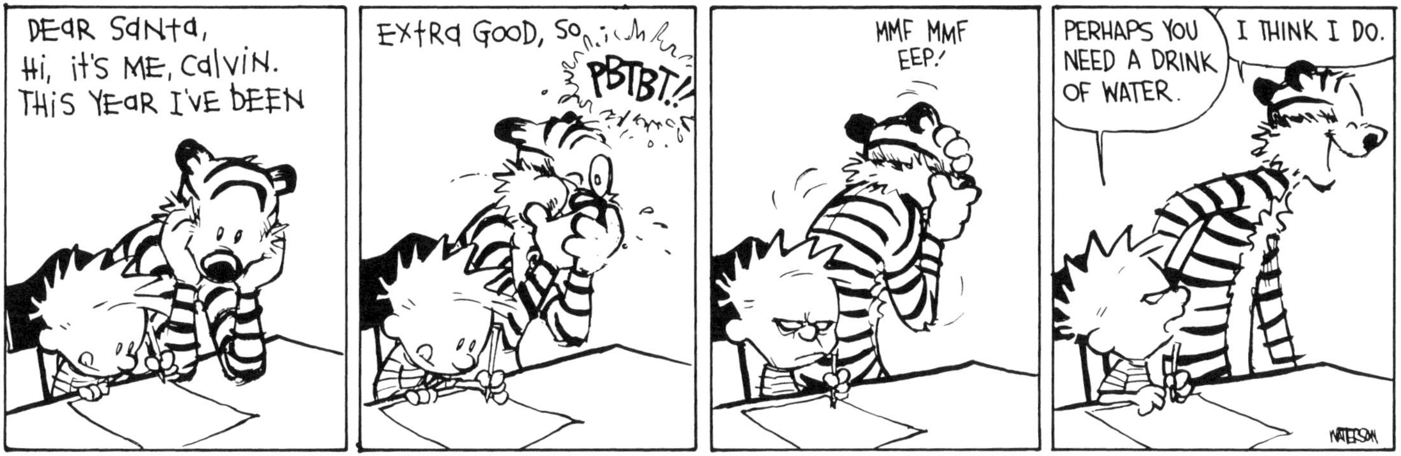
Dear Santa,
Hi, it's me, Calvin.
This year I've been
Extra good, so
PBTBT!!
MMF MMF EEP!
PERHAPS YOU NEED A DRINK OF WATER.
I THINK I DO.
WATTERSON

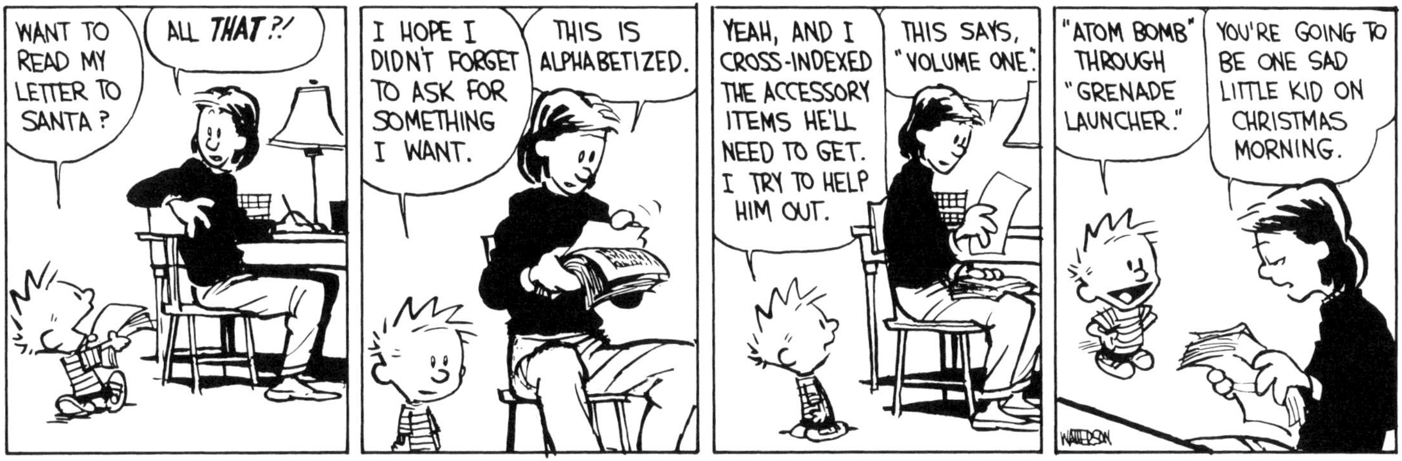
WANT TO READ MY LETTER TO SANTA ?
ALL *THAT* ?!
I HOPE I DIDN'T FORGET TO ASK FOR SOMETHING I WANT.
THIS IS ALPHABETIZED.
YEAH, AND I CROSS-INDEXED THE ACCESSORY ITEMS HE'LL NEED TO GET. I TRY TO HELP HIM OUT.
THIS SAYS, "VOLUME ONE."
"ATOM BOMB" THROUGH "GRENADE LAUNCHER."
YOU'RE GOING TO BE ONE SAD LITTLE KID ON CHRISTMAS MORNING.
WATTERSON

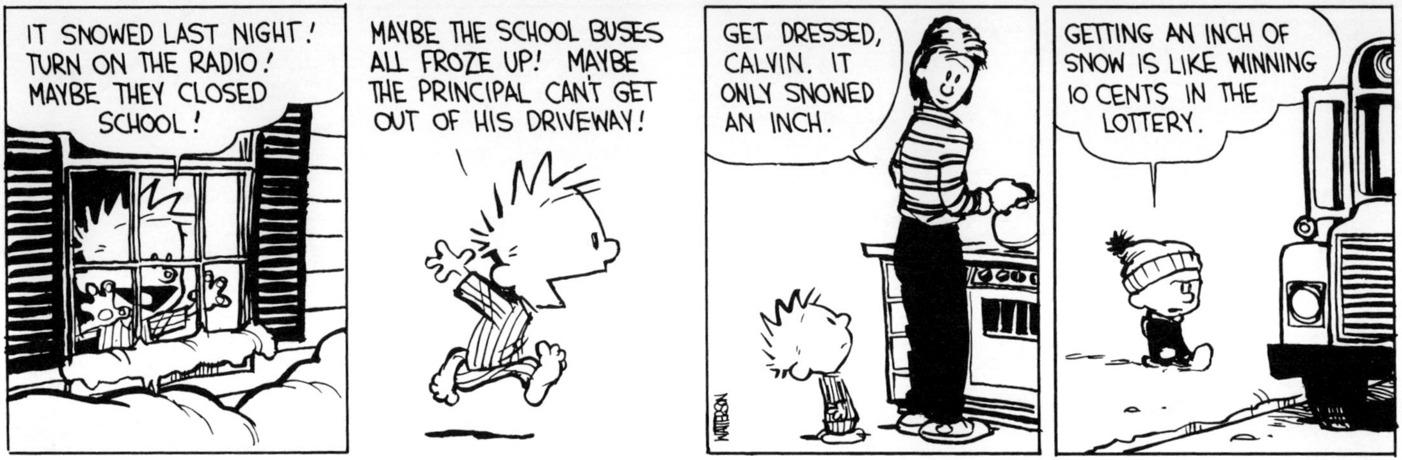
IT SNOWED LAST NIGHT! TURN ON THE RADIO! MAYBE THEY CLOSED SCHOOL!
MAYBE THE SCHOOL BUSES ALL FROZE UP! MAYBE THE PRINCIPAL CAN'T GET OUT OF HIS DRIVEWAY!
GET DRESSED, CALVIN. IT ONLY SNOWED AN INCH.
GETTING AN INCH OF SNOW IS LIKE WINNING 10 CENTS IN THE LOTTERY.

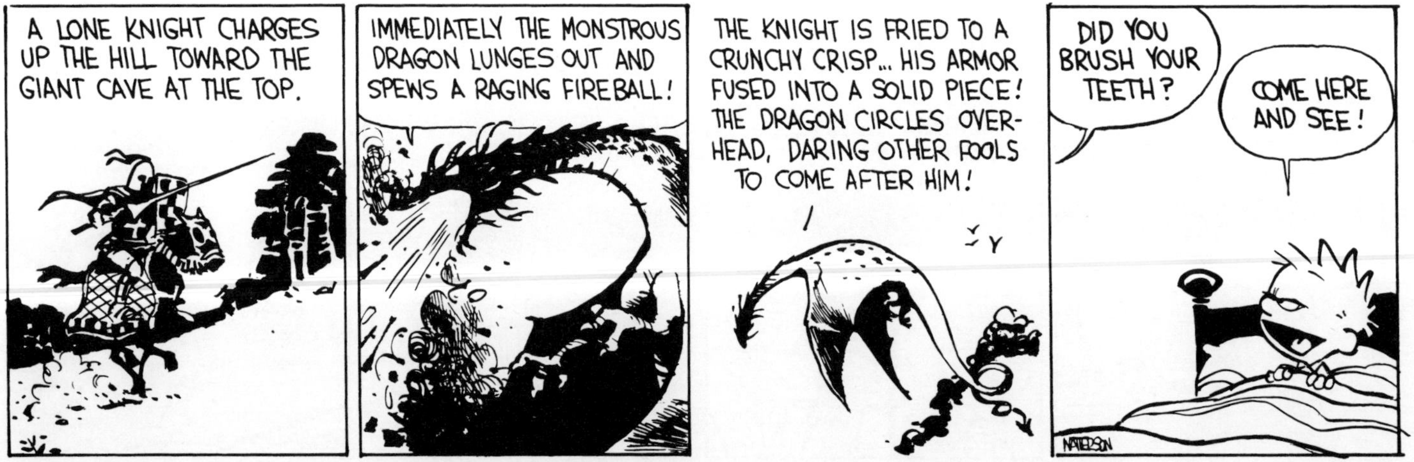
A LONE KNIGHT CHARGES UP THE HILL TOWARD THE GIANT CAVE AT THE TOP.
IMMEDIATELY THE MONSTROUS DRAGON LUNGES OUT AND SPEWS A RAGING FIREBALL!
THE KNIGHT IS FRIED TO A CRUNCHY CRISP... HIS ARMOR FUSED INTO A SOLID PIECE! THE DRAGON CIRCLES OVERHEAD, DARING OTHER FOOLS TO COME AFTER HIM!
DID YOU BRUSH YOUR TEETH?
COME HERE AND SEE!

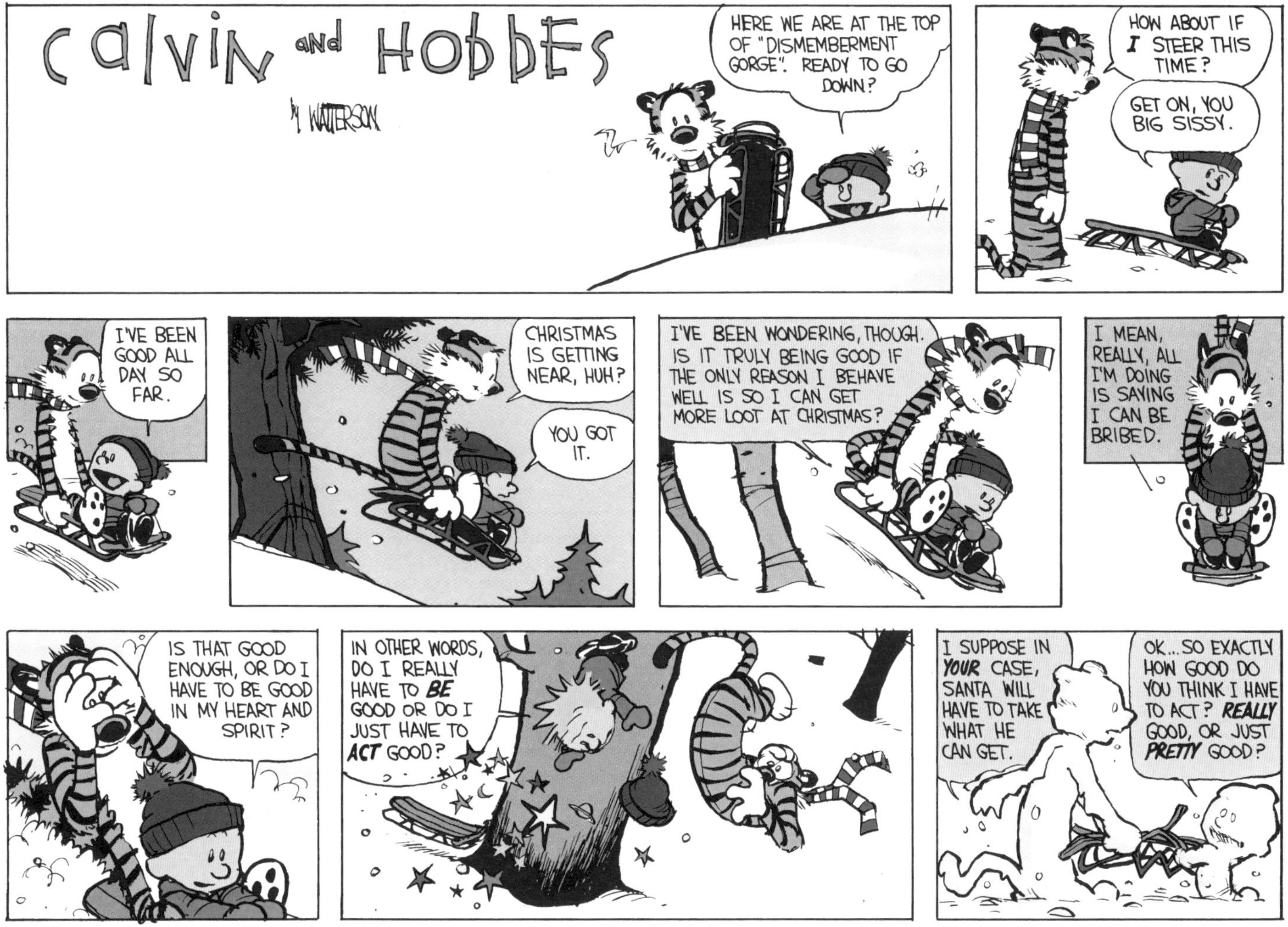
Calvin and HobbES
by WATTERSON
HERE WE ARE AT THE TOP OF "DISMEMBERMENT GORGE". READY TO GO DOWN?
HOW ABOUT IF I STEER THIS TIME?
GET ON, YOU BIG SISSY.
I'VE BEEN GOOD ALL DAY SO FAR.
CHRISTMAS IS GETTING NEAR, HUH?
YOU GOT IT.
I'VE BEEN WONDERING, THOUGH. IS IT TRULY BEING GOOD IF THE ONLY REASON I BEHAVE WELL IS SO I CAN GET MORE LOOT AT CHRISTMAS?
I MEAN, REALLY, ALL I'M DOING IS SAYING I CAN BE BRIBED.
IS THAT GOOD ENOUGH, OR DO I HAVE TO BE GOOD IN MY HEART AND SPIRIT?
IN OTHER WORDS, DO I REALLY HAVE TO BE GOOD OR DO I JUST HAVE TO ACT GOOD?
I SUPPOSE IN YOUR CASE, SANTA WILL HAVE TO TAKE WHAT HE CAN GET.
OK... SO EXACTLY HOW GOOD DO YOU THINK I HAVE TO ACT? REALLY GOOD, OR JUST PRETTY GOOD?

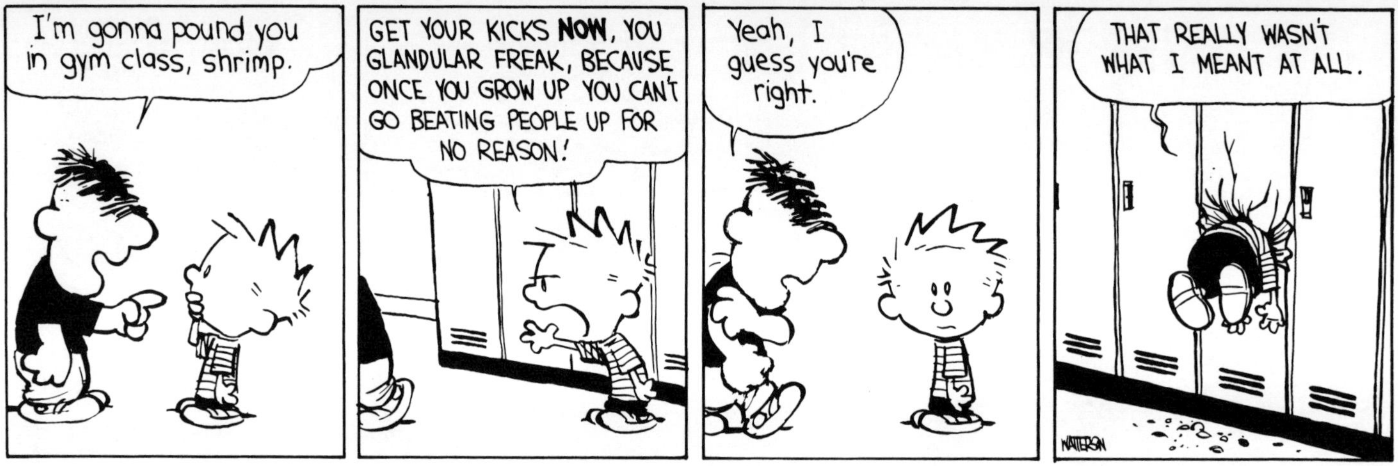
I'm gonna pound you in gym class, shrimp.
GET YOUR KICKS **NOW**, YOU GLANDULAR FREAK, BECAUSE ONCE YOU GROW UP YOU CAN'T GO BEATING PEOPLE UP FOR NO REASON!
Yeah, I guess you're right.
THAT REALLY WASN'T WHAT I MEANT AT ALL.
WATTERSON

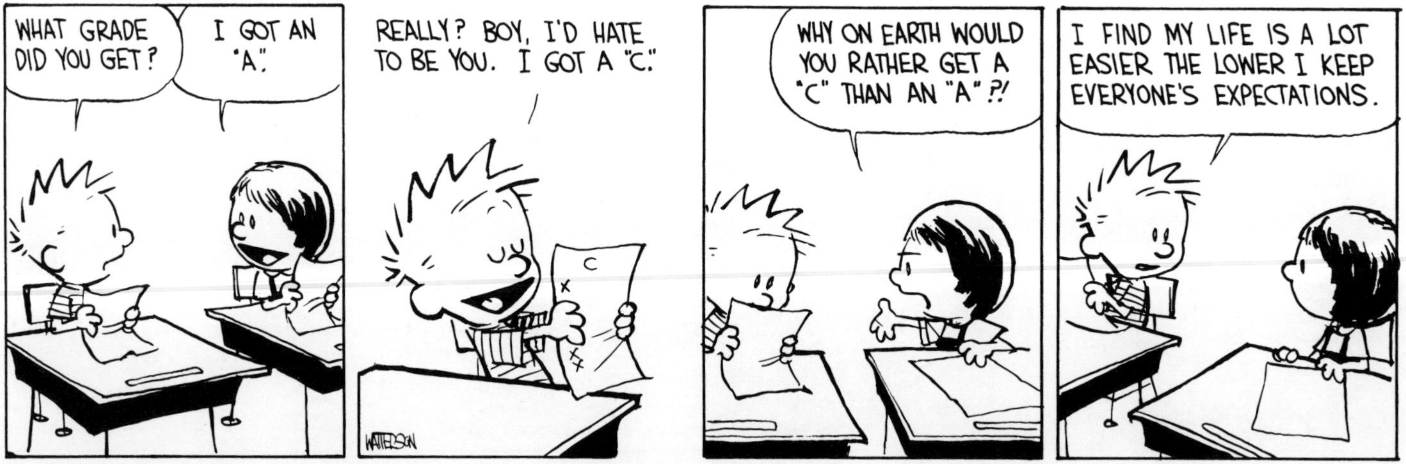
WHAT GRADE DID YOU GET?
I GOT AN "A".
REALLY? BOY, I'D HATE TO BE YOU. I GOT A "C."
WATTERSON
WHY ON EARTH WOULD YOU RATHER GET A "C" THAN AN "A"?!
I FIND MY LIFE IS A LOT EASIER THE LOWER I KEEP EVERYONE'S EXPECTATIONS.

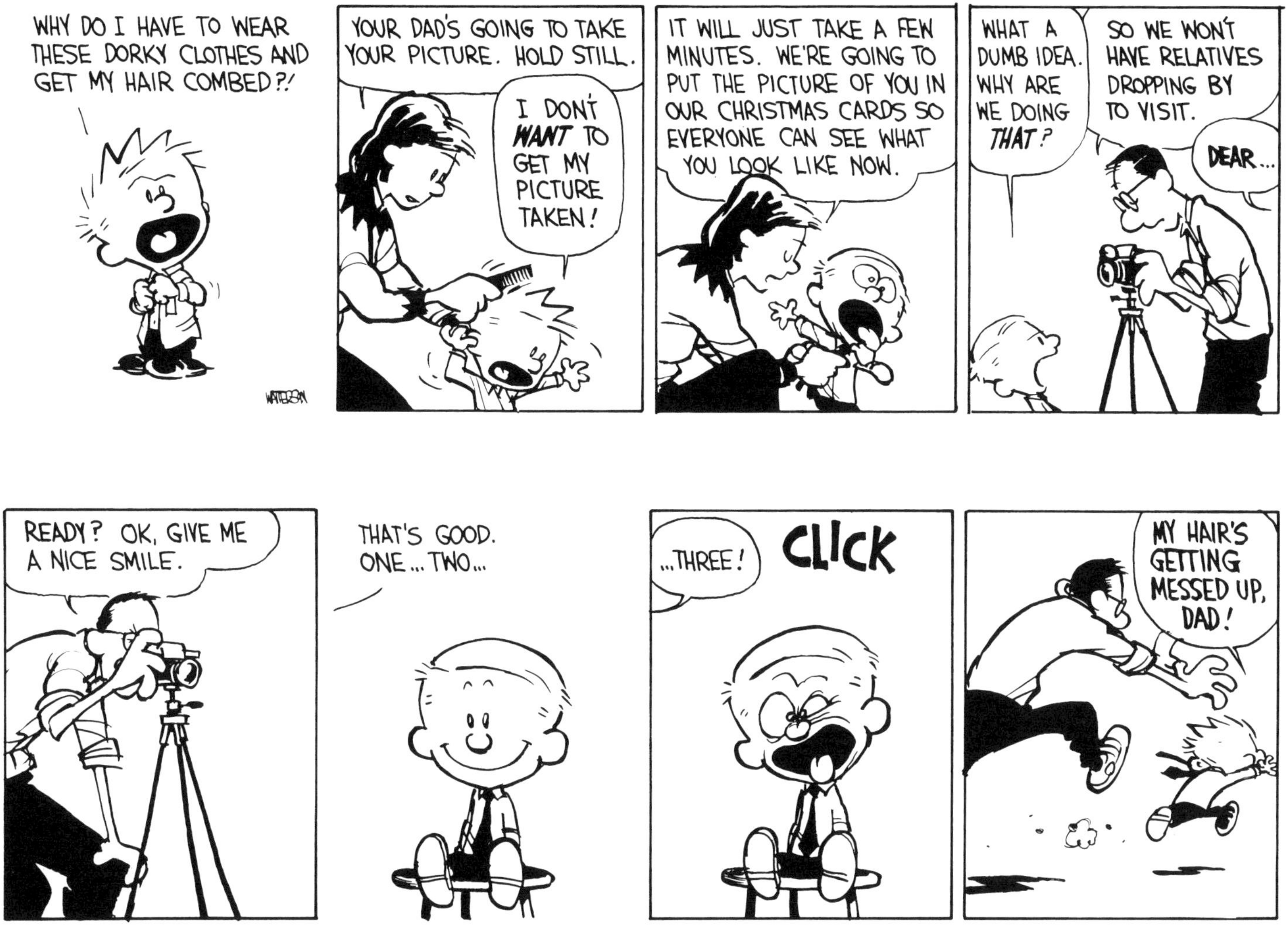

WHY DO I HAVE TO WEAR THESE DORKY CLOTHES AND GET MY HAIR COMBED?!
YOUR DAD'S GOING TO TAKE YOUR PICTURE. HOLD STILL.
I DON'T WANT TO GET MY PICTURE TAKEN!
IT WILL JUST TAKE A FEW MINUTES. WE'RE GOING TO PUT THE PICTURE OF YOU IN OUR CHRISTMAS CARDS SO EVERYONE CAN SEE WHAT YOU LOOK LIKE NOW.
WHAT A DUMB IDEA. WHY ARE WE DOING THAT?
SO WE WON'T HAVE RELATIVES DROPPING BY TO VISIT.
DEAR...
READY? OK, GIVE ME A NICE SMILE.
THAT'S GOOD. ONE... TWO...
...THREE!
CLICK
MY HAIR'S GETTING MESSED UP, DAD!

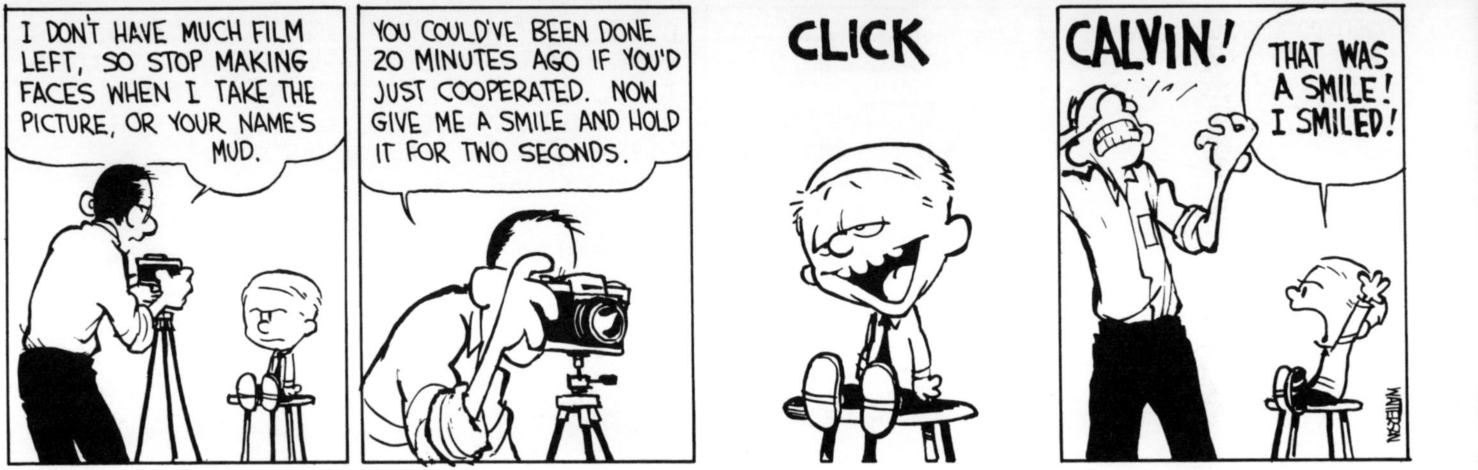
I DON'T HAVE MUCH FILM LEFT, SO STOP MAKING FACES WHEN I TAKE THE PICTURE, OR YOUR NAME'S MUD.
YOU COULD'VE BEEN DONE 20 MINUTES AGO IF YOU'D JUST COOPERATED. NOW GIVE ME A SMILE AND HOLD IT FOR TWO SECONDS.
CLICK
CALVIN!
THAT WAS A SMILE! I SMILED!
WATTERSON

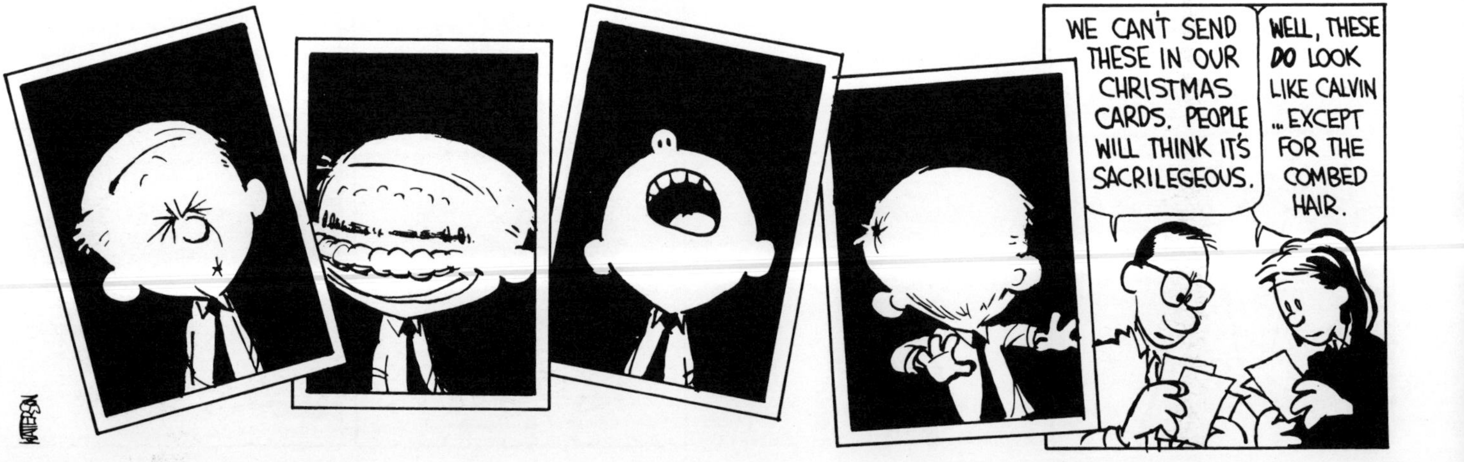
WATTERSON
WE CAN'T SEND THESE IN OUR CHRISTMAS CARDS. PEOPLE WILL THINK IT'S SACRILEGEOUS.
WELL, THESE DO LOOK LIKE CALVIN ... EXCEPT FOR THE COMBED HAIR.

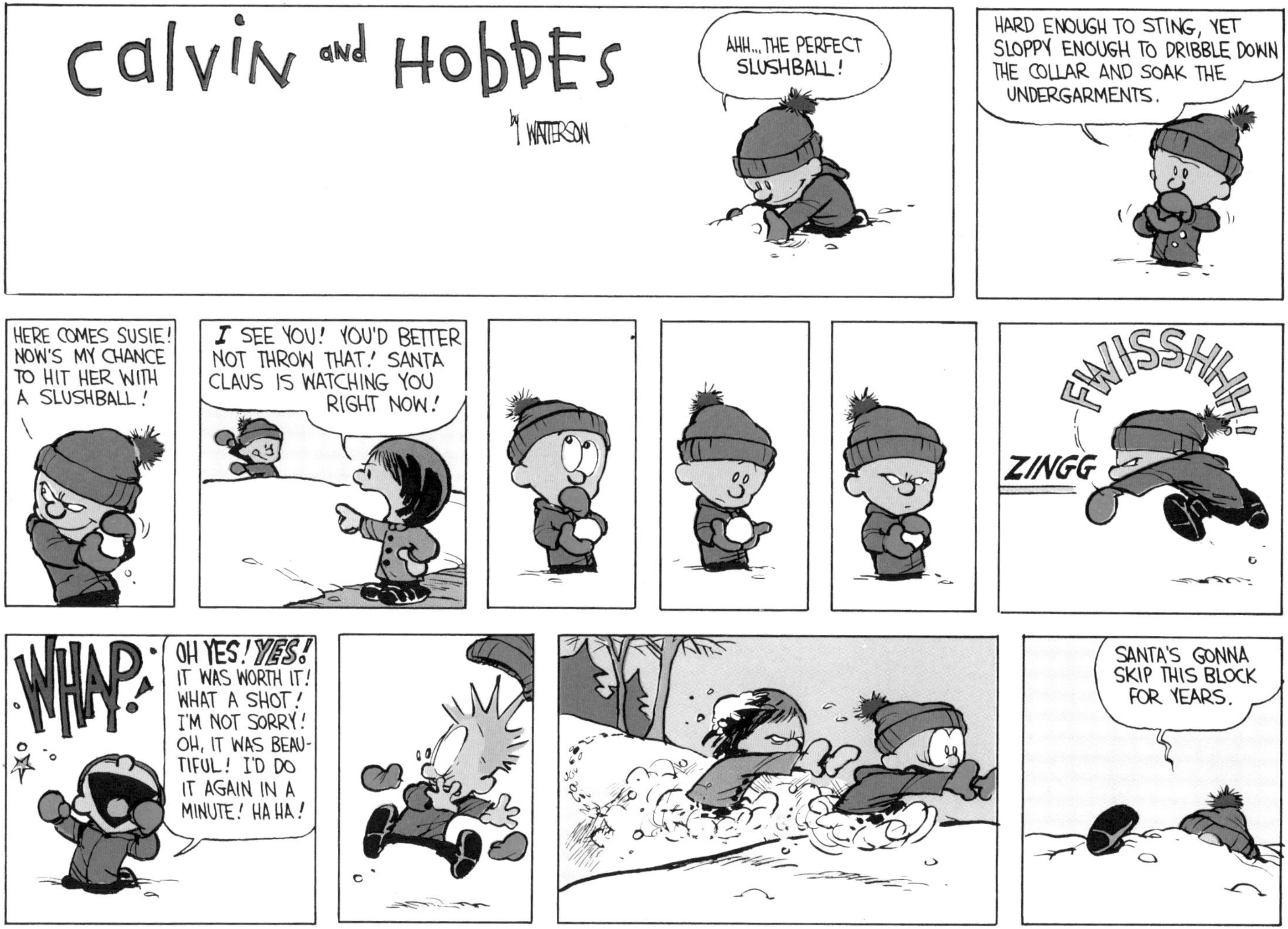
Calvin and Hobbes
by WATTERSON
AHH... THE PERFECT SLUSHBALL!
HARD ENOUGH TO STING, YET SLOPPY ENOUGH TO DRIBBLE DOWN THE COLLAR AND SOAK THE UNDERGARMENTS.
HERE COMES SUSIE! NOW'S MY CHANCE TO HIT HER WITH A SLUSHBALL!
I SEE YOU! YOU'D BETTER NOT THROW THAT! SANTA CLAUS IS WATCHING YOU RIGHT NOW!
FWISSHHH!
ZINGG
WHAP!
OH YES! YES! IT WAS WORTH IT! WHAT A SHOT! I'M NOT SORRY! OH, IT WAS BEAUTIFUL! I'D DO IT AGAIN IN A MINUTE! HA HA!
SANTA'S GONNA SKIP THIS BLOCK FOR YEARS.

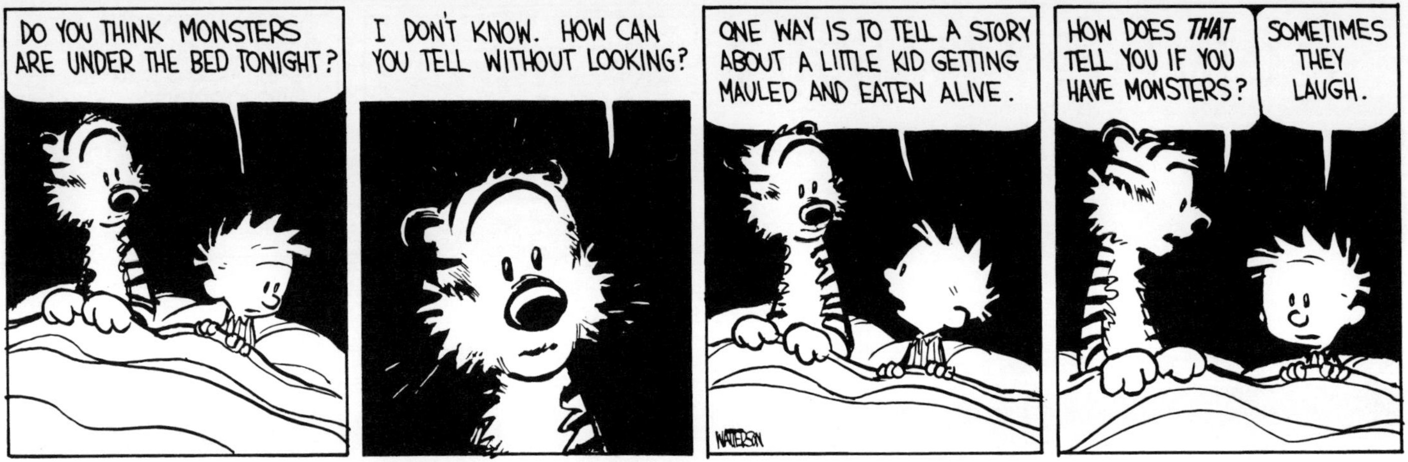
DO YOU THINK MONSTERS ARE UNDER THE BED TONIGHT?
I DON'T KNOW. HOW CAN YOU TELL WITHOUT LOOKING?
ONE WAY IS TO TELL A STORY ABOUT A LITTLE KID GETTING MAULED AND EATEN ALIVE.
WATTERSON
HOW DOES *THAT* TELL YOU IF YOU HAVE MONSTERS?
SOMETIMES THEY LAUGH.

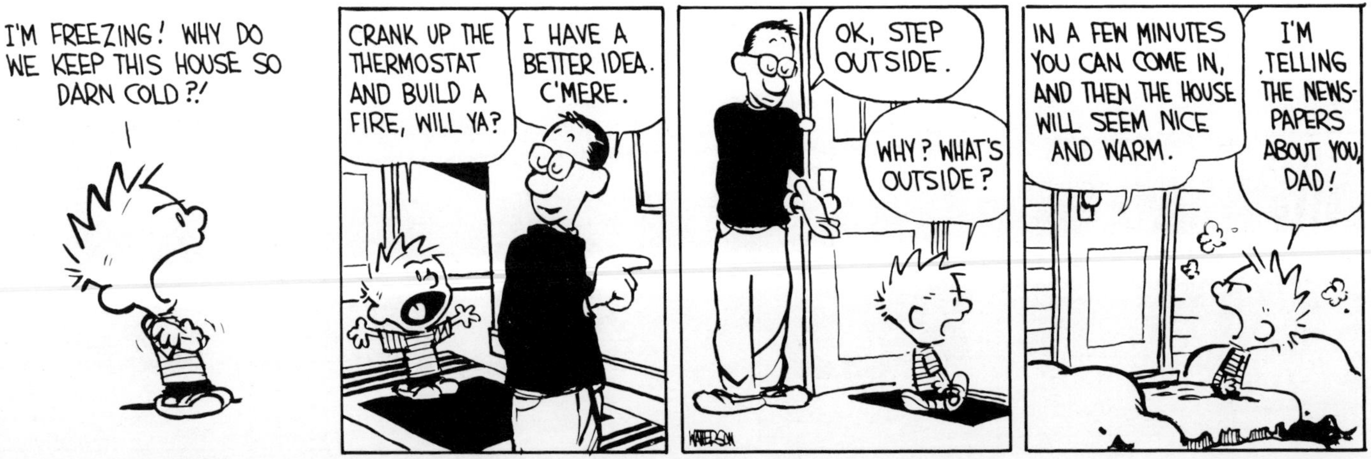
I'M FREEZING! WHY DO WE KEEP THIS HOUSE SO DARN COLD?!
CRANK UP THE THERMOSTAT AND BUILD A FIRE, WILL YA?
I HAVE A BETTER IDEA. C'MERE.
OK, STEP OUTSIDE.
WHY? WHAT'S OUTSIDE?
WATTERSON
IN A FEW MINUTES YOU CAN COME IN, AND THEN THE HOUSE WILL SEEM NICE AND WARM.
I'M TELLING THE NEWS-PAPERS ABOUT YOU, DAD!

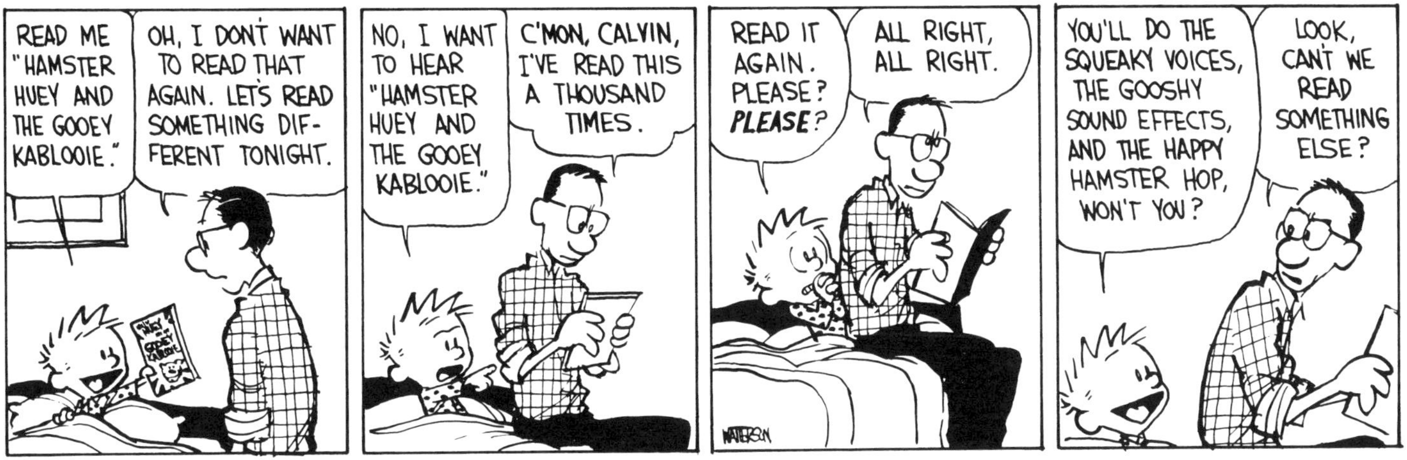
READ ME "HAMSTER HUEY AND THE GOOEY KABLOOIE."
OH, I DON'T WANT TO READ THAT AGAIN. LET'S READ SOMETHING DIF-FERENT TONIGHT.
NO, I WANT TO HEAR "HAMSTER HUEY AND THE GOOEY KABLOOIE."
C'MON, CALVIN, I'VE READ THIS A THOUSAND TIMES.
READ IT AGAIN. PLEASE? *PLEASE*?
ALL RIGHT, ALL RIGHT.
YOU'LL DO THE SQUEAKY VOICES, THE GOOSHY SOUND EFFECTS, AND THE HAPPY HAMSTER HOP, WON'T YOU?
LOOK, CAN'T WE READ SOMETHING ELSE?

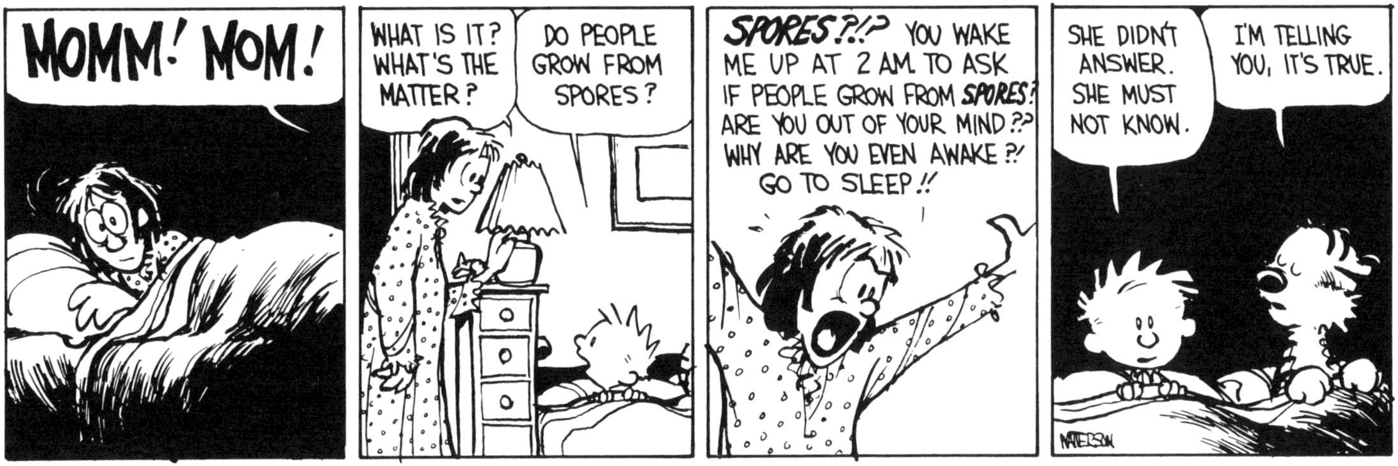
MOMM! MOM!
WHAT IS IT? WHAT'S THE MATTER?
DO PEOPLE GROW FROM SPORES?
SPORES?!? YOU WAKE ME UP AT 2 AM. TO ASK IF PEOPLE GROW FROM *SPORES?* ARE YOU OUT OF YOUR MIND?? WHY ARE YOU EVEN AWAKE?! GO TO SLEEP!!
SHE DIDN'T ANSWER. SHE MUST NOT KNOW.
I'M TELLING YOU, IT'S TRUE.

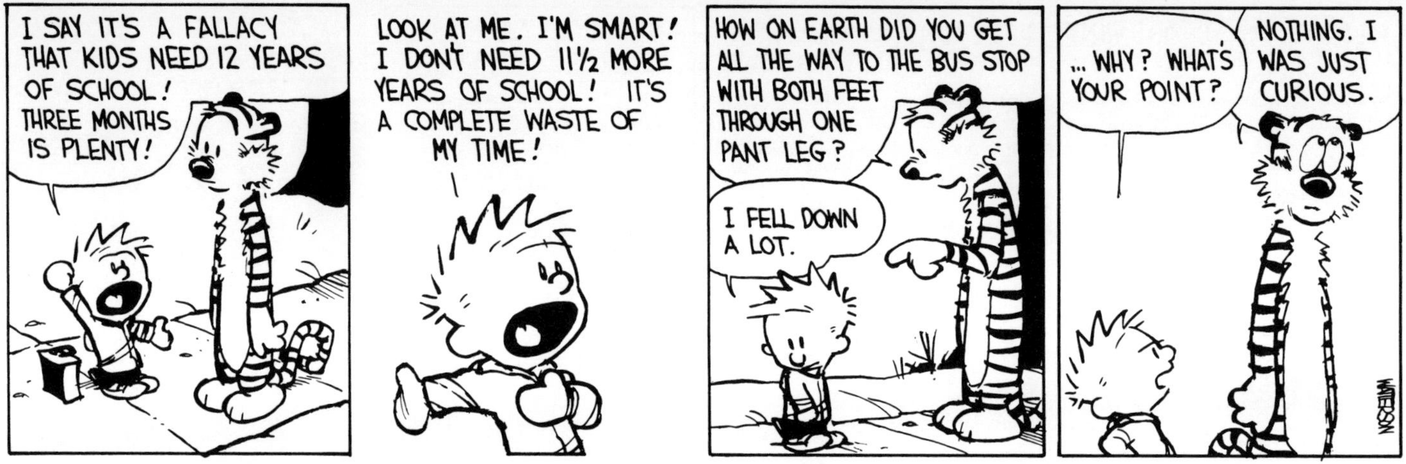
I SAY IT'S A FALLACY THAT KIDS NEED 12 YEARS OF SCHOOL! THREE MONTHS IS PLENTY!
LOOK AT ME. I'M SMART! I DON'T NEED 11½ MORE YEARS OF SCHOOL! IT'S A COMPLETE WASTE OF MY TIME!
HOW ON EARTH DID YOU GET ALL THE WAY TO THE BUS STOP WITH BOTH FEET THROUGH ONE PANT LEG?
I FELL DOWN A LOT.
... WHY? WHAT'S YOUR POINT?
NOTHING. I WAS JUST CURIOUS.

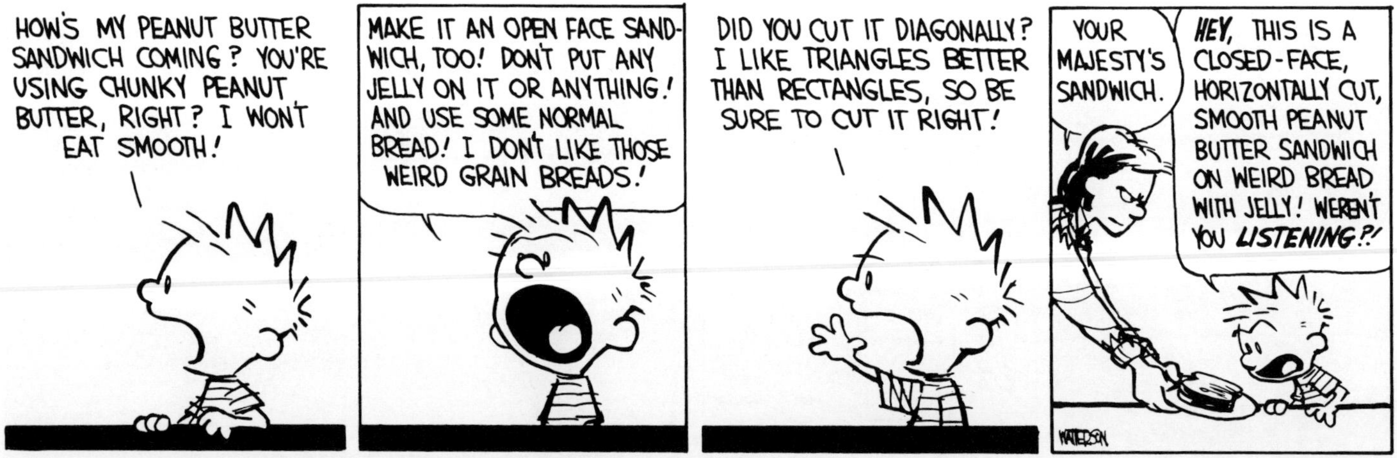
HOW'S MY PEANUT BUTTER SANDWICH COMING? YOU'RE USING CHUNKY PEANUT BUTTER, RIGHT? I WON'T EAT SMOOTH!
MAKE IT AN OPEN FACE SANDWICH, TOO! DON'T PUT ANY JELLY ON IT OR ANYTHING! AND USE SOME NORMAL BREAD! I DON'T LIKE THOSE WEIRD GRAIN BREADS!
DID YOU CUT IT DIAGONALLY? I LIKE TRIANGLES BETTER THAN RECTANGLES, SO BE SURE TO CUT IT RIGHT!
YOUR MAJESTY'S SANDWICH.
HEY, THIS IS A CLOSED-FACE, HORIZONTALLY CUT, SMOOTH PEANUT BUTTER SANDWICH ON WEIRD BREAD WITH JELLY! WEREN'T YOU LISTENING?!

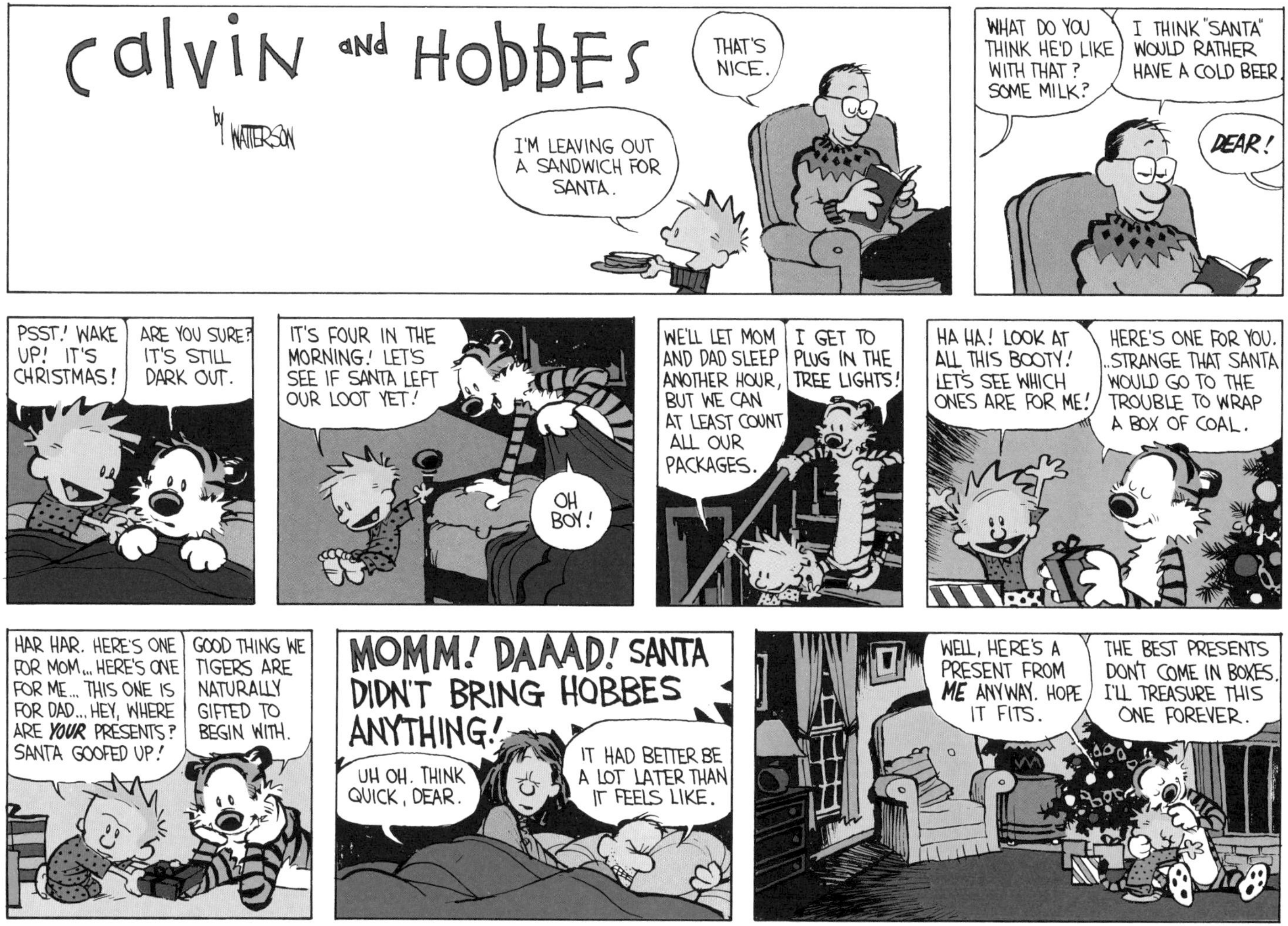
Calvin and Hobbes
by WATTERSON
I'M LEAVING OUT A SANDWICH FOR SANTA.
THAT'S NICE.
WHAT DO YOU THINK HE'D LIKE WITH THAT? SOME MILK?
I THINK "SANTA" WOULD RATHER HAVE A COLD BEER.
DEAR!
PSST! WAKE UP! IT'S CHRISTMAS!
ARE YOU SURE? IT'S STILL DARK OUT.
IT'S FOUR IN THE MORNING! LET'S SEE IF SANTA LEFT OUR LOOT YET!
OH BOY!
WE'LL LET MOM AND DAD SLEEP ANOTHER HOUR, BUT WE CAN AT LEAST COUNT ALL OUR PACKAGES.
I GET TO PLUG IN THE TREE LIGHTS!
HA HA! LOOK AT ALL THIS BOOTY! LET'S SEE WHICH ONES ARE FOR ME!
HERE'S ONE FOR YOU. ..STRANGE THAT SANTA WOULD GO TO THE TROUBLE TO WRAP A BOX OF COAL.
HAR HAR. HERE'S ONE FOR MOM... HERE'S ONE FOR ME... THIS ONE IS FOR DAD... HEY, WHERE ARE YOUR PRESENTS? SANTA GOOFED UP!
GOOD THING WE TIGERS ARE NATURALLY GIFTED TO BEGIN WITH.
MOMM! DAAAD! SANTA DIDN'T BRING HOBBES ANYTHING!
UH OH. THINK QUICK, DEAR.
IT HAD BETTER BE A LOT LATER THAN IT FEELS LIKE.
WELL, HERE'S A PRESENT FROM ME ANYWAY. HOPE IT FITS.
THE BEST PRESENTS DON'T COME IN BOXES. I'LL TREASURE THIS ONE FOREVER.

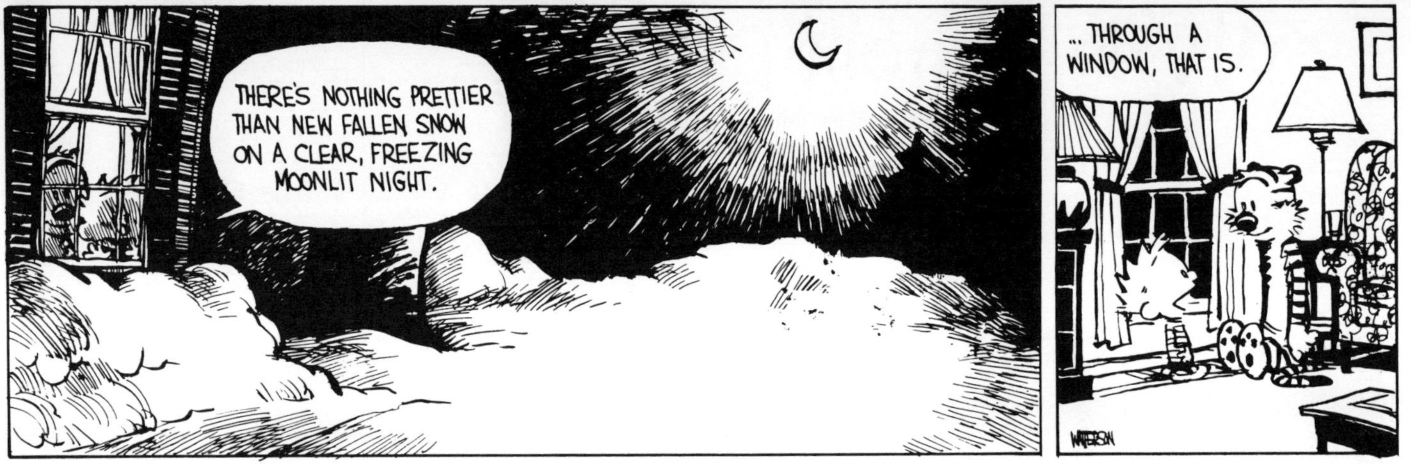
THERE'S NOTHING PRETTIER THAN NEW FALLEN SNOW ON A CLEAR, FREEZING MOONLIT NIGHT.
... THROUGH A WINDOW, THAT IS.

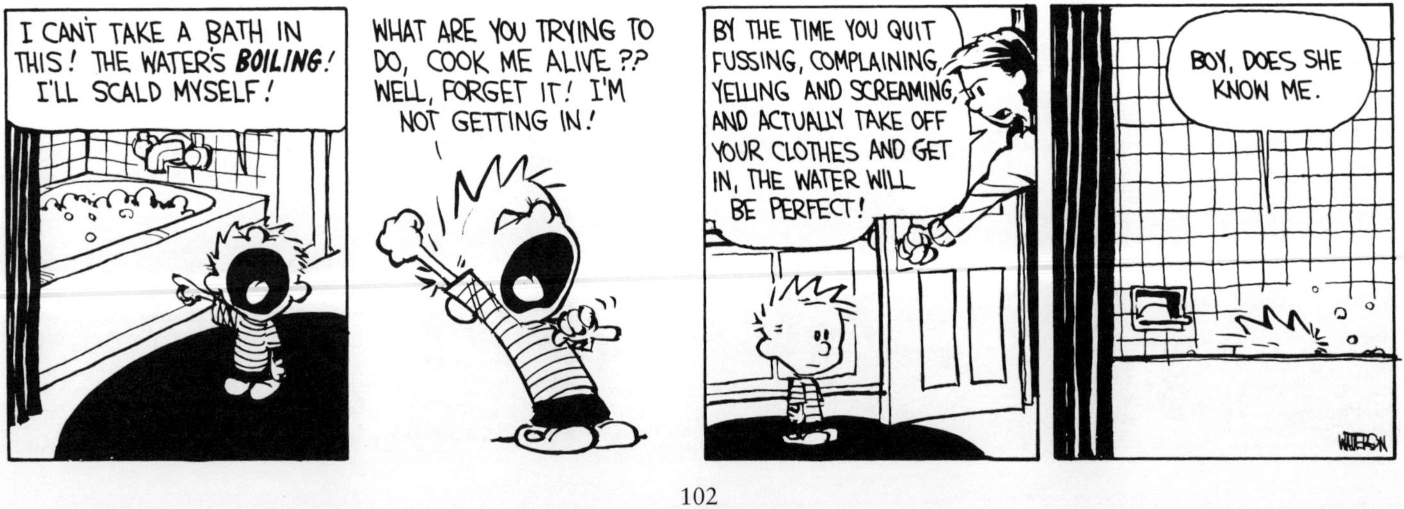
I CAN'T TAKE A BATH IN THIS! THE WATER'S **BOILING**! I'LL SCALD MYSELF!
WHAT ARE YOU TRYING TO DO, COOK ME ALIVE ?? WELL, FORGET IT! I'M NOT GETTING IN!
BY THE TIME YOU QUIT FUSSING, COMPLAINING, YELLING AND SCREAMING, AND ACTUALLY TAKE OFF YOUR CLOTHES AND GET IN, THE WATER WILL BE PERFECT!
BOY, DOES SHE KNOW ME.

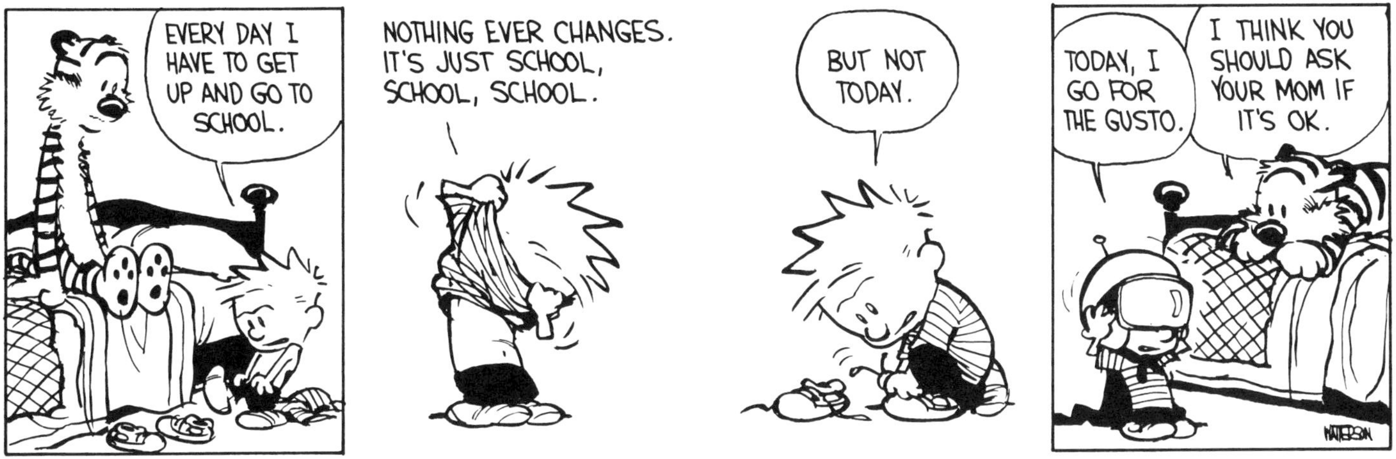
EVERY DAY I HAVE TO GET UP AND GO TO SCHOOL.
NOTHING EVER CHANGES. IT'S JUST SCHOOL, SCHOOL, SCHOOL.
BUT NOT TODAY.
TODAY, I GO FOR THE GUSTO.
I THINK YOU SHOULD ASK YOUR MOM IF IT'S OK.
WATERSON

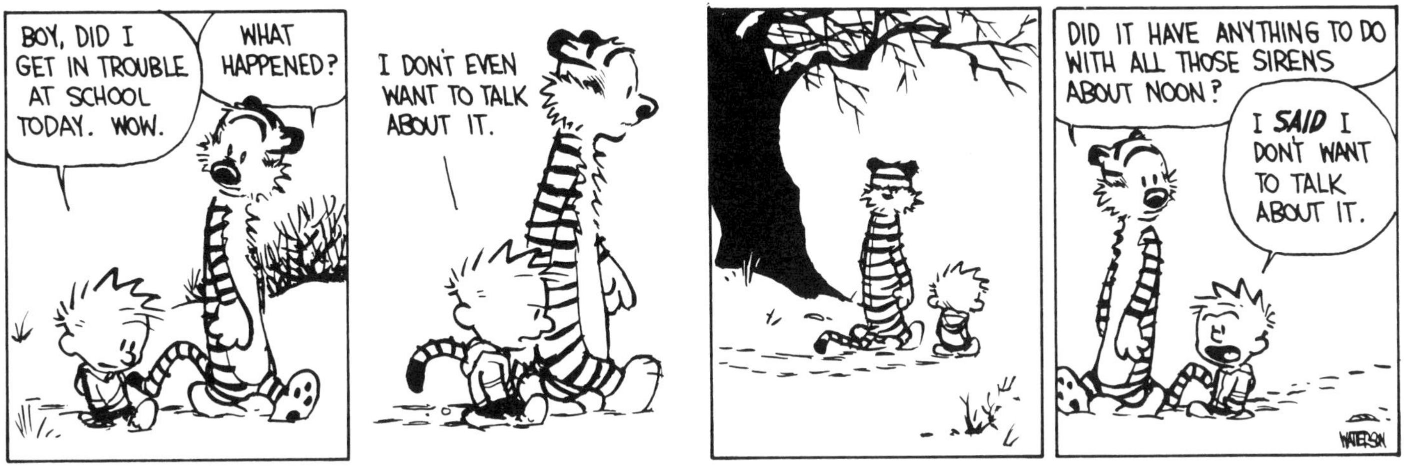
BOY, DID I GET IN TROUBLE AT SCHOOL TODAY. WOW.
WHAT HAPPENED?
I DON'T EVEN WANT TO TALK ABOUT IT.
DID IT HAVE ANYTHING TO DO WITH ALL THOSE SIRENS ABOUT NOON?
I SAID I DON'T WANT TO TALK ABOUT IT.
WATERSON

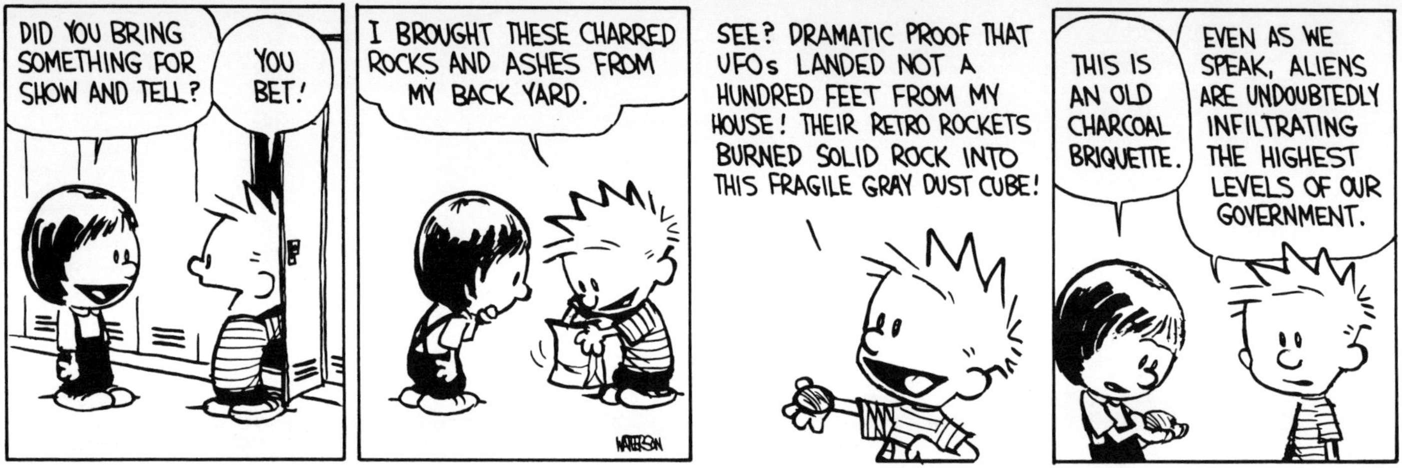
DID YOU BRING SOMETHING FOR SHOW AND TELL?
YOU BET!
I BROUGHT THESE CHARRED ROCKS AND ASHES FROM MY BACK YARD.
SEE? DRAMATIC PROOF THAT UFOs LANDED NOT A HUNDRED FEET FROM MY HOUSE! THEIR RETRO ROCKETS BURNED SOLID ROCK INTO THIS FRAGILE GRAY DUST CUBE!
THIS IS AN OLD CHARCOAL BRIQUETTE.
EVEN AS WE SPEAK, ALIENS ARE UNDOUBTEDLY INFILTRATING THE HIGHEST LEVELS OF OUR GOVERNMENT.

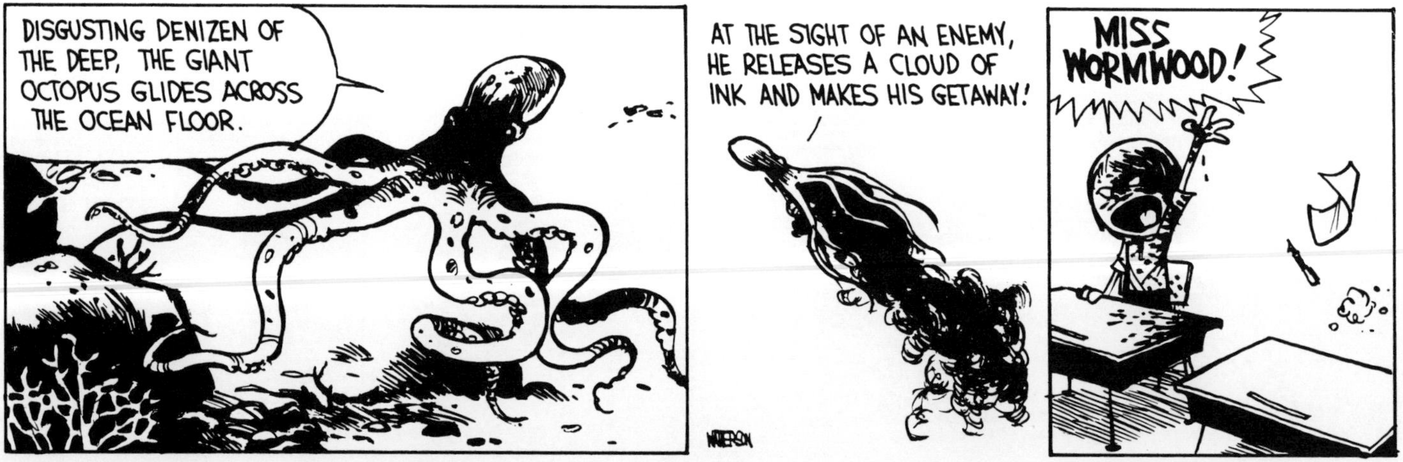
DISGUSTING DENIZEN OF THE DEEP, THE GIANT OCTOPUS GLIDES ACROSS THE OCEAN FLOOR.
AT THE SIGHT OF AN ENEMY, HE RELEASES A CLOUD OF INK AND MAKES HIS GETAWAY!
MISS WORMWOOD!

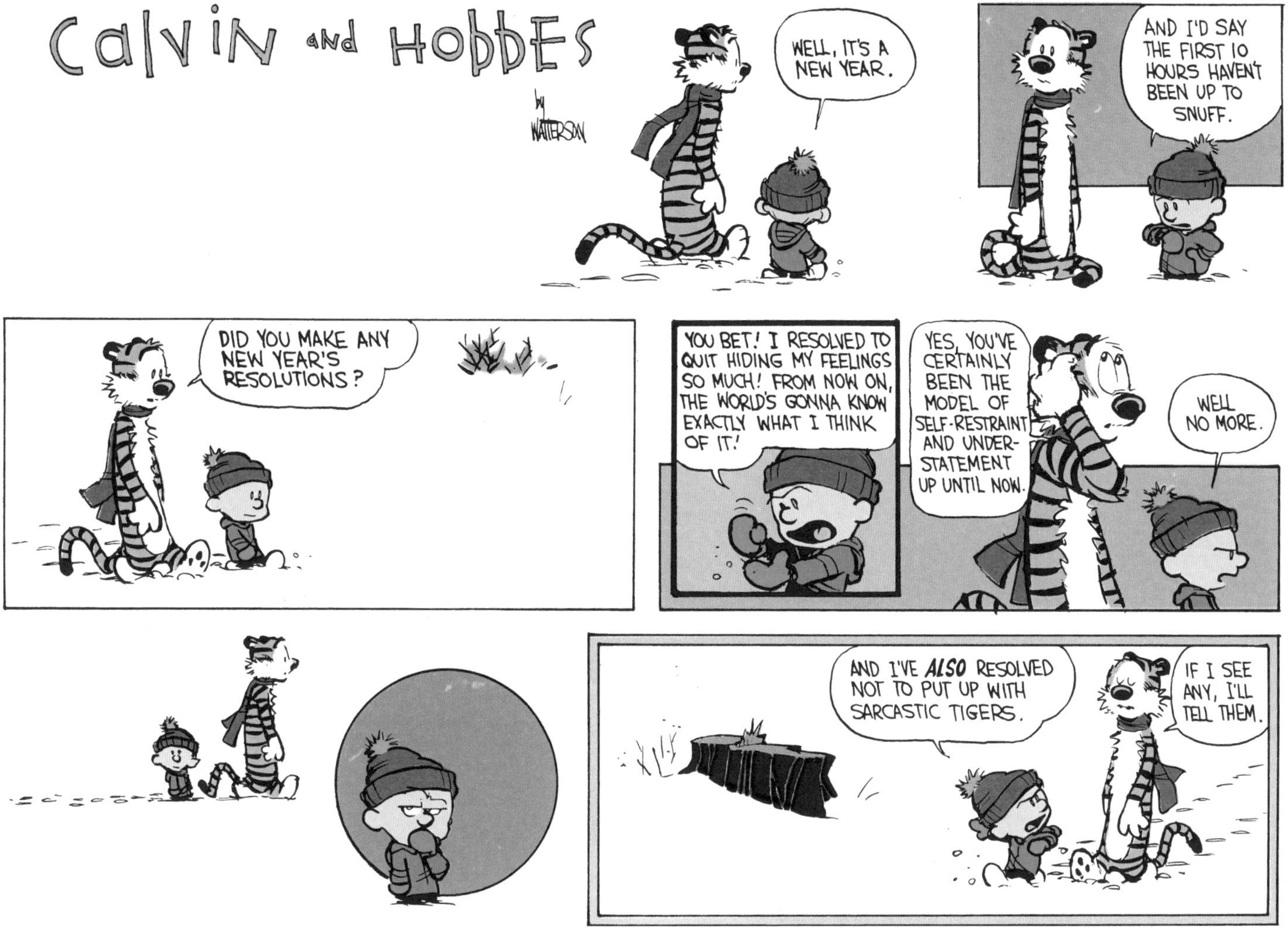
Calvin and HOBBES
by WATTERSON
WELL, IT'S A NEW YEAR.
AND I'D SAY THE FIRST 10 HOURS HAVEN'T BEEN UP TO SNUFF.
DID YOU MAKE ANY NEW YEAR'S RESOLUTIONS?
YOU BET! I RESOLVED TO QUIT HIDING MY FEELINGS SO MUCH! FROM NOW ON, THE WORLD'S GONNA KNOW EXACTLY WHAT I THINK OF IT!
YES, YOU'VE CERTAINLY BEEN THE MODEL OF SELF-RESTRAINT AND UNDER-STATEMENT UP UNTIL NOW.
WELL NO MORE.
AND I'VE ALSO RESOLVED NOT TO PUT UP WITH SARCASTIC TIGERS.
IF I SEE ANY, I'LL TELL THEM.

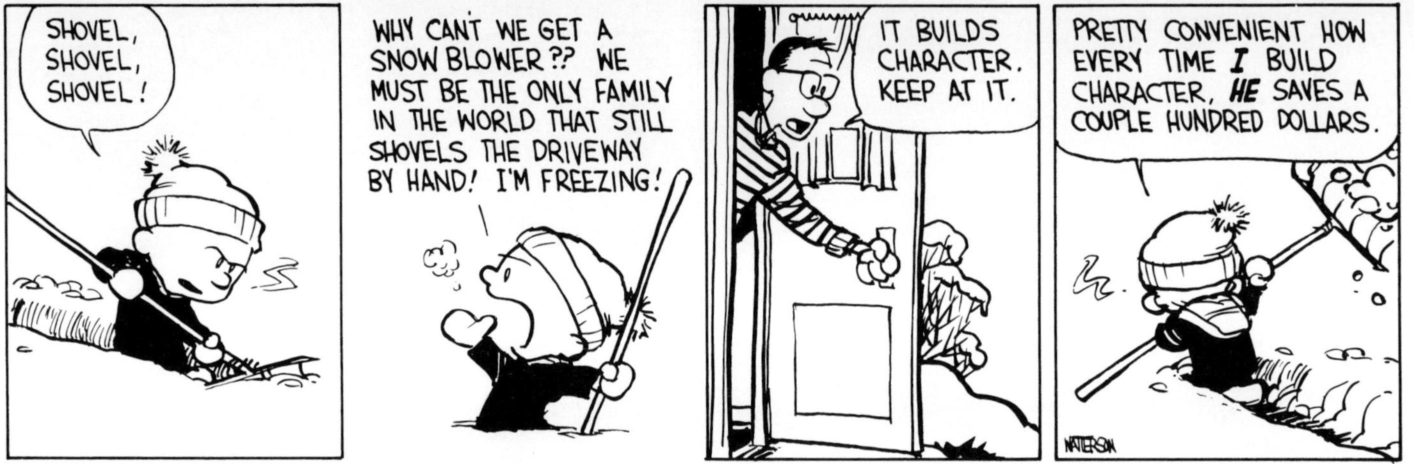
SHOVEL, SHOVEL, SHOVEL!
WHY CAN'T WE GET A SNOW BLOWER?? WE MUST BE THE ONLY FAMILY IN THE WORLD THAT STILL SHOVELS THE DRIVEWAY BY HAND! I'M FREEZING!
IT BUILDS CHARACTER. KEEP AT IT.
PRETTY CONVENIENT HOW EVERY TIME I BUILD CHARACTER, HE SAVES A COUPLE HUNDRED DOLLARS.
WATTERSON

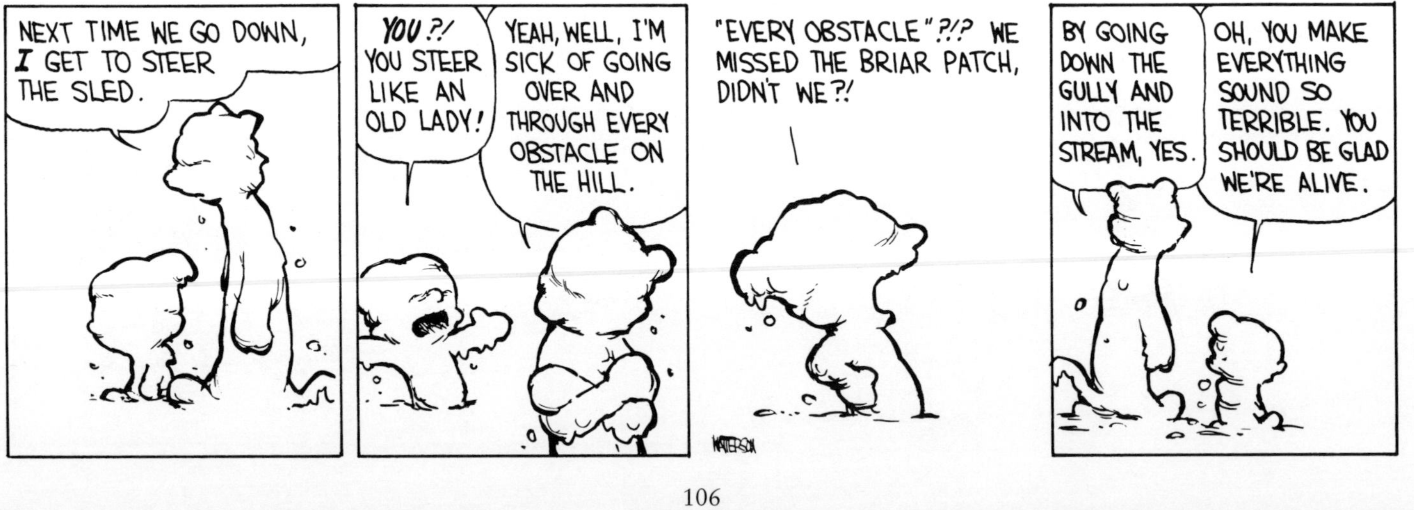
NEXT TIME WE GO DOWN, I GET TO STEER THE SLED.
YOU?! YOU STEER LIKE AN OLD LADY!
YEAH, WELL, I'M SICK OF GOING OVER AND THROUGH EVERY OBSTACLE ON THE HILL.
"EVERY OBSTACLE"?!? WE MISSED THE BRIAR PATCH, DIDN'T WE?!
WATTERSON
BY GOING DOWN THE GULLY AND INTO THE STREAM, YES.
OH, YOU MAKE EVERYTHING SOUND SO TERRIBLE. YOU SHOULD BE GLAD WE'RE ALIVE.

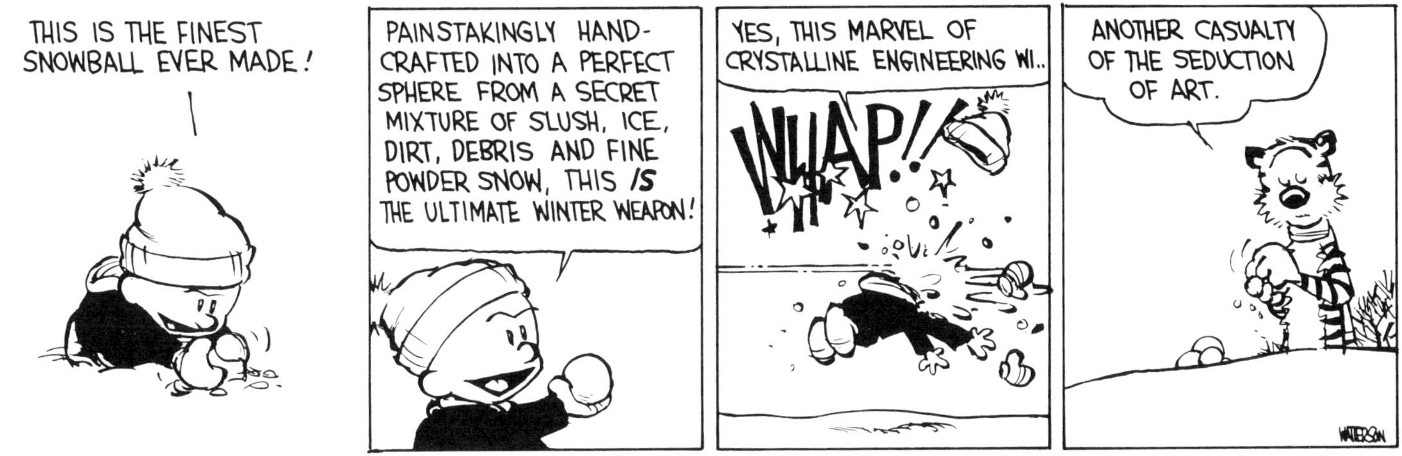
THIS IS THE FINEST SNOWBALL EVER MADE!
PAINSTAKINGLY HAND-CRAFTED INTO A PERFECT SPHERE FROM A SECRET MIXTURE OF SLUSH, ICE, DIRT, DEBRIS AND FINE POWDER SNOW, THIS *IS* THE ULTIMATE WINTER WEAPON!
YES, THIS MARVEL OF CRYSTALLINE ENGINEERING WI..
WHAP!!
ANOTHER CASUALTY OF THE SEDUCTION OF ART.

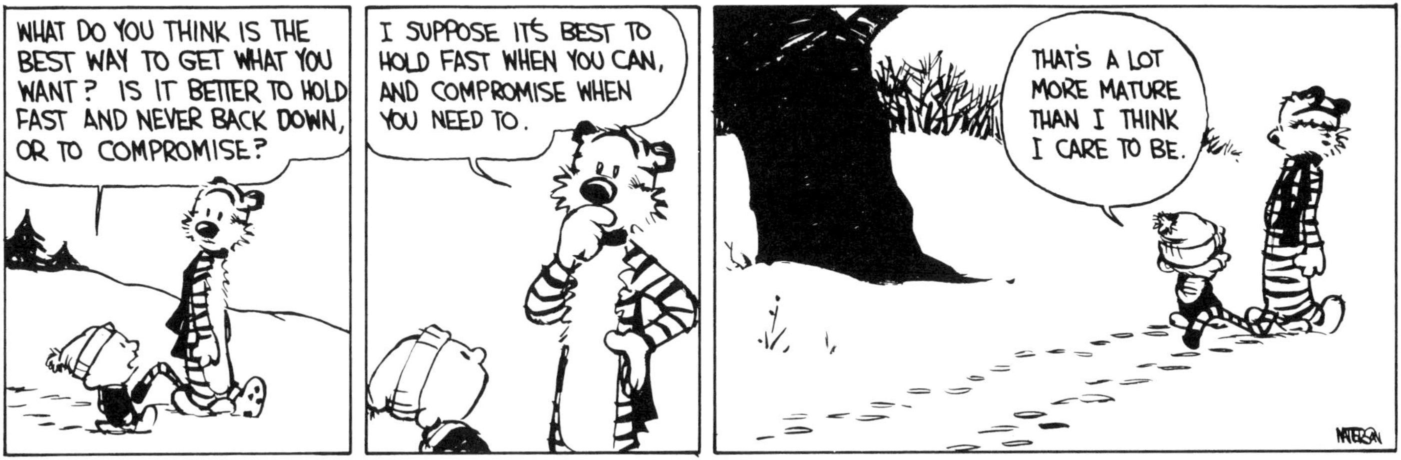
WHAT DO YOU THINK IS THE BEST WAY TO GET WHAT YOU WANT? IS IT BETTER TO HOLD FAST AND NEVER BACK DOWN, OR TO COMPROMISE?
I SUPPOSE IT'S BEST TO HOLD FAST WHEN YOU CAN, AND COMPROMISE WHEN YOU NEED TO.
THAT'S A LOT MORE MATURE THAN I THINK I CARE TO BE.

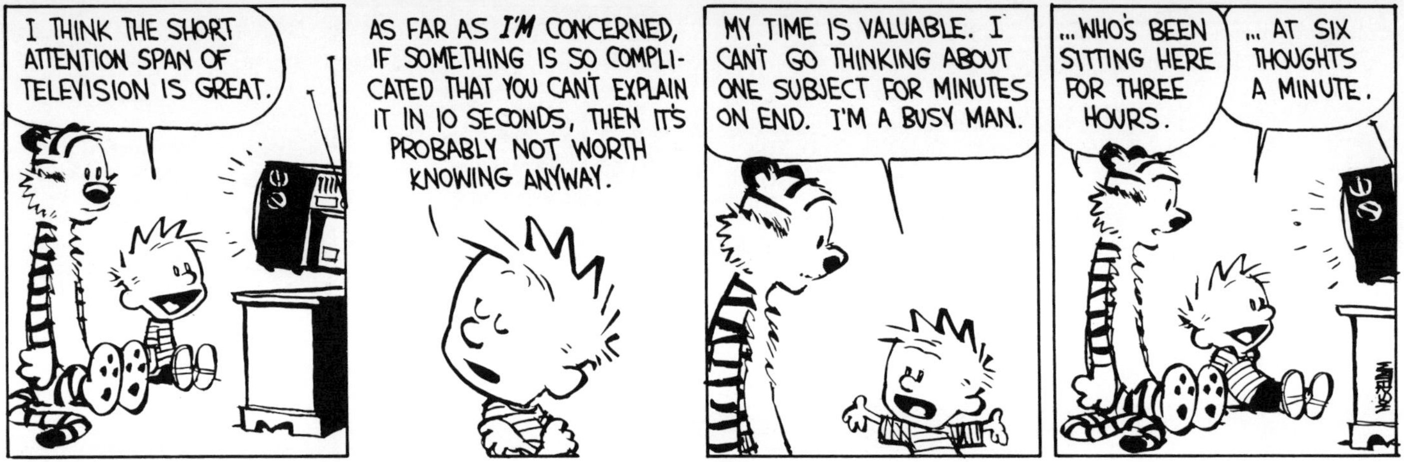
I THINK THE SHORT ATTENTION SPAN OF TELEVISION IS GREAT.
AS FAR AS *I'M* CONCERNED, IF SOMETHING IS SO COMPLICATED THAT YOU CAN'T EXPLAIN IT IN 10 SECONDS, THEN IT'S PROBABLY NOT WORTH KNOWING ANYWAY.
MY TIME IS VALUABLE. I CAN'T GO THINKING ABOUT ONE SUBJECT FOR MINUTES ON END. I'M A BUSY MAN.
...WHO'S BEEN SITTING HERE FOR THREE HOURS.
... AT SIX THOUGHTS A MINUTE.

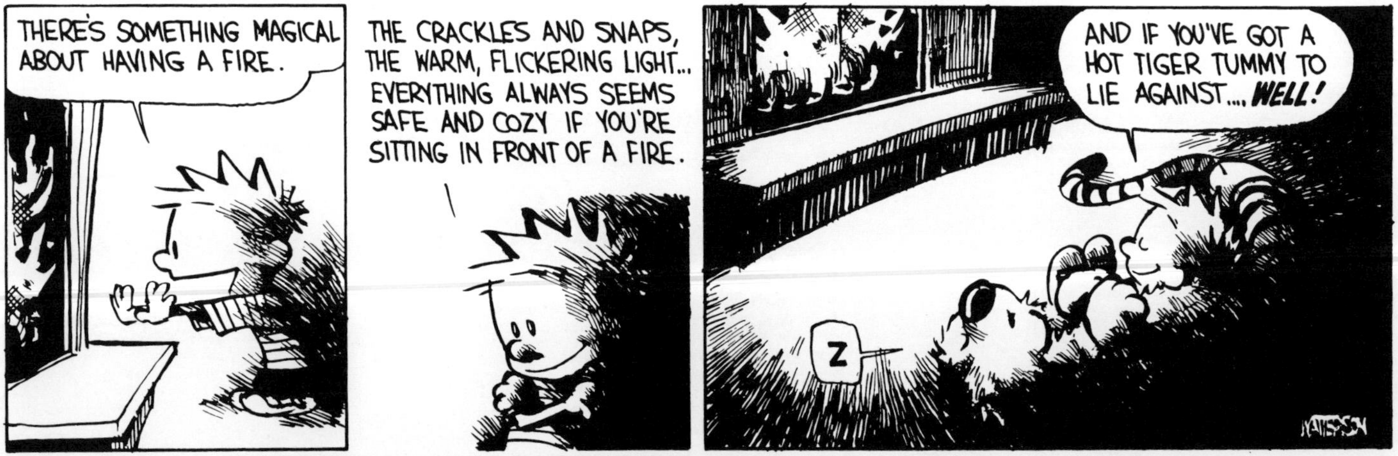
THERE'S SOMETHING MAGICAL ABOUT HAVING A FIRE.
THE CRACKLES AND SNAPS, THE WARM, FLICKERING LIGHT... EVERYTHING ALWAYS SEEMS SAFE AND COZY IF YOU'RE SITTING IN FRONT OF A FIRE.
AND IF YOU'VE GOT A HOT TIGER TUMMY TO LIE AGAINST.... ***WELL!***
Z

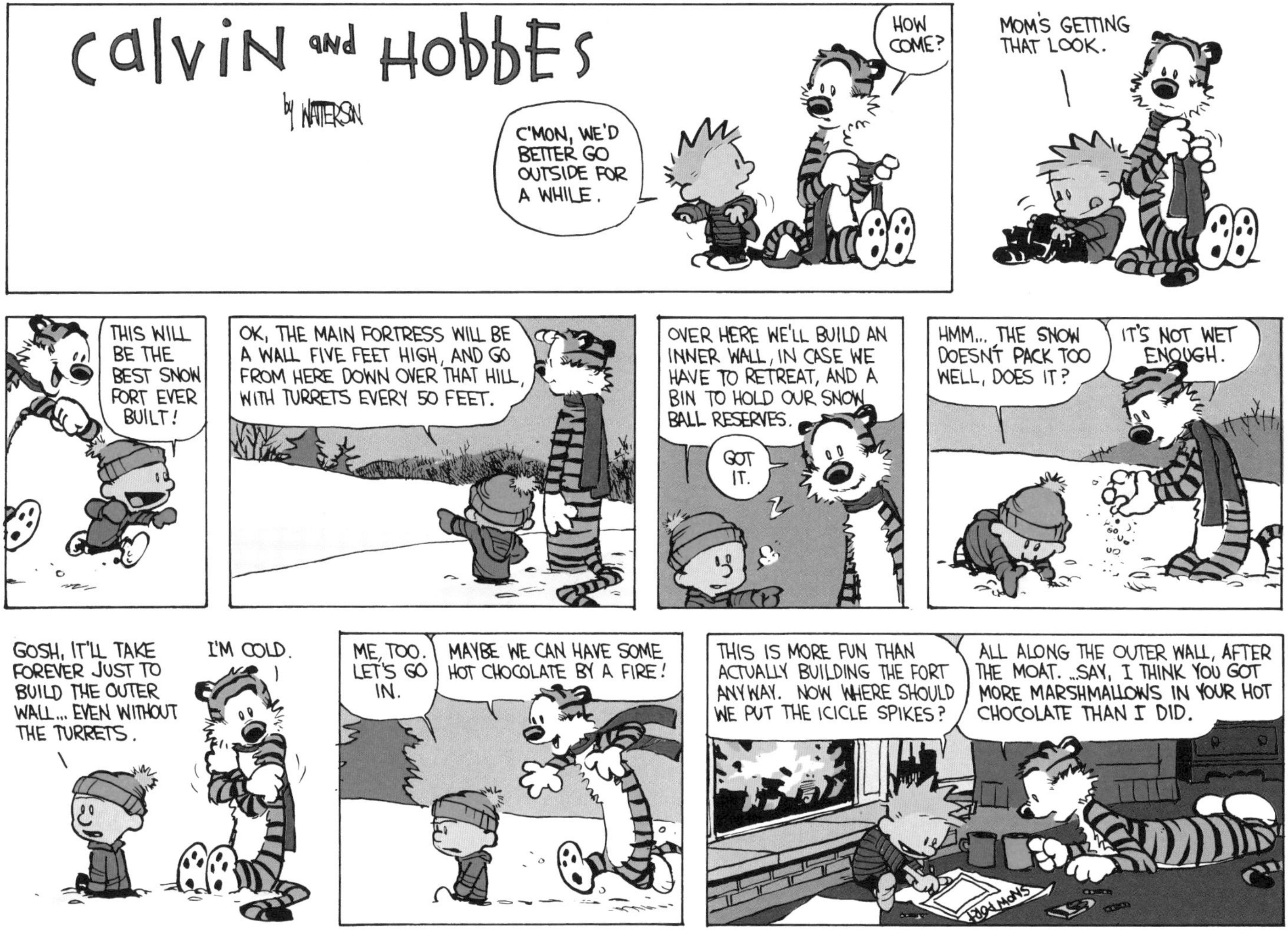
Calvin and HOBBES
by WATTERSON
C'MON, WE'D BETTER GO OUTSIDE FOR A WHILE.
HOW COME?
MOM'S GETTING THAT LOOK.
THIS WILL BE THE BEST SNOW FORT EVER BUILT!
OK, THE MAIN FORTRESS WILL BE A WALL FIVE FEET HIGH, AND GO FROM HERE DOWN OVER THAT HILL, WITH TURRETS EVERY 50 FEET.
OVER HERE WE'LL BUILD AN INNER WALL, IN CASE WE HAVE TO RETREAT, AND A BIN TO HOLD OUR SNOW BALL RESERVES.
GOT IT.
HMM... THE SNOW DOESN'T PACK TOO WELL, DOES IT?
IT'S NOT WET ENOUGH.
GOSH, IT'LL TAKE FOREVER JUST TO BUILD THE OUTER WALL... EVEN WITHOUT THE TURRETS.
I'M COLD.
ME, TOO. LET'S GO IN.
MAYBE WE CAN HAVE SOME HOT CHOCOLATE BY A FIRE!
THIS IS MORE FUN THAN ACTUALLY BUILDING THE FORT ANYWAY. NOW WHERE SHOULD WE PUT THE ICICLE SPIKES?
ALL ALONG THE OUTER WALL, AFTER THE MOAT. ...SAY, I THINK YOU GOT MORE MARSHMALLOWS IN YOUR HOT CHOCOLATE THAN I DID.
SNOW FORT

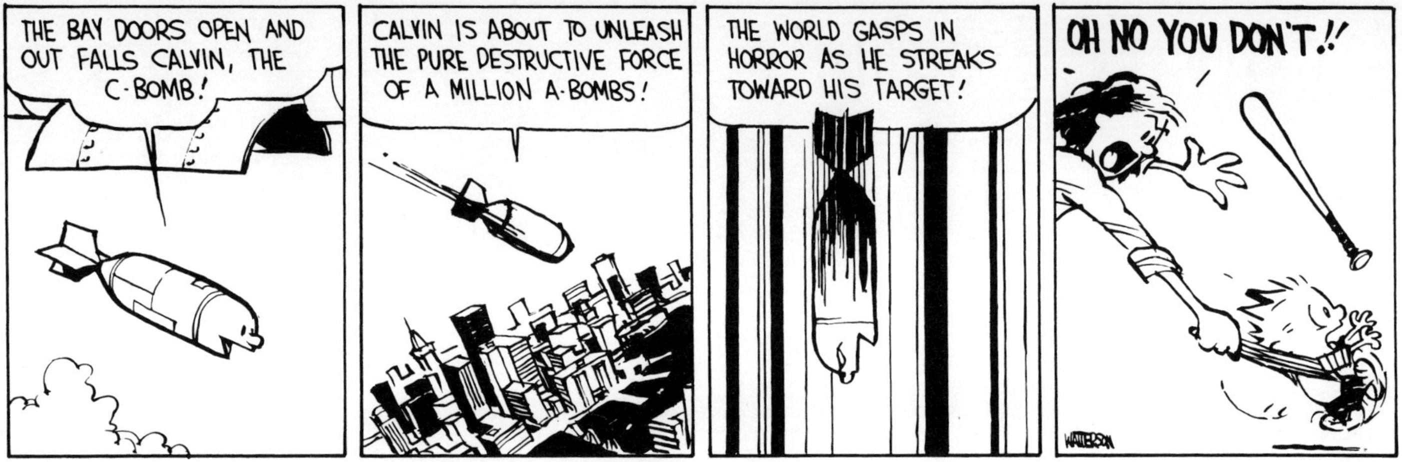
THE BAY DOORS OPEN AND OUT FALLS CALVIN, THE C-BOMB!
CALVIN IS ABOUT TO UNLEASH THE PURE DESTRUCTIVE FORCE OF A MILLION A-BOMBS!
THE WORLD GASPS IN HORROR AS HE STREAKS TOWARD HIS TARGET!
OH NO YOU DON'T!!
WATTERSON

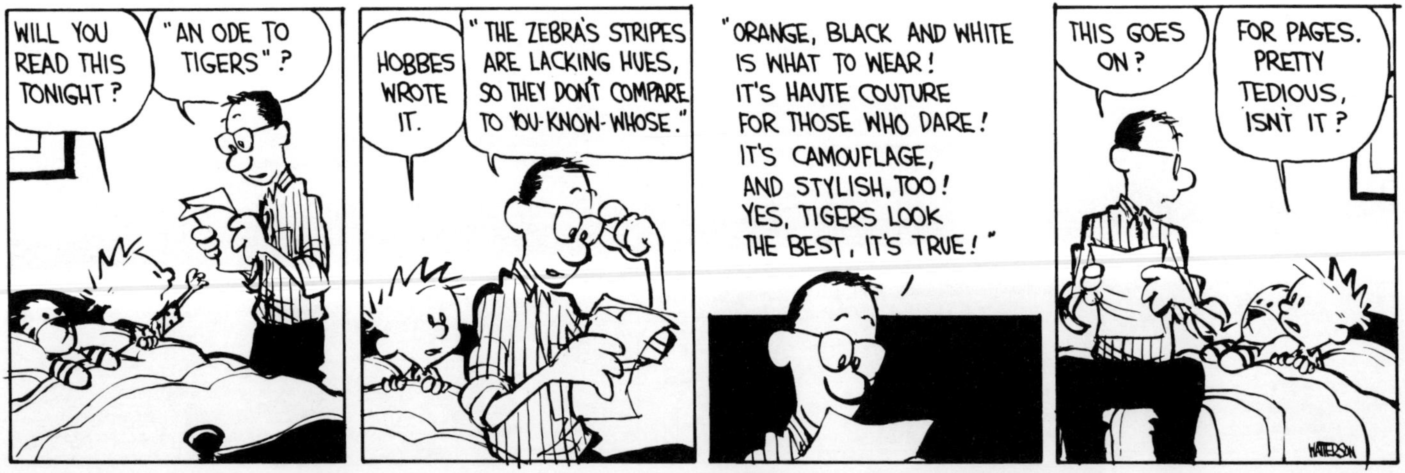
WILL YOU READ THIS TONIGHT?
"AN ODE TO TIGERS"?
HOBBES WROTE IT.
"THE ZEBRA'S STRIPES ARE LACKING HUES, SO THEY DON'T COMPARE TO YOU-KNOW-WHOSE."
"ORANGE, BLACK AND WHITE IS WHAT TO WEAR! IT'S HAUTE COUTURE FOR THOSE WHO DARE! IT'S CAMOUFLAGE, AND STYLISH, TOO! YES, TIGERS LOOK THE BEST, IT'S TRUE!"
THIS GOES ON?
FOR PAGES. PRETTY TEDIOUS, ISN'T IT?
WATTERSON

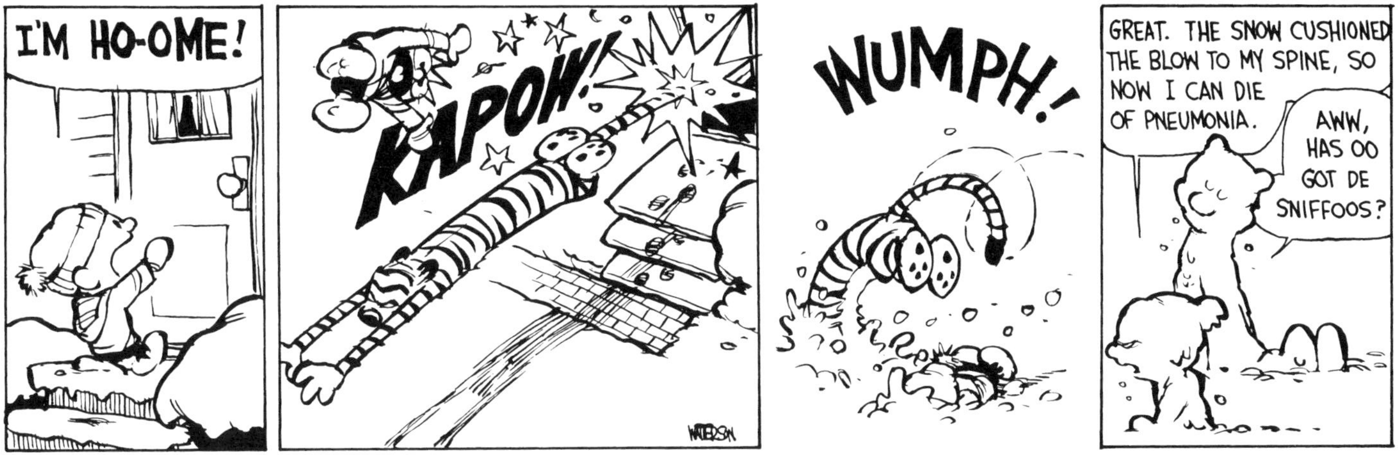
I'M HO-OME!
KAPOW!
WUMPH!
GREAT. THE SNOW CUSHIONED THE BLOW TO MY SPINE, SO NOW I CAN DIE OF PNEUMONIA.
AWW, HAS OO GOT DE SNIFFOOS?

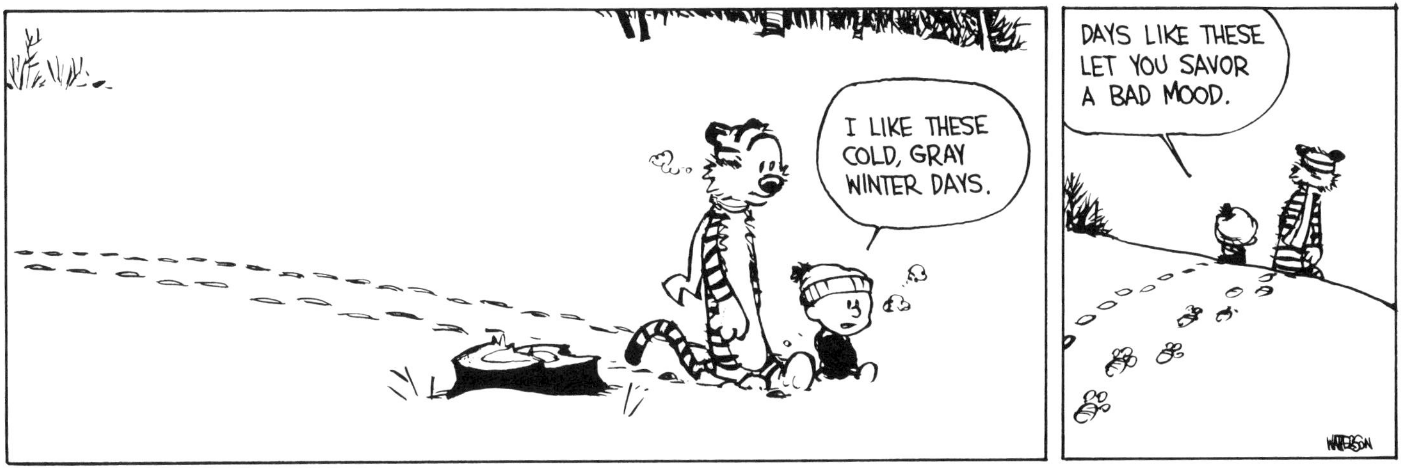
I LIKE THESE COLD, GRAY WINTER DAYS.
DAYS LIKE THESE LET YOU SAVOR A BAD MOOD.

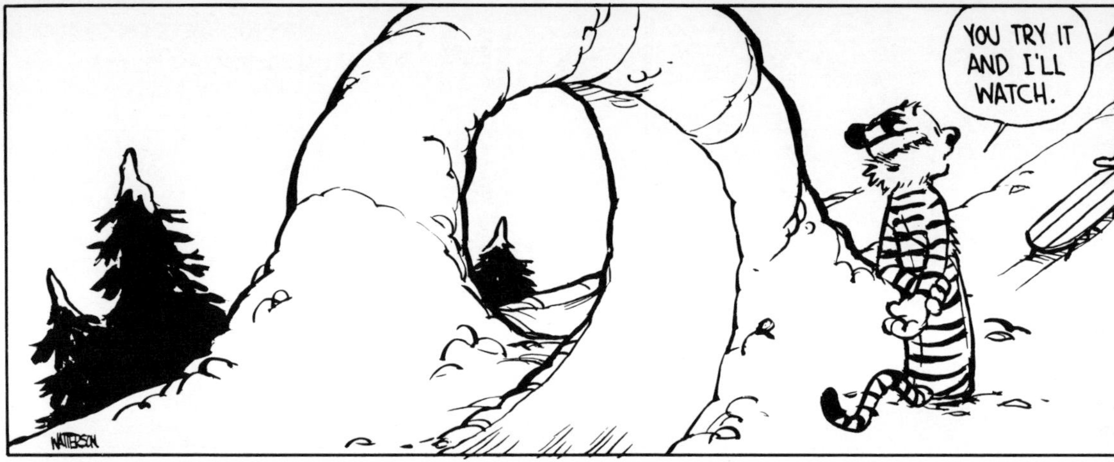
YOU TRY IT AND I'LL WATCH.
SISSY.

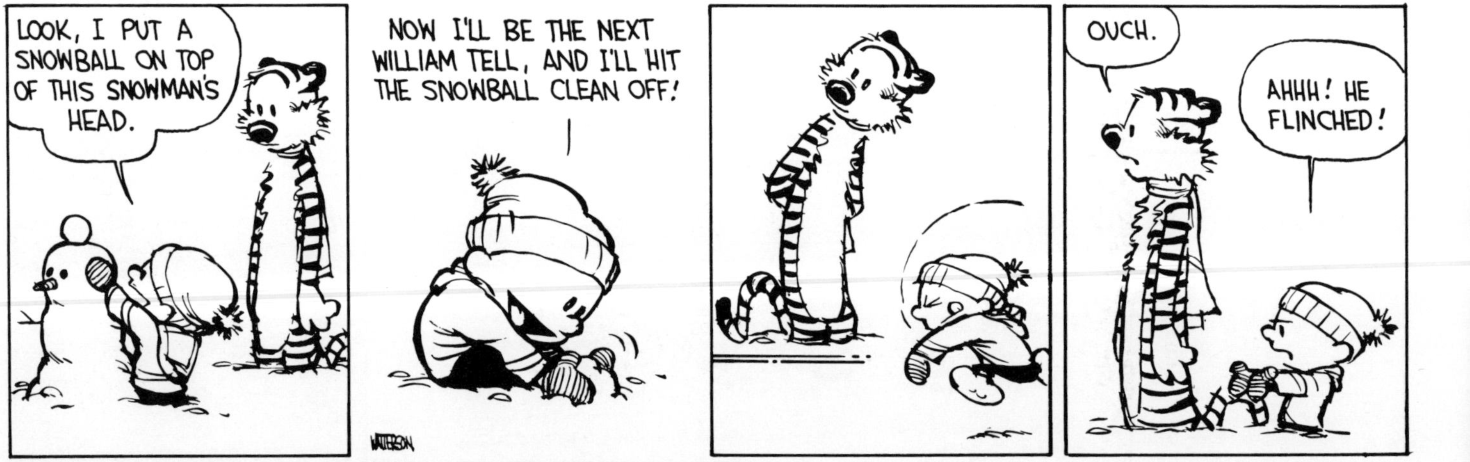
LOOK, I PUT A SNOWBALL ON TOP OF THIS SNOWMAN'S HEAD.
NOW I'LL BE THE NEXT WILLIAM TELL, AND I'LL HIT THE SNOWBALL CLEAN OFF!
OUCH.
AHHH! HE FLINCHED!

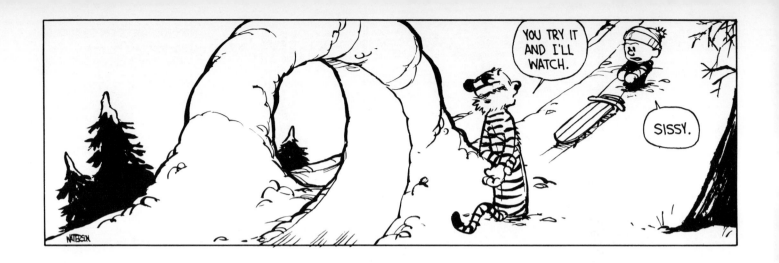

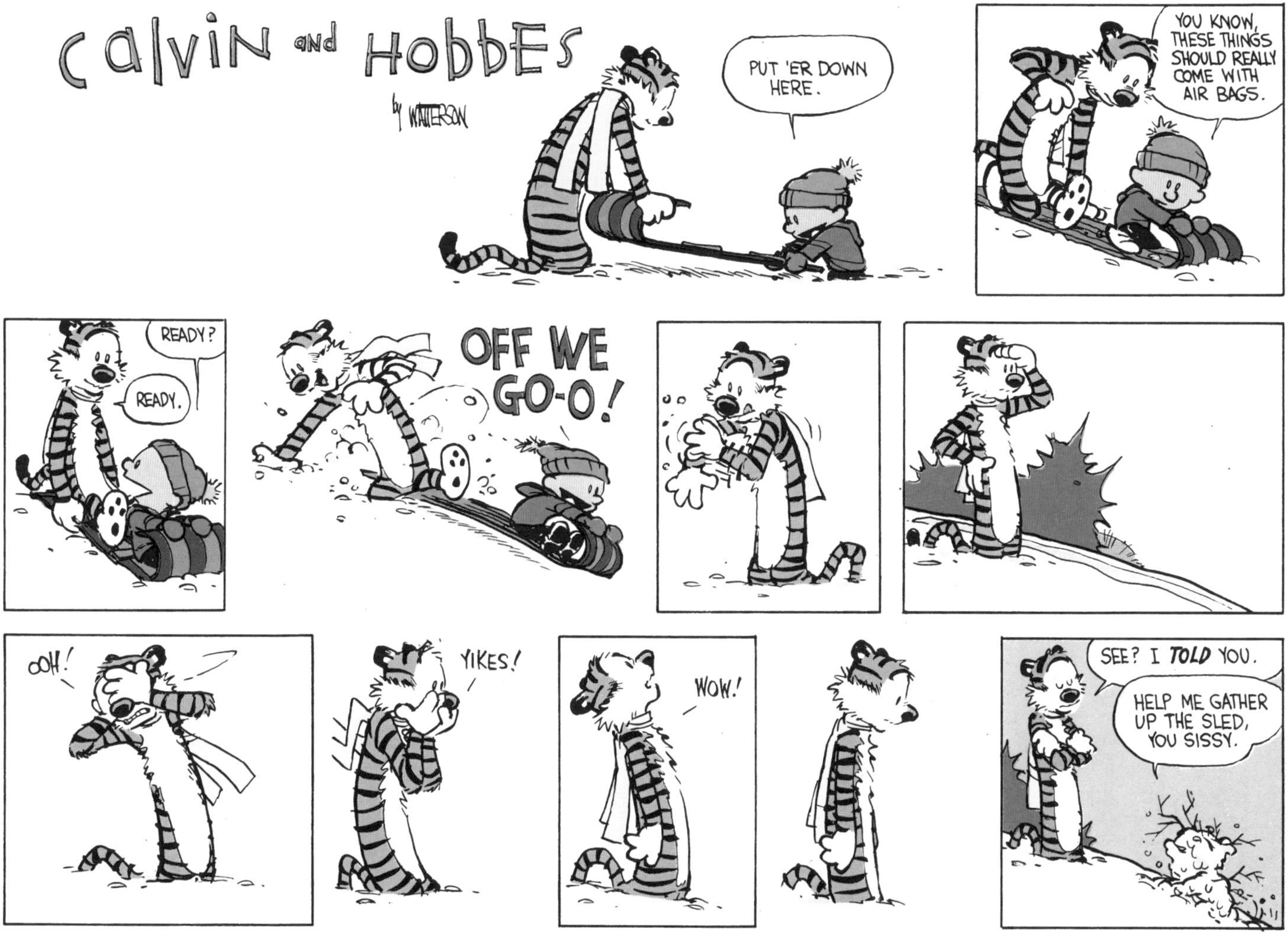
Calvin and Hobbes
by WATTERSON
PUT 'ER DOWN HERE.
YOU KNOW, THESE THINGS SHOULD REALLY COME WITH AIR BAGS.
READY?
READY.
OFF WE GO-O!
OOH!
YIKES!
WOW!
SEE? I TOLD YOU.
HELP ME GATHER UP THE SLED, YOU SISSY.

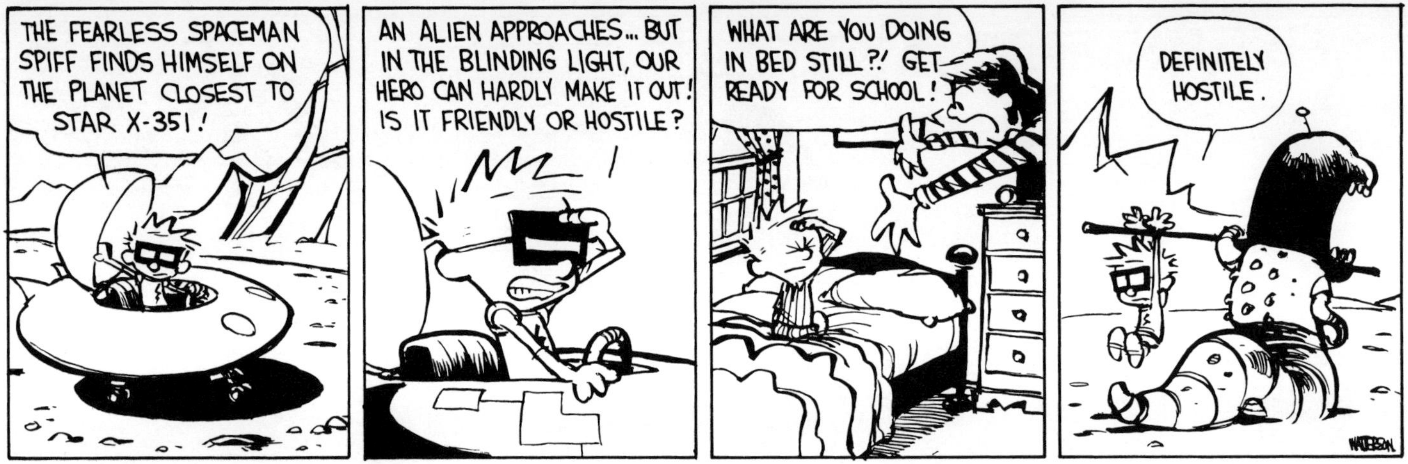
THE FEARLESS SPACEMAN SPIFF FINDS HIMSELF ON THE PLANET CLOSEST TO STAR X-351!
AN ALIEN APPROACHES... BUT IN THE BLINDING LIGHT, OUR HERO CAN HARDLY MAKE IT OUT! IS IT FRIENDLY OR HOSTILE?
WHAT ARE YOU DOING IN BED STILL?! GET READY FOR SCHOOL!
DEFINITELY HOSTILE.

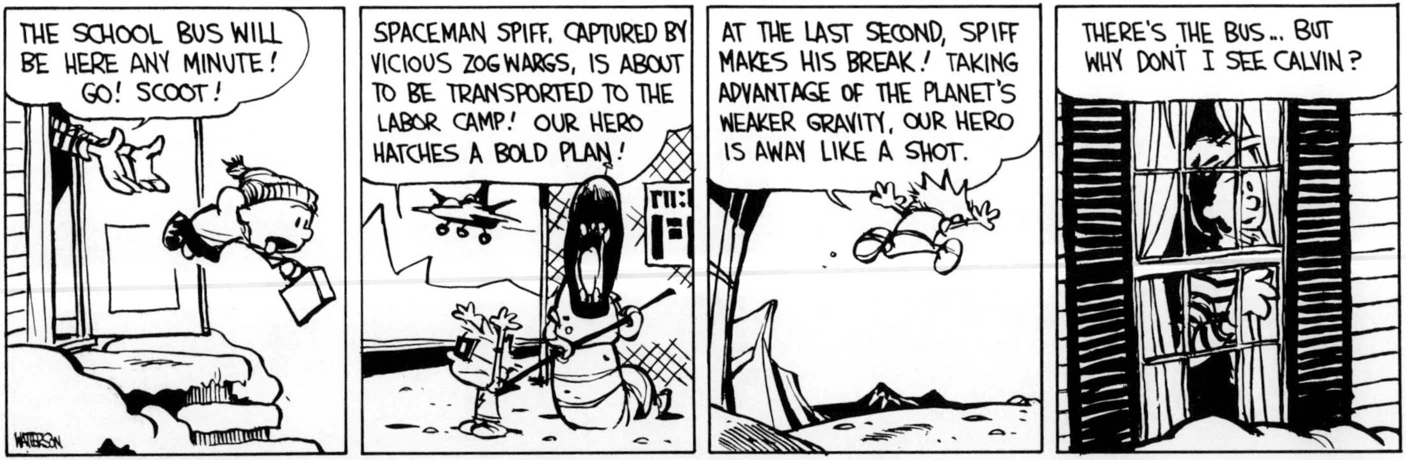
THE SCHOOL BUS WILL BE HERE ANY MINUTE! GO! SCOOT!
SPACEMAN SPIFF, CAPTURED BY VICIOUS ZOG WARGS, IS ABOUT TO BE TRANSPORTED TO THE LABOR CAMP! OUR HERO HATCHES A BOLD PLAN!
AT THE LAST SECOND, SPIFF MAKES HIS BREAK! TAKING ADVANTAGE OF THE PLANET'S WEAKER GRAVITY, OUR HERO IS AWAY LIKE A SHOT.
THERE'S THE BUS... BUT WHY DON'T I SEE CALVIN?

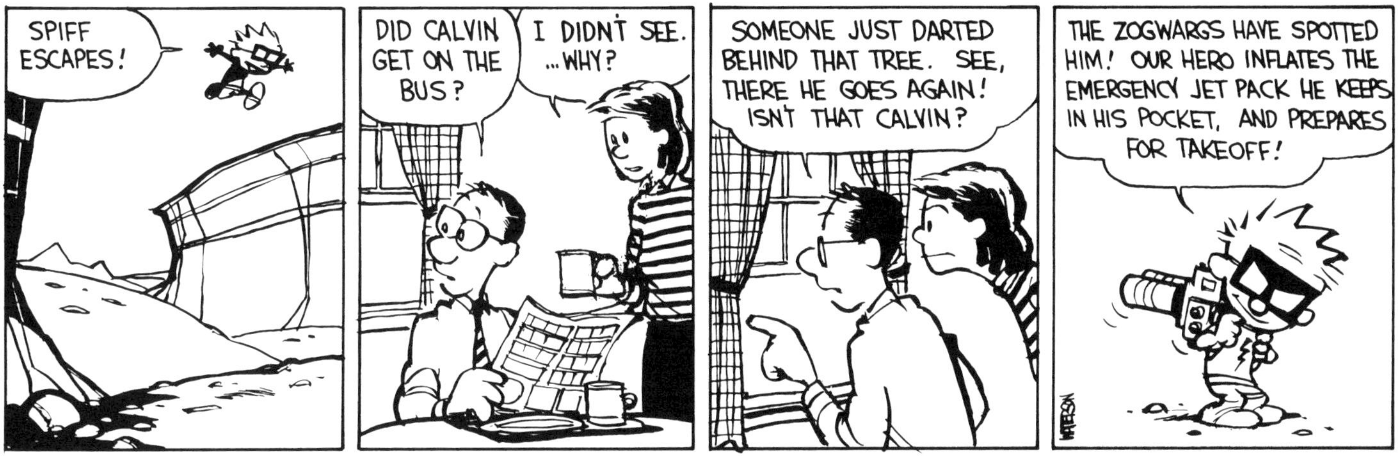
SPIFF ESCAPES!
DID CALVIN GET ON THE BUS?
I DIDN'T SEE. ...WHY?
SOMEONE JUST DARTED BEHIND THAT TREE. SEE, THERE HE GOES AGAIN! ISN'T THAT CALVIN?
THE ZOGWARGS HAVE SPOTTED HIM! OUR HERO INFLATES THE EMERGENCY JET PACK HE KEEPS IN HIS POCKET, AND PREPARES FOR TAKEOFF!

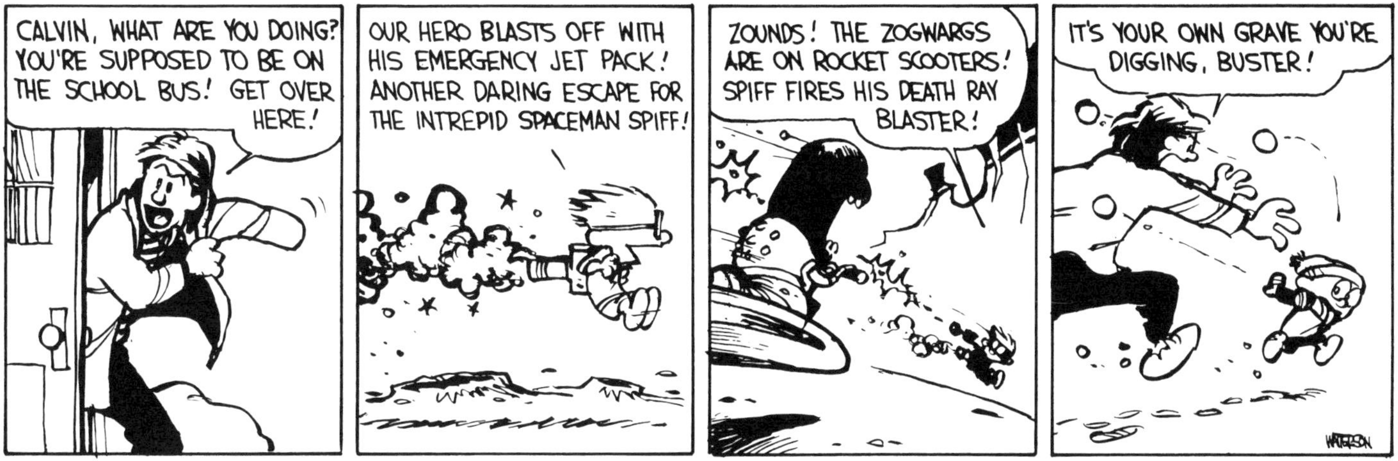
CALVIN, WHAT ARE YOU DOING? YOU'RE SUPPOSED TO BE ON THE SCHOOL BUS! GET OVER HERE!
OUR HERO BLASTS OFF WITH HIS EMERGENCY JET PACK! ANOTHER DARING ESCAPE FOR THE INTREPID SPACEMAN SPIFF!
ZOUNDS! THE ZOGWARGS ARE ON ROCKET SCOOTERS! SPIFF FIRES HIS DEATH RAY BLASTER!
IT'S YOUR OWN GRAVE YOU'RE DIGGING, BUSTER!

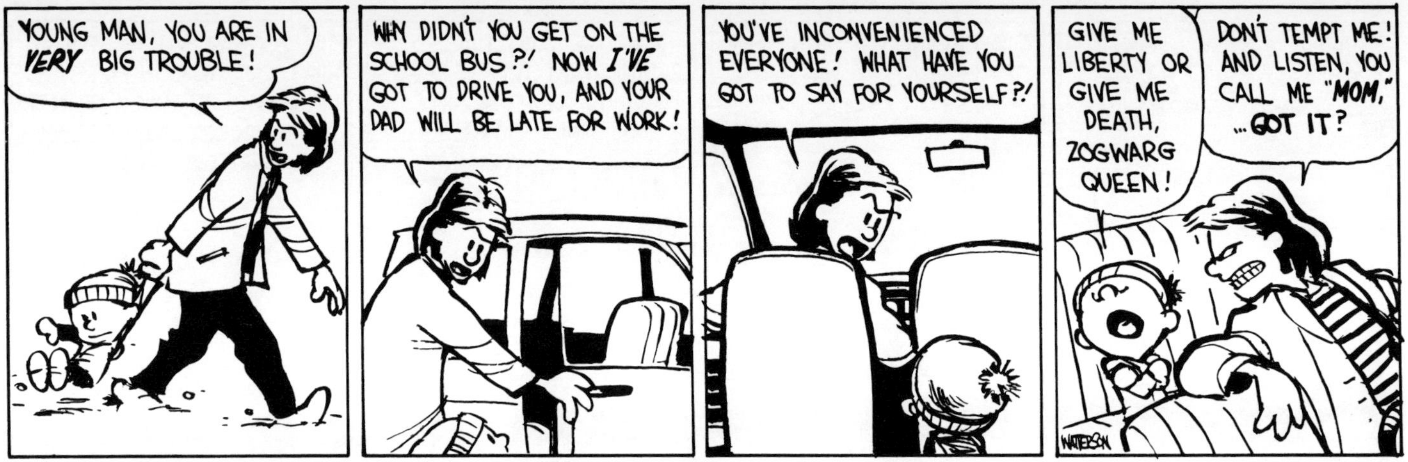
YOUNG MAN, YOU ARE IN VERY BIG TROUBLE!
WHY DIDN'T YOU GET ON THE SCHOOL BUS?! NOW I'VE GOT TO DRIVE YOU, AND YOUR DAD WILL BE LATE FOR WORK!
YOU'VE INCONVENIENCED EVERYONE! WHAT HAVE YOU GOT TO SAY FOR YOURSELF?!
GIVE ME LIBERTY OR GIVE ME DEATH, ZOGWARG QUEEN!
DON'T TEMPT ME! AND LISTEN, YOU CALL ME "MOM," ...GOT IT?

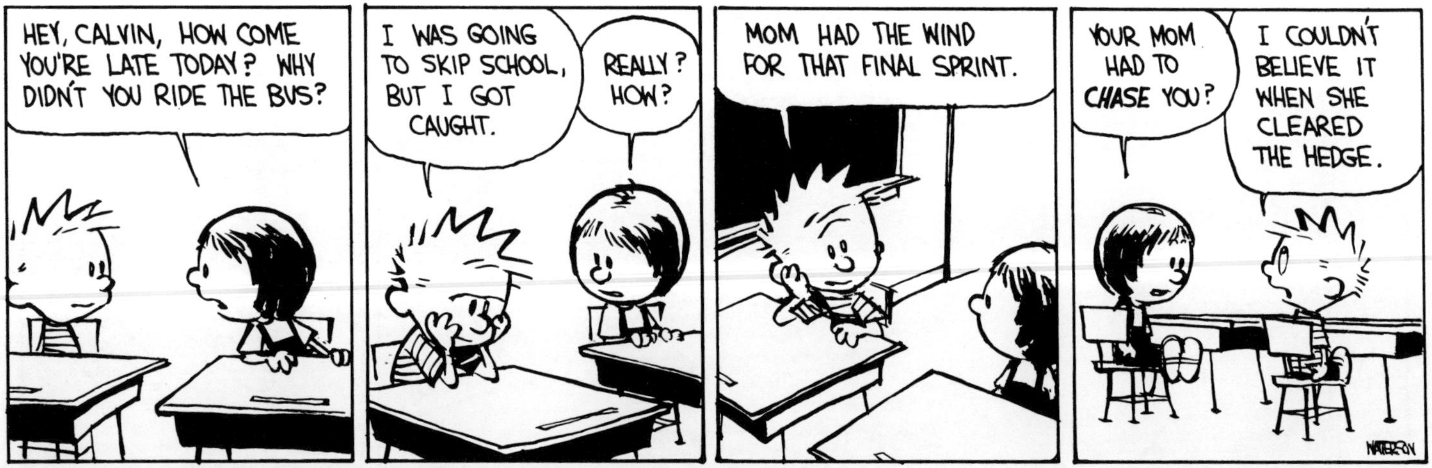
HEY, CALVIN, HOW COME YOU'RE LATE TODAY? WHY DIDN'T YOU RIDE THE BUS?
I WAS GOING TO SKIP SCHOOL, BUT I GOT CAUGHT.
REALLY? HOW?
MOM HAD THE WIND FOR THAT FINAL SPRINT.
YOUR MOM HAD TO CHASE YOU?
I COULDN'T BELIEVE IT WHEN SHE CLEARED THE HEDGE.

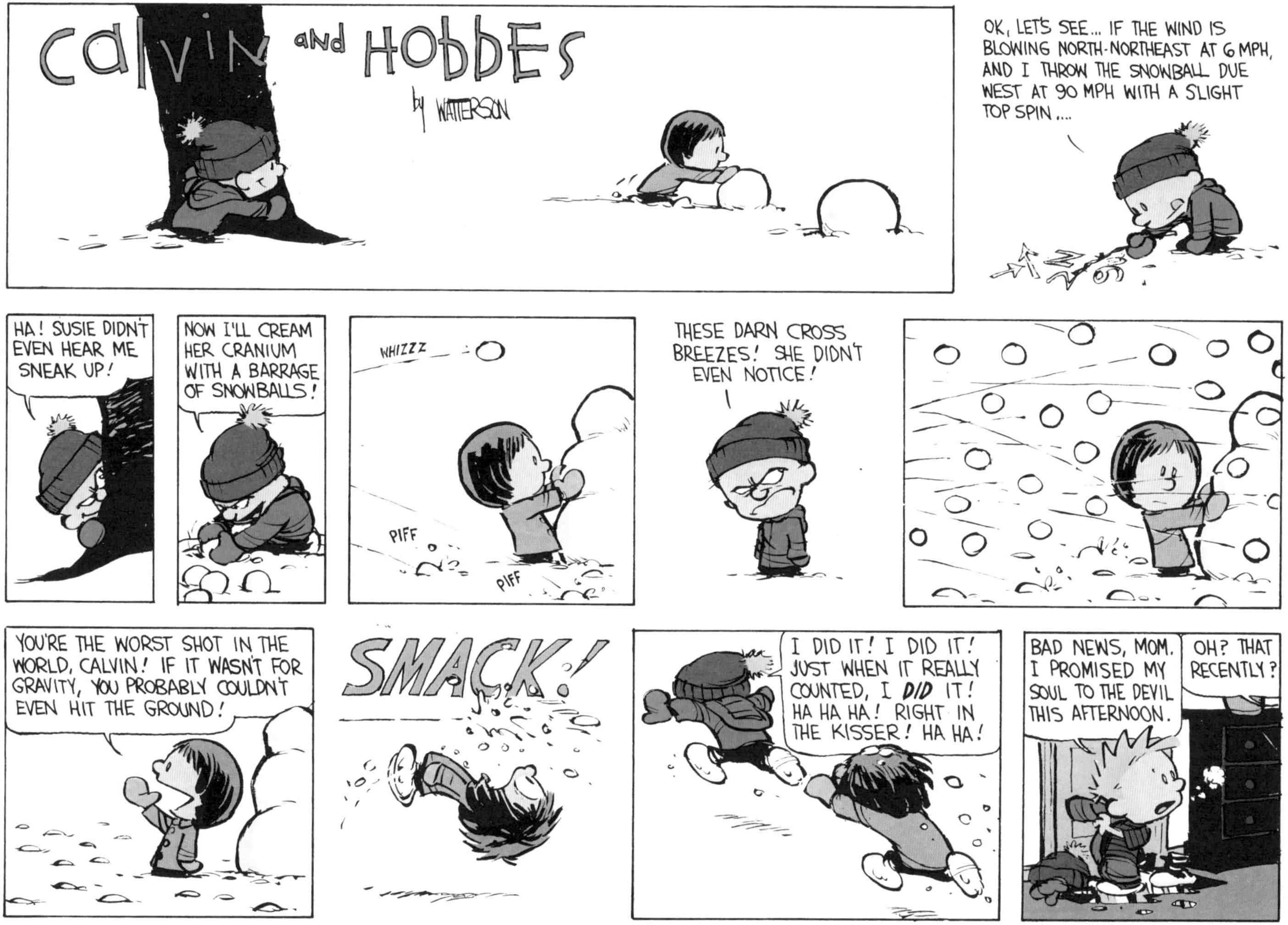
Calvin and HOBBES
by WATTERSON
OK, LET'S SEE... IF THE WIND IS BLOWING NORTH-NORTHEAST AT 6 MPH, AND I THROW THE SNOWBALL DUE WEST AT 90 MPH WITH A SLIGHT TOP SPIN....
HA! SUSIE DIDN'T EVEN HEAR ME SNEAK UP!
NOW I'LL CREAM HER CRANIUM WITH A BARRAGE OF SNOWBALLS!
WHIZZZ
PIFF
PIFF
THESE DARN CROSS BREEZES! SHE DIDN'T EVEN NOTICE!
YOU'RE THE WORST SHOT IN THE WORLD, CALVIN! IF IT WASN'T FOR GRAVITY, YOU PROBABLY COULDN'T EVEN HIT THE GROUND!
SMACK!
I DID IT! I DID IT! JUST WHEN IT REALLY COUNTED, I DID IT! HA HA HA! RIGHT IN THE KISSER! HA HA!
BAD NEWS, MOM. I PROMISED MY SOUL TO THE DEVIL THIS AFTERNOON.
OH? THAT RECENTLY?

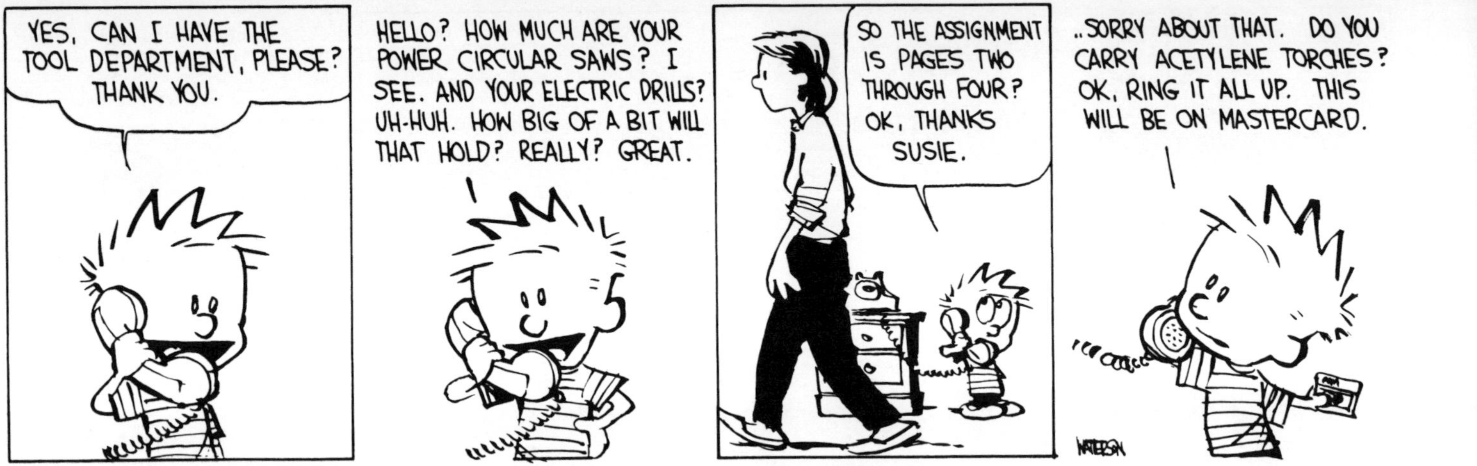

YES, CAN I HAVE THE TOOL DEPARTMENT, PLEASE? THANK YOU.
HELLO? HOW MUCH ARE YOUR POWER CIRCULAR SAWS? I SEE. AND YOUR ELECTRIC DRILLS? UH-HUH. HOW BIG OF A BIT WILL THAT HOLD? REALLY? GREAT.
SO THE ASSIGNMENT IS PAGES TWO THROUGH FOUR? OK, THANKS SUSIE.
..SORRY ABOUT THAT. DO YOU CARRY ACETYLENE TORCHES? OK, RING IT ALL UP. THIS WILL BE ON MASTERCARD.

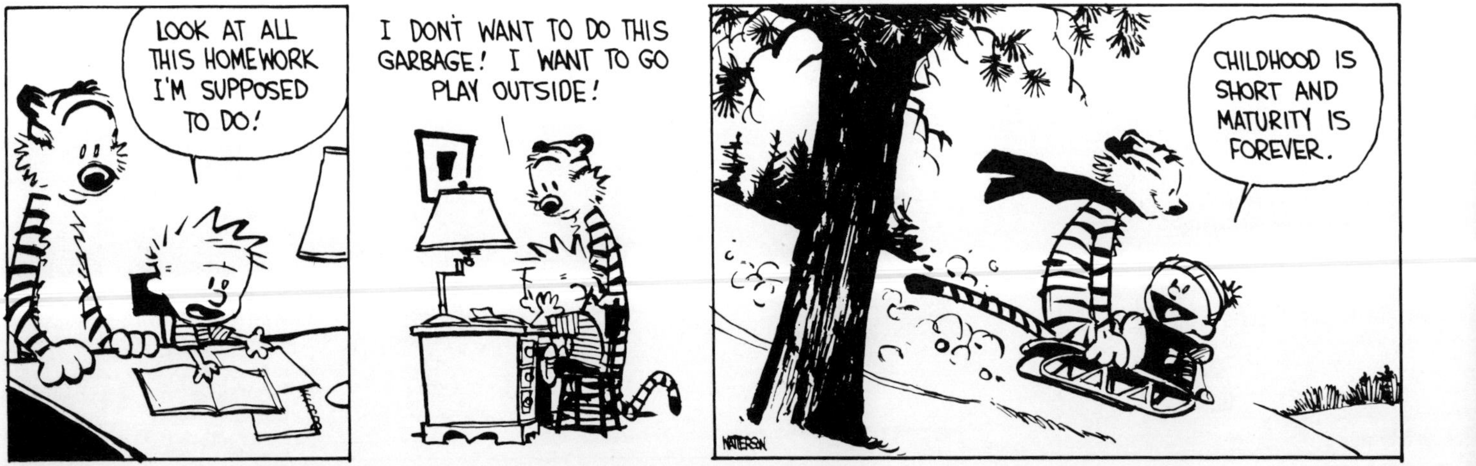

LOOK AT ALL THIS HOMEWORK I'M SUPPOSED TO DO!
I DON'T WANT TO DO THIS GARBAGE! I WANT TO GO PLAY OUTSIDE!
CHILDHOOD IS SHORT AND MATURITY IS FOREVER.

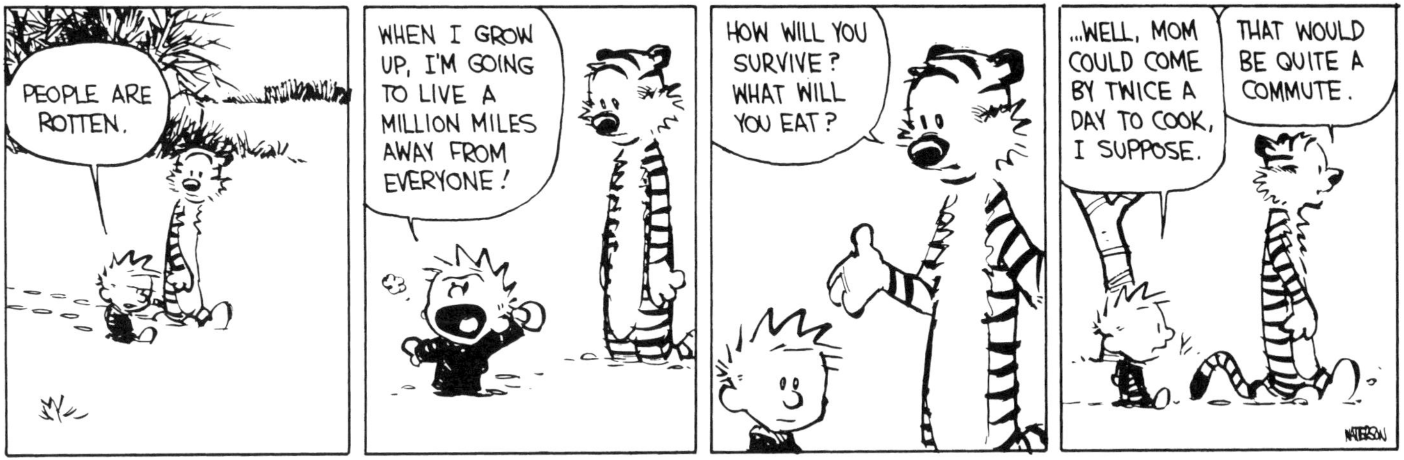
PEOPLE ARE ROTTEN.
WHEN I GROW UP, I'M GOING TO LIVE A MILLION MILES AWAY FROM EVERYONE!
HOW WILL YOU SURVIVE? WHAT WILL YOU EAT?
...WELL, MOM COULD COME BY TWICE A DAY TO COOK, I SUPPOSE.
THAT WOULD BE QUITE A COMMUTE.

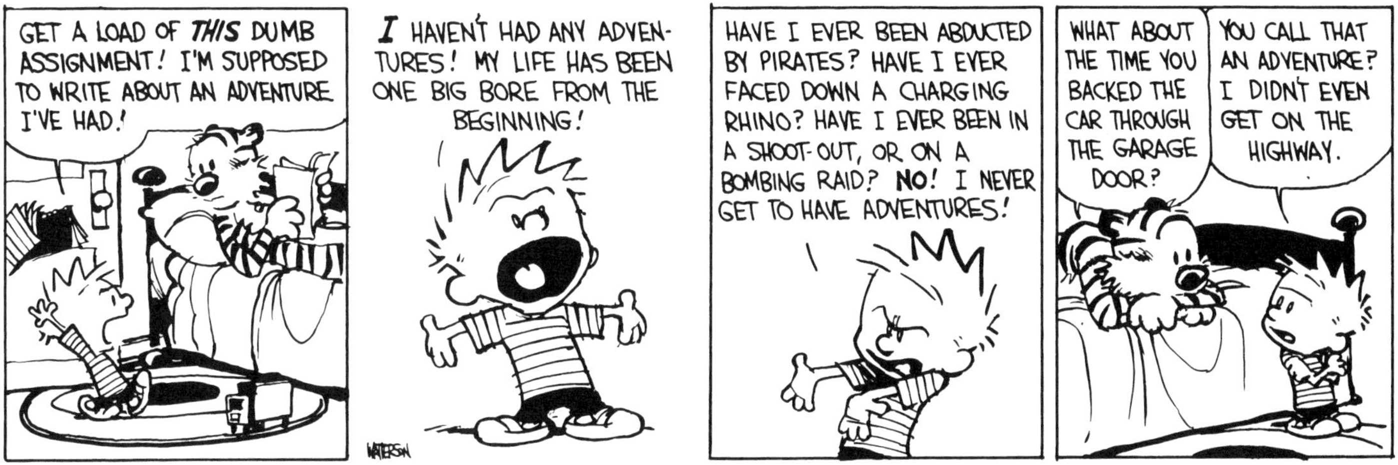
GET A LOAD OF *THIS* DUMB ASSIGNMENT! I'M SUPPOSED TO WRITE ABOUT AN ADVENTURE I'VE HAD!
I HAVEN'T HAD ANY ADVENTURES! MY LIFE HAS BEEN ONE BIG BORE FROM THE BEGINNING!
HAVE I EVER BEEN ABDUCTED BY PIRATES? HAVE I EVER FACED DOWN A CHARGING RHINO? HAVE I EVER BEEN IN A SHOOT-OUT, OR ON A BOMBING RAID? **NO**! I NEVER GET TO HAVE ADVENTURES!
WHAT ABOUT THE TIME YOU BACKED THE CAR THROUGH THE GARAGE DOOR?
YOU CALL THAT AN ADVENTURE? I DIDN'T EVEN GET ON THE HIGHWAY.

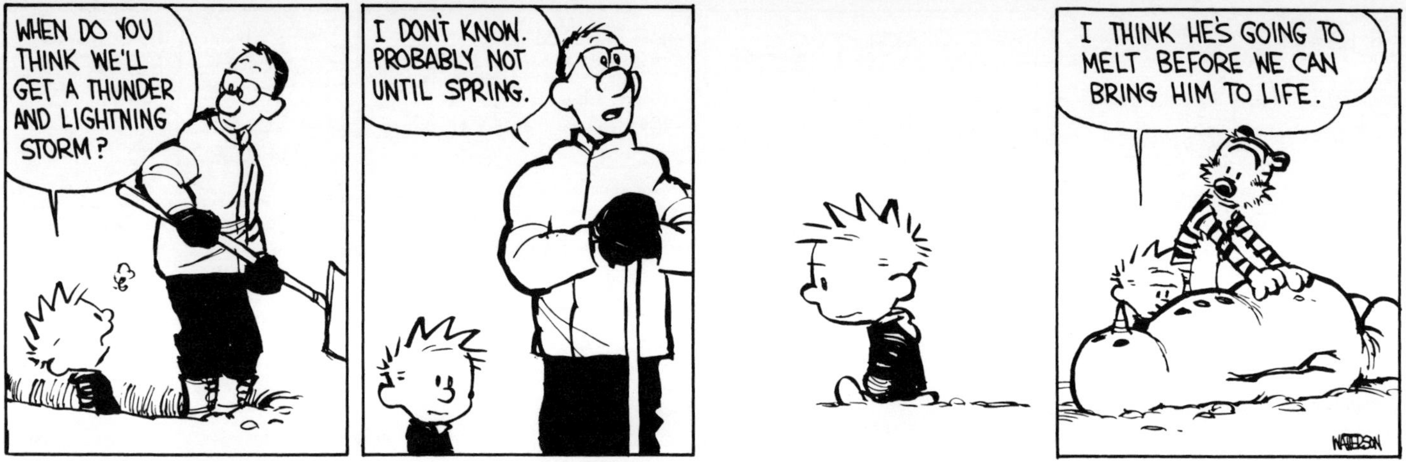
WHEN DO YOU THINK WE'LL GET A THUNDER AND LIGHTNING STORM?
I DON'T KNOW. PROBABLY NOT UNTIL SPRING.
I THINK HE'S GOING TO MELT BEFORE WE CAN BRING HIM TO LIFE.

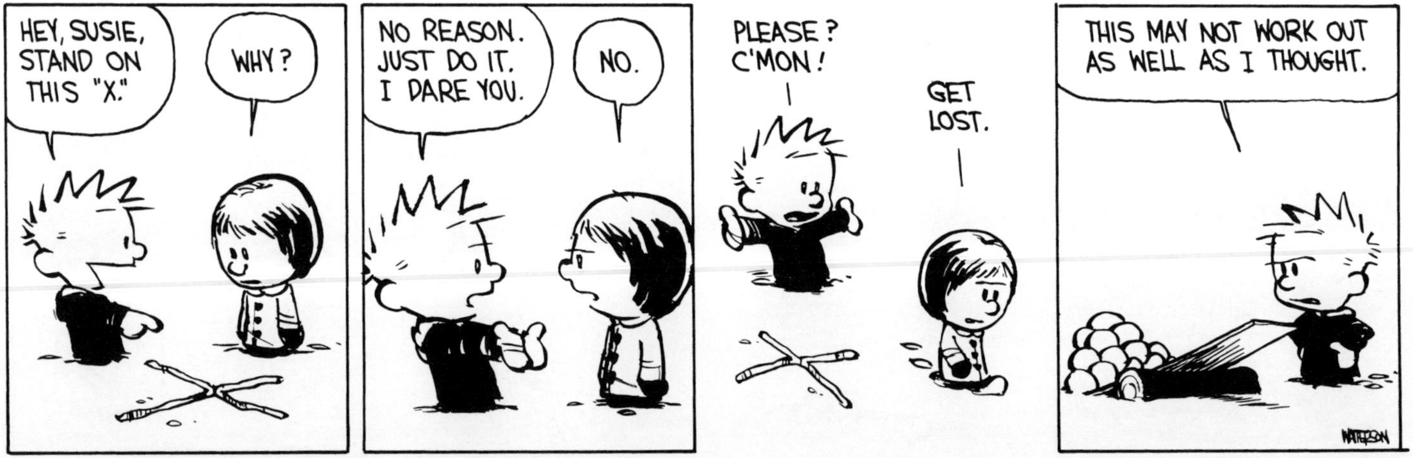
HEY, SUSIE, STAND ON THIS "X."
WHY?
NO REASON. JUST DO IT. I DARE YOU.
NO.
PLEASE? C'MON!
GET LOST.
THIS MAY NOT WORK OUT AS WELL AS I THOUGHT.

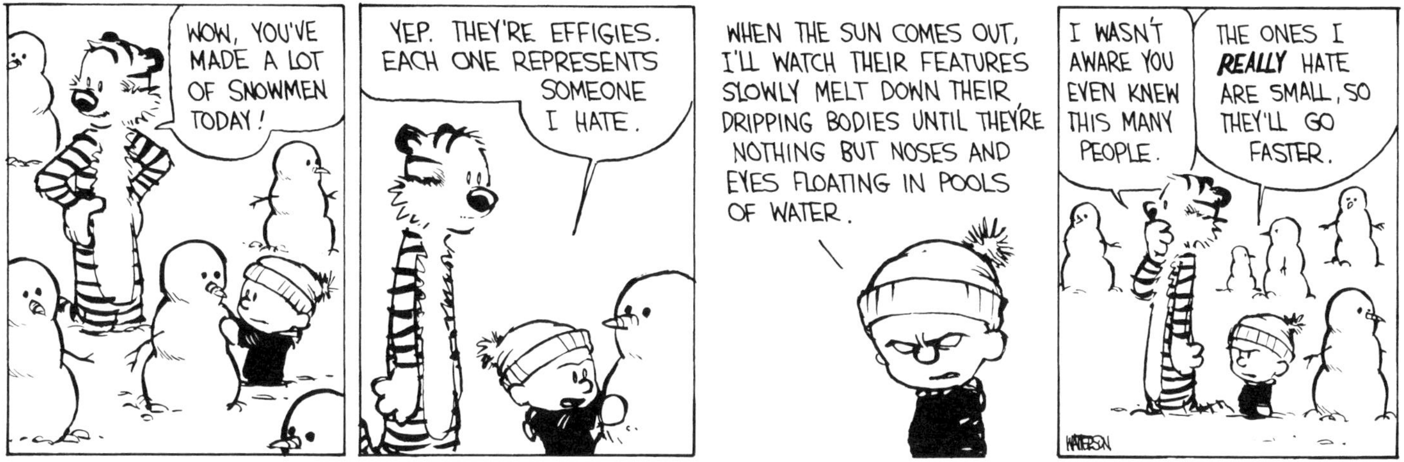
WOW, YOU'VE MADE A LOT OF SNOWMEN TODAY!
YEP. THEY'RE EFFIGIES. EACH ONE REPRESENTS SOMEONE I HATE.
WHEN THE SUN COMES OUT, I'LL WATCH THEIR FEATURES SLOWLY MELT DOWN THEIR DRIPPING BODIES UNTIL THEY'RE NOTHING BUT NOSES AND EYES FLOATING IN POOLS OF WATER.
I WASN'T AWARE YOU EVEN KNEW THIS MANY PEOPLE.
THE ONES I **REALLY** HATE ARE SMALL, SO THEY'LL GO FASTER.

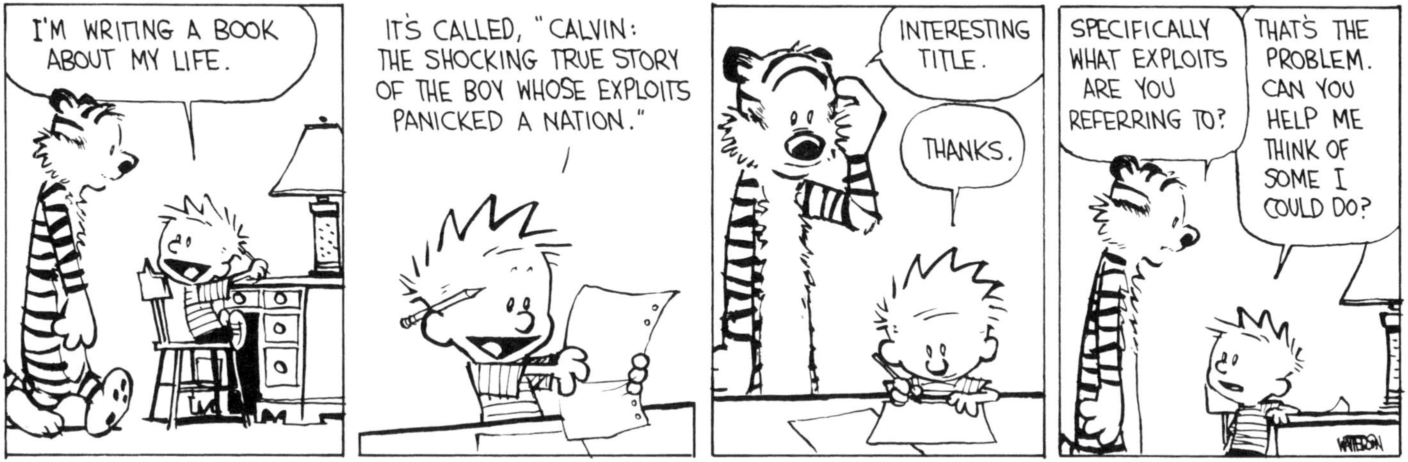
I'M WRITING A BOOK ABOUT MY LIFE.
IT'S CALLED, "CALVIN: THE SHOCKING TRUE STORY OF THE BOY WHOSE EXPLOITS PANICKED A NATION."
INTERESTING TITLE.
THANKS.
SPECIFICALLY WHAT EXPLOITS ARE YOU REFERRING TO?
THAT'S THE PROBLEM. CAN YOU HELP ME THINK OF SOME I COULD DO?

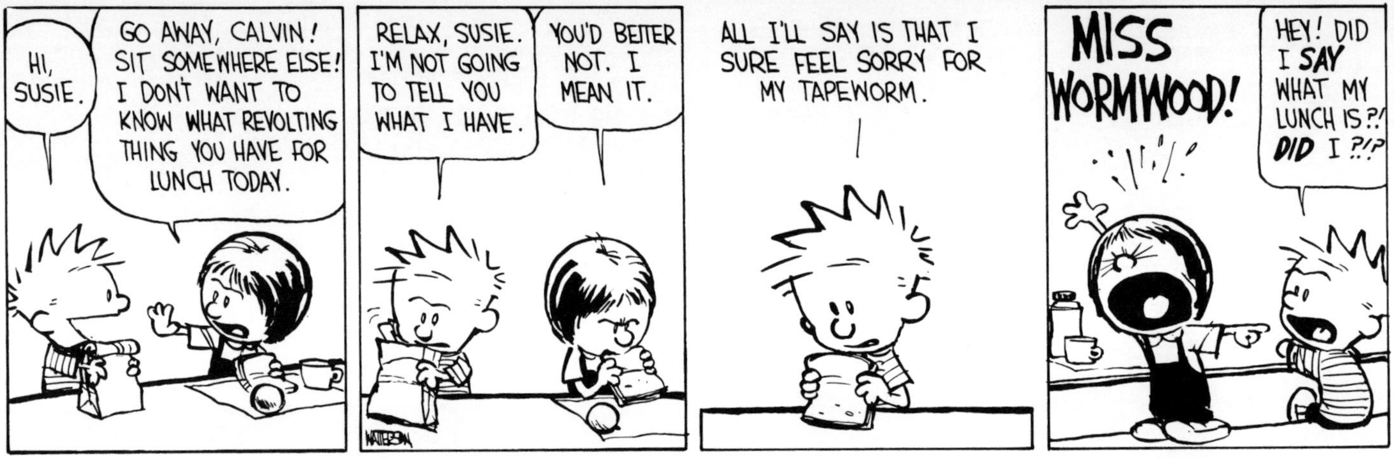
HI, SUSIE.
GO AWAY, CALVIN! SIT SOMEWHERE ELSE! I DON'T WANT TO KNOW WHAT REVOLTING THING YOU HAVE FOR LUNCH TODAY.
RELAX, SUSIE. I'M NOT GOING TO TELL YOU WHAT I HAVE.
YOU'D BETTER NOT. I MEAN IT.
ALL I'LL SAY IS THAT I SURE FEEL SORRY FOR MY TAPEWORM.
MISS WORMWOOD!
HEY! DID I SAY WHAT MY LUNCH IS?! DID I ?!?

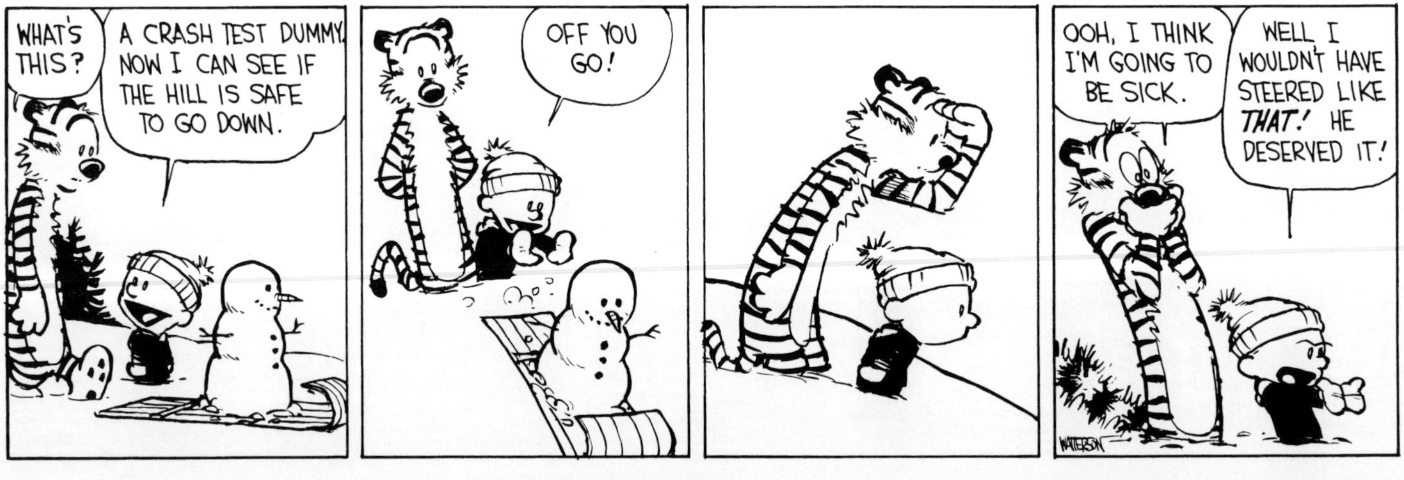
WHAT'S THIS?
A CRASH TEST DUMMY. NOW I CAN SEE IF THE HILL IS SAFE TO GO DOWN.
OFF YOU GO!
OOH, I THINK I'M GOING TO BE SICK.
WELL I WOULDN'T HAVE STEERED LIKE THAT! HE DESERVED IT!

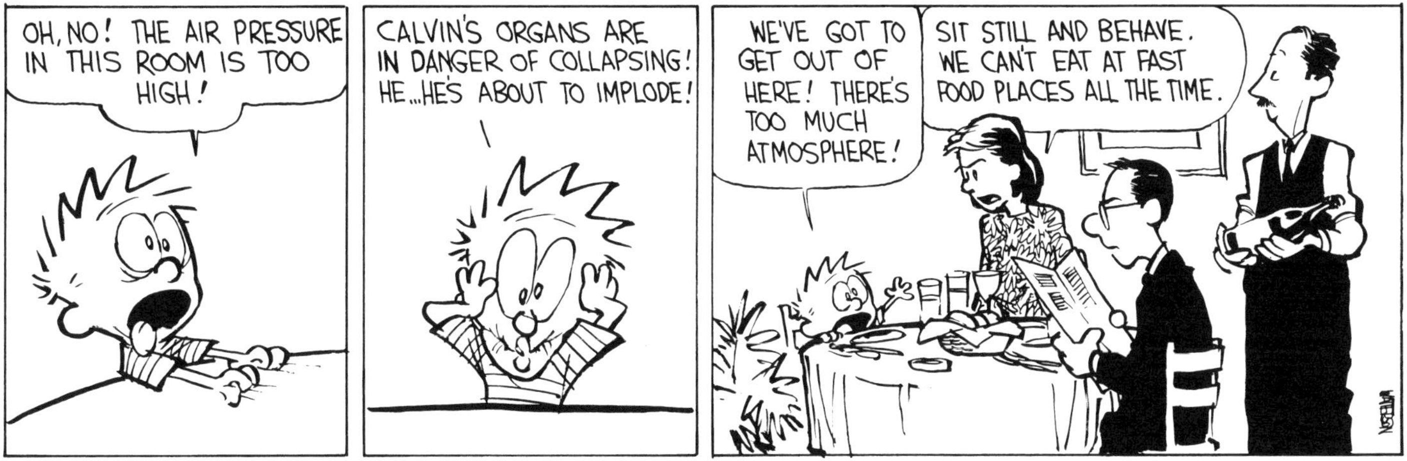
OH, NO! THE AIR PRESSURE IN THIS ROOM IS TOO HIGH!
CALVIN'S ORGANS ARE IN DANGER OF COLLAPSING! HE...HE'S ABOUT TO IMPLODE!
WE'VE GOT TO GET OUT OF HERE! THERE'S TOO MUCH ATMOSPHERE!
SIT STILL AND BEHAVE. WE CAN'T EAT AT FAST FOOD PLACES ALL THE TIME.

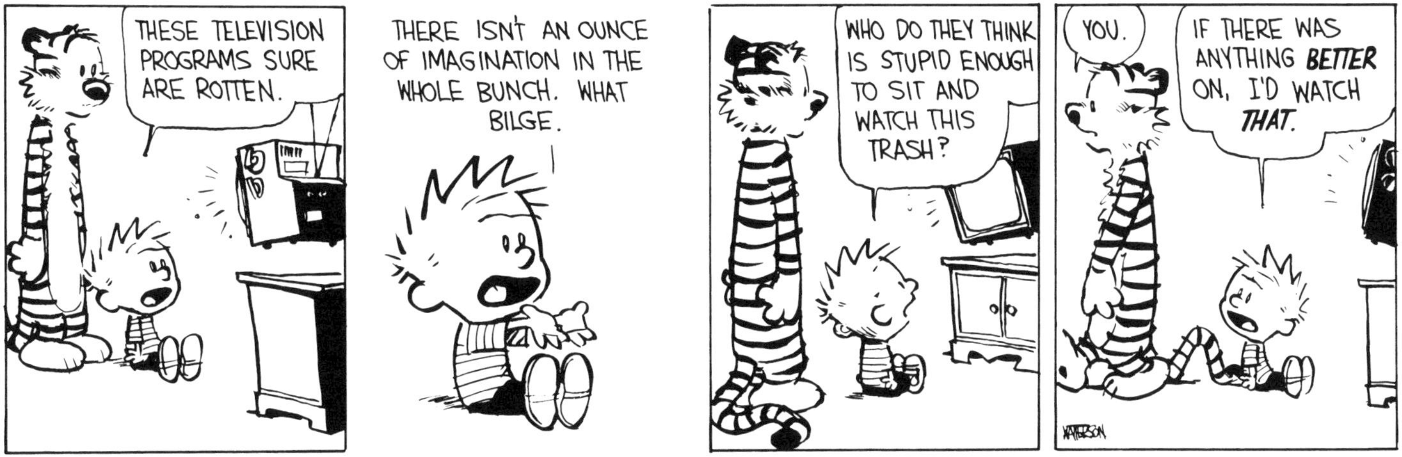
THESE TELEVISION PROGRAMS SURE ARE ROTTEN.
THERE ISN'T AN OUNCE OF IMAGINATION IN THE WHOLE BUNCH. WHAT BILGE.
WHO DO THEY THINK IS STUPID ENOUGH TO SIT AND WATCH THIS TRASH?
YOU.
IF THERE WAS ANYTHING **BETTER** ON, I'D WATCH ***THAT.***

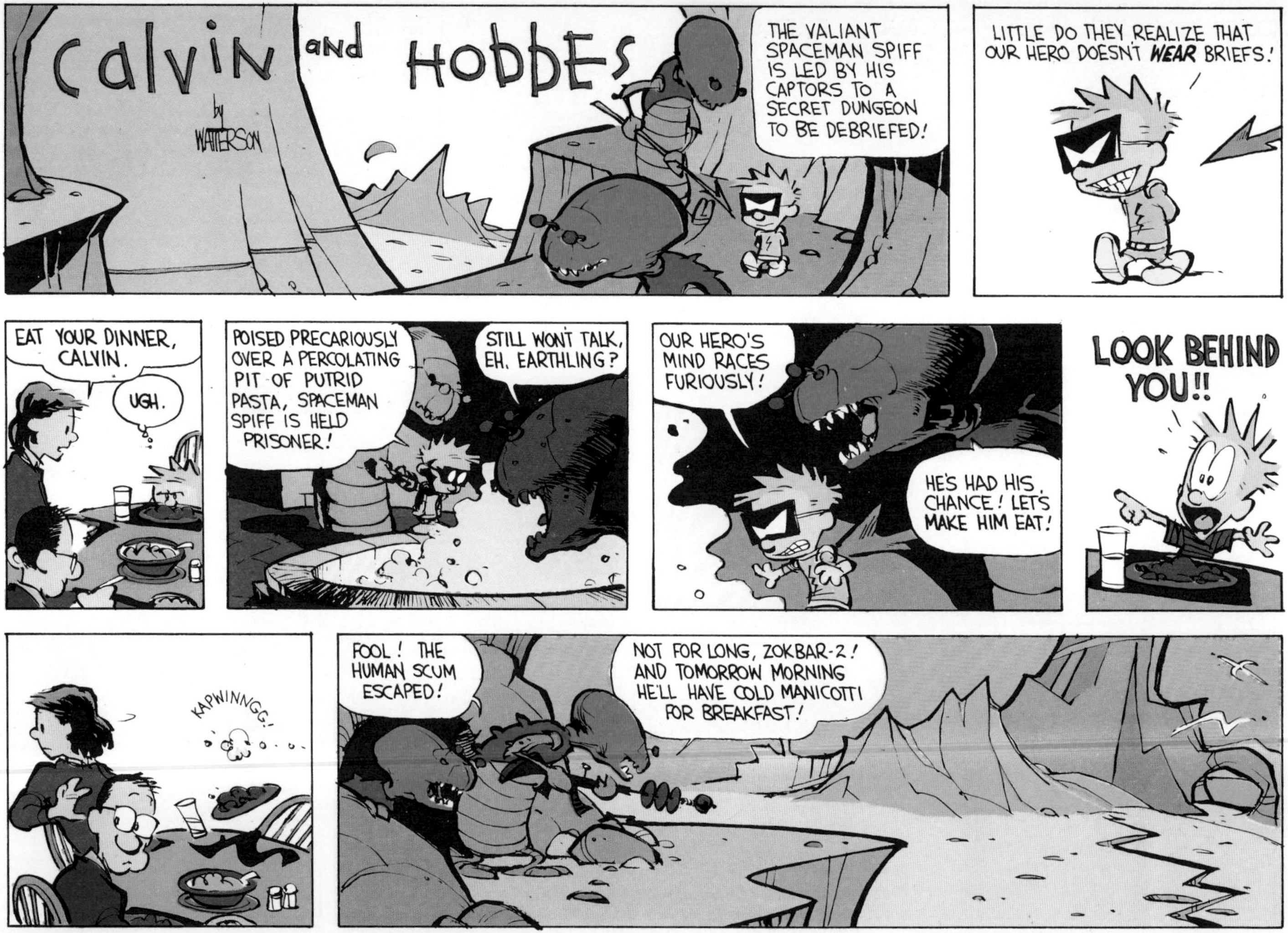
Calvin and HOBBES
by WATTERSON
THE VALIANT SPACEMAN SPIFF IS LED BY HIS CAPTORS TO A SECRET DUNGEON TO BE DEBRIEFED!
LITTLE DO THEY REALIZE THAT OUR HERO DOESN'T WEAR BRIEFS!
EAT YOUR DINNER, CALVIN.
UGH.
POISED PRECARIOUSLY OVER A PERCOLATING PIT OF PUTRID PASTA, SPACEMAN SPIFF IS HELD PRISONER!
STILL WON'T TALK, EH, EARTHLING?
OUR HERO'S MIND RACES FURIOUSLY!
HE'S HAD HIS CHANCE! LET'S MAKE HIM EAT!
LOOK BEHIND YOU!!
KAPWINNGG!
FOOL! THE HUMAN SCUM ESCAPED!
NOT FOR LONG, ZOKBAR-2! AND TOMORROW MORNING HE'LL HAVE COLD MANICOTTI FOR BREAKFAST!

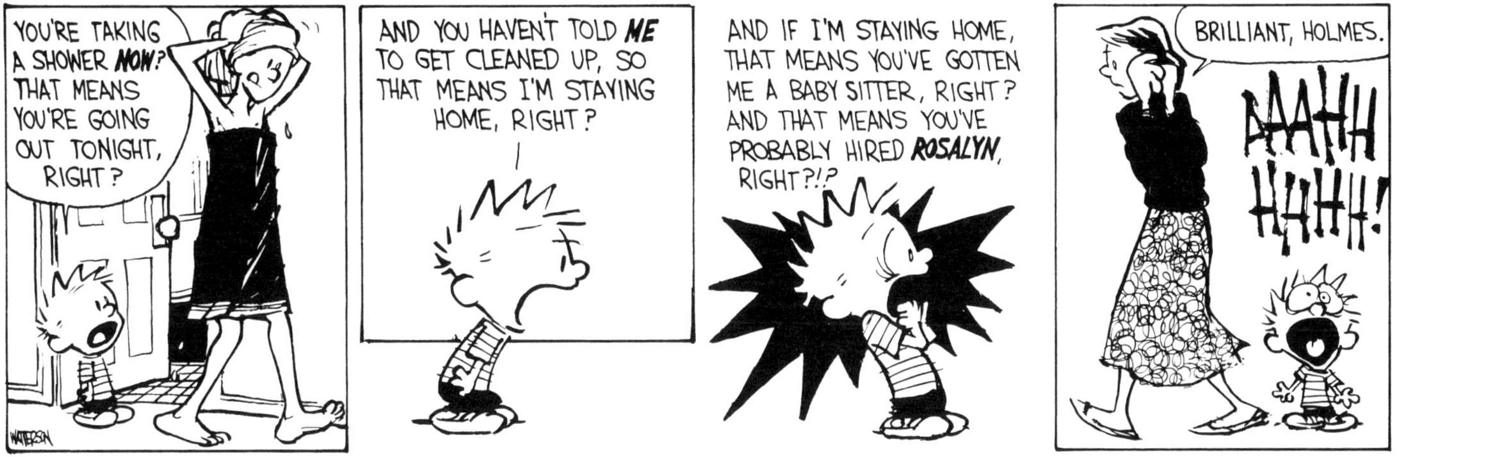
YOU'RE TAKING A SHOWER NOW? THAT MEANS YOU'RE GOING OUT TONIGHT, RIGHT?
WATTERSON
AND YOU HAVEN'T TOLD ME TO GET CLEANED UP, SO THAT MEANS I'M STAYING HOME, RIGHT?
AND IF I'M STAYING HOME, THAT MEANS YOU'VE GOTTEN ME A BABY SITTER, RIGHT? AND THAT MEANS YOU'VE PROBABLY HIRED ROSALYN, RIGHT?!?
BRILLIANT, HOLMES.
AAAHHHHHH!

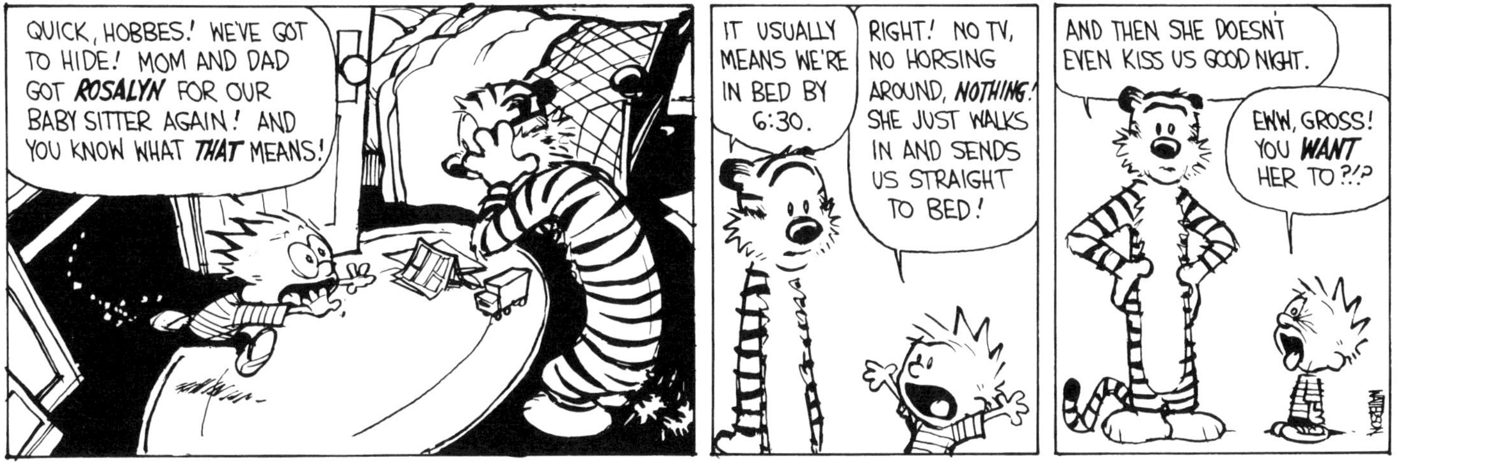
QUICK, HOBBES! WE'VE GOT TO HIDE! MOM AND DAD GOT ROSALYN FOR OUR BABY SITTER AGAIN! AND YOU KNOW WHAT THAT MEANS!
IT USUALLY MEANS WE'RE IN BED BY 6:30.
RIGHT! NO TV, NO HORSING AROUND, NOTHING! SHE JUST WALKS IN AND SENDS US STRAIGHT TO BED!
AND THEN SHE DOESN'T EVEN KISS US GOOD NIGHT.
EWW, GROSS! YOU WANT HER TO?!?
WATTERSON

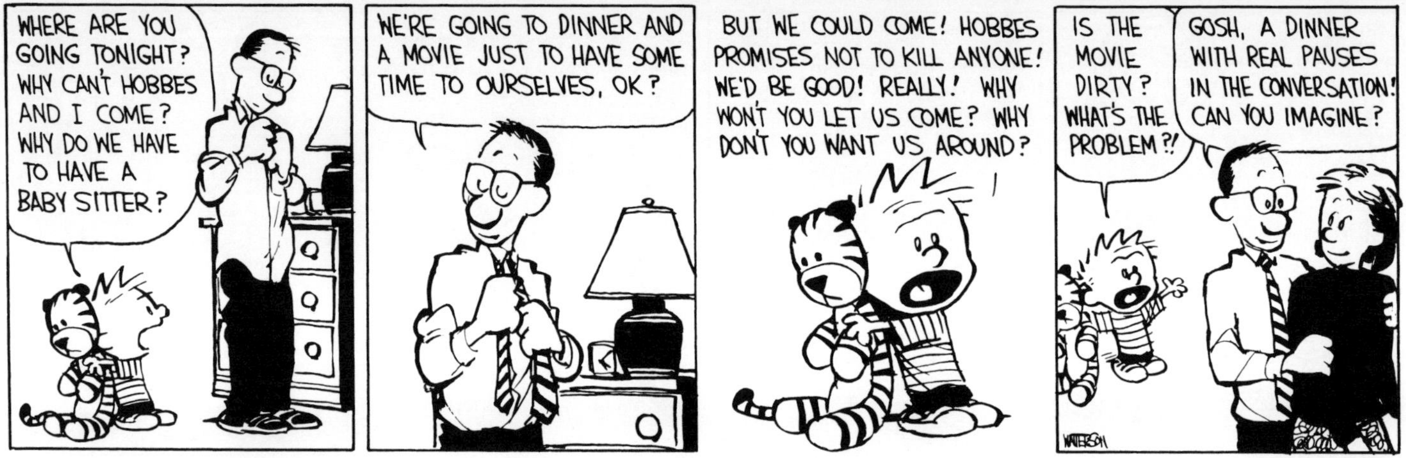
WHERE ARE YOU GOING TONIGHT? WHY CAN'T HOBBES AND I COME? WHY DO WE HAVE TO HAVE A BABY SITTER?
WE'RE GOING TO DINNER AND A MOVIE JUST TO HAVE SOME TIME TO OURSELVES, OK?
BUT WE COULD COME! HOBBES PROMISES NOT TO KILL ANYONE! WE'D BE GOOD! REALLY! WHY WON'T YOU LET US COME? WHY DON'T YOU WANT US AROUND?
IS THE MOVIE DIRTY? WHAT'S THE PROBLEM?!
GOSH, A DINNER WITH REAL PAUSES IN THE CONVERSATION! CAN YOU IMAGINE?
WATTERSON

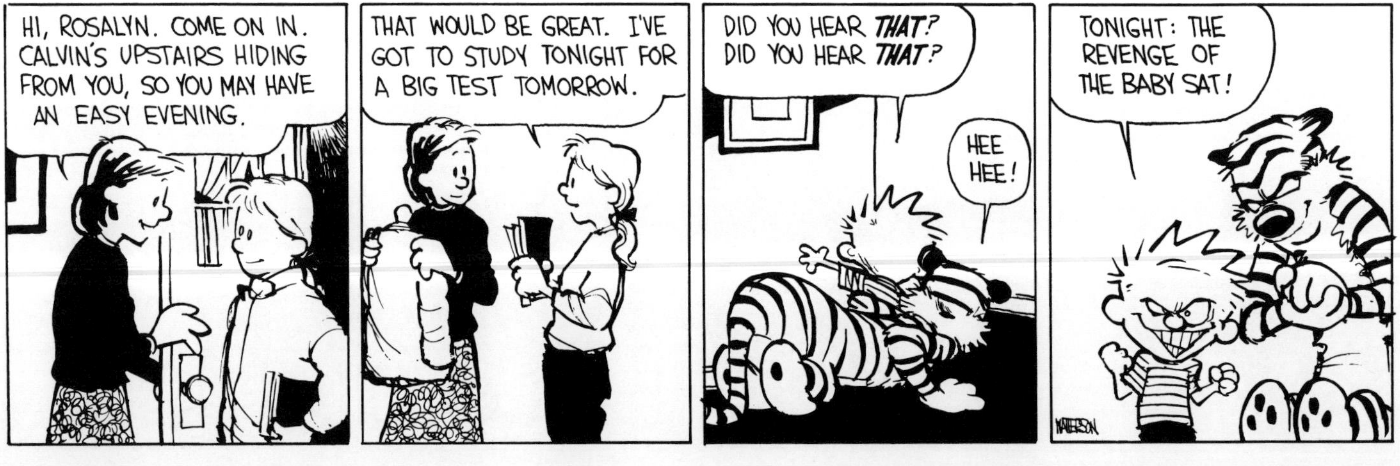
HI, ROSALYN. COME ON IN. CALVIN'S UPSTAIRS HIDING FROM YOU, SO YOU MAY HAVE AN EASY EVENING.
THAT WOULD BE GREAT. I'VE GOT TO STUDY TONIGHT FOR A BIG TEST TOMORROW.
DID YOU HEAR ***THAT***? DID YOU HEAR ***THAT***?
HEE HEE!
TONIGHT: THE REVENGE OF THE BABY SAT!
WATTERSON

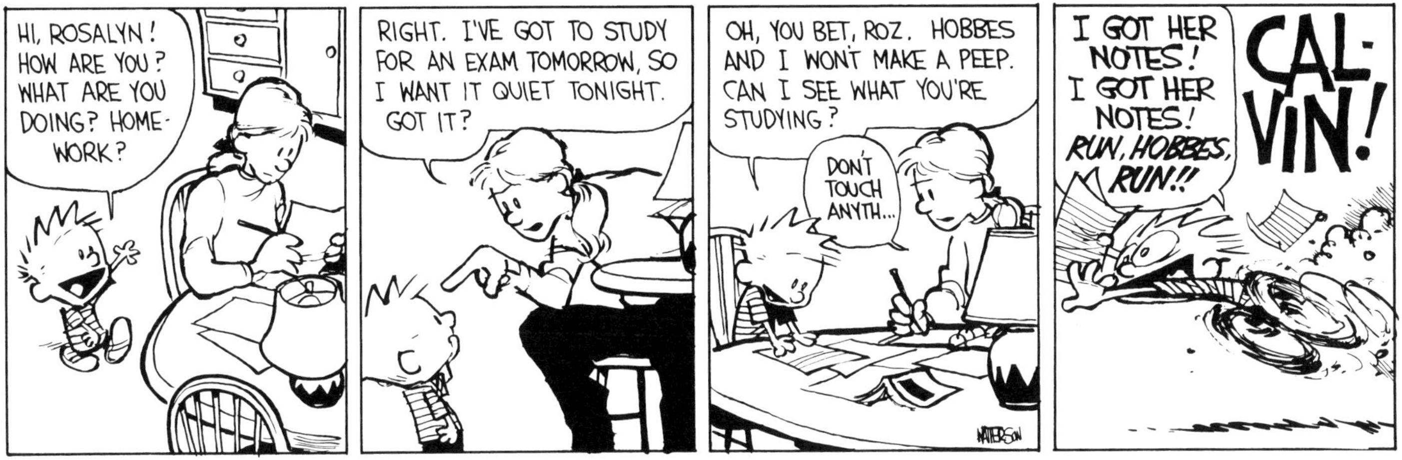
HI, ROSALYN! HOW ARE YOU? WHAT ARE YOU DOING? HOME-WORK?
RIGHT. I'VE GOT TO STUDY FOR AN EXAM TOMORROW, SO I WANT IT QUIET TONIGHT. GOT IT?
OH, YOU BET, ROZ. HOBBES AND I WON'T MAKE A PEEP. CAN I SEE WHAT YOU'RE STUDYING?
DON'T TOUCH ANYTH...
I GOT HER NOTES! I GOT HER NOTES! RUN, HOBBES, RUN!!
CAL-VIN!

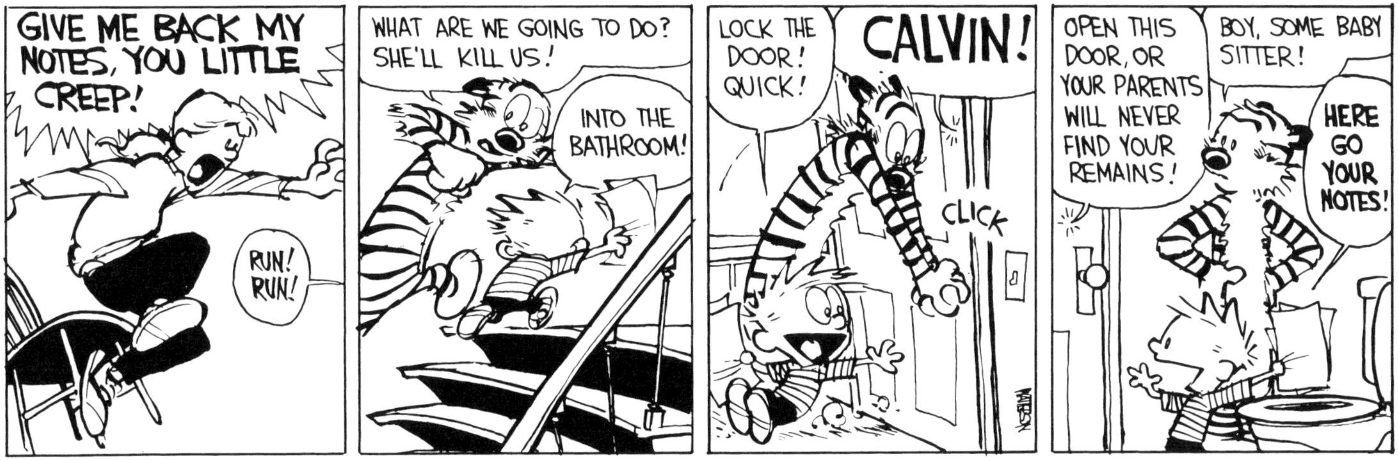
GIVE ME BACK MY NOTES, YOU LITTLE CREEP!
RUN! RUN!
WHAT ARE WE GOING TO DO? SHE'LL KILL US!
INTO THE BATHROOM!
LOCK THE DOOR! QUICK!
CALVIN!
CLICK
OPEN THIS DOOR, OR YOUR PARENTS WILL NEVER FIND YOUR REMAINS!
BOY, SOME BABY SITTER!
HERE GO YOUR NOTES!

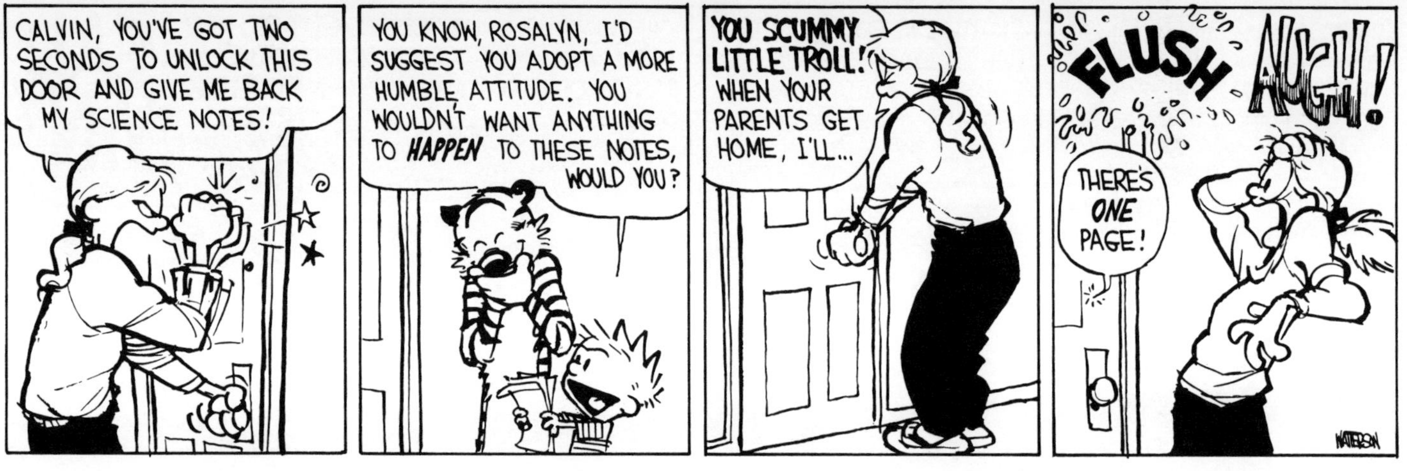
CALVIN, YOU'VE GOT TWO SECONDS TO UNLOCK THIS DOOR AND GIVE ME BACK MY SCIENCE NOTES!
YOU KNOW, ROSALYN, I'D SUGGEST YOU ADOPT A MORE HUMBLE ATTITUDE. YOU WOULDN'T WANT ANYTHING TO HAPPEN TO THESE NOTES, WOULD YOU?
YOU SCUMMY LITTLE TROLL! WHEN YOUR PARENTS GET HOME, I'LL...
FLUSH
AUGH!
THERE'S ONE PAGE!

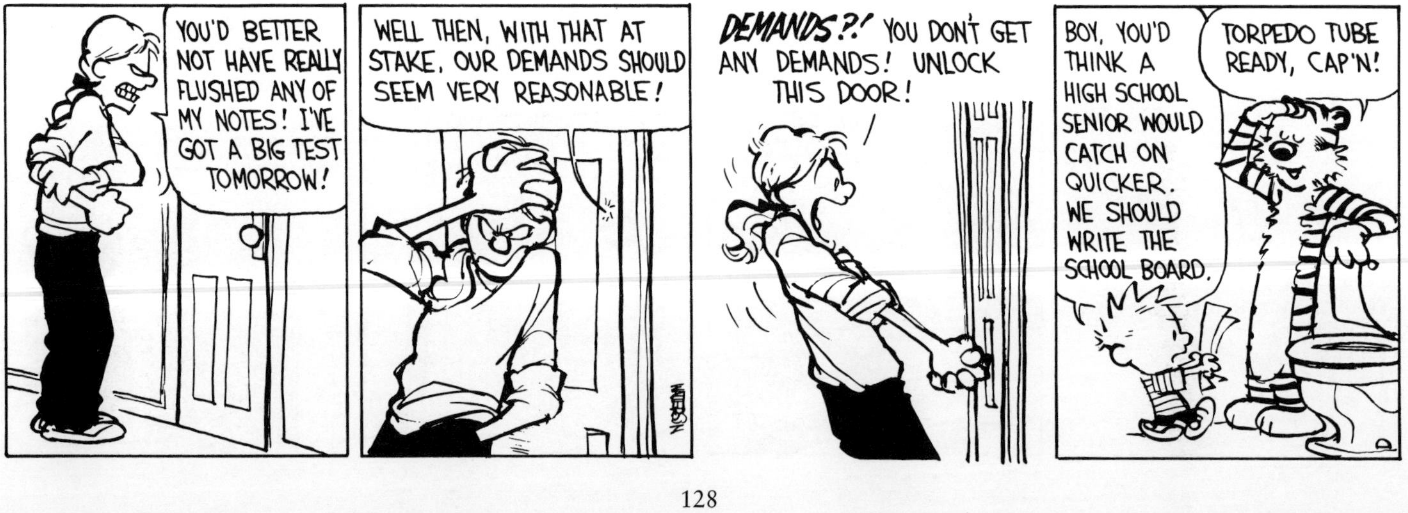
YOU'D BETTER NOT HAVE REALLY FLUSHED ANY OF MY NOTES! I'VE GOT A BIG TEST TOMORROW!
WELL THEN, WITH THAT AT STAKE, OUR DEMANDS SHOULD SEEM VERY REASONABLE!
DEMANDS?! YOU DON'T GET ANY DEMANDS! UNLOCK THIS DOOR!
BOY, YOU'D THINK A HIGH SCHOOL SENIOR WOULD CATCH ON QUICKER. WE SHOULD WRITE THE SCHOOL BOARD.
TORPEDO TUBE READY, CAP'N!

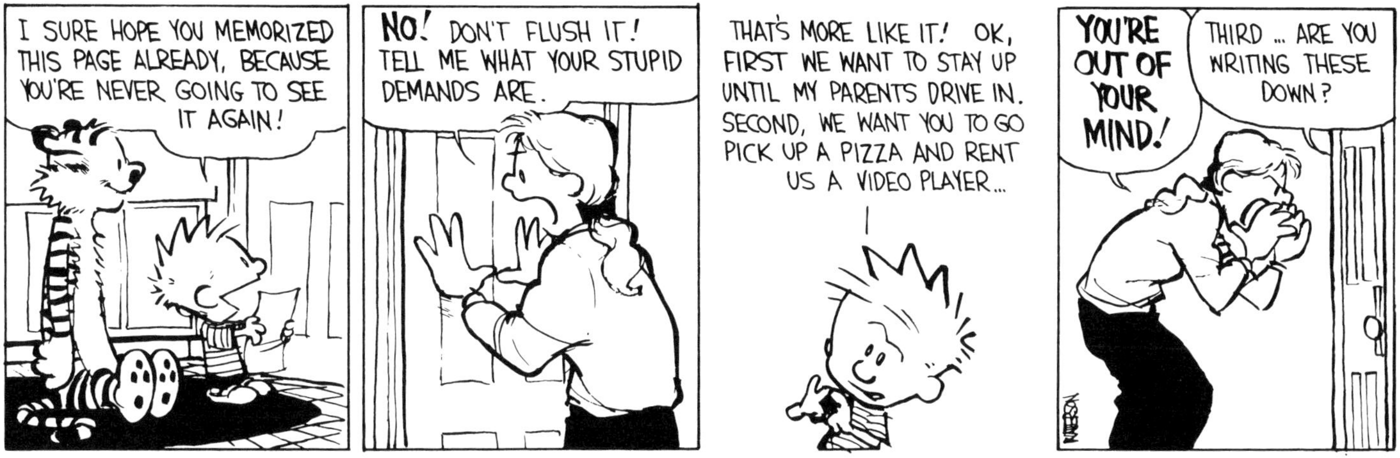
I SURE HOPE YOU MEMORIZED THIS PAGE ALREADY, BECAUSE YOU'RE NEVER GOING TO SEE IT AGAIN!
NO! DON'T FLUSH IT! TELL ME WHAT YOUR STUPID DEMANDS ARE.
THAT'S MORE LIKE IT! OK, FIRST WE WANT TO STAY UP UNTIL MY PARENTS DRIVE IN. SECOND, WE WANT YOU TO GO PICK UP A PIZZA AND RENT US A VIDEO PLAYER...
YOU'RE OUT OF YOUR MIND!
THIRD ... ARE YOU WRITING THESE DOWN?
WATTERSON

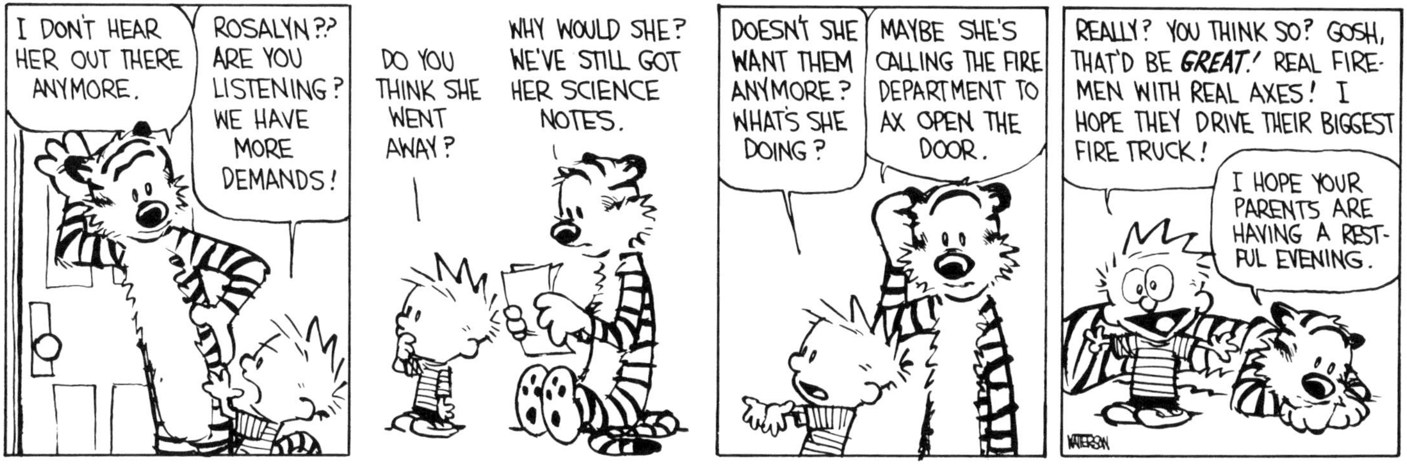
I DON'T HEAR HER OUT THERE ANYMORE.
ROSALYN?? ARE YOU LISTENING? WE HAVE MORE DEMANDS!
DO YOU THINK SHE WENT AWAY?
WHY WOULD SHE? WE'VE STILL GOT HER SCIENCE NOTES.
DOESN'T SHE WANT THEM ANYMORE? WHAT'S SHE DOING?
MAYBE SHE'S CALLING THE FIRE DEPARTMENT TO AX OPEN THE DOOR.
REALLY? YOU THINK SO? GOSH, THAT'D BE GREAT! REAL FIREMEN WITH REAL AXES! I HOPE THEY DRIVE THEIR BIGGEST FIRE TRUCK!
I HOPE YOUR PARENTS ARE HAVING A RESTFUL EVENING.
WATTERSON

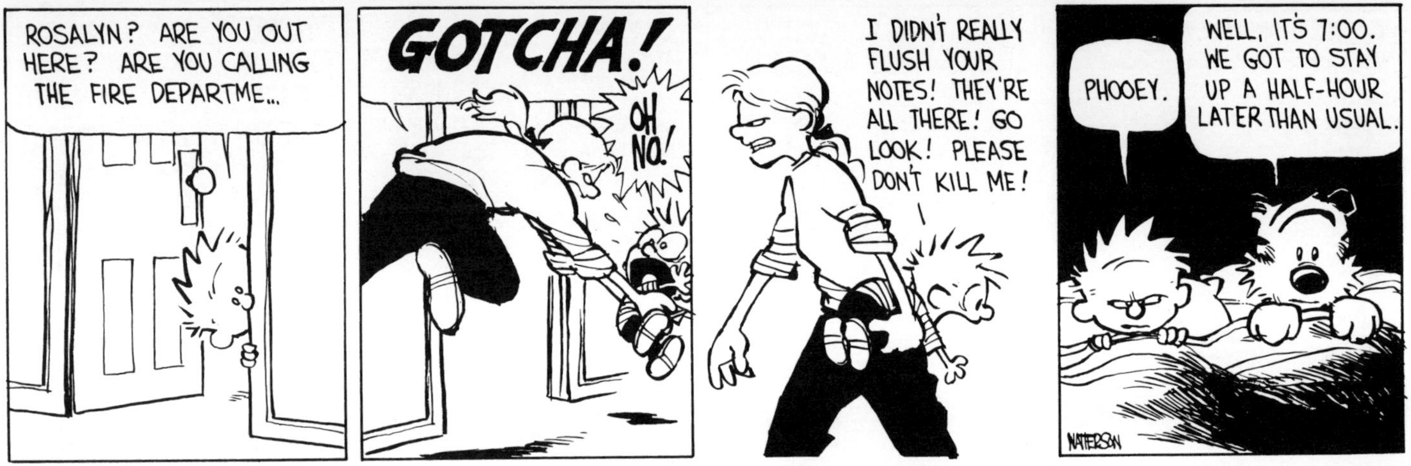
ROSALYN? ARE YOU OUT HERE? ARE YOU CALLING THE FIRE DEPARTME...
GOTCHA!
OH NO!
I DIDN'T REALLY FLUSH YOUR NOTES! THEY'RE ALL THERE! GO LOOK! PLEASE DON'T KILL ME!
PHOOEY.
WELL, IT'S 7:00. WE GOT TO STAY UP A HALF-HOUR LATER THAN USUAL.

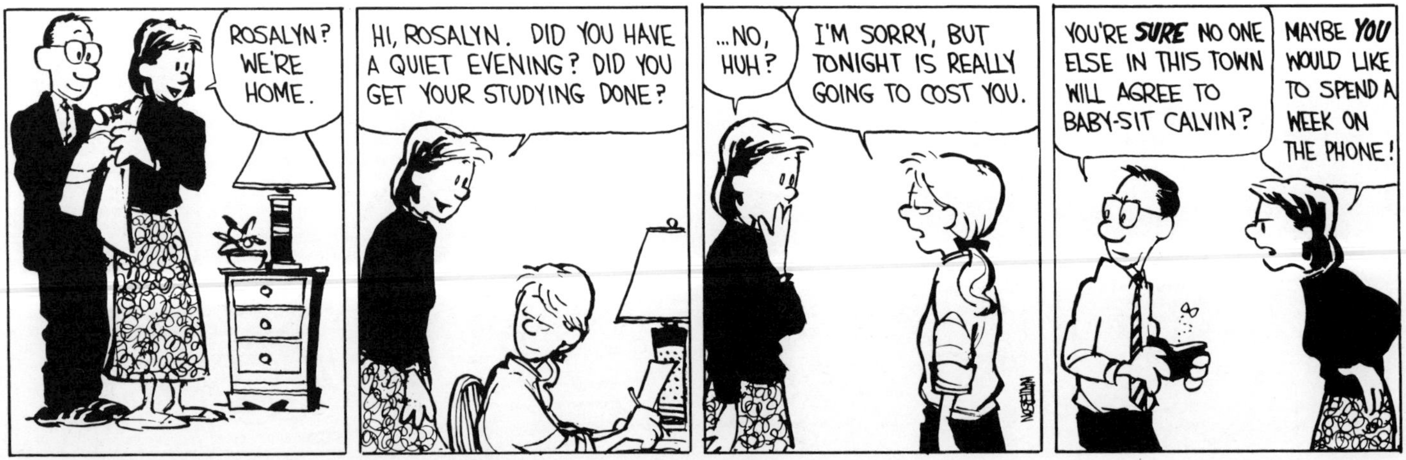
ROSALYN? WE'RE HOME.
HI, ROSALYN. DID YOU HAVE A QUIET EVENING? DID YOU GET YOUR STUDYING DONE?
...NO, HUH?
I'M SORRY, BUT TONIGHT IS REALLY GOING TO COST YOU.
YOU'RE SURE NO ONE ELSE IN THIS TOWN WILL AGREE TO BABY-SIT CALVIN?
MAYBE YOU WOULD LIKE TO SPEND A WEEK ON THE PHONE!

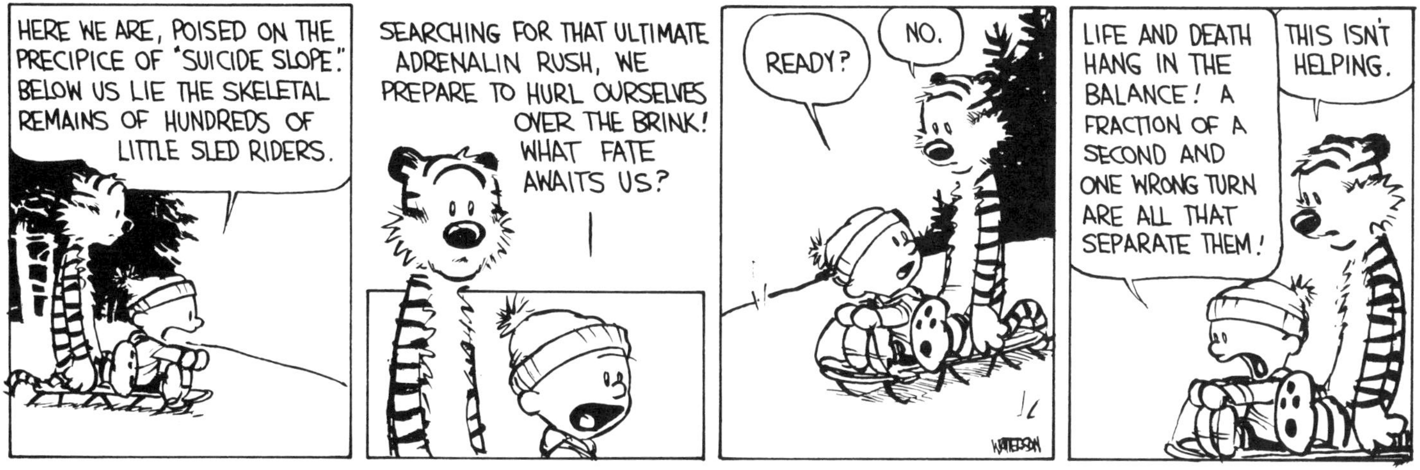
HERE WE ARE, POISED ON THE PRECIPICE OF "SUICIDE SLOPE." BELOW US LIE THE SKELETAL REMAINS OF HUNDREDS OF LITTLE SLED RIDERS.
SEARCHING FOR THAT ULTIMATE ADRENALIN RUSH, WE PREPARE TO HURL OURSELVES OVER THE BRINK! WHAT FATE AWAITS US?
READY?
NO.
LIFE AND DEATH HANG IN THE BALANCE! A FRACTION OF A SECOND AND ONE WRONG TURN ARE ALL THAT SEPARATE THEM!
THIS ISN'T HELPING.

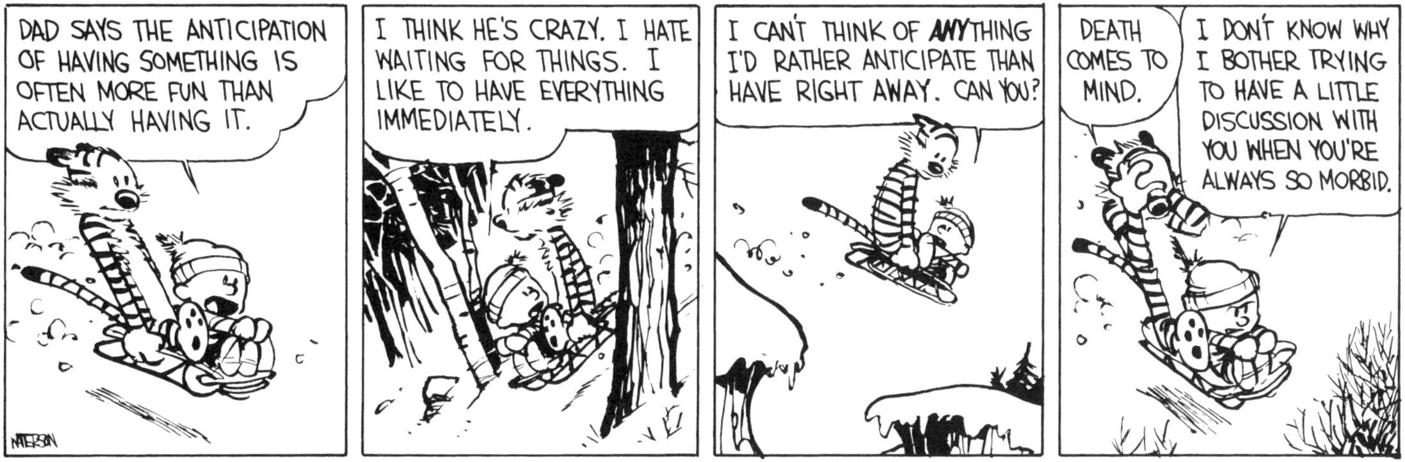
DAD SAYS THE ANTICIPATION OF HAVING SOMETHING IS OFTEN MORE FUN THAN ACTUALLY HAVING IT.
I THINK HE'S CRAZY. I HATE WAITING FOR THINGS. I LIKE TO HAVE EVERYTHING IMMEDIATELY.
I CAN'T THINK OF ANYTHING I'D RATHER ANTICIPATE THAN HAVE RIGHT AWAY. CAN YOU?
DEATH COMES TO MIND.
I DON'T KNOW WHY I BOTHER TRYING TO HAVE A LITTLE DISCUSSION WITH YOU WHEN YOU'RE ALWAYS SO MORBID.

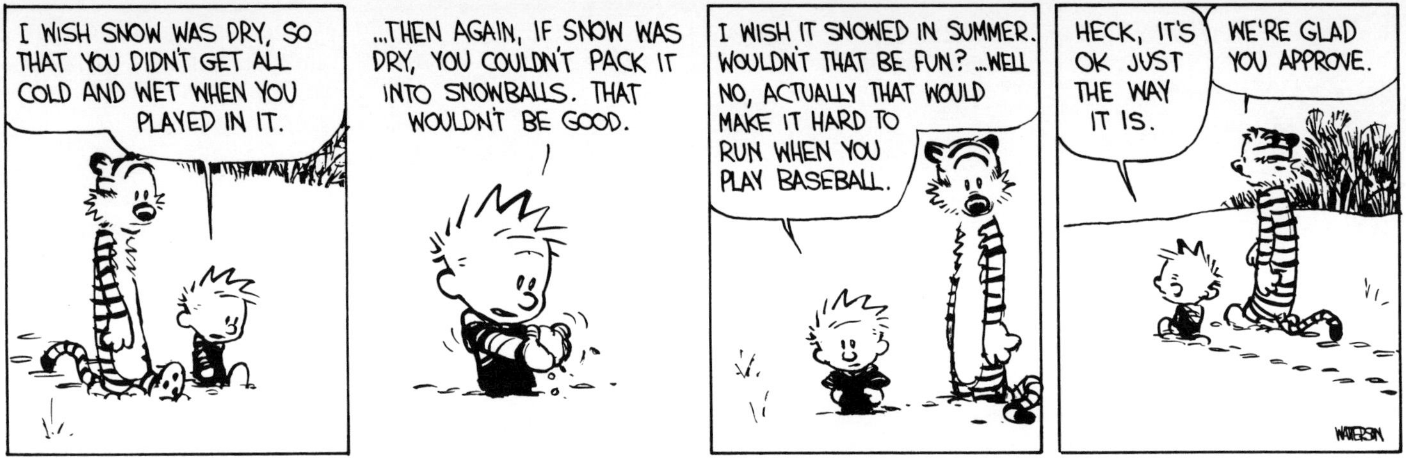
I WISH SNOW WAS DRY, SO THAT YOU DIDN'T GET ALL COLD AND WET WHEN YOU PLAYED IN IT.
...THEN AGAIN, IF SNOW WAS DRY, YOU COULDN'T PACK IT INTO SNOWBALLS. THAT WOULDN'T BE GOOD.
I WISH IT SNOWED IN SUMMER. WOULDN'T THAT BE FUN? ...WELL NO, ACTUALLY THAT WOULD MAKE IT HARD TO RUN WHEN YOU PLAY BASEBALL.
HECK, IT'S OK JUST THE WAY IT IS.
WE'RE GLAD YOU APPROVE.
WATTERSON

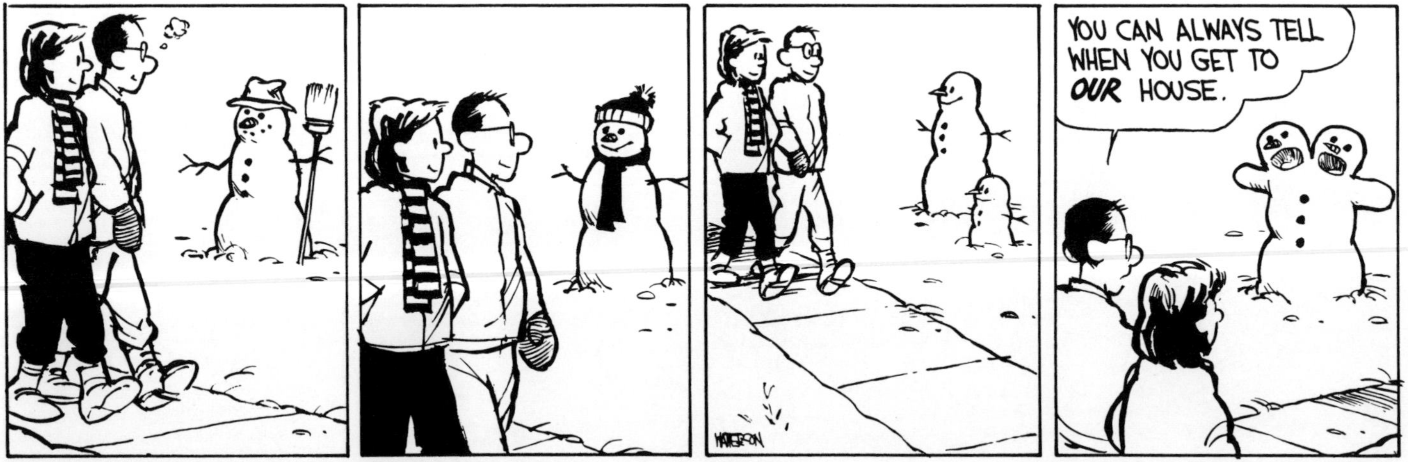
WATTERSON
YOU CAN ALWAYS TELL WHEN YOU GET TO ***OUR*** HOUSE.

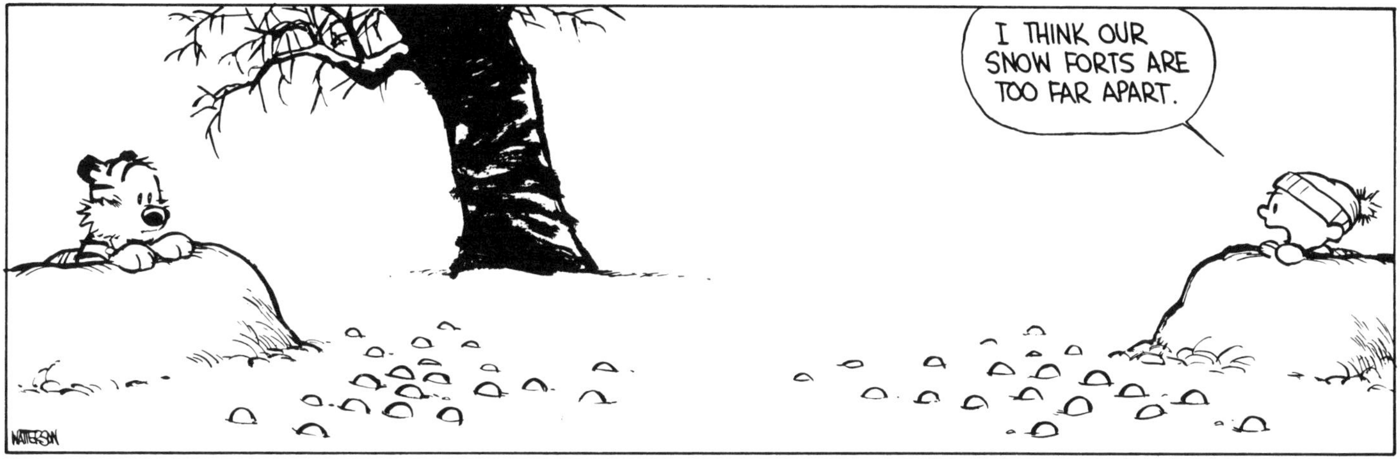
I THINK OUR SNOW FORTS ARE TOO FAR APART.

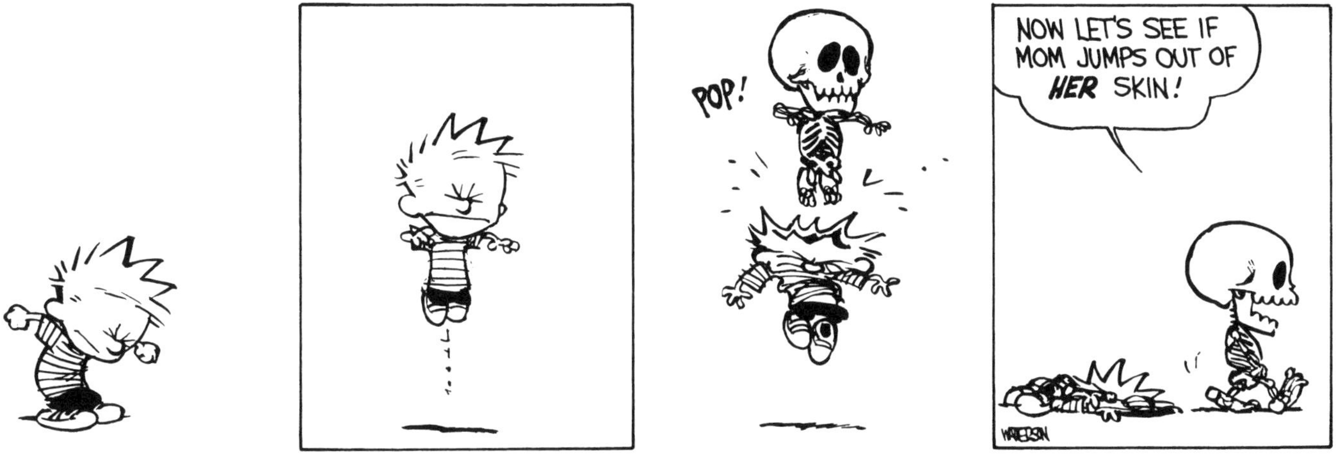
POP!
NOW LET'S SEE IF MOM JUMPS OUT OF **HER** SKIN!

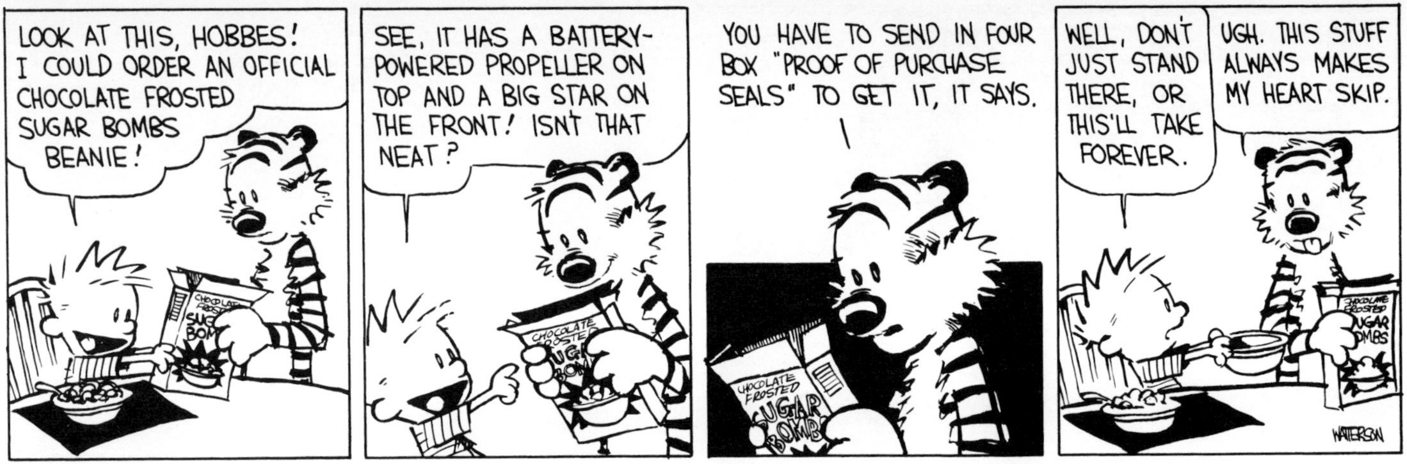
LOOK AT THIS, HOBBES! I COULD ORDER AN OFFICIAL CHOCOLATE FROSTED SUGAR BOMBS BEANIE!
SEE, IT HAS A BATTERY-POWERED PROPELLER ON TOP AND A BIG STAR ON THE FRONT! ISN'T THAT NEAT?
YOU HAVE TO SEND IN FOUR BOX "PROOF OF PURCHASE SEALS" TO GET IT, IT SAYS.
CHOCOLATE FROSTED SUGAR BOMBS
WELL, DON'T JUST STAND THERE, OR THIS'LL TAKE FOREVER.
UGH. THIS STUFF ALWAYS MAKES MY HEART SKIP.
WATERSON

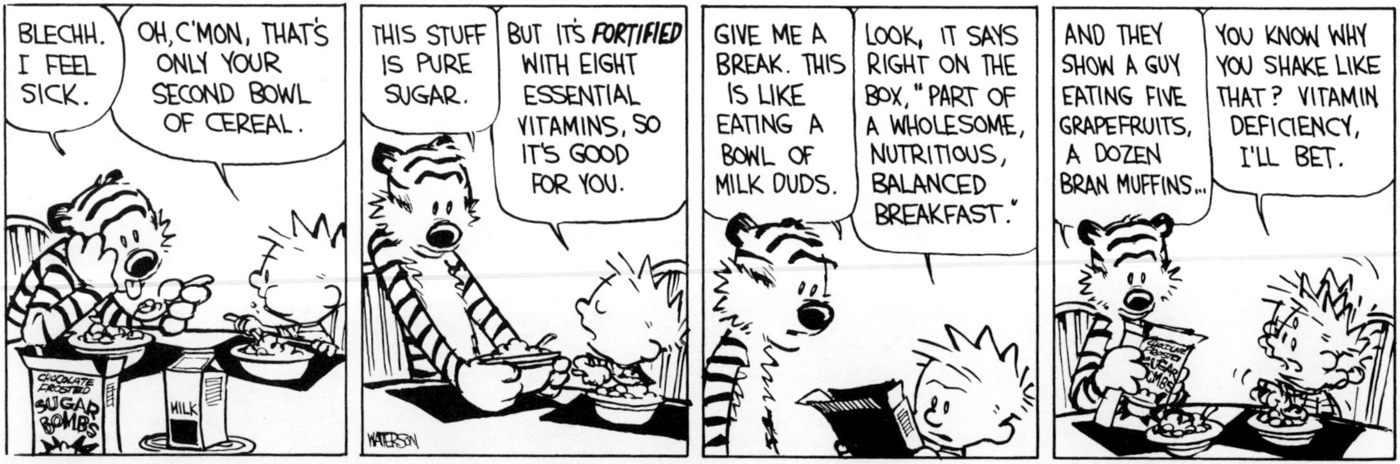
BLECHH. I FEEL SICK.
OH, C'MON, THAT'S ONLY YOUR SECOND BOWL OF CEREAL.
CHOCOLATE FROSTED SUGAR BOMBS
MILK
THIS STUFF IS PURE SUGAR.
BUT IT'S FORTIFIED WITH EIGHT ESSENTIAL VITAMINS, SO IT'S GOOD FOR YOU.
WATERSON
GIVE ME A BREAK. THIS IS LIKE EATING A BOWL OF MILK DUDS.
LOOK, IT SAYS RIGHT ON THE BOX, "PART OF A WHOLESOME, NUTRITIOUS, BALANCED BREAKFAST."
AND THEY SHOW A GUY EATING FIVE GRAPEFRUITS, A DOZEN BRAN MUFFINS...
YOU KNOW WHY YOU SHAKE LIKE THAT? VITAMIN DEFICIENCY, I'LL BET.

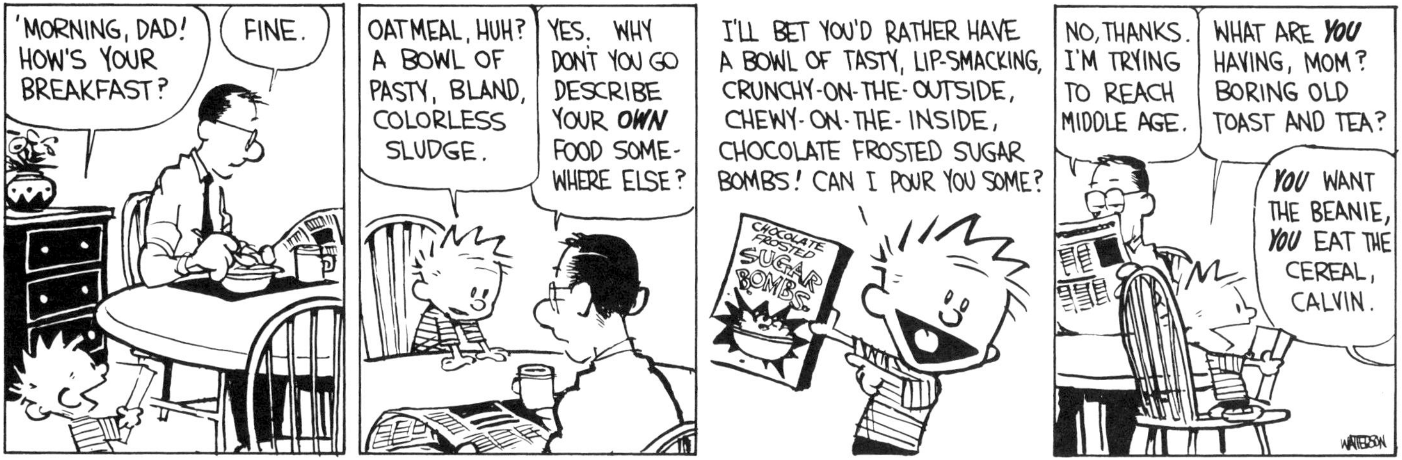
'MORNING, DAD! HOW'S YOUR BREAKFAST?
FINE.
OATMEAL, HUH? A BOWL OF PASTY, BLAND, COLORLESS SLUDGE.
YES. WHY DON'T YOU GO DESCRIBE YOUR **OWN** FOOD SOME-WHERE ELSE?
I'LL BET YOU'D RATHER HAVE A BOWL OF TASTY, LIP-SMACKING, CRUNCHY-ON-THE-OUTSIDE, CHEWY-ON-THE-INSIDE, CHOCOLATE FROSTED SUGAR BOMBS! CAN I POUR YOU SOME?
CHOCOLATE FROSTED SUGAR BOMBS
NO, THANKS. I'M TRYING TO REACH MIDDLE AGE.
WHAT ARE **YOU** HAVING, MOM? BORING OLD TOAST AND TEA?
YOU WANT THE BEANIE, **YOU** EAT THE CEREAL, CALVIN.
WATTERSON

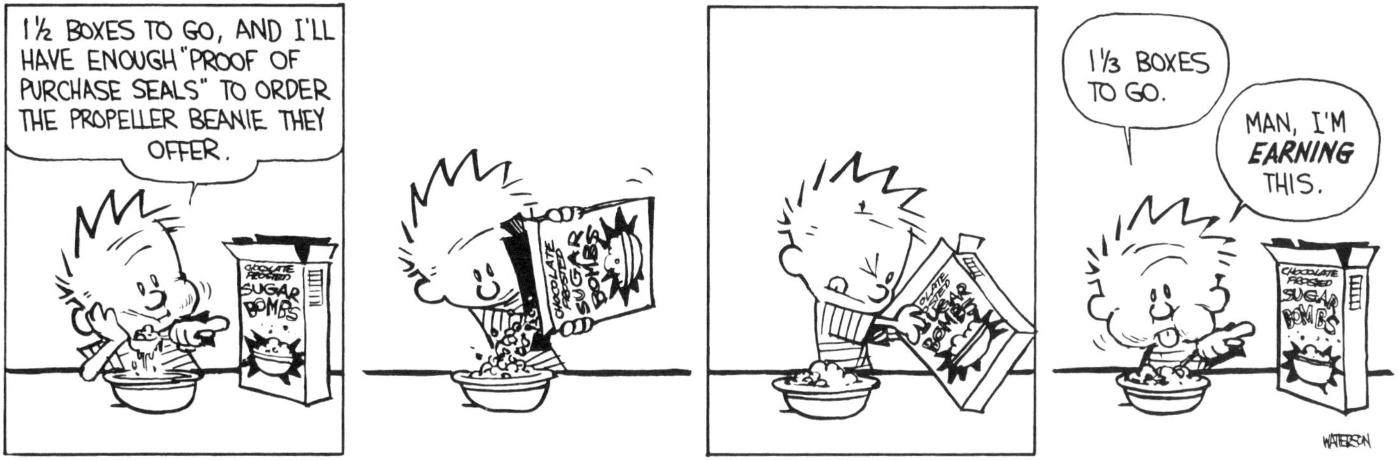
1½ BOXES TO GO, AND I'LL HAVE ENOUGH "PROOF OF PURCHASE SEALS" TO ORDER THE PROPELLER BEANIE THEY OFFER.
CHOCOLATE FROSTED SUGAR BOMBS
1⅓ BOXES TO GO.
MAN, I'M ***EARNING*** THIS.
WATTERSON

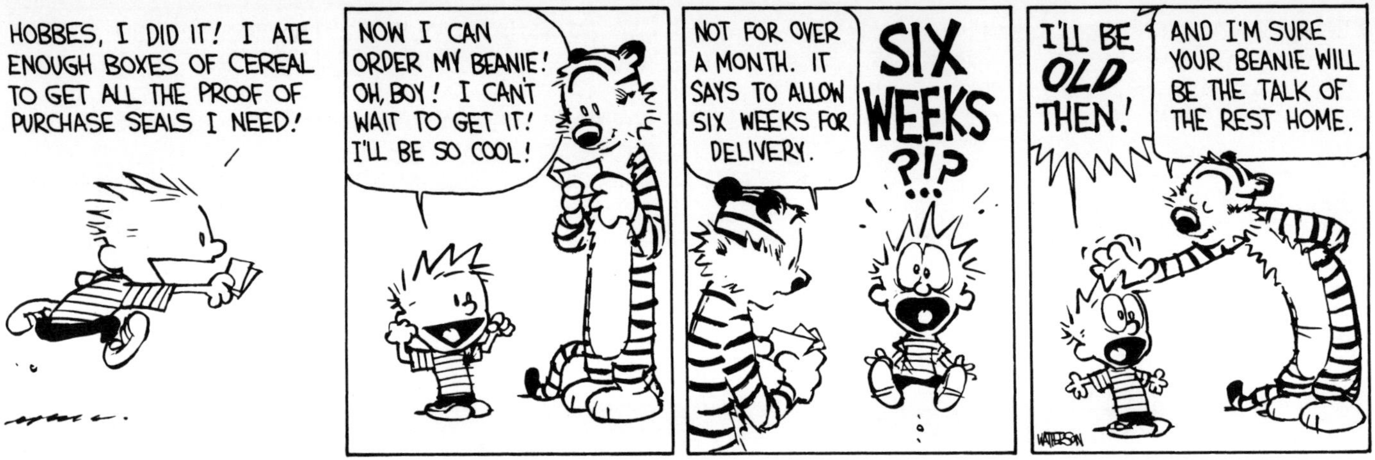
HOBBES, I DID IT! I ATE ENOUGH BOXES OF CEREAL TO GET ALL THE PROOF OF PURCHASE SEALS I NEED!
NOW I CAN ORDER MY BEANIE! OH, BOY! I CAN'T WAIT TO GET IT! I'LL BE SO COOL!
NOT FOR OVER A MONTH. IT SAYS TO ALLOW SIX WEEKS FOR DELIVERY.
SIX WEEKS ?!?
I'LL BE OLD THEN!
AND I'M SURE YOUR BEANIE WILL BE THE TALK OF THE REST HOME.
WATTERSON

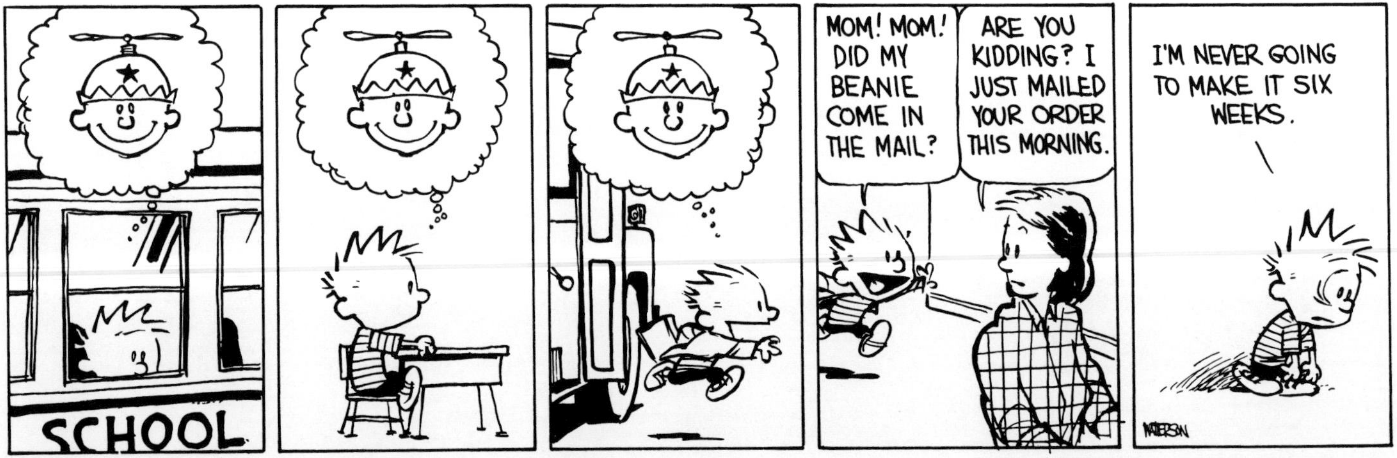
SCHOOL
MOM! MOM! DID MY BEANIE COME IN THE MAIL?
ARE YOU KIDDING? I JUST MAILED YOUR ORDER THIS MORNING.
I'M NEVER GOING TO MAKE IT SIX WEEKS.
WATTERSON

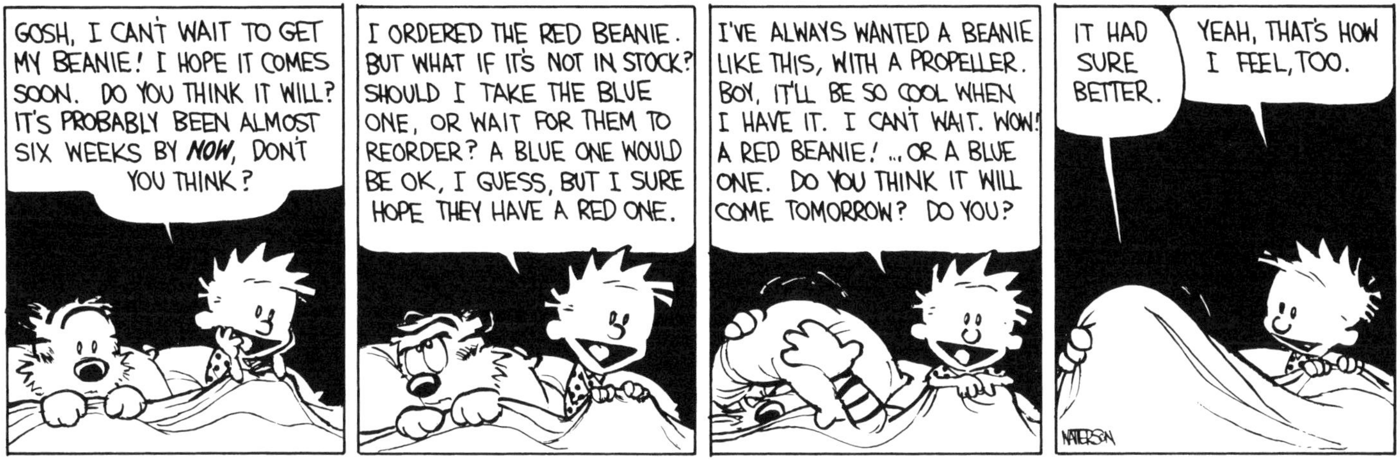
GOSH, I CAN'T WAIT TO GET MY BEANIE! I HOPE IT COMES SOON. DO YOU THINK IT WILL? IT'S PROBABLY BEEN ALMOST SIX WEEKS BY *NOW*, DON'T YOU THINK?
I ORDERED THE RED BEANIE. BUT WHAT IF IT'S NOT IN STOCK? SHOULD I TAKE THE BLUE ONE, OR WAIT FOR THEM TO REORDER? A BLUE ONE WOULD BE OK, I GUESS, BUT I SURE HOPE THEY HAVE A RED ONE.
I'VE ALWAYS WANTED A BEANIE LIKE THIS, WITH A PROPELLER. BOY, IT'LL BE SO COOL WHEN I HAVE IT. I CAN'T WAIT. WOW! A RED BEANIE! ...OR A BLUE ONE. DO YOU THINK IT WILL COME TOMORROW? DO YOU?
IT HAD SURE BETTER.
YEAH, THAT'S HOW I FEEL, TOO.

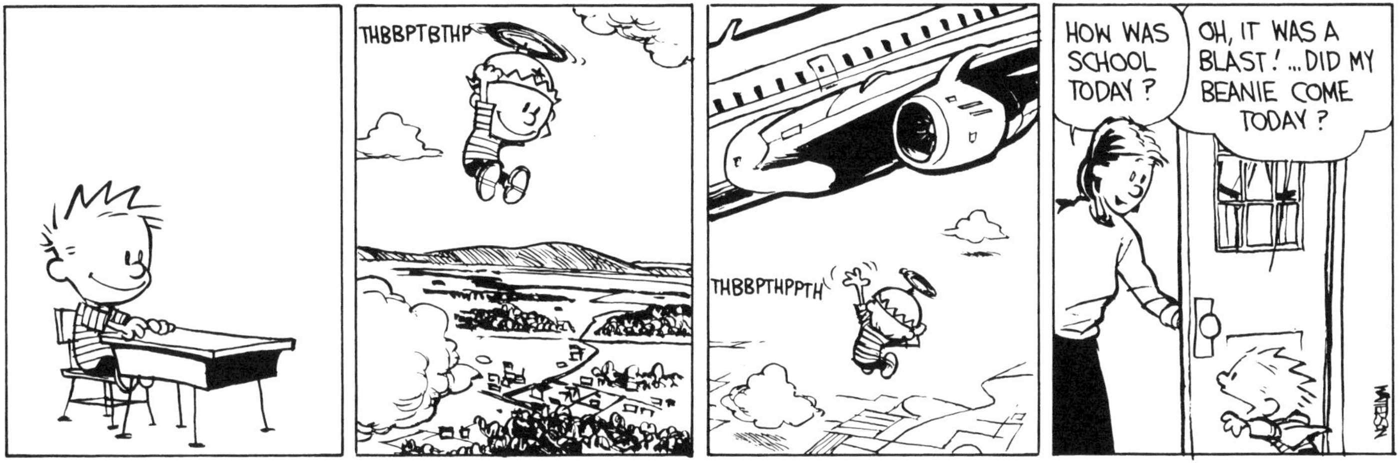
THBBPTBTHP
THBBPTHPPTH
HOW WAS SCHOOL TODAY?
OH, IT WAS A BLAST! ...DID MY BEANIE COME TODAY?

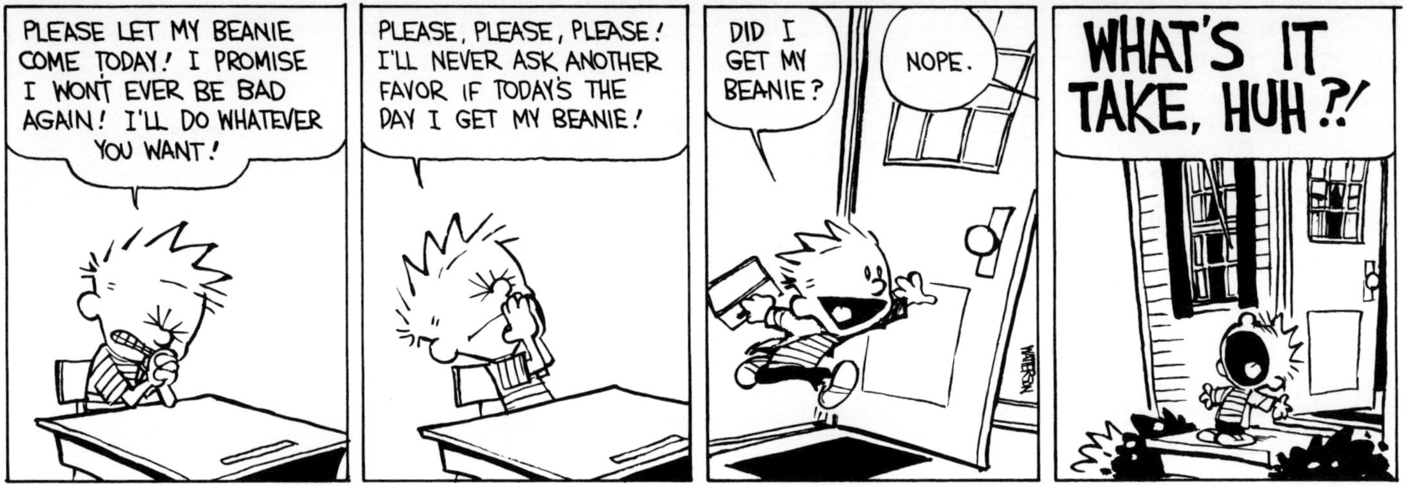
PLEASE LET MY BEANIE COME TODAY! I PROMISE I WON'T EVER BE BAD AGAIN! I'LL DO WHATEVER YOU WANT!
PLEASE, PLEASE, PLEASE! I'LL NEVER ASK ANOTHER FAVOR IF TODAY'S THE DAY I GET MY BEANIE!
DID I GET MY BEANIE?
NOPE.
WHAT'S IT TAKE, HUH?!
WATERSON

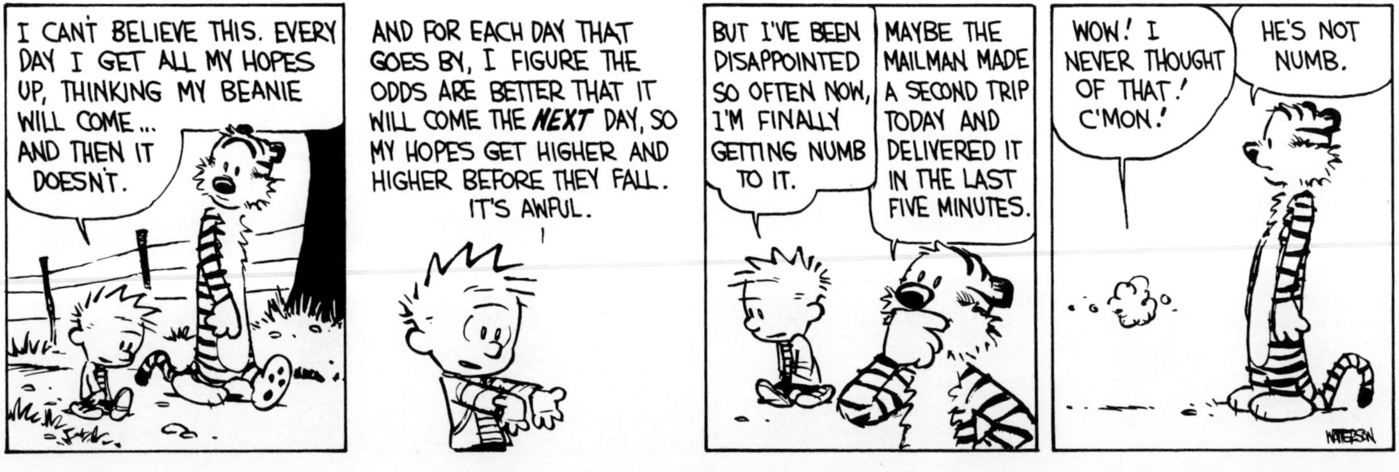
I CAN'T BELIEVE THIS. EVERY DAY I GET ALL MY HOPES UP, THINKING MY BEANIE WILL COME... AND THEN IT DOESN'T.
AND FOR EACH DAY THAT GOES BY, I FIGURE THE ODDS ARE BETTER THAT IT WILL COME THE NEXT DAY, SO MY HOPES GET HIGHER AND HIGHER BEFORE THEY FALL. IT'S AWFUL.
BUT I'VE BEEN DISAPPOINTED SO OFTEN NOW, I'M FINALLY GETTING NUMB TO IT.
MAYBE THE MAILMAN MADE A SECOND TRIP TODAY AND DELIVERED IT IN THE LAST FIVE MINUTES.
WOW! I NEVER THOUGHT OF THAT! C'MON!
HE'S NOT NUMB.
WATERSON

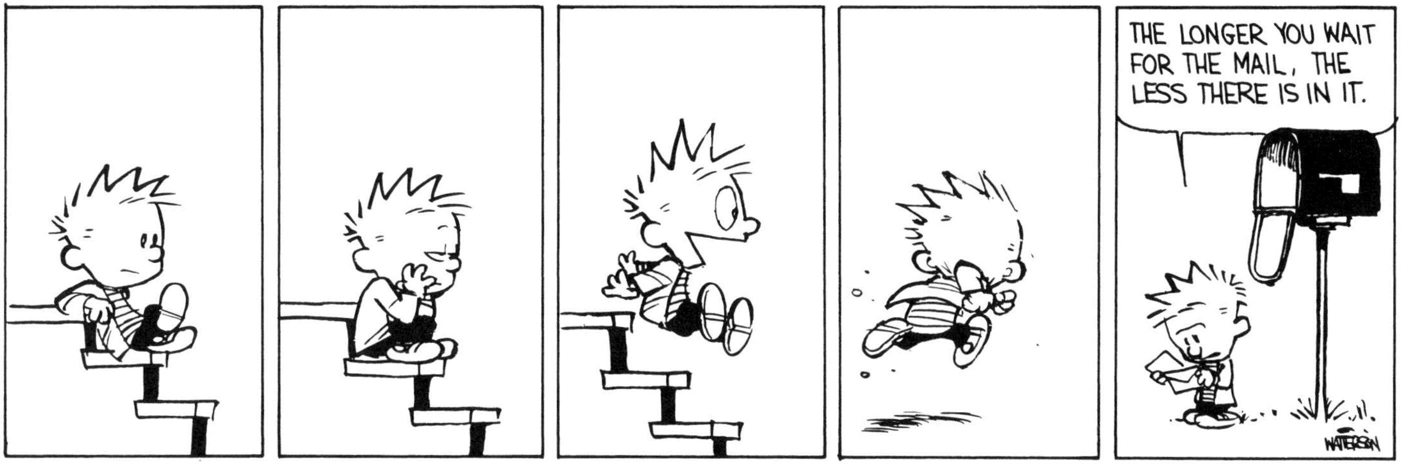
THE LONGER YOU WAIT FOR THE MAIL, THE LESS THERE IS IN IT.

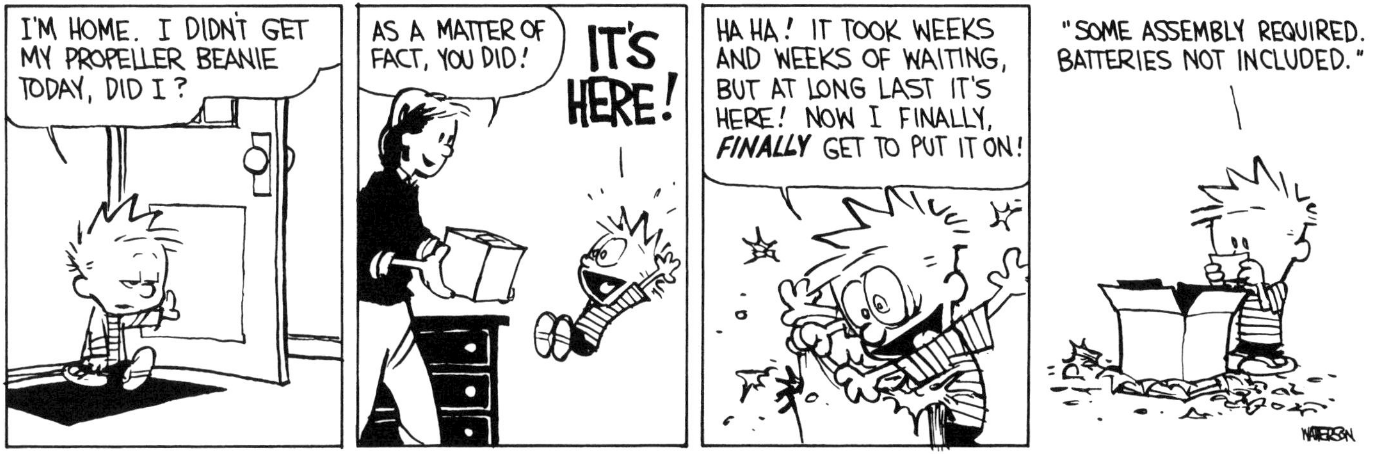
I'M HOME. I DIDN'T GET MY PROPELLER BEANIE TODAY, DID I?
AS A MATTER OF FACT, YOU DID!
IT'S HERE!
HA HA! IT TOOK WEEKS AND WEEKS OF WAITING, BUT AT LONG LAST IT'S HERE! NOW I FINALLY, *FINALLY* GET TO PUT IT ON!
"SOME ASSEMBLY REQUIRED. BATTERIES NOT INCLUDED."

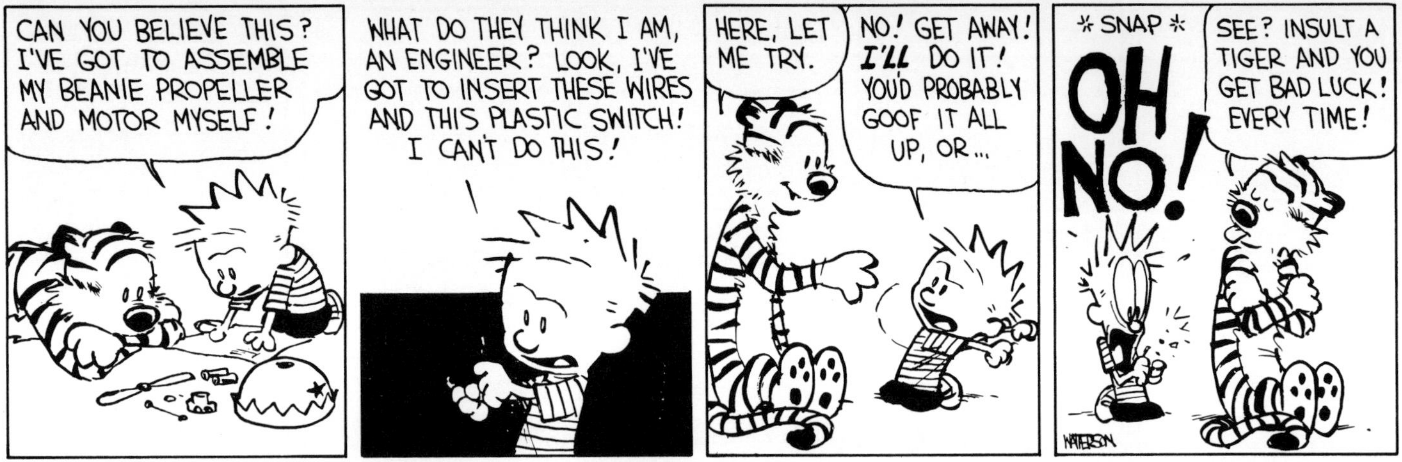
CAN YOU BELIEVE THIS? I'VE GOT TO ASSEMBLE MY BEANIE PROPELLER AND MOTOR MYSELF!
WHAT DO THEY THINK I AM, AN ENGINEER? LOOK, I'VE GOT TO INSERT THESE WIRES AND THIS PLASTIC SWITCH! I CAN'T DO THIS!
HERE, LET ME TRY.
NO! GET AWAY! I'LL DO IT! YOU'D PROBABLY GOOF IT ALL UP, OR...
SNAP
OH NO!
SEE? INSULT A TIGER AND YOU GET BAD LUCK! EVERY TIME!
WATTERSON

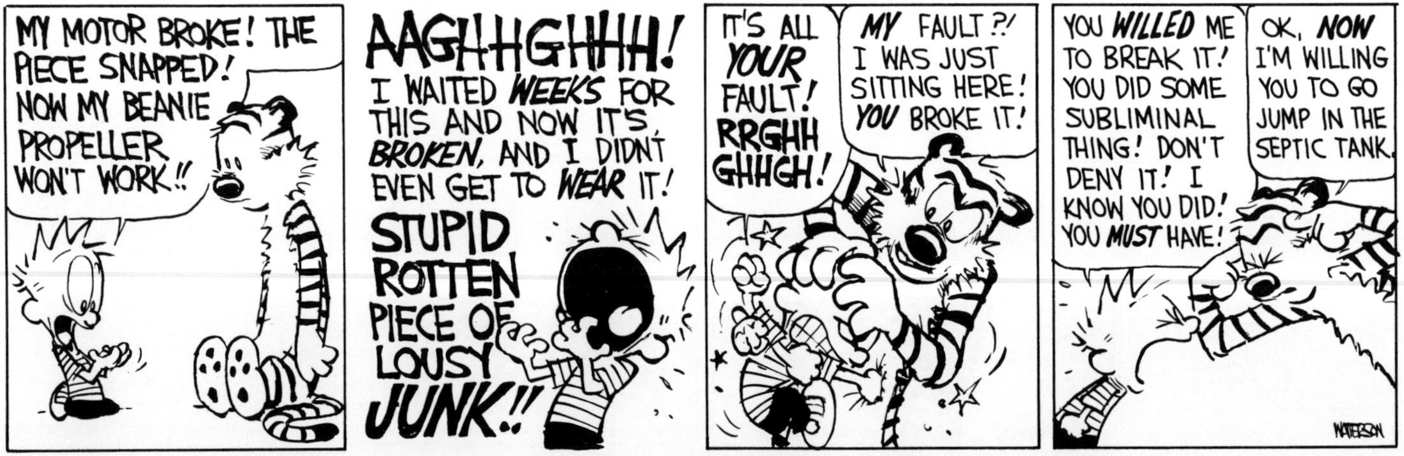
MY MOTOR BROKE! THE PIECE SNAPPED! NOW MY BEANIE PROPELLER WON'T WORK!!
AAGHHGHHH! I WAITED WEEKS FOR THIS AND NOW IT'S BROKEN, AND I DIDN'T EVEN GET TO WEAR IT!
STUPID ROTTEN PIECE OF LOUSY JUNK!!
IT'S ALL YOUR FAULT! RRGHH GHHGH!
MY FAULT?! I WAS JUST SITTING HERE! YOU BROKE IT!
YOU WILLED ME TO BREAK IT! YOU DID SOME SUBLIMINAL THING! DON'T DENY IT! I KNOW YOU DID! YOU MUST HAVE!
OK, NOW I'M WILLING YOU TO GO JUMP IN THE SEPTIC TANK.
WATTERSON

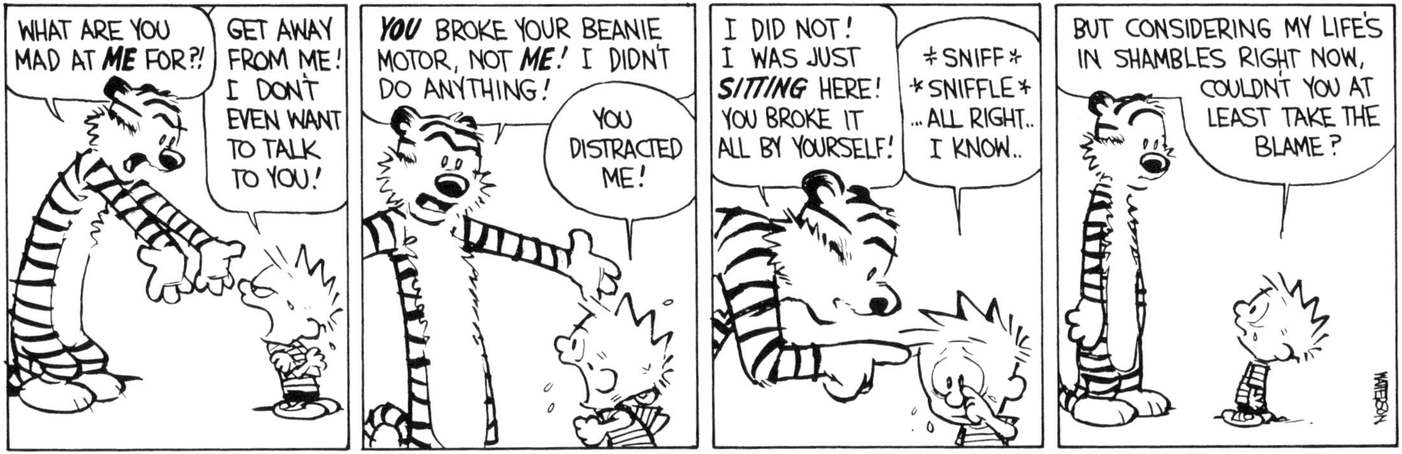
WHAT ARE YOU MAD AT ME FOR?!
GET AWAY FROM ME! I DON'T EVEN WANT TO TALK TO YOU!
YOU BROKE YOUR BEANIE MOTOR, NOT ME! I DIDN'T DO ANYTHING!
YOU DISTRACTED ME!
I DID NOT! I WAS JUST SITTING HERE! YOU BROKE IT ALL BY YOURSELF!
SNIFF *SNIFFLE* ...ALL RIGHT.. I KNOW..
BUT CONSIDERING MY LIFE'S IN SHAMBLES RIGHT NOW, COULDN'T YOU AT LEAST TAKE THE BLAME?
WATTERSON

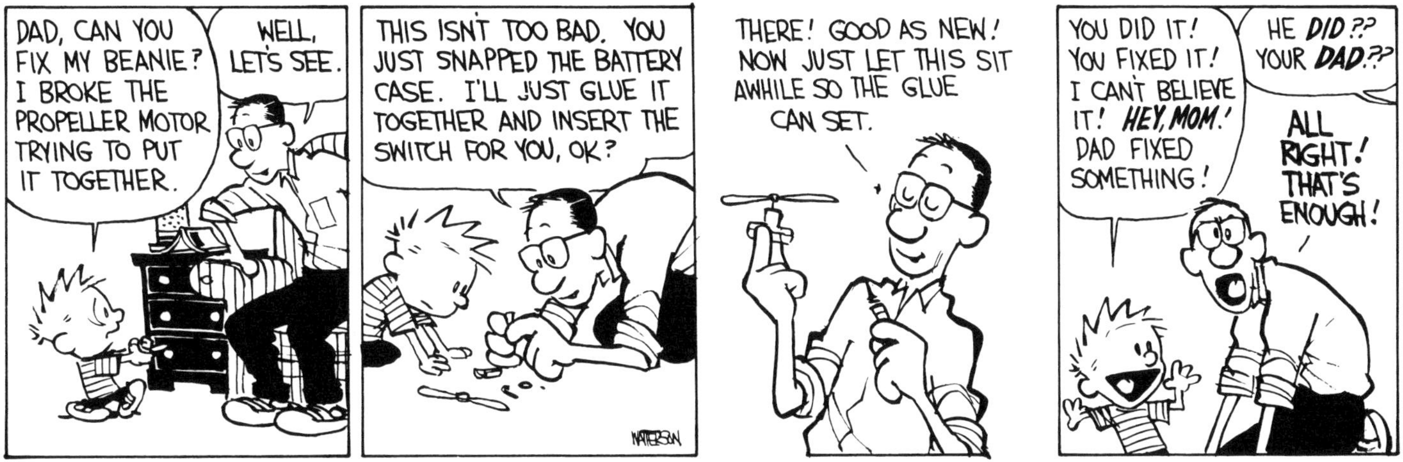
DAD, CAN YOU FIX MY BEANIE? I BROKE THE PROPELLER MOTOR TRYING TO PUT IT TOGETHER.
WELL, LET'S SEE.
THIS ISN'T TOO BAD. YOU JUST SNAPPED THE BATTERY CASE. I'LL JUST GLUE IT TOGETHER AND INSERT THE SWITCH FOR YOU, OK?
WATTERSON
THERE! GOOD AS NEW! NOW JUST LET THIS SIT AWHILE SO THE GLUE CAN SET.
YOU DID IT! YOU FIXED IT! I CAN'T BELIEVE IT! HEY, MOM! DAD FIXED SOMETHING!
HE DID?? YOUR DAD??
ALL RIGHT! THAT'S ENOUGH!

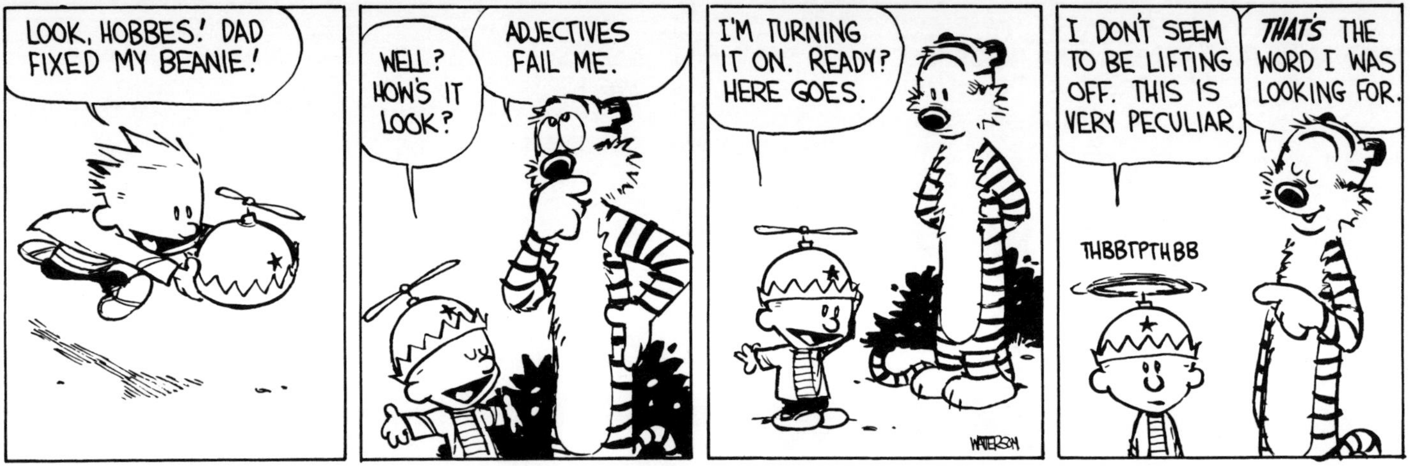
LOOK, HOBBES! DAD FIXED MY BEANIE!
WELL? HOW'S IT LOOK?
ADJECTIVES FAIL ME.
I'M TURNING IT ON. READY? HERE GOES.
THBBTPTHBB
I DON'T SEEM TO BE LIFTING OFF. THIS IS VERY PECULIAR.
THAT'S THE WORD I WAS LOOKING FOR.
WATTERSON

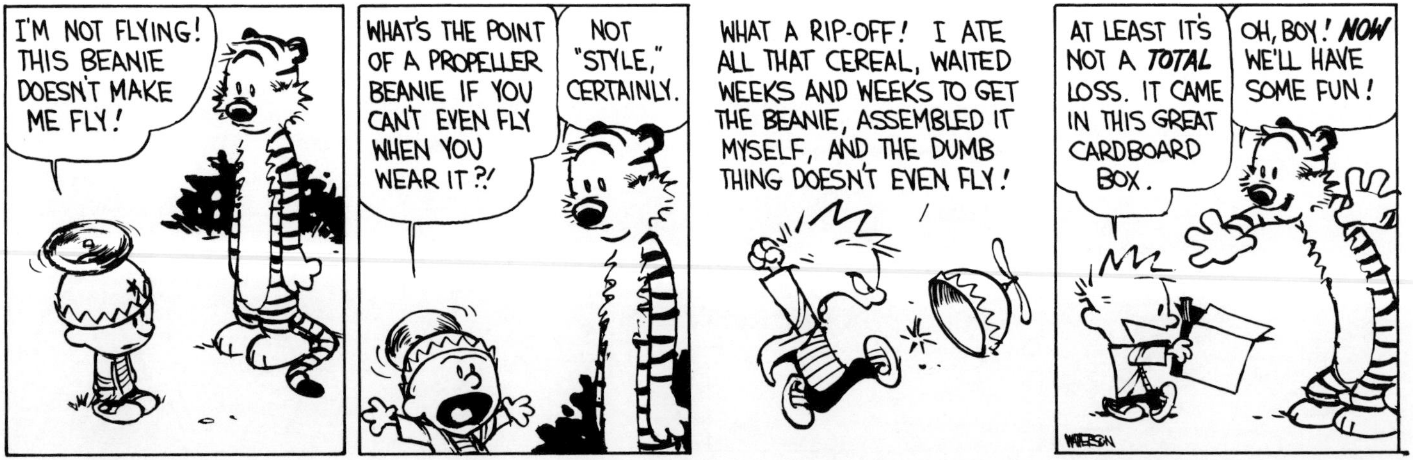
I'M NOT FLYING! THIS BEANIE DOESN'T MAKE ME FLY!
WHAT'S THE POINT OF A PROPELLER BEANIE IF YOU CAN'T EVEN FLY WHEN YOU WEAR IT?!
NOT "STYLE," CERTAINLY.
WHAT A RIP-OFF! I ATE ALL THAT CEREAL, WAITED WEEKS AND WEEKS TO GET THE BEANIE, ASSEMBLED IT MYSELF, AND THE DUMB THING DOESN'T EVEN FLY!
AT LEAST IT'S NOT A TOTAL LOSS. IT CAME IN THIS GREAT CARDBOARD BOX.
OH, BOY! NOW WE'LL HAVE SOME FUN!
WATTERSON

Andrews McMeel Publishing
a division of Andrews McMeel Universal
1130 Walnut Street, Kansas City, Missouri 64106

www.andrewsmcmeel.com

24 25 26 27 28 SDB 10 9 8 7 6 5 4 3 2 1

ISBN: 978-1-5248-8807-7

Library of Congress Control Number: 2024936289

ATTENTION: SCHOOLS AND BUSINESSES
Andrews McMeel books are available at quantity discounts with bulk purchase for educational, business, or sales promotional use.
For information, please e-mail the Andrews McMeel Publishing Special Sales Department: sales@amuniversal.com.

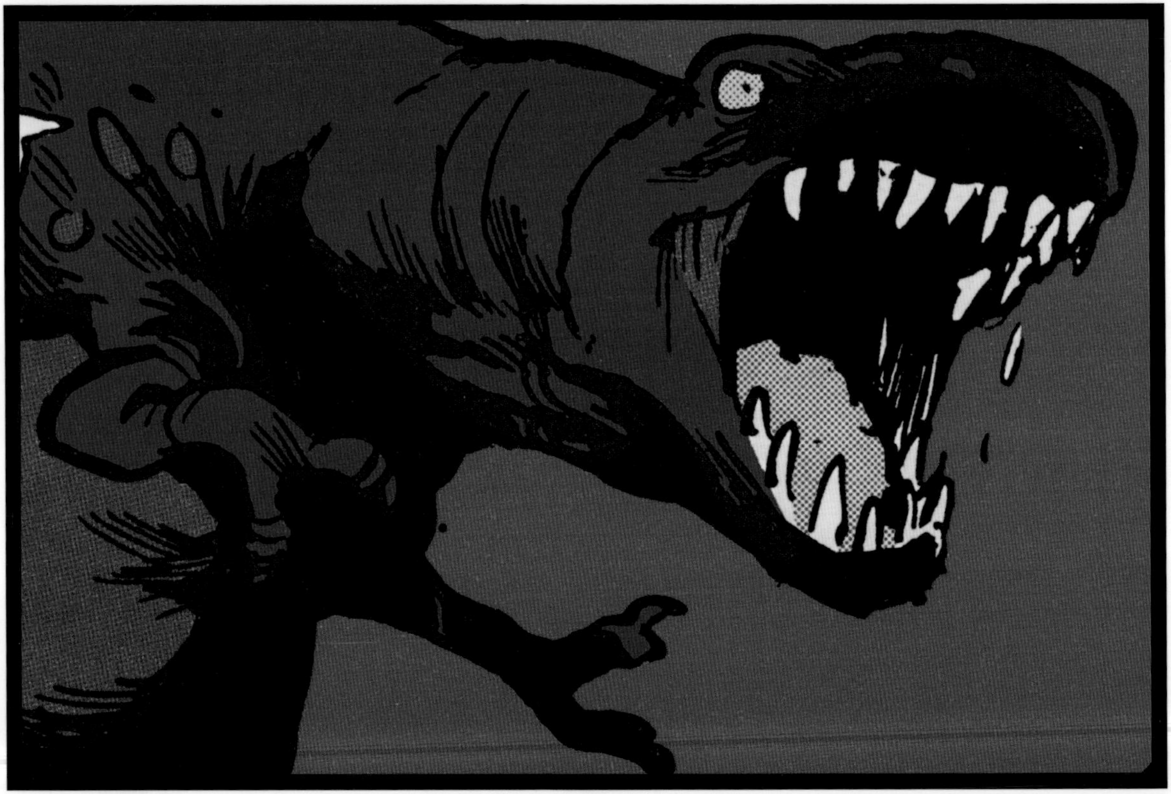

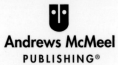

Andrews McMeel
PUBLISHING®
www.andrewsmcmeel.com

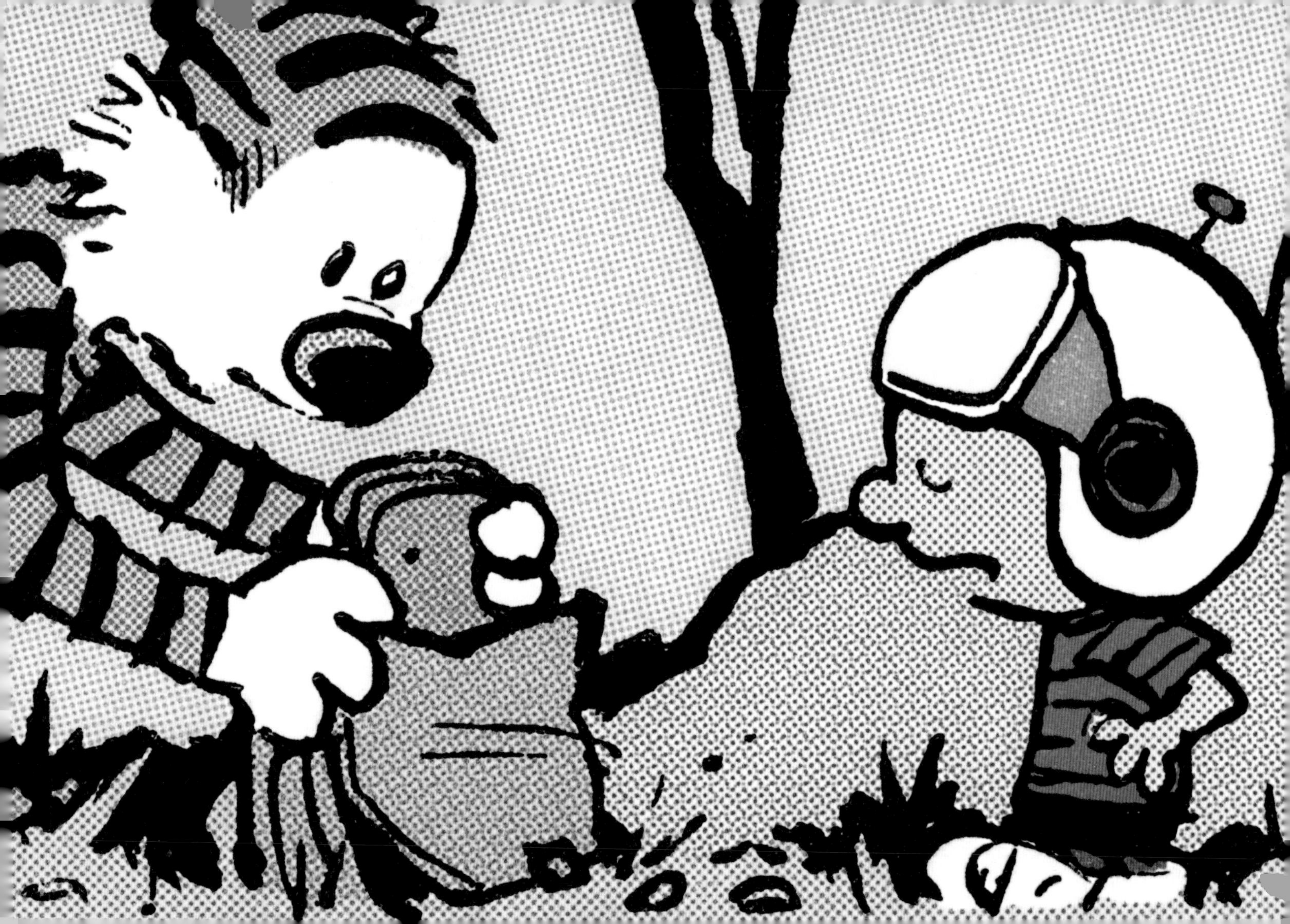

THE
Calvin and Hobbes
PORTABLE COMPENDIUM

BOOK 6

BILL WATTERSON

Andrews McMeel
PUBLISHING®

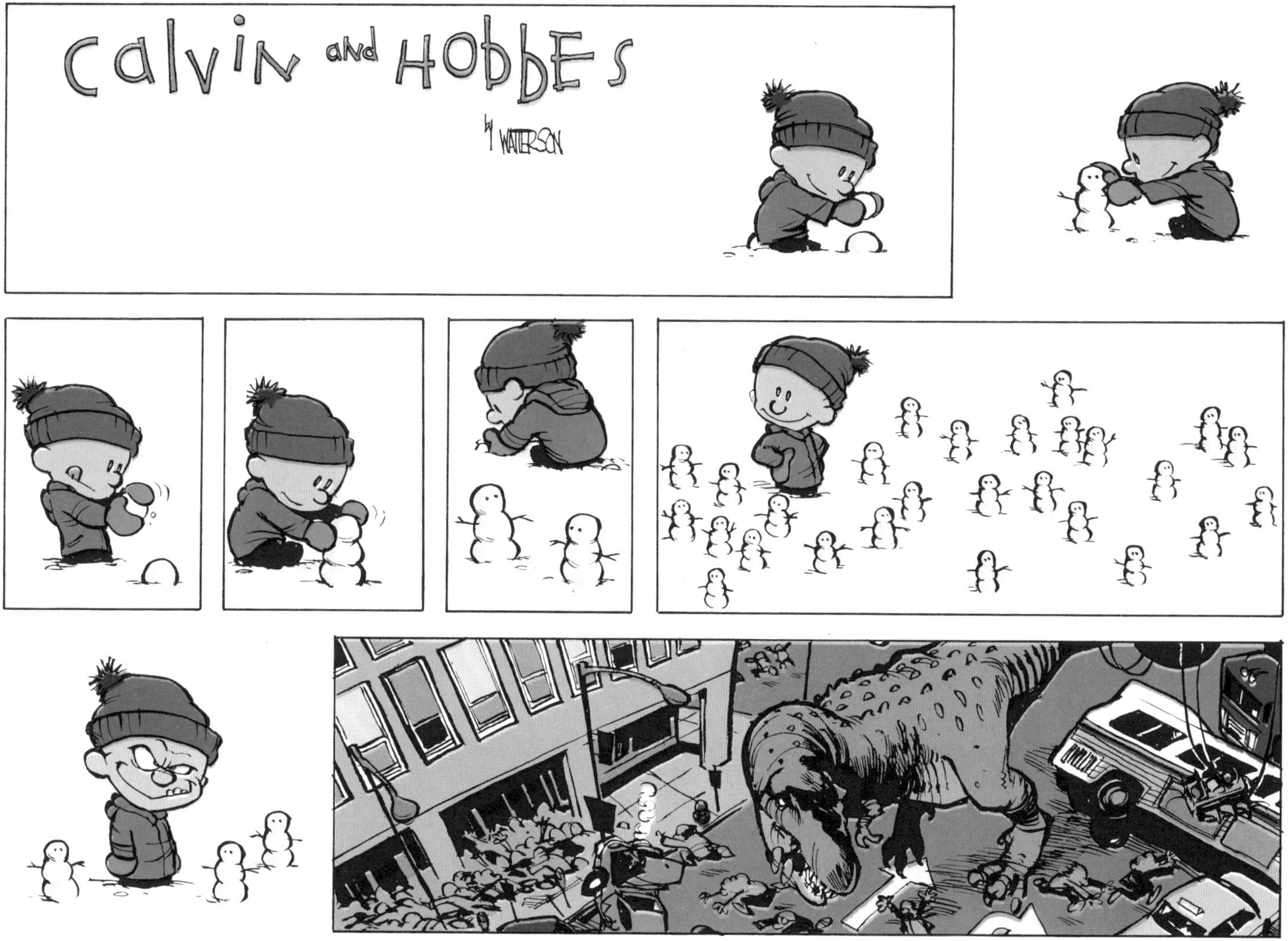
Calvin and HOBBES
by WATTERSON

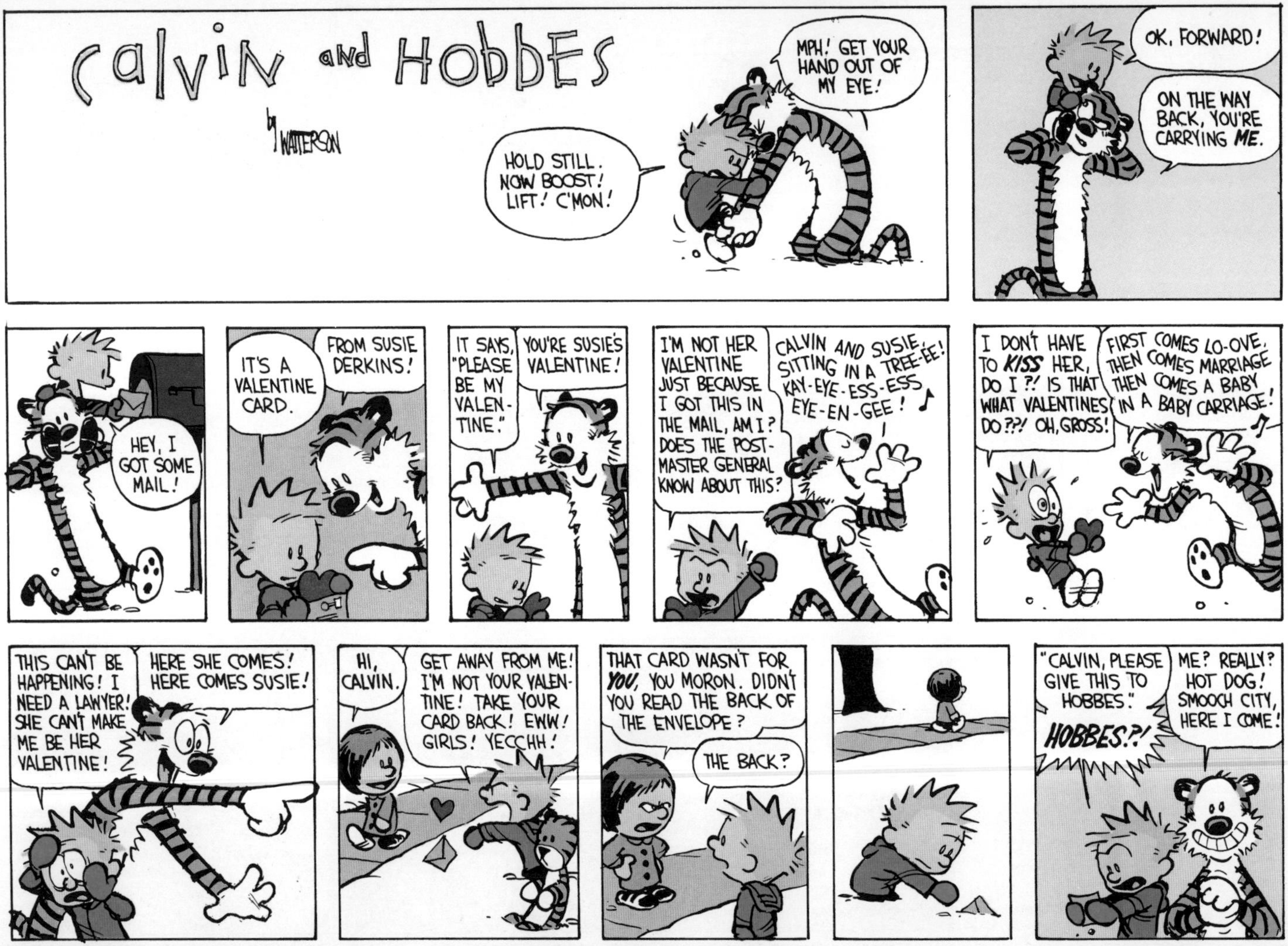
Calvin and HobbES
by WATTERSON
HOLD STILL. NOW BOOST! LIFT! C'MON!
MPH! GET YOUR HAND OUT OF MY EYE!
OK, FORWARD!
ON THE WAY BACK, YOU'RE CARRYING ME.
HEY, I GOT SOME MAIL!
IT'S A VALENTINE CARD.
FROM SUSIE DERKINS!
IT SAYS, "PLEASE BE MY VALENTINE."
YOU'RE SUSIE'S VALENTINE!
I'M NOT HER VALENTINE JUST BECAUSE I GOT THIS IN THE MAIL, AM I? DOES THE POSTMASTER GENERAL KNOW ABOUT THIS?
CALVIN AND SUSIE, SITTING IN A TREE-EE! KAY-EYE-ESS-ESS EYE-EN-GEE!
I DON'T HAVE TO KISS HER, DO I ?! IS THAT WHAT VALENTINES DO ?!?! OH, GROSS!
FIRST COMES LO-OVE, THEN COMES MARRIAGE THEN COMES A BABY IN A BABY CARRIAGE!
THIS CAN'T BE HAPPENING! I NEED A LAWYER! SHE CAN'T MAKE ME BE HER VALENTINE!
HERE SHE COMES! HERE COMES SUSIE!
HI, CALVIN.
GET AWAY FROM ME! I'M NOT YOUR VALENTINE! TAKE YOUR CARD BACK! EWW! GIRLS! YECCHH!
THAT CARD WASN'T FOR YOU, YOU MORON. DIDN'T YOU READ THE BACK OF THE ENVELOPE?
THE BACK?
"CALVIN, PLEASE GIVE THIS TO HOBBES."
HOBBES?!
ME? REALLY? HOT DOG! SMOOCH CITY, HERE I COME!

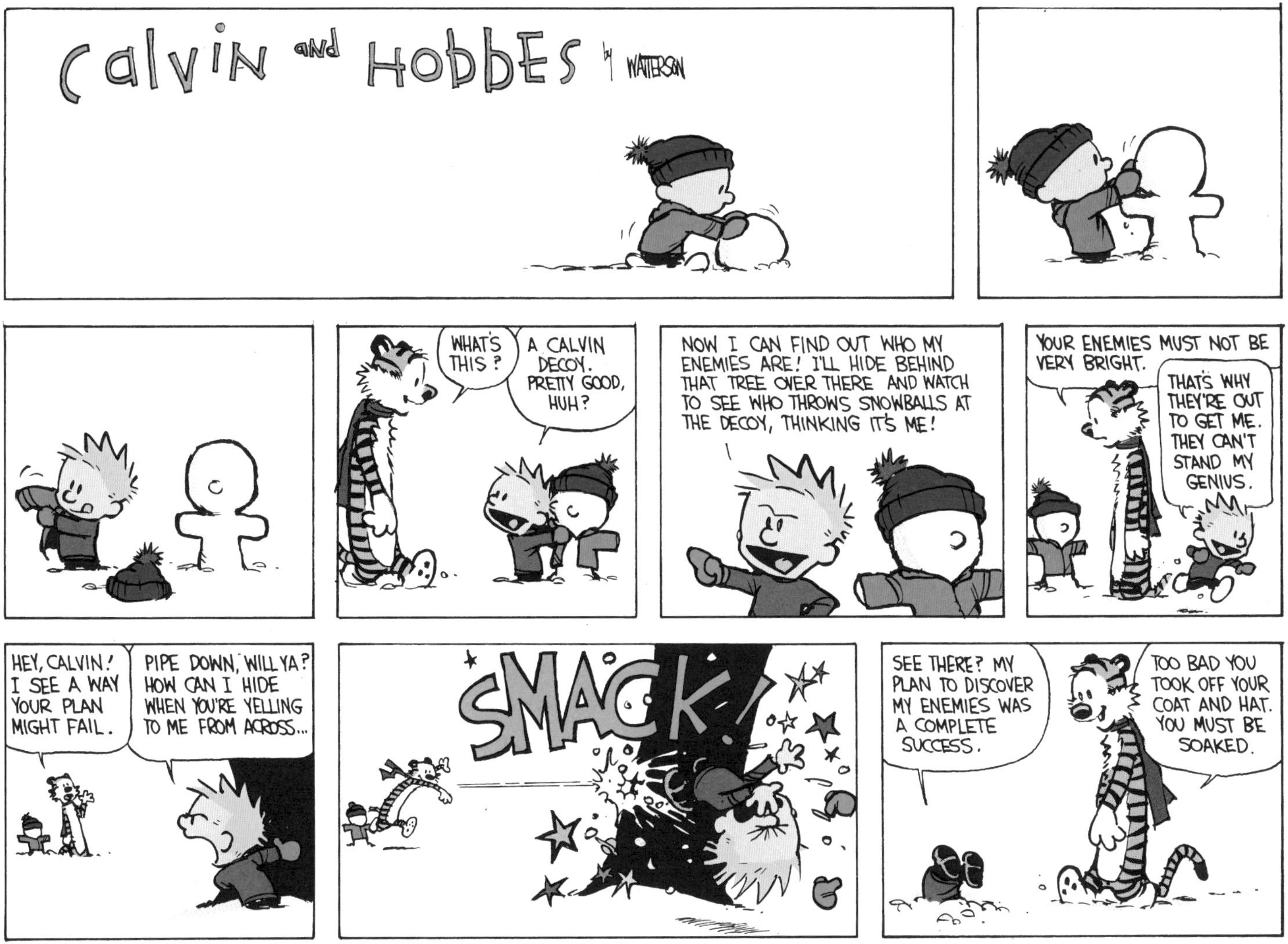
Calvin and HOBBES by WATTERSON
WHAT'S THIS?
A CALVIN DECOY. PRETTY GOOD, HUH?
NOW I CAN FIND OUT WHO MY ENEMIES ARE! I'LL HIDE BEHIND THAT TREE OVER THERE AND WATCH TO SEE WHO THROWS SNOWBALLS AT THE DECOY, THINKING IT'S ME!
YOUR ENEMIES MUST NOT BE VERY BRIGHT.
THAT'S WHY THEY'RE OUT TO GET ME. THEY CAN'T STAND MY GENIUS.
HEY, CALVIN! I SEE A WAY YOUR PLAN MIGHT FAIL.
PIPE DOWN, WILL YA? HOW CAN I HIDE WHEN YOU'RE YELLING TO ME FROM ACROSS...
SMACK!
SEE THERE? MY PLAN TO DISCOVER MY ENEMIES WAS A COMPLETE SUCCESS.
TOO BAD YOU TOOK OFF YOUR COAT AND HAT. YOU MUST BE SOAKED.

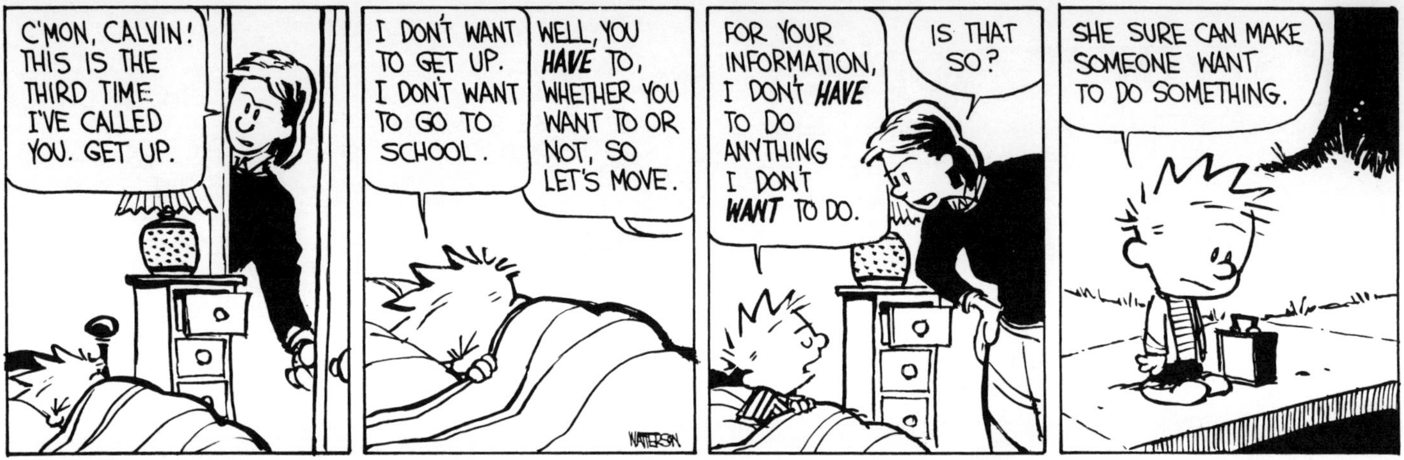
C'MON, CALVIN! THIS IS THE THIRD TIME I'VE CALLED YOU. GET UP.
I DON'T WANT TO GET UP. I DON'T WANT TO GO TO SCHOOL.
WELL, YOU **HAVE** TO, WHETHER YOU WANT TO OR NOT, SO LET'S MOVE.
WATTERSON
FOR YOUR INFORMATION, I DON'T **HAVE** TO DO ANYTHING I DON'T **WANT** TO DO.
IS THAT SO?
SHE SURE CAN MAKE SOMEONE WANT TO DO SOMETHING.

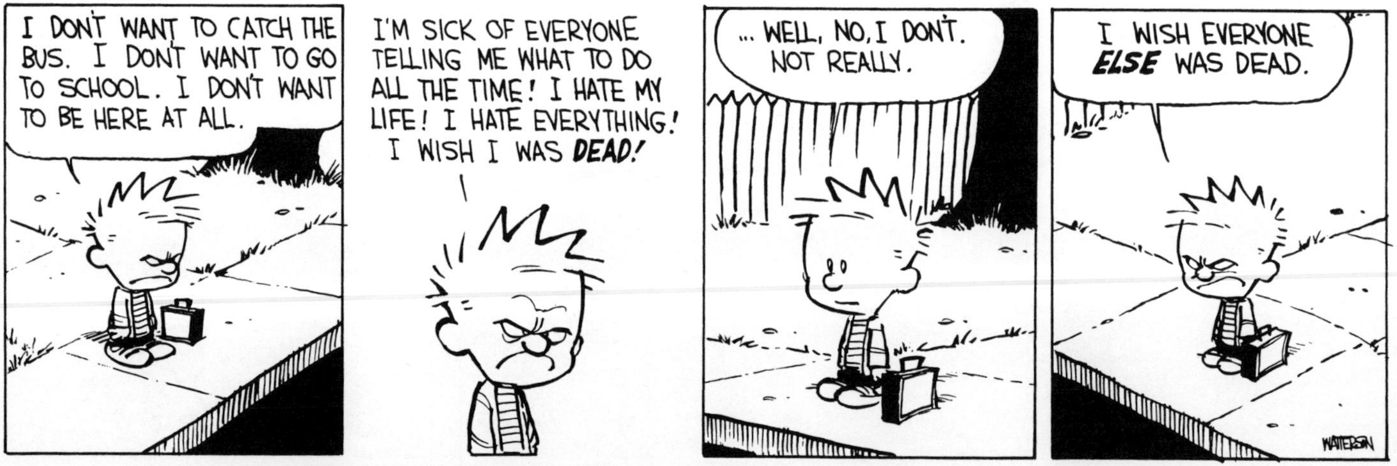
I DON'T WANT TO CATCH THE BUS. I DON'T WANT TO GO TO SCHOOL. I DON'T WANT TO BE HERE AT ALL.
I'M SICK OF EVERYONE TELLING ME WHAT TO DO ALL THE TIME! I HATE MY LIFE! I HATE EVERYTHING! I WISH I WAS **DEAD!**
... WELL, NO, I DON'T. NOT REALLY.
I WISH EVERYONE **ELSE** WAS DEAD.
WATTERSON

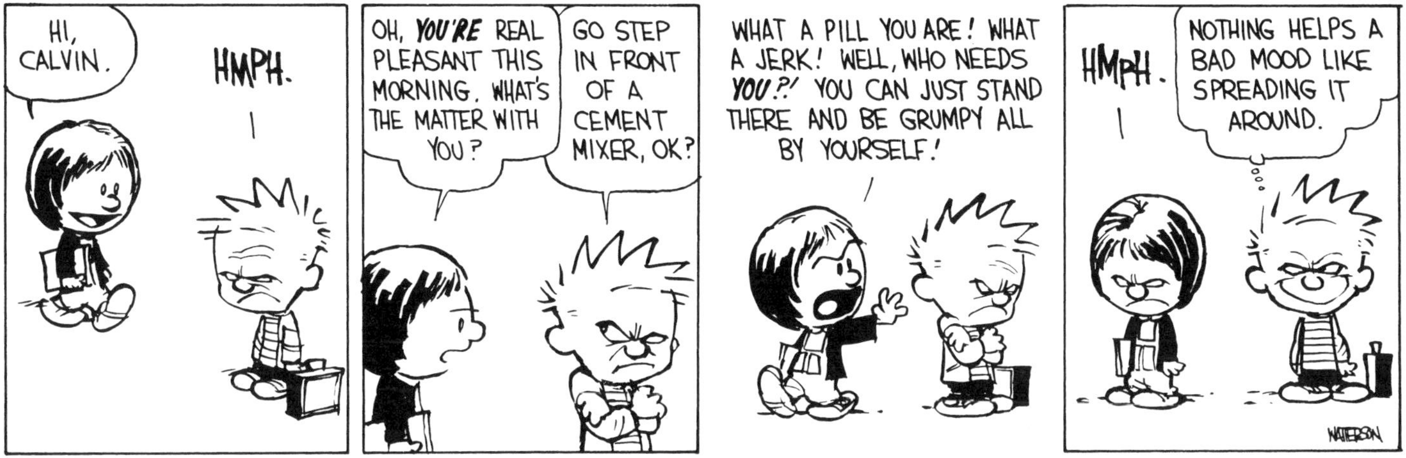
HI, CALVIN.
HMPH.
OH, ***YOU'RE*** REAL PLEASANT THIS MORNING. WHAT'S THE MATTER WITH YOU?
GO STEP IN FRONT OF A CEMENT MIXER, OK?
WHAT A PILL YOU ARE! WHAT A JERK! WELL, WHO NEEDS ***YOU?!*** YOU CAN JUST STAND THERE AND BE GRUMPY ALL BY YOURSELF!
HMPH.
NOTHING HELPS A BAD MOOD LIKE SPREADING IT AROUND.
WATTERSON

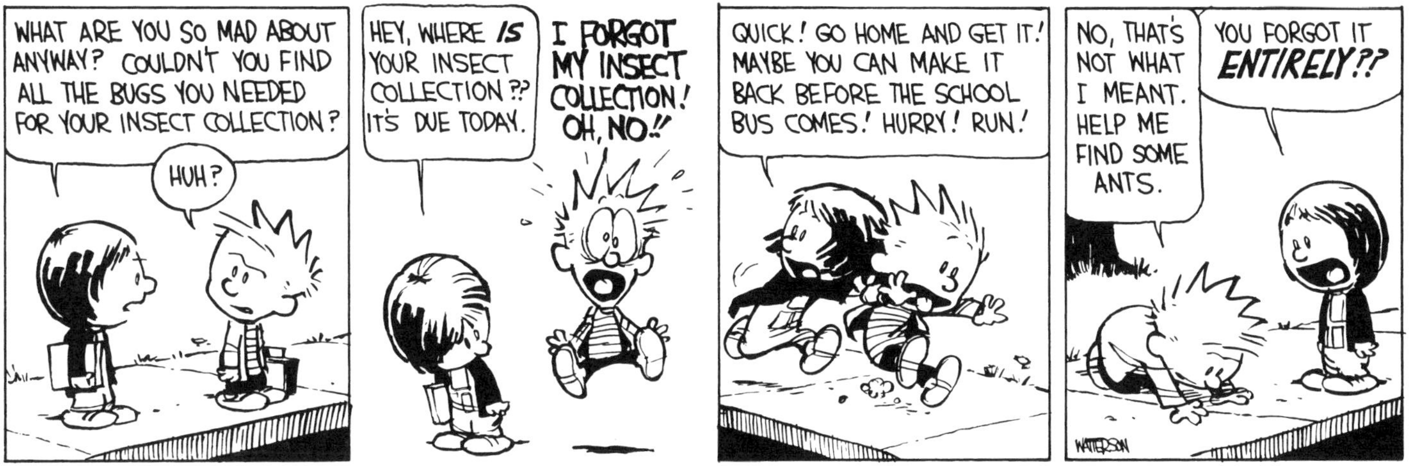
WHAT ARE YOU SO MAD ABOUT ANYWAY? COULDN'T YOU FIND ALL THE BUGS YOU NEEDED FOR YOUR INSECT COLLECTION?
HUH?
HEY, WHERE ***IS*** YOUR INSECT COLLECTION?? IT'S DUE TODAY.
I FORGOT MY INSECT COLLECTION! OH, NO!!
QUICK! GO HOME AND GET IT! MAYBE YOU CAN MAKE IT BACK BEFORE THE SCHOOL BUS COMES! HURRY! RUN!
NO, THAT'S NOT WHAT I MEANT. HELP ME FIND SOME ANTS.
YOU FORGOT IT ***ENTIRELY??***
WATTERSON

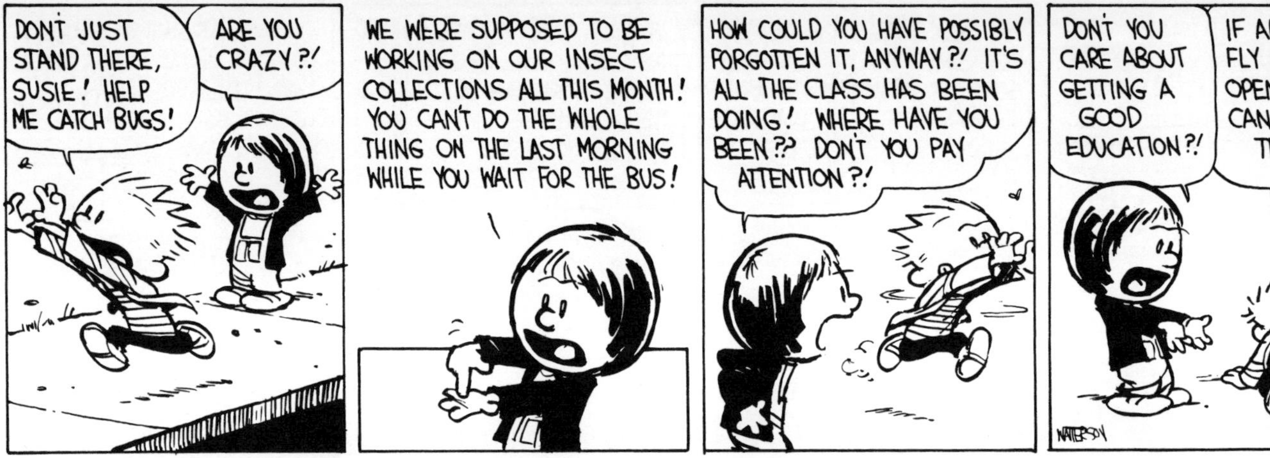
DON'T JUST STAND THERE, SUSIE! HELP ME CATCH BUGS!
ARE YOU CRAZY?!
WE WERE SUPPOSED TO BE WORKING ON OUR INSECT COLLECTIONS ALL THIS MONTH! YOU CAN'T DO THE WHOLE THING ON THE LAST MORNING WHILE YOU WAIT FOR THE BUS!
HOW COULD YOU HAVE POSSIBLY FORGOTTEN IT, ANYWAY?! IT'S ALL THE CLASS HAS BEEN DOING! WHERE HAVE YOU BEEN?? DON'T YOU PAY ATTENTION?!
DON'T YOU CARE ABOUT GETTING A GOOD EDUCATION?!
IF ANY BUGS FLY IN YOUR OPEN MOUTH, CAN I HAVE THEM?
WATTERSON

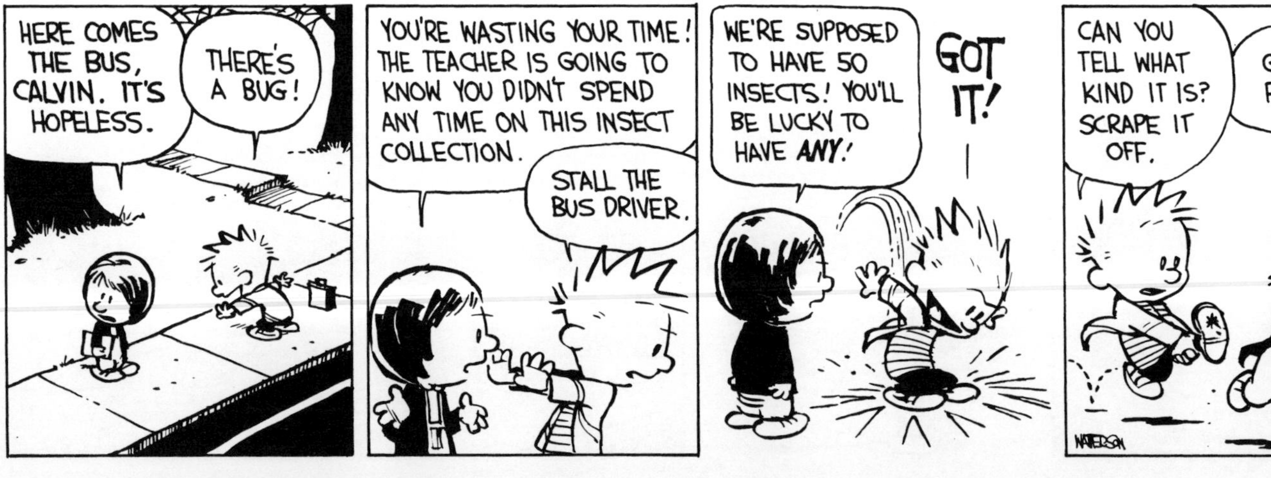
HERE COMES THE BUS, CALVIN. IT'S HOPELESS.
THERE'S A BUG!
YOU'RE WASTING YOUR TIME! THE TEACHER IS GOING TO KNOW YOU DIDN'T SPEND ANY TIME ON THIS INSECT COLLECTION.
STALL THE BUS DRIVER.
WE'RE SUPPOSED TO HAVE 50 INSECTS! YOU'LL BE LUCKY TO HAVE *ANY*!
GOT IT!
CAN YOU TELL WHAT KIND IT IS? SCRAPE IT OFF.
GET AWAY FROM ME!
WATTERSON

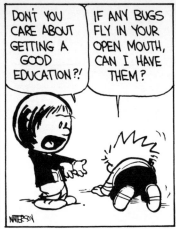

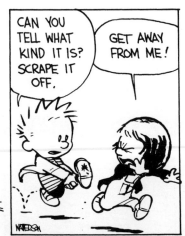

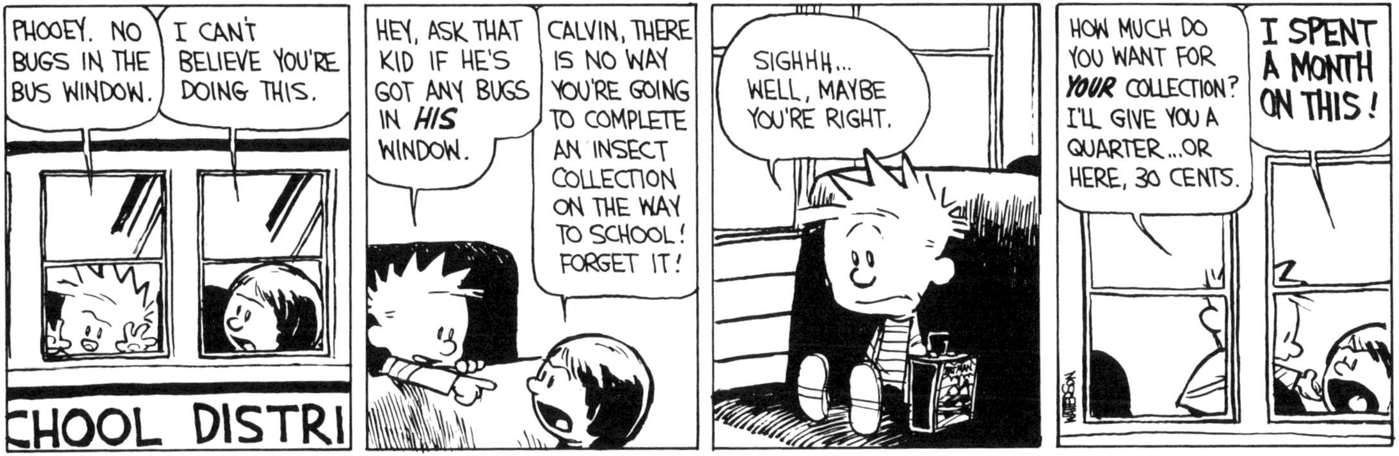
PHOOEY. NO BUGS IN THE BUS WINDOW.
I CAN'T BELIEVE YOU'RE DOING THIS.
CHOOL DISTRI
HEY, ASK THAT KID IF HE'S GOT ANY BUGS IN *HIS* WINDOW.
CALVIN, THERE IS NO WAY YOU'RE GOING TO COMPLETE AN INSECT COLLECTION ON THE WAY TO SCHOOL! FORGET IT!
SIGHHH... WELL, MAYBE YOU'RE RIGHT.
HOW MUCH DO YOU WANT FOR ***YOUR*** COLLECTION? I'LL GIVE YOU A QUARTER...OR HERE, 30 CENTS.
I SPENT A MONTH ON THIS!

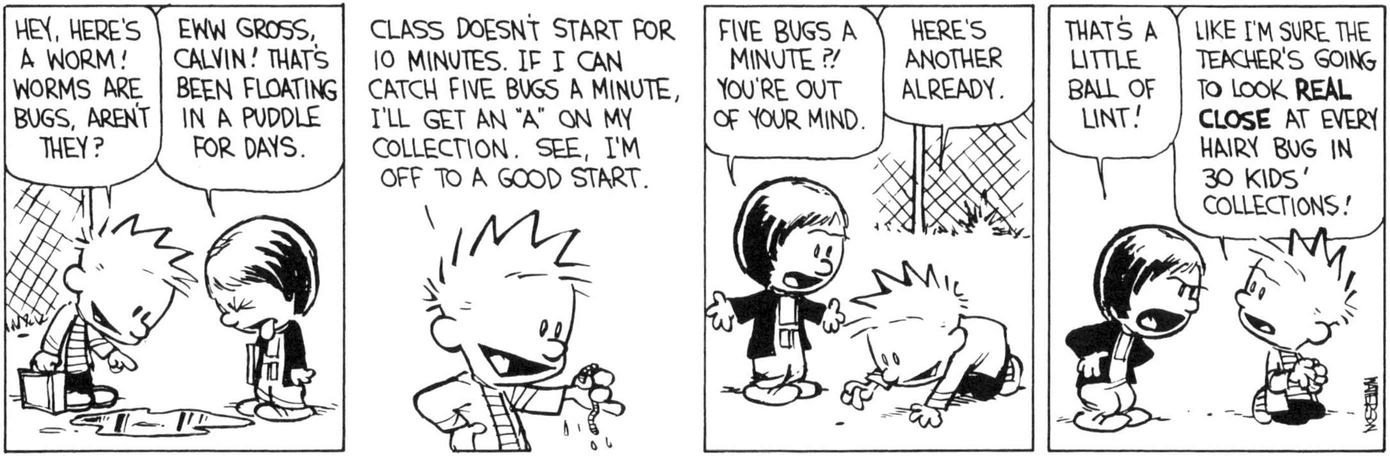
HEY, HERE'S A WORM! WORMS ARE BUGS, AREN'T THEY?
EWW GROSS, CALVIN! THAT'S BEEN FLOATING IN A PUDDLE FOR DAYS.
CLASS DOESN'T START FOR 10 MINUTES. IF I CAN CATCH FIVE BUGS A MINUTE, I'LL GET AN "A" ON MY COLLECTION. SEE, I'M OFF TO A GOOD START.
FIVE BUGS A MINUTE?! YOU'RE OUT OF YOUR MIND.
HERE'S ANOTHER ALREADY.
THAT'S A LITTLE BALL OF LINT!
LIKE I'M SURE THE TEACHER'S GOING TO LOOK **REAL CLOSE** AT EVERY HAIRY BUG IN 30 KIDS' COLLECTIONS!

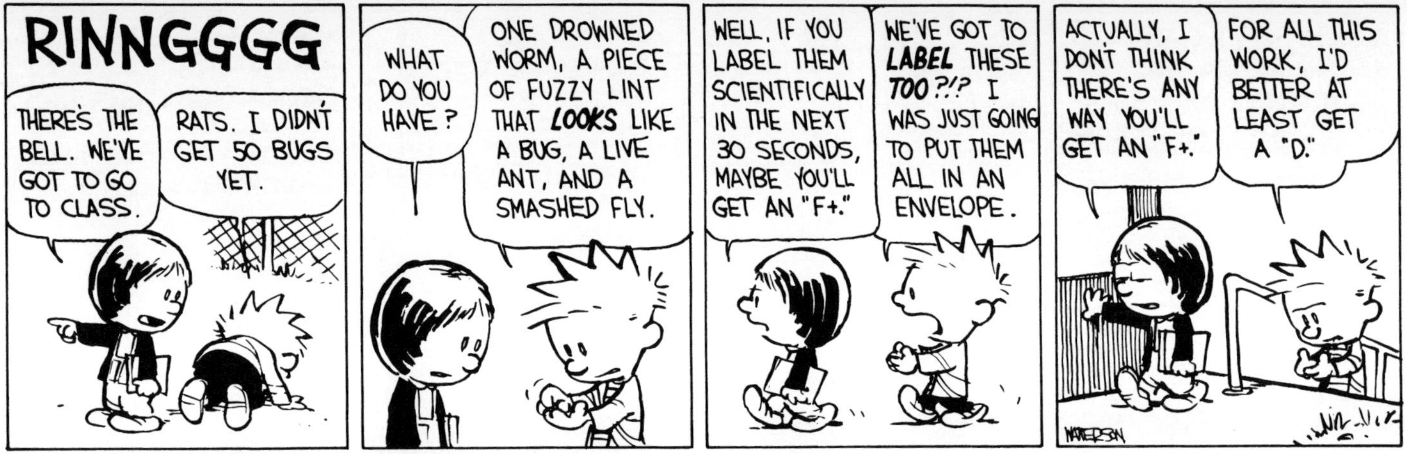
RINNGGGG
THERE'S THE BELL. WE'VE GOT TO GO TO CLASS.
RATS. I DIDN'T GET 50 BUGS YET.
WHAT DO YOU HAVE?
ONE DROWNED WORM, A PIECE OF FUZZY LINT THAT LOOKS LIKE A BUG, A LIVE ANT, AND A SMASHED FLY.
WELL, IF YOU LABEL THEM SCIENTIFICALLY IN THE NEXT 30 SECONDS, MAYBE YOU'LL GET AN "F+."
WE'VE GOT TO LABEL THESE TOO?!? I WAS JUST GOING TO PUT THEM ALL IN AN ENVELOPE.
ACTUALLY, I DON'T THINK THERE'S ANY WAY YOU'LL GET AN "F+."
FOR ALL THIS WORK, I'D BETTER AT LEAST GET A "D."
WATTERSON

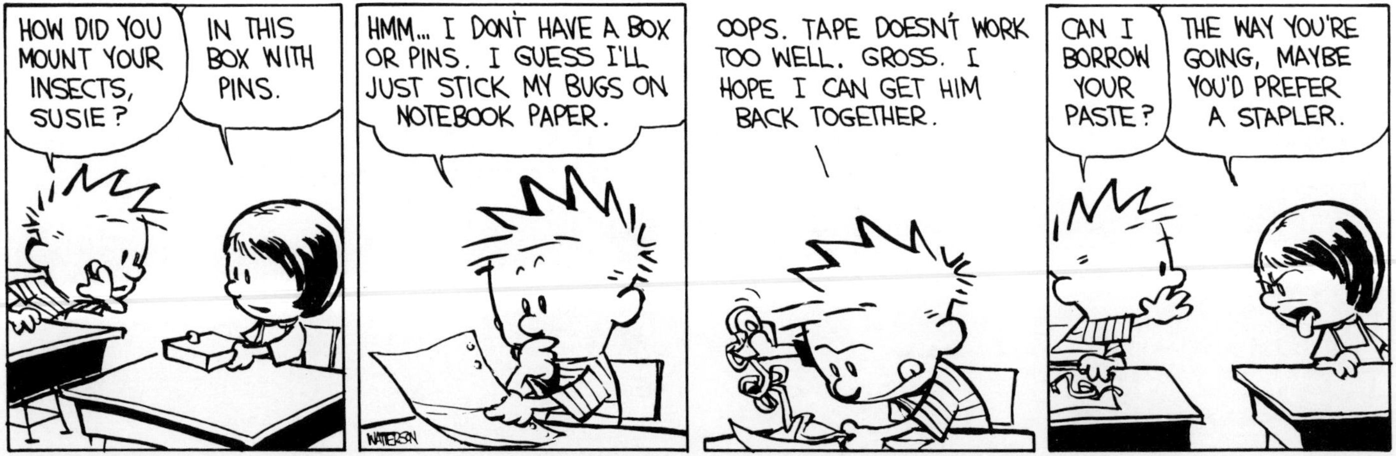
HOW DID YOU MOUNT YOUR INSECTS, SUSIE?
IN THIS BOX WITH PINS.
HMM... I DON'T HAVE A BOX OR PINS. I GUESS I'LL JUST STICK MY BUGS ON NOTEBOOK PAPER.
OOPS. TAPE DOESN'T WORK TOO WELL. GROSS. I HOPE I CAN GET HIM BACK TOGETHER.
CAN I BORROW YOUR PASTE?
THE WAY YOU'RE GOING, MAYBE YOU'D PREFER A STAPLER.
WATTERSON

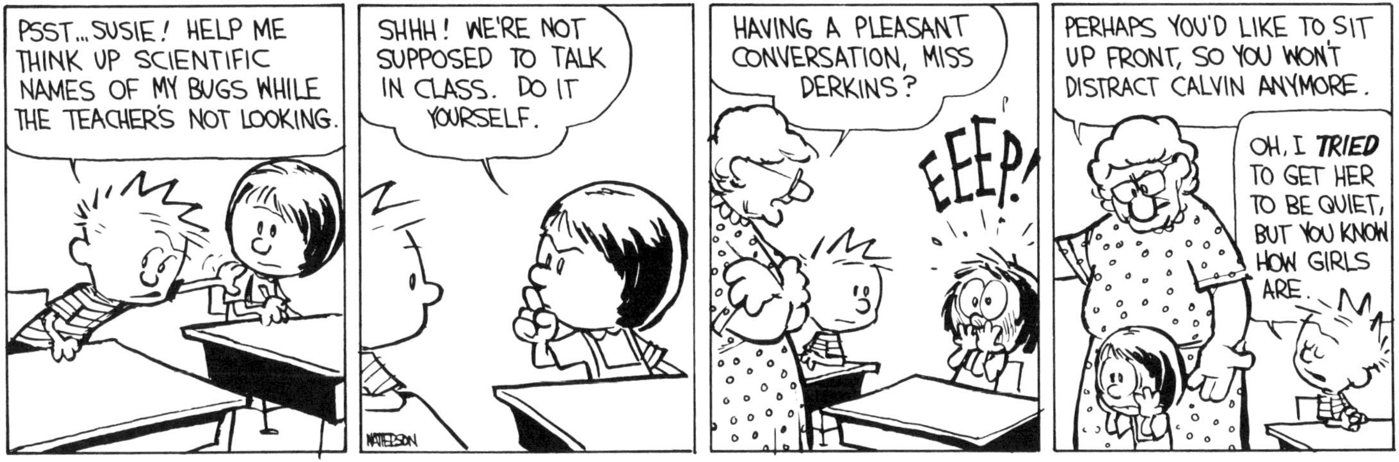
PSST... SUSIE! HELP ME THINK UP SCIENTIFIC NAMES OF MY BUGS WHILE THE TEACHER'S NOT LOOKING.
SHHH! WE'RE NOT SUPPOSED TO TALK IN CLASS. DO IT YOURSELF.
HAVING A PLEASANT CONVERSATION, MISS DERKINS?
EEEP!
PERHAPS YOU'D LIKE TO SIT UP FRONT, SO YOU WON'T DISTRACT CALVIN ANYMORE.
OH, I TRIED TO GET HER TO BE QUIET, BUT YOU KNOW HOW GIRLS ARE.

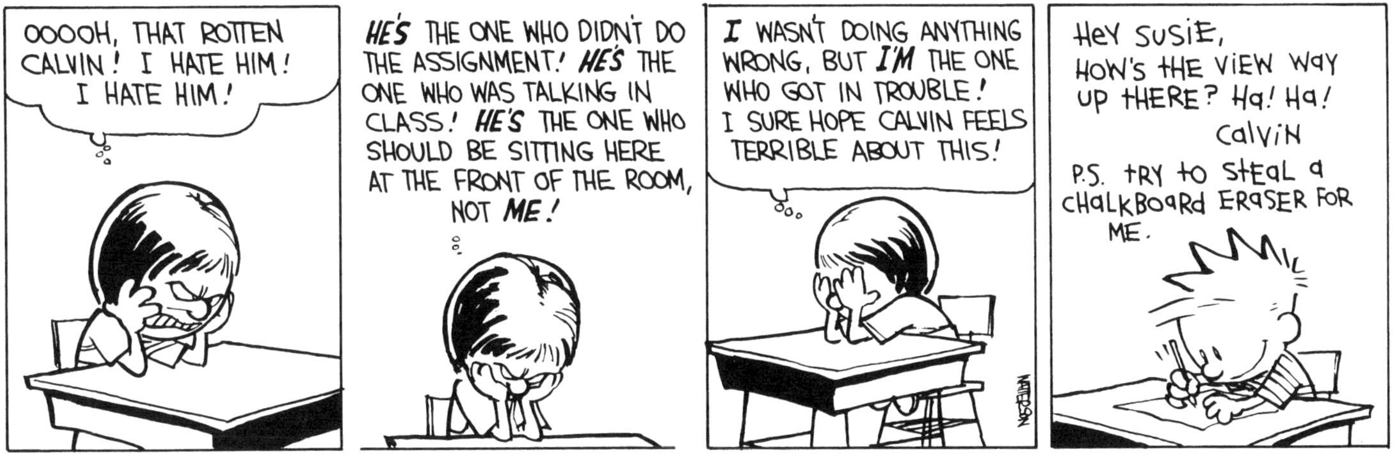
OOOOH, THAT ROTTEN CALVIN! I HATE HIM! I HATE HIM!
HE'S THE ONE WHO DIDN'T DO THE ASSIGNMENT! HE'S THE ONE WHO WAS TALKING IN CLASS! HE'S THE ONE WHO SHOULD BE SITTING HERE AT THE FRONT OF THE ROOM, NOT ME!
I WASN'T DOING ANYTHING WRONG, BUT I'M THE ONE WHO GOT IN TROUBLE! I SURE HOPE CALVIN FEELS TERRIBLE ABOUT THIS!
Hey SUSIE,
HOW'S THE VIEW WAY UP THERE? Ha! Ha!
Calvin
P.S. TRY TO STEAL a CHALKBOARD ERASER FOR ME.

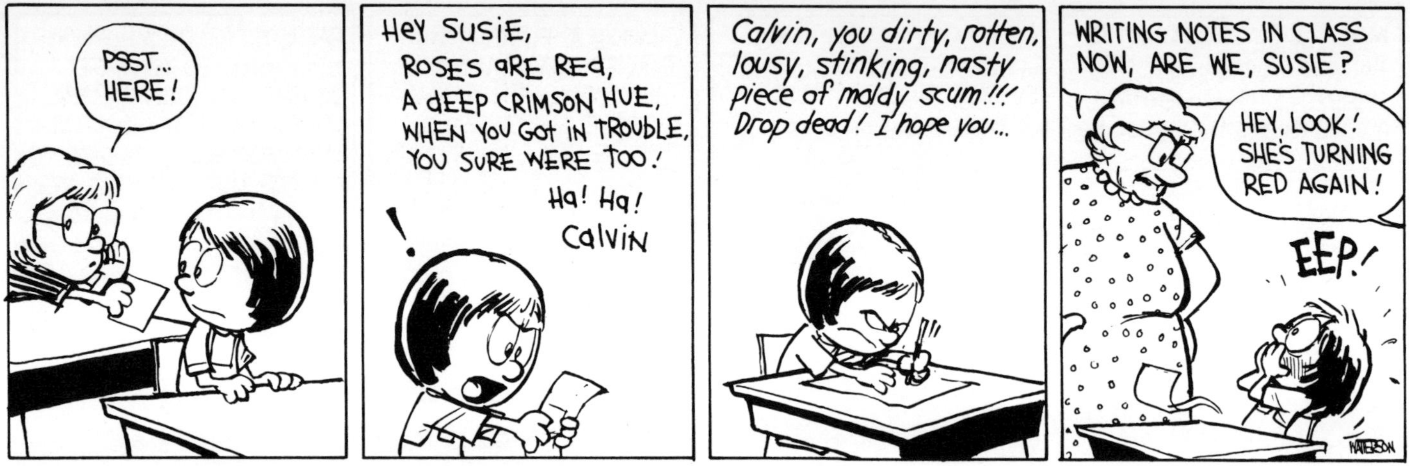
PSST... HERE!
Hey Susie,
Roses are Red,
A deep crimson hue,
When you got in trouble,
You sure were too!
Ha! Ha!
Calvin
!
Calvin, you dirty, rotten, lousy, stinking, nasty piece of moldy scum!!! Drop dead! I hope you...
WRITING NOTES IN CLASS NOW, ARE WE, SUSIE?
HEY, LOOK! SHE'S TURNING RED AGAIN!
EEP!
WATTERSON

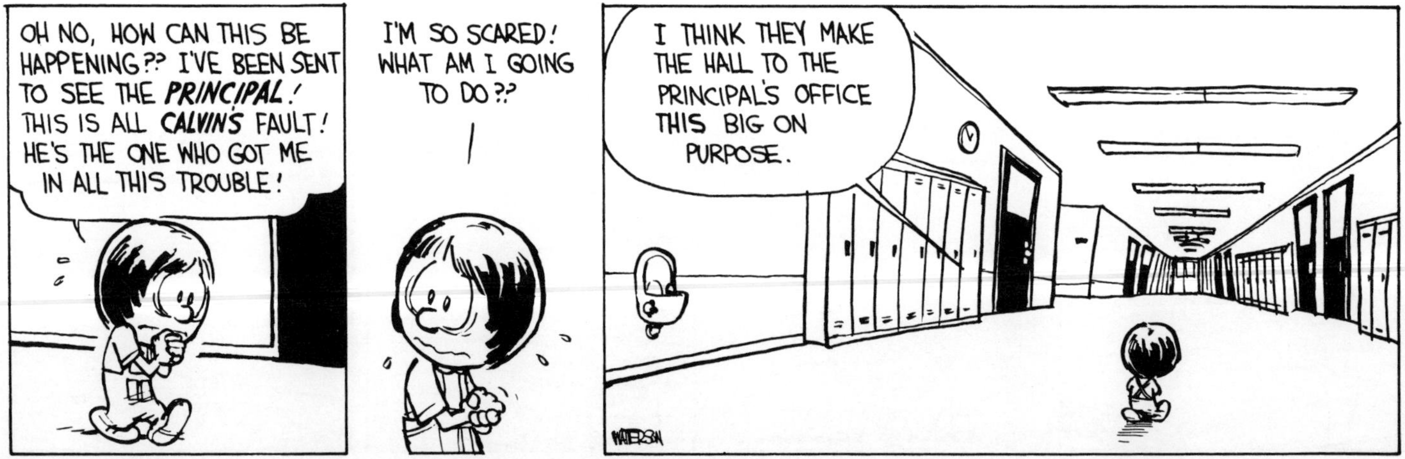
OH NO, HOW CAN THIS BE HAPPENING?? I'VE BEEN SENT TO SEE THE PRINCIPAL! THIS IS ALL CALVIN'S FAULT! HE'S THE ONE WHO GOT ME IN ALL THIS TROUBLE!
I'M SO SCARED! WHAT AM I GOING TO DO??
I THINK THEY MAKE THE HALL TO THE PRINCIPAL'S OFFICE THIS BIG ON PURPOSE.
WATTERSON

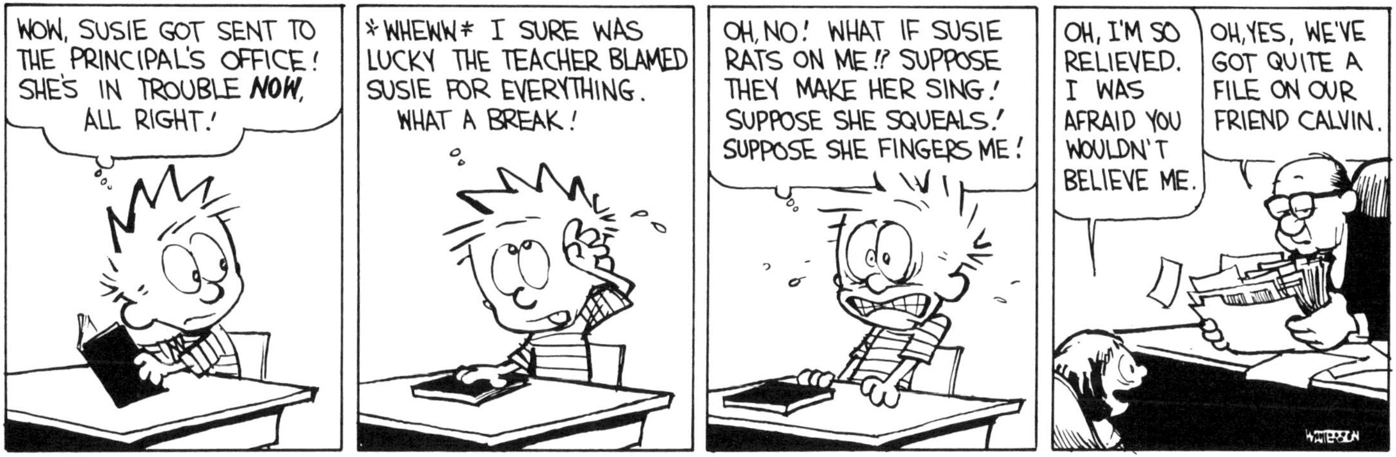
WOW, SUSIE GOT SENT TO THE PRINCIPAL'S OFFICE! SHE'S IN TROUBLE NOW, ALL RIGHT!
WHEWW I SURE WAS LUCKY THE TEACHER BLAMED SUSIE FOR EVERYTHING. WHAT A BREAK!
OH, NO! WHAT IF SUSIE RATS ON ME!? SUPPOSE THEY MAKE HER SING! SUPPOSE SHE SQUEALS! SUPPOSE SHE FINGERS ME!
OH, I'M SO RELIEVED. I WAS AFRAID YOU WOULDN'T BELIEVE ME.
OH, YES, WE'VE GOT QUITE A FILE ON OUR FRIEND CALVIN.
WATTERSON

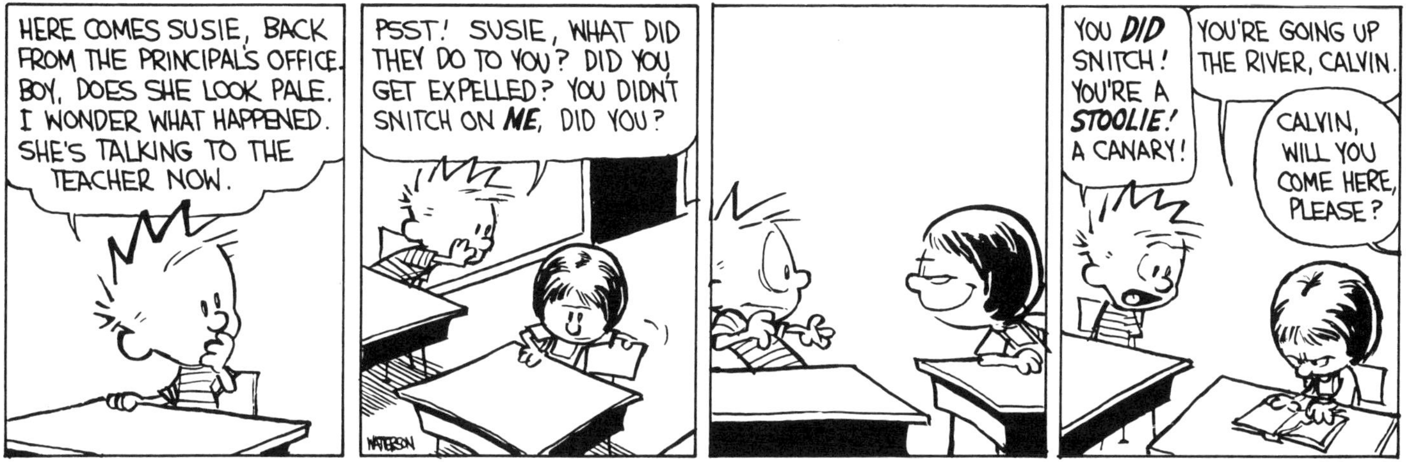
HERE COMES SUSIE, BACK FROM THE PRINCIPAL'S OFFICE. BOY, DOES SHE LOOK PALE. I WONDER WHAT HAPPENED. SHE'S TALKING TO THE TEACHER NOW.
PSST! SUSIE, WHAT DID THEY DO TO YOU? DID YOU GET EXPELLED? YOU DIDN'T SNITCH ON ME, DID YOU?
WATTERSON
YOU DID SNITCH! YOU'RE A STOOLIE! A CANARY!
YOU'RE GOING UP THE RIVER, CALVIN.
CALVIN, WILL YOU COME HERE, PLEASE?

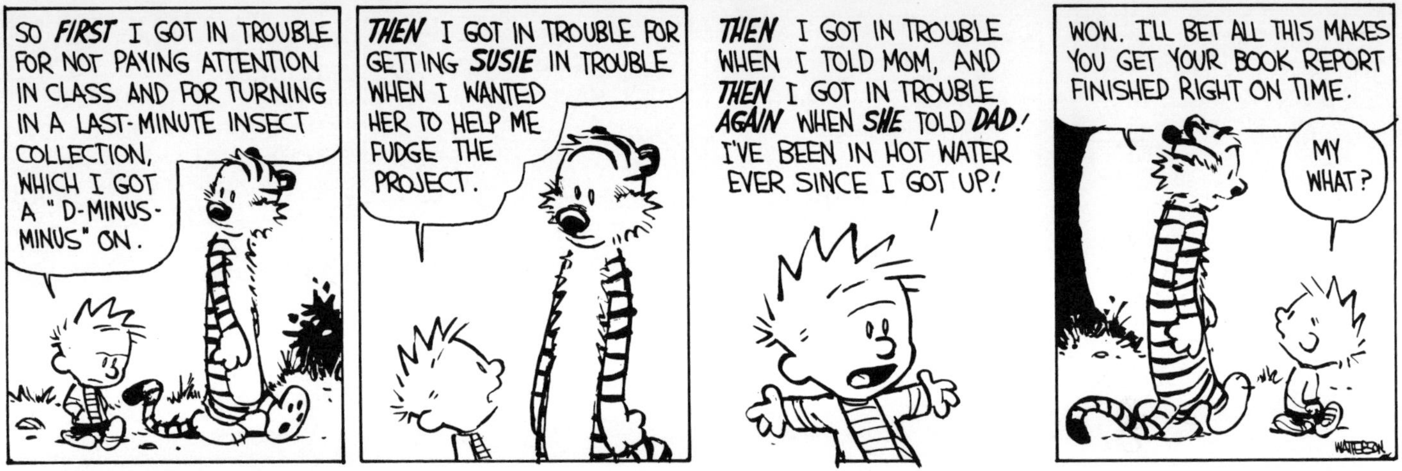
SO FIRST I GOT IN TROUBLE FOR NOT PAYING ATTENTION IN CLASS AND FOR TURNING IN A LAST-MINUTE INSECT COLLECTION, WHICH I GOT A "D-MINUS-MINUS" ON.
THEN I GOT IN TROUBLE FOR GETTING SUSIE IN TROUBLE WHEN I WANTED HER TO HELP ME FUDGE THE PROJECT.
THEN I GOT IN TROUBLE WHEN I TOLD MOM, AND THEN I GOT IN TROUBLE AGAIN WHEN SHE TOLD DAD! I'VE BEEN IN HOT WATER EVER SINCE I GOT UP!
WOW. I'LL BET ALL THIS MAKES YOU GET YOUR BOOK REPORT FINISHED RIGHT ON TIME.
MY WHAT?
WATTERSON

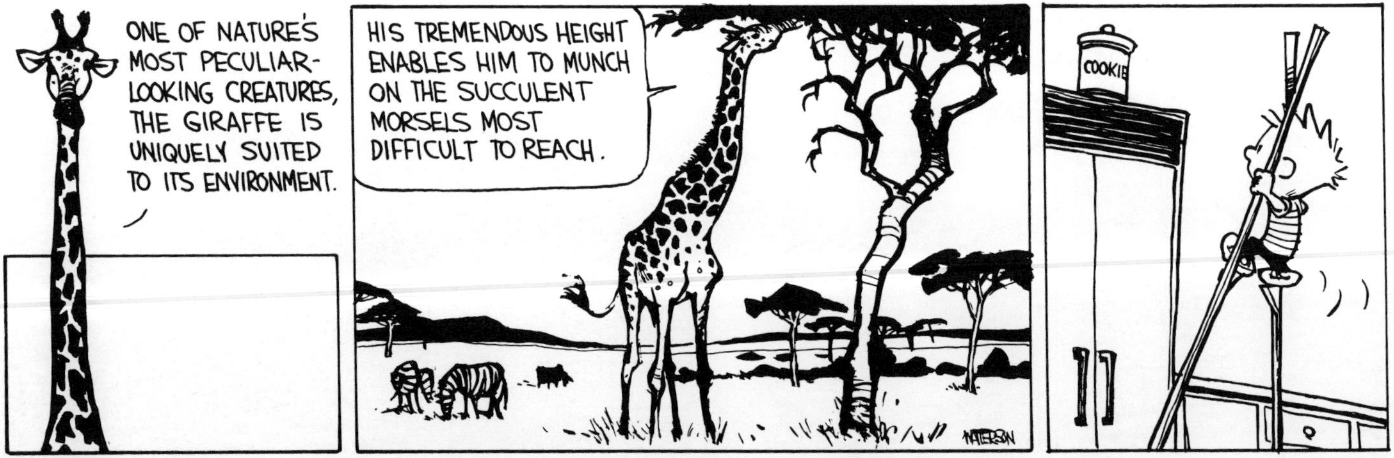
ONE OF NATURE'S MOST PECULIAR-LOOKING CREATURES, THE GIRAFFE IS UNIQUELY SUITED TO ITS ENVIRONMENT.
HIS TREMENDOUS HEIGHT ENABLES HIM TO MUNCH ON THE SUCCULENT MORSELS MOST DIFFICULT TO REACH.
WATTERSON
COOKIE

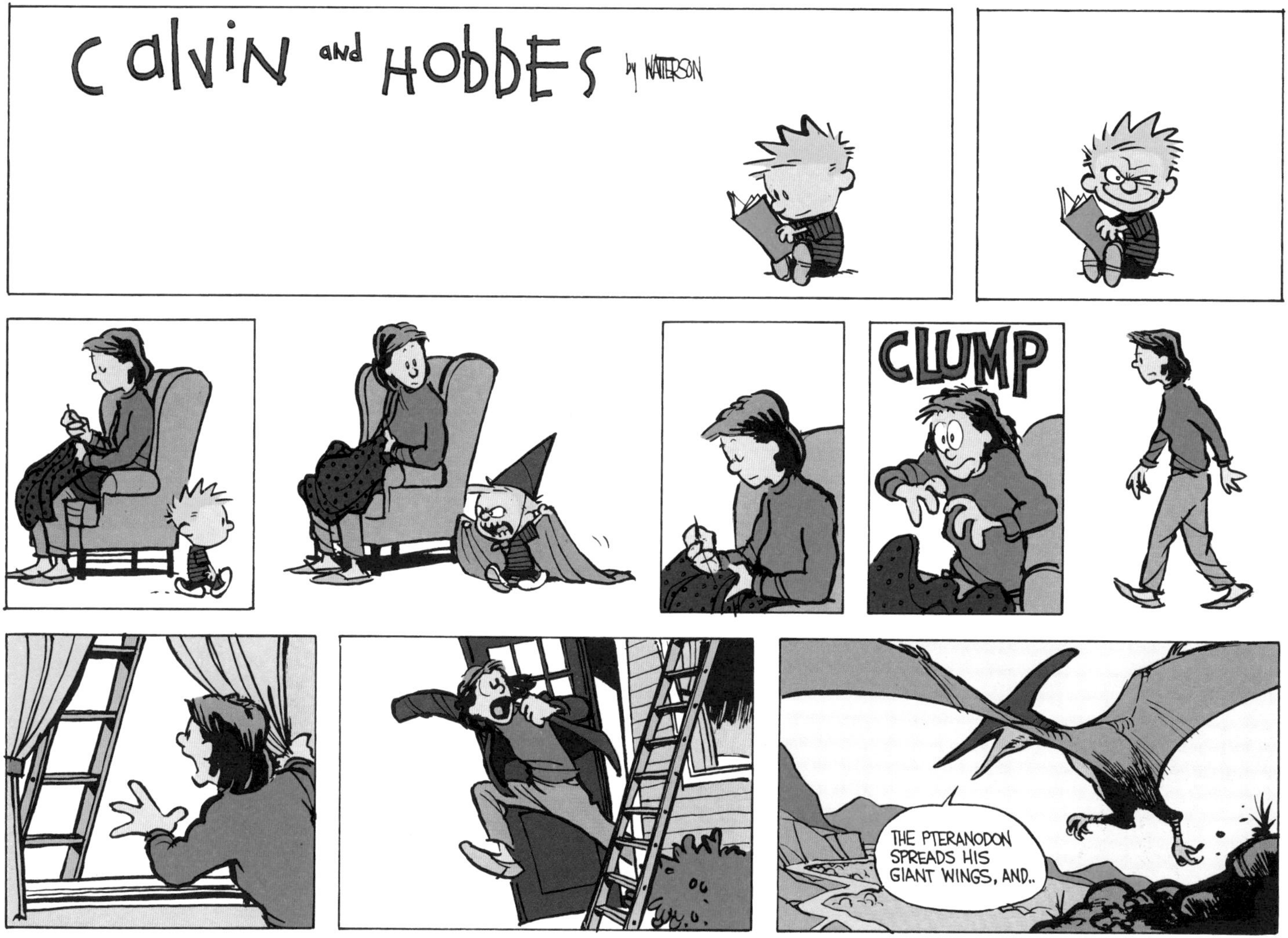
Calvin and HOBBES
by WATTERSON
CLUMP
THE PTERANODON SPREADS HIS GIANT WINGS, AND..

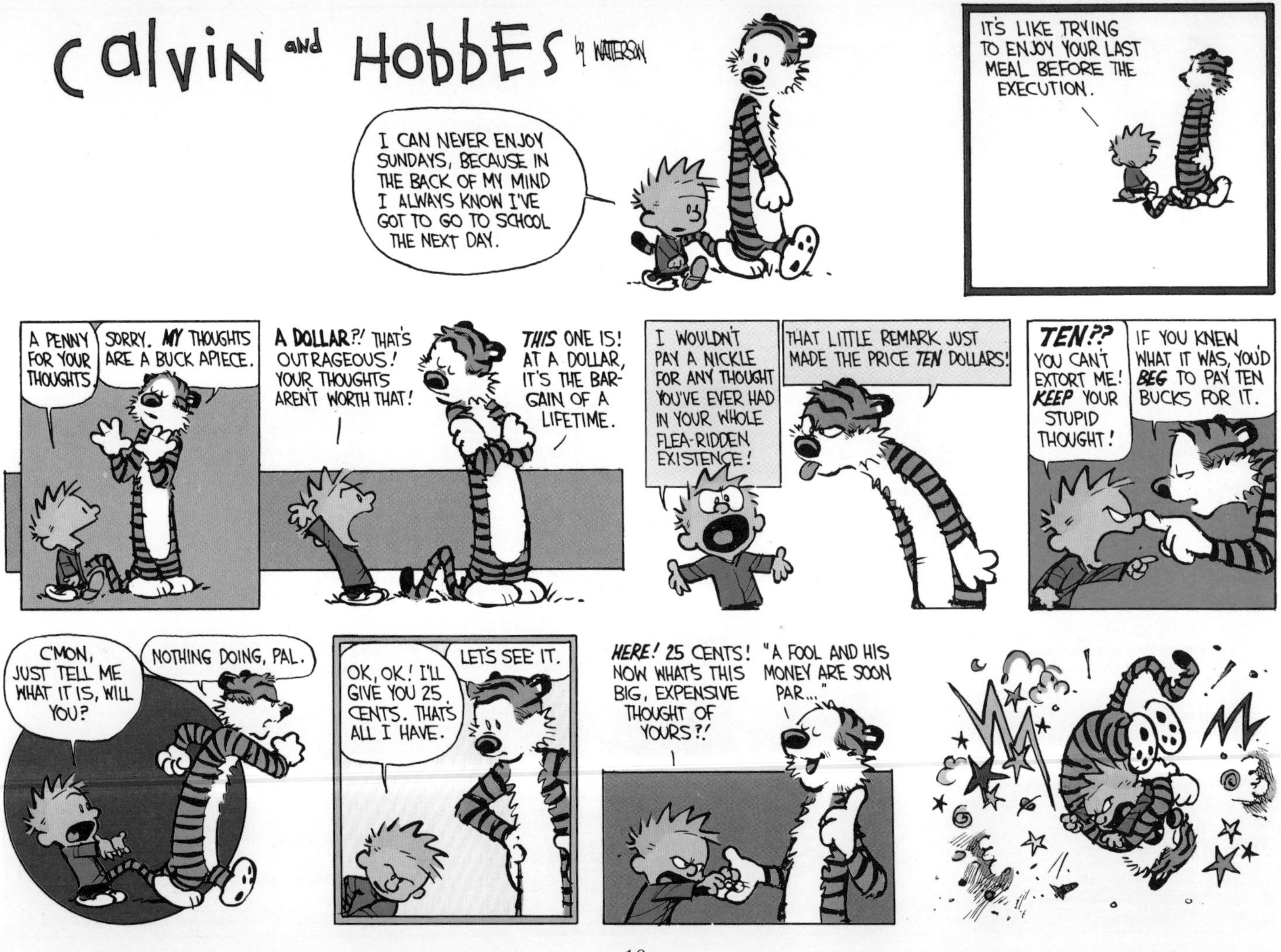
Calvin and HOBBES by WATTERSON
I CAN NEVER ENJOY SUNDAYS, BECAUSE IN THE BACK OF MY MIND I ALWAYS KNOW I'VE GOT TO GO TO SCHOOL THE NEXT DAY.
IT'S LIKE TRYING TO ENJOY YOUR LAST MEAL BEFORE THE EXECUTION.
A PENNY FOR YOUR THOUGHTS.
SORRY. MY THOUGHTS ARE A BUCK APIECE.
A DOLLAR?! THAT'S OUTRAGEOUS! YOUR THOUGHTS AREN'T WORTH THAT!
THIS ONE IS! AT A DOLLAR, IT'S THE BARGAIN OF A LIFETIME.
I WOULDN'T PAY A NICKLE FOR ANY THOUGHT YOU'VE EVER HAD IN YOUR WHOLE FLEA-RIDDEN EXISTENCE!
THAT LITTLE REMARK JUST MADE THE PRICE TEN DOLLARS!
TEN?? YOU CAN'T EXTORT ME! KEEP YOUR STUPID THOUGHT!
IF YOU KNEW WHAT IT WAS, YOU'D BEG TO PAY TEN BUCKS FOR IT.
C'MON, JUST TELL ME WHAT IT IS, WILL YOU?
NOTHING DOING, PAL.
OK, OK! I'LL GIVE YOU 25 CENTS. THAT'S ALL I HAVE.
LET'S SEE IT.
HERE! 25 CENTS! NOW WHAT'S THIS BIG, EXPENSIVE THOUGHT OF YOURS?!
"A FOOL AND HIS MONEY ARE SOON PAR..."

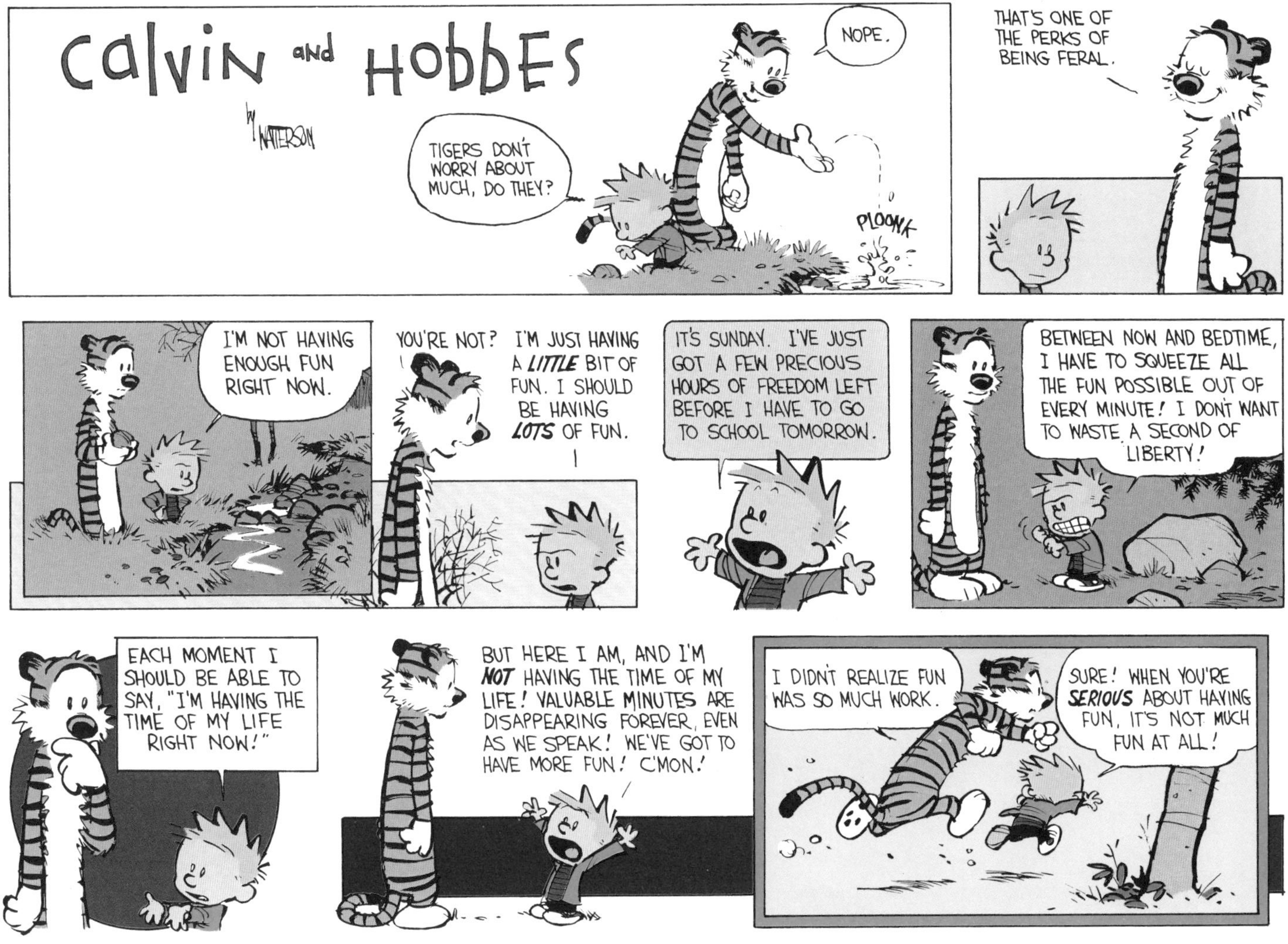
Calvin and HOBBES
by WATTERSON
TIGERS DON'T WORRY ABOUT MUCH, DO THEY?
NOPE.
PLOONK
THAT'S ONE OF THE PERKS OF BEING FERAL.
I'M NOT HAVING ENOUGH FUN RIGHT NOW.
YOU'RE NOT?
I'M JUST HAVING A LITTLE BIT OF FUN. I SHOULD BE HAVING LOTS OF FUN.
IT'S SUNDAY. I'VE JUST GOT A FEW PRECIOUS HOURS OF FREEDOM LEFT BEFORE I HAVE TO GO TO SCHOOL TOMORROW.
BETWEEN NOW AND BEDTIME, I HAVE TO SQUEEZE ALL THE FUN POSSIBLE OUT OF EVERY MINUTE! I DON'T WANT TO WASTE A SECOND OF LIBERTY!
EACH MOMENT I SHOULD BE ABLE TO SAY, "I'M HAVING THE TIME OF MY LIFE RIGHT NOW!"
BUT HERE I AM, AND I'M NOT HAVING THE TIME OF MY LIFE! VALUABLE MINUTES ARE DISAPPEARING FOREVER, EVEN AS WE SPEAK! WE'VE GOT TO HAVE MORE FUN! C'MON!
I DIDN'T REALIZE FUN WAS SO MUCH WORK.
SURE! WHEN YOU'RE SERIOUS ABOUT HAVING FUN, IT'S NOT MUCH FUN AT ALL!

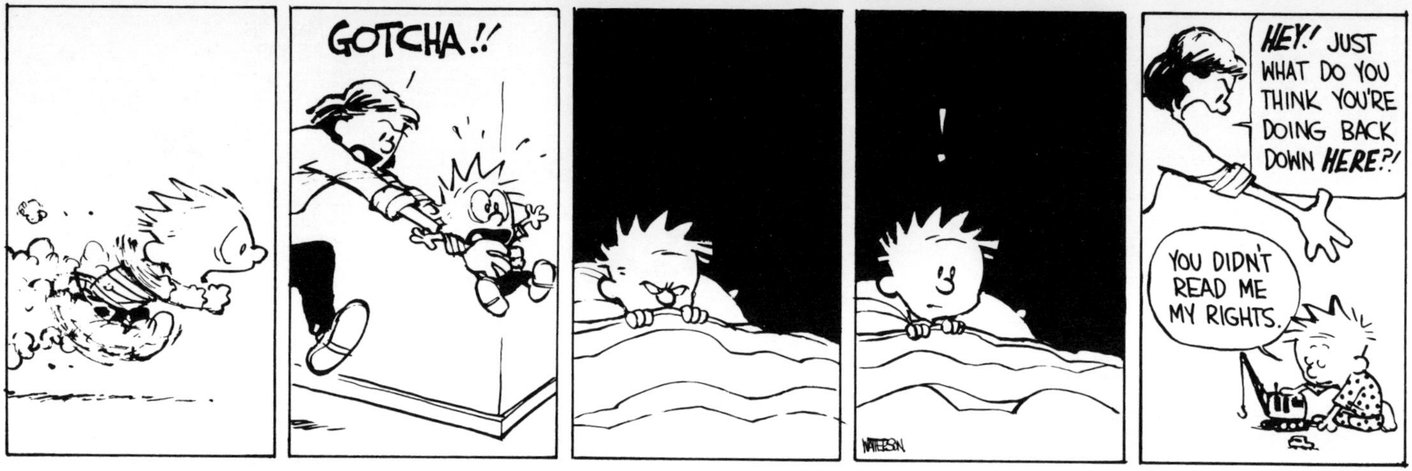
GOTCHA!!
!
HEY! JUST WHAT DO YOU THINK YOU'RE DOING BACK DOWN HERE?!
YOU DIDN'T READ ME MY RIGHTS.

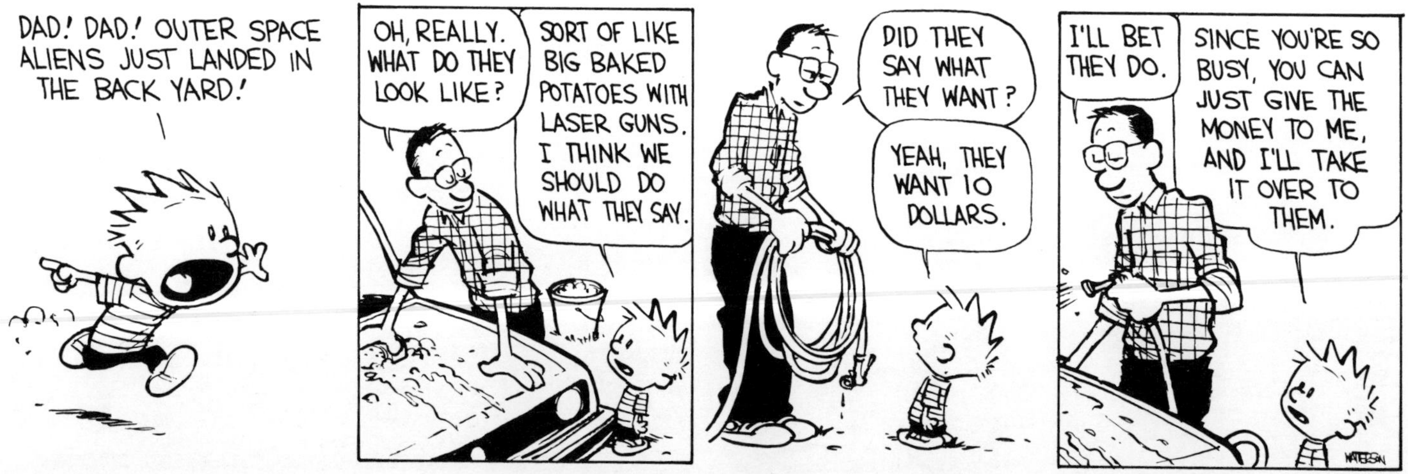
DAD! DAD! OUTER SPACE ALIENS JUST LANDED IN THE BACK YARD!
OH, REALLY. WHAT DO THEY LOOK LIKE?
SORT OF LIKE BIG BAKED POTATOES WITH LASER GUNS. I THINK WE SHOULD DO WHAT THEY SAY.
DID THEY SAY WHAT THEY WANT?
YEAH, THEY WANT 10 DOLLARS.
I'LL BET THEY DO.
SINCE YOU'RE SO BUSY, YOU CAN JUST GIVE THE MONEY TO ME, AND I'LL TAKE IT OVER TO THEM.

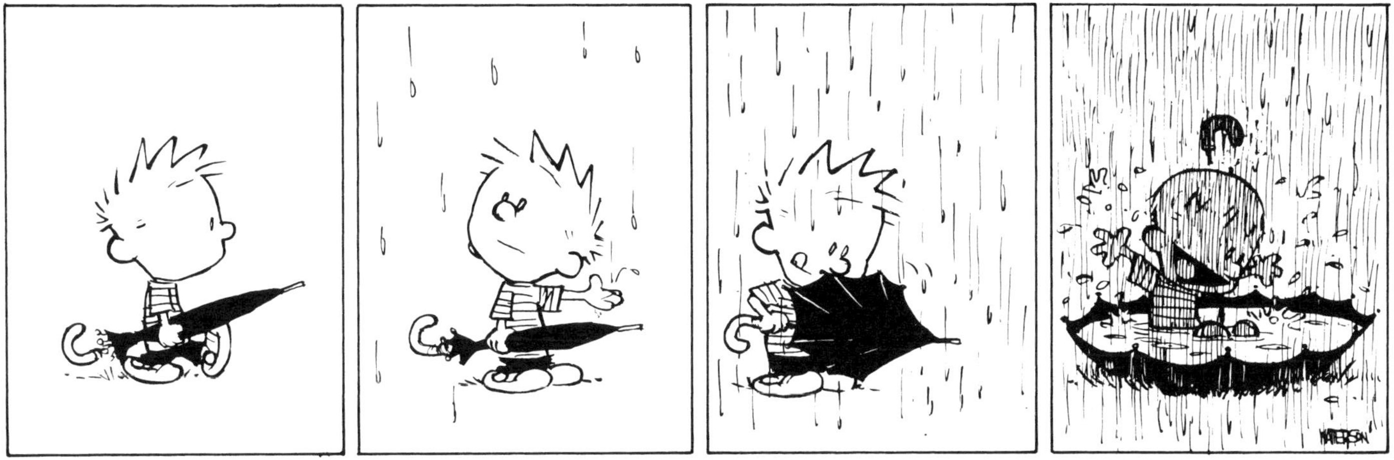

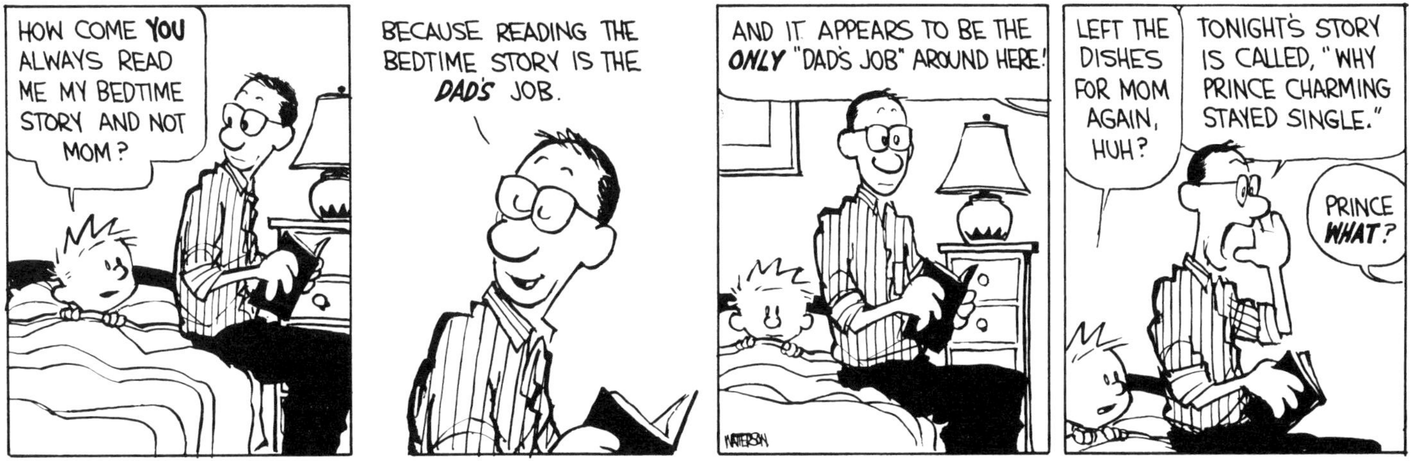

HOW COME **YOU** ALWAYS READ ME MY BEDTIME STORY AND NOT MOM?
BECAUSE READING THE BEDTIME STORY IS THE ***DAD'S*** JOB.
AND IT APPEARS TO BE THE ***ONLY*** "DAD'S JOB" AROUND HERE!
LEFT THE DISHES FOR MOM AGAIN, HUH?
TONIGHT'S STORY IS CALLED, "WHY PRINCE CHARMING STAYED SINGLE."
PRINCE ***WHAT***?

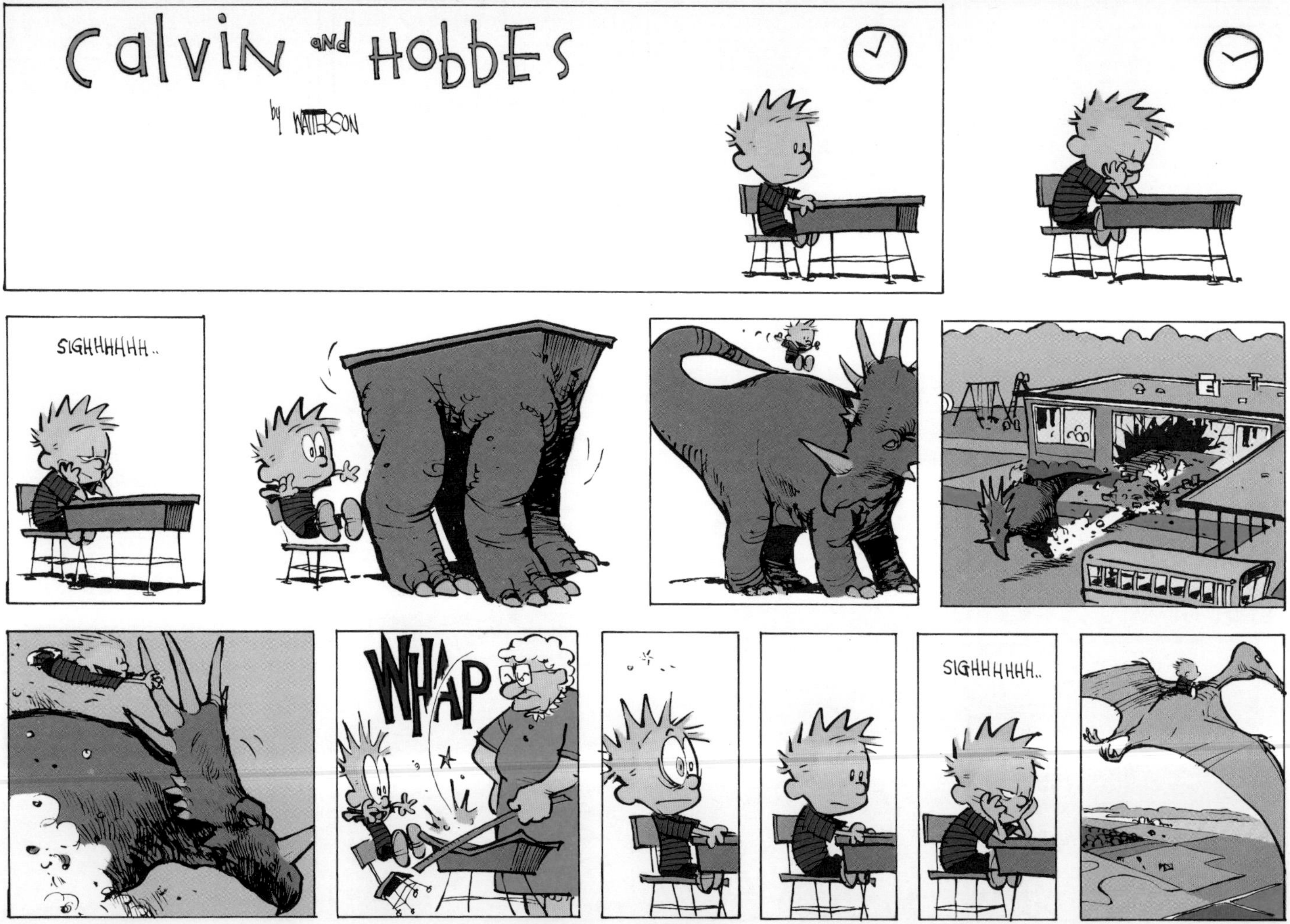
Calvin and Hobbes
by WATTERSON
SIGHHHHHH..
WHAP
SIGHHHHHH..

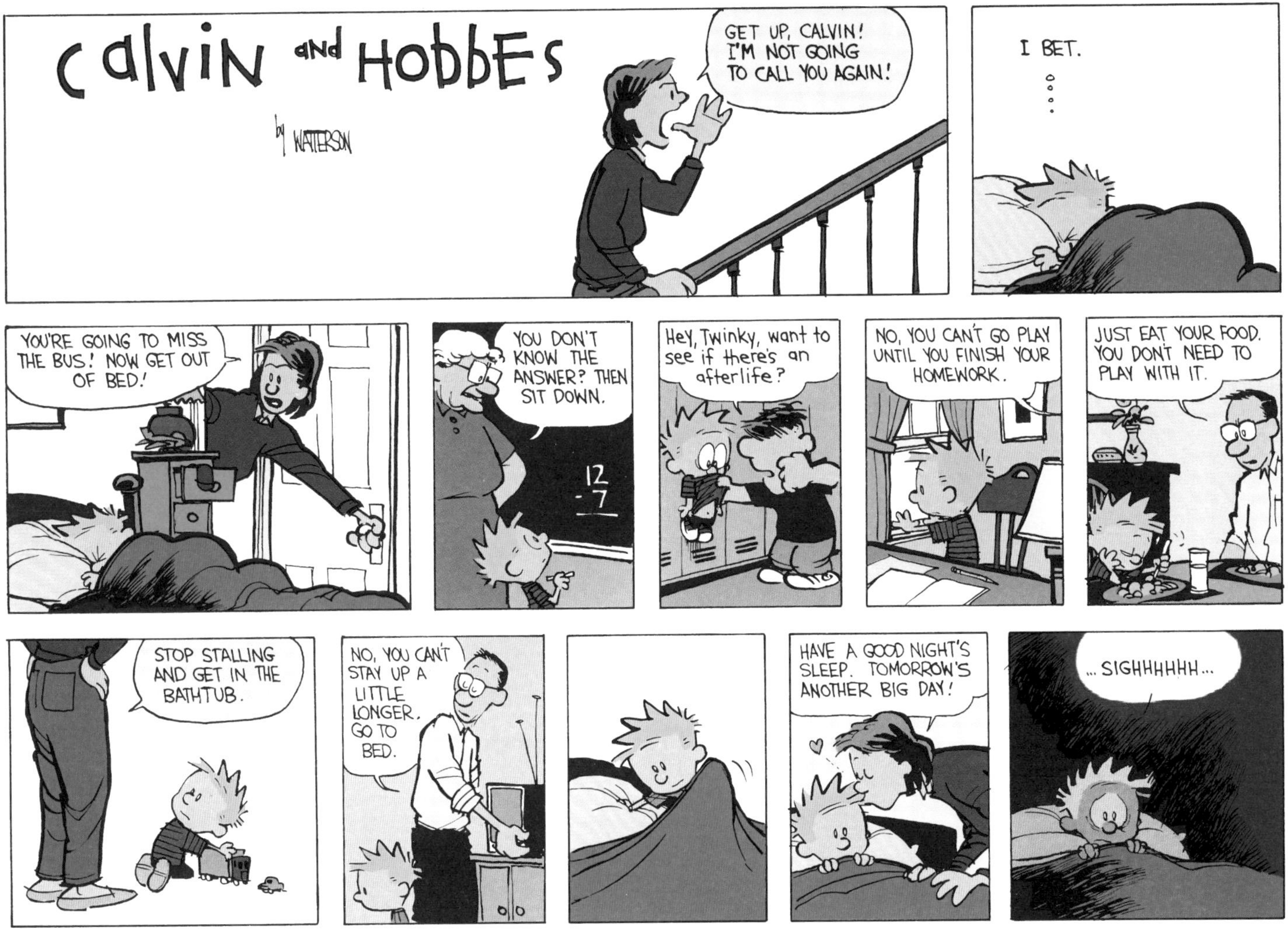
Calvin and HOBBES
by WATTERSON
GET UP, CALVIN! I'M NOT GOING TO CALL YOU AGAIN!
I BET.
YOU'RE GOING TO MISS THE BUS! NOW GET OUT OF BED!
YOU DON'T KNOW THE ANSWER? THEN SIT DOWN.
12
- 7
Hey, Twinky, want to see if there's an afterlife?
NO, YOU CAN'T GO PLAY UNTIL YOU FINISH YOUR HOMEWORK.
JUST EAT YOUR FOOD. YOU DON'T NEED TO PLAY WITH IT.
STOP STALLING AND GET IN THE BATHTUB.
NO, YOU CAN'T STAY UP A LITTLE LONGER. GO TO BED.
HAVE A GOOD NIGHT'S SLEEP. TOMORROW'S ANOTHER BIG DAY!
... SIGHHHHHH ...

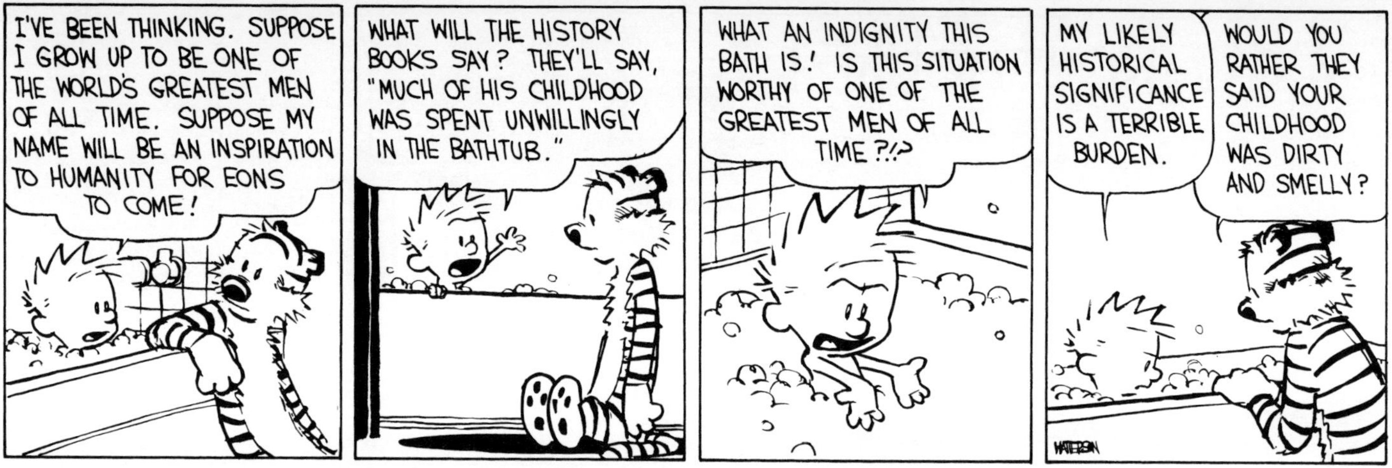
I'VE BEEN THINKING. SUPPOSE I GROW UP TO BE ONE OF THE WORLD'S GREATEST MEN OF ALL TIME. SUPPOSE MY NAME WILL BE AN INSPIRATION TO HUMANITY FOR EONS TO COME!
WHAT WILL THE HISTORY BOOKS SAY? THEY'LL SAY, "MUCH OF HIS CHILDHOOD WAS SPENT UNWILLINGLY IN THE BATHTUB."
WHAT AN INDIGNITY THIS BATH IS! IS THIS SITUATION WORTHY OF ONE OF THE GREATEST MEN OF ALL TIME?!?
MY LIKELY HISTORICAL SIGNIFICANCE IS A TERRIBLE BURDEN.
WOULD YOU RATHER THEY SAID YOUR CHILDHOOD WAS DIRTY AND SMELLY?
WATTERSON

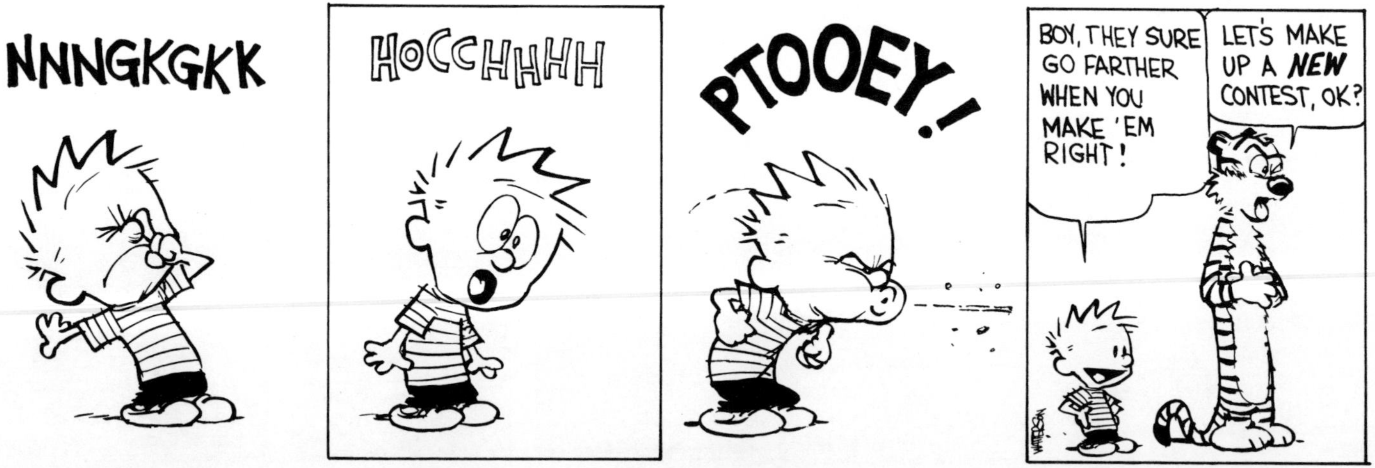
NNNGKGKK
HOCCHHHH
PTOOEY!
BOY, THEY SURE GO FARTHER WHEN YOU MAKE 'EM RIGHT!
LET'S MAKE UP A *NEW* CONTEST, OK?
WATTERSON

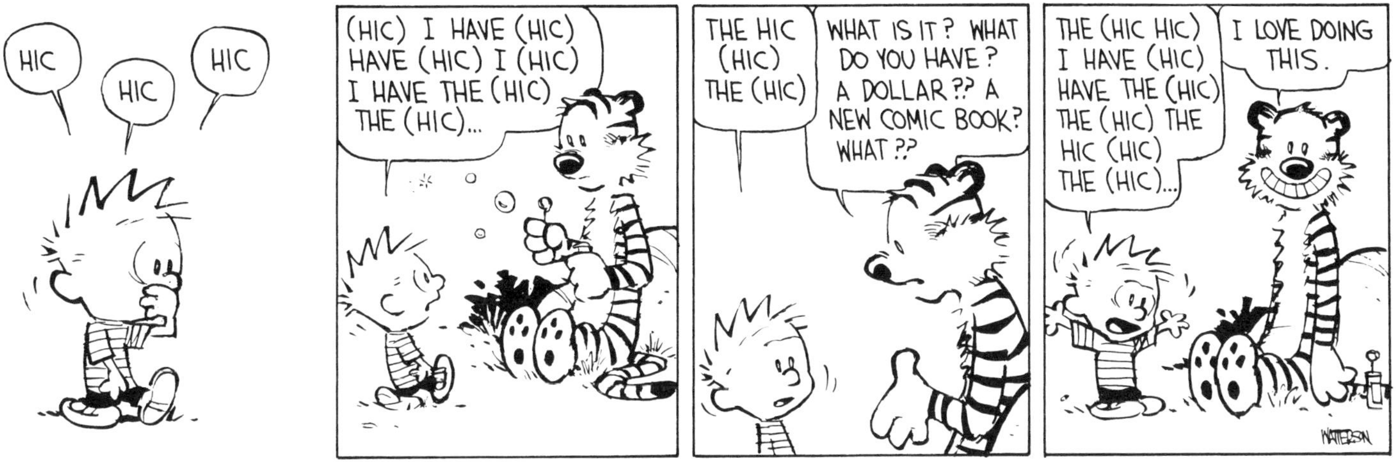
HIC
HIC
HIC
(HIC) I HAVE (HIC) HAVE (HIC) I (HIC) I HAVE THE (HIC) THE (HIC)...
THE HIC (HIC) THE (HIC)
WHAT IS IT? WHAT DO YOU HAVE? A DOLLAR?? A NEW COMIC BOOK? WHAT??
THE (HIC HIC) I HAVE (HIC) HAVE THE (HIC) THE (HIC) THE HIC (HIC) THE (HIC)...
I LOVE DOING THIS.
WATTERSON

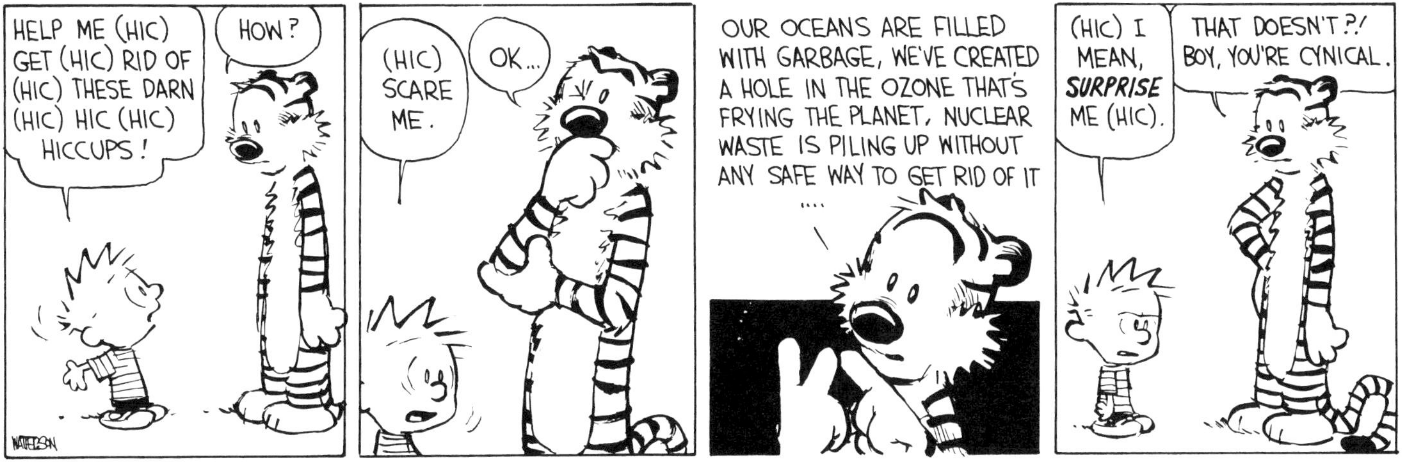
HELP ME (HIC) GET (HIC) RID OF (HIC) THESE DARN (HIC) HIC (HIC) HICCUPS!
HOW?
(HIC) SCARE ME.
OK...
OUR OCEANS ARE FILLED WITH GARBAGE, WE'VE CREATED A HOLE IN THE OZONE THAT'S FRYING THE PLANET, NUCLEAR WASTE IS PILING UP WITHOUT ANY SAFE WAY TO GET RID OF IT ....
(HIC) I MEAN, ***SURPRISE*** ME (HIC).
THAT DOESN'T?! BOY, YOU'RE CYNICAL.
WATTERSON

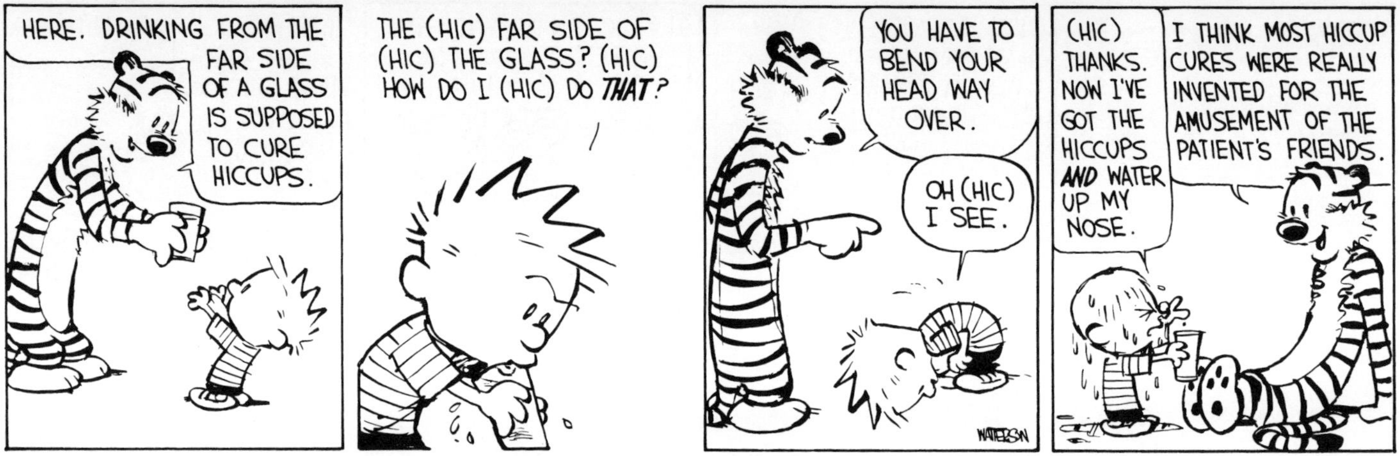
HERE. DRINKING FROM THE FAR SIDE OF A GLASS IS SUPPOSED TO CURE HICCUPS.
THE (HIC) FAR SIDE OF (HIC) THE GLASS? (HIC) HOW DO I (HIC) DO *THAT*?
YOU HAVE TO BEND YOUR HEAD WAY OVER.
OH (HIC) I SEE.
WATTERSON
(HIC) THANKS. NOW I'VE GOT THE HICCUPS *AND* WATER UP MY NOSE.
I THINK MOST HICCUP CURES WERE REALLY INVENTED FOR THE AMUSEMENT OF THE PATIENT'S FRIENDS.

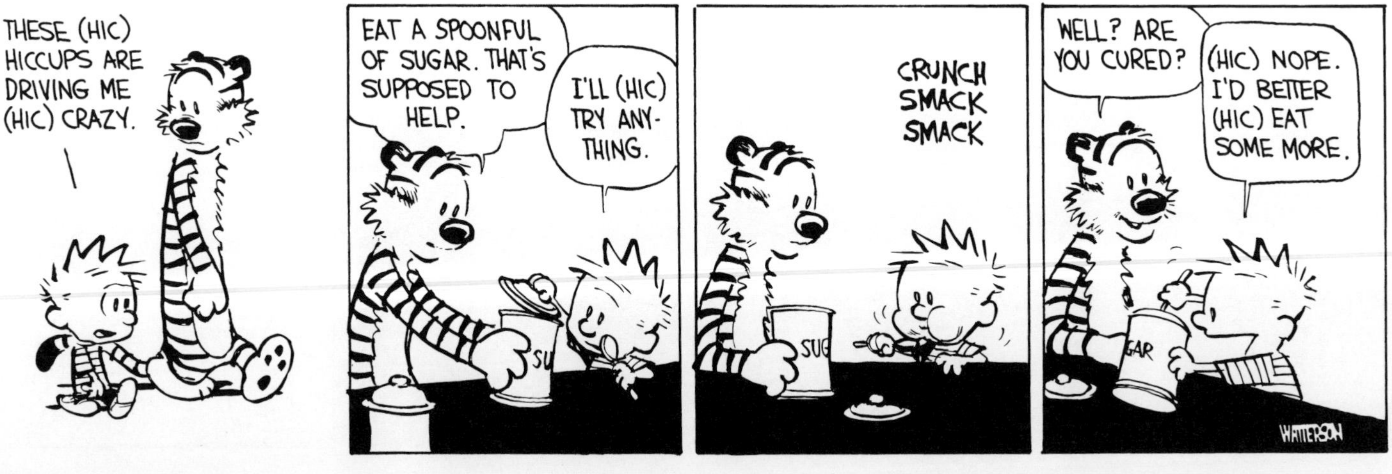
THESE (HIC) HICCUPS ARE DRIVING ME (HIC) CRAZY.
EAT A SPOONFUL OF SUGAR. THAT'S SUPPOSED TO HELP.
I'LL (HIC) TRY ANY-THING.
SU
CRUNCH SMACK SMACK
SUG
WELL? ARE YOU CURED?
(HIC) NOPE. I'D BETTER (HIC) EAT SOME MORE.
GAR
WATTERSON

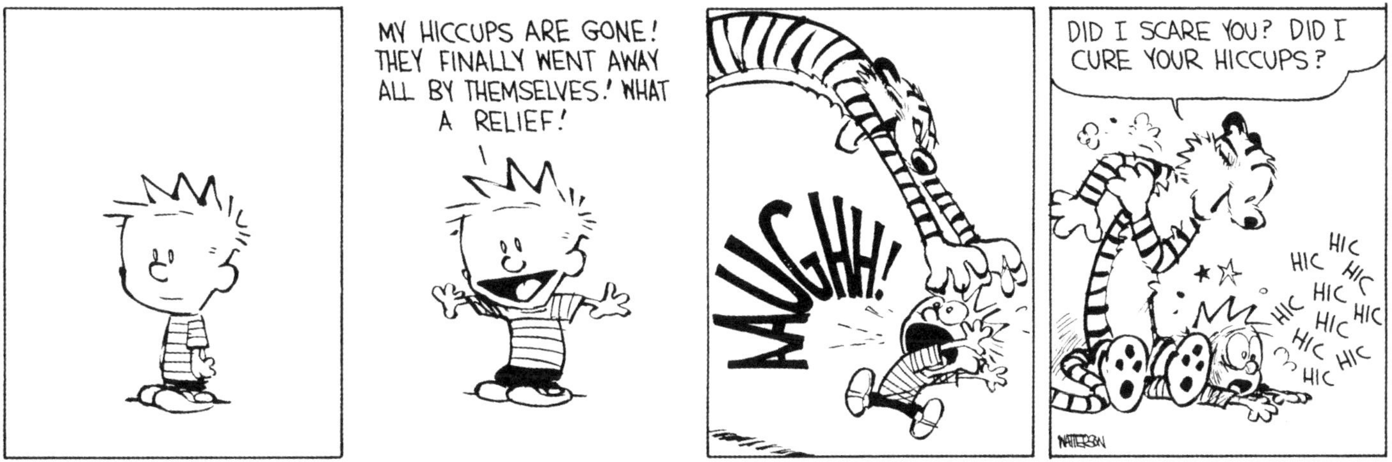
MY HICCUPS ARE GONE! THEY FINALLY WENT AWAY ALL BY THEMSELVES! WHAT A RELIEF!
MAUGHH!
DID I SCARE YOU? DID I CURE YOUR HICCUPS?
HIC HIC HIC HIC HIC HIC HIC HIC HIC HIC HIC
WATTERSON

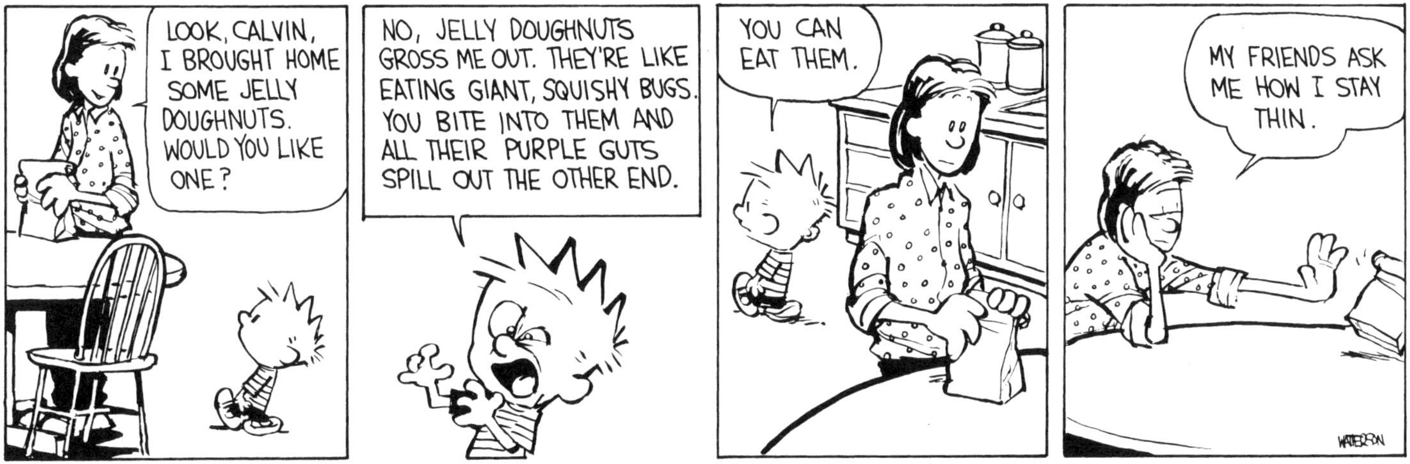
LOOK, CALVIN, I BROUGHT HOME SOME JELLY DOUGHNUTS. WOULD YOU LIKE ONE?
NO, JELLY DOUGHNUTS GROSS ME OUT. THEY'RE LIKE EATING GIANT, SQUISHY BUGS. YOU BITE INTO THEM AND ALL THEIR PURPLE GUTS SPILL OUT THE OTHER END.
YOU CAN EAT THEM.
MY FRIENDS ASK ME HOW I STAY THIN.
WATTERSON

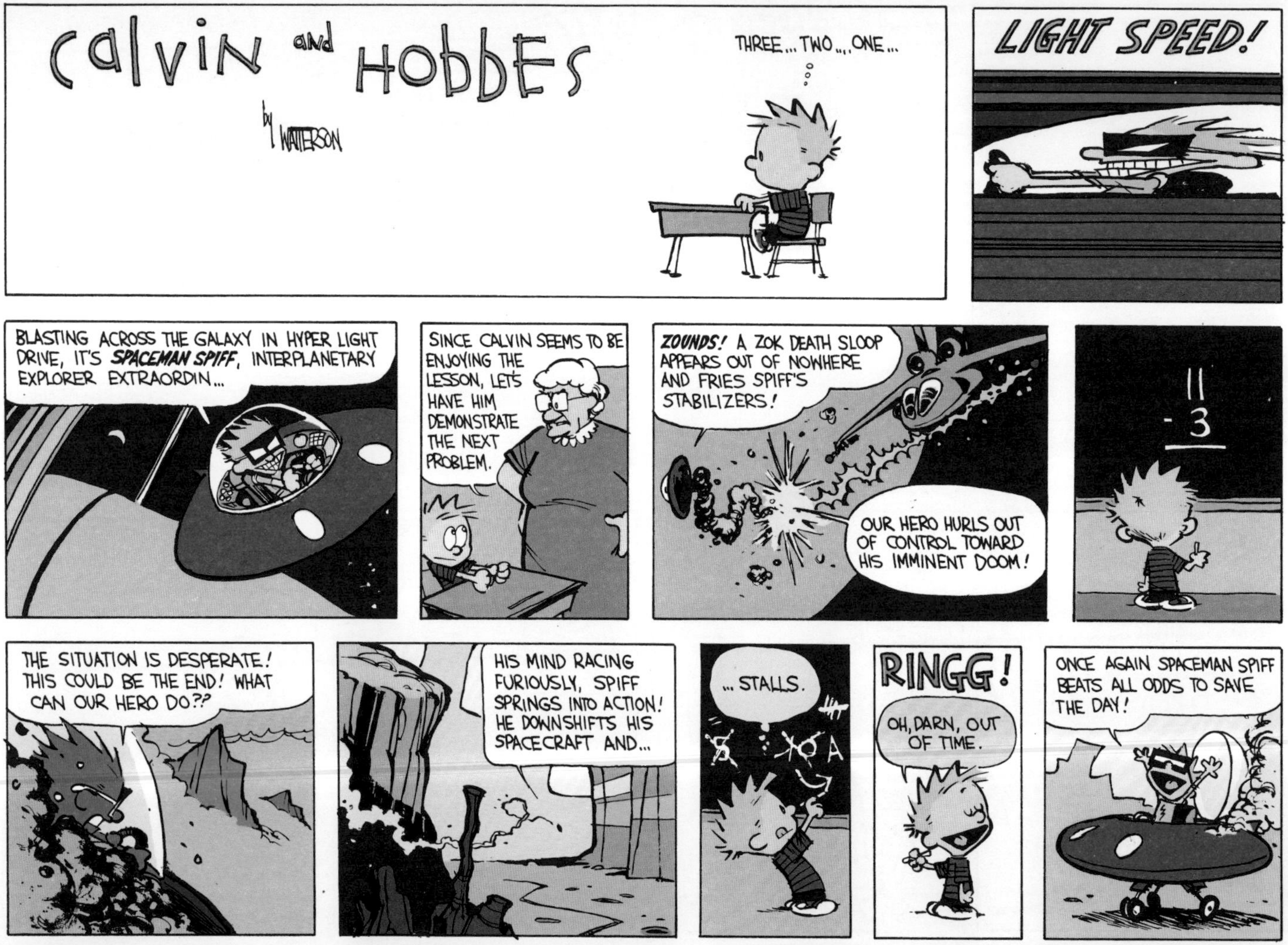
Calvin and Hobbes
by WATTERSON
THREE... TWO..., ONE...
LIGHT SPEED!
BLASTING ACROSS THE GALAXY IN HYPER LIGHT DRIVE, IT'S SPACEMAN SPIFF, INTERPLANETARY EXPLORER EXTRAORDIN...
SINCE CALVIN SEEMS TO BE ENJOYING THE LESSON, LET'S HAVE HIM DEMONSTRATE THE NEXT PROBLEM.
ZOUNDS! A ZOK DEATH SLOOP APPEARS OUT OF NOWHERE AND FRIES SPIFF'S STABILIZERS!
OUR HERO HURLS OUT OF CONTROL TOWARD HIS IMMINENT DOOM!
11
- 3
THE SITUATION IS DESPERATE! THIS COULD BE THE END! WHAT CAN OUR HERO DO??
HIS MIND RACING FURIOUSLY, SPIFF SPRINGS INTO ACTION! HE DOWNSHIFTS HIS SPACECRAFT AND...
... STALLS.
RINGG!
OH, DARN, OUT OF TIME.
ONCE AGAIN SPACEMAN SPIFF BEATS ALL ODDS TO SAVE THE DAY!

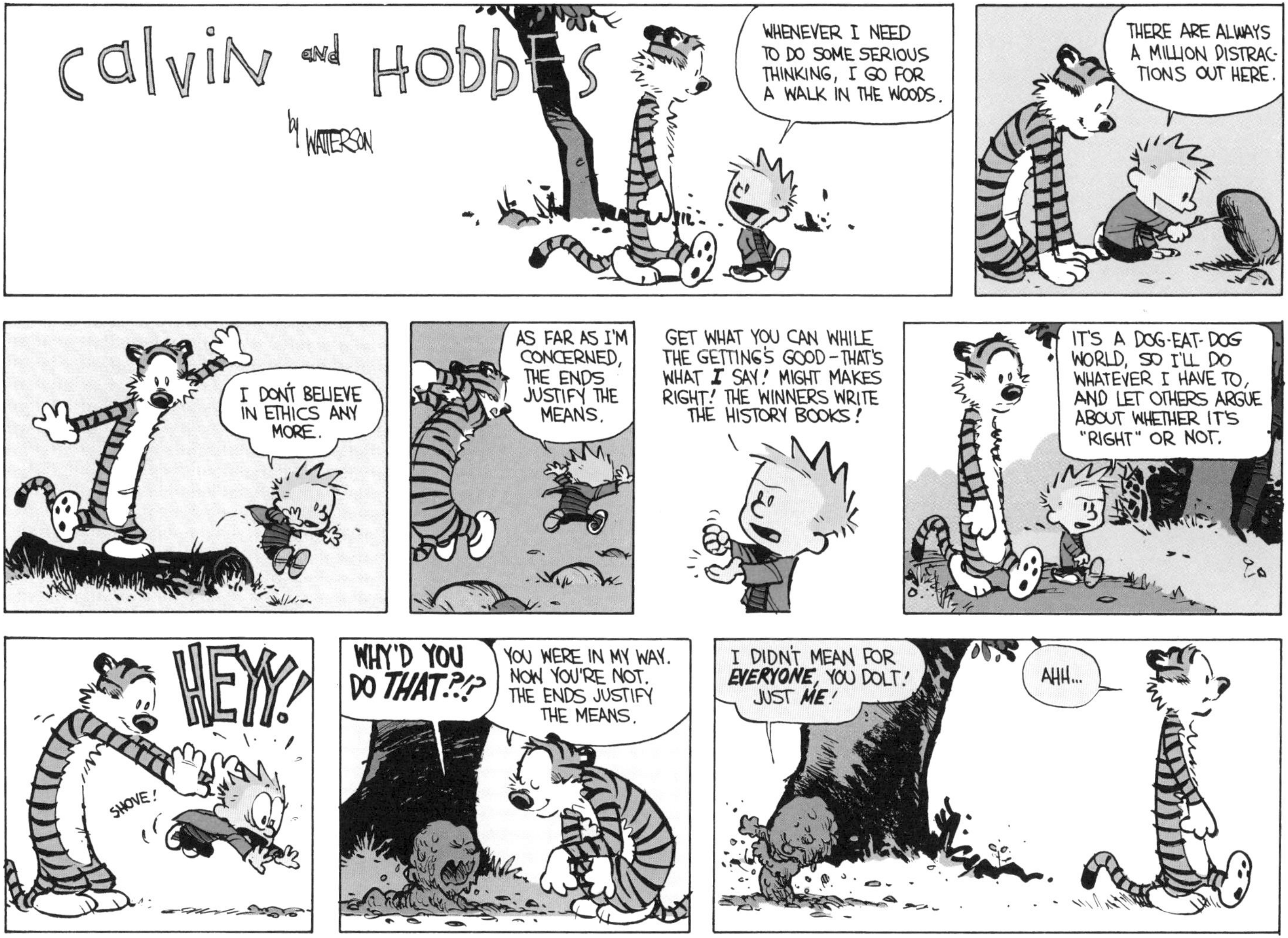
Calvin and HOBBES
by WATTERSON
WHENEVER I NEED TO DO SOME SERIOUS THINKING, I GO FOR A WALK IN THE WOODS.
THERE ARE ALWAYS A MILLION DISTRACTIONS OUT HERE.
I DON'T BELIEVE IN ETHICS ANY MORE.
AS FAR AS I'M CONCERNED, THE ENDS JUSTIFY THE MEANS.
GET WHAT YOU CAN WHILE THE GETTING'S GOOD – THAT'S WHAT I SAY! MIGHT MAKES RIGHT! THE WINNERS WRITE THE HISTORY BOOKS!
IT'S A DOG-EAT-DOG WORLD, SO I'LL DO WHATEVER I HAVE TO, AND LET OTHERS ARGUE ABOUT WHETHER IT'S "RIGHT" OR NOT.
HEYY!
SHOVE!
WHY'D YOU DO THAT?!?
YOU WERE IN MY WAY. NOW YOU'RE NOT. THE ENDS JUSTIFY THE MEANS.
I DIDN'T MEAN FOR EVERYONE, YOU DOLT! JUST ME!
AHH...

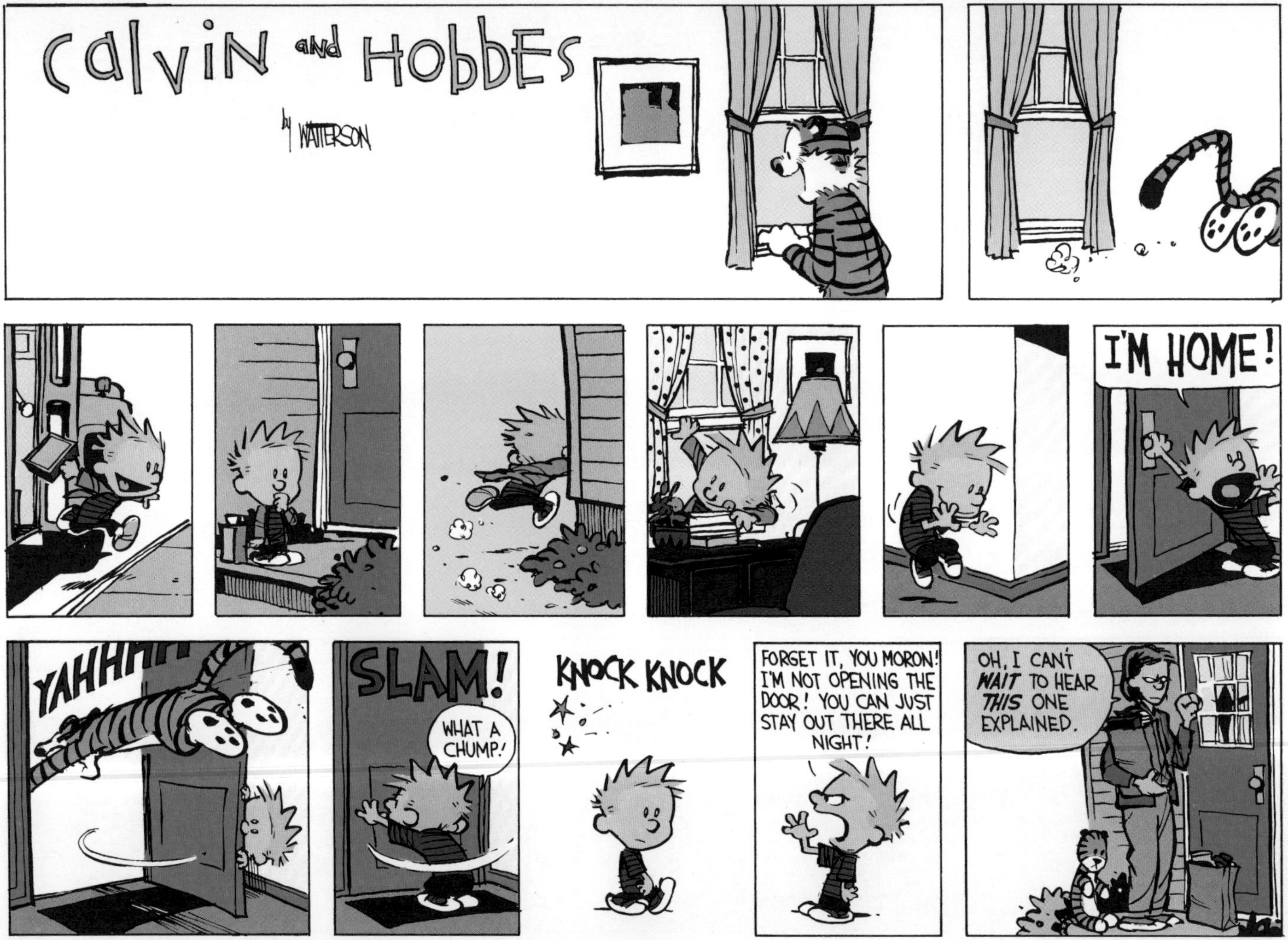
Calvin and HOBBES
by WATTERSON
I'M HOME!
YAHHHH
SLAM!
WHAT A CHUMP!
KNOCK KNOCK
FORGET IT, YOU MORON! I'M NOT OPENING THE DOOR! YOU CAN JUST STAY OUT THERE ALL NIGHT!
OH, I CAN'T WAIT TO HEAR THIS ONE EXPLAINED.

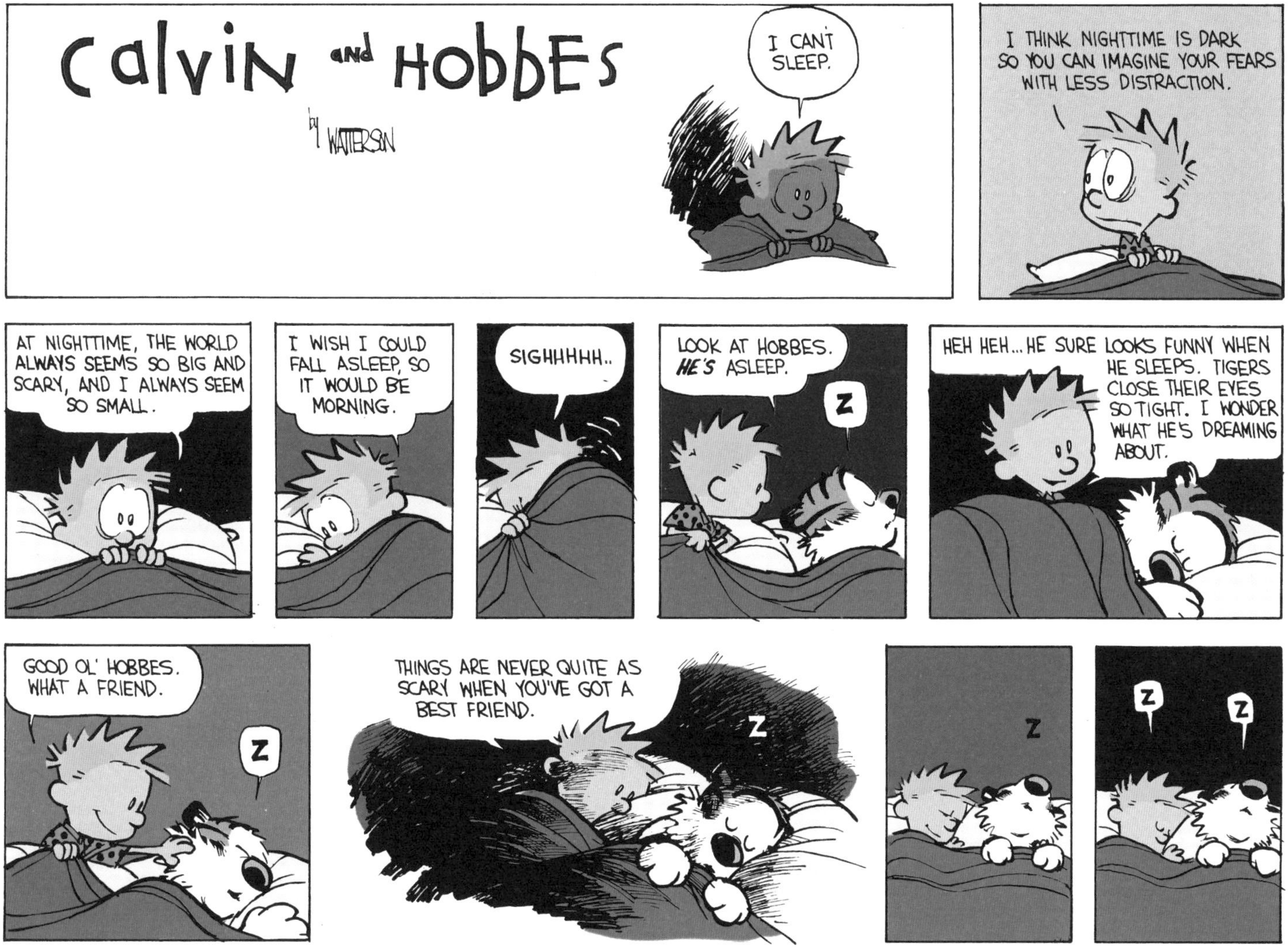
Calvin and HOBBES
by WATTERSON
I CAN'T SLEEP.
I THINK NIGHTTIME IS DARK SO YOU CAN IMAGINE YOUR FEARS WITH LESS DISTRACTION.
AT NIGHTTIME, THE WORLD ALWAYS SEEMS SO BIG AND SCARY, AND I ALWAYS SEEM SO SMALL.
I WISH I COULD FALL ASLEEP, SO IT WOULD BE MORNING.
SIGHHHHH..
LOOK AT HOBBES. HE'S ASLEEP.
Z
HEH HEH... HE SURE LOOKS FUNNY WHEN HE SLEEPS. TIGERS CLOSE THEIR EYES SO TIGHT. I WONDER WHAT HE'S DREAMING ABOUT.
GOOD OL' HOBBES. WHAT A FRIEND.
Z
THINGS ARE NEVER QUITE AS SCARY WHEN YOU'VE GOT A BEST FRIEND.
Z
Z
Z
Z

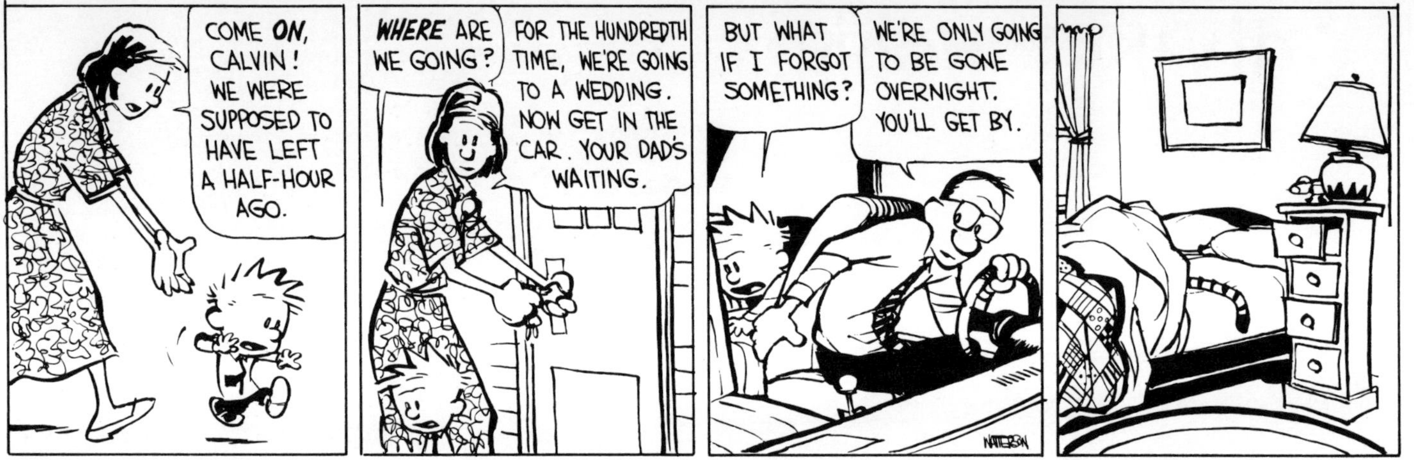
COME **ON**, CALVIN! WE WERE SUPPOSED TO HAVE LEFT A HALF-HOUR AGO.
WHERE ARE WE GOING?
FOR THE HUNDREDTH TIME, WE'RE GOING TO A WEDDING. NOW GET IN THE CAR. YOUR DAD'S WAITING.
BUT WHAT IF I FORGOT SOMETHING?
WE'RE ONLY GOING TO BE GONE OVERNIGHT. YOU'LL GET BY.

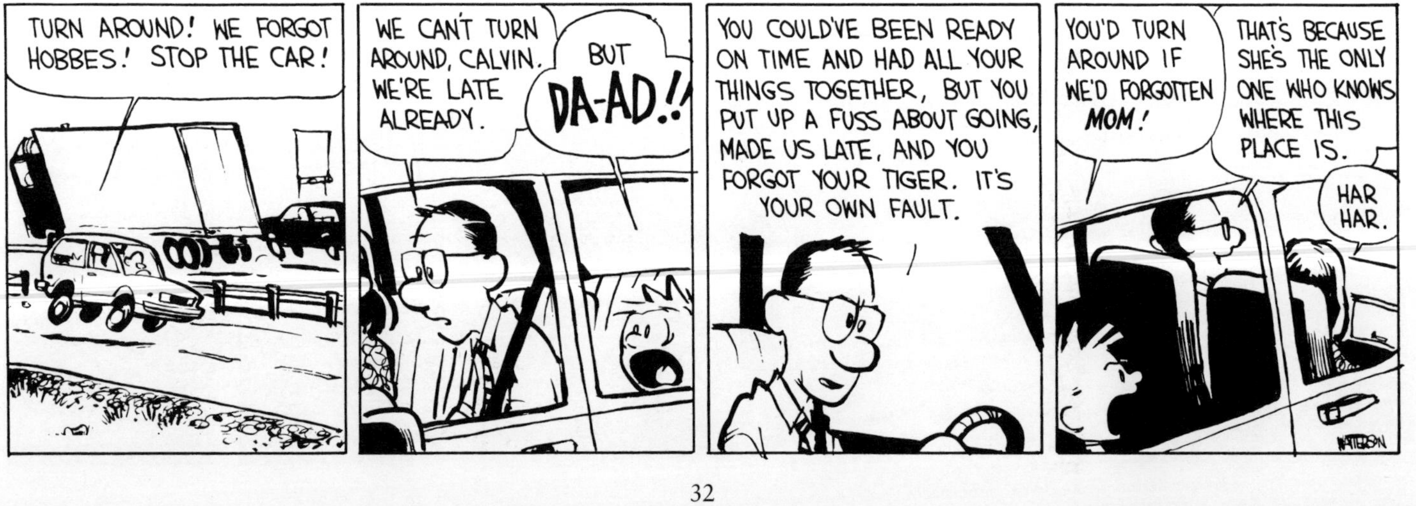
TURN AROUND! WE FORGOT HOBBES! STOP THE CAR!
WE CAN'T TURN AROUND, CALVIN. WE'RE LATE ALREADY.
BUT DA-AD!!
YOU COULD'VE BEEN READY ON TIME AND HAD ALL YOUR THINGS TOGETHER, BUT YOU PUT UP A FUSS ABOUT GOING, MADE US LATE, AND YOU FORGOT YOUR TIGER. IT'S YOUR OWN FAULT.
YOU'D TURN AROUND IF WE'D FORGOTTEN **MOM**!
THAT'S BECAUSE SHE'S THE ONLY ONE WHO KNOWS WHERE THIS PLACE IS.
HAR HAR.

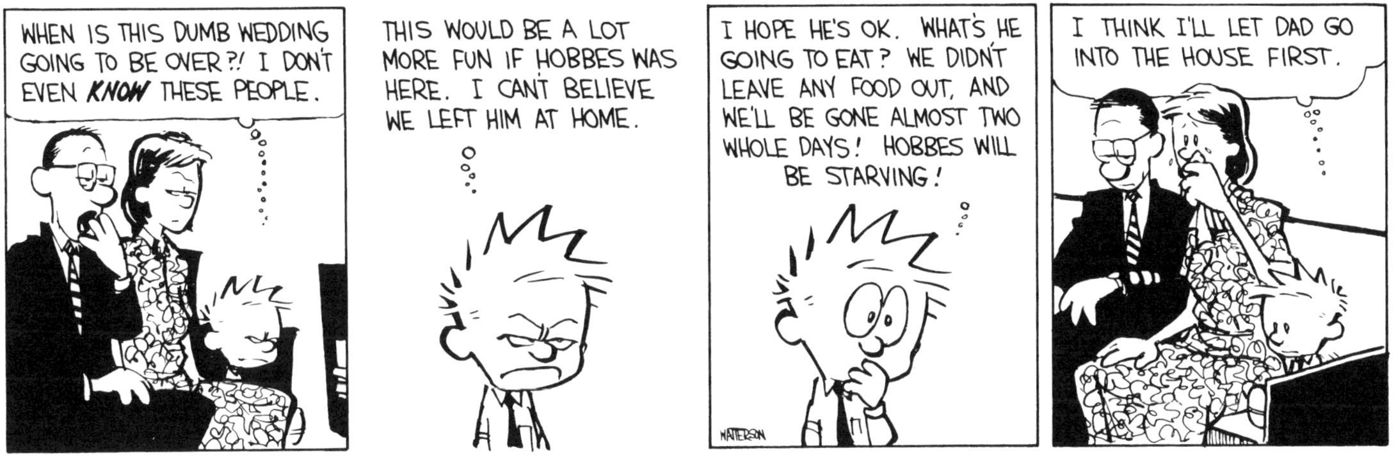
WHEN IS THIS DUMB WEDDING GOING TO BE OVER?! I DON'T EVEN *KNOW* THESE PEOPLE.
THIS WOULD BE A LOT MORE FUN IF HOBBES WAS HERE. I CAN'T BELIEVE WE LEFT HIM AT HOME.
I HOPE HE'S OK. WHAT'S HE GOING TO EAT? WE DIDN'T LEAVE ANY FOOD OUT, AND WE'LL BE GONE ALMOST TWO WHOLE DAYS! HOBBES WILL BE STARVING!
I THINK I'LL LET DAD GO INTO THE HOUSE FIRST.

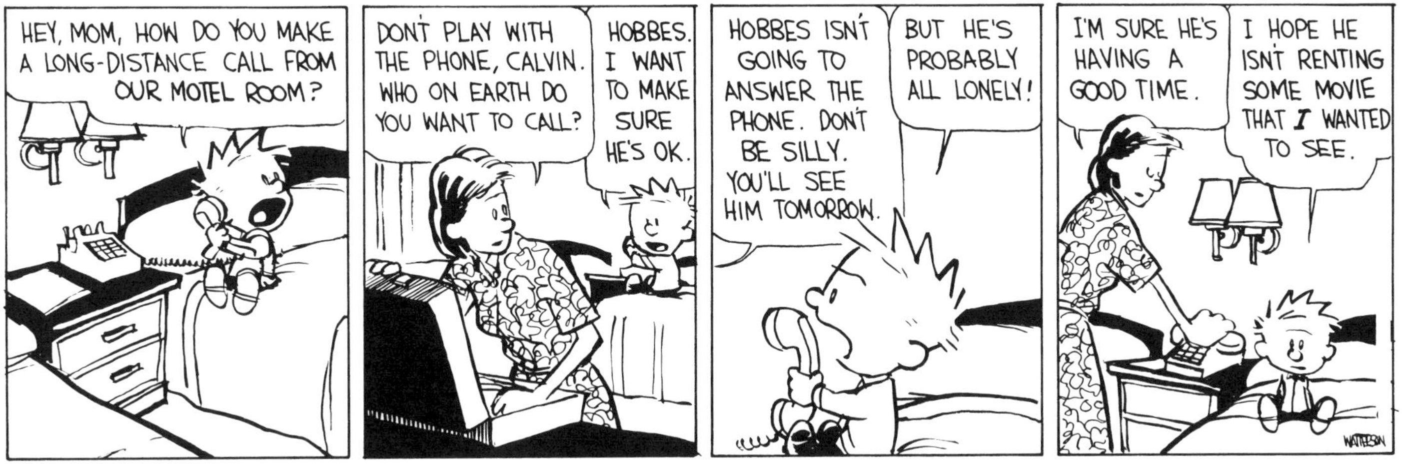
HEY, MOM, HOW DO YOU MAKE A LONG-DISTANCE CALL FROM OUR MOTEL ROOM?
DON'T PLAY WITH THE PHONE, CALVIN. WHO ON EARTH DO YOU WANT TO CALL?
HOBBES. I WANT TO MAKE SURE HE'S OK.
HOBBES ISN'T GOING TO ANSWER THE PHONE. DON'T BE SILLY. YOU'LL SEE HIM TOMORROW.
BUT HE'S PROBABLY ALL LONELY!
I'M SURE HE'S HAVING A GOOD TIME.
I HOPE HE ISN'T RENTING SOME MOVIE THAT *I* WANTED TO SEE.

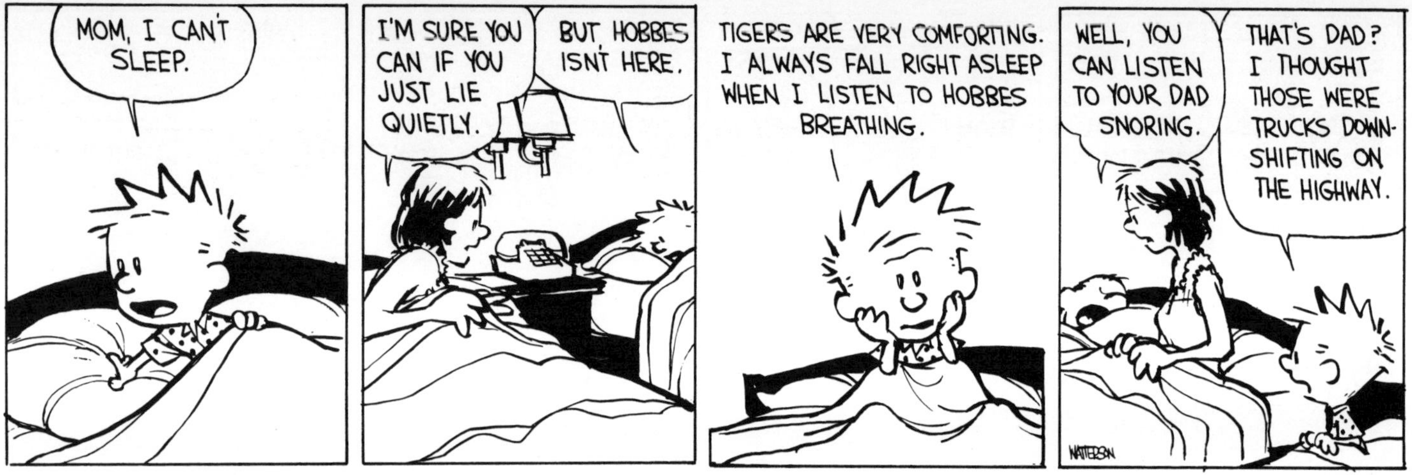
MOM, I CAN'T SLEEP.
I'M SURE YOU CAN IF YOU JUST LIE QUIETLY.
BUT, HOBBES ISN'T HERE.
TIGERS ARE VERY COMFORTING. I ALWAYS FALL RIGHT ASLEEP WHEN I LISTEN TO HOBBES BREATHING.
WELL, YOU CAN LISTEN TO YOUR DAD SNORING.
THAT'S DAD? I THOUGHT THOSE WERE TRUCKS DOWN-SHIFTING ON THE HIGHWAY.

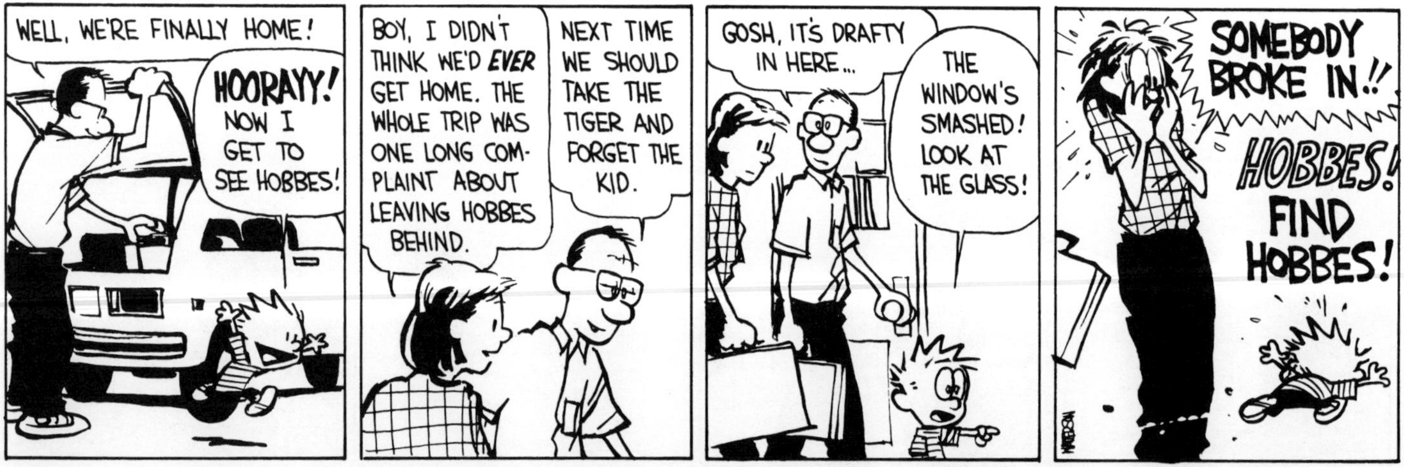
WELL, WE'RE FINALLY HOME!
HOORAYY! NOW I GET TO SEE HOBBES!
BOY, I DIDN'T THINK WE'D EVER GET HOME. THE WHOLE TRIP WAS ONE LONG COM-PLAINT ABOUT LEAVING HOBBES BEHIND.
NEXT TIME WE SHOULD TAKE THE TIGER AND FORGET THE KID.
GOSH, IT'S DRAFTY IN HERE...
THE WINDOW'S SMASHED! LOOK AT THE GLASS!
SOMEBODY BROKE IN!!
HOBBES! FIND HOBBES!

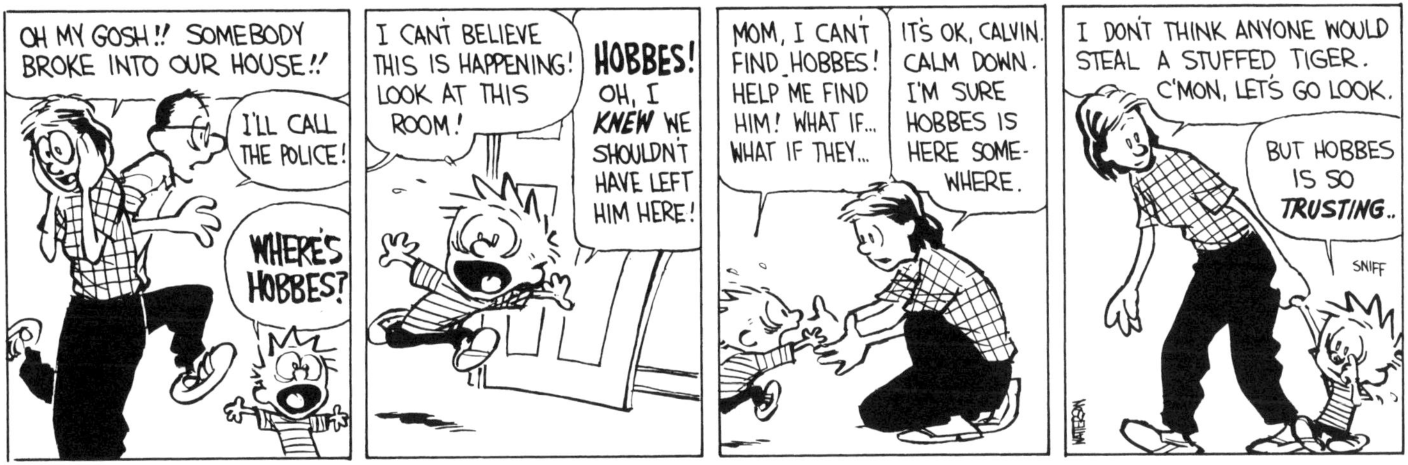
OH MY GOSH!! SOMEBODY BROKE INTO OUR HOUSE!!
I'LL CALL THE POLICE!
WHERE'S HOBBES?
I CAN'T BELIEVE THIS IS HAPPENING! LOOK AT THIS ROOM!
HOBBES! OH, I KNEW WE SHOULDN'T HAVE LEFT HIM HERE!
MOM, I CAN'T FIND HOBBES! HELP ME FIND HIM! WHAT IF... WHAT IF THEY...
IT'S OK, CALVIN. CALM DOWN. I'M SURE HOBBES IS HERE SOMEWHERE.
I DON'T THINK ANYONE WOULD STEAL A STUFFED TIGER. C'MON, LET'S GO LOOK.
BUT HOBBES IS SO TRUSTING..
SNIFF

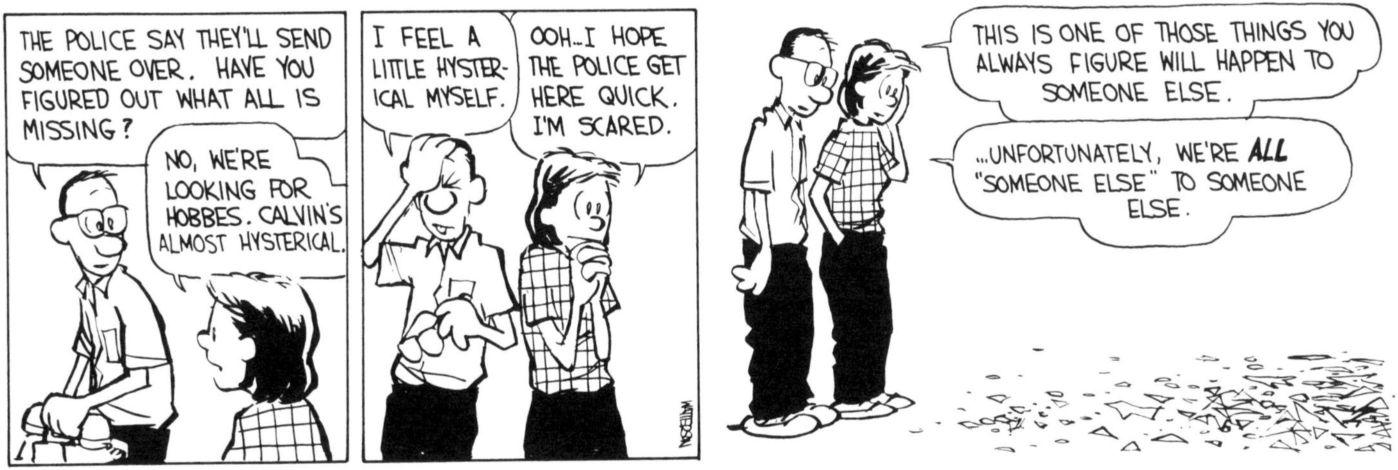
THE POLICE SAY THEY'LL SEND SOMEONE OVER. HAVE YOU FIGURED OUT WHAT ALL IS MISSING?
NO, WE'RE LOOKING FOR HOBBES. CALVIN'S ALMOST HYSTERICAL.
I FEEL A LITTLE HYSTERICAL MYSELF.
OOH...I HOPE THE POLICE GET HERE QUICK. I'M SCARED.
THIS IS ONE OF THOSE THINGS YOU ALWAYS FIGURE WILL HAPPEN TO SOMEONE ELSE.
...UNFORTUNATELY, WE'RE ALL "SOMEONE ELSE" TO SOMEONE ELSE.

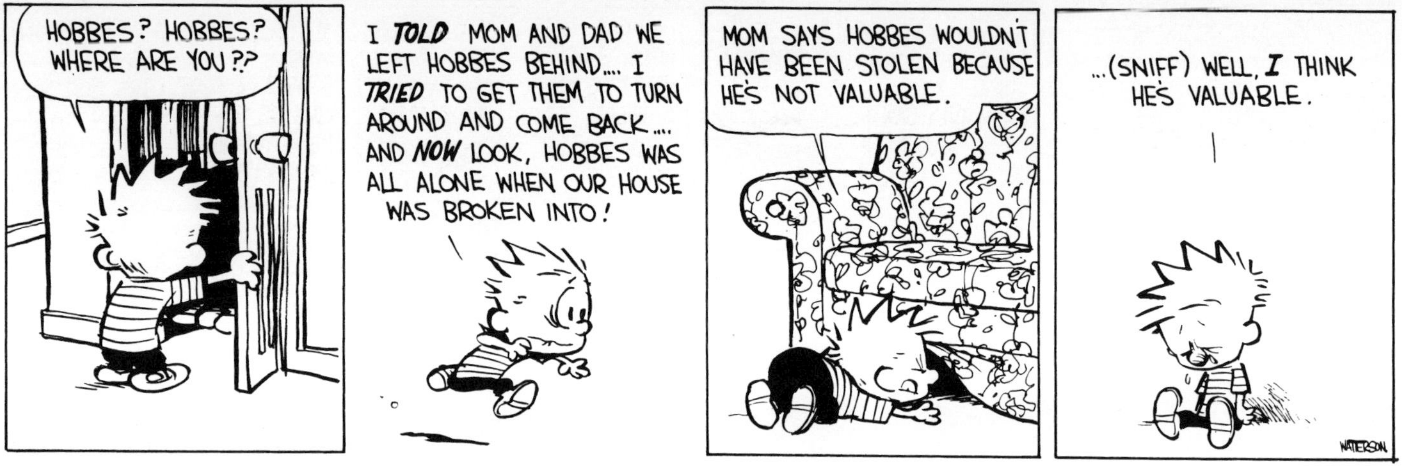
HOBBES? HOBBES? WHERE ARE YOU??
I TOLD MOM AND DAD WE LEFT HOBBES BEHIND.... I TRIED TO GET THEM TO TURN AROUND AND COME BACK.... AND NOW LOOK, HOBBES WAS ALL ALONE WHEN OUR HOUSE WAS BROKEN INTO!
MOM SAYS HOBBES WOULDN'T HAVE BEEN STOLEN BECAUSE HE'S NOT VALUABLE.
...(SNIFF) WELL, I THINK HE'S VALUABLE.

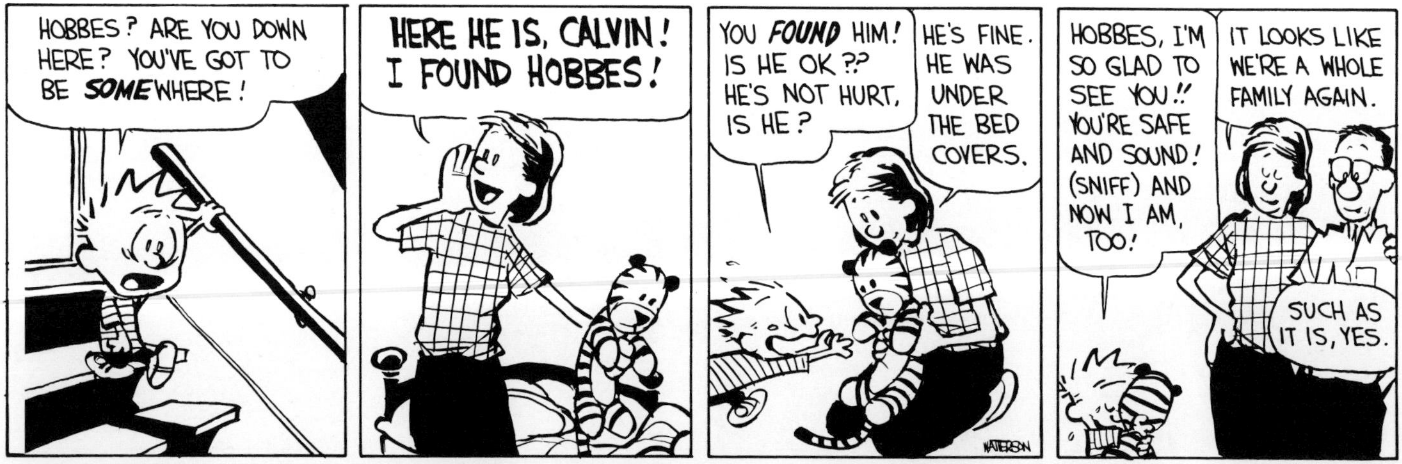
HOBBES? ARE YOU DOWN HERE? YOU'VE GOT TO BE SOMEWHERE!
HERE HE IS, CALVIN! I FOUND HOBBES!
YOU FOUND HIM! IS HE OK?? HE'S NOT HURT, IS HE?
HE'S FINE. HE WAS UNDER THE BED COVERS.
HOBBES, I'M SO GLAD TO SEE YOU!! YOU'RE SAFE AND SOUND! (SNIFF) AND NOW I AM, TOO!
IT LOOKS LIKE WE'RE A WHOLE FAMILY AGAIN.
SUCH AS IT IS, YES.

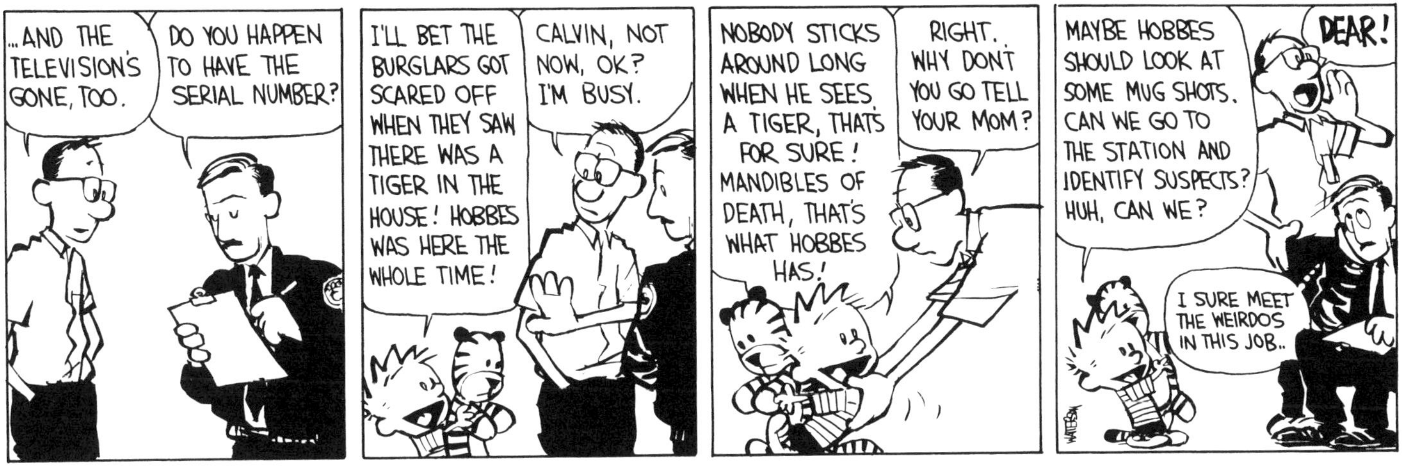
...AND THE TELEVISION'S GONE, TOO.
DO YOU HAPPEN TO HAVE THE SERIAL NUMBER?
I'LL BET THE BURGLARS GOT SCARED OFF WHEN THEY SAW THERE WAS A TIGER IN THE HOUSE! HOBBES WAS HERE THE WHOLE TIME!
CALVIN, NOT NOW, OK? I'M BUSY.
NOBODY STICKS AROUND LONG WHEN HE SEES A TIGER, THAT'S FOR SURE! MANDIBLES OF DEATH, THAT'S WHAT HOBBES HAS!
RIGHT. WHY DON'T YOU GO TELL YOUR MOM?
MAYBE HOBBES SHOULD LOOK AT SOME MUG SHOTS. CAN WE GO TO THE STATION AND IDENTIFY SUSPECTS? HUH, CAN WE?
DEAR!
I SURE MEET THE WEIRDOS IN THIS JOB..
WATTERSON

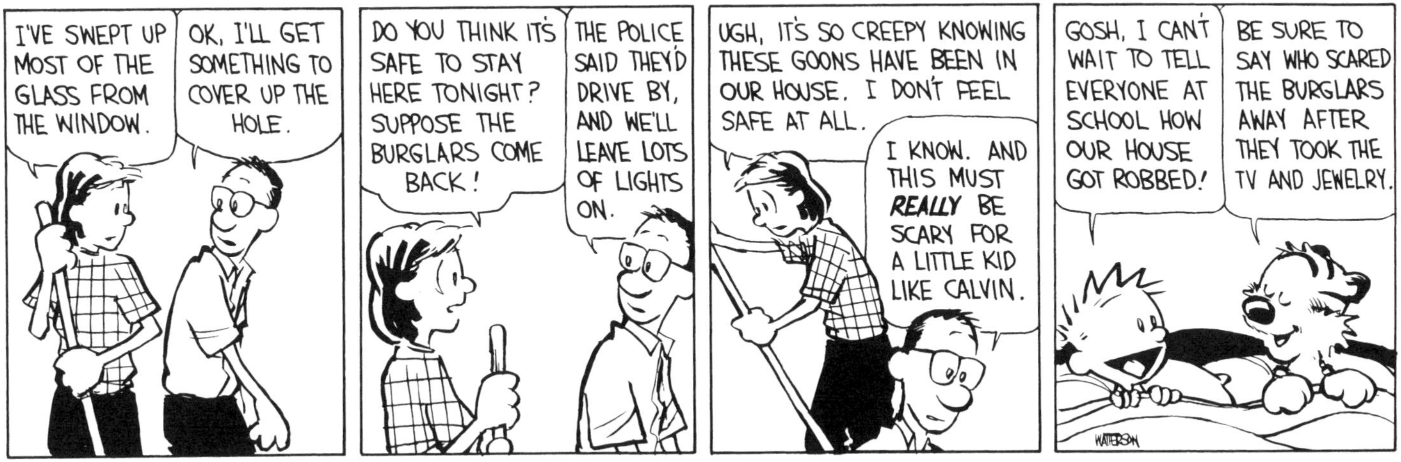
I'VE SWEPT UP MOST OF THE GLASS FROM THE WINDOW.
OK, I'LL GET SOMETHING TO COVER UP THE HOLE.
DO YOU THINK IT'S SAFE TO STAY HERE TONIGHT? SUPPOSE THE BURGLARS COME BACK!
THE POLICE SAID THEY'D DRIVE BY, AND WE'LL LEAVE LOTS OF LIGHTS ON.
UGH, IT'S SO CREEPY KNOWING THESE GOONS HAVE BEEN IN OUR HOUSE. I DON'T FEEL SAFE AT ALL.
I KNOW. AND THIS MUST REALLY BE SCARY FOR A LITTLE KID LIKE CALVIN.
GOSH, I CAN'T WAIT TO TELL EVERYONE AT SCHOOL HOW OUR HOUSE GOT ROBBED!
BE SURE TO SAY WHO SCARED THE BURGLARS AWAY AFTER THEY TOOK THE TV AND JEWELRY.
WATTERSON

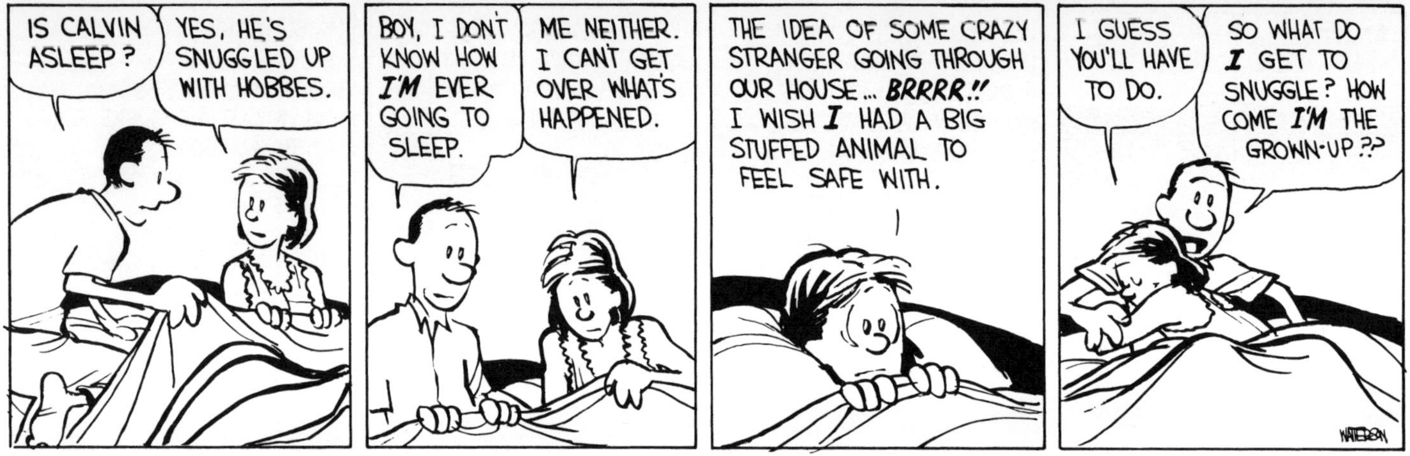
IS CALVIN ASLEEP?
YES, HE'S SNUGGLED UP WITH HOBBES.
BOY, I DON'T KNOW HOW *I'M* EVER GOING TO SLEEP.
ME NEITHER. I CAN'T GET OVER WHAT'S HAPPENED.
THE IDEA OF SOME CRAZY STRANGER GOING THROUGH OUR HOUSE... **BRRRR.!!** I WISH *I* HAD A BIG STUFFED ANIMAL TO FEEL SAFE WITH.
I GUESS YOU'LL HAVE TO DO.
SO WHAT DO *I* GET TO SNUGGLE? HOW COME *I'M* THE GROWN-UP??
WATTERSON

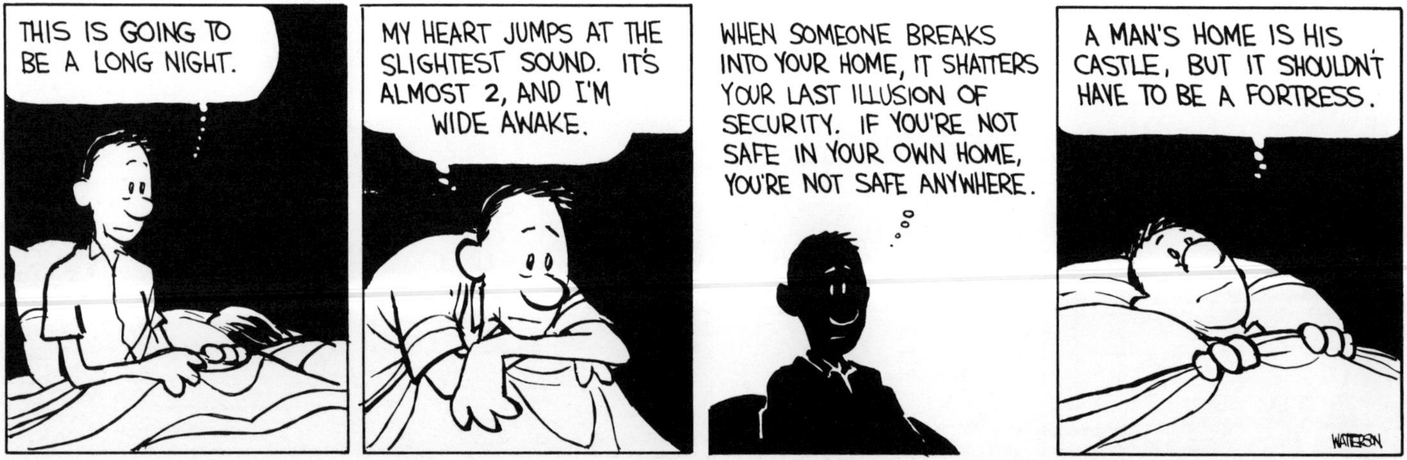
THIS IS GOING TO BE A LONG NIGHT.
MY HEART JUMPS AT THE SLIGHTEST SOUND. IT'S ALMOST 2, AND I'M WIDE AWAKE.
WHEN SOMEONE BREAKS INTO YOUR HOME, IT SHATTERS YOUR LAST ILLUSION OF SECURITY. IF YOU'RE NOT SAFE IN YOUR OWN HOME, YOU'RE NOT SAFE ANYWHERE.
A MAN'S HOME IS HIS CASTLE, BUT IT SHOULDN'T HAVE TO BE A FORTRESS.
WATTERSON

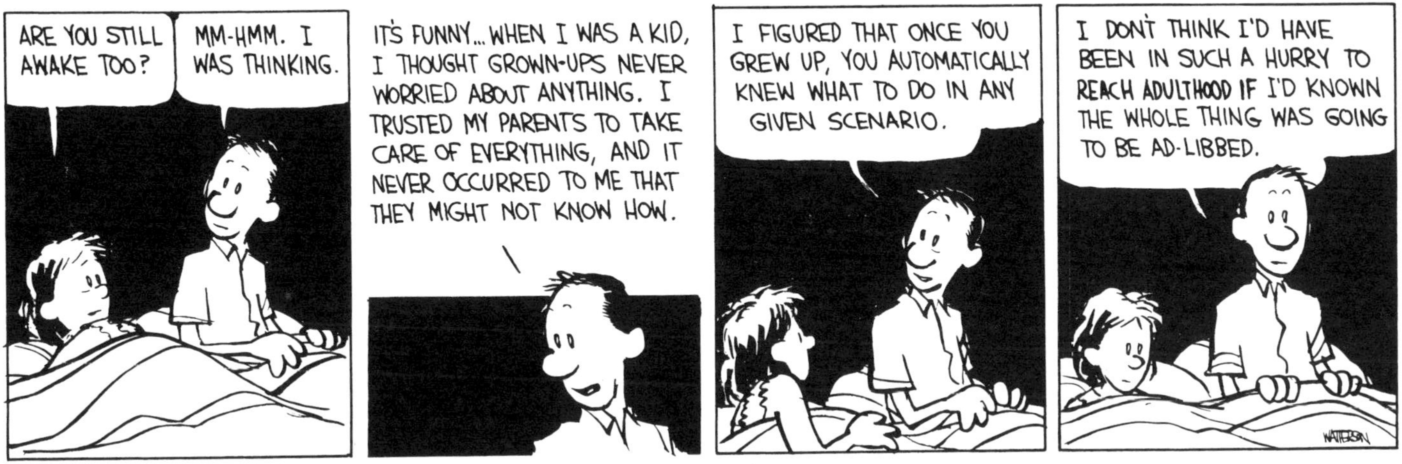
ARE YOU STILL AWAKE TOO?
MM-HMM. I WAS THINKING.
IT'S FUNNY... WHEN I WAS A KID, I THOUGHT GROWN-UPS NEVER WORRIED ABOUT ANYTHING. I TRUSTED MY PARENTS TO TAKE CARE OF EVERYTHING, AND IT NEVER OCCURRED TO ME THAT THEY MIGHT NOT KNOW HOW.
I FIGURED THAT ONCE YOU GREW UP, YOU AUTOMATICALLY KNEW WHAT TO DO IN ANY GIVEN SCENARIO.
I DON'T THINK I'D HAVE BEEN IN SUCH A HURRY TO REACH ADULTHOOD IF I'D KNOWN THE WHOLE THING WAS GOING TO BE AD-LIBBED.
WATTERSON

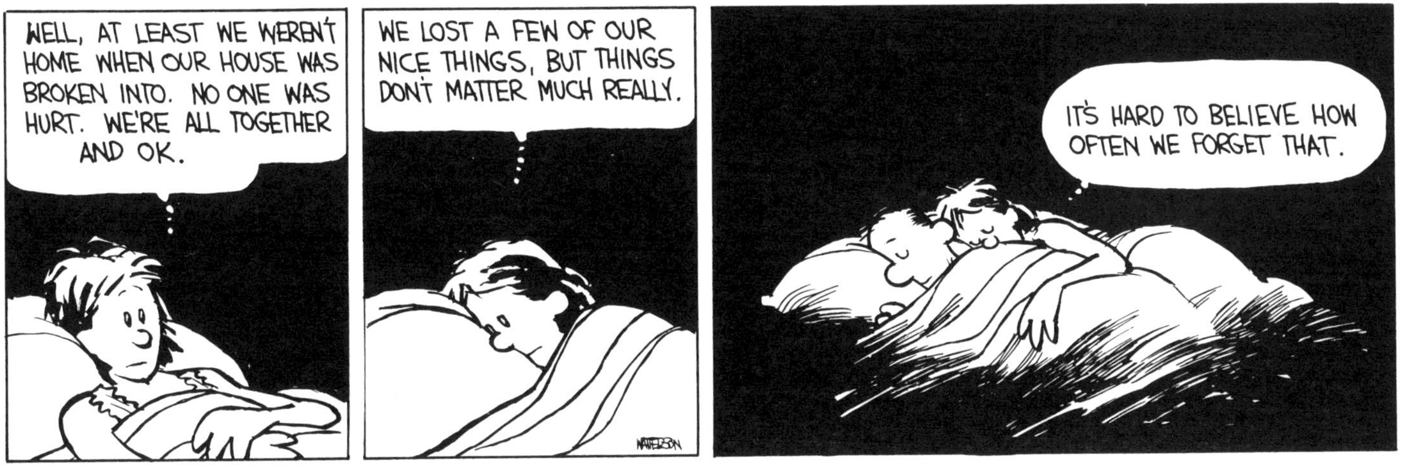
WELL, AT LEAST WE WEREN'T HOME WHEN OUR HOUSE WAS BROKEN INTO. NO ONE WAS HURT. WE'RE ALL TOGETHER AND OK.
WE LOST A FEW OF OUR NICE THINGS, BUT THINGS DON'T MATTER MUCH REALLY.
WATTERSON
IT'S HARD TO BELIEVE HOW OFTEN WE FORGET THAT.

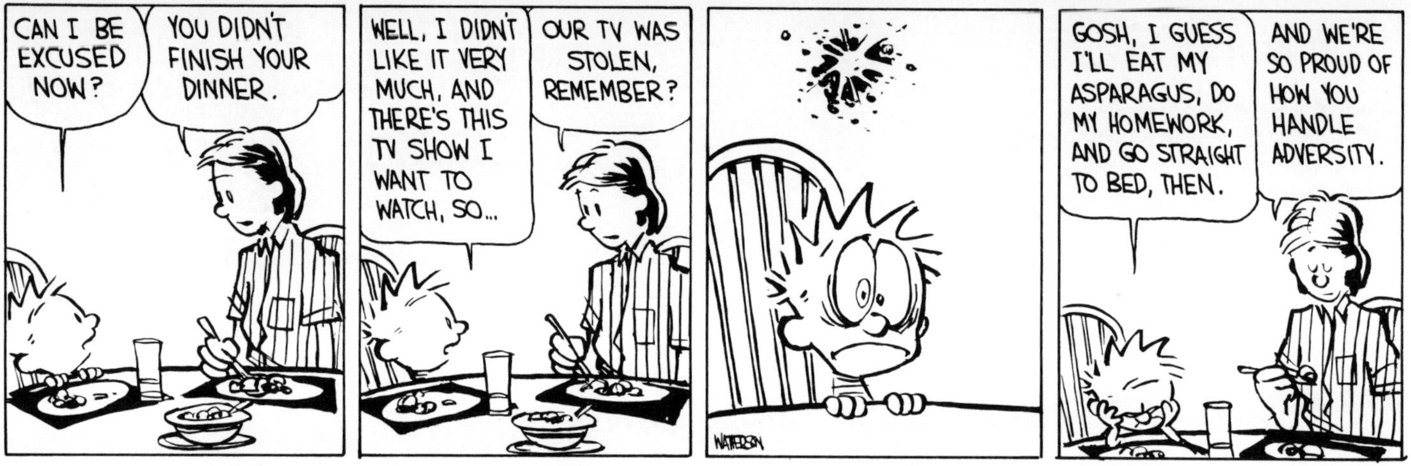
CAN I BE EXCUSED NOW?
YOU DIDN'T FINISH YOUR DINNER.
WELL, I DIDN'T LIKE IT VERY MUCH, AND THERE'S THIS TV SHOW I WANT TO WATCH, SO...
OUR TV WAS STOLEN, REMEMBER?
GOSH, I GUESS I'LL EAT MY ASPARAGUS, DO MY HOMEWORK, AND GO STRAIGHT TO BED, THEN.
AND WE'RE SO PROUD OF HOW YOU HANDLE ADVERSITY.

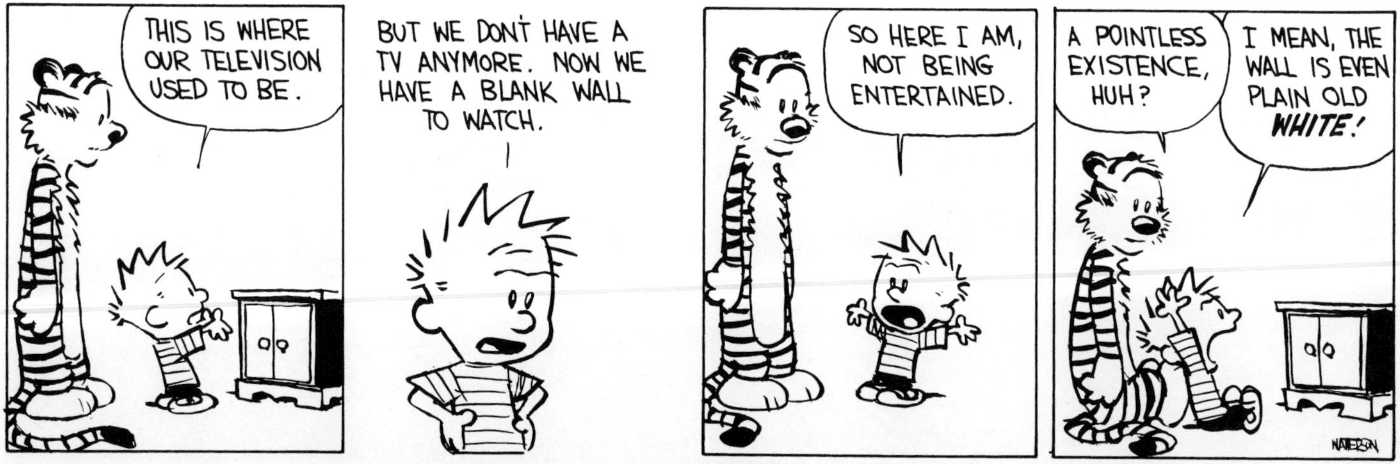
THIS IS WHERE OUR TELEVISION USED TO BE.
BUT WE DON'T HAVE A TV ANYMORE. NOW WE HAVE A BLANK WALL TO WATCH.
SO HERE I AM, NOT BEING ENTERTAINED.
A POINTLESS EXISTENCE, HUH?
I MEAN, THE WALL IS EVEN PLAIN OLD ***WHITE!***

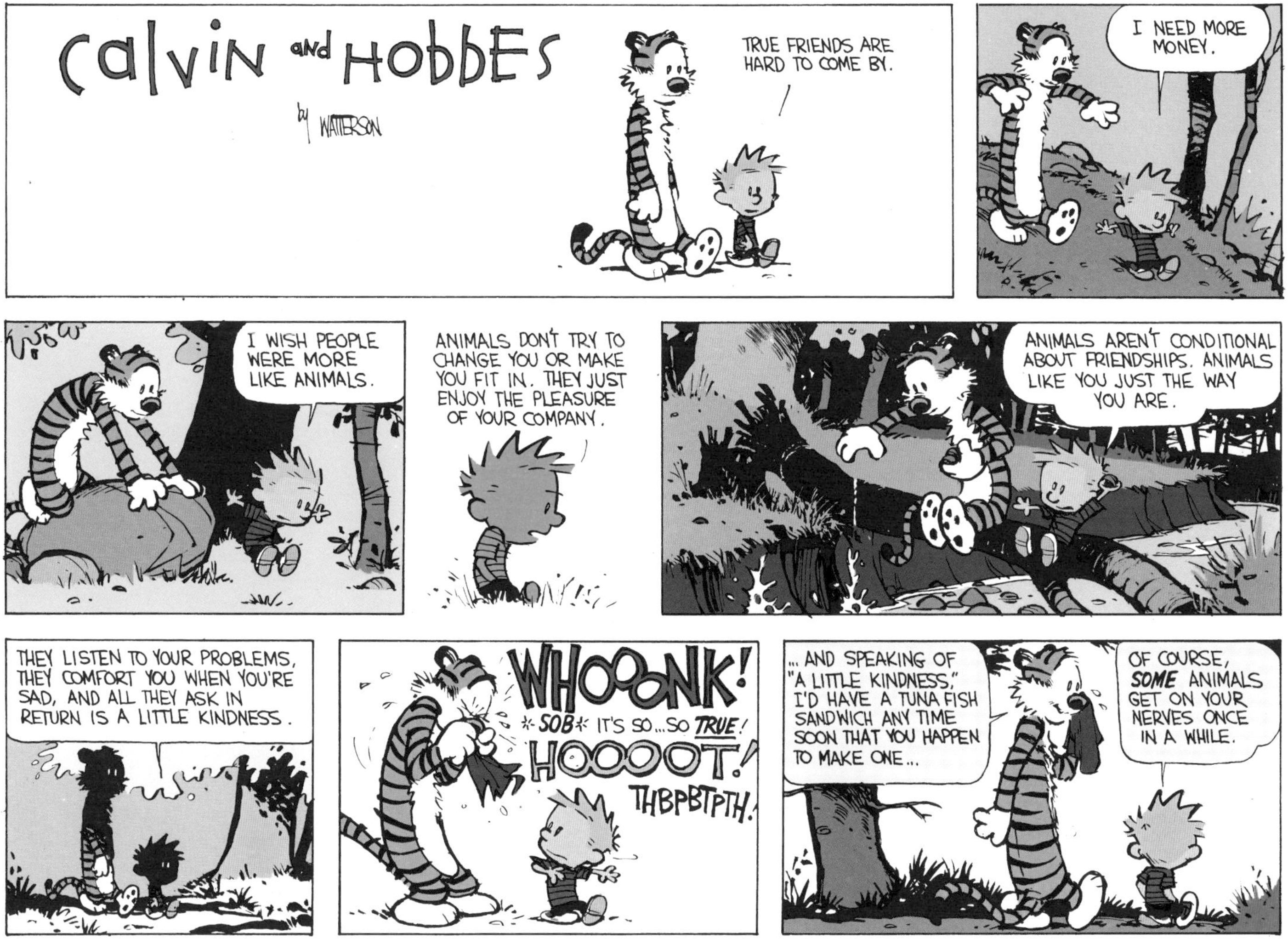
Calvin and Hobbes
by WATTERSON
TRUE FRIENDS ARE HARD TO COME BY.
I NEED MORE MONEY.
I WISH PEOPLE WERE MORE LIKE ANIMALS.
ANIMALS DON'T TRY TO CHANGE YOU OR MAKE YOU FIT IN. THEY JUST ENJOY THE PLEASURE OF YOUR COMPANY.
ANIMALS AREN'T CONDITIONAL ABOUT FRIENDSHIPS. ANIMALS LIKE YOU JUST THE WAY YOU ARE.
THEY LISTEN TO YOUR PROBLEMS, THEY COMFORT YOU WHEN YOU'RE SAD, AND ALL THEY ASK IN RETURN IS A LITTLE KINDNESS.
WHOOONK!
SOB IT'S SO...SO TRUE!
HOOOOT!
THBPBTPTH!
...AND SPEAKING OF "A LITTLE KINDNESS," I'D HAVE A TUNA FISH SANDWICH ANY TIME SOON THAT YOU HAPPEN TO MAKE ONE...
OF COURSE, SOME ANIMALS GET ON YOUR NERVES ONCE IN A WHILE.

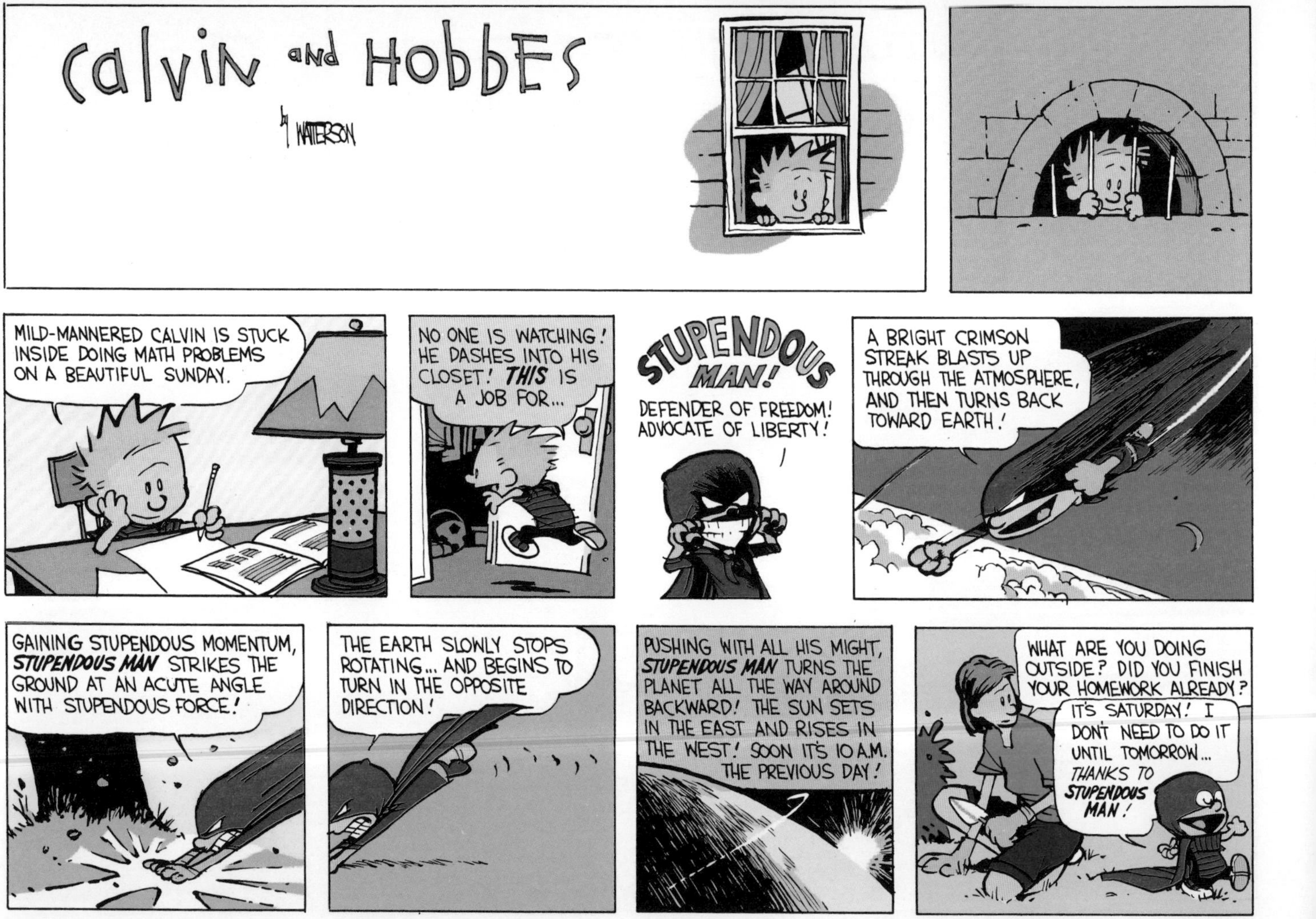
Calvin and HOBBES
by WATTERSON
MILD-MANNERED CALVIN IS STUCK INSIDE DOING MATH PROBLEMS ON A BEAUTIFUL SUNDAY.
NO ONE IS WATCHING! HE DASHES INTO HIS CLOSET! THIS IS A JOB FOR...
STUPENDOUS MAN!
DEFENDER OF FREEDOM! ADVOCATE OF LIBERTY!
A BRIGHT CRIMSON STREAK BLASTS UP THROUGH THE ATMOSPHERE, AND THEN TURNS BACK TOWARD EARTH!
GAINING STUPENDOUS MOMENTUM, STUPENDOUS MAN STRIKES THE GROUND AT AN ACUTE ANGLE WITH STUPENDOUS FORCE!
THE EARTH SLOWLY STOPS ROTATING... AND BEGINS TO TURN IN THE OPPOSITE DIRECTION!
PUSHING WITH ALL HIS MIGHT, STUPENDOUS MAN TURNS THE PLANET ALL THE WAY AROUND BACKWARD! THE SUN SETS IN THE EAST AND RISES IN THE WEST! SOON IT'S 10 A.M. THE PREVIOUS DAY!
WHAT ARE YOU DOING OUTSIDE? DID YOU FINISH YOUR HOMEWORK ALREADY?
IT'S SATURDAY! I DON'T NEED TO DO IT UNTIL TOMORROW... THANKS TO STUPENDOUS MAN!

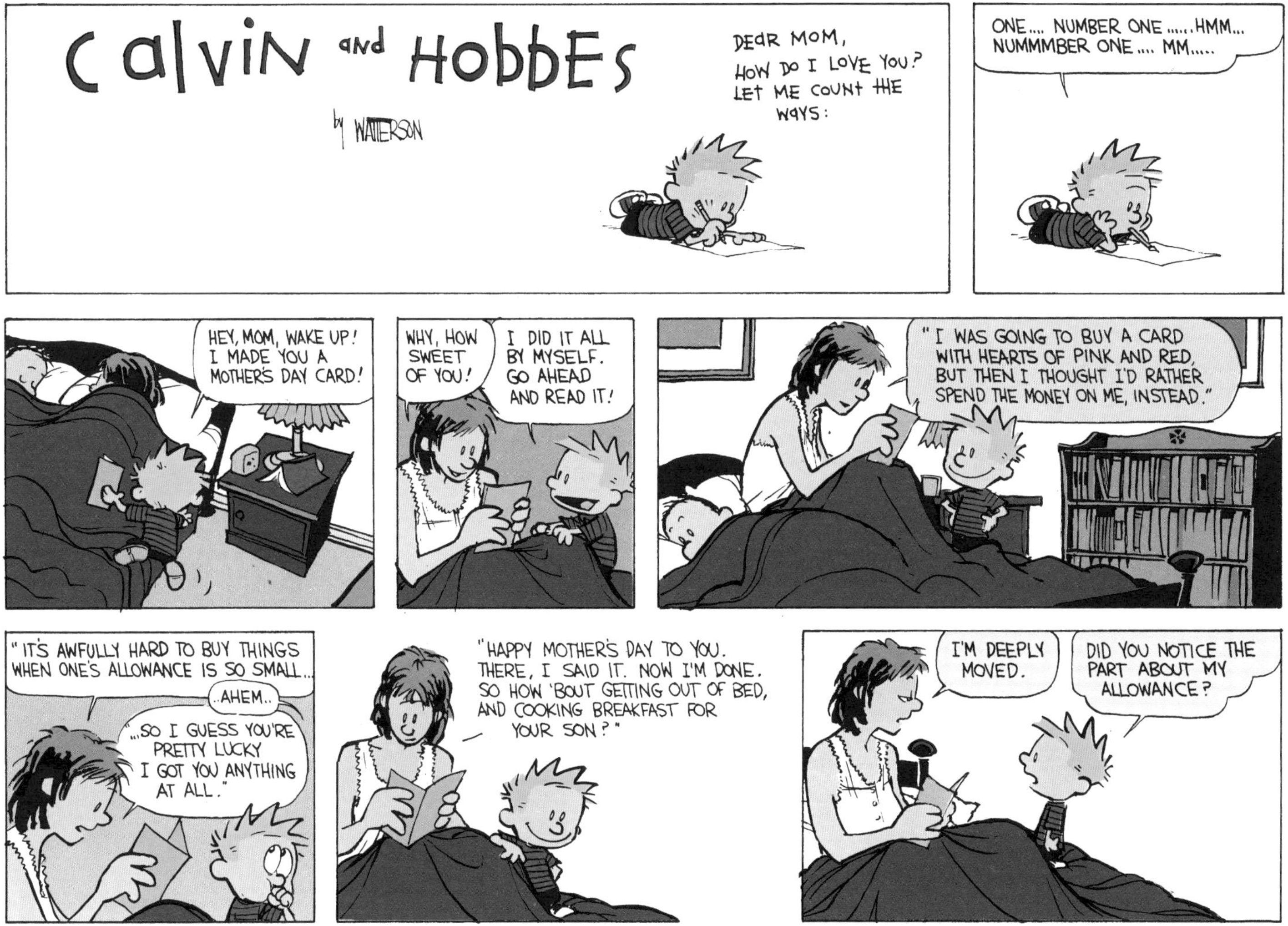
Calvin and HobbEs
by WATTERSON
DEAR MOM,
HOW DO I LOVE YOU? LET ME COUNT THE WAYS:
ONE.... NUMBER ONE ......HMM... NUMMMBER ONE..... MM.....
HEY, MOM, WAKE UP! I MADE YOU A MOTHER'S DAY CARD!
WHY, HOW SWEET OF YOU!
I DID IT ALL BY MYSELF. GO AHEAD AND READ IT!
"I WAS GOING TO BUY A CARD WITH HEARTS OF PINK AND RED, BUT THEN I THOUGHT I'D RATHER SPEND THE MONEY ON ME, INSTEAD."
"IT'S AWFULLY HARD TO BUY THINGS WHEN ONE'S ALLOWANCE IS SO SMALL...
..AHEM..
...SO I GUESS YOU'RE PRETTY LUCKY I GOT YOU ANYTHING AT ALL."
"HAPPY MOTHER'S DAY TO YOU. THERE, I SAID IT. NOW I'M DONE. SO HOW 'BOUT GETTING OUT OF BED, AND COOKING BREAKFAST FOR YOUR SON?"
I'M DEEPLY MOVED.
DID YOU NOTICE THE PART ABOUT MY ALLOWANCE?

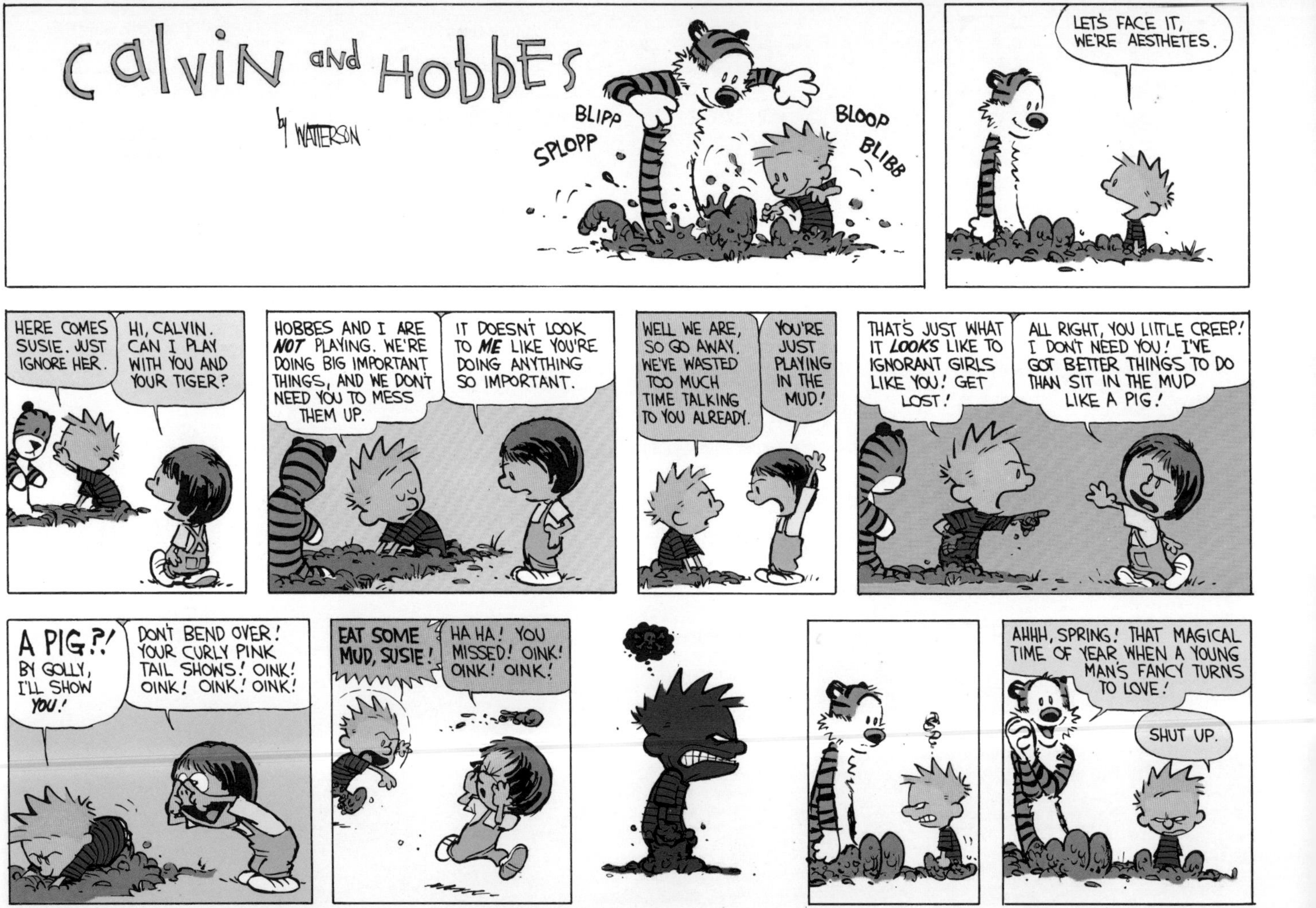

Calvin and HOBBES
by WATTERSON
BLIPP
SPLOPP
BLOOP
BLIBB
LET'S FACE IT, WE'RE AESTHETES.
HERE COMES SUSIE. JUST IGNORE HER.
HI, CALVIN. CAN I PLAY WITH YOU AND YOUR TIGER?
HOBBES AND I ARE NOT PLAYING. WE'RE DOING BIG IMPORTANT THINGS, AND WE DON'T NEED YOU TO MESS THEM UP.
IT DOESN'T LOOK TO ME LIKE YOU'RE DOING ANYTHING SO IMPORTANT.
WELL WE ARE, SO GO AWAY. WE'VE WASTED TOO MUCH TIME TALKING TO YOU ALREADY.
YOU'RE JUST PLAYING IN THE MUD!
THAT'S JUST WHAT IT LOOKS LIKE TO IGNORANT GIRLS LIKE YOU! GET LOST!
ALL RIGHT, YOU LITTLE CREEP! I DON'T NEED YOU! I'VE GOT BETTER THINGS TO DO THAN SIT IN THE MUD LIKE A PIG!
A PIG?! BY GOLLY, I'LL SHOW YOU!
DON'T BEND OVER! YOUR CURLY PINK TAIL SHOWS! OINK! OINK! OINK! OINK!
EAT SOME MUD, SUSIE!
HA HA! YOU MISSED! OINK! OINK! OINK!
AHHH, SPRING! THAT MAGICAL TIME OF YEAR WHEN A YOUNG MAN'S FANCY TURNS TO LOVE!
SHUT UP.

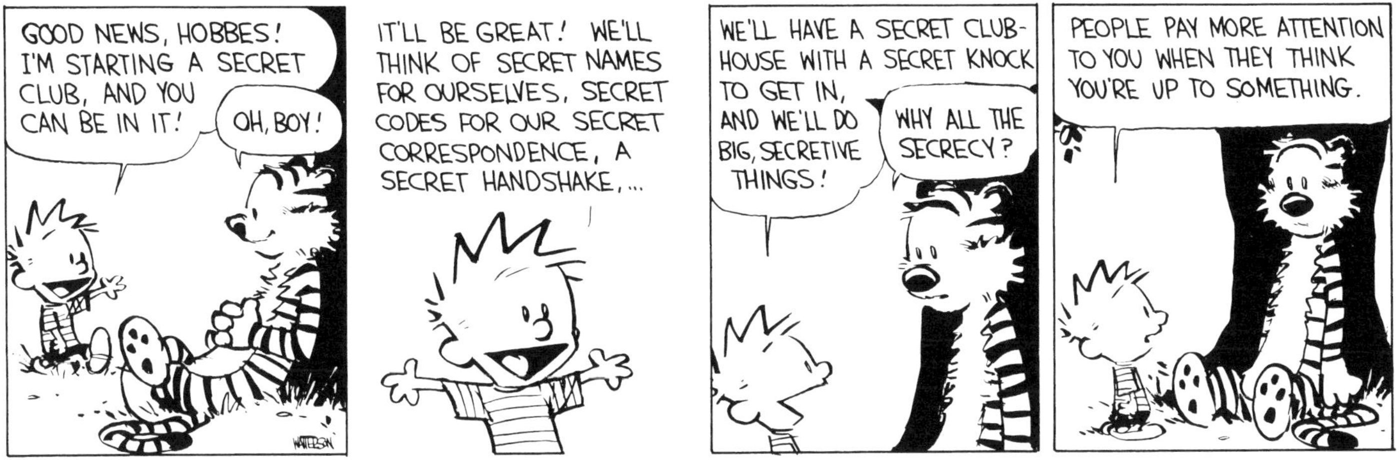
GOOD NEWS, HOBBES! I'M STARTING A SECRET CLUB, AND YOU CAN BE IN IT!
OH, BOY!
IT'LL BE GREAT! WE'LL THINK OF SECRET NAMES FOR OURSELVES, SECRET CODES FOR OUR SECRET CORRESPONDENCE, A SECRET HANDSHAKE,...
WE'LL HAVE A SECRET CLUB-HOUSE WITH A SECRET KNOCK TO GET IN, AND WE'LL DO BIG, SECRETIVE THINGS!
WHY ALL THE SECRECY?
PEOPLE PAY MORE ATTENTION TO YOU WHEN THEY THINK YOU'RE UP TO SOMETHING.

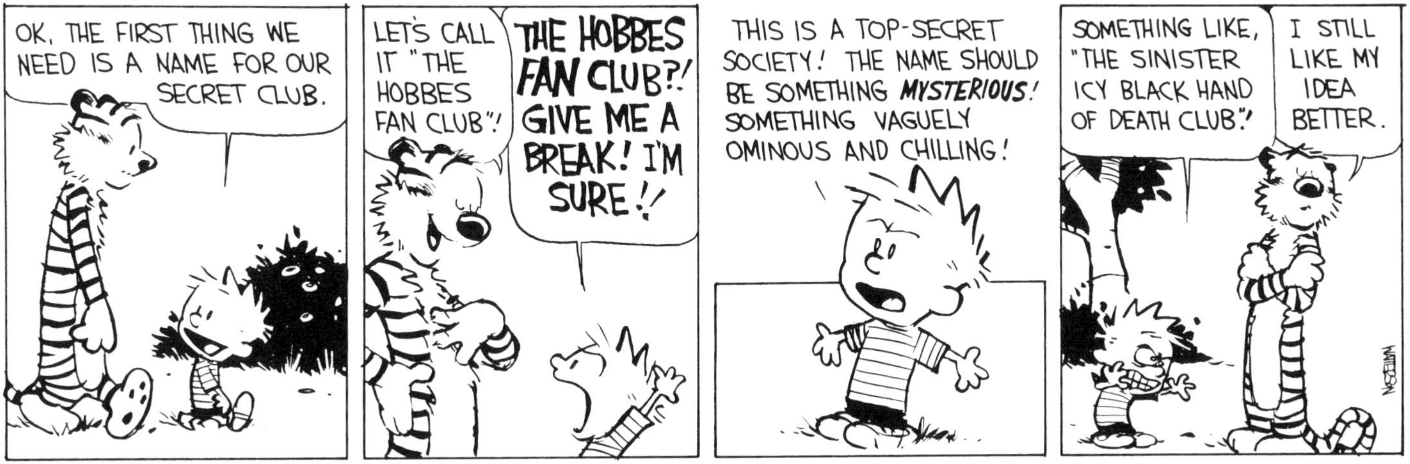
OK, THE FIRST THING WE NEED IS A NAME FOR OUR SECRET CLUB.
LET'S CALL IT "THE HOBBES FAN CLUB"!
THE HOBBES FAN CLUB?! GIVE ME A BREAK! I'M SURE!!
THIS IS A TOP-SECRET SOCIETY! THE NAME SHOULD BE SOMETHING *MYSTERIOUS*! SOMETHING VAGUELY OMINOUS AND CHILLING!
SOMETHING LIKE, "THE SINISTER ICY BLACK HAND OF DEATH CLUB"!
I STILL LIKE MY IDEA BETTER.

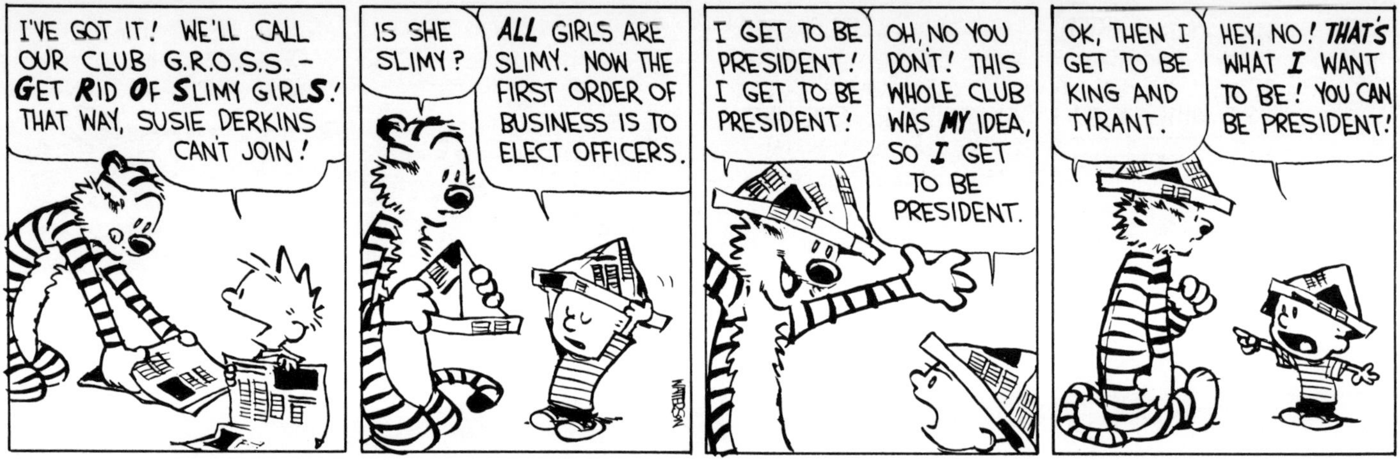
I'VE GOT IT! WE'LL CALL OUR CLUB G.R.O.S.S.– GET RID OF SLIMY GIRLS! THAT WAY, SUSIE DERKINS CAN'T JOIN!
IS SHE SLIMY?
ALL GIRLS ARE SLIMY. NOW THE FIRST ORDER OF BUSINESS IS TO ELECT OFFICERS.
WATTERSON
I GET TO BE PRESIDENT! I GET TO BE PRESIDENT!
OH, NO YOU DON'T! THIS WHOLE CLUB WAS MY IDEA, SO I GET TO BE PRESIDENT.
OK, THEN I GET TO BE KING AND TYRANT.
HEY, NO! THAT'S WHAT I WANT TO BE! YOU CAN BE PRESIDENT!

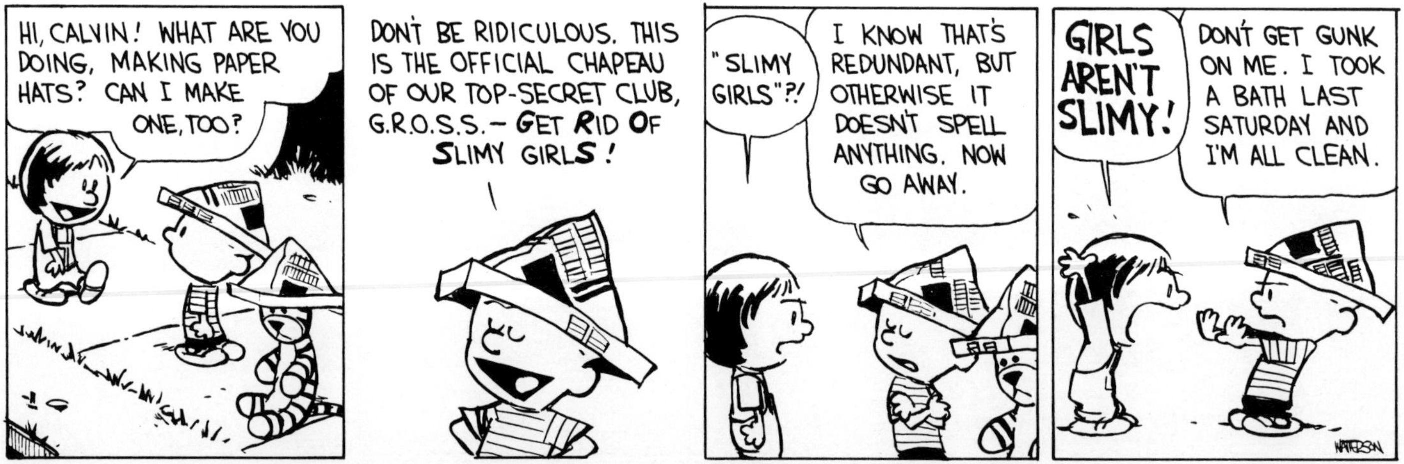
HI, CALVIN! WHAT ARE YOU DOING, MAKING PAPER HATS? CAN I MAKE ONE, TOO?
DON'T BE RIDICULOUS. THIS IS THE OFFICIAL CHAPEAU OF OUR TOP-SECRET CLUB, G.R.O.S.S.– GET RID OF SLIMY GIRLS!
"SLIMY GIRLS"?!
I KNOW THAT'S REDUNDANT, BUT OTHERWISE IT DOESN'T SPELL ANYTHING. NOW GO AWAY.
GIRLS AREN'T SLIMY!
DON'T GET GUNK ON ME. I TOOK A BATH LAST SATURDAY AND I'M ALL CLEAN.
WATTERSON

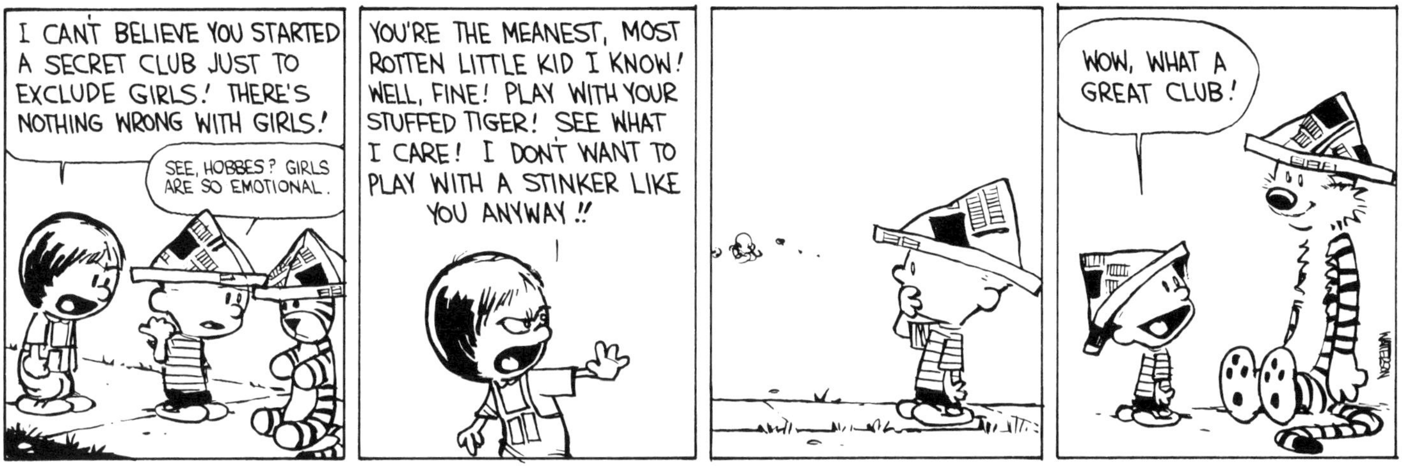
I CAN'T BELIEVE YOU STARTED A SECRET CLUB JUST TO EXCLUDE GIRLS! THERE'S NOTHING WRONG WITH GIRLS!
SEE, HOBBES? GIRLS ARE SO EMOTIONAL.
YOU'RE THE MEANEST, MOST ROTTEN LITTLE KID I KNOW! WELL, FINE! PLAY WITH YOUR STUFFED TIGER! SEE WHAT I CARE! I DON'T WANT TO PLAY WITH A STINKER LIKE YOU ANYWAY!!
WOW, WHAT A GREAT CLUB!

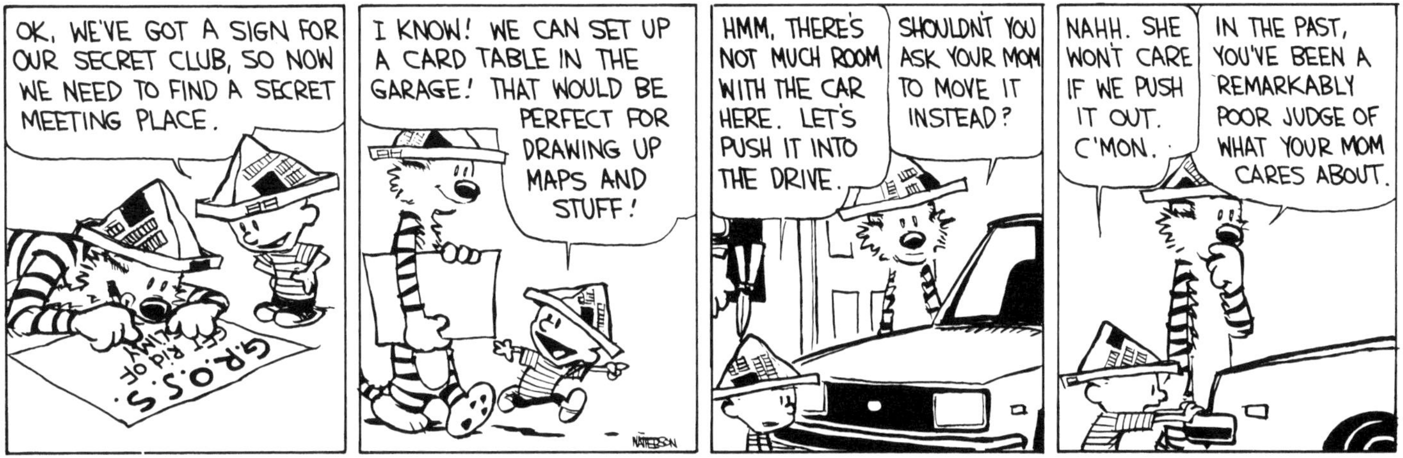
OK, WE'VE GOT A SIGN FOR OUR SECRET CLUB, SO NOW WE NEED TO FIND A SECRET MEETING PLACE.
G.R.O.S.S.
I KNOW! WE CAN SET UP A CARD TABLE IN THE GARAGE! THAT WOULD BE PERFECT FOR DRAWING UP MAPS AND STUFF!
HMM, THERE'S NOT MUCH ROOM WITH THE CAR HERE. LET'S PUSH IT INTO THE DRIVE.
SHOULDN'T YOU ASK YOUR MOM TO MOVE IT INSTEAD?
NAHH. SHE WON'T CARE IF WE PUSH IT OUT. C'MON.
IN THE PAST, YOU'VE BEEN A REMARKABLY POOR JUDGE OF WHAT YOUR MOM CARES ABOUT.

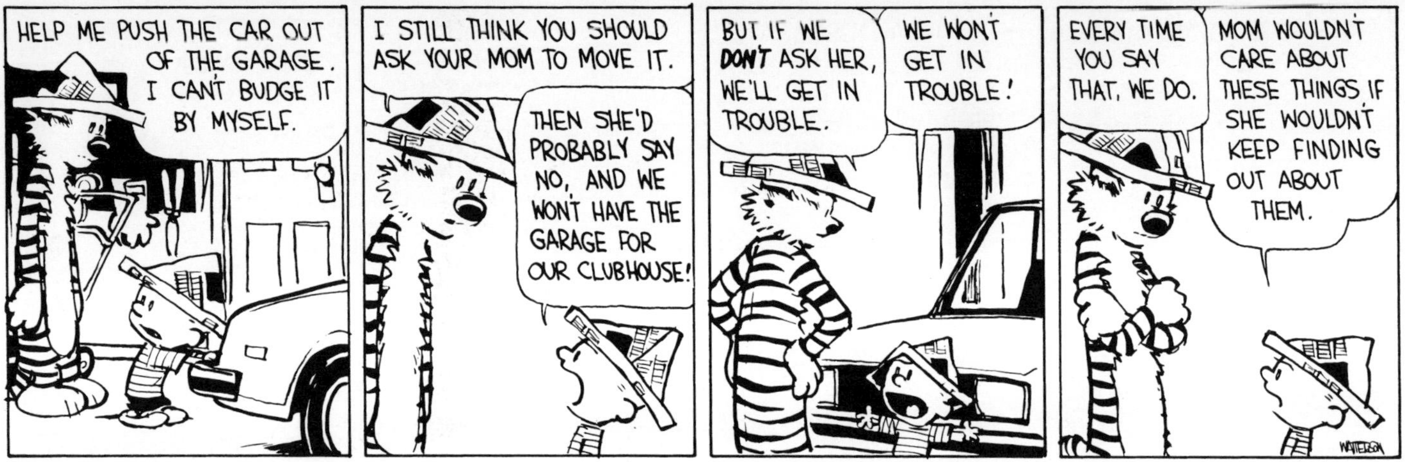
HELP ME PUSH THE CAR OUT OF THE GARAGE. I CAN'T BUDGE IT BY MYSELF.
I STILL THINK YOU SHOULD ASK YOUR MOM TO MOVE IT.
THEN SHE'D PROBABLY SAY NO, AND WE WON'T HAVE THE GARAGE FOR OUR CLUBHOUSE!
BUT IF WE **DON'T** ASK HER, WE'LL GET IN TROUBLE.
WE WON'T GET IN TROUBLE!
EVERY TIME YOU SAY THAT, WE DO.
MOM WOULDN'T CARE ABOUT THESE THINGS IF SHE WOULDN'T KEEP FINDING OUT ABOUT THEM.
WATTERSON

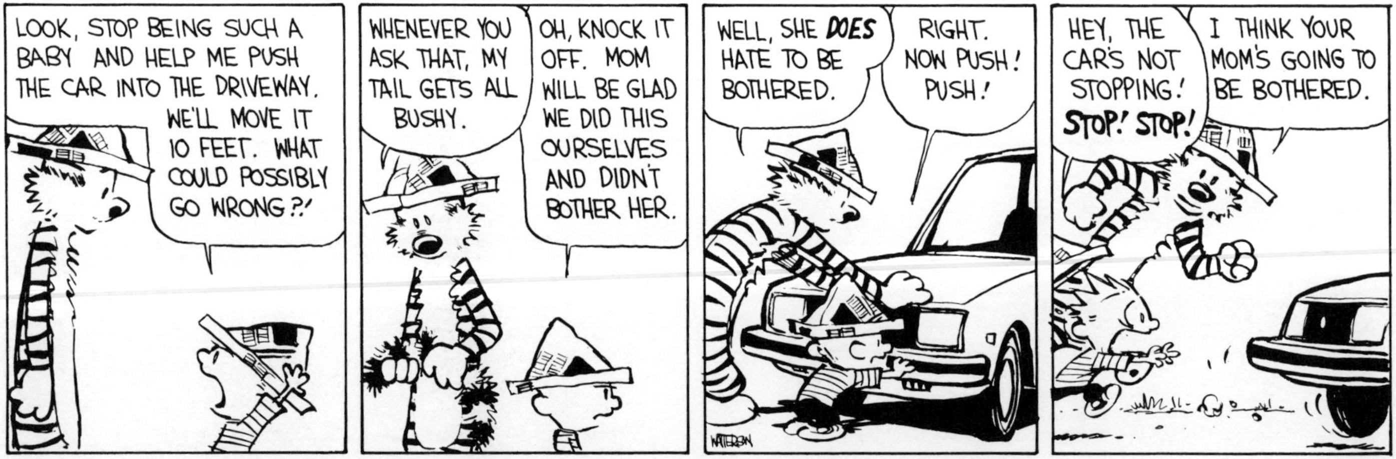
LOOK, STOP BEING SUCH A BABY AND HELP ME PUSH THE CAR INTO THE DRIVEWAY. WE'LL MOVE IT 10 FEET. WHAT COULD POSSIBLY GO WRONG?!
WHENEVER YOU ASK THAT, MY TAIL GETS ALL BUSHY.
OH, KNOCK IT OFF. MOM WILL BE GLAD WE DID THIS OURSELVES AND DIDN'T BOTHER HER.
WELL, SHE **DOES** HATE TO BE BOTHERED.
RIGHT. NOW PUSH! PUSH!
WATTERSON
HEY, THE CAR'S NOT STOPPING! **STOP! STOP!**
I THINK YOUR MOM'S GOING TO BE BOTHERED.

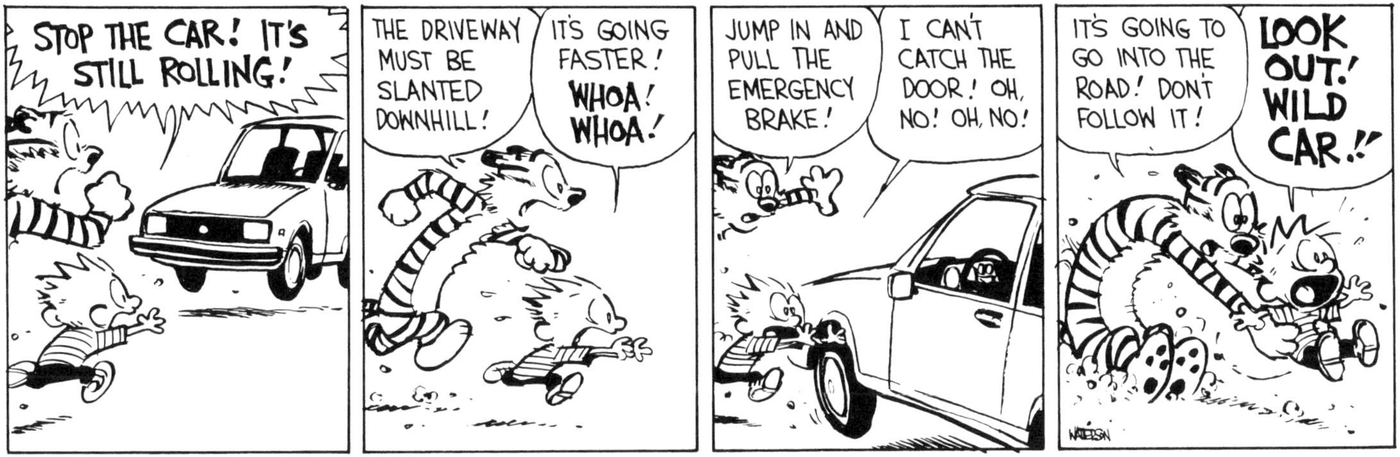
STOP THE CAR! IT'S STILL ROLLING!
THE DRIVEWAY MUST BE SLANTED DOWNHILL!
IT'S GOING FASTER! WHOA! WHOA!
JUMP IN AND PULL THE EMERGENCY BRAKE!
I CAN'T CATCH THE DOOR! OH, NO! OH, NO!
IT'S GOING TO GO INTO THE ROAD! DON'T FOLLOW IT!
LOOK OUT! WILD CAR.!!

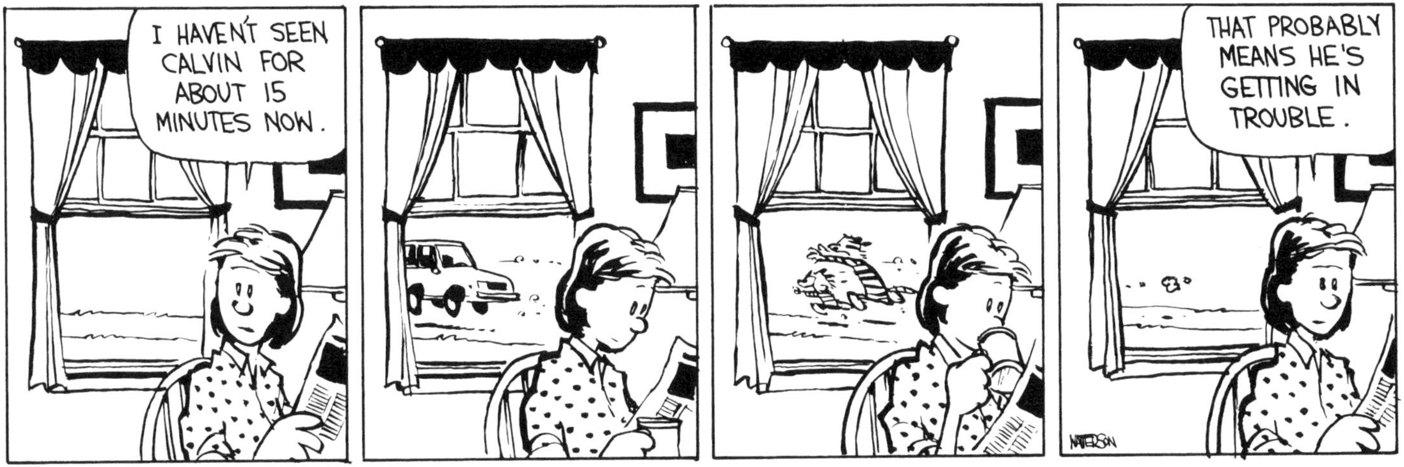
I HAVEN'T SEEN CALVIN FOR ABOUT 15 MINUTES NOW.
THAT PROBABLY MEANS HE'S GETTING IN TROUBLE.

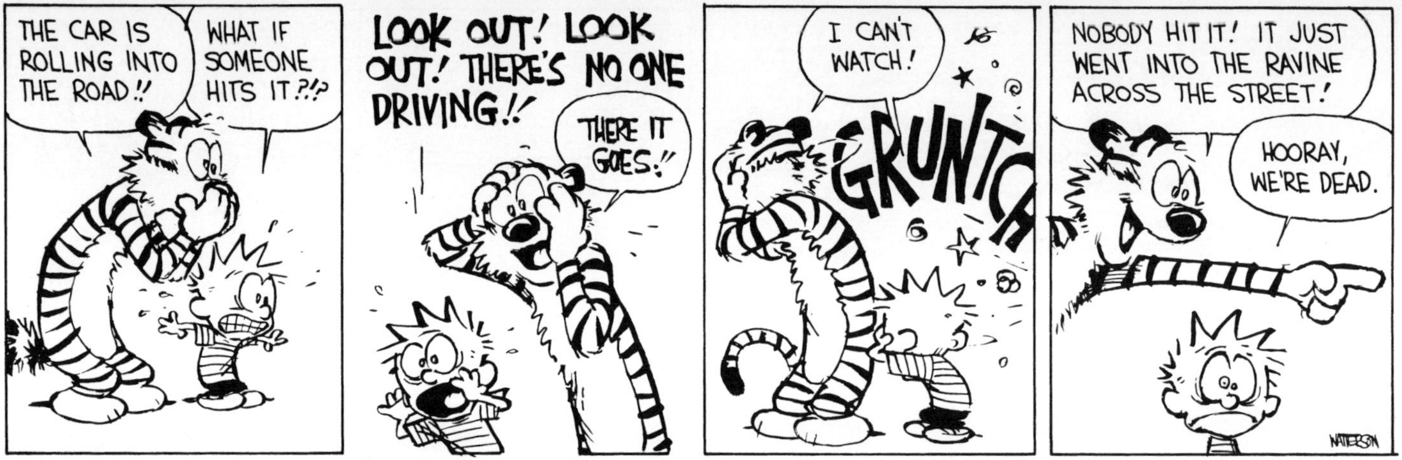
THE CAR IS ROLLING INTO THE ROAD!!
WHAT IF SOMEONE HITS IT?!?
LOOK OUT! LOOK OUT! THERE'S NO ONE DRIVING!!
THERE IT GOES!!
I CAN'T WATCH!
GRUNTCH
NOBODY HIT IT! IT JUST WENT INTO THE RAVINE ACROSS THE STREET!
HOORAY, WE'RE DEAD.
WATTERSON

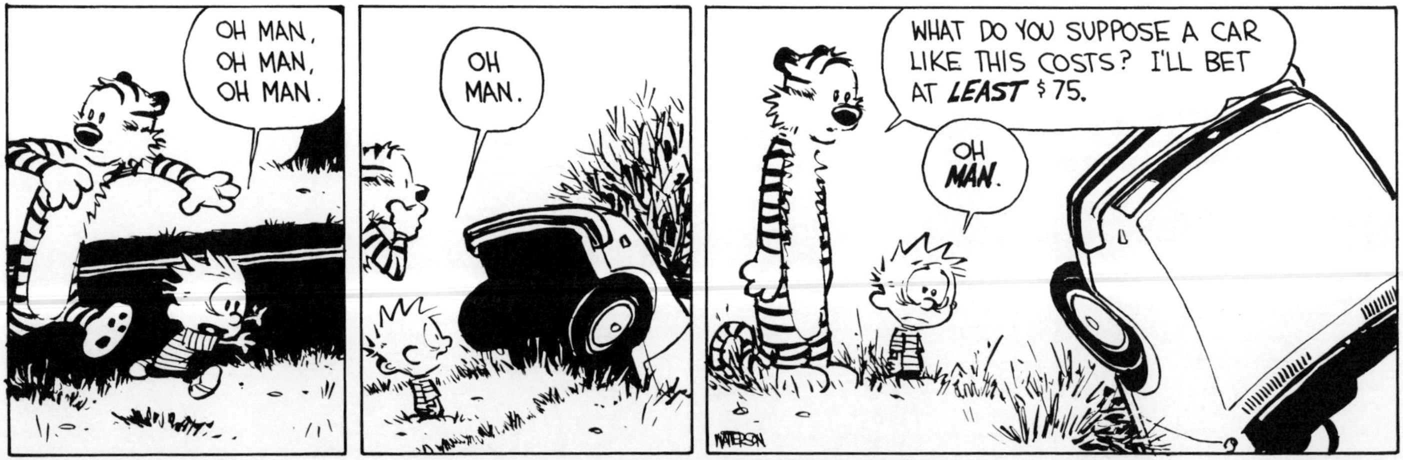
OH MAN, OH MAN, OH MAN.
OH MAN.
WHAT DO YOU SUPPOSE A CAR LIKE THIS COSTS? I'LL BET AT LEAST $75.
OH MAN.
WATTERSON

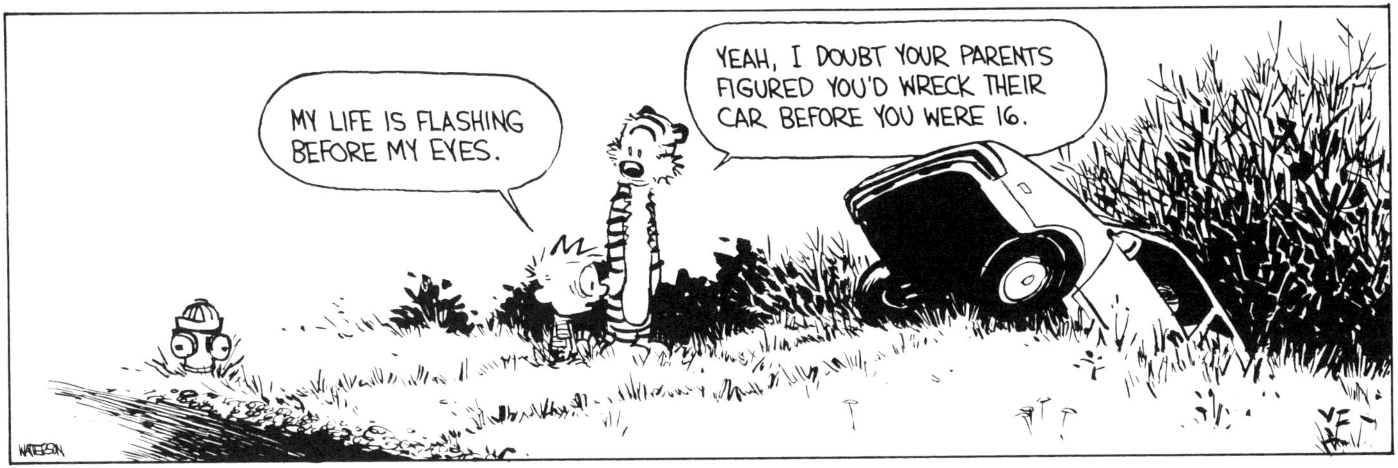
MY LIFE IS FLASHING BEFORE MY EYES.
YEAH, I DOUBT YOUR PARENTS FIGURED YOU'D WRECK THEIR CAR BEFORE YOU WERE 16.

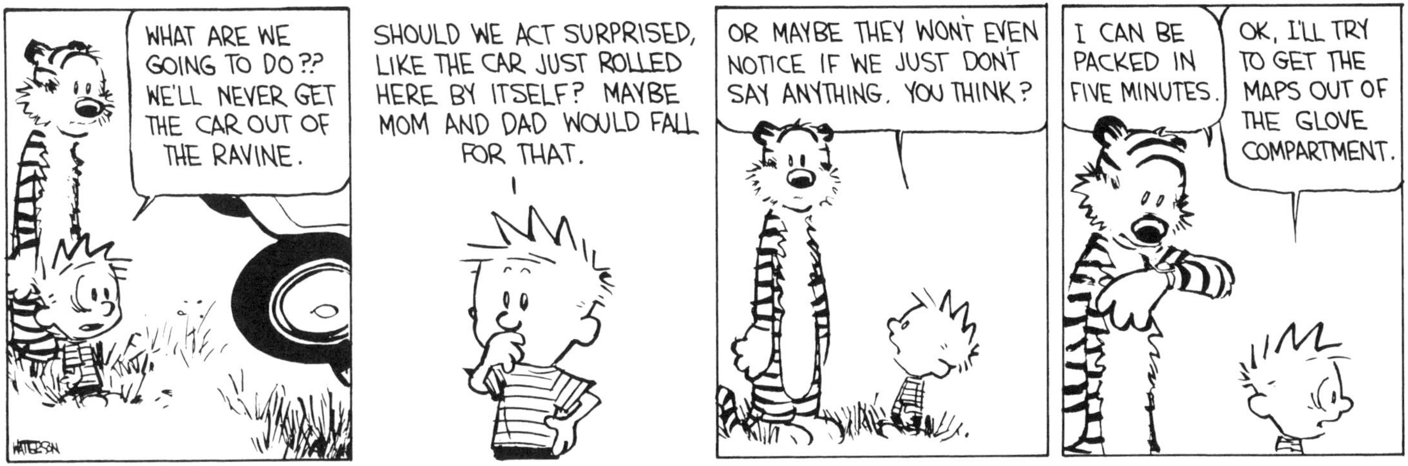
WHAT ARE WE GOING TO DO?? WE'LL NEVER GET THE CAR OUT OF THE RAVINE.
SHOULD WE ACT SURPRISED, LIKE THE CAR JUST ROLLED HERE BY ITSELF? MAYBE MOM AND DAD WOULD FALL FOR THAT.
OR MAYBE THEY WON'T EVEN NOTICE IF WE JUST DON'T SAY ANYTHING. YOU THINK?
I CAN BE PACKED IN FIVE MINUTES.
OK, I'LL TRY TO GET THE MAPS OUT OF THE GLOVE COMPARTMENT.

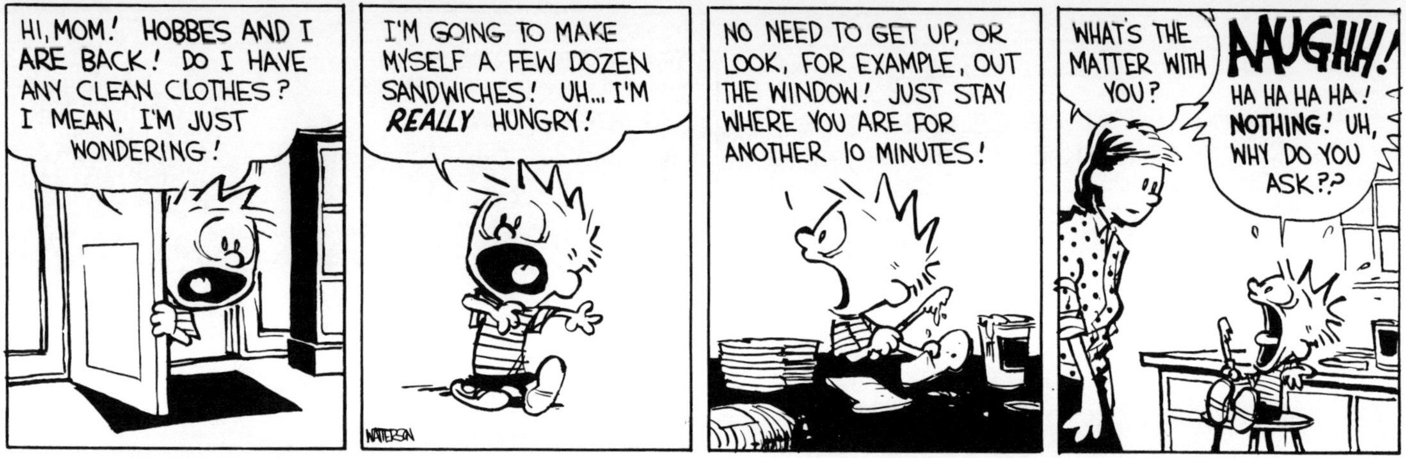
HI, MOM! HOBBES AND I ARE BACK! DO I HAVE ANY CLEAN CLOTHES? I MEAN, I'M JUST WONDERING!
I'M GOING TO MAKE MYSELF A FEW DOZEN SANDWICHES! UH... I'M *REALLY* HUNGRY!
WATTERSON
NO NEED TO GET UP, OR LOOK, FOR EXAMPLE, OUT THE WINDOW! JUST STAY WHERE YOU ARE FOR ANOTHER 10 MINUTES!
WHAT'S THE MATTER WITH YOU?
AAUGHH!
HA HA HA HA! NOTHING! UH, WHY DO YOU ASK??

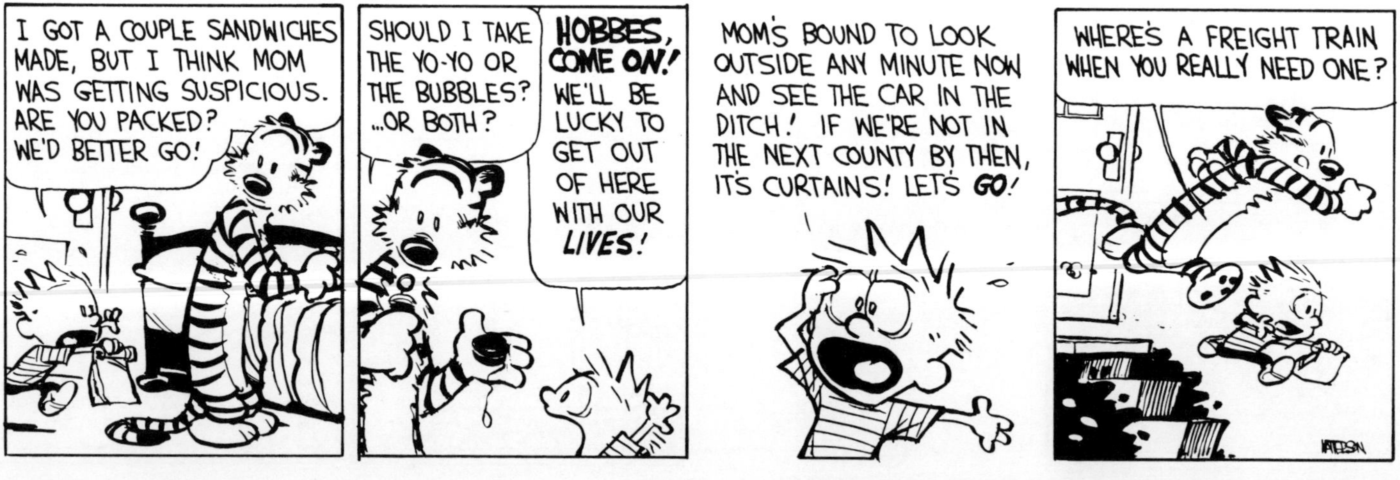
I GOT A COUPLE SANDWICHES MADE, BUT I THINK MOM WAS GETTING SUSPICIOUS. ARE YOU PACKED? WE'D BETTER GO!
SHOULD I TAKE THE YO-YO OR THE BUBBLES? ...OR BOTH?
HOBBES, COME ON! WE'LL BE LUCKY TO GET OUT OF HERE WITH OUR *LIVES*!
MOM'S BOUND TO LOOK OUTSIDE ANY MINUTE NOW AND SEE THE CAR IN THE DITCH! IF WE'RE NOT IN THE NEXT COUNTY BY THEN, IT'S CURTAINS! LET'S *GO*!
WHERE'S A FREIGHT TRAIN WHEN YOU REALLY NEED ONE?
WATTERSON

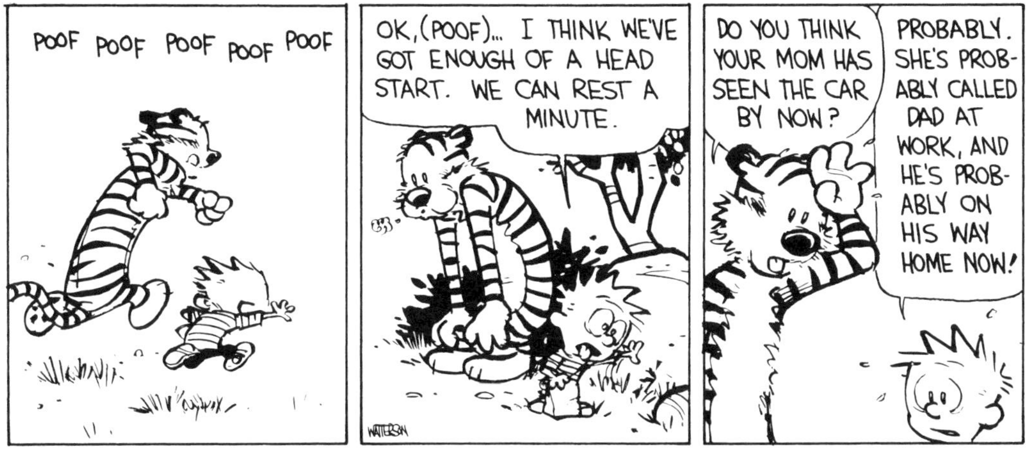
POOF POOF POOF POOF POOF
OK, (POOF)... I THINK WE'VE GOT ENOUGH OF A HEAD START. WE CAN REST A MINUTE.
DO YOU THINK YOUR MOM HAS SEEN THE CAR BY NOW?
PROBABLY. SHE'S PROBABLY CALLED DAD AT WORK, AND HE'S PROBABLY ON HIS WAY HOME NOW!

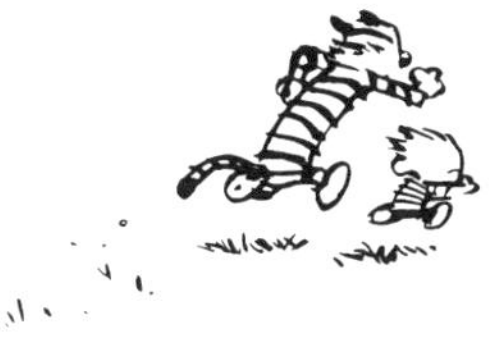

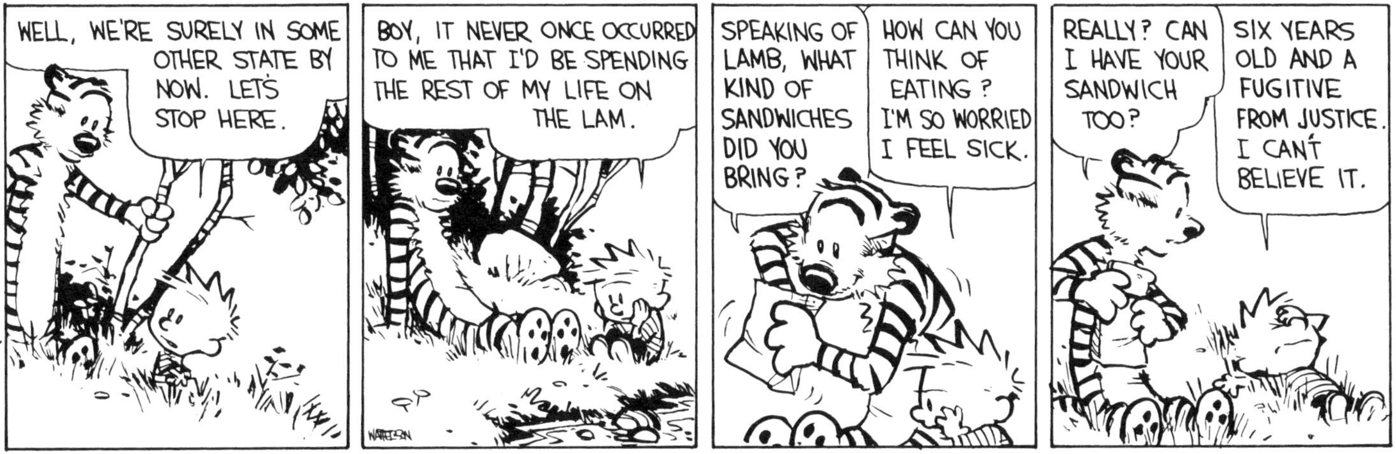
WELL, WE'RE SURELY IN SOME OTHER STATE BY NOW. LET'S STOP HERE.
BOY, IT NEVER ONCE OCCURRED TO ME THAT I'D BE SPENDING THE REST OF MY LIFE ON THE LAM.
SPEAKING OF LAMB, WHAT KIND OF SANDWICHES DID YOU BRING?
HOW CAN YOU THINK OF EATING? I'M SO WORRIED I FEEL SICK.
REALLY? CAN I HAVE YOUR SANDWICH TOO?
SIX YEARS OLD AND A FUGITIVE FROM JUSTICE. I CAN'T BELIEVE IT.

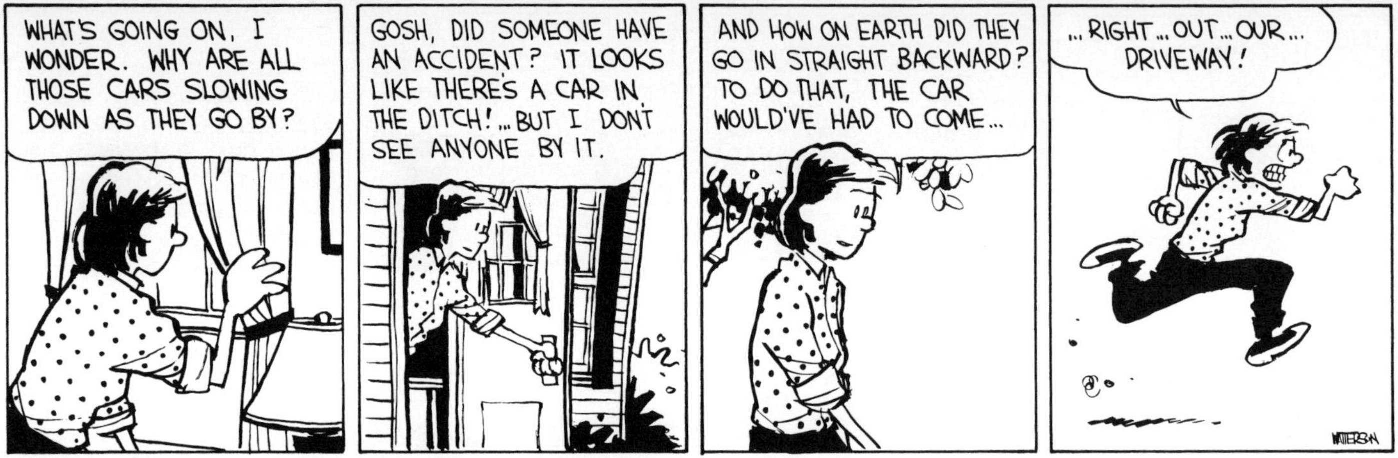
WHAT'S GOING ON, I WONDER. WHY ARE ALL THOSE CARS SLOWING DOWN AS THEY GO BY?
GOSH, DID SOMEONE HAVE AN ACCIDENT? IT LOOKS LIKE THERE'S A CAR IN THE DITCH! ... BUT I DON'T SEE ANYONE BY IT.
AND HOW ON EARTH DID THEY GO IN STRAIGHT BACKWARD? TO DO THAT, THE CAR WOULD'VE HAD TO COME...
... RIGHT... OUT... OUR... DRIVEWAY!
WATTERSON

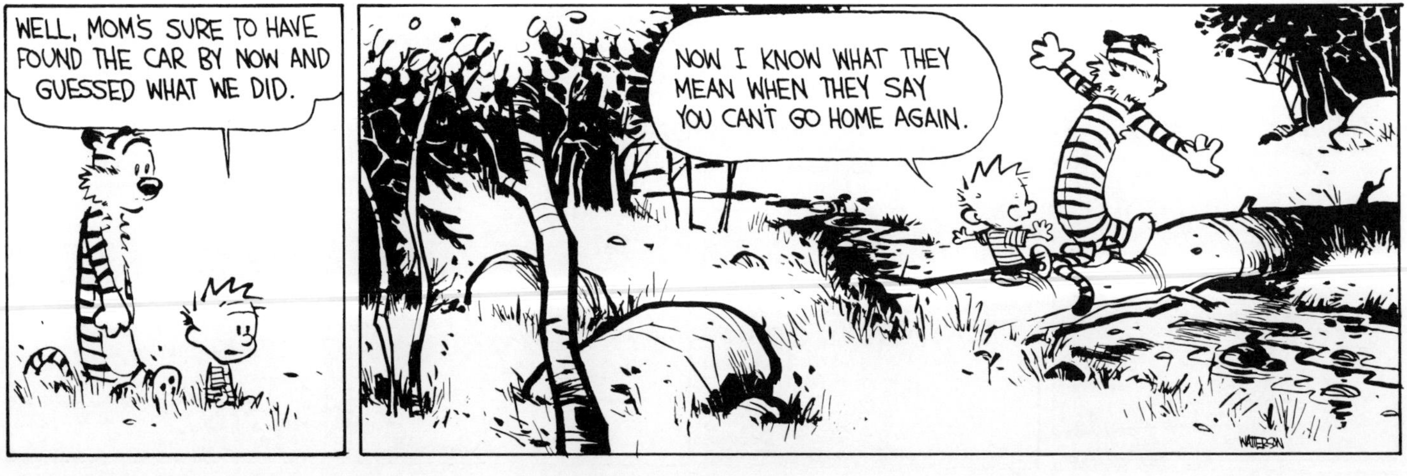
WELL, MOM'S SURE TO HAVE FOUND THE CAR BY NOW AND GUESSED WHAT WE DID.
NOW I KNOW WHAT THEY MEAN WHEN THEY SAY YOU CAN'T GO HOME AGAIN.
WATTERSON

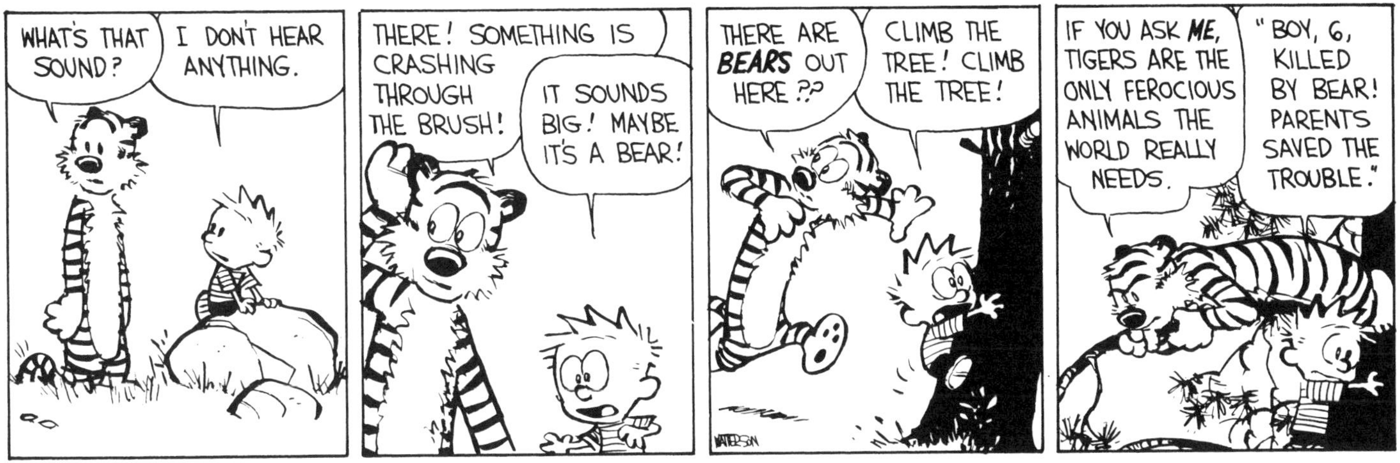
WHAT'S THAT SOUND?
I DON'T HEAR ANYTHING.
THERE! SOMETHING IS CRASHING THROUGH THE BRUSH!
IT SOUNDS BIG! MAYBE IT'S A BEAR!
THERE ARE **BEARS** OUT HERE??
CLIMB THE TREE! CLIMB THE TREE!
IF YOU ASK **ME**, TIGERS ARE THE ONLY FEROCIOUS ANIMALS THE WORLD REALLY NEEDS.
"BOY, 6, KILLED BY BEAR! PARENTS SAVED THE TROUBLE."

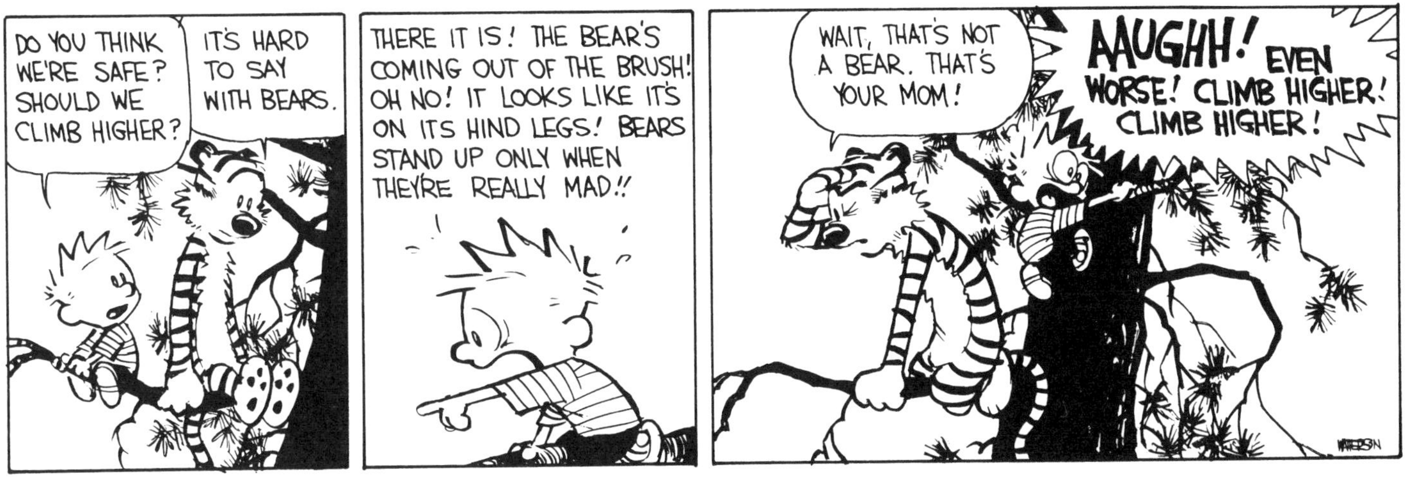
DO YOU THINK WE'RE SAFE? SHOULD WE CLIMB HIGHER?
IT'S HARD TO SAY WITH BEARS.
THERE IT IS! THE BEAR'S COMING OUT OF THE BRUSH! OH NO! IT LOOKS LIKE IT'S ON ITS HIND LEGS! BEARS STAND UP ONLY WHEN THEY'RE REALLY MAD!!
WAIT, THAT'S NOT A BEAR. THAT'S YOUR MOM!
AAUGHH! EVEN WORSE! CLIMB HIGHER! CLIMB HIGHER!

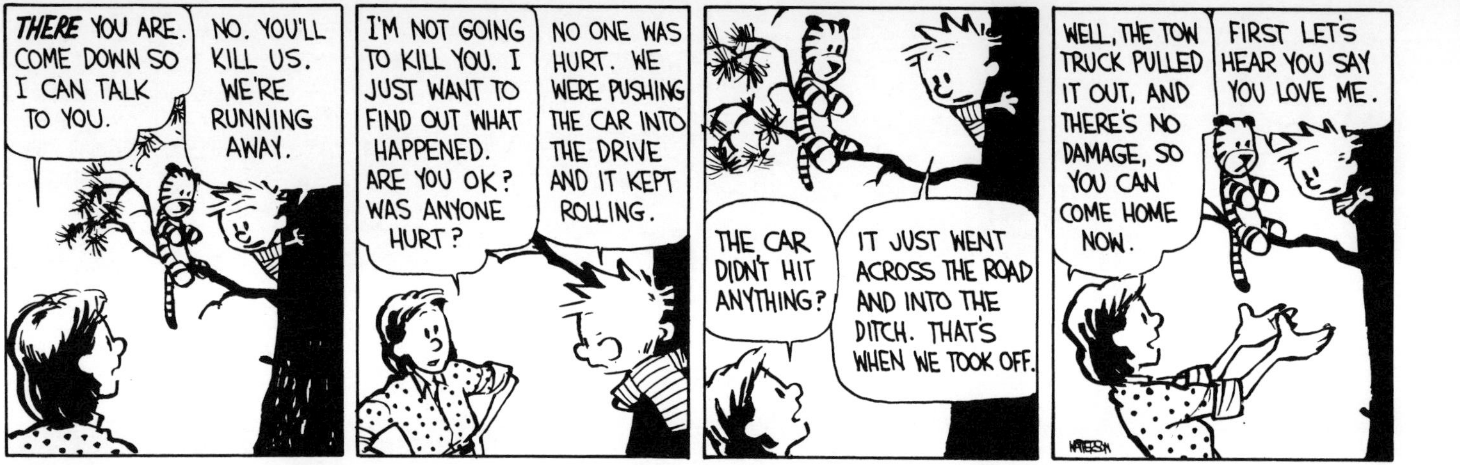
THERE YOU ARE. COME DOWN SO I CAN TALK TO YOU.
NO. YOU'LL KILL US. WE'RE RUNNING AWAY.
I'M NOT GOING TO KILL YOU. I JUST WANT TO FIND OUT WHAT HAPPENED. ARE YOU OK? WAS ANYONE HURT?
NO ONE WAS HURT. WE WERE PUSHING THE CAR INTO THE DRIVE AND IT KEPT ROLLING.
THE CAR DIDN'T HIT ANYTHING?
IT JUST WENT ACROSS THE ROAD AND INTO THE DITCH. THAT'S WHEN WE TOOK OFF.
WELL, THE TOW TRUCK PULLED IT OUT, AND THERE'S NO DAMAGE, SO YOU CAN COME HOME NOW.
FIRST LET'S HEAR YOU SAY YOU LOVE ME.
WATTERSON

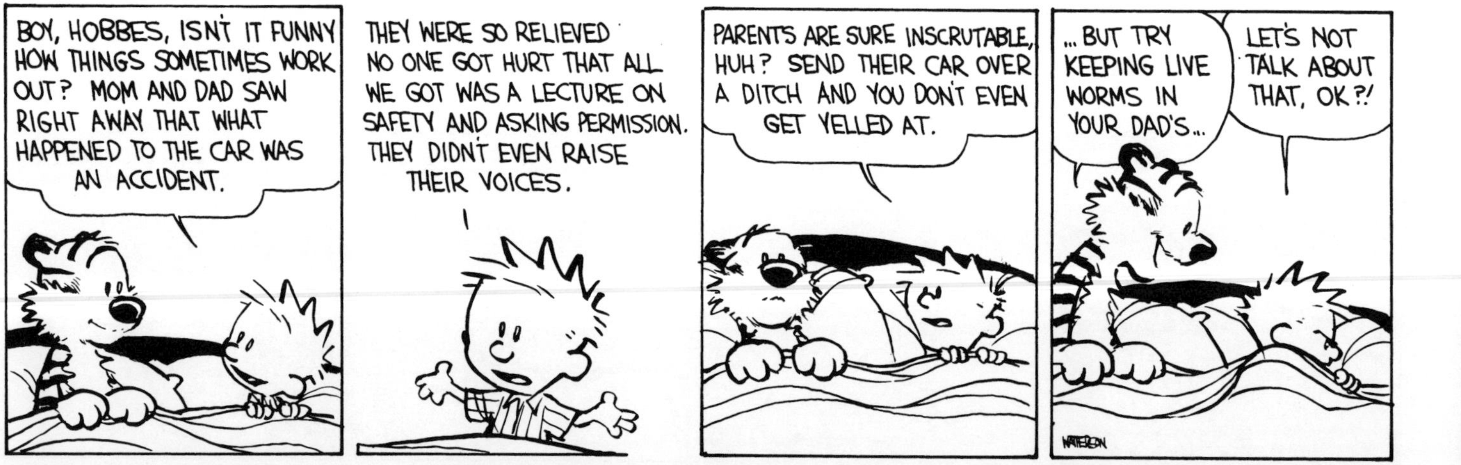
BOY, HOBBES, ISN'T IT FUNNY HOW THINGS SOMETIMES WORK OUT? MOM AND DAD SAW RIGHT AWAY THAT WHAT HAPPENED TO THE CAR WAS AN ACCIDENT.
THEY WERE SO RELIEVED NO ONE GOT HURT THAT ALL WE GOT WAS A LECTURE ON SAFETY AND ASKING PERMISSION. THEY DIDN'T EVEN RAISE THEIR VOICES.
PARENTS ARE SURE INSCRUTABLE, HUH? SEND THEIR CAR OVER A DITCH AND YOU DON'T EVEN GET YELLED AT.
... BUT TRY KEEPING LIVE WORMS IN YOUR DAD'S...
LET'S NOT TALK ABOUT THAT, OK?!
WATTERSON

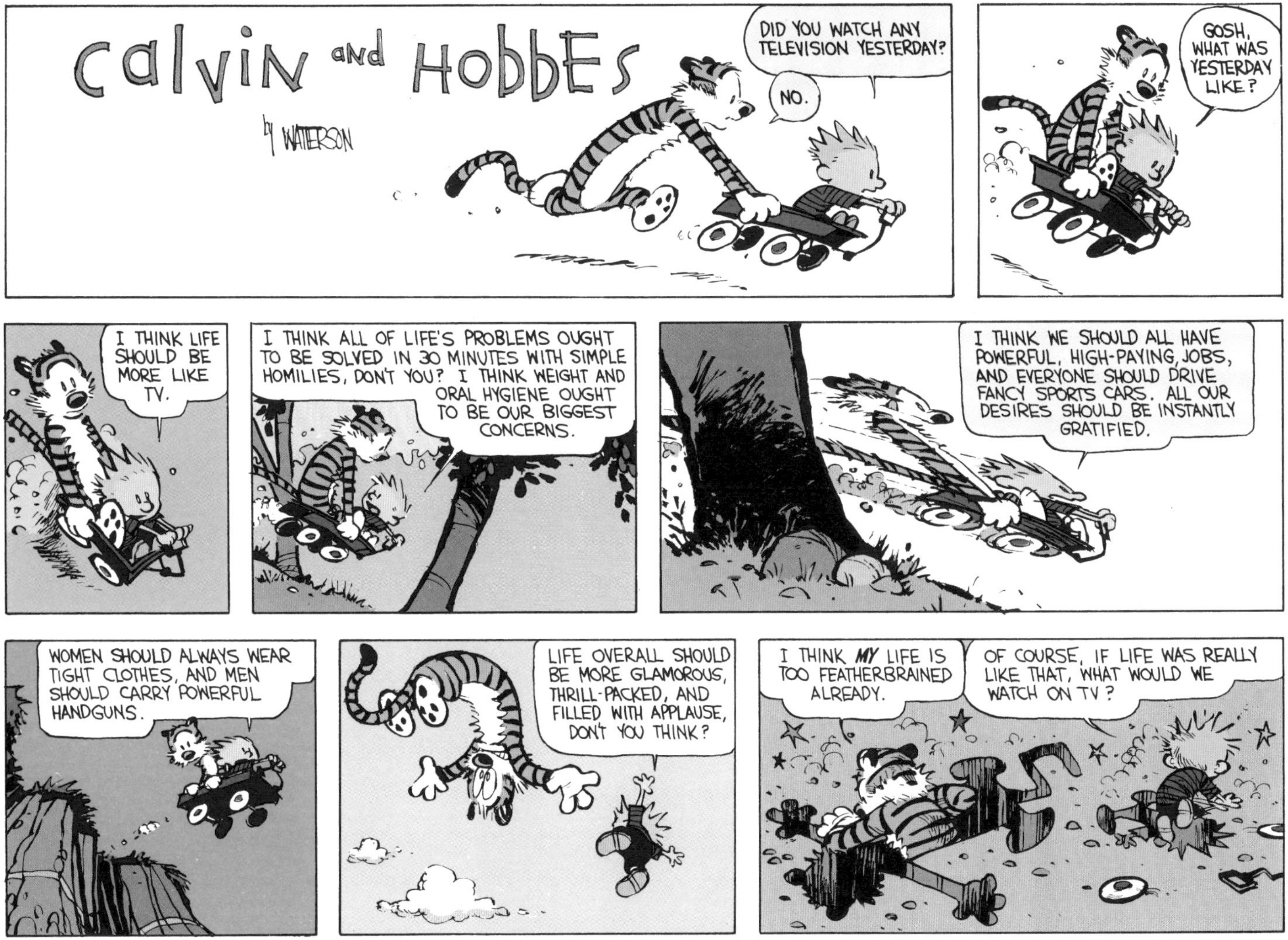

Calvin and Hobbes
by WATTERSON
DID YOU WATCH ANY TELEVISION YESTERDAY?
NO.
GOSH, WHAT WAS YESTERDAY LIKE?
I THINK LIFE SHOULD BE MORE LIKE TV.
I THINK ALL OF LIFE'S PROBLEMS OUGHT TO BE SOLVED IN 30 MINUTES WITH SIMPLE HOMILIES, DON'T YOU? I THINK WEIGHT AND ORAL HYGIENE OUGHT TO BE OUR BIGGEST CONCERNS.
by WATTERSON
I THINK WE SHOULD ALL HAVE POWERFUL, HIGH-PAYING JOBS, AND EVERYONE SHOULD DRIVE FANCY SPORTS CARS. ALL OUR DESIRES SHOULD BE INSTANTLY GRATIFIED.
WOMEN SHOULD ALWAYS WEAR TIGHT CLOTHES, AND MEN SHOULD CARRY POWERFUL HANDGUNS.
LIFE OVERALL SHOULD BE MORE GLAMOROUS, THRILL-PACKED, AND FILLED WITH APPLAUSE, DON'T YOU THINK?
I THINK *MY* LIFE IS TOO FEATHERBRAINED ALREADY.
OF COURSE, IF LIFE WAS REALLY LIKE THAT, WHAT WOULD WE WATCH ON TV?

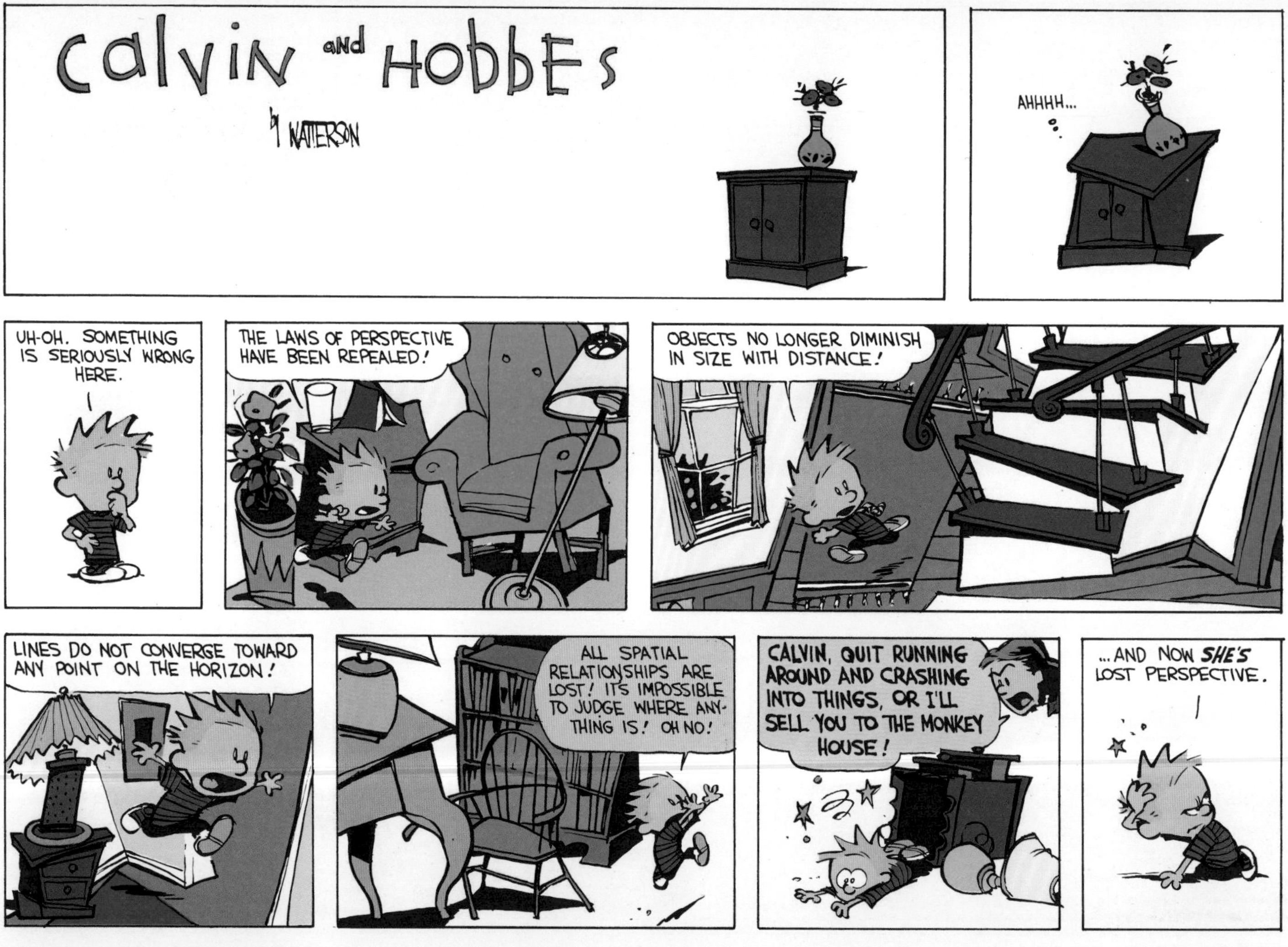
Calvin and HOBBES
by WATTERSON
AHHHH...
UH-OH. SOMETHING IS SERIOUSLY WRONG HERE.
THE LAWS OF PERSPECTIVE HAVE BEEN REPEALED!
OBJECTS NO LONGER DIMINISH IN SIZE WITH DISTANCE!
LINES DO NOT CONVERGE TOWARD ANY POINT ON THE HORIZON!
ALL SPATIAL RELATIONSHIPS ARE LOST! IT'S IMPOSSIBLE TO JUDGE WHERE ANYTHING IS! OH NO!
CALVIN, QUIT RUNNING AROUND AND CRASHING INTO THINGS, OR I'LL SELL YOU TO THE MONKEY HOUSE!
...AND NOW SHE'S LOST PERSPECTIVE.

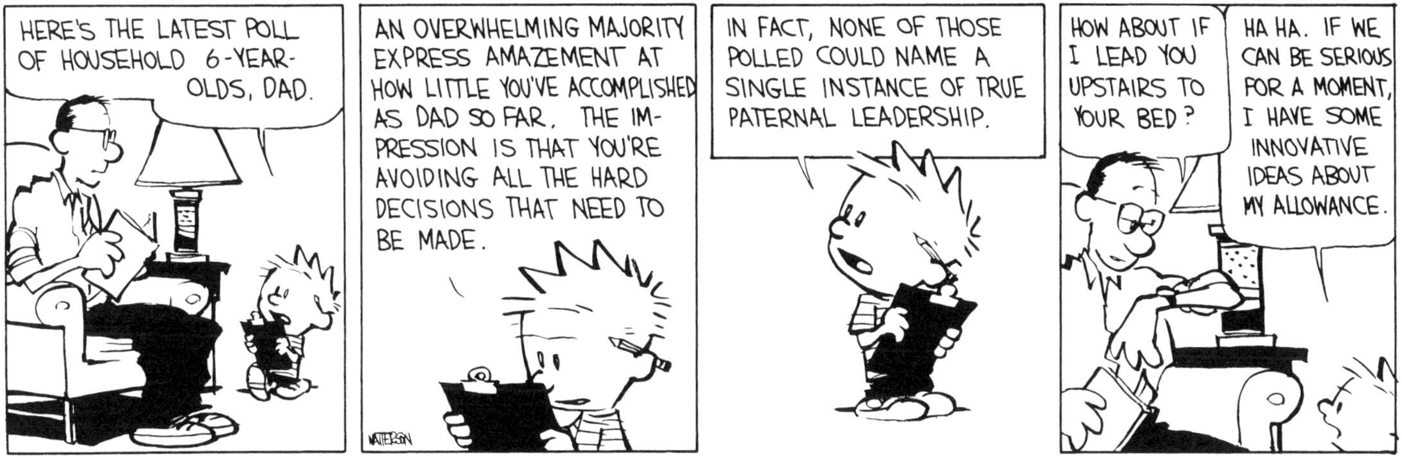
HERE'S THE LATEST POLL OF HOUSEHOLD 6-YEAR-OLDS, DAD.
AN OVERWHELMING MAJORITY EXPRESS AMAZEMENT AT HOW LITTLE YOU'VE ACCOMPLISHED AS DAD SO FAR. THE IMPRESSION IS THAT YOU'RE AVOIDING ALL THE HARD DECISIONS THAT NEED TO BE MADE.
WATTERSON
IN FACT, NONE OF THOSE POLLED COULD NAME A SINGLE INSTANCE OF TRUE PATERNAL LEADERSHIP.
HOW ABOUT IF I LEAD YOU UPSTAIRS TO YOUR BED?
HA HA. IF WE CAN BE SERIOUS FOR A MOMENT, I HAVE SOME INNOVATIVE IDEAS ABOUT MY ALLOWANCE.

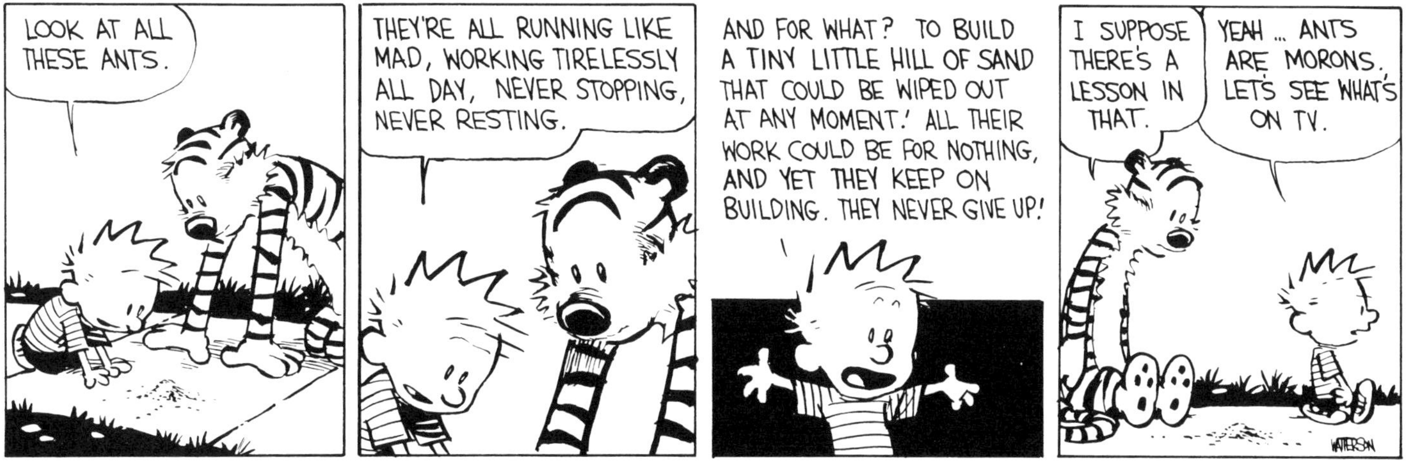
LOOK AT ALL THESE ANTS.
THEY'RE ALL RUNNING LIKE MAD, WORKING TIRELESSLY ALL DAY, NEVER STOPPING, NEVER RESTING.
AND FOR WHAT? TO BUILD A TINY LITTLE HILL OF SAND THAT COULD BE WIPED OUT AT ANY MOMENT! ALL THEIR WORK COULD BE FOR NOTHING, AND YET THEY KEEP ON BUILDING. THEY NEVER GIVE UP!
I SUPPOSE THERE'S A LESSON IN THAT.
YEAH ... ANTS ARE MORONS. LET'S SEE WHAT'S ON TV.
WATTERSON

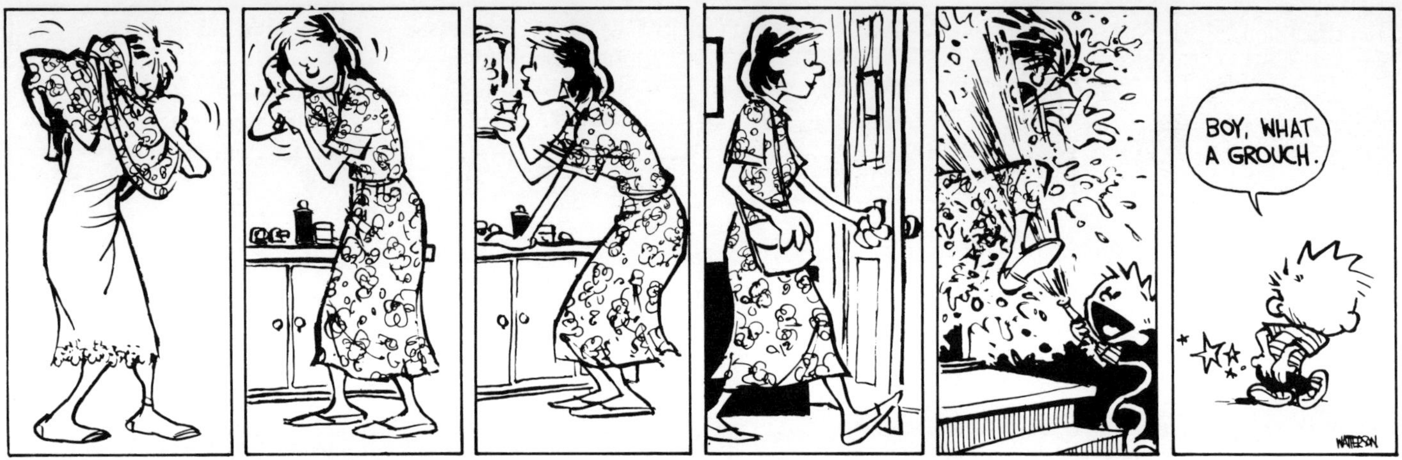
BOY, WHAT A GROUCH.

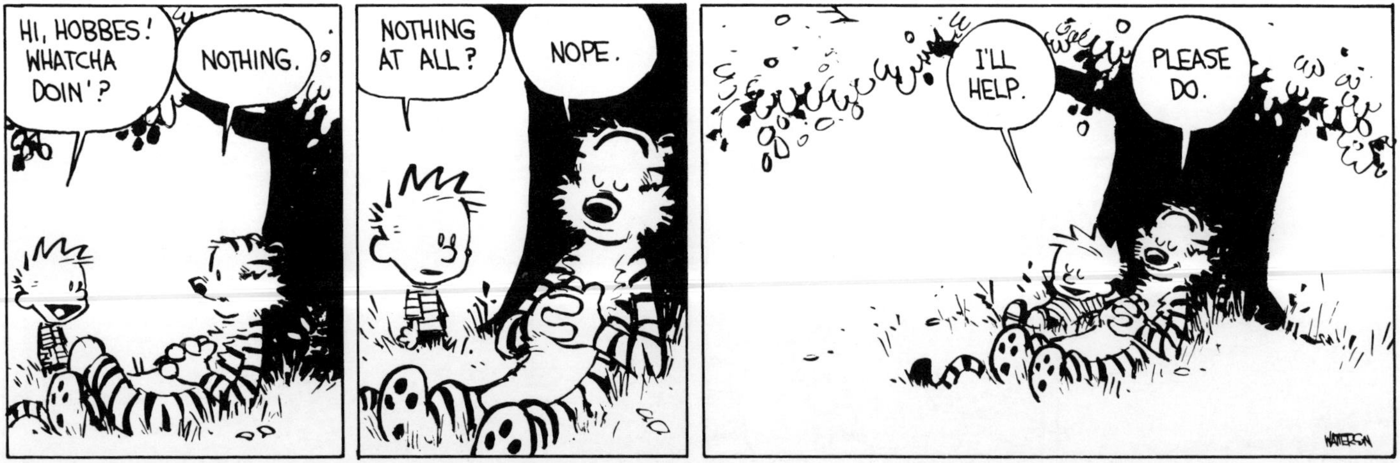
HI, HOBBES! WHATCHA DOIN'?
NOTHING.
NOTHING AT ALL?
NOPE.
I'LL HELP.
PLEASE DO.

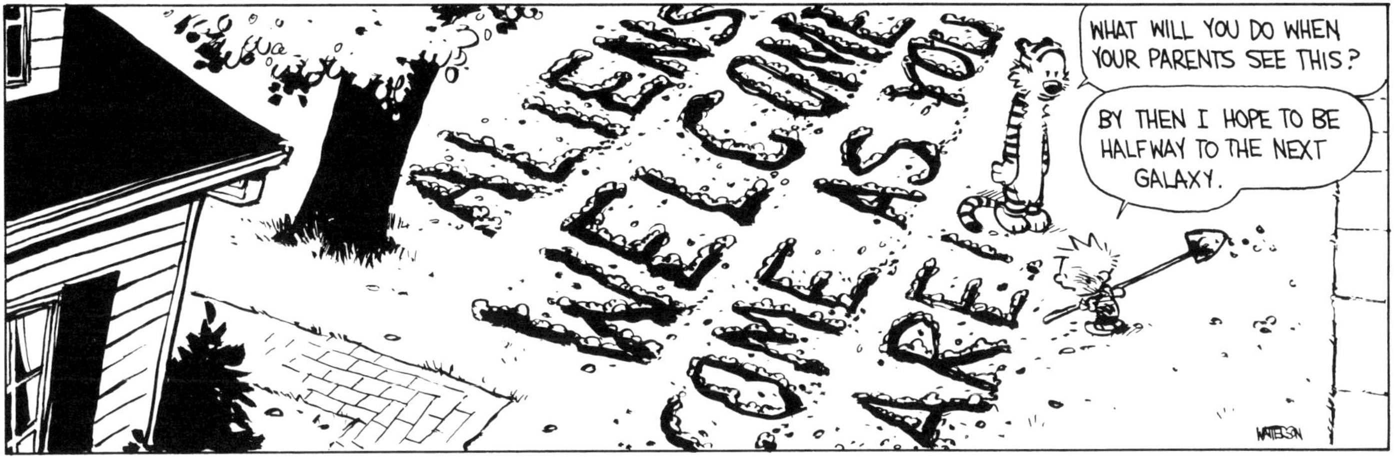
ALIENS WELCOME COME AS YOU ARE!
WHAT WILL YOU DO WHEN YOUR PARENTS SEE THIS?
BY THEN I HOPE TO BE HALFWAY TO THE NEXT GALAXY.
WATTERSON

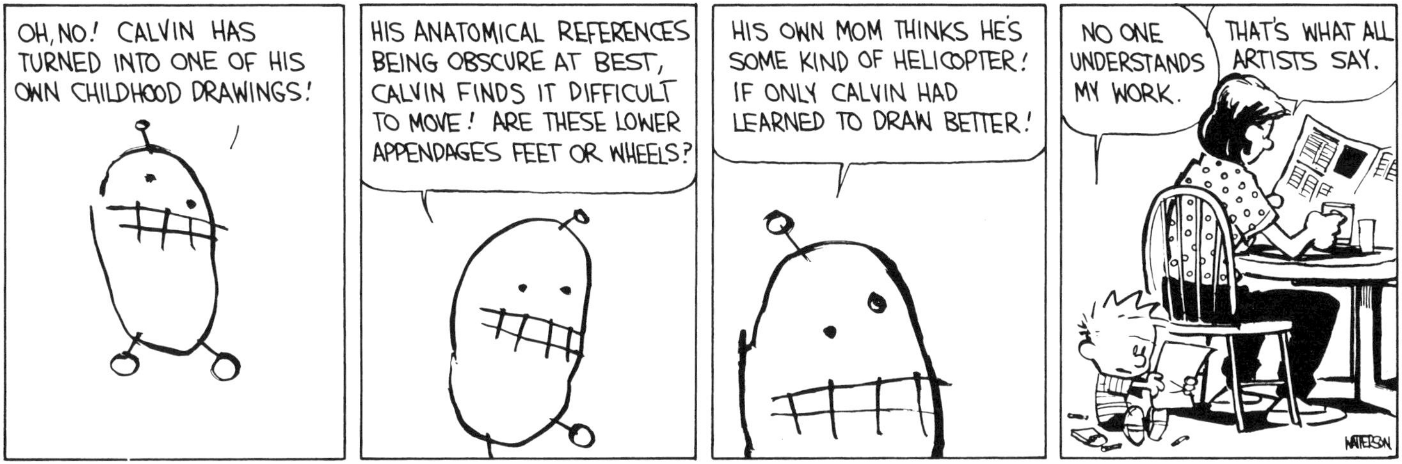
OH, NO! CALVIN HAS TURNED INTO ONE OF HIS OWN CHILDHOOD DRAWINGS!
HIS ANATOMICAL REFERENCES BEING OBSCURE AT BEST, CALVIN FINDS IT DIFFICULT TO MOVE! ARE THESE LOWER APPENDAGES FEET OR WHEELS?
HIS OWN MOM THINKS HE'S SOME KIND OF HELICOPTER! IF ONLY CALVIN HAD LEARNED TO DRAW BETTER!
NO ONE UNDERSTANDS MY WORK.
THAT'S WHAT ALL ARTISTS SAY.
WATTERSON

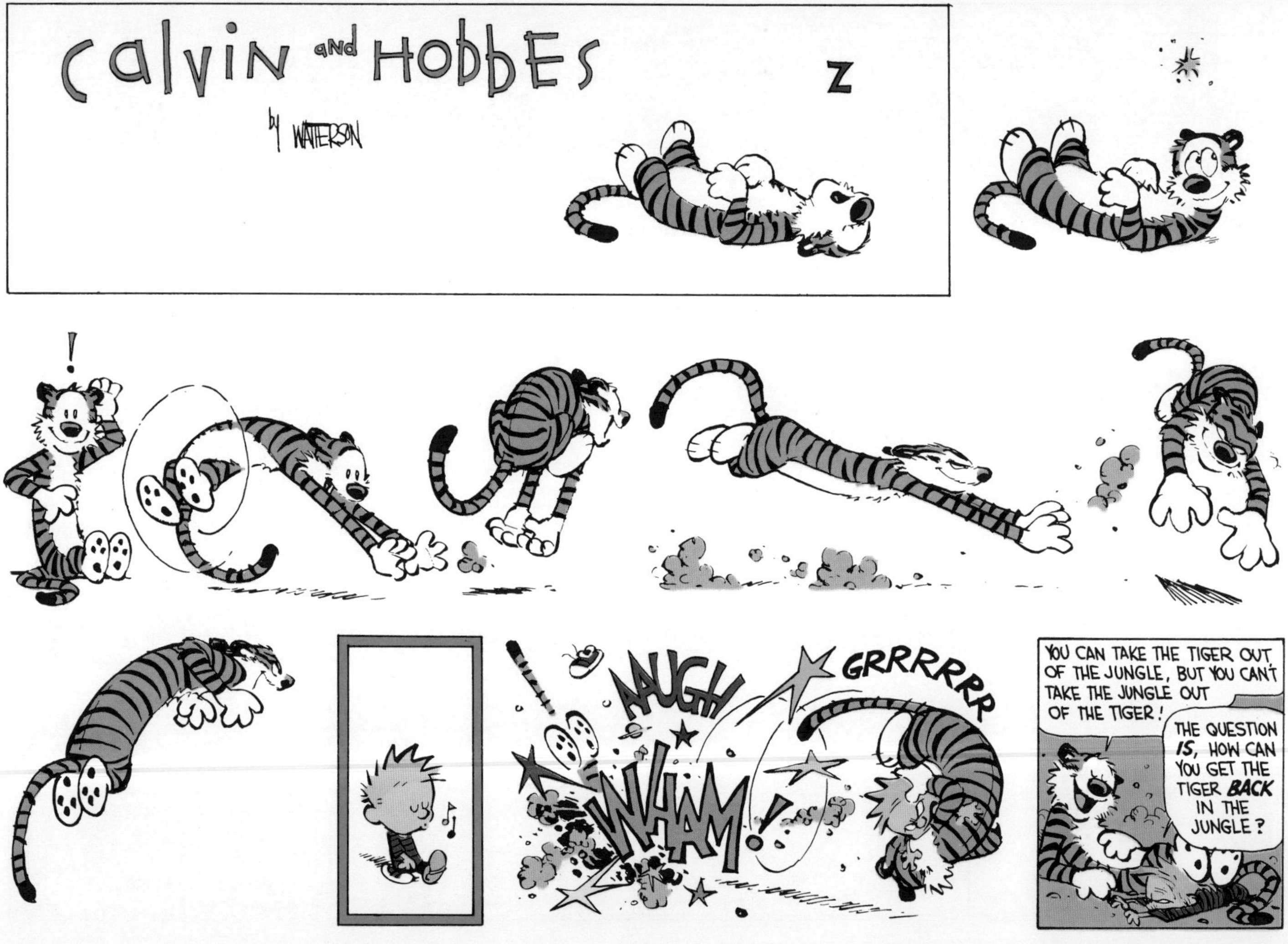
Calvin and HOBBES
by WATTERSON
Z
!
AAUGH
WHAM!
GRRRRRR
YOU CAN TAKE THE TIGER OUT OF THE JUNGLE, BUT YOU CAN'T TAKE THE JUNGLE OUT OF THE TIGER!
THE QUESTION *IS*, HOW CAN YOU GET THE TIGER *BACK* IN THE JUNGLE?

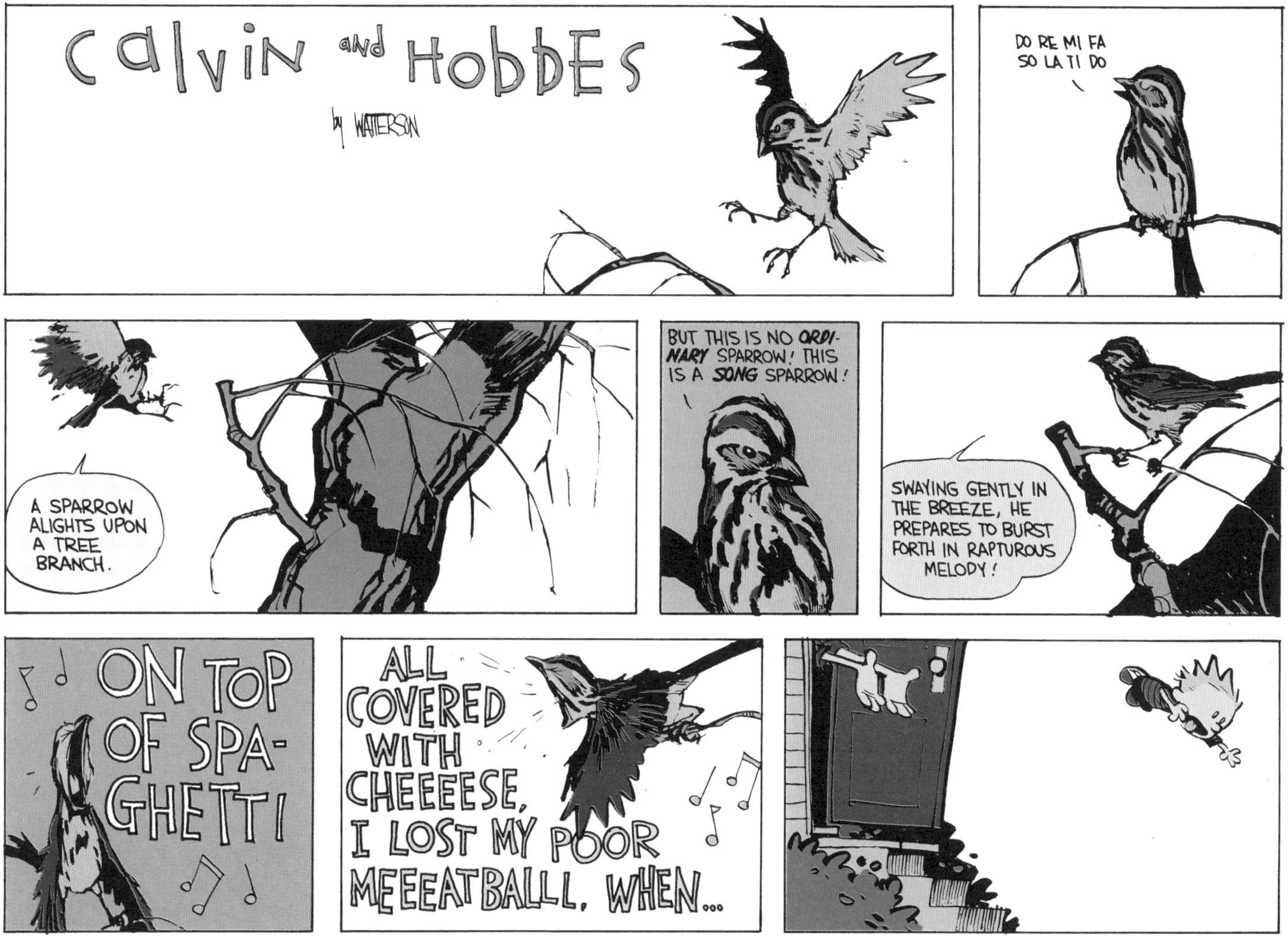
Calvin and Hobbes
by WATTERSON
DO RE MI FA SO LA TI DO
A SPARROW ALIGHTS UPON A TREE BRANCH.
BUT THIS IS NO ORDINARY SPARROW! THIS IS A SONG SPARROW!
SWAYING GENTLY IN THE BREEZE, HE PREPARES TO BURST FORTH IN RAPTUROUS MELODY!
ON TOP OF SPA-GHETTI
ALL COVERED WITH CHEEEESE, I LOST MY POOR MEEEATBALLL, WHEN...

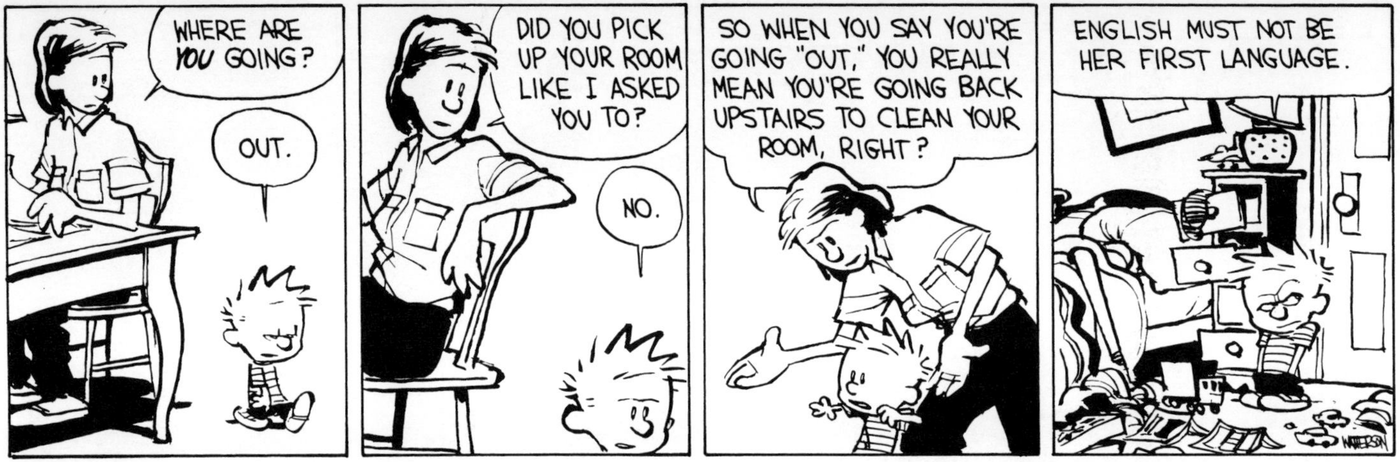
WHERE ARE *YOU* GOING?
OUT.
DID YOU PICK UP YOUR ROOM LIKE I ASKED YOU TO?
NO.
SO WHEN YOU SAY YOU'RE GOING "OUT," YOU REALLY MEAN YOU'RE GOING BACK UPSTAIRS TO CLEAN YOUR ROOM, RIGHT?
ENGLISH MUST NOT BE HER FIRST LANGUAGE.
WATTERSON

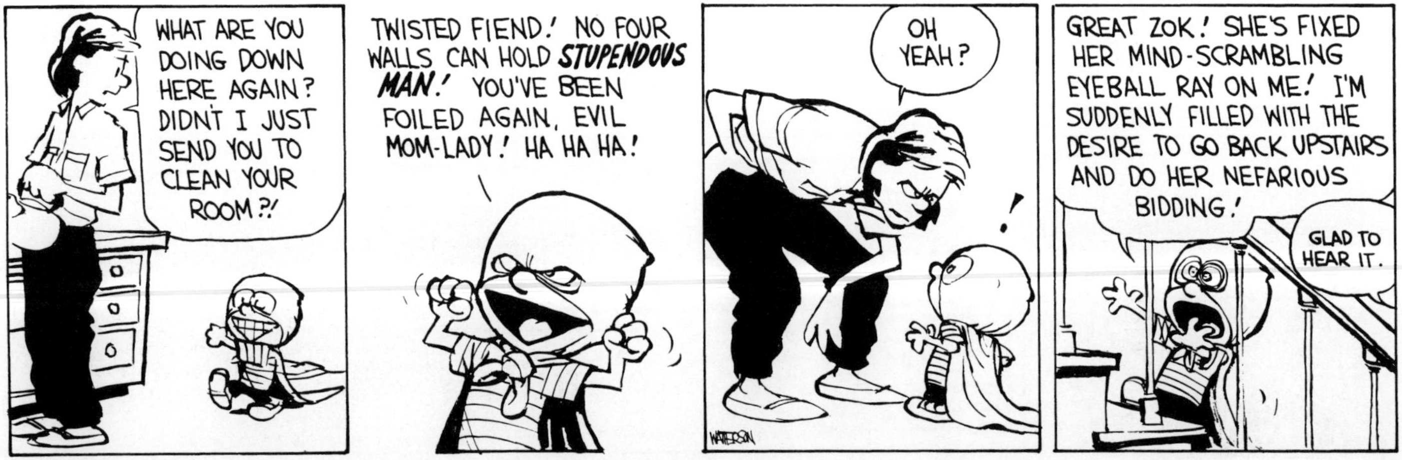
WHAT ARE YOU DOING DOWN HERE AGAIN? DIDN'T I JUST SEND YOU TO CLEAN YOUR ROOM?!
TWISTED FIEND! NO FOUR WALLS CAN HOLD **STUPENDOUS MAN**! YOU'VE BEEN FOILED AGAIN, EVIL MOM-LADY! HA HA HA!
OH YEAH?
!
WATTERSON
GREAT ZOK! SHE'S FIXED HER MIND-SCRAMBLING EYEBALL RAY ON ME! I'M SUDDENLY FILLED WITH THE DESIRE TO GO BACK UPSTAIRS AND DO HER NEFARIOUS BIDDING!
GLAD TO HEAR IT.

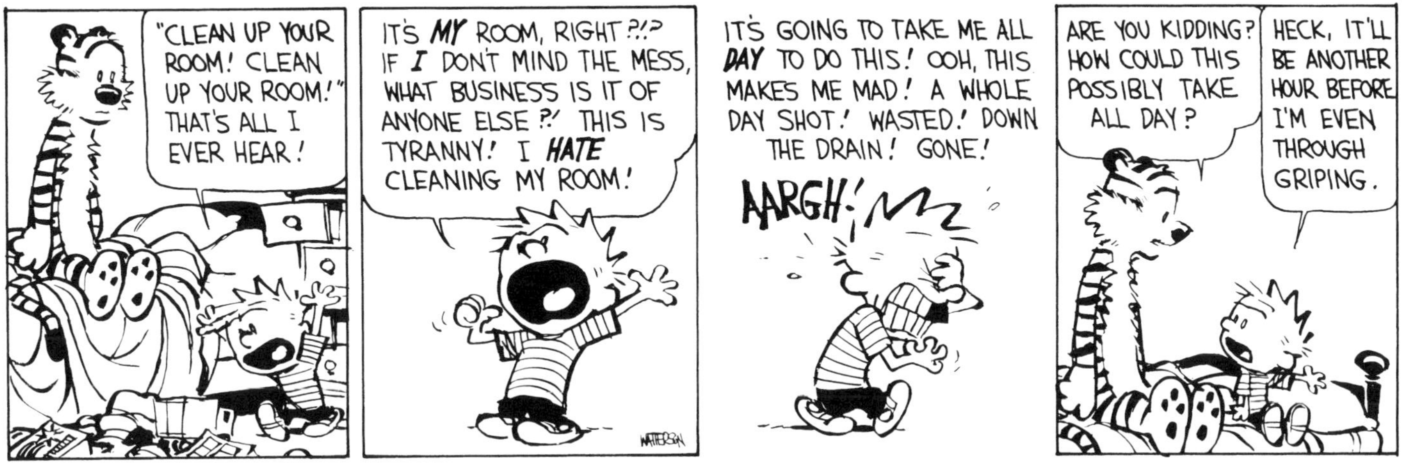
"CLEAN UP YOUR ROOM! CLEAN UP YOUR ROOM!" THAT'S ALL I EVER HEAR!
IT'S MY ROOM, RIGHT?!? IF I DON'T MIND THE MESS, WHAT BUSINESS IS IT OF ANYONE ELSE?! THIS IS TYRANNY! I HATE CLEANING MY ROOM!
WATTERSON
IT'S GOING TO TAKE ME ALL DAY TO DO THIS! OOH, THIS MAKES ME MAD! A WHOLE DAY SHOT! WASTED! DOWN THE DRAIN! GONE!
AARGH!
ARE YOU KIDDING? HOW COULD THIS POSSIBLY TAKE ALL DAY?
HECK, IT'LL BE ANOTHER HOUR BEFORE I'M EVEN THROUGH GRIPING.

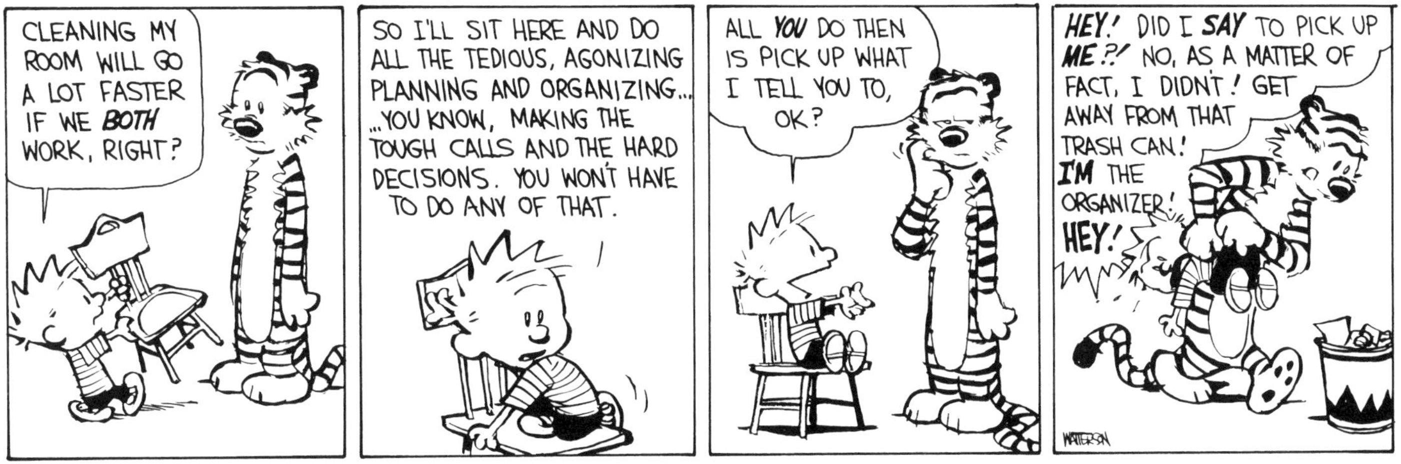
CLEANING MY ROOM WILL GO A LOT FASTER IF WE BOTH WORK, RIGHT?
SO I'LL SIT HERE AND DO ALL THE TEDIOUS, AGONIZING PLANNING AND ORGANIZING... ...YOU KNOW, MAKING THE TOUGH CALLS AND THE HARD DECISIONS. YOU WON'T HAVE TO DO ANY OF THAT.
ALL YOU DO THEN IS PICK UP WHAT I TELL YOU TO, OK?
HEY! DID I SAY TO PICK UP ME?! NO, AS A MATTER OF FACT, I DIDN'T! GET AWAY FROM THAT TRASH CAN! I'M THE ORGANIZER! HEY!
WATTERSON

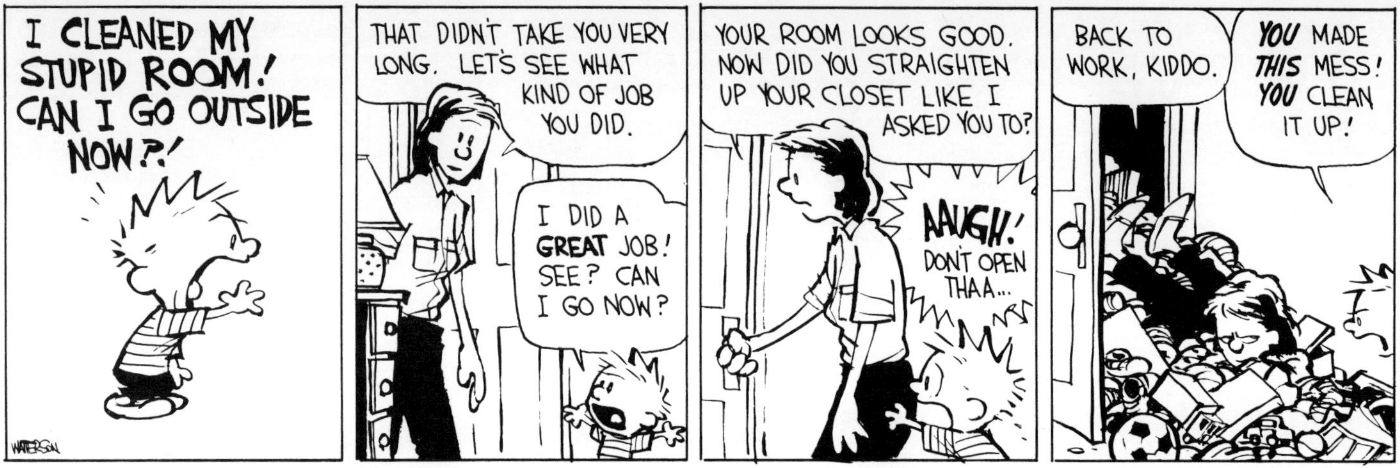
I CLEANED MY STUPID ROOM! CAN I GO OUTSIDE NOW?!
WATTERSON
THAT DIDN'T TAKE YOU VERY LONG. LET'S SEE WHAT KIND OF JOB YOU DID.
I DID A GREAT JOB! SEE? CAN I GO NOW?
YOUR ROOM LOOKS GOOD. NOW DID YOU STRAIGHTEN UP YOUR CLOSET LIKE I ASKED YOU TO?
AAUGH! DON'T OPEN THAA...
BACK TO WORK, KIDDO.
YOU MADE THIS MESS! YOU CLEAN IT UP!

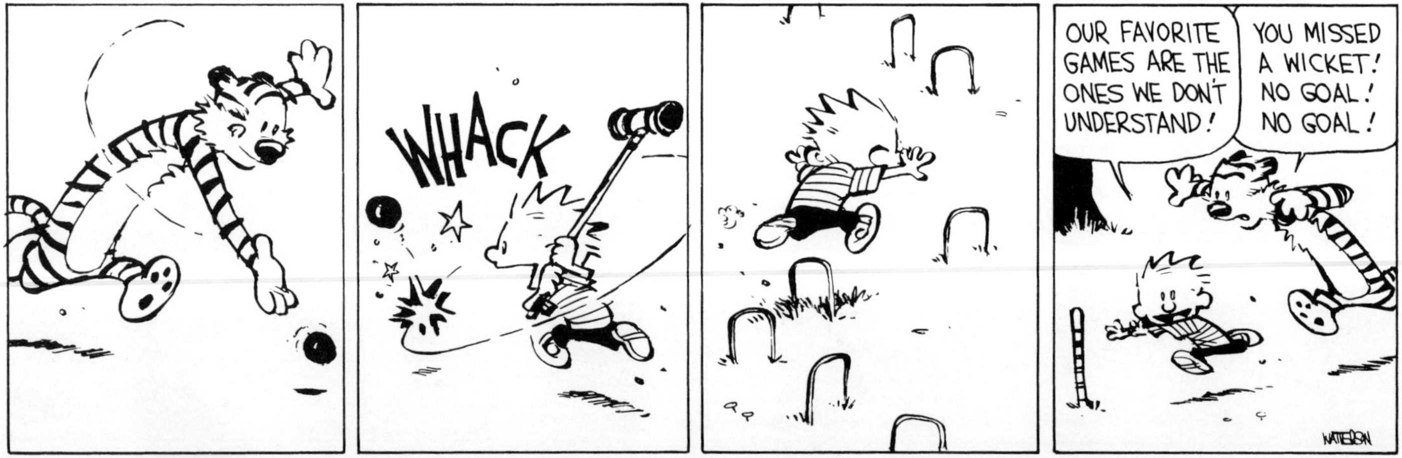
WHACK
OUR FAVORITE GAMES ARE THE ONES WE DON'T UNDERSTAND!
YOU MISSED A WICKET! NO GOAL! NO GOAL!
WATTERSON

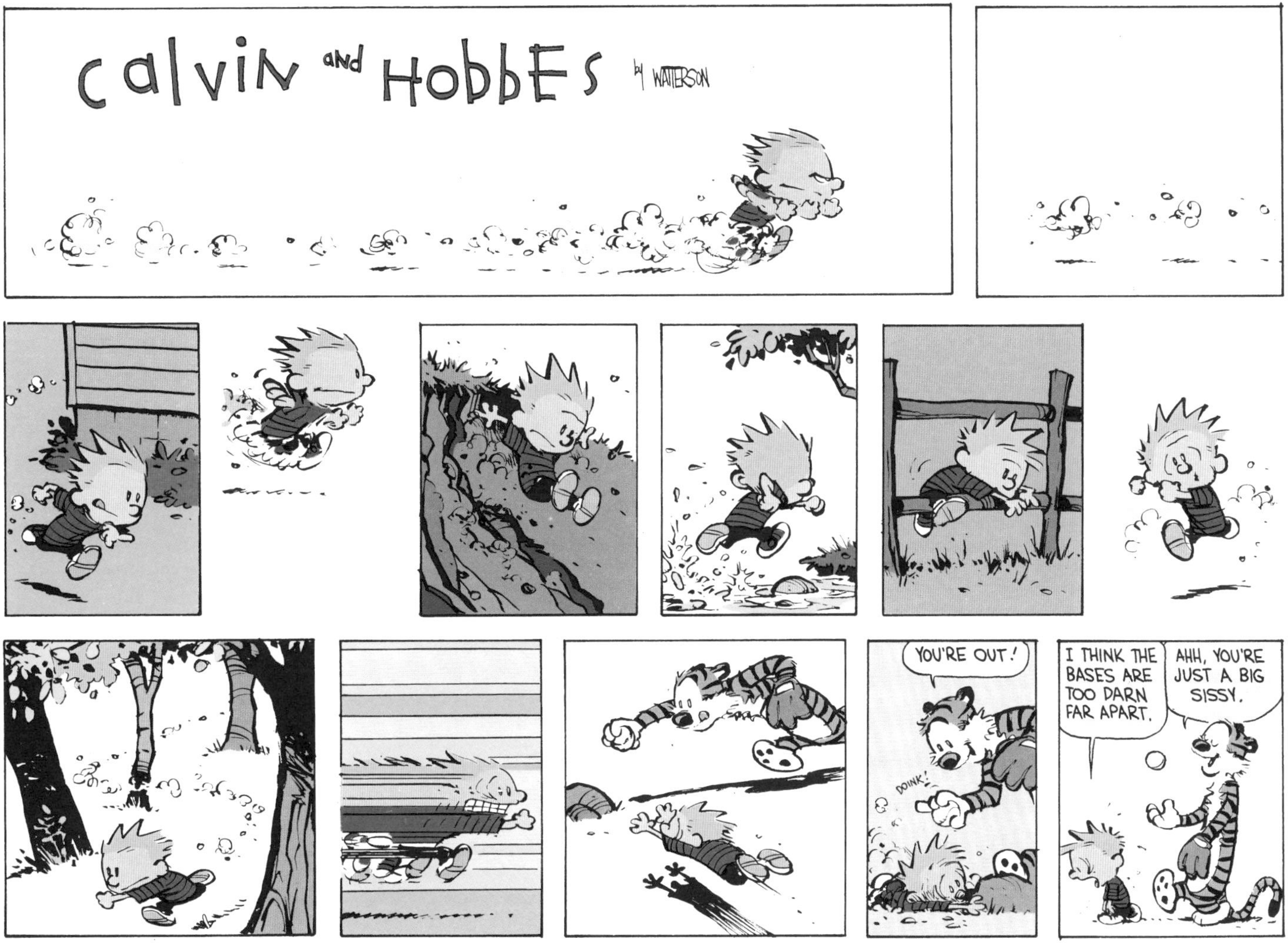
Calvin and HobbEs
by WATTERSON
YOU'RE OUT!
DOINK!
I THINK THE BASES ARE TOO DARN FAR APART.
AHH, YOU'RE JUST A BIG SISSY.

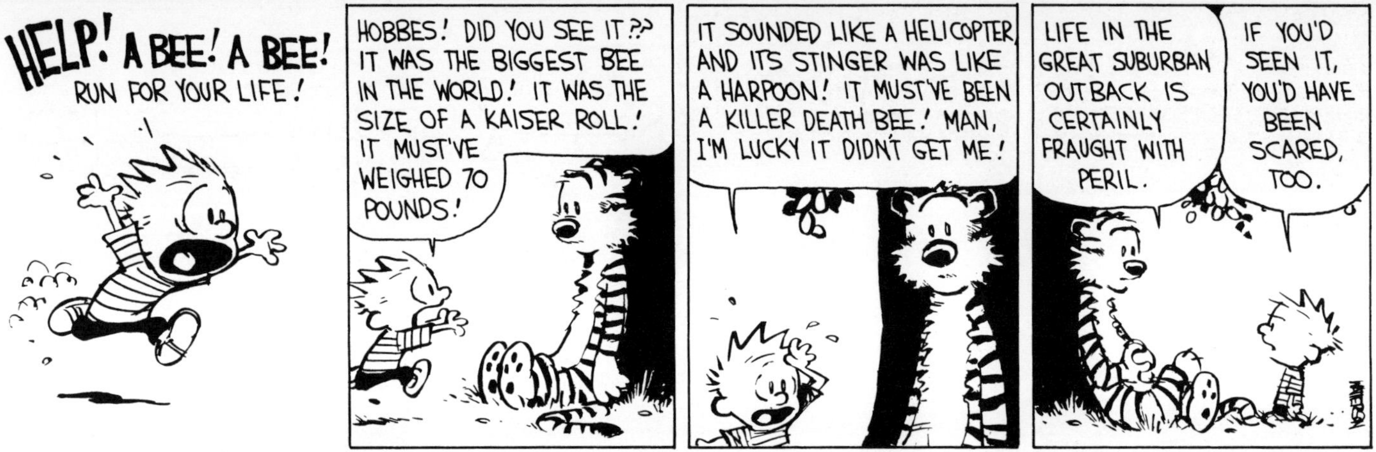
HELP! A BEE! A BEE!
RUN FOR YOUR LIFE!
HOBBES! DID YOU SEE IT?? IT WAS THE BIGGEST BEE IN THE WORLD! IT WAS THE SIZE OF A KAISER ROLL! IT MUST'VE WEIGHED 70 POUNDS!
IT SOUNDED LIKE A HELICOPTER, AND ITS STINGER WAS LIKE A HARPOON! IT MUST'VE BEEN A KILLER DEATH BEE! MAN, I'M LUCKY IT DIDN'T GET ME!
LIFE IN THE GREAT SUBURBAN OUTBACK IS CERTAINLY FRAUGHT WITH PERIL.
IF YOU'D SEEN IT, YOU'D HAVE BEEN SCARED, TOO.

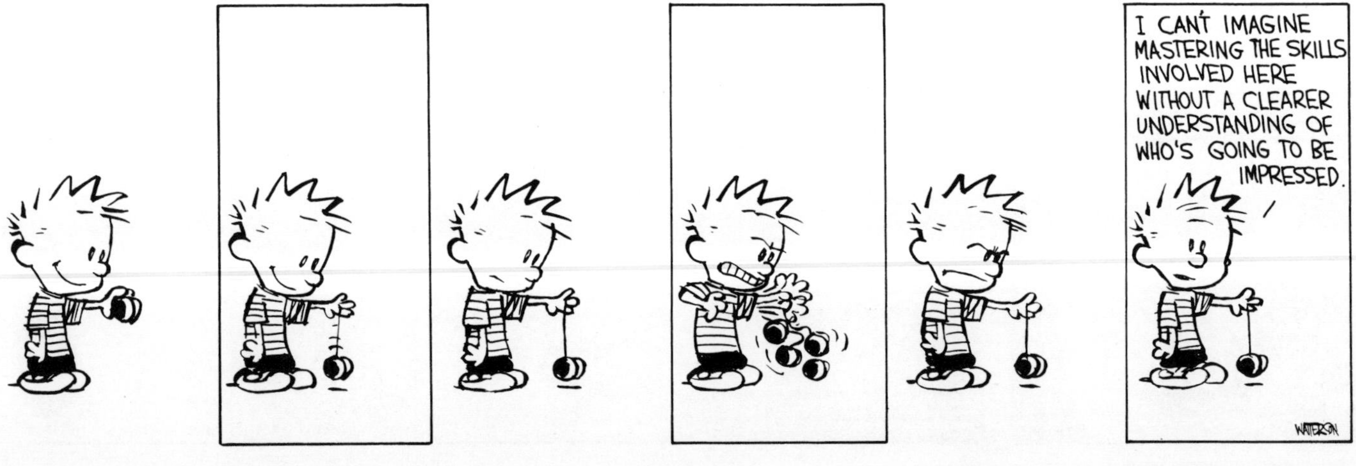
I CAN'T IMAGINE MASTERING THE SKILLS INVOLVED HERE WITHOUT A CLEARER UNDERSTANDING OF WHO'S GOING TO BE IMPRESSED.

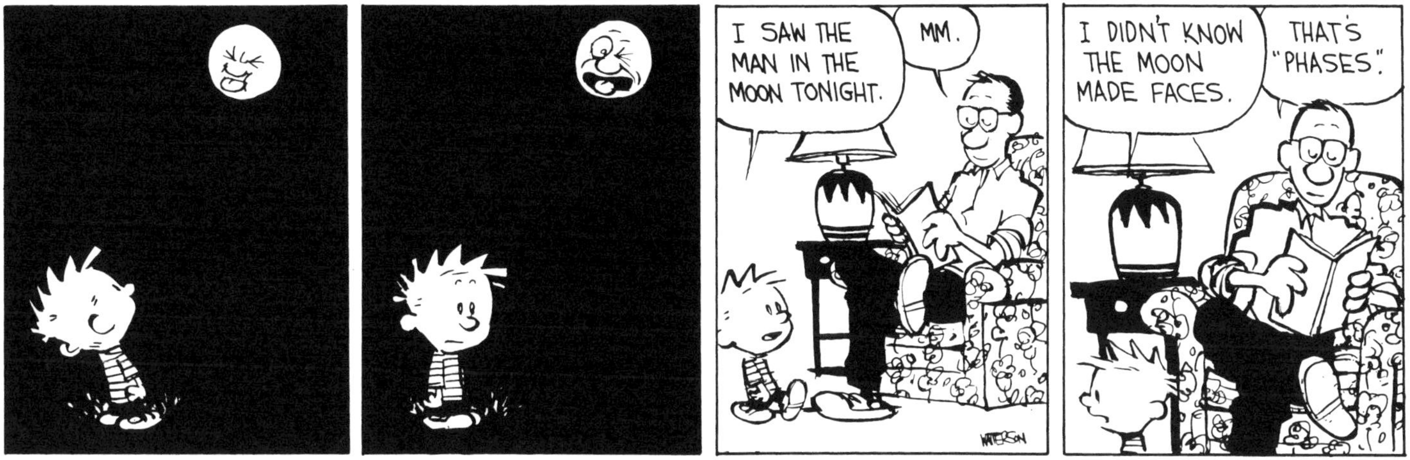
I SAW THE MAN IN THE MOON TONIGHT.
MM.
I DIDN'T KNOW THE MOON MADE FACES.
THAT'S "PHASES".
WATTERSON

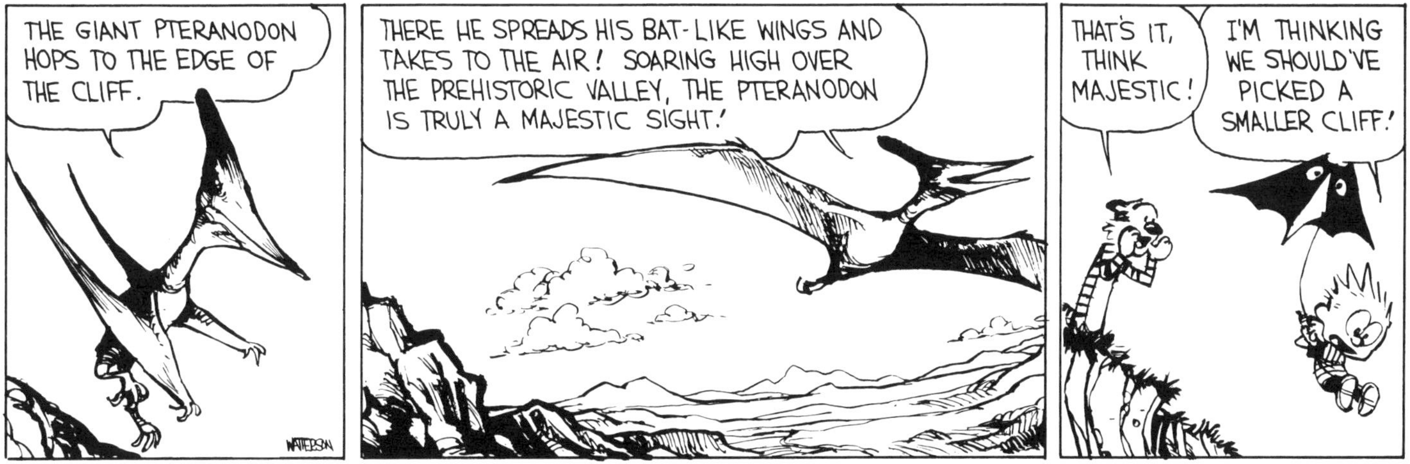
THE GIANT PTERANODON HOPS TO THE EDGE OF THE CLIFF.
WATTERSON
THERE HE SPREADS HIS BAT-LIKE WINGS AND TAKES TO THE AIR! SOARING HIGH OVER THE PREHISTORIC VALLEY, THE PTERANODON IS TRULY A MAJESTIC SIGHT!
THAT'S IT, THINK MAJESTIC!
I'M THINKING WE SHOULD'VE PICKED A SMALLER CLIFF!

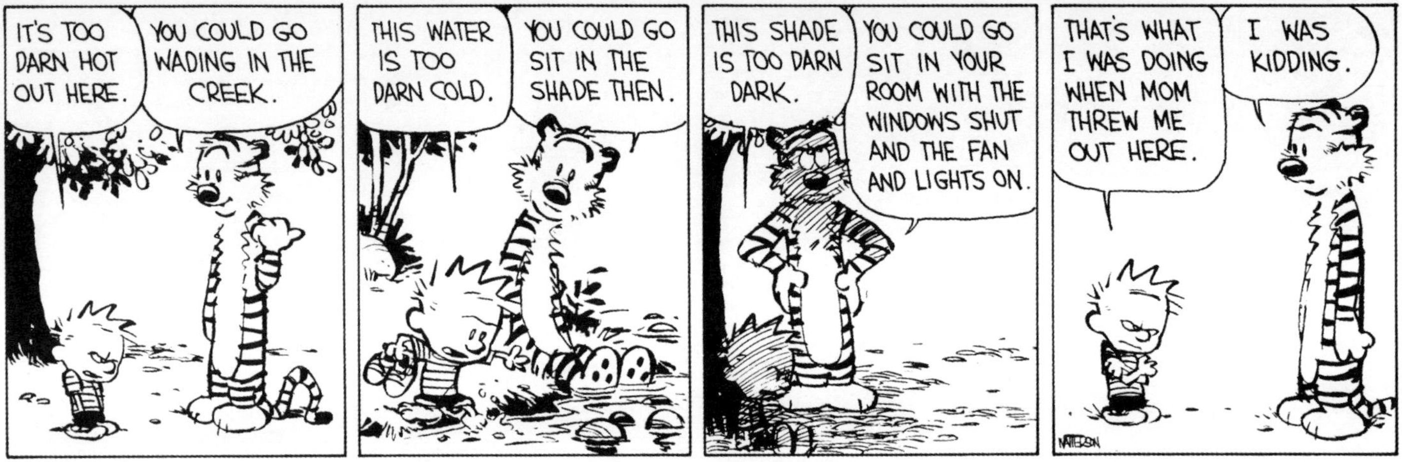
IT'S TOO DARN HOT OUT HERE.
YOU COULD GO WADING IN THE CREEK.
THIS WATER IS TOO DARN COLD.
YOU COULD GO SIT IN THE SHADE THEN.
THIS SHADE IS TOO DARN DARK.
YOU COULD GO SIT IN YOUR ROOM WITH THE WINDOWS SHUT AND THE FAN AND LIGHTS ON.
THAT'S WHAT I WAS DOING WHEN MOM THREW ME OUT HERE.
I WAS KIDDING.
WATTERSON

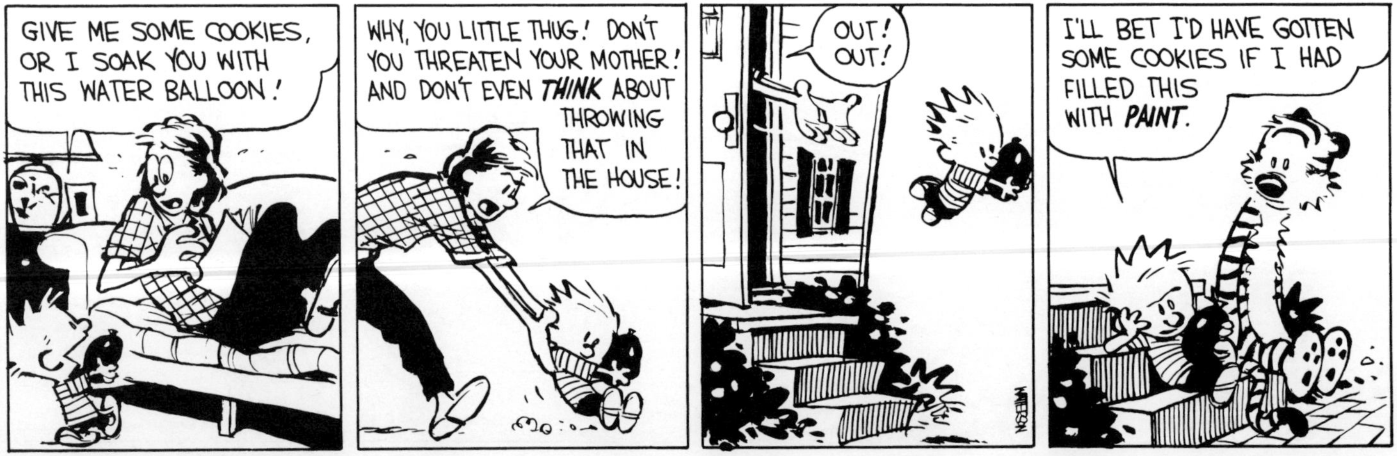
GIVE ME SOME COOKIES, OR I SOAK YOU WITH THIS WATER BALLOON!
WHY, YOU LITTLE THUG! DON'T YOU THREATEN YOUR MOTHER! AND DON'T EVEN THINK ABOUT THROWING THAT IN THE HOUSE!
OUT! OUT!
WATTERSON
I'LL BET I'D HAVE GOTTEN SOME COOKIES IF I HAD FILLED THIS WITH PAINT.

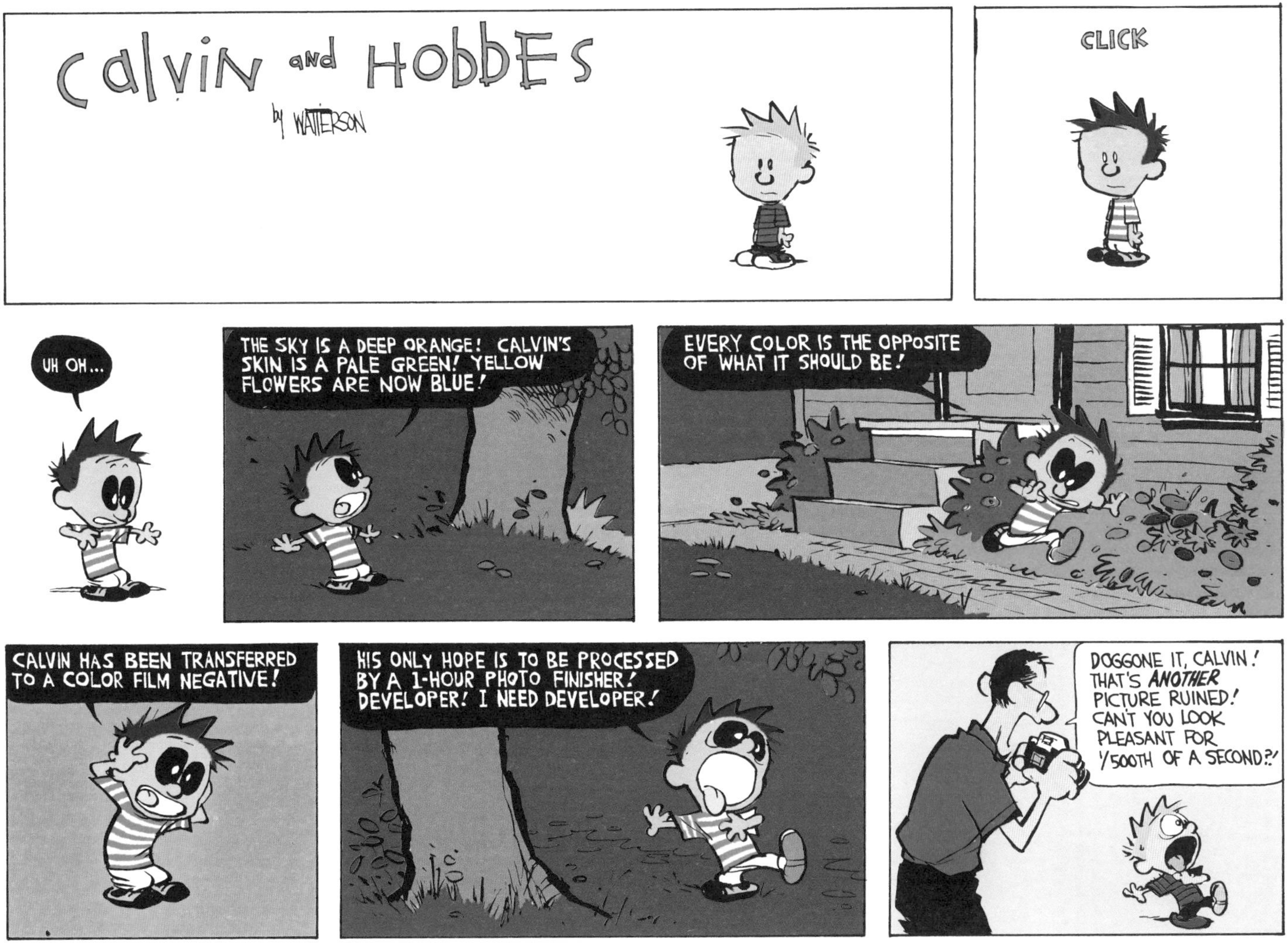
Calvin and HOBBES
by WATTERSON
CLICK
UH OH...
THE SKY IS A DEEP ORANGE! CALVIN'S SKIN IS A PALE GREEN! YELLOW FLOWERS ARE NOW BLUE!
EVERY COLOR IS THE OPPOSITE OF WHAT IT SHOULD BE!
CALVIN HAS BEEN TRANSFERRED TO A COLOR FILM NEGATIVE!
HIS ONLY HOPE IS TO BE PROCESSED BY A 1-HOUR PHOTO FINISHER! DEVELOPER! I NEED DEVELOPER!
DOGGONE IT, CALVIN! THAT'S ANOTHER PICTURE RUINED! CAN'T YOU LOOK PLEASANT FOR 1/500TH OF A SECOND?!

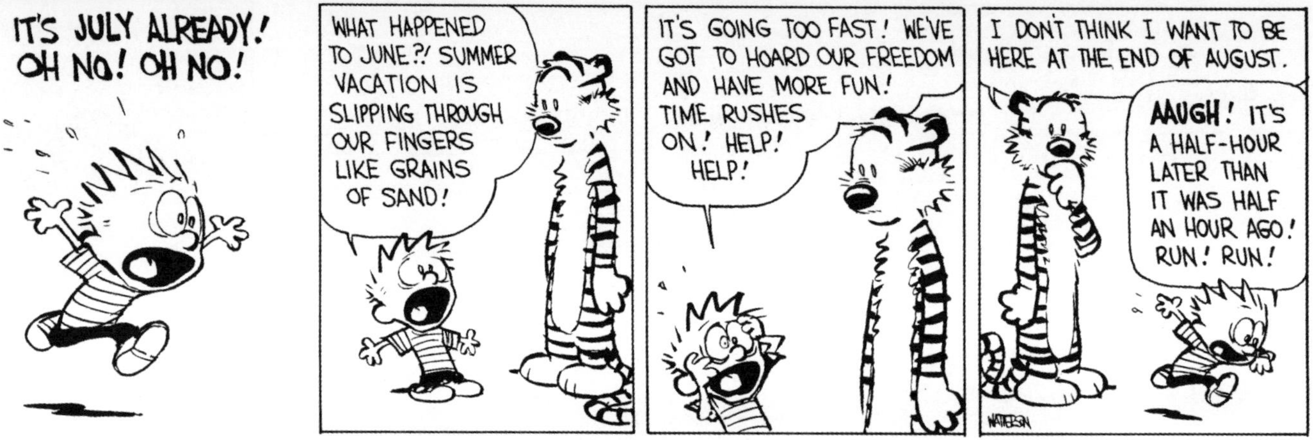
IT'S JULY ALREADY! OH NO! OH NO!
WHAT HAPPENED TO JUNE?! SUMMER VACATION IS SLIPPING THROUGH OUR FINGERS LIKE GRAINS OF SAND!
IT'S GOING TOO FAST! WE'VE GOT TO HOARD OUR FREEDOM AND HAVE MORE FUN! TIME RUSHES ON! HELP! HELP!
I DON'T THINK I WANT TO BE HERE AT THE END OF AUGUST.
AAUGH! IT'S A HALF-HOUR LATER THAN IT WAS HALF AN HOUR AGO! RUN! RUN!
WATTERSON

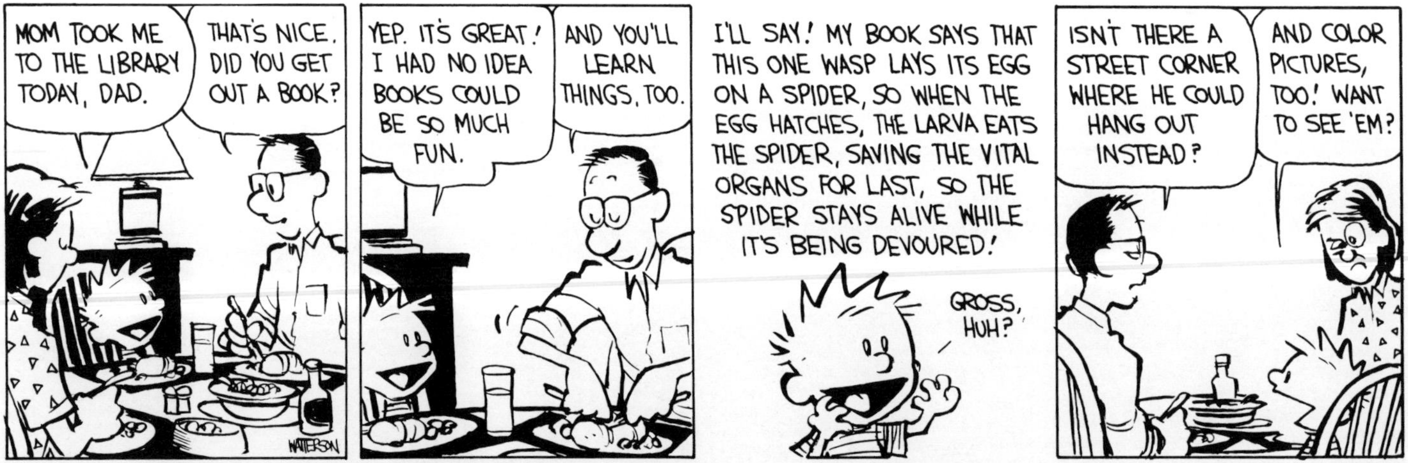
MOM TOOK ME TO THE LIBRARY TODAY, DAD.
THAT'S NICE. DID YOU GET OUT A BOOK?
WATTERSON
YEP. IT'S GREAT! I HAD NO IDEA BOOKS COULD BE SO MUCH FUN.
AND YOU'LL LEARN THINGS, TOO.
I'LL SAY! MY BOOK SAYS THAT THIS ONE WASP LAYS ITS EGG ON A SPIDER, SO WHEN THE EGG HATCHES, THE LARVA EATS THE SPIDER, SAVING THE VITAL ORGANS FOR LAST, SO THE SPIDER STAYS ALIVE WHILE IT'S BEING DEVOURED!
GROSS, HUH?
ISN'T THERE A STREET CORNER WHERE HE COULD HANG OUT INSTEAD?
AND COLOR PICTURES, TOO! WANT TO SEE 'EM?

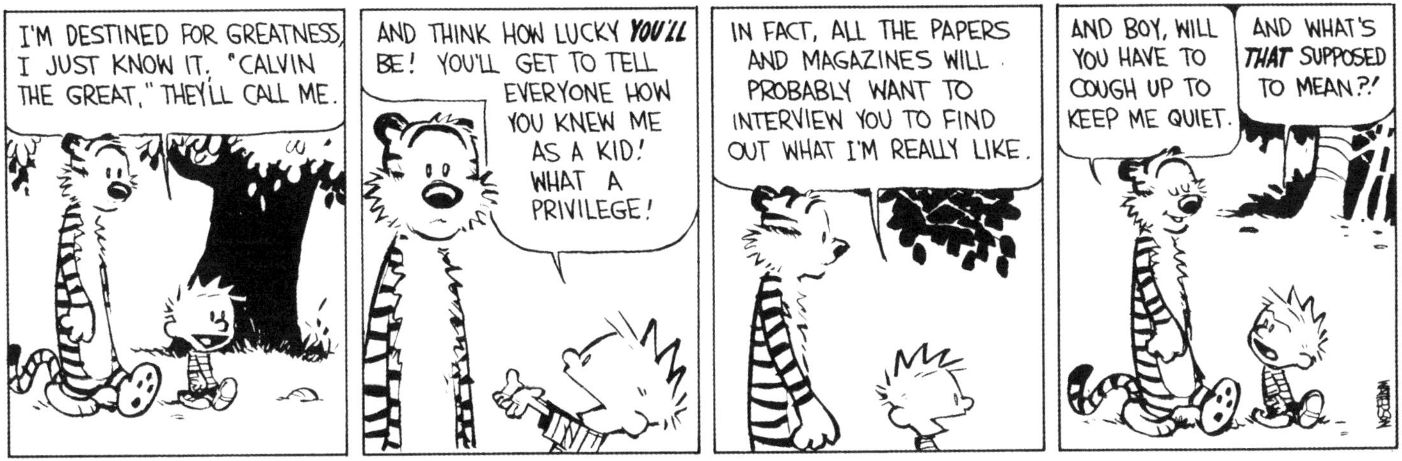

I'M DESTINED FOR GREATNESS, I JUST KNOW IT. "CALVIN THE GREAT," THEY'LL CALL ME.
AND THINK HOW LUCKY YOU'LL BE! YOU'LL GET TO TELL EVERYONE HOW YOU KNEW ME AS A KID! WHAT A PRIVILEGE!
IN FACT, ALL THE PAPERS AND MAGAZINES WILL PROBABLY WANT TO INTERVIEW YOU TO FIND OUT WHAT I'M REALLY LIKE.
AND BOY, WILL YOU HAVE TO COUGH UP TO KEEP ME QUIET.
AND WHAT'S THAT SUPPOSED TO MEAN?!

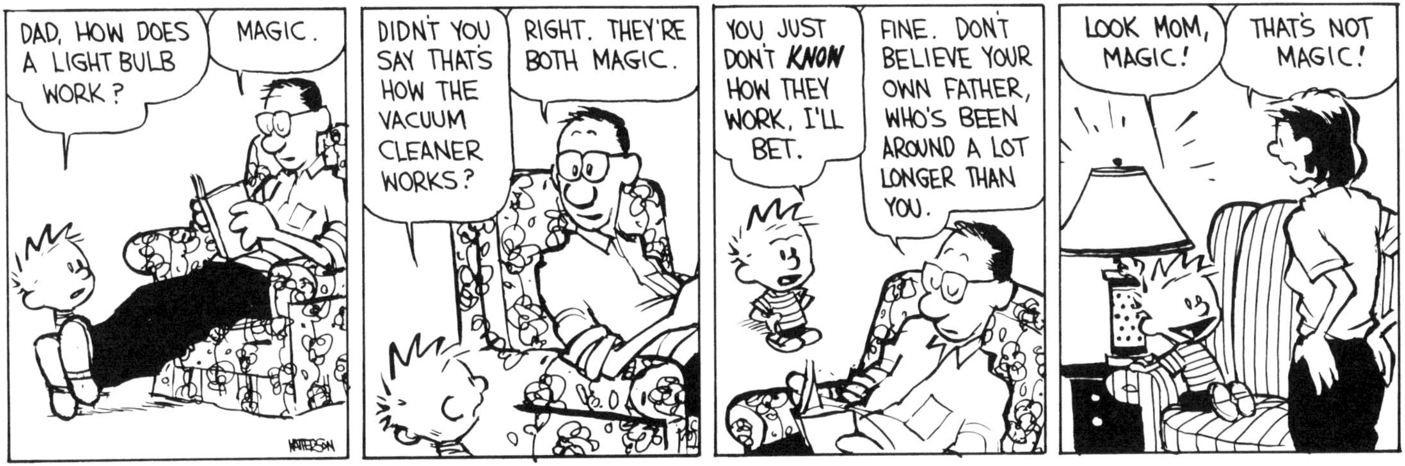

DAD, HOW DOES A LIGHT BULB WORK?
MAGIC.
DIDN'T YOU SAY THAT'S HOW THE VACUUM CLEANER WORKS?
RIGHT. THEY'RE BOTH MAGIC.
YOU JUST DON'T KNOW HOW THEY WORK, I'LL BET.
FINE. DON'T BELIEVE YOUR OWN FATHER, WHO'S BEEN AROUND A LOT LONGER THAN YOU.
LOOK MOM, MAGIC!
THAT'S NOT MAGIC!

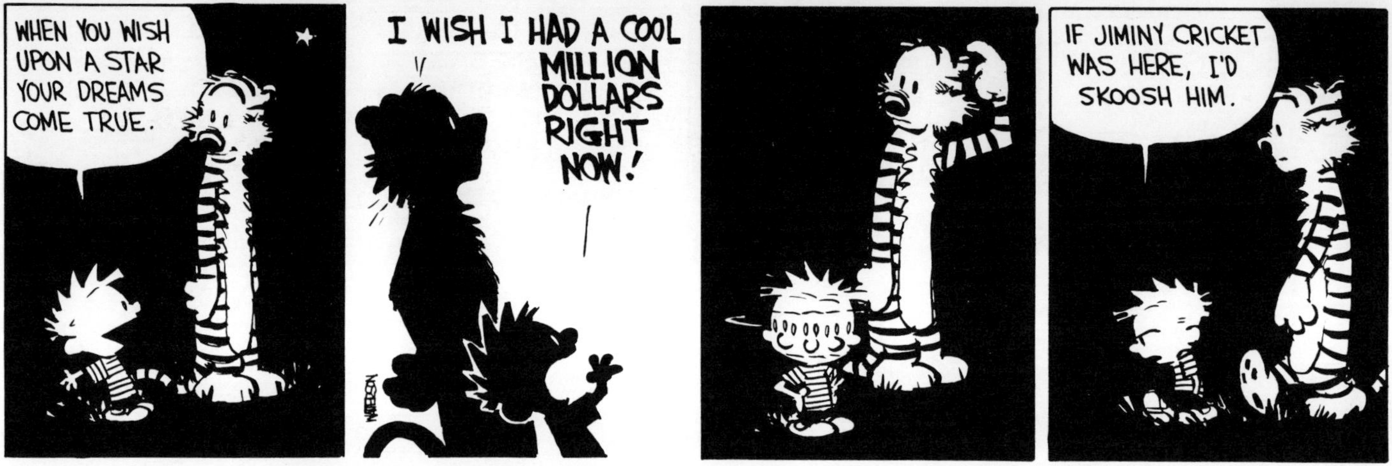
WHEN YOU WISH UPON A STAR YOUR DREAMS COME TRUE.
I WISH I HAD A COOL MILLION DOLLARS RIGHT NOW!
IF JIMINY CRICKET WAS HERE, I'D SKOOSH HIM.

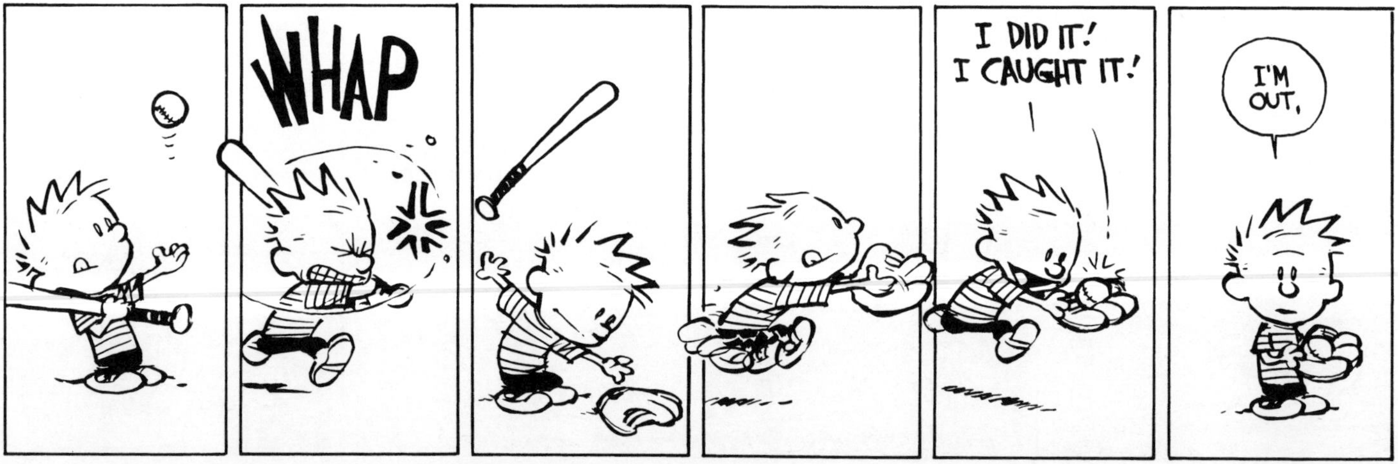
WHAP
I DID IT! I CAUGHT IT!
I'M OUT.

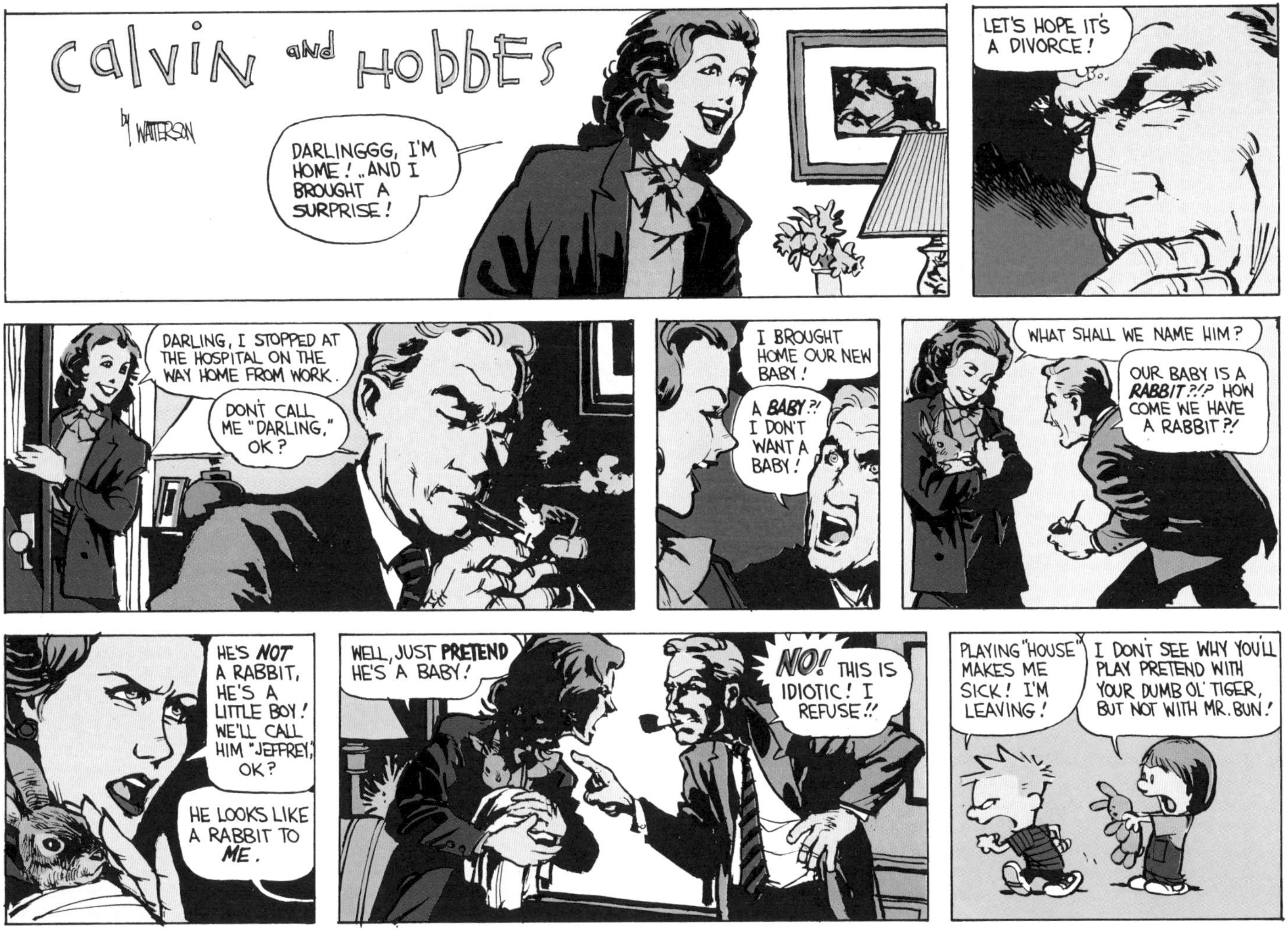
Calvin and Hobbes
by WATTERSON
DARLINGGG, I'M HOME! ..AND I BROUGHT A SURPRISE!
LET'S HOPE IT'S A DIVORCE!
DARLING, I STOPPED AT THE HOSPITAL ON THE WAY HOME FROM WORK.
DON'T CALL ME "DARLING," OK?
I BROUGHT HOME OUR NEW BABY!
A BABY?! I DON'T WANT A BABY!
WHAT SHALL WE NAME HIM?
OUR BABY IS A RABBIT?!? HOW COME WE HAVE A RABBIT?!
HE'S NOT A RABBIT, HE'S A LITTLE BOY! WE'LL CALL HIM "JEFFREY," OK?
HE LOOKS LIKE A RABBIT TO ME.
WELL, JUST PRETEND HE'S A BABY!
NO! THIS IS IDIOTIC! I REFUSE!!
PLAYING "HOUSE" MAKES ME SICK! I'M LEAVING!
I DON'T SEE WHY YOU'LL PLAY PRETEND WITH YOUR DUMB OL' TIGER, BUT NOT WITH MR. BUN!

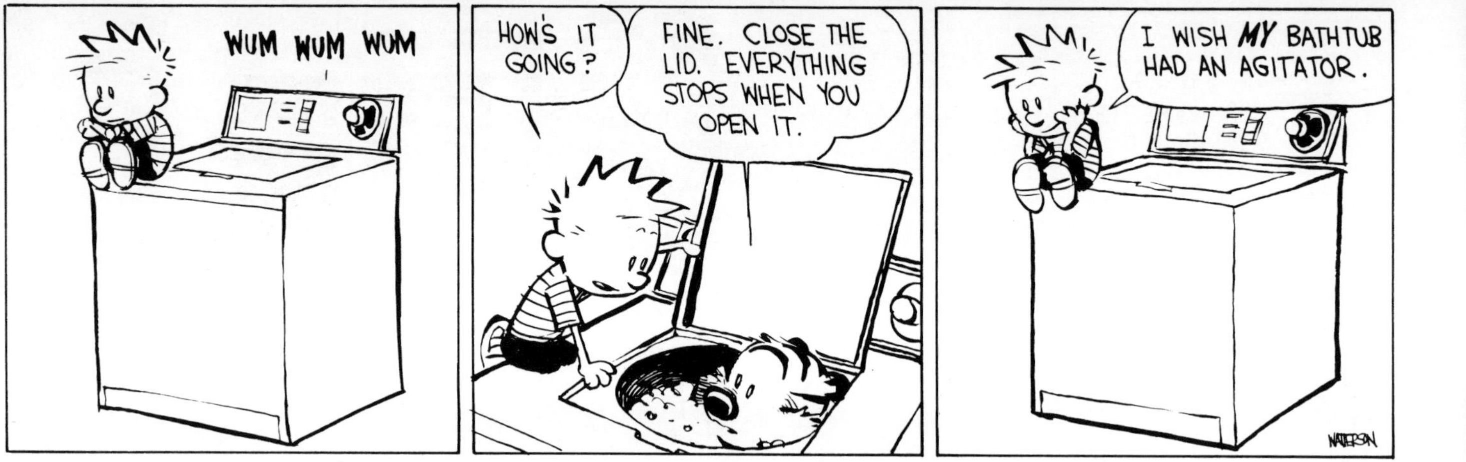
WUM WUM WUM
HOW'S IT GOING?
FINE. CLOSE THE LID. EVERYTHING STOPS WHEN YOU OPEN IT.
I WISH MY BATHTUB HAD AN AGITATOR.
WATTERSON

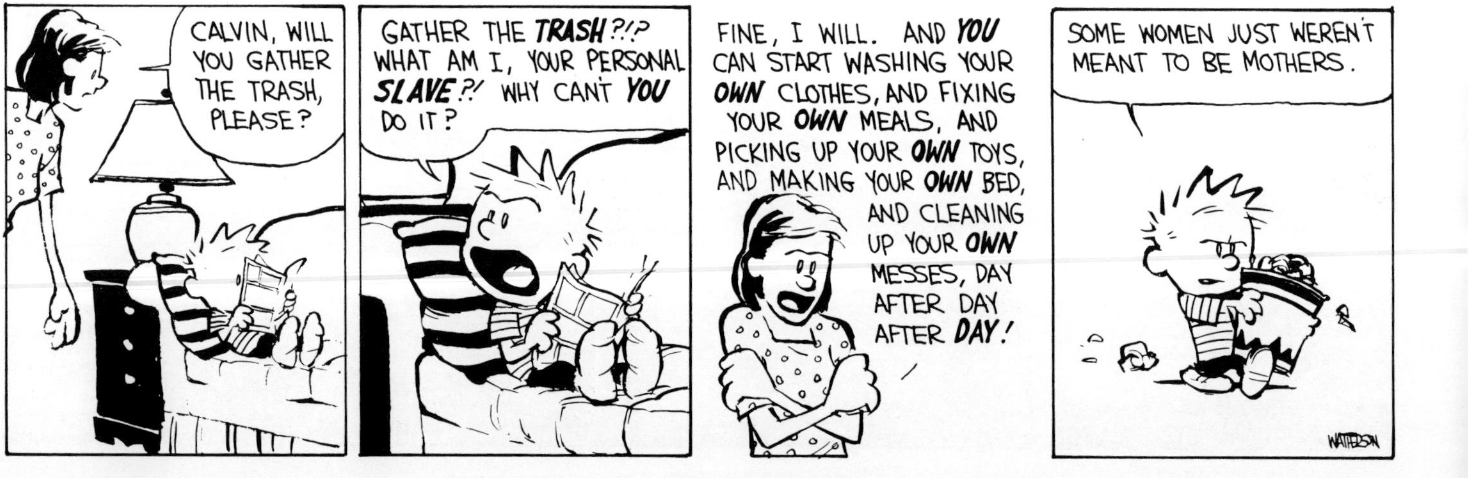
CALVIN, WILL YOU GATHER THE TRASH, PLEASE?
GATHER THE TRASH?!? WHAT AM I, YOUR PERSONAL SLAVE?! WHY CAN'T YOU DO IT?
FINE, I WILL. AND YOU CAN START WASHING YOUR OWN CLOTHES, AND FIXING YOUR OWN MEALS, AND PICKING UP YOUR OWN TOYS, AND MAKING YOUR OWN BED, AND CLEANING UP YOUR OWN MESSES, DAY AFTER DAY AFTER DAY!
SOME WOMEN JUST WEREN'T MEANT TO BE MOTHERS.
WATTERSON

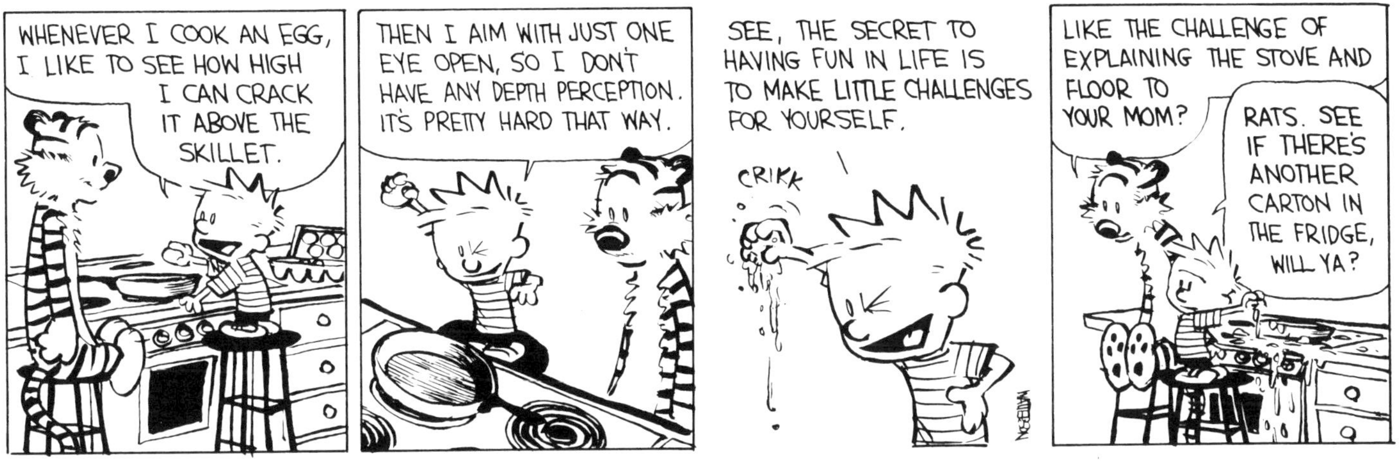
WHENEVER I COOK AN EGG, I LIKE TO SEE HOW HIGH I CAN CRACK IT ABOVE THE SKILLET.
THEN I AIM WITH JUST ONE EYE OPEN, SO I DON'T HAVE ANY DEPTH PERCEPTION. IT'S PRETTY HARD THAT WAY.
SEE, THE SECRET TO HAVING FUN IN LIFE IS TO MAKE LITTLE CHALLENGES FOR YOURSELF.
CRIKK
LIKE THE CHALLENGE OF EXPLAINING THE STOVE AND FLOOR TO YOUR MOM?
RATS. SEE IF THERE'S ANOTHER CARTON IN THE FRIDGE, WILL YA?

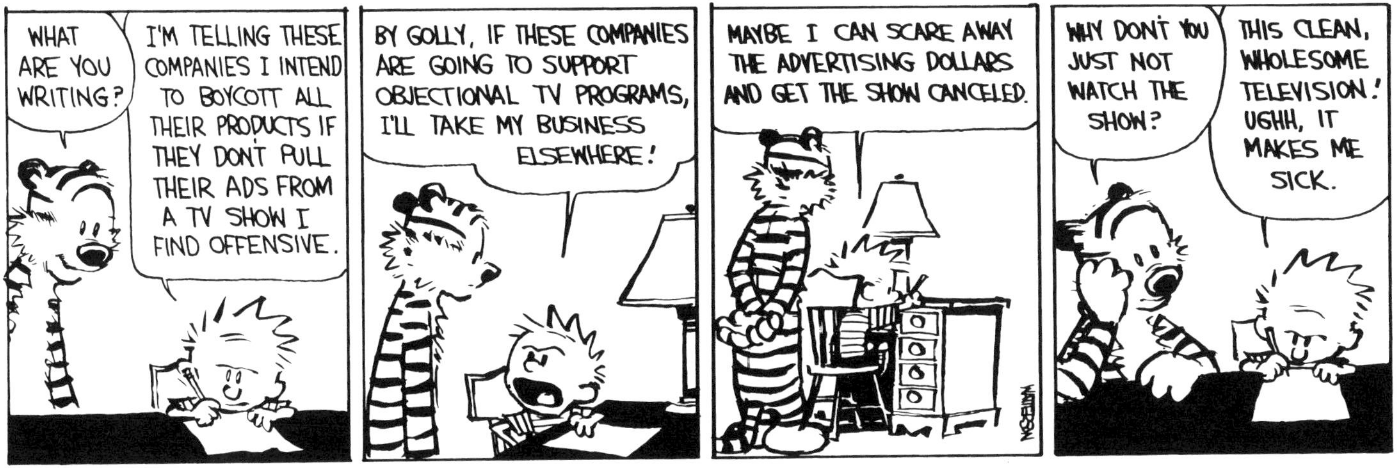
WHAT ARE YOU WRITING?
I'M TELLING THESE COMPANIES I INTEND TO BOYCOTT ALL THEIR PRODUCTS IF THEY DON'T PULL THEIR ADS FROM A TV SHOW I FIND OFFENSIVE.
BY GOLLY, IF THESE COMPANIES ARE GOING TO SUPPORT OBJECTIONAL TV PROGRAMS, I'LL TAKE MY BUSINESS ELSEWHERE!
MAYBE I CAN SCARE AWAY THE ADVERTISING DOLLARS AND GET THE SHOW CANCELED.
WHY DON'T YOU JUST NOT WATCH THE SHOW?
THIS CLEAN, WHOLESOME TELEVISION! UGHH, IT MAKES ME SICK.

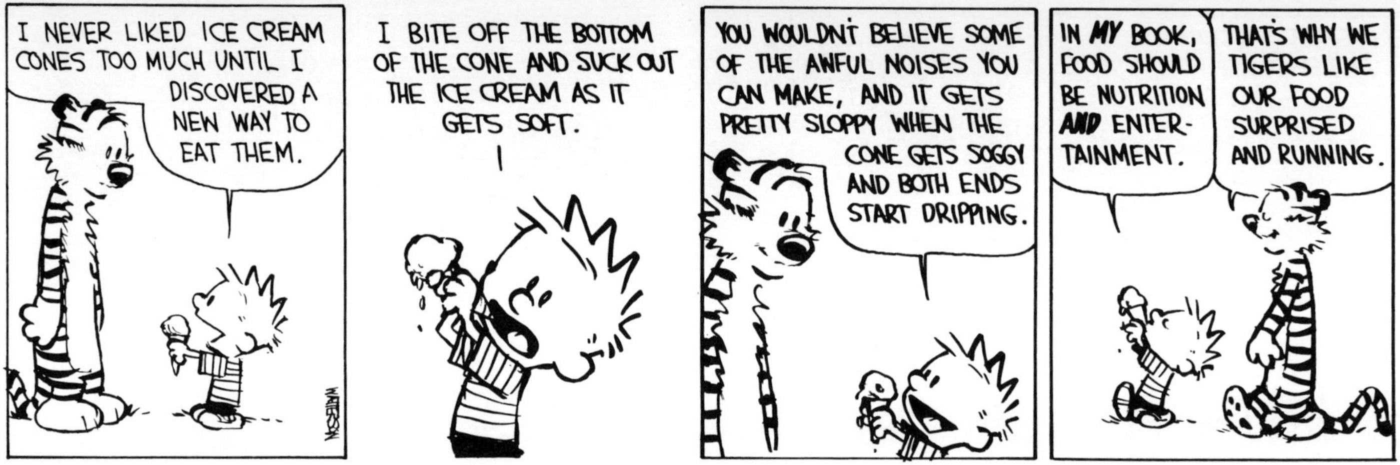
I NEVER LIKED ICE CREAM CONES TOO MUCH UNTIL I DISCOVERED A NEW WAY TO EAT THEM.
I BITE OFF THE BOTTOM OF THE CONE AND SUCK OUT THE ICE CREAM AS IT GETS SOFT.
YOU WOULDN'T BELIEVE SOME OF THE AWFUL NOISES YOU CAN MAKE, AND IT GETS PRETTY SLOPPY WHEN THE CONE GETS SOGGY AND BOTH ENDS START DRIPPING.
IN MY BOOK, FOOD SHOULD BE NUTRITION AND ENTERTAINMENT.
THAT'S WHY WE TIGERS LIKE OUR FOOD SURPRISED AND RUNNING.

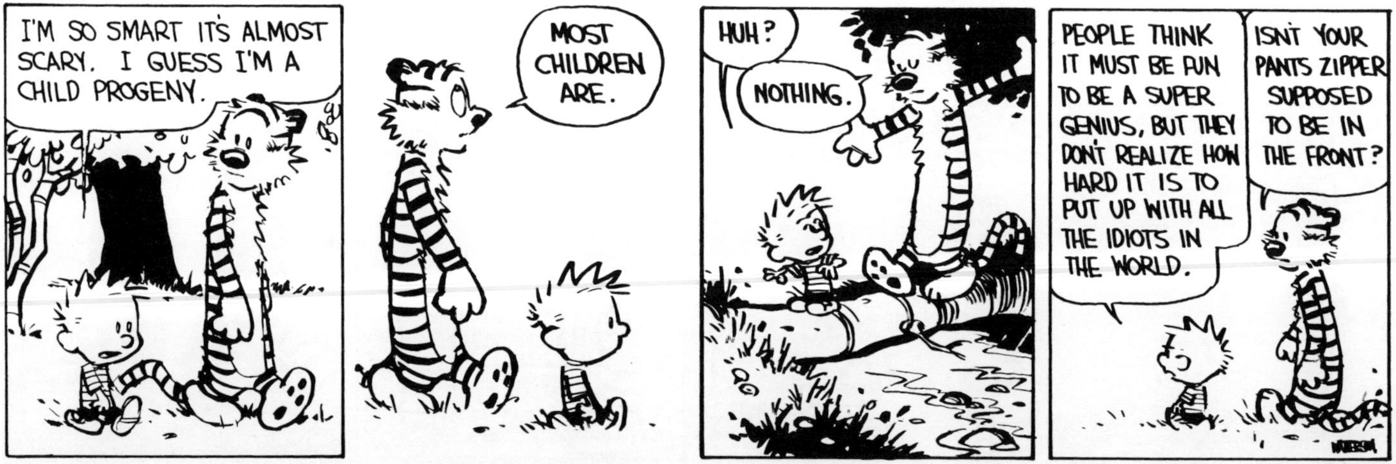
I'M SO SMART IT'S ALMOST SCARY. I GUESS I'M A CHILD PROGENY.
MOST CHILDREN ARE.
HUH?
NOTHING.
PEOPLE THINK IT MUST BE FUN TO BE A SUPER GENIUS, BUT THEY DON'T REALIZE HOW HARD IT IS TO PUT UP WITH ALL THE IDIOTS IN THE WORLD.
ISN'T YOUR PANTS ZIPPER SUPPOSED TO BE IN THE FRONT?

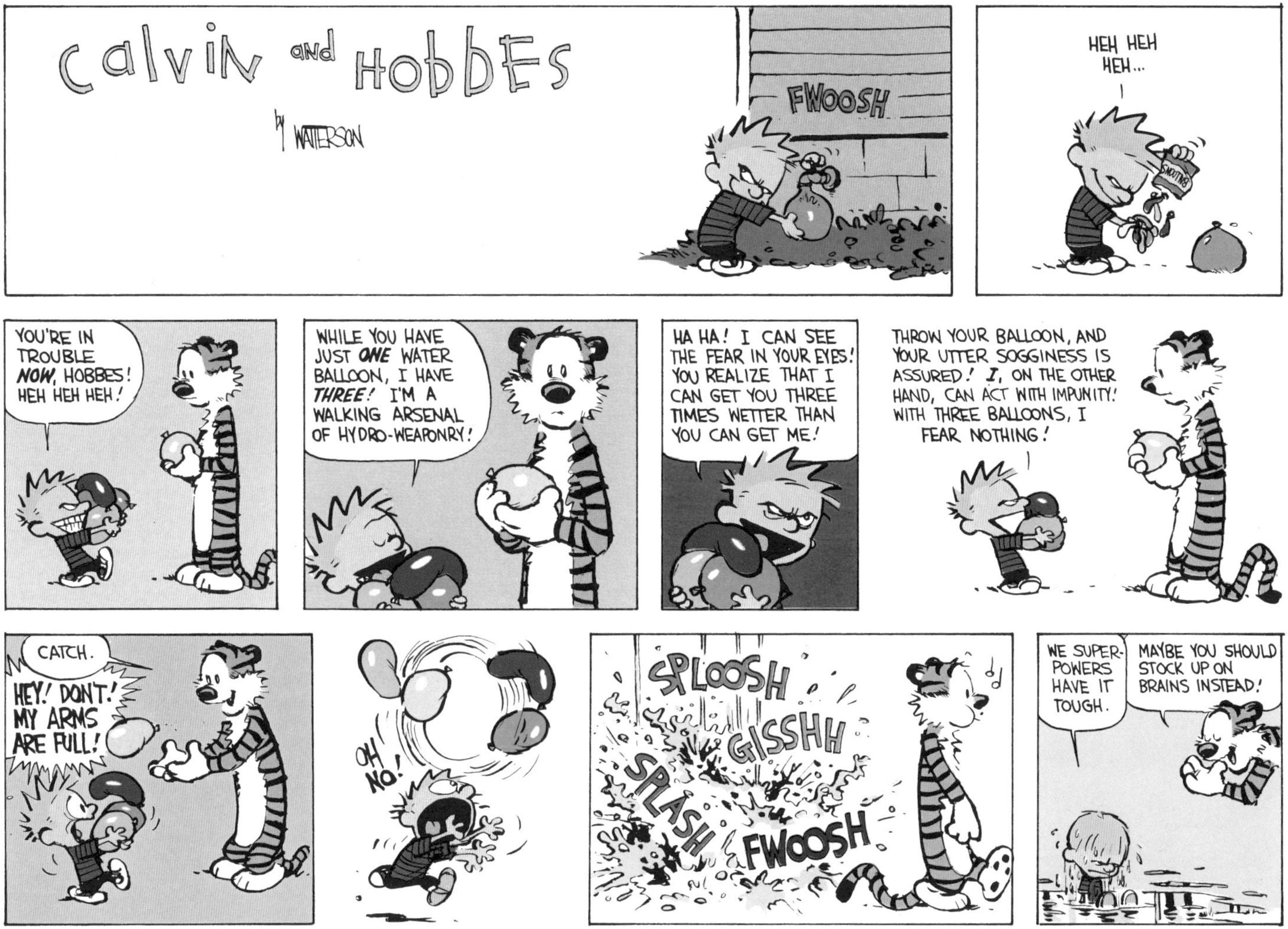
Calvin and HOBBES
by WATTERSON
FWOOSH
HEH HEH HEH...
SMOOTHIES
YOU'RE IN TROUBLE NOW, HOBBES! HEH HEH HEH!
WHILE YOU HAVE JUST ONE WATER BALLOON, I HAVE THREE! I'M A WALKING ARSENAL OF HYDRO-WEAPONRY!
HA HA! I CAN SEE THE FEAR IN YOUR EYES! YOU REALIZE THAT I CAN GET YOU THREE TIMES WETTER THAN YOU CAN GET ME!
THROW YOUR BALLOON, AND YOUR UTTER SOGGINESS IS ASSURED! I, ON THE OTHER HAND, CAN ACT WITH IMPUNITY! WITH THREE BALLOONS, I FEAR NOTHING!
CATCH.
HEY! DON'T! MY ARMS ARE FULL!
OH NO!
SPLOOSH
GISSHH
SPLASH
FWOOSH
WE SUPER-POWERS HAVE IT TOUGH.
MAYBE YOU SHOULD STOCK UP ON BRAINS INSTEAD!

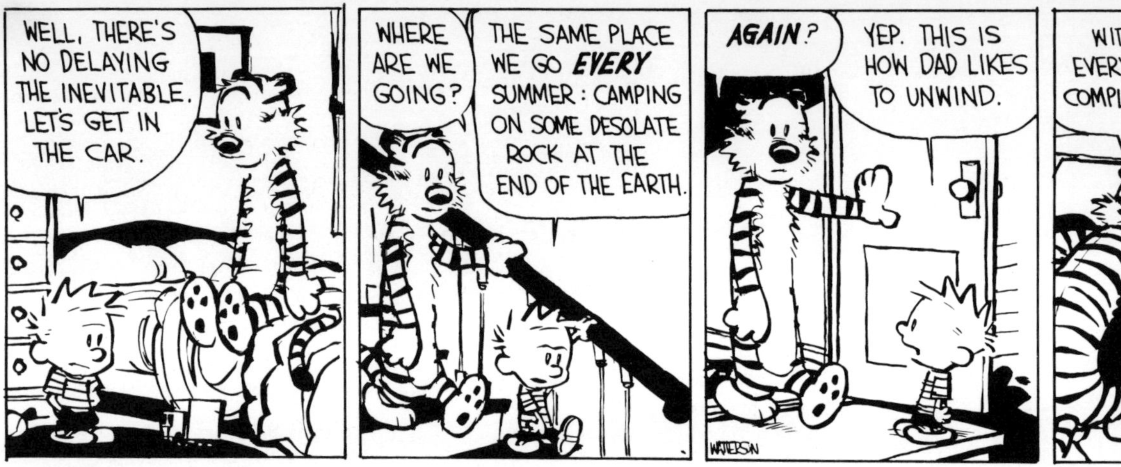
WELL, THERE'S NO DELAYING THE INEVITABLE. LET'S GET IN THE CAR.
WHERE ARE WE GOING?
THE SAME PLACE WE GO **EVERY** SUMMER: CAMPING ON SOME DESOLATE ROCK AT THE END OF THE EARTH.
AGAIN?
YEP. THIS IS HOW DAD LIKES TO UNWIND.
WITH EVERYONE COMPLAINING?
RIGHT. HE LIKES TO WATCH US ALL SUFFER.

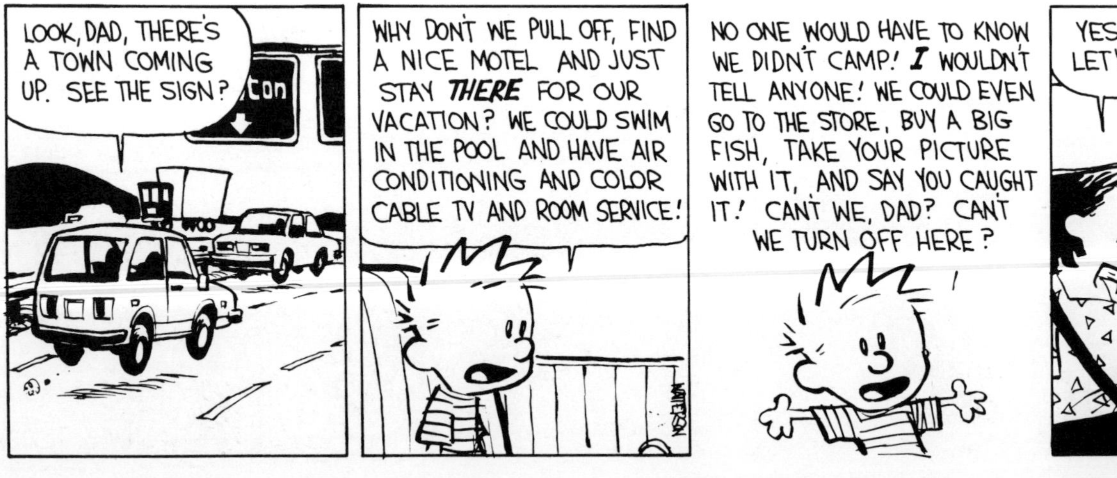
LOOK, DAD, THERE'S A TOWN COMING UP. SEE THE SIGN?
WHY DON'T WE PULL OFF, FIND A NICE MOTEL AND JUST STAY **THERE** FOR OUR VACATION? WE COULD SWIM IN THE POOL AND HAVE AIR CONDITIONING AND COLOR CABLE TV AND ROOM SERVICE!
NO ONE WOULD HAVE TO KNOW WE DIDN'T CAMP! **I** WOULDN'T TELL ANYONE! WE COULD EVEN GO TO THE STORE, BUY A BIG FISH, TAKE YOUR PICTURE WITH IT, AND SAY YOU CAUGHT IT! CAN'T WE, DAD? CAN'T WE TURN OFF HERE?
YES, LET'S!
NOW DON'T **YOU** START!

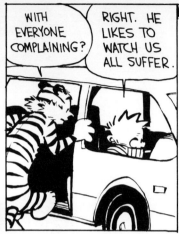

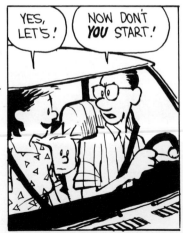

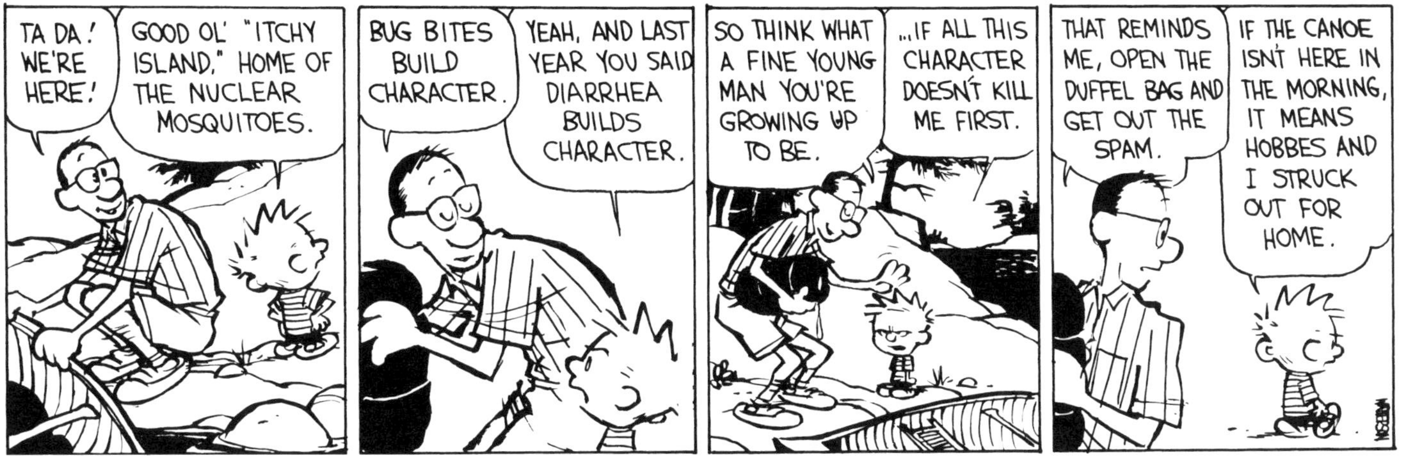
TA DA! WE'RE HERE!
GOOD OL' "ITCHY ISLAND," HOME OF THE NUCLEAR MOSQUITOES.
BUG BITES BUILD CHARACTER.
YEAH, AND LAST YEAR YOU SAID DIARRHEA BUILDS CHARACTER.
SO THINK WHAT A FINE YOUNG MAN YOU'RE GROWING UP TO BE.
...IF ALL THIS CHARACTER DOESN'T KILL ME FIRST.
THAT REMINDS ME, OPEN THE DUFFEL BAG AND GET OUT THE SPAM.
IF THE CANOE ISN'T HERE IN THE MORNING, IT MEANS HOBBES AND I STRUCK OUT FOR HOME.

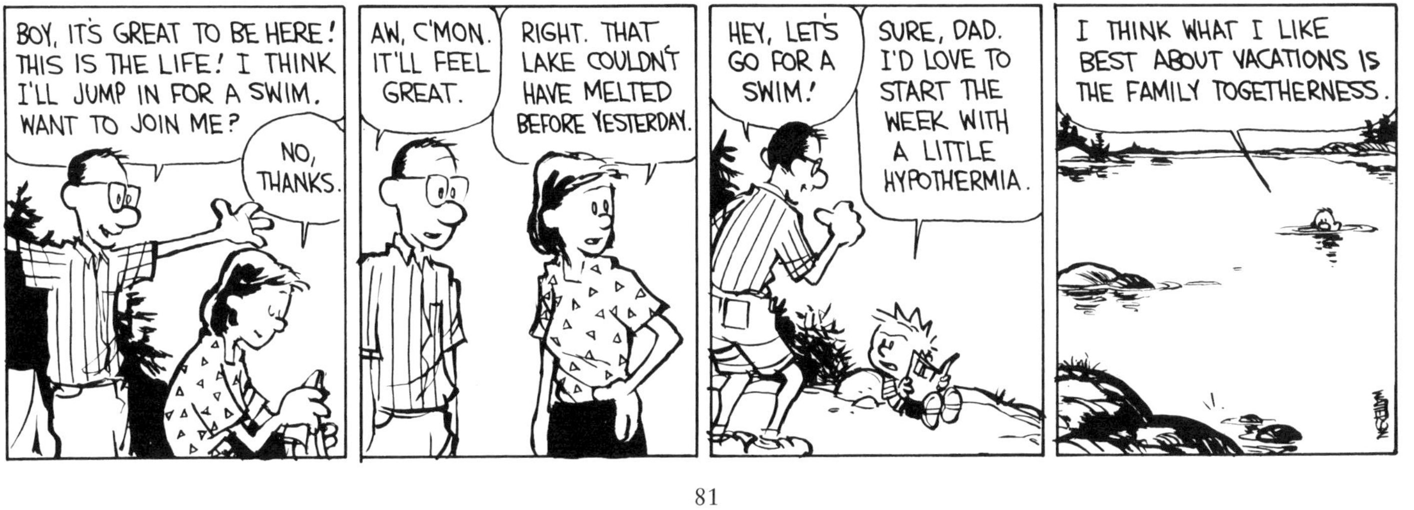
BOY, IT'S GREAT TO BE HERE! THIS IS THE LIFE! I THINK I'LL JUMP IN FOR A SWIM. WANT TO JOIN ME?
NO, THANKS.
AW, C'MON. IT'LL FEEL GREAT.
RIGHT. THAT LAKE COULDN'T HAVE MELTED BEFORE YESTERDAY.
HEY, LET'S GO FOR A SWIM!
SURE, DAD. I'D LOVE TO START THE WEEK WITH A LITTLE HYPOTHERMIA.
I THINK WHAT I LIKE BEST ABOUT VACATIONS IS THE FAMILY TOGETHERNESS.

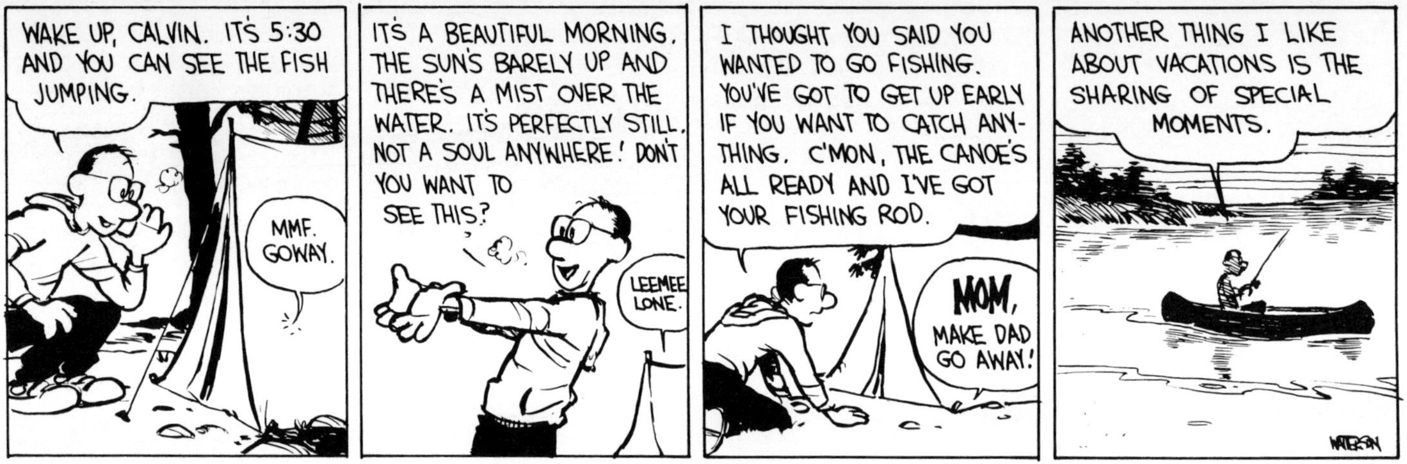
WAKE UP, CALVIN. IT'S 5:30 AND YOU CAN SEE THE FISH JUMPING.
MMF. GOWAY.
IT'S A BEAUTIFUL MORNING. THE SUN'S BARELY UP AND THERE'S A MIST OVER THE WATER. IT'S PERFECTLY STILL. NOT A SOUL ANYWHERE! DON'T YOU WANT TO SEE THIS?
LEEMEE LONE.
I THOUGHT YOU SAID YOU WANTED TO GO FISHING. YOU'VE GOT TO GET UP EARLY IF YOU WANT TO CATCH ANYTHING. C'MON, THE CANOE'S ALL READY AND I'VE GOT YOUR FISHING ROD.
MOM, MAKE DAD GO AWAY!
ANOTHER THING I LIKE ABOUT VACATIONS IS THE SHARING OF SPECIAL MOMENTS.

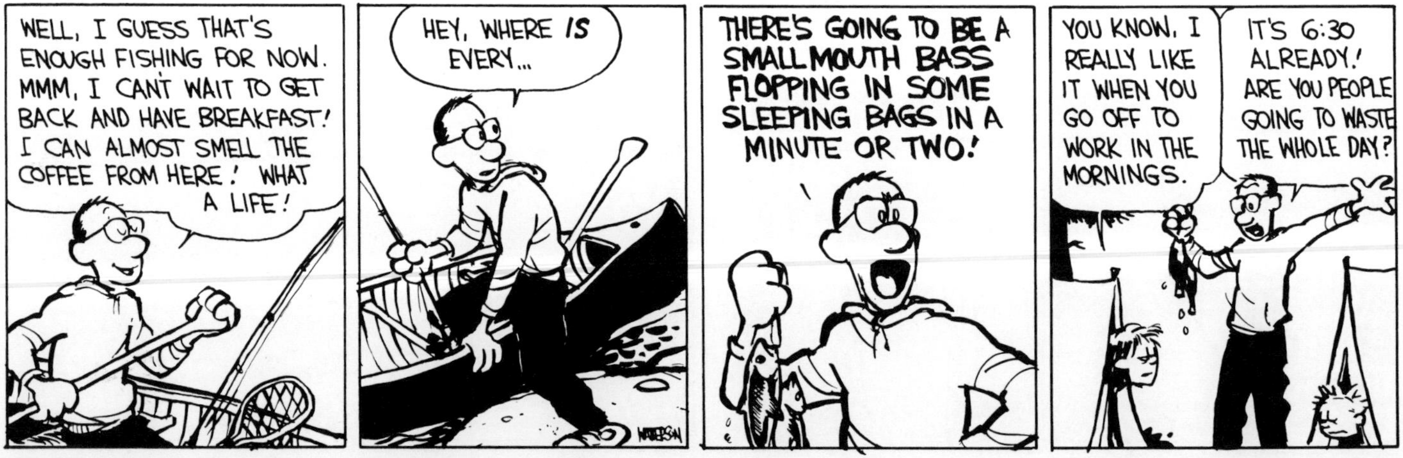
WELL, I GUESS THAT'S ENOUGH FISHING FOR NOW. MMM, I CAN'T WAIT TO GET BACK AND HAVE BREAKFAST! I CAN ALMOST SMELL THE COFFEE FROM HERE! WHAT A LIFE!
HEY, WHERE *IS* EVERY...
THERE'S GOING TO BE A SMALLMOUTH BASS FLOPPING IN SOME SLEEPING BAGS IN A MINUTE OR TWO!
YOU KNOW, I REALLY LIKE IT WHEN YOU GO OFF TO WORK IN THE MORNINGS.
IT'S 6:30 ALREADY! ARE YOU PEOPLE GOING TO WASTE THE WHOLE DAY?

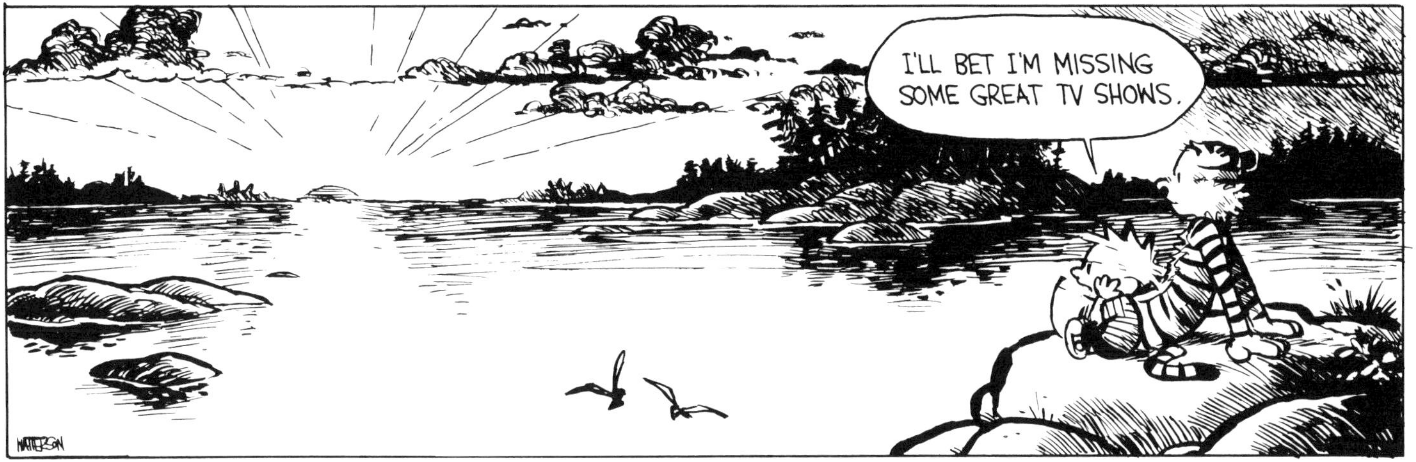
I'LL BET I'M MISSING SOME GREAT TV SHOWS.

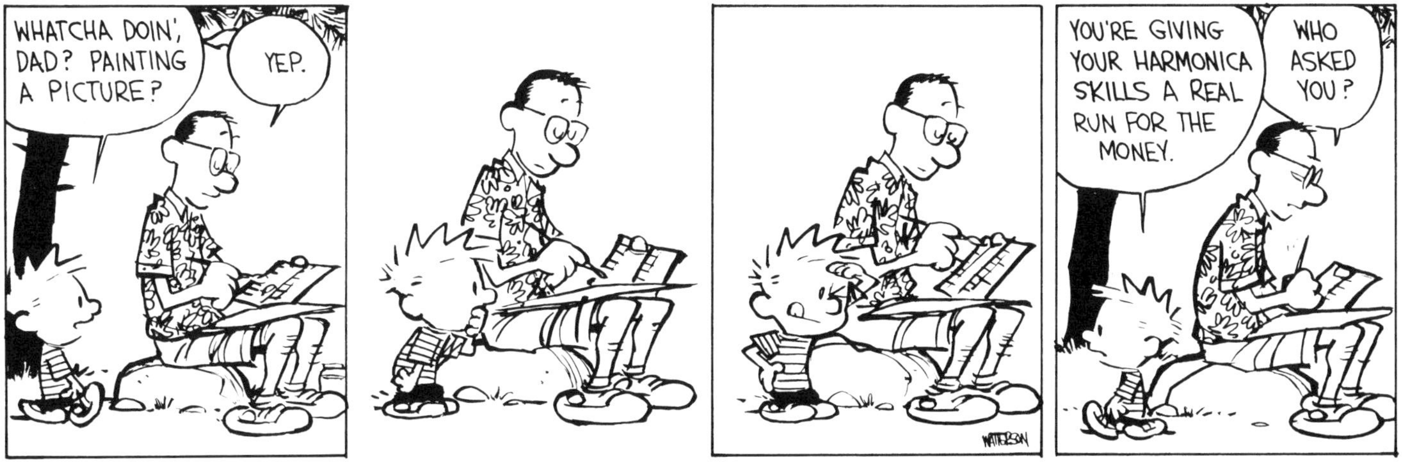
WHATCHA DOIN', DAD? PAINTING A PICTURE?
YEP.
YOU'RE GIVING YOUR HARMONICA SKILLS A REAL RUN FOR THE MONEY.
WHO ASKED YOU?

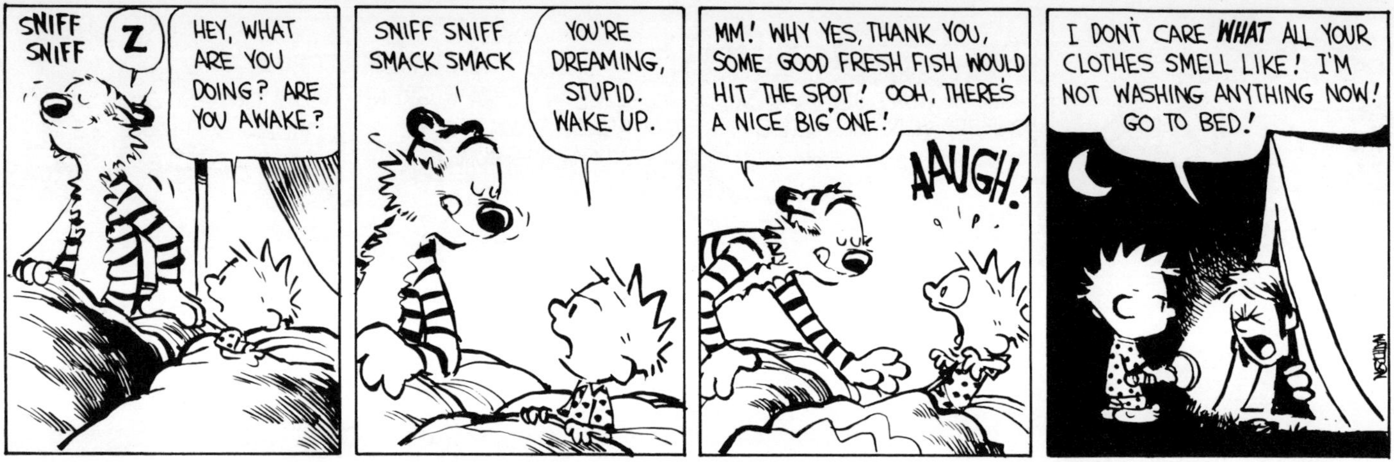
SNIFF SNIFF
Z
HEY, WHAT ARE YOU DOING? ARE YOU AWAKE?
SNIFF SNIFF SMACK SMACK
YOU'RE DREAMING, STUPID. WAKE UP.
MM! WHY YES, THANK YOU, SOME GOOD FRESH FISH WOULD HIT THE SPOT! OOH, THERE'S A NICE BIG ONE!
AAUGH!
I DON'T CARE WHAT ALL YOUR CLOTHES SMELL LIKE! I'M NOT WASHING ANYTHING NOW! GO TO BED!

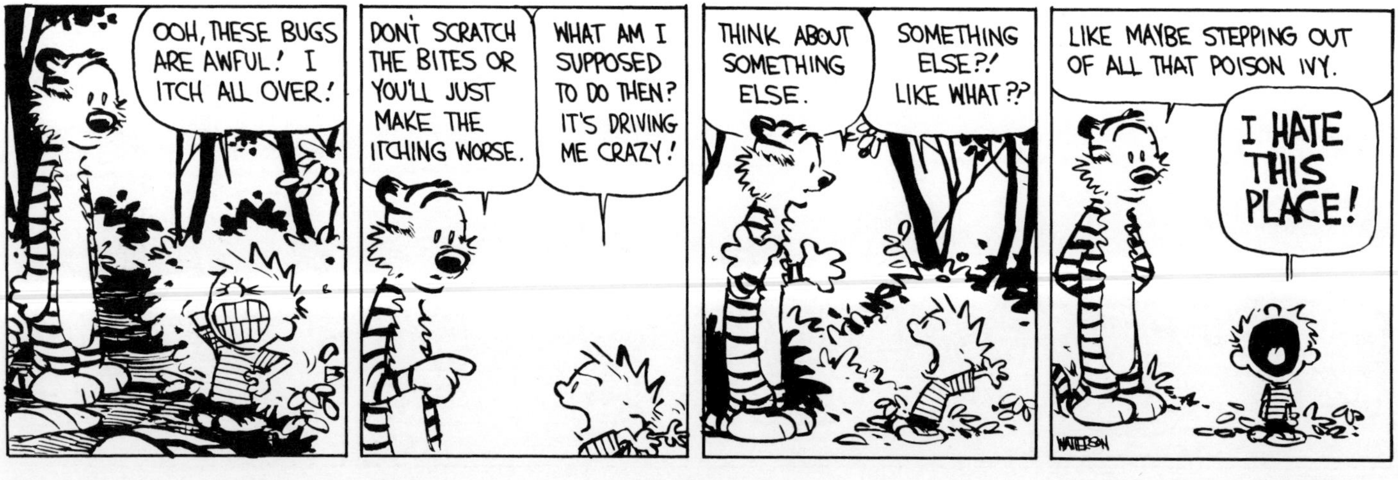
OOH, THESE BUGS ARE AWFUL! I ITCH ALL OVER!
DON'T SCRATCH THE BITES OR YOU'LL JUST MAKE THE ITCHING WORSE.
WHAT AM I SUPPOSED TO DO THEN? IT'S DRIVING ME CRAZY!
THINK ABOUT SOMETHING ELSE.
SOMETHING ELSE?! LIKE WHAT??
LIKE MAYBE STEPPING OUT OF ALL THAT POISON IVY.
I HATE THIS PLACE!

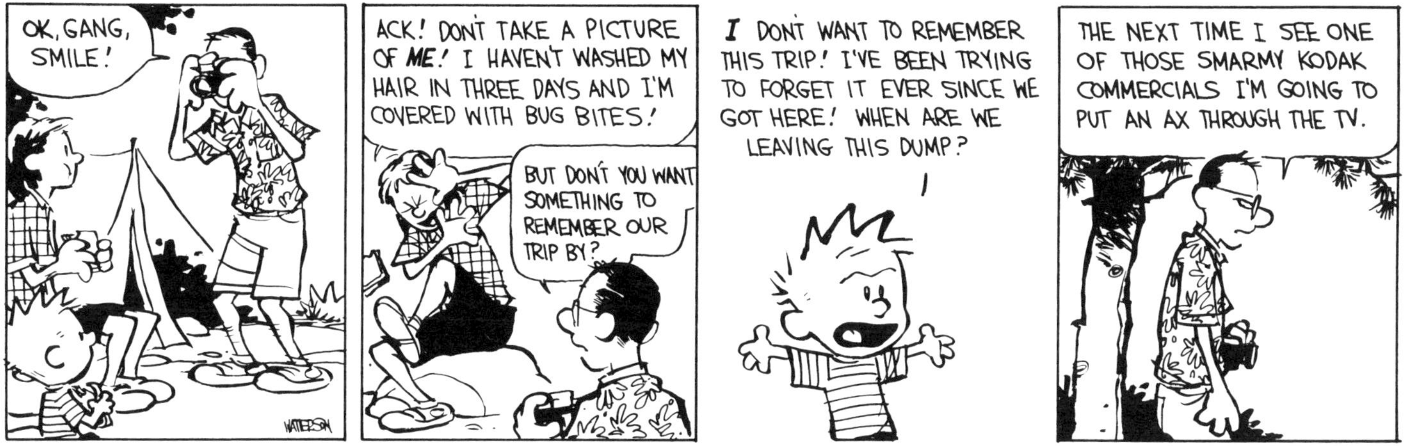
OK, GANG, SMILE!
ACK! DON'T TAKE A PICTURE OF ME! I HAVEN'T WASHED MY HAIR IN THREE DAYS AND I'M COVERED WITH BUG BITES!
BUT DON'T YOU WANT SOMETHING TO REMEMBER OUR TRIP BY?
I DON'T WANT TO REMEMBER THIS TRIP! I'VE BEEN TRYING TO FORGET IT EVER SINCE WE GOT HERE! WHEN ARE WE LEAVING THIS DUMP?
THE NEXT TIME I SEE ONE OF THOSE SMARMY KODAK COMMERCIALS I'M GOING TO PUT AN AX THROUGH THE TV.
WATTERSON

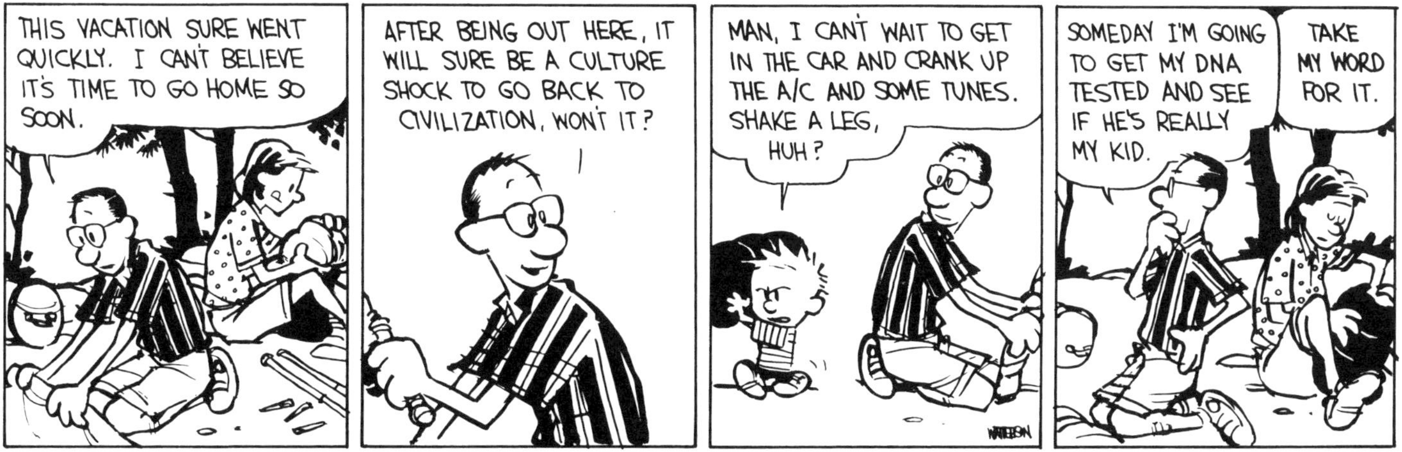
THIS VACATION SURE WENT QUICKLY. I CAN'T BELIEVE IT'S TIME TO GO HOME SO SOON.
AFTER BEING OUT HERE, IT WILL SURE BE A CULTURE SHOCK TO GO BACK TO CIVILIZATION, WON'T IT?
MAN, I CAN'T WAIT TO GET IN THE CAR AND CRANK UP THE A/C AND SOME TUNES. SHAKE A LEG, HUH?
SOMEDAY I'M GOING TO GET MY DNA TESTED AND SEE IF HE'S REALLY MY KID.
TAKE MY WORD FOR IT.
WATTERSON

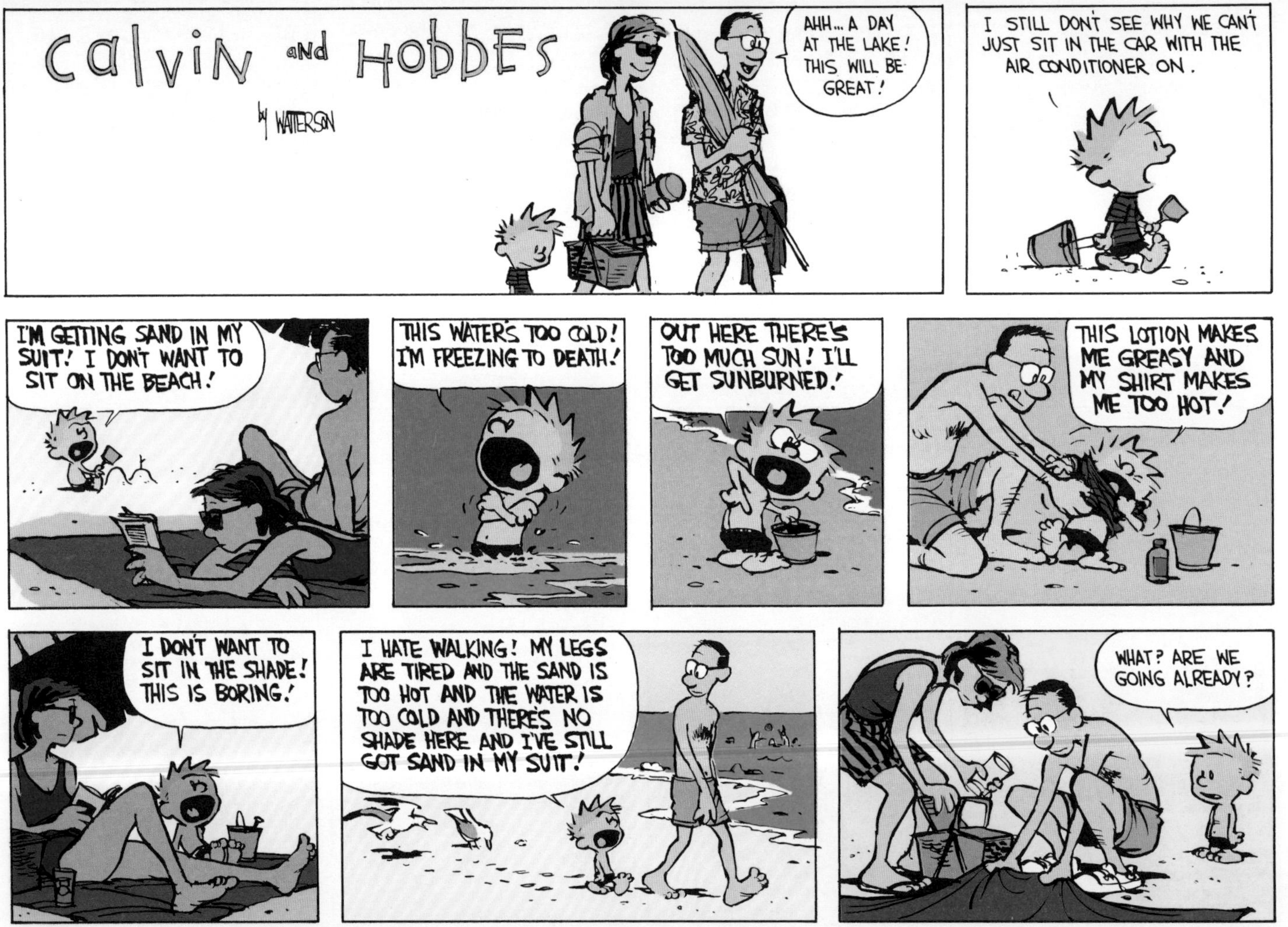
Calvin and HobbEs
by WATTERSON
AHH... A DAY AT THE LAKE! THIS WILL BE GREAT!
I STILL DON'T SEE WHY WE CAN'T JUST SIT IN THE CAR WITH THE AIR CONDITIONER ON.
I'M GETTING SAND IN MY SUIT! I DON'T WANT TO SIT ON THE BEACH!
THIS WATER'S TOO COLD! I'M FREEZING TO DEATH!
OUT HERE THERE'S TOO MUCH SUN! I'LL GET SUNBURNED!
THIS LOTION MAKES ME GREASY AND MY SHIRT MAKES ME TOO HOT!
I DON'T WANT TO SIT IN THE SHADE! THIS IS BORING!
I HATE WALKING! MY LEGS ARE TIRED AND THE SAND IS TOO HOT AND THE WATER IS TOO COLD AND THERE'S NO SHADE HERE AND I'VE STILL GOT SAND IN MY SUIT!
WHAT? ARE WE GOING ALREADY?

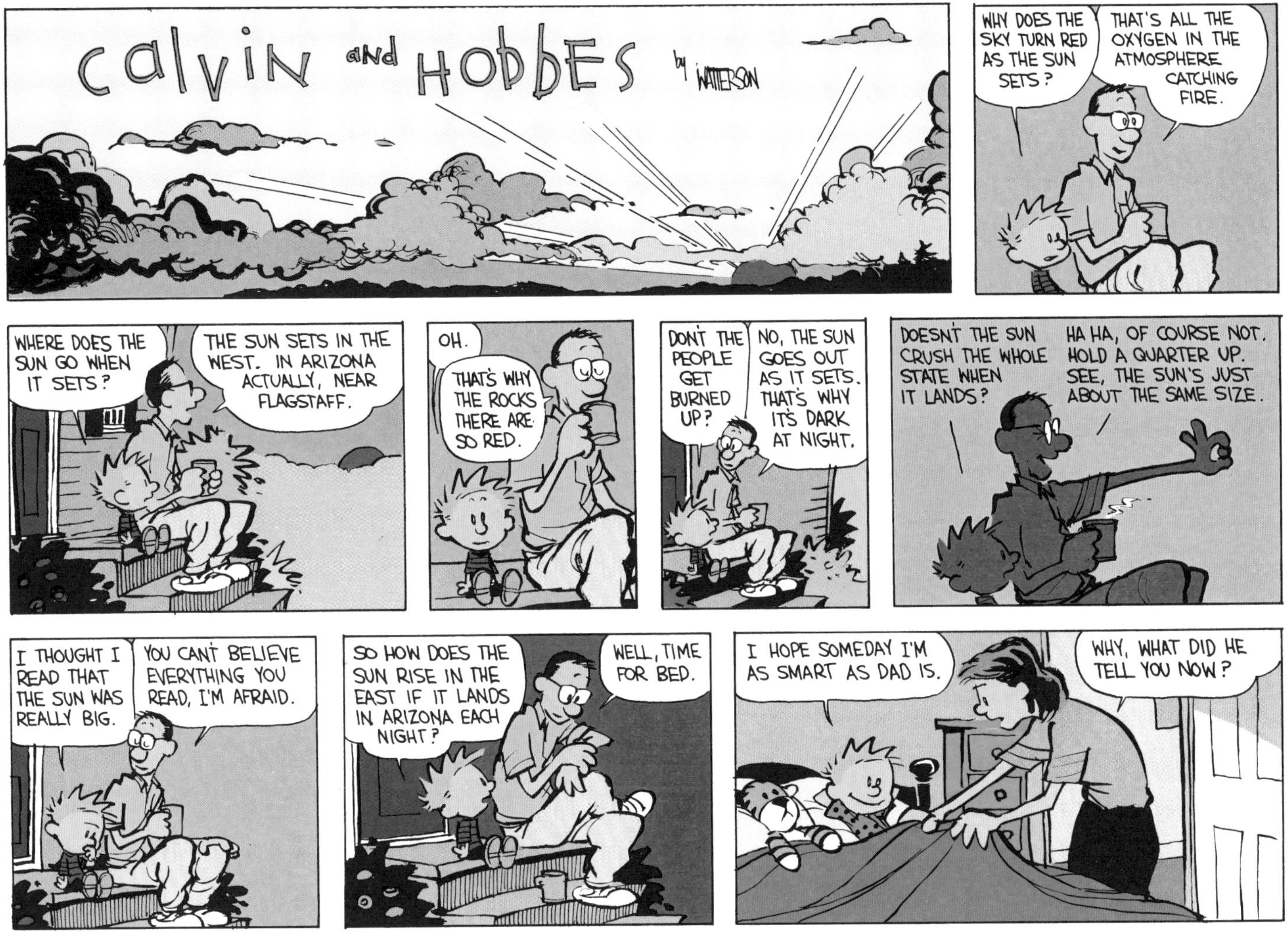
Calvin and HOBBES
by WATTERSON
WHY DOES THE SKY TURN RED AS THE SUN SETS?
THAT'S ALL THE OXYGEN IN THE ATMOSPHERE CATCHING FIRE.
WHERE DOES THE SUN GO WHEN IT SETS?
THE SUN SETS IN THE WEST. IN ARIZONA ACTUALLY, NEAR FLAGSTAFF.
OH.
THAT'S WHY THE ROCKS THERE ARE SO RED.
DON'T THE PEOPLE GET BURNED UP?
NO, THE SUN GOES OUT AS IT SETS. THAT'S WHY IT'S DARK AT NIGHT.
DOESN'T THE SUN CRUSH THE WHOLE STATE WHEN IT LANDS?
HA HA, OF COURSE NOT. HOLD A QUARTER UP. SEE, THE SUN'S JUST ABOUT THE SAME SIZE.
I THOUGHT I READ THAT THE SUN WAS REALLY BIG.
YOU CAN'T BELIEVE EVERYTHING YOU READ, I'M AFRAID.
SO HOW DOES THE SUN RISE IN THE EAST IF IT LANDS IN ARIZONA EACH NIGHT?
WELL, TIME FOR BED.
I HOPE SOMEDAY I'M AS SMART AS DAD IS.
WHY, WHAT DID HE TELL YOU NOW?

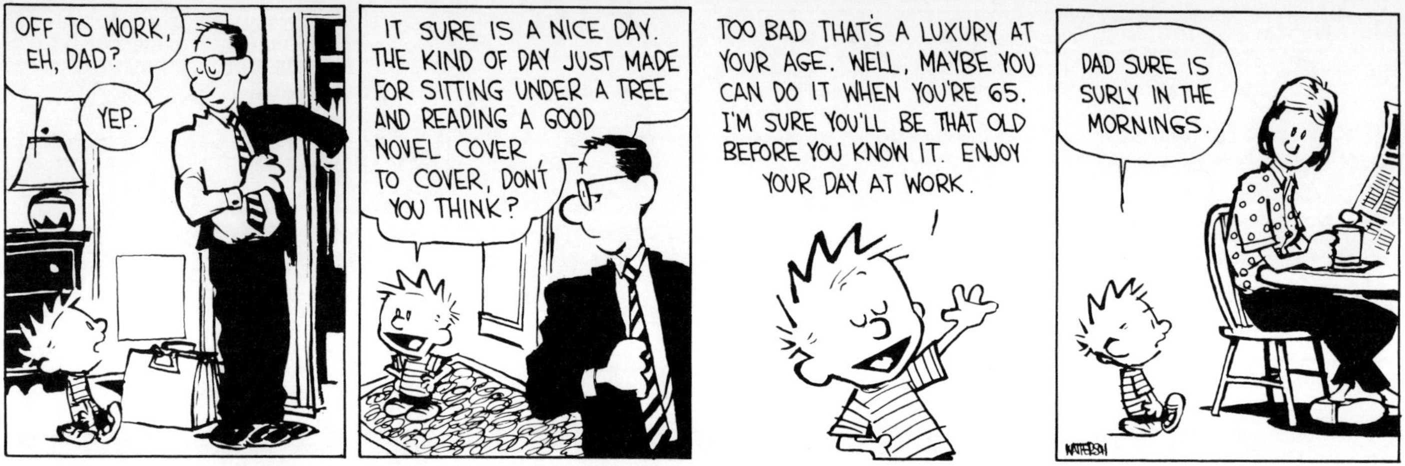
OFF TO WORK, EH, DAD?
YEP.
IT SURE IS A NICE DAY. THE KIND OF DAY JUST MADE FOR SITTING UNDER A TREE AND READING A GOOD NOVEL COVER TO COVER, DON'T YOU THINK?
TOO BAD THAT'S A LUXURY AT YOUR AGE. WELL, MAYBE YOU CAN DO IT WHEN YOU'RE 65. I'M SURE YOU'LL BE THAT OLD BEFORE YOU KNOW IT. ENJOY YOUR DAY AT WORK.
DAD SURE IS SURLY IN THE MORNINGS.
WATTERSON

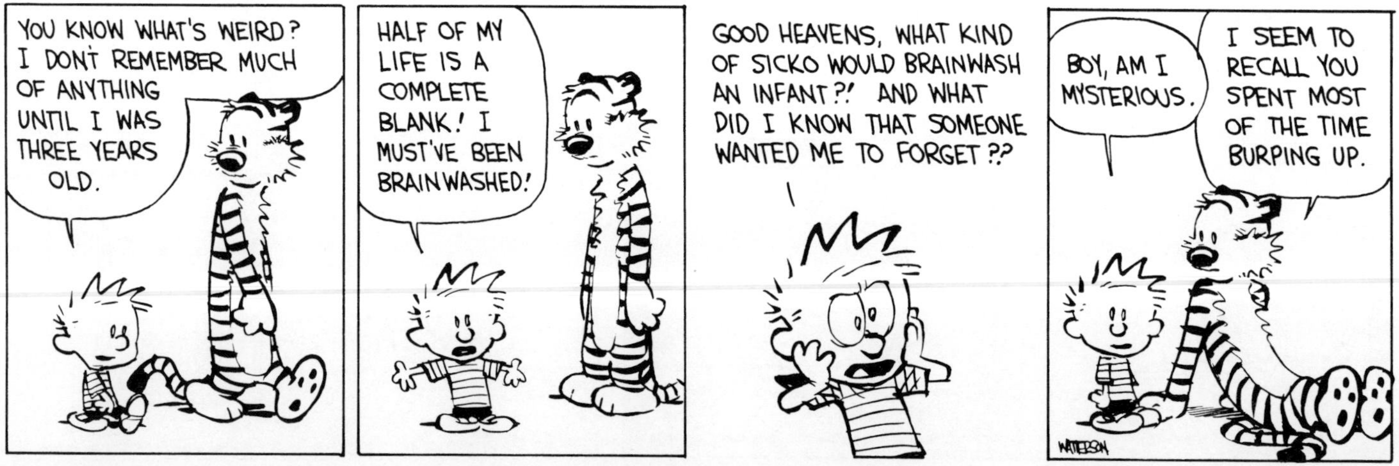
YOU KNOW WHAT'S WEIRD? I DON'T REMEMBER MUCH OF ANYTHING UNTIL I WAS THREE YEARS OLD.
HALF OF MY LIFE IS A COMPLETE BLANK! I MUST'VE BEEN BRAINWASHED!
GOOD HEAVENS, WHAT KIND OF SICKO WOULD BRAINWASH AN INFANT?! AND WHAT DID I KNOW THAT SOMEONE WANTED ME TO FORGET??
BOY, AM I MYSTERIOUS.
I SEEM TO RECALL YOU SPENT MOST OF THE TIME BURPING UP.
WATTERSON

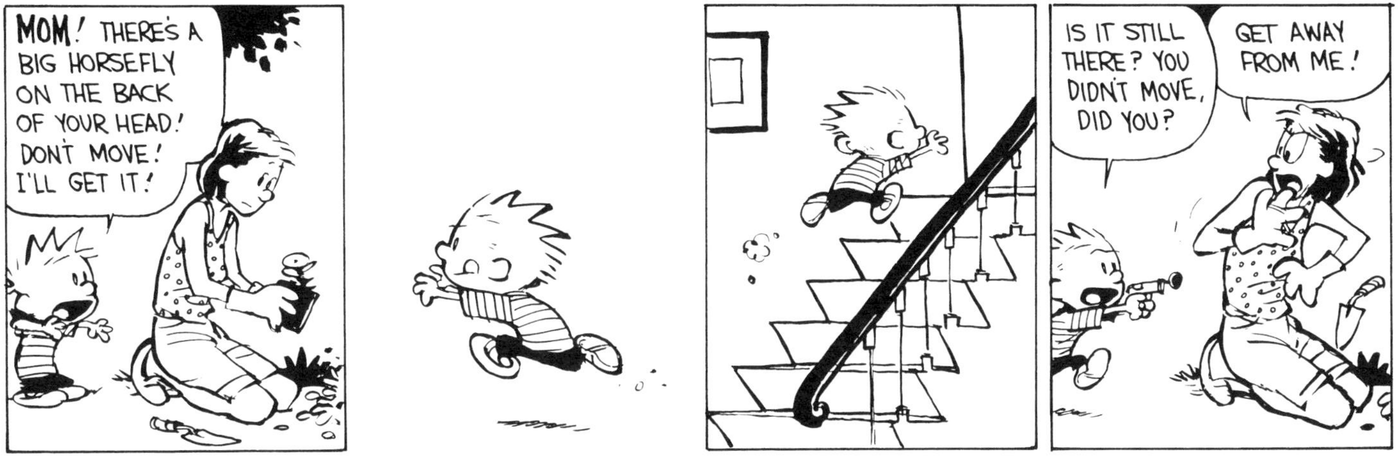
MOM! THERE'S A BIG HORSEFLY ON THE BACK OF YOUR HEAD! DON'T MOVE! I'LL GET IT!
IS IT STILL THERE? YOU DIDN'T MOVE, DID YOU?
GET AWAY FROM ME!

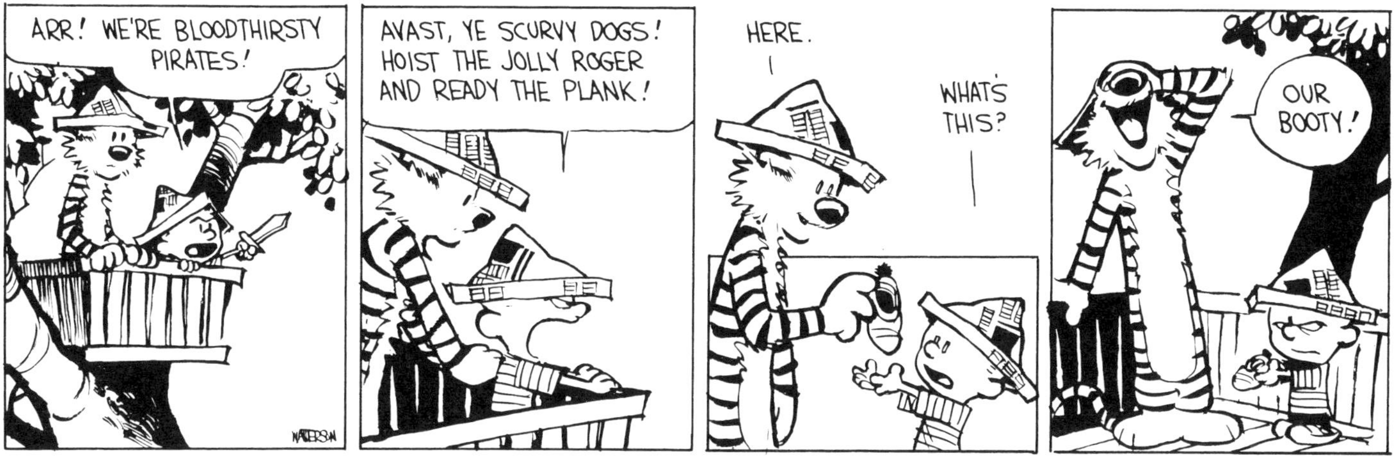
ARR! WE'RE BLOODTHIRSTY PIRATES!
AVAST, YE SCURVY DOGS! HOIST THE JOLLY ROGER AND READY THE PLANK!
HERE.
WHAT'S THIS?
OUR BOOTY!

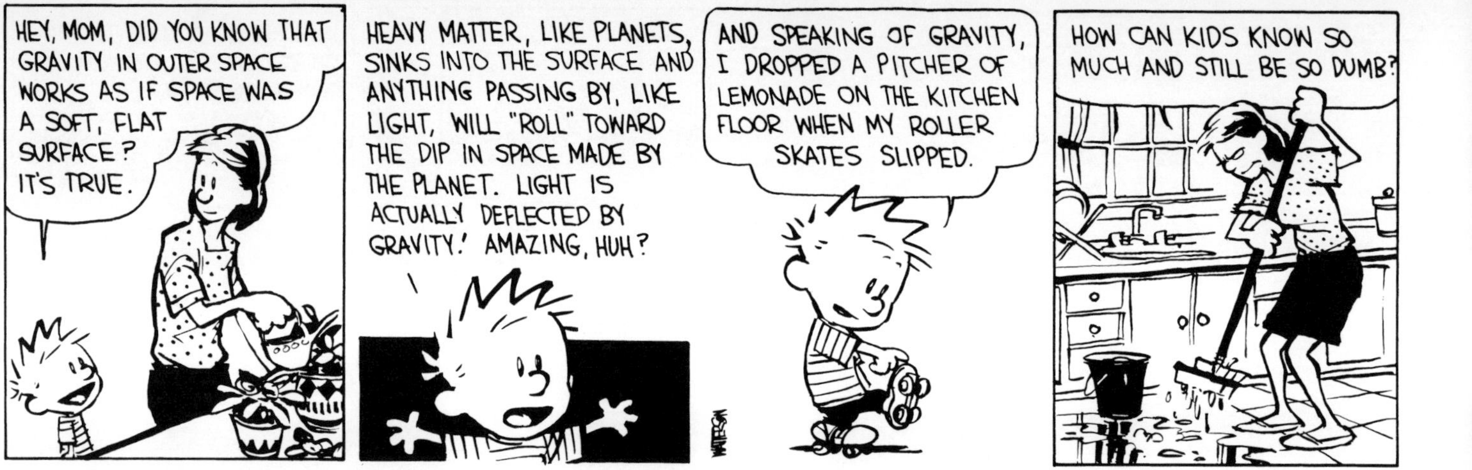
HEY, MOM, DID YOU KNOW THAT GRAVITY IN OUTER SPACE WORKS AS IF SPACE WAS A SOFT, FLAT SURFACE? IT'S TRUE.
HEAVY MATTER, LIKE PLANETS, SINKS INTO THE SURFACE AND ANYTHING PASSING BY, LIKE LIGHT, WILL "ROLL" TOWARD THE DIP IN SPACE MADE BY THE PLANET. LIGHT IS ACTUALLY DEFLECTED BY GRAVITY! AMAZING, HUH?
AND SPEAKING OF GRAVITY, I DROPPED A PITCHER OF LEMONADE ON THE KITCHEN FLOOR WHEN MY ROLLER SKATES SLIPPED.
HOW CAN KIDS KNOW SO MUCH AND STILL BE SO DUMB?

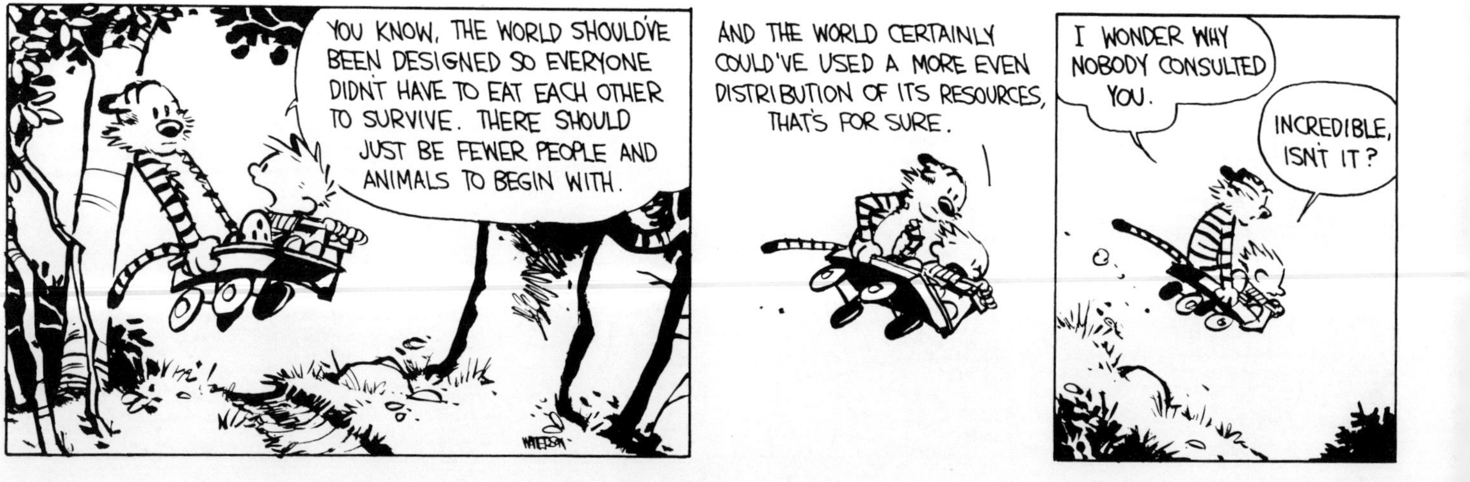
YOU KNOW, THE WORLD SHOULD'VE BEEN DESIGNED SO EVERYONE DIDN'T HAVE TO EAT EACH OTHER TO SURVIVE. THERE SHOULD JUST BE FEWER PEOPLE AND ANIMALS TO BEGIN WITH.
AND THE WORLD CERTAINLY COULD'VE USED A MORE EVEN DISTRIBUTION OF ITS RESOURCES, THAT'S FOR SURE.
I WONDER WHY NOBODY CONSULTED YOU.
INCREDIBLE, ISN'T IT?

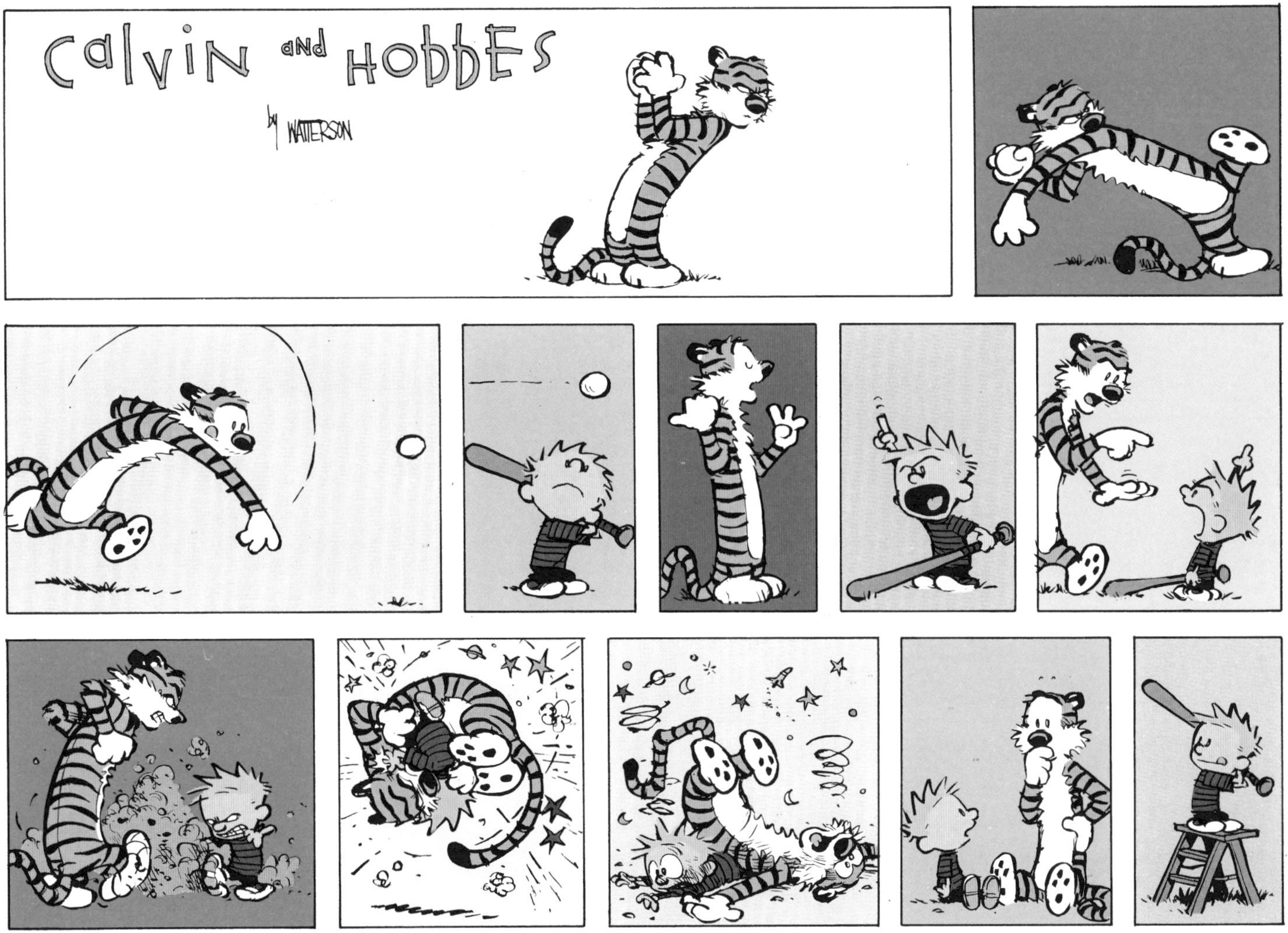
Calvin and HOBBES
by WATTERSON

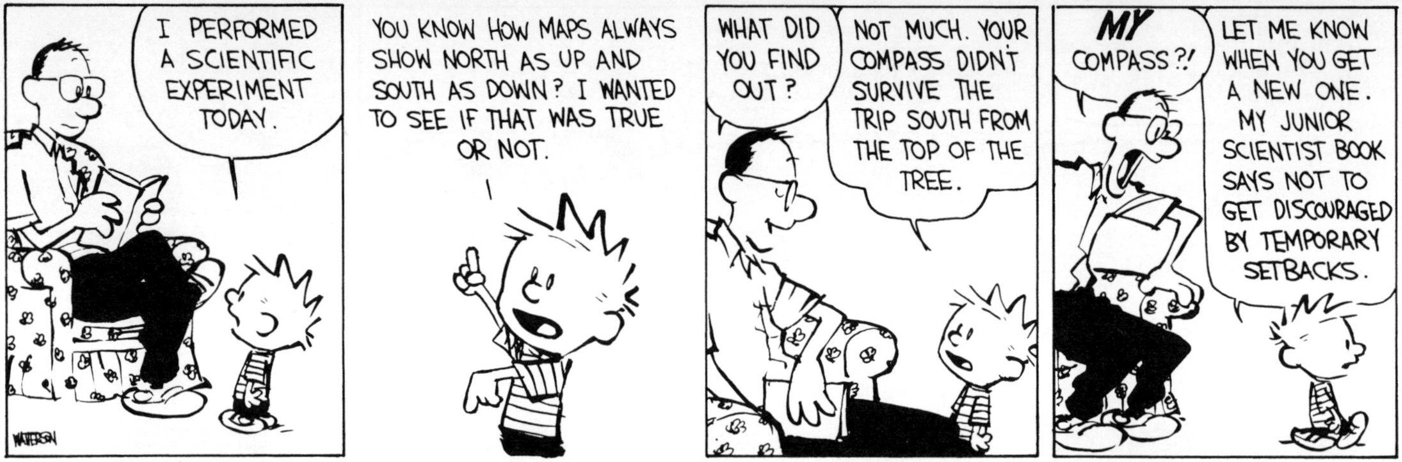
I PERFORMED A SCIENTIFIC EXPERIMENT TODAY.
WATTERSON
YOU KNOW HOW MAPS ALWAYS SHOW NORTH AS UP AND SOUTH AS DOWN? I WANTED TO SEE IF THAT WAS TRUE OR NOT.
WHAT DID YOU FIND OUT?
NOT MUCH. YOUR COMPASS DIDN'T SURVIVE THE TRIP SOUTH FROM THE TOP OF THE TREE.
MY COMPASS?!
LET ME KNOW WHEN YOU GET A NEW ONE. MY JUNIOR SCIENTIST BOOK SAYS NOT TO GET DISCOURAGED BY TEMPORARY SETBACKS.

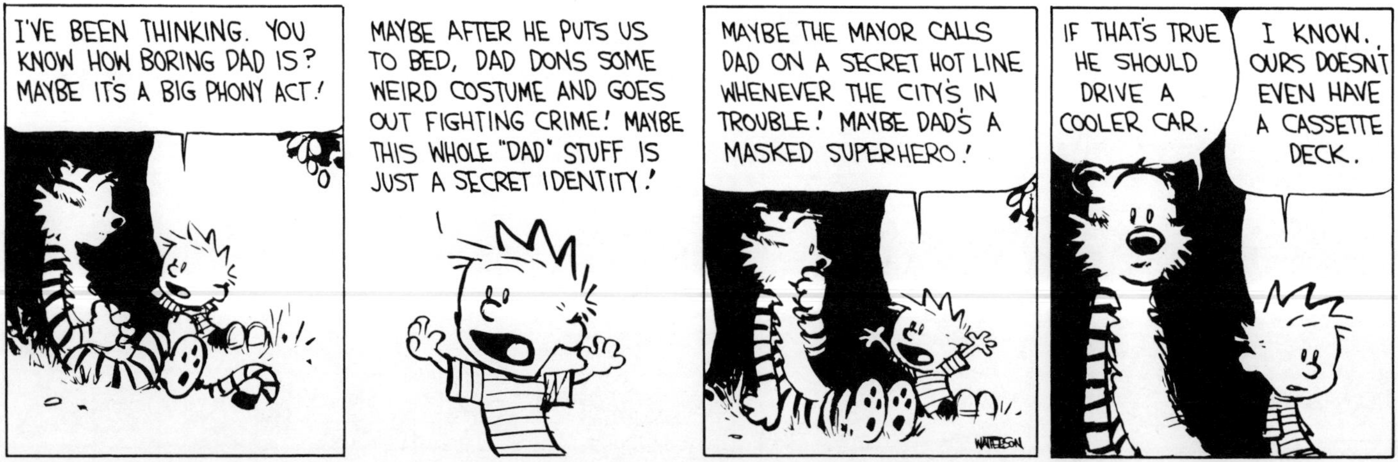
I'VE BEEN THINKING. YOU KNOW HOW BORING DAD IS? MAYBE IT'S A BIG PHONY ACT!
MAYBE AFTER HE PUTS US TO BED, DAD DONS SOME WEIRD COSTUME AND GOES OUT FIGHTING CRIME! MAYBE THIS WHOLE "DAD" STUFF IS JUST A SECRET IDENTITY!
MAYBE THE MAYOR CALLS DAD ON A SECRET HOT LINE WHENEVER THE CITY'S IN TROUBLE! MAYBE DAD'S A MASKED SUPERHERO!
WATTERSON
IF THAT'S TRUE HE SHOULD DRIVE A COOLER CAR.
I KNOW. OURS DOESN'T EVEN HAVE A CASSETTE DECK.

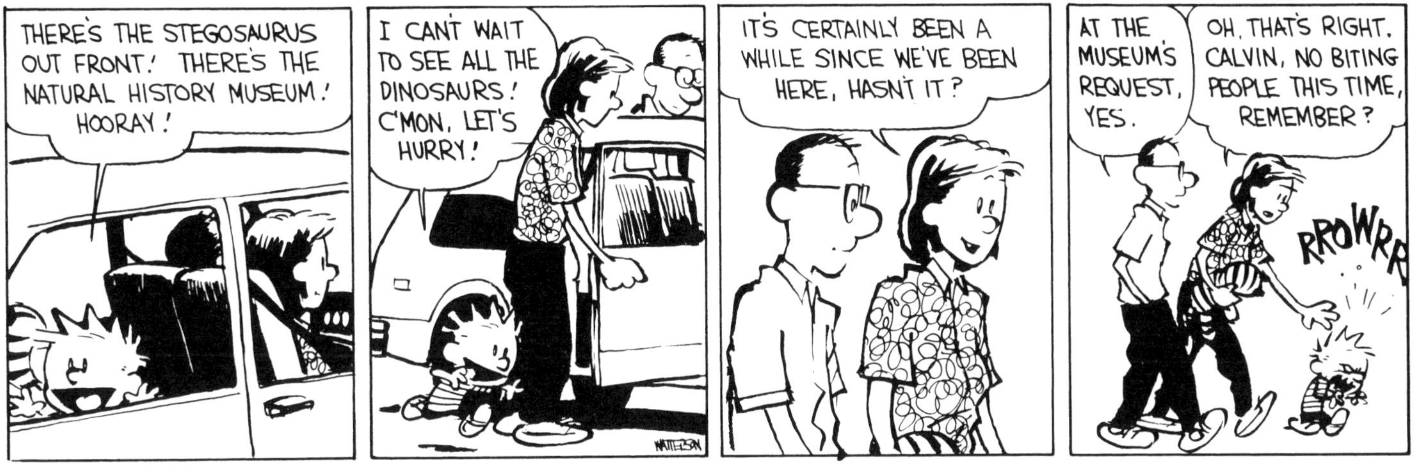
THERE'S THE STEGOSAURUS OUT FRONT! THERE'S THE NATURAL HISTORY MUSEUM! HOORAY!
I CAN'T WAIT TO SEE ALL THE DINOSAURS! C'MON, LET'S HURRY!
IT'S CERTAINLY BEEN A WHILE SINCE WE'VE BEEN HERE, HASN'T IT?
AT THE MUSEUM'S REQUEST, YES.
OH, THAT'S RIGHT. CALVIN, NO BITING PEOPLE THIS TIME, REMEMBER?
RROWRR

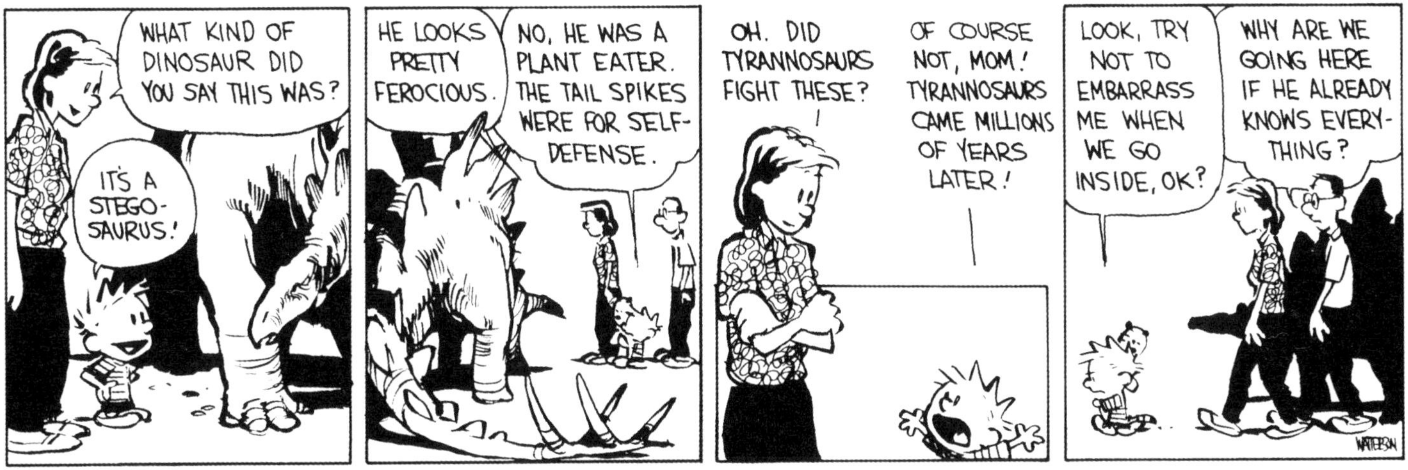
WHAT KIND OF DINOSAUR DID YOU SAY THIS WAS?
IT'S A STEGO-SAURUS!
HE LOOKS PRETTY FEROCIOUS.
NO, HE WAS A PLANT EATER. THE TAIL SPIKES WERE FOR SELF-DEFENSE.
OH. DID TYRANNOSAURS FIGHT THESE?
OF COURSE NOT, MOM! TYRANNOSAURS CAME MILLIONS OF YEARS LATER!
LOOK, TRY NOT TO EMBARRASS ME WHEN WE GO INSIDE, OK?
WHY ARE WE GOING HERE IF HE ALREADY KNOWS EVERY-THING?

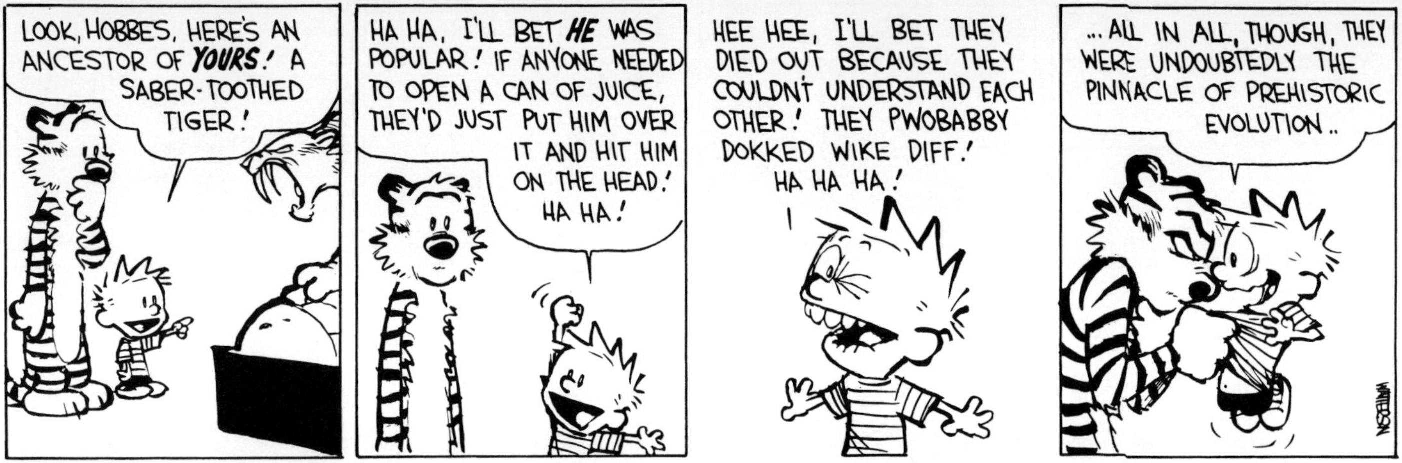
LOOK, HOBBES, HERE'S AN ANCESTOR OF YOURS! A SABER-TOOTHED TIGER!
HA HA, I'LL BET HE WAS POPULAR! IF ANYONE NEEDED TO OPEN A CAN OF JUICE, THEY'D JUST PUT HIM OVER IT AND HIT HIM ON THE HEAD! HA HA!
HEE HEE, I'LL BET THEY DIED OUT BECAUSE THEY COULDN'T UNDERSTAND EACH OTHER! THEY PWOBABBY DOKKED WIKE DIFF! HA HA HA!
...ALL IN ALL, THOUGH, THEY WERE UNDOUBTEDLY THE PINNACLE OF PREHISTORIC EVOLUTION..

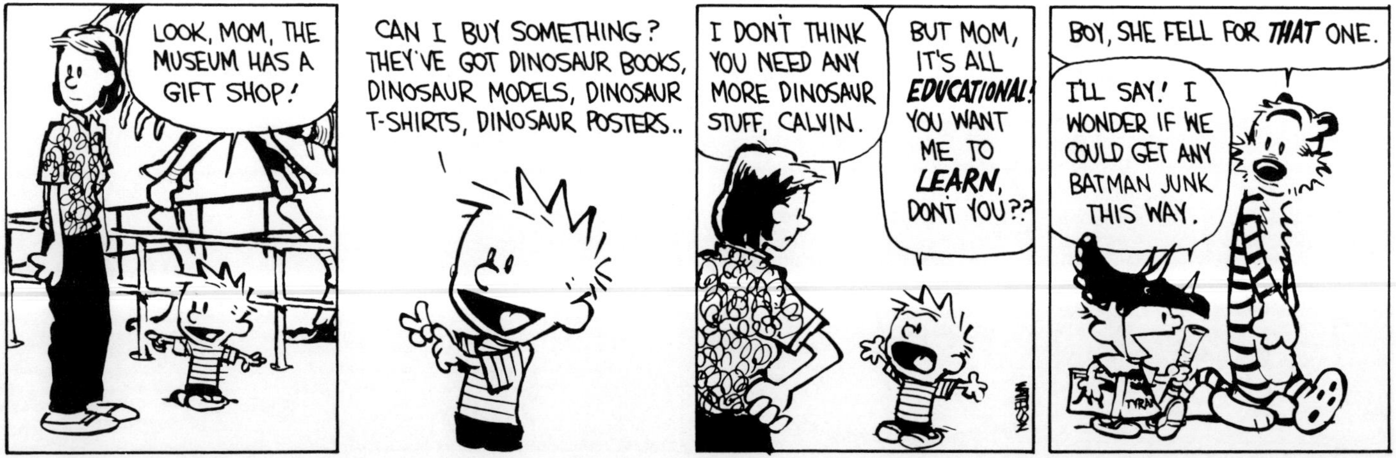
LOOK, MOM, THE MUSEUM HAS A GIFT SHOP!
CAN I BUY SOMETHING? THEY'VE GOT DINOSAUR BOOKS, DINOSAUR MODELS, DINOSAUR T-SHIRTS, DINOSAUR POSTERS..
I DON'T THINK YOU NEED ANY MORE DINOSAUR STUFF, CALVIN.
BUT MOM, IT'S ALL EDUCATIONAL! YOU WANT ME TO LEARN, DON'T YOU??
BOY, SHE FELL FOR THAT ONE.
I'LL SAY! I WONDER IF WE COULD GET ANY BATMAN JUNK THIS WAY.

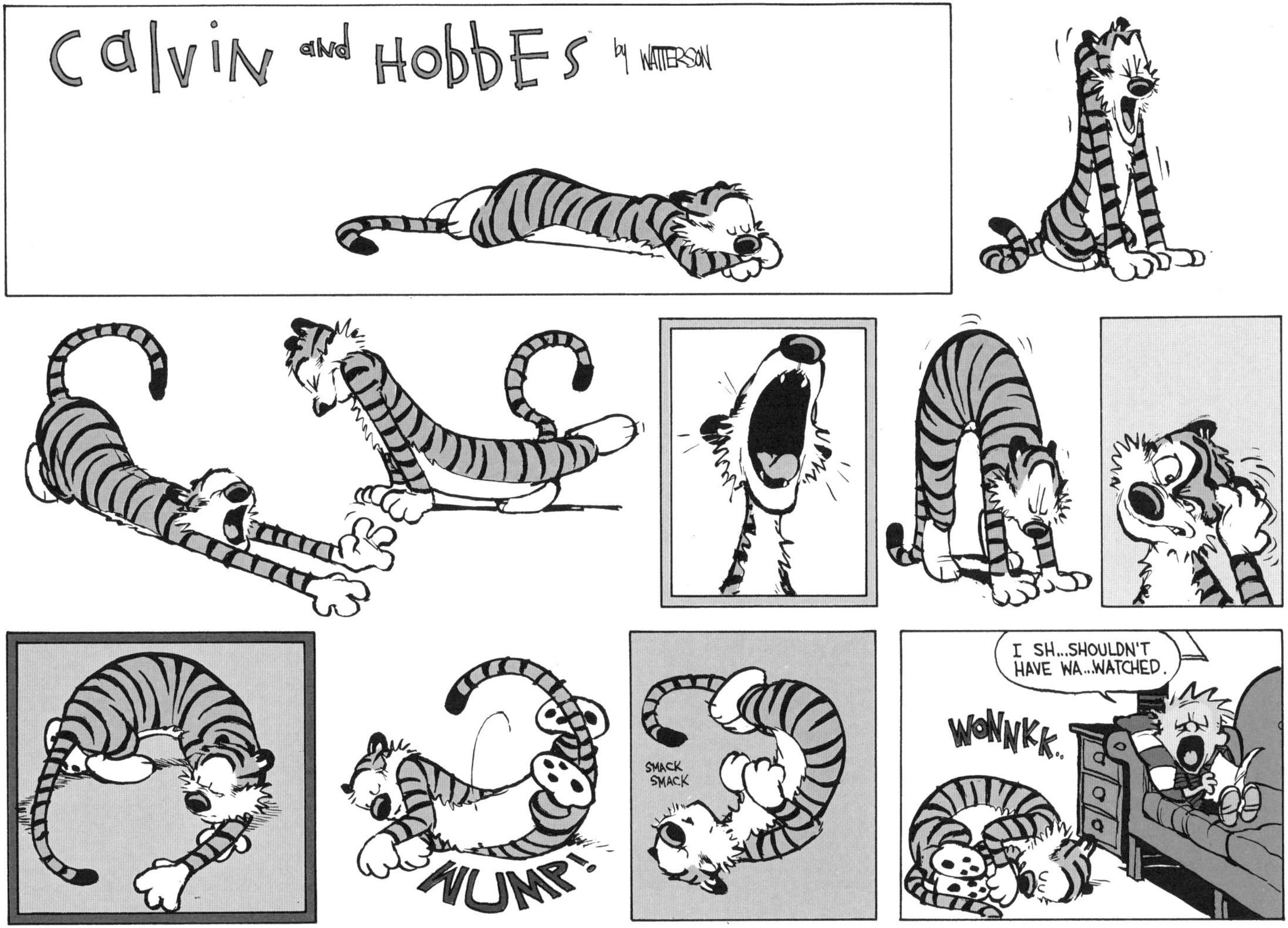
Calvin and Hobbes
by WATTERSON
WUMP!
SMACK SMACK
WONNKK..
I SH...SHOULDN'T HAVE WA...WATCHED.

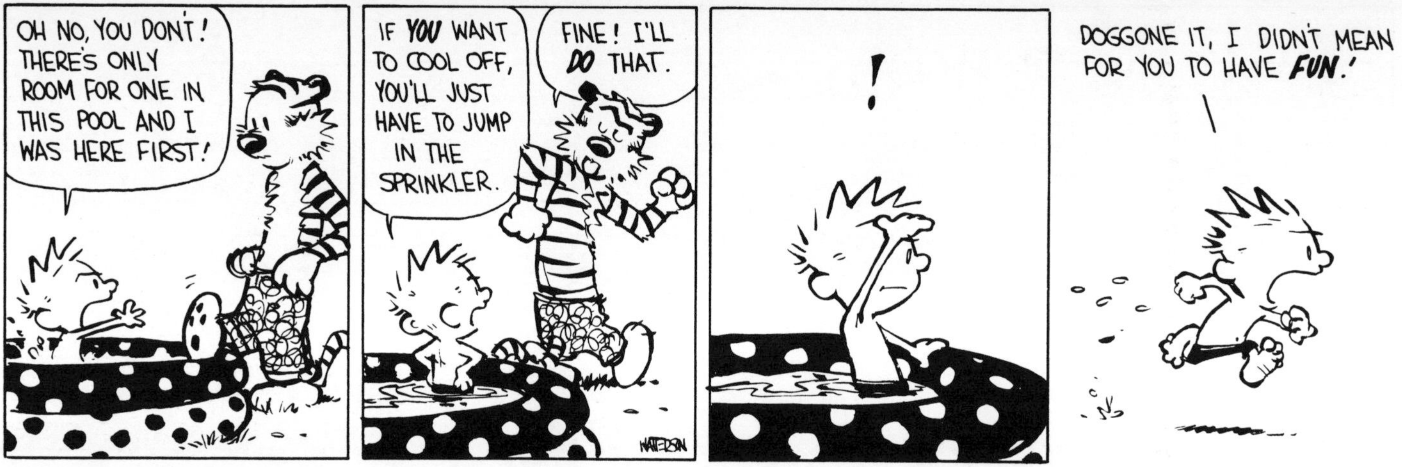
OH NO, YOU DON'T! THERE'S ONLY ROOM FOR ONE IN THIS POOL AND I WAS HERE FIRST!
IF YOU WANT TO COOL OFF, YOU'LL JUST HAVE TO JUMP IN THE SPRINKLER.
FINE! I'LL DO THAT.
!
DOGGONE IT, I DIDN'T MEAN FOR YOU TO HAVE FUN!

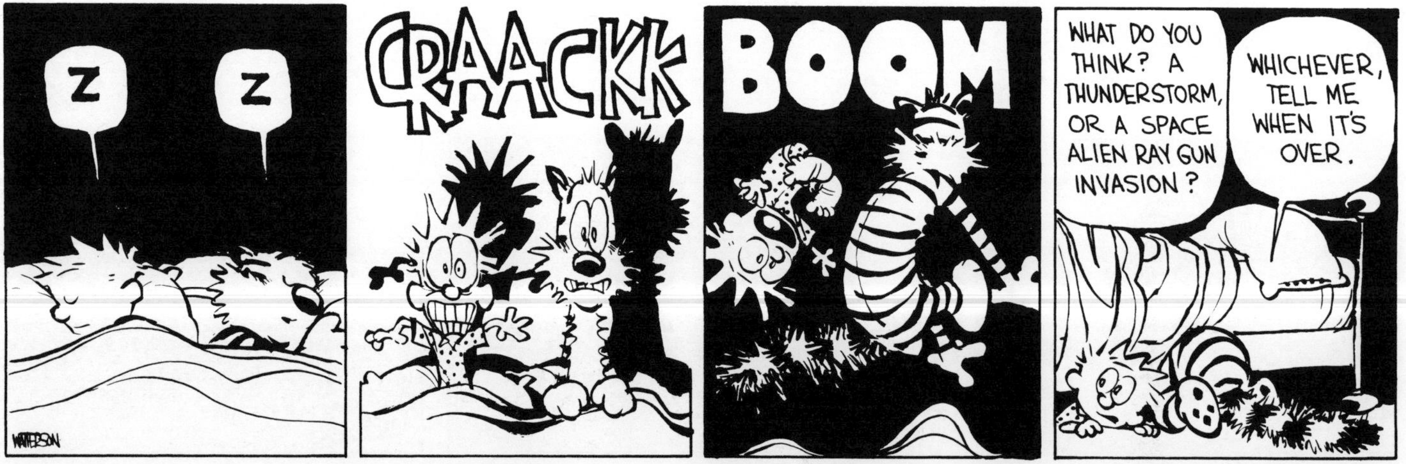
Z
Z
CRAACKK
BOOM
WHAT DO YOU THINK? A THUNDERSTORM, OR A SPACE ALIEN RAY GUN INVASION?
WHICHEVER, TELL ME WHEN IT'S OVER.

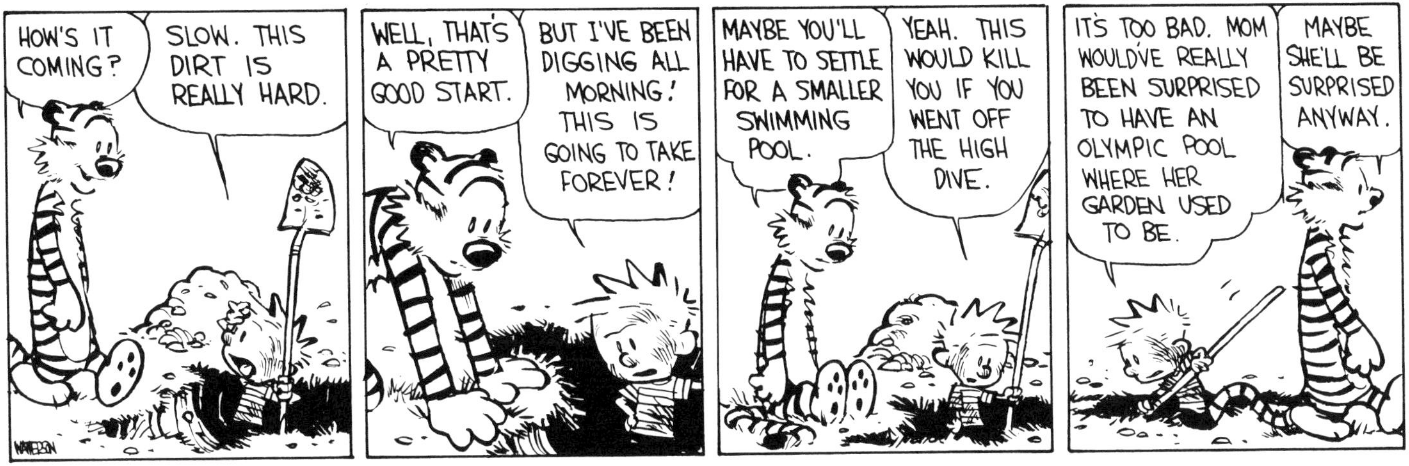
HOW'S IT COMING?
SLOW. THIS DIRT IS REALLY HARD.
WELL, THAT'S A PRETTY GOOD START.
BUT I'VE BEEN DIGGING ALL MORNING! THIS IS GOING TO TAKE FOREVER!
MAYBE YOU'LL HAVE TO SETTLE FOR A SMALLER SWIMMING POOL.
YEAH. THIS WOULD KILL YOU IF YOU WENT OFF THE HIGH DIVE.
IT'S TOO BAD. MOM WOULD'VE REALLY BEEN SURPRISED TO HAVE AN OLYMPIC POOL WHERE HER GARDEN USED TO BE.
MAYBE SHE'LL BE SURPRISED ANYWAY.

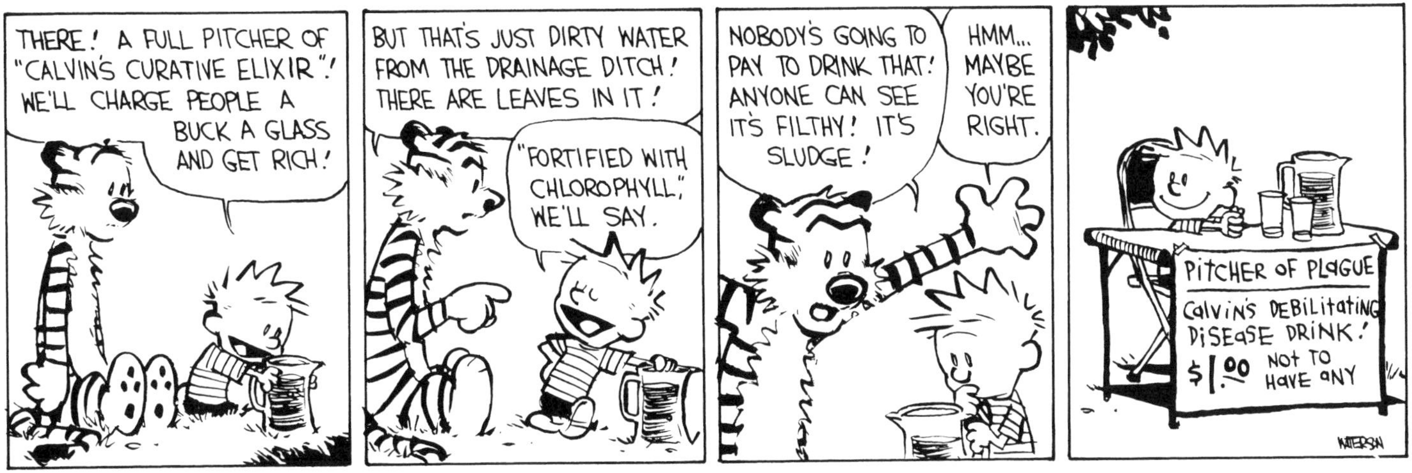
THERE! A FULL PITCHER OF "CALVIN'S CURATIVE ELIXIR"! WE'LL CHARGE PEOPLE A BUCK A GLASS AND GET RICH!
BUT THAT'S JUST DIRTY WATER FROM THE DRAINAGE DITCH! THERE ARE LEAVES IN IT!
"FORTIFIED WITH CHLOROPHYLL," WE'LL SAY.
NOBODY'S GOING TO PAY TO DRINK THAT! ANYONE CAN SEE IT'S FILTHY! IT'S SLUDGE!
HMM... MAYBE YOU'RE RIGHT.
PITCHER OF PLAGUE
Calvin's DEBILITATING DISEASE DRINK!
$1.00 Not TO HAVE ANY

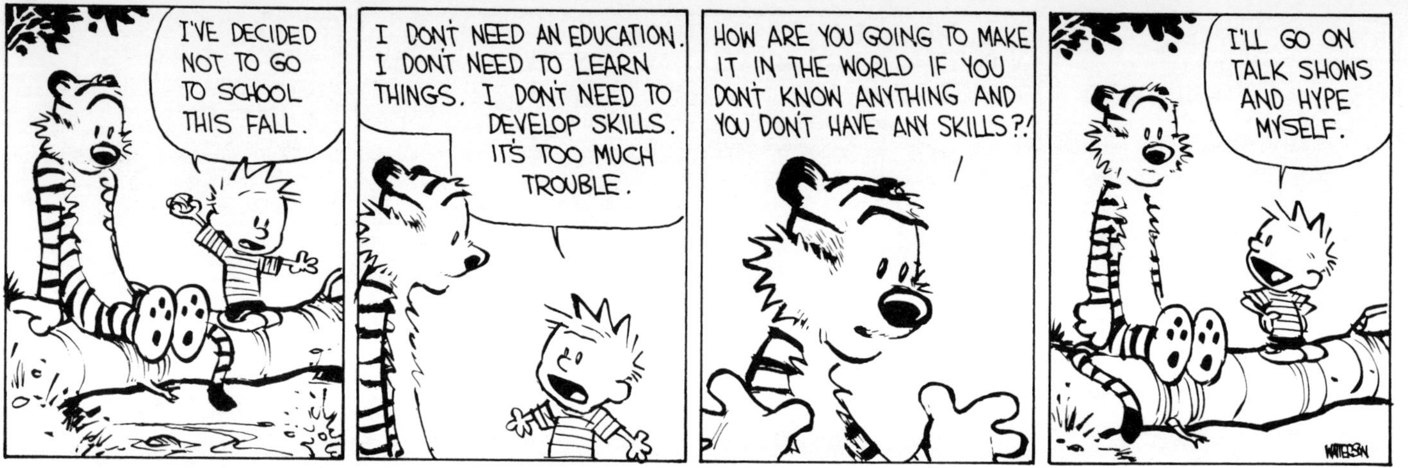
I'VE DECIDED NOT TO GO TO SCHOOL THIS FALL.
I DON'T NEED AN EDUCATION. I DON'T NEED TO LEARN THINGS. I DON'T NEED TO DEVELOP SKILLS. IT'S TOO MUCH TROUBLE.
HOW ARE YOU GOING TO MAKE IT IN THE WORLD IF YOU DON'T KNOW ANYTHING AND YOU DON'T HAVE ANY SKILLS?!
I'LL GO ON TALK SHOWS AND HYPE MYSELF.
WATTERSON

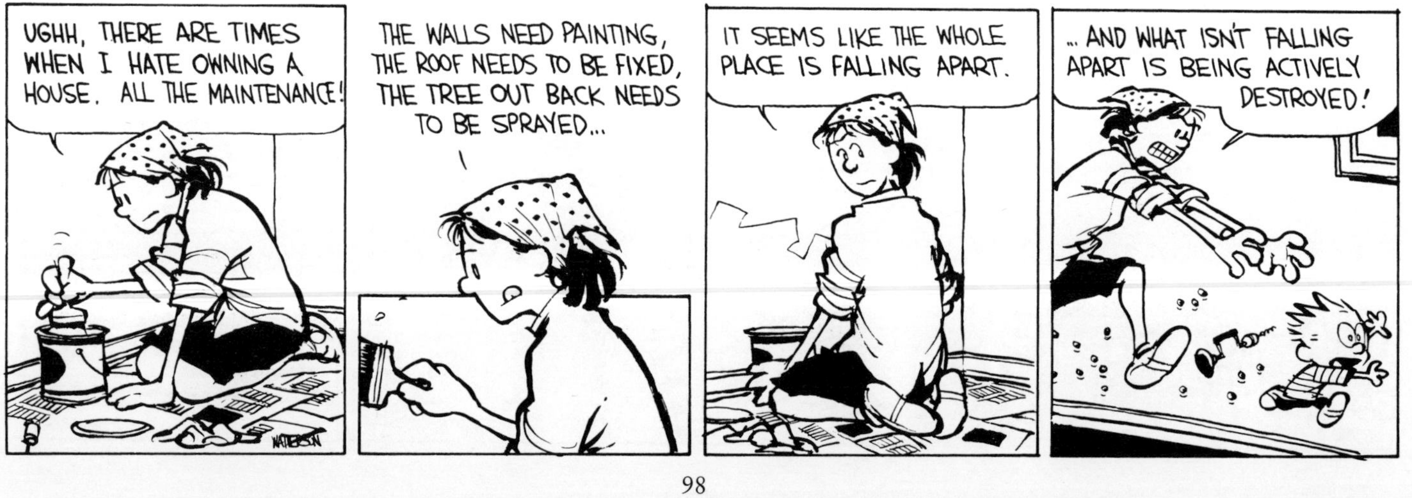
UGHH, THERE ARE TIMES WHEN I HATE OWNING A HOUSE. ALL THE MAINTENANCE!
WATTERSON
THE WALLS NEED PAINTING, THE ROOF NEEDS TO BE FIXED, THE TREE OUT BACK NEEDS TO BE SPRAYED...
IT SEEMS LIKE THE WHOLE PLACE IS FALLING APART.
... AND WHAT ISN'T FALLING APART IS BEING ACTIVELY DESTROYED!

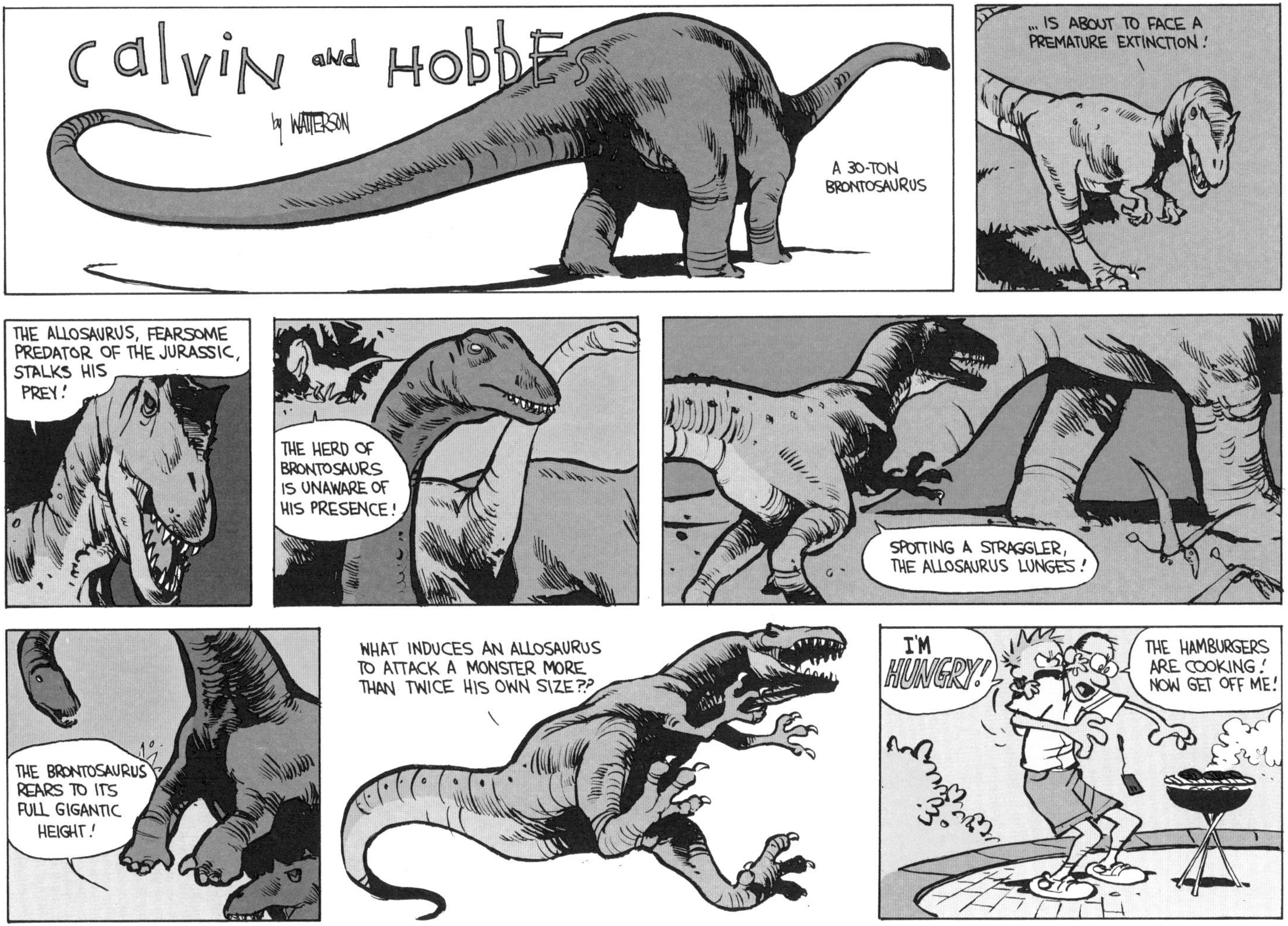
Calvin and Hobbes
by WATTERSON
A 30-TON BRONTOSAURUS
... IS ABOUT TO FACE A PREMATURE EXTINCTION!
THE ALLOSAURUS, FEARSOME PREDATOR OF THE JURASSIC, STALKS HIS PREY!
THE HERD OF BRONTOSAURS IS UNAWARE OF HIS PRESENCE!
SPOTTING A STRAGGLER, THE ALLOSAURUS LUNGES!
THE BRONTOSAURUS REARS TO ITS FULL GIGANTIC HEIGHT!
WHAT INDUCES AN ALLOSAURUS TO ATTACK A MONSTER MORE THAN TWICE HIS OWN SIZE??
I'M HUNGRY!
THE HAMBURGERS ARE COOKING! NOW GET OFF ME!

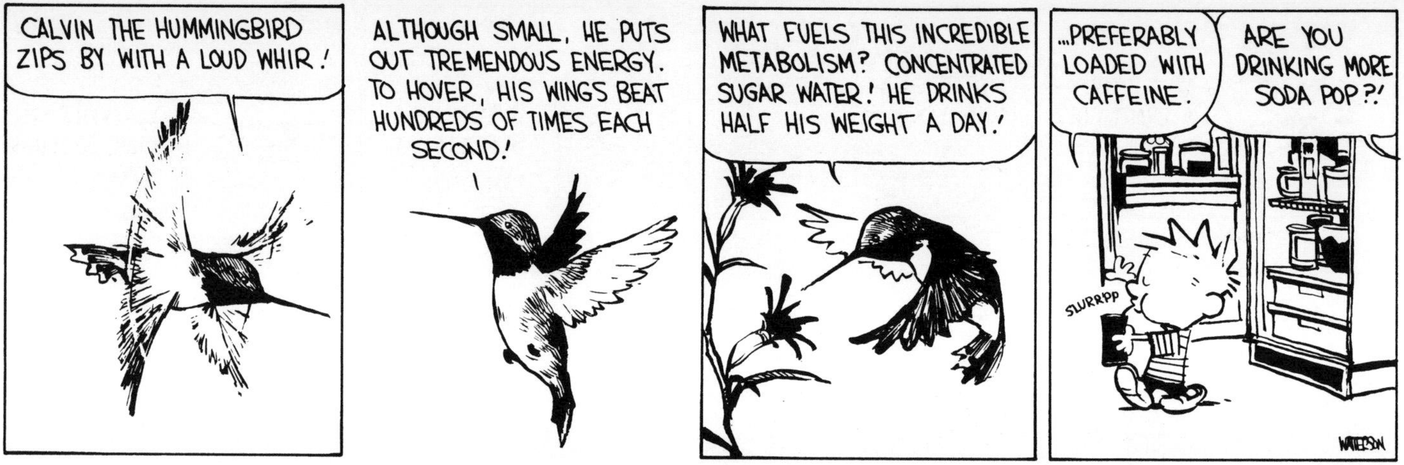
CALVIN THE HUMMINGBIRD ZIPS BY WITH A LOUD WHIR!
ALTHOUGH SMALL, HE PUTS OUT TREMENDOUS ENERGY. TO HOVER, HIS WINGS BEAT HUNDREDS OF TIMES EACH SECOND!
WHAT FUELS THIS INCREDIBLE METABOLISM? CONCENTRATED SUGAR WATER! HE DRINKS HALF HIS WEIGHT A DAY!
...PREFERABLY LOADED WITH CAFFEINE.
ARE YOU DRINKING MORE SODA POP?!
SLURRPP
WATTERSON

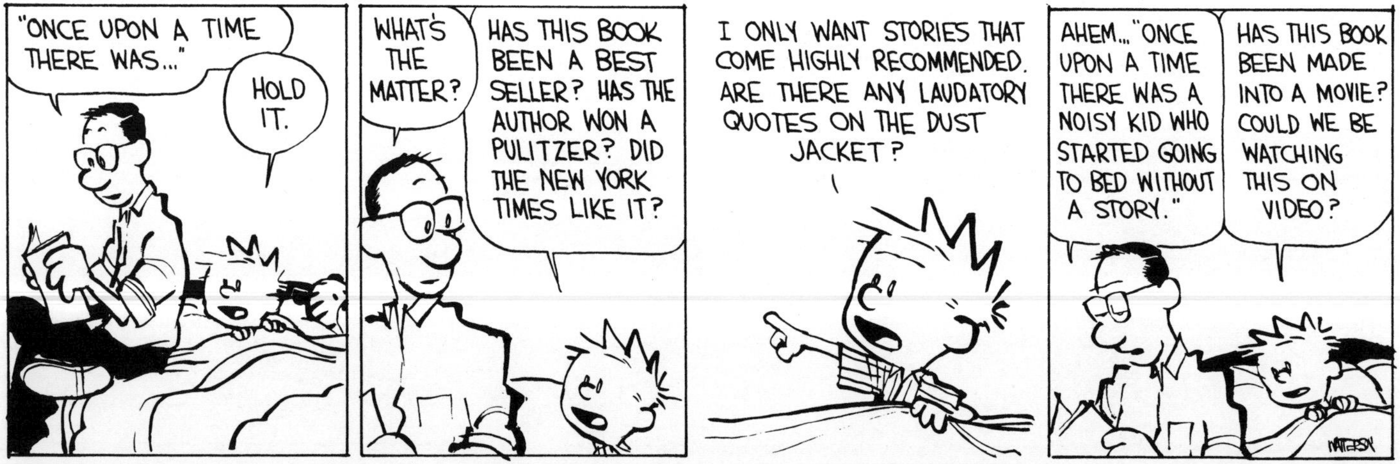
"ONCE UPON A TIME THERE WAS..."
HOLD IT.
WHAT'S THE MATTER?
HAS THIS BOOK BEEN A BEST SELLER? HAS THE AUTHOR WON A PULITZER? DID THE NEW YORK TIMES LIKE IT?
I ONLY WANT STORIES THAT COME HIGHLY RECOMMENDED. ARE THERE ANY LAUDATORY QUOTES ON THE DUST JACKET?
AHEM... "ONCE UPON A TIME THERE WAS A NOISY KID WHO STARTED GOING TO BED WITHOUT A STORY."
HAS THIS BOOK BEEN MADE INTO A MOVIE? COULD WE BE WATCHING THIS ON VIDEO?
WATTERSON

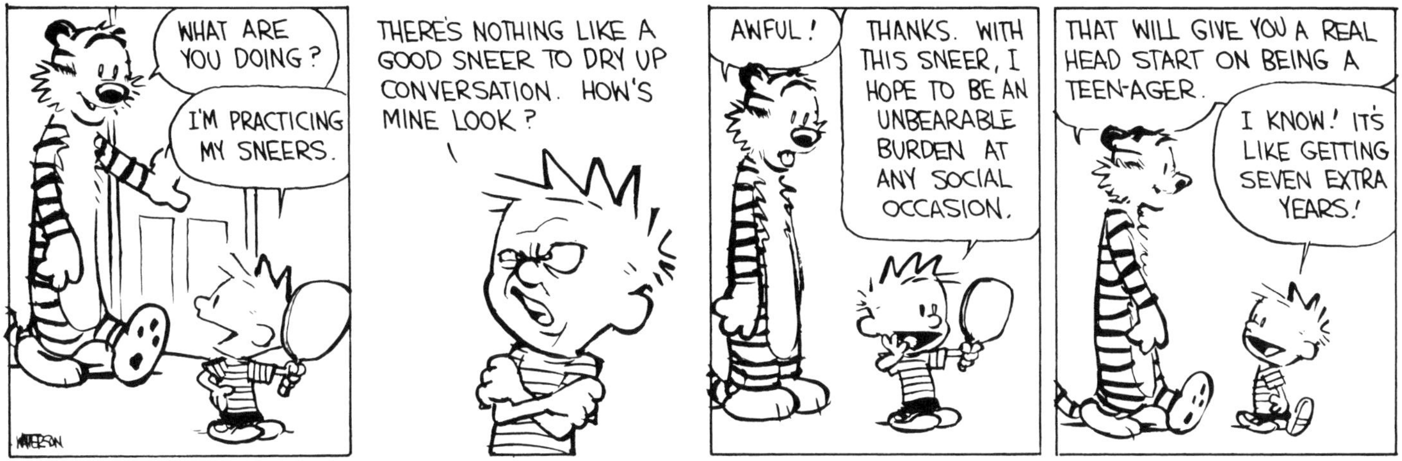
WHAT ARE YOU DOING?
I'M PRACTICING MY SNEERS.
THERE'S NOTHING LIKE A GOOD SNEER TO DRY UP CONVERSATION. HOW'S MINE LOOK?
AWFUL!
THANKS. WITH THIS SNEER, I HOPE TO BE AN UNBEARABLE BURDEN AT ANY SOCIAL OCCASION.
THAT WILL GIVE YOU A REAL HEAD START ON BEING A TEEN-AGER.
I KNOW! IT'S LIKE GETTING SEVEN EXTRA YEARS!

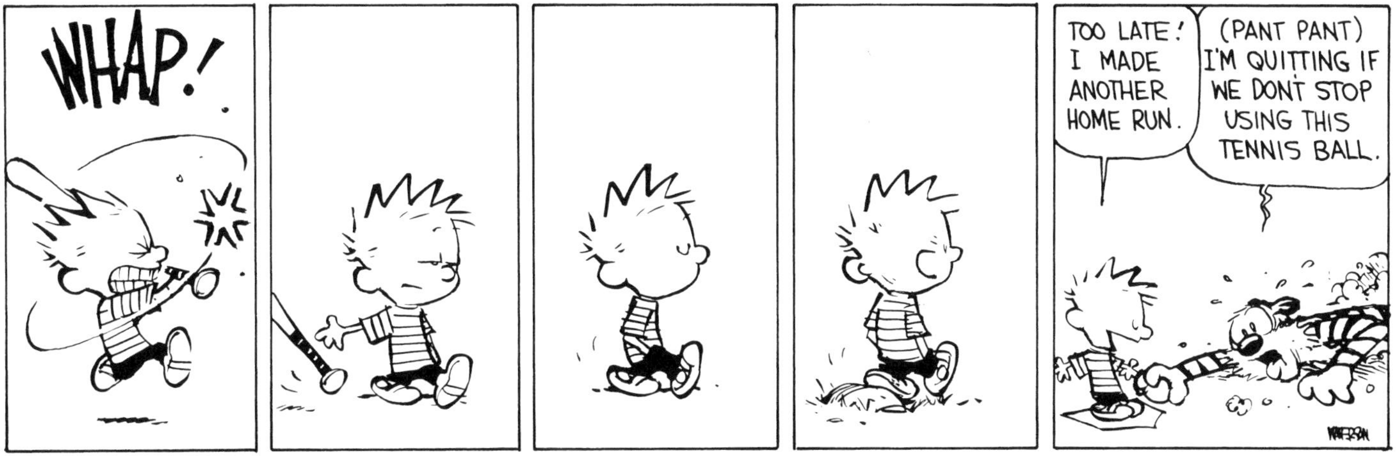
WHAP!
TOO LATE! I MADE ANOTHER HOME RUN.
(PANT PANT) I'M QUITTING IF WE DON'T STOP USING THIS TENNIS BALL.

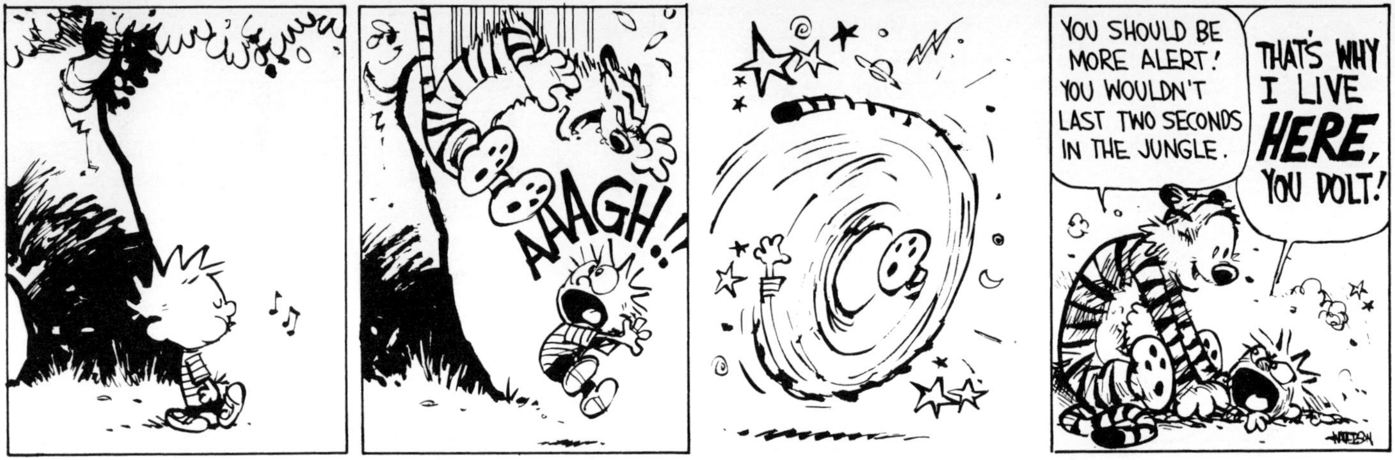
AAAGH!!
YOU SHOULD BE MORE ALERT! YOU WOULDN'T LAST TWO SECONDS IN THE JUNGLE.
THAT'S WHY I LIVE HERE, YOU DOLT!
WATTERSON

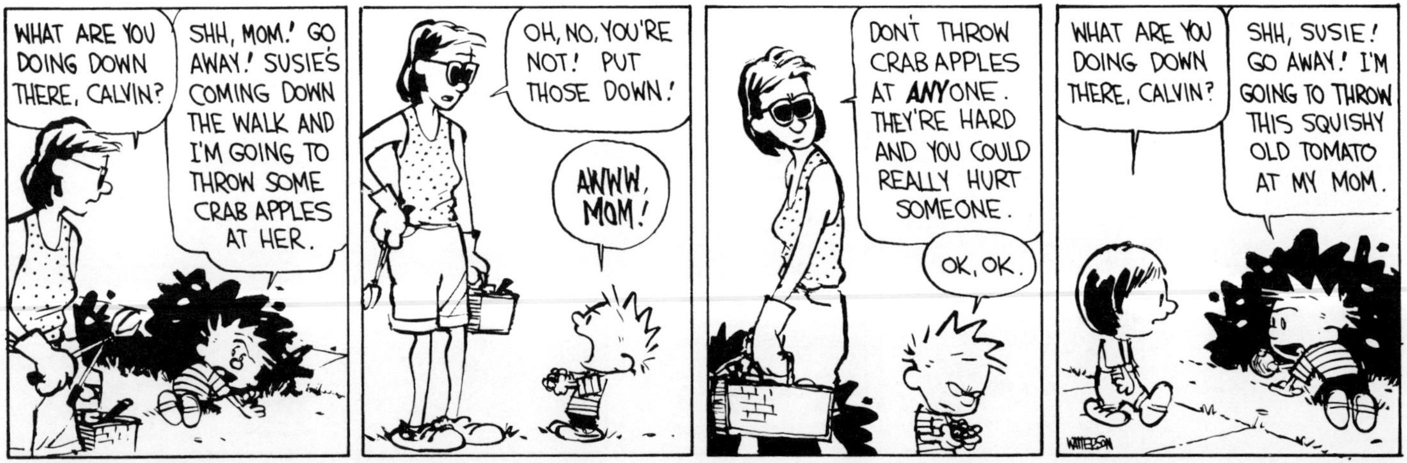
WHAT ARE YOU DOING DOWN THERE, CALVIN?
SHH, MOM! GO AWAY! SUSIE'S COMING DOWN THE WALK AND I'M GOING TO THROW SOME CRAB APPLES AT HER.
OH, NO, YOU'RE NOT! PUT THOSE DOWN!
AWWW, MOM!
DON'T THROW CRAB APPLES AT ANYONE. THEY'RE HARD AND YOU COULD REALLY HURT SOMEONE.
OK, OK.
WHAT ARE YOU DOING DOWN THERE, CALVIN?
SHH, SUSIE! GO AWAY! I'M GOING TO THROW THIS SQUISHY OLD TOMATO AT MY MOM.
WATTERSON

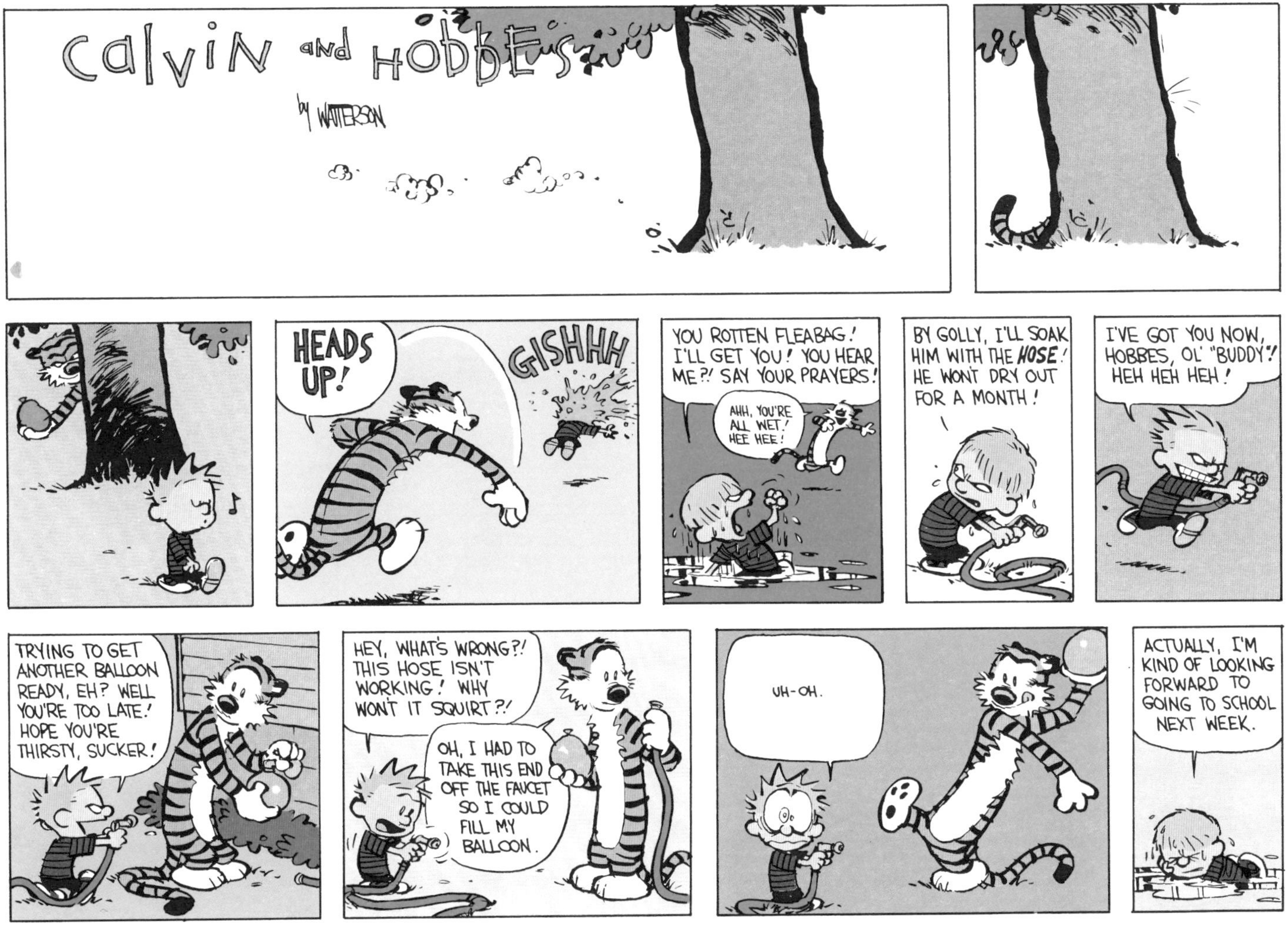
Calvin and Hobbes
by WATTERSON
HEADS UP!
GISHHH
YOU ROTTEN FLEABAG! I'LL GET YOU! YOU HEAR ME?! SAY YOUR PRAYERS!
AHH, YOU'RE ALL WET! HEE HEE!
BY GOLLY, I'LL SOAK HIM WITH THE HOSE! HE WON'T DRY OUT FOR A MONTH!
I'VE GOT YOU NOW, HOBBES, OL' "BUDDY"! HEH HEH HEH!
TRYING TO GET ANOTHER BALLOON READY, EH? WELL YOU'RE TOO LATE! HOPE YOU'RE THIRSTY, SUCKER!
HEY, WHAT'S WRONG?! THIS HOSE ISN'T WORKING! WHY WON'T IT SQUIRT?!
OH, I HAD TO TAKE THIS END OFF THE FAUCET SO I COULD FILL MY BALLOON.
UH-OH.
ACTUALLY, I'M KIND OF LOOKING FORWARD TO GOING TO SCHOOL NEXT WEEK.

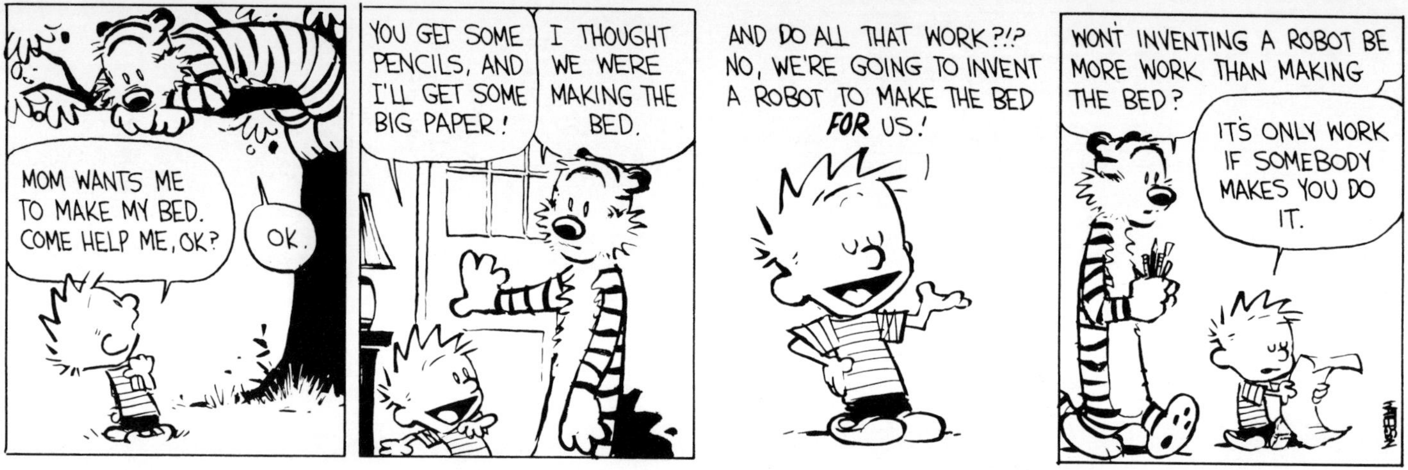
MOM WANTS ME TO MAKE MY BED. COME HELP ME, OK?
OK.
YOU GET SOME PENCILS, AND I'LL GET SOME BIG PAPER!
I THOUGHT WE WERE MAKING THE BED.
AND DO ALL THAT WORK?!? NO, WE'RE GOING TO INVENT A ROBOT TO MAKE THE BED **FOR** US!
WON'T INVENTING A ROBOT BE MORE WORK THAN MAKING THE BED?
IT'S ONLY WORK IF SOMEBODY MAKES YOU DO IT.

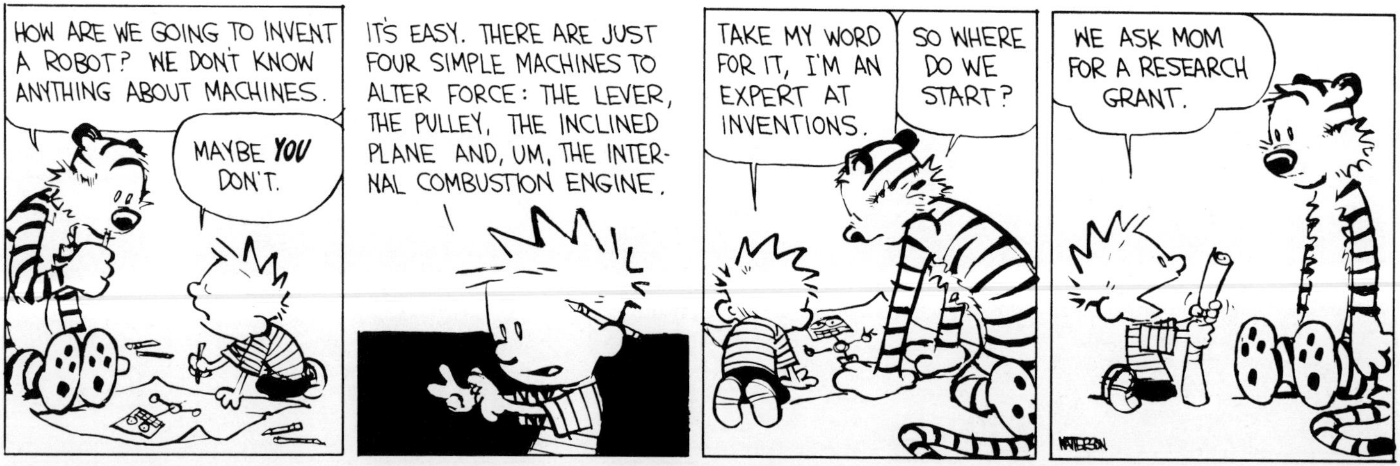
HOW ARE WE GOING TO INVENT A ROBOT? WE DON'T KNOW ANYTHING ABOUT MACHINES.
MAYBE **YOU** DON'T.
IT'S EASY. THERE ARE JUST FOUR SIMPLE MACHINES TO ALTER FORCE: THE LEVER, THE PULLEY, THE INCLINED PLANE AND, UM, THE INTERNAL COMBUSTION ENGINE.
TAKE MY WORD FOR IT, I'M AN EXPERT AT INVENTIONS.
SO WHERE DO WE START?
WE ASK MOM FOR A RESEARCH GRANT.

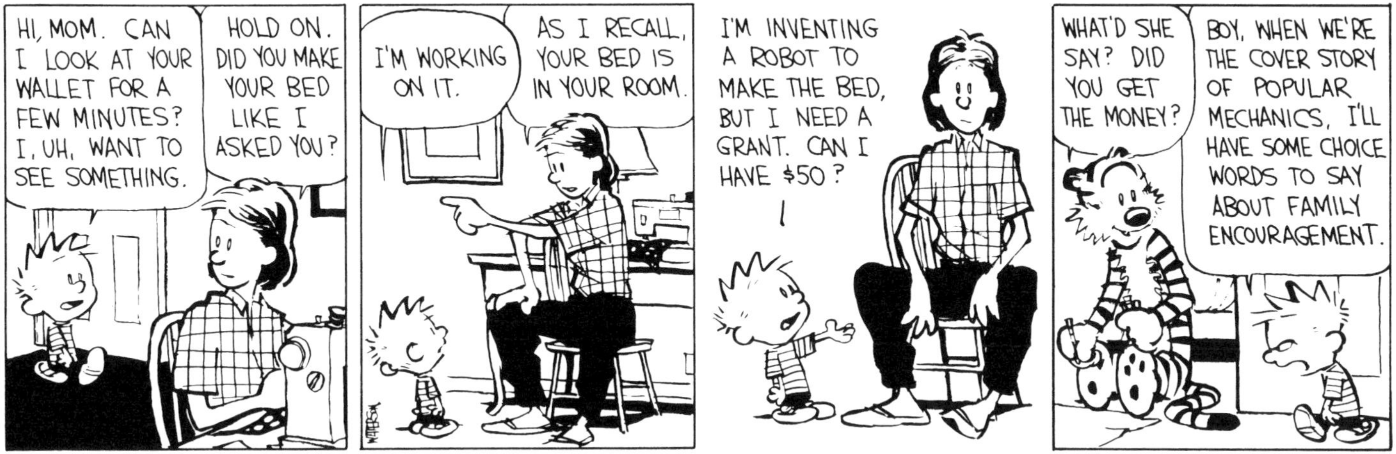
HI, MOM. CAN I LOOK AT YOUR WALLET FOR A FEW MINUTES? I, UH, WANT TO SEE SOMETHING.
HOLD ON. DID YOU MAKE YOUR BED LIKE I ASKED YOU?
I'M WORKING ON IT.
AS I RECALL, YOUR BED IS IN YOUR ROOM.
I'M INVENTING A ROBOT TO MAKE THE BED, BUT I NEED A GRANT. CAN I HAVE $50?
WHAT'D SHE SAY? DID YOU GET THE MONEY?
BOY, WHEN WE'RE THE COVER STORY OF POPULAR MECHANICS, I'LL HAVE SOME CHOICE WORDS TO SAY ABOUT FAMILY ENCOURAGEMENT.

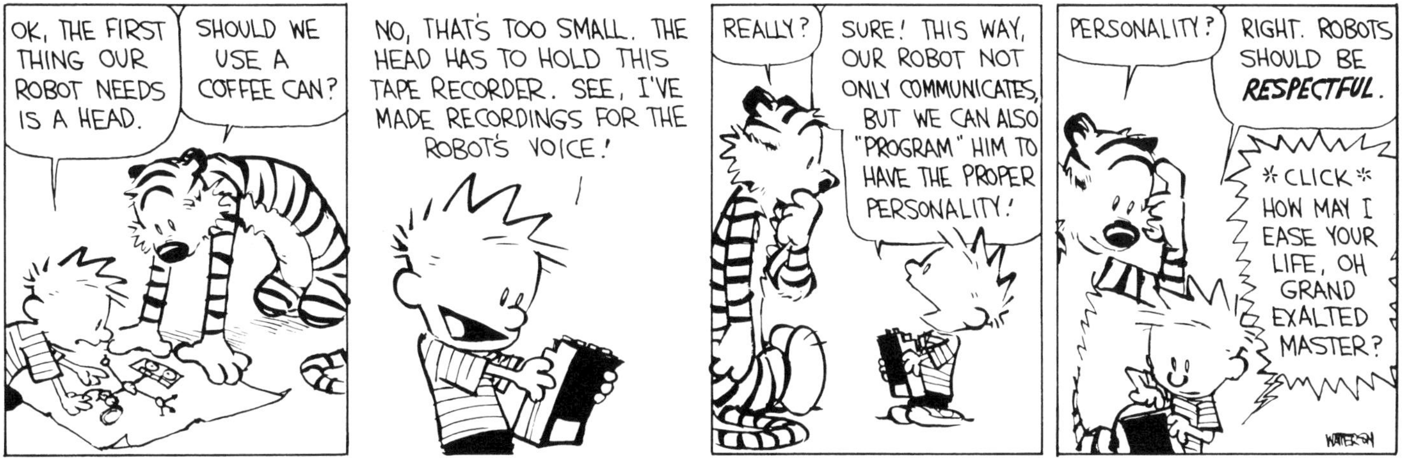
OK, THE FIRST THING OUR ROBOT NEEDS IS A HEAD.
SHOULD WE USE A COFFEE CAN?
NO, THAT'S TOO SMALL. THE HEAD HAS TO HOLD THIS TAPE RECORDER. SEE, I'VE MADE RECORDINGS FOR THE ROBOT'S VOICE!
REALLY?
SURE! THIS WAY, OUR ROBOT NOT ONLY COMMUNICATES, BUT WE CAN ALSO "PROGRAM" HIM TO HAVE THE PROPER PERSONALITY!
PERSONALITY?
RIGHT. ROBOTS SHOULD BE ***RESPECTFUL***.
CLICK HOW MAY I EASE YOUR LIFE, OH GRAND EXALTED MASTER?

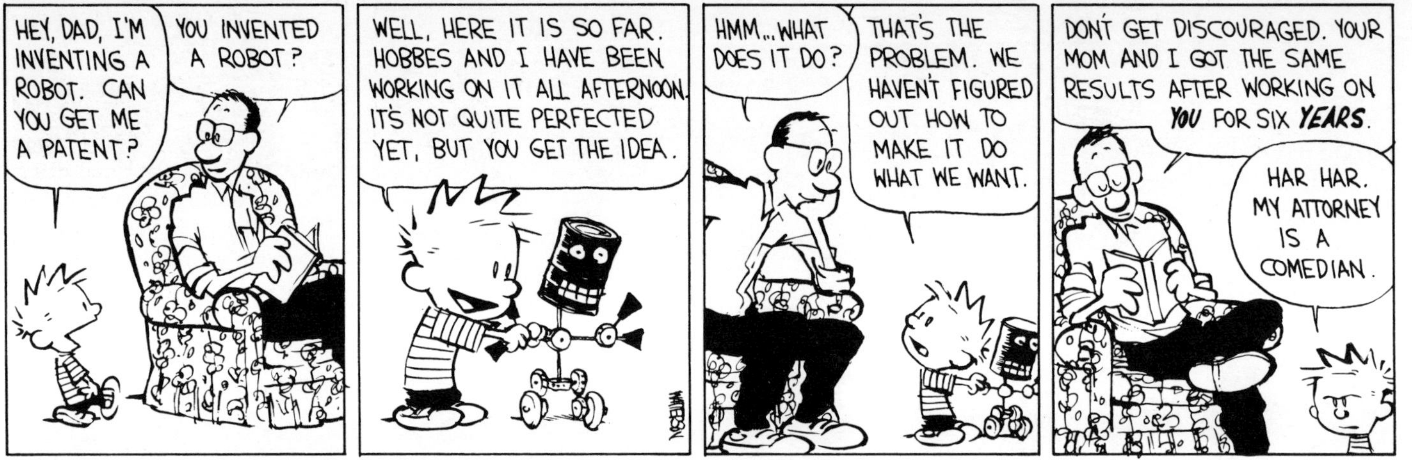
HEY, DAD, I'M INVENTING A ROBOT. CAN YOU GET ME A PATENT?
YOU INVENTED A ROBOT?
WELL, HERE IT IS SO FAR. HOBBES AND I HAVE BEEN WORKING ON IT ALL AFTERNOON. IT'S NOT QUITE PERFECTED YET, BUT YOU GET THE IDEA.
HMM... WHAT DOES IT DO?
THAT'S THE PROBLEM. WE HAVEN'T FIGURED OUT HOW TO MAKE IT DO WHAT WE WANT.
DON'T GET DISCOURAGED. YOUR MOM AND I GOT THE SAME RESULTS AFTER WORKING ON **YOU** FOR SIX **YEARS**.
HAR HAR. MY ATTORNEY IS A COMEDIAN.

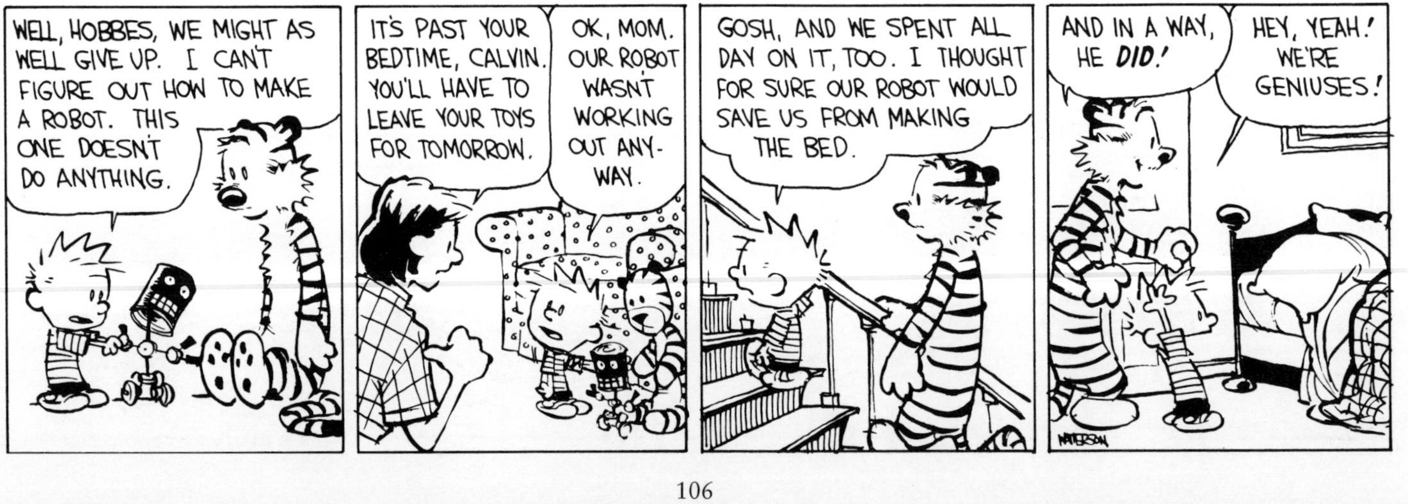
WELL, HOBBES, WE MIGHT AS WELL GIVE UP. I CAN'T FIGURE OUT HOW TO MAKE A ROBOT. THIS ONE DOESN'T DO ANYTHING.
IT'S PAST YOUR BEDTIME, CALVIN. YOU'LL HAVE TO LEAVE YOUR TOYS FOR TOMORROW.
OK, MOM. OUR ROBOT WASN'T WORKING OUT ANYWAY.
GOSH, AND WE SPENT ALL DAY ON IT, TOO. I THOUGHT FOR SURE OUR ROBOT WOULD SAVE US FROM MAKING THE BED.
AND IN A WAY, HE **DID**!
HEY, YEAH! WE'RE GENIUSES!

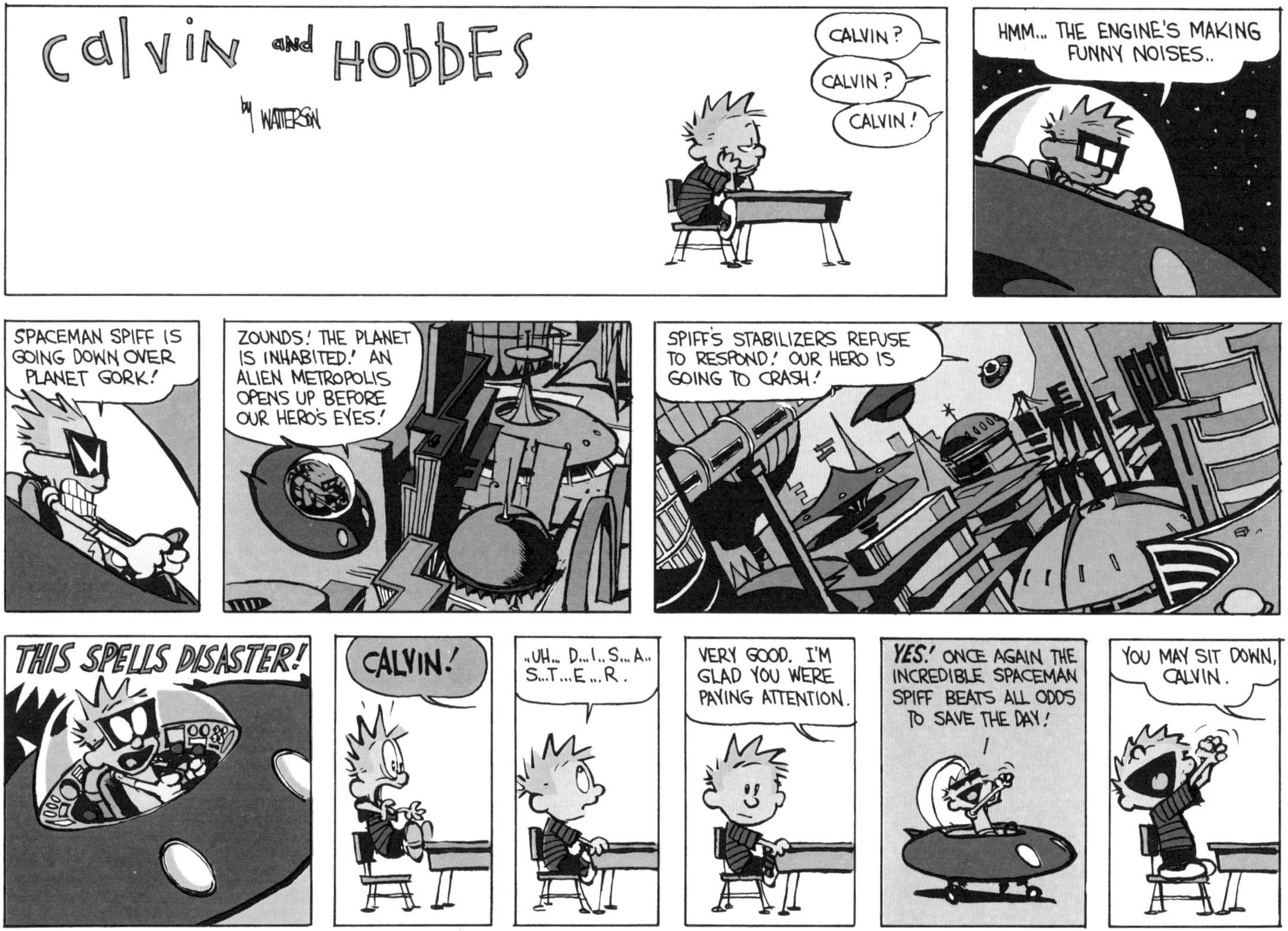
Calvin and HOBBES
by WATTERSON
CALVIN?
CALVIN?
CALVIN!
HMM... THE ENGINE'S MAKING FUNNY NOISES..
SPACEMAN SPIFF IS GOING DOWN OVER PLANET GORK!
ZOUNDS! THE PLANET IS INHABITED! AN ALIEN METROPOLIS OPENS UP BEFORE OUR HERO'S EYES!
SPIFF'S STABILIZERS REFUSE TO RESPOND! OUR HERO IS GOING TO CRASH!
THIS SPELLS DISASTER!
CALVIN!
..UH... D...I...S...A... S...T...E...R.
VERY GOOD. I'M GLAD YOU WERE PAYING ATTENTION.
YES! ONCE AGAIN THE INCREDIBLE SPACEMAN SPIFF BEATS ALL ODDS TO SAVE THE DAY!
YOU MAY SIT DOWN, CALVIN.

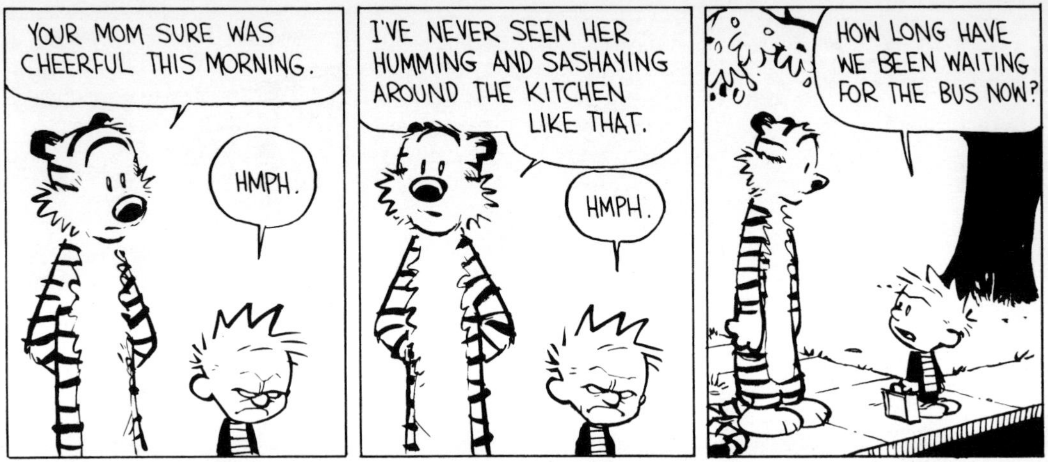
YOUR MOM SURE WAS CHEERFUL THIS MORNING.
HMPH.
I'VE NEVER SEEN HER HUMMING AND SASHAYING AROUND THE KITCHEN LIKE THAT.
HMPH.
HOW LONG HAVE WE BEEN WAITING FOR THE BUS NOW?
ABOUT TWO AND A HALF HOURS.
I THINK MOM PUT ME OUT HERE THIS EARLY ON ***PURPOSE***.

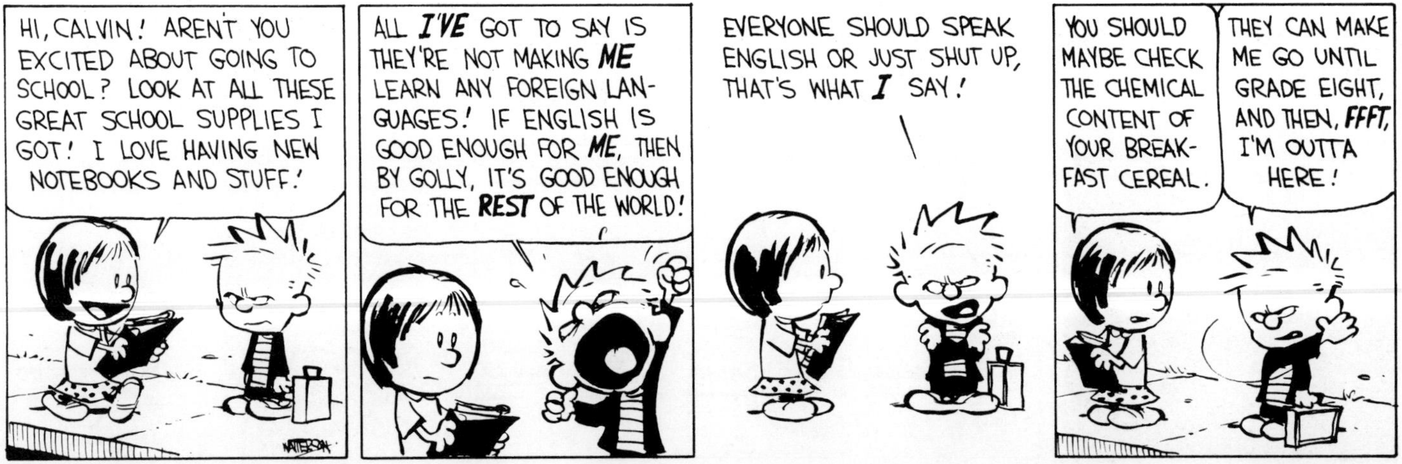
HI, CALVIN! AREN'T YOU EXCITED ABOUT GOING TO SCHOOL? LOOK AT ALL THESE GREAT SCHOOL SUPPLIES I GOT! I LOVE HAVING NEW NOTEBOOKS AND STUFF!
ALL ***I'VE*** GOT TO SAY IS THEY'RE NOT MAKING ***ME*** LEARN ANY FOREIGN LANGUAGES! IF ENGLISH IS GOOD ENOUGH FOR ***ME***, THEN BY GOLLY, IT'S GOOD ENOUGH FOR THE ***REST*** OF THE WORLD!
EVERYONE SHOULD SPEAK ENGLISH OR JUST SHUT UP, THAT'S WHAT ***I*** SAY!
YOU SHOULD MAYBE CHECK THE CHEMICAL CONTENT OF YOUR BREAKFAST CEREAL.
THEY CAN MAKE ME GO UNTIL GRADE EIGHT, AND THEN, ***FFFT,*** I'M OUTTA HERE!

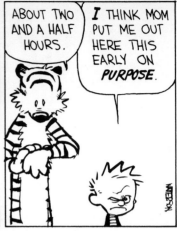

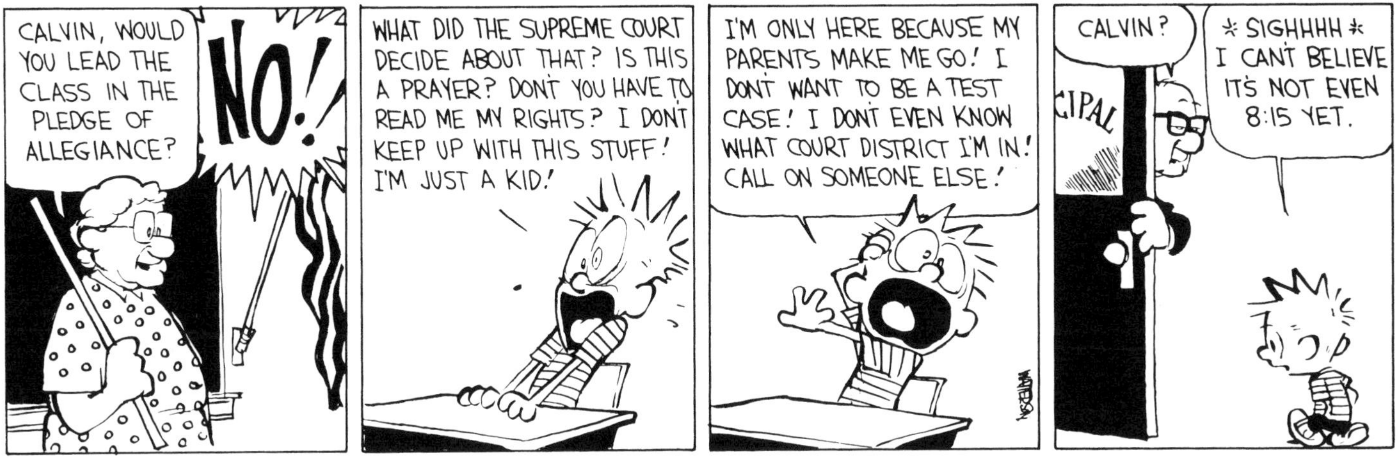
CALVIN, WOULD YOU LEAD THE CLASS IN THE PLEDGE OF ALLEGIANCE?
NO!!
WHAT DID THE SUPREME COURT DECIDE ABOUT THAT? IS THIS A PRAYER? DON'T YOU HAVE TO READ ME MY RIGHTS? I DON'T KEEP UP WITH THIS STUFF! I'M JUST A KID!
I'M ONLY HERE BECAUSE MY PARENTS MAKE ME GO! I DON'T WANT TO BE A TEST CASE! I DON'T EVEN KNOW WHAT COURT DISTRICT I'M IN! CALL ON SOMEONE ELSE!
CALVIN?
SIGHHHH I CAN'T BELIEVE IT'S NOT EVEN 8:15 YET.

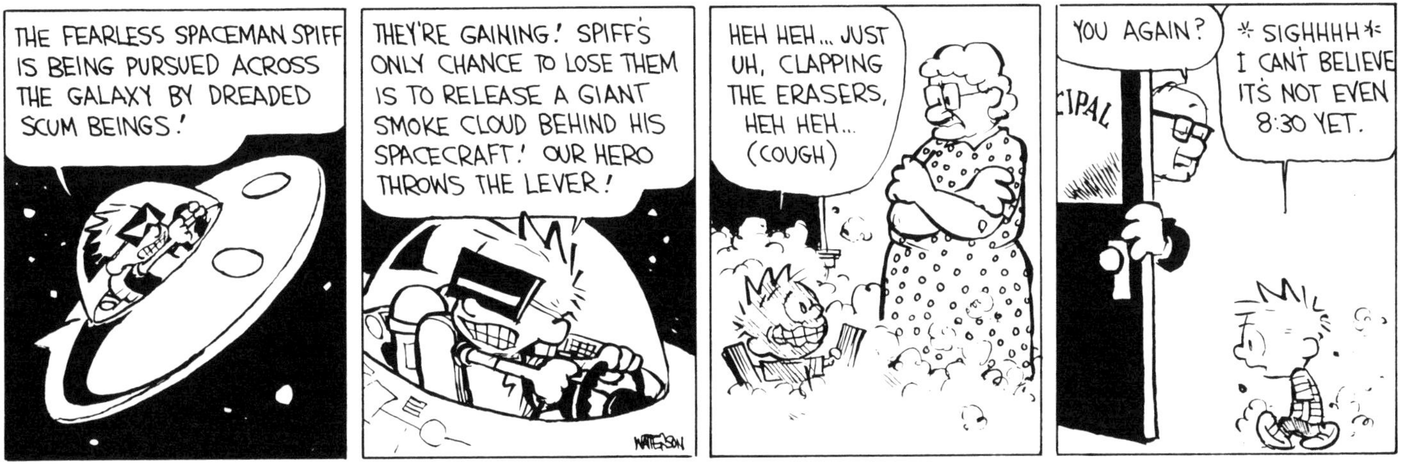
THE FEARLESS SPACEMAN SPIFF IS BEING PURSUED ACROSS THE GALAXY BY DREADED SCUM BEINGS!
THEY'RE GAINING! SPIFF'S ONLY CHANCE TO LOSE THEM IS TO RELEASE A GIANT SMOKE CLOUD BEHIND HIS SPACECRAFT! OUR HERO THROWS THE LEVER!
WATTERSON
HEH HEH... JUST UH, CLAPPING THE ERASERS, HEH HEH... (COUGH)
YOU AGAIN?
SIGHHHH I CAN'T BELIEVE IT'S NOT EVEN 8:30 YET.

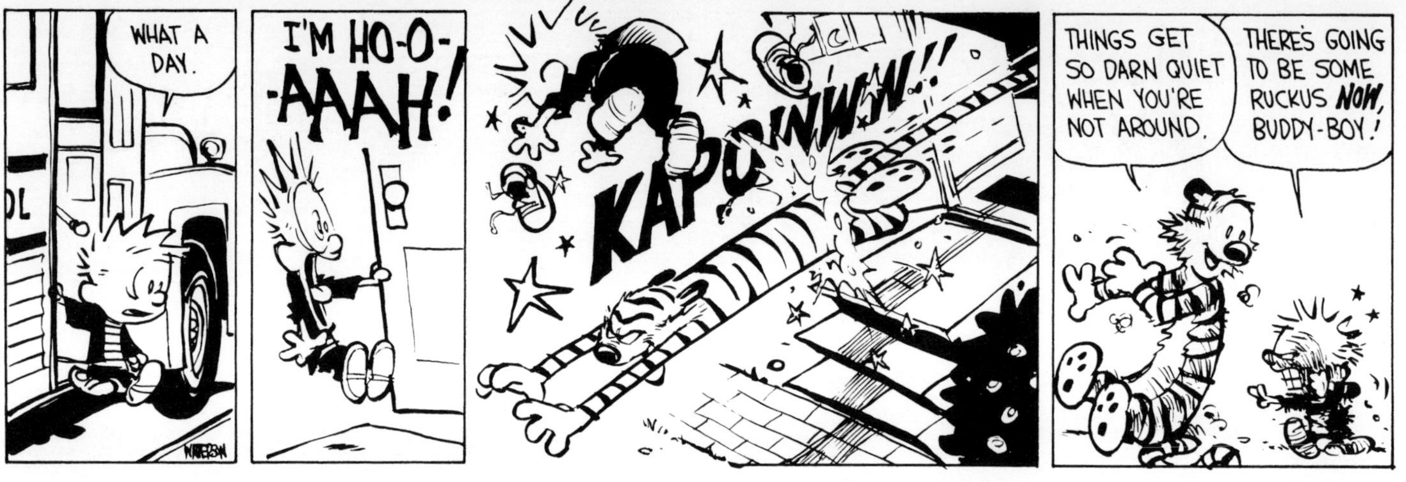
WHAT A DAY.
I'M HO-O-O-AAAH!
KAPOINWWN!!
THINGS GET SO DARN QUIET WHEN YOU'RE NOT AROUND.
THERE'S GOING TO BE SOME RUCKUS **NOW**, BUDDY-BOY!

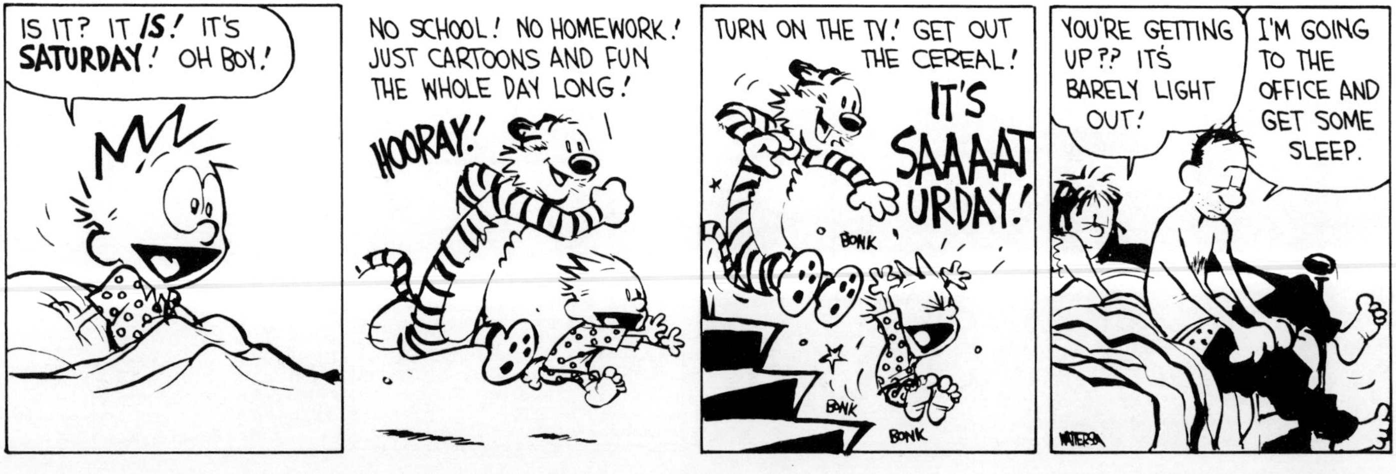
IS IT? IT **IS**! IT'S **SATURDAY**! OH BOY!
NO SCHOOL! NO HOMEWORK! JUST CARTOONS AND FUN THE WHOLE DAY LONG!
HOORAY!
TURN ON THE TV! GET OUT THE CEREAL!
IT'S SAAAAT URDAY!
BONK
BONK
BONK
YOU'RE GETTING UP?? IT'S BARELY LIGHT OUT!
I'M GOING TO THE OFFICE AND GET SOME SLEEP.

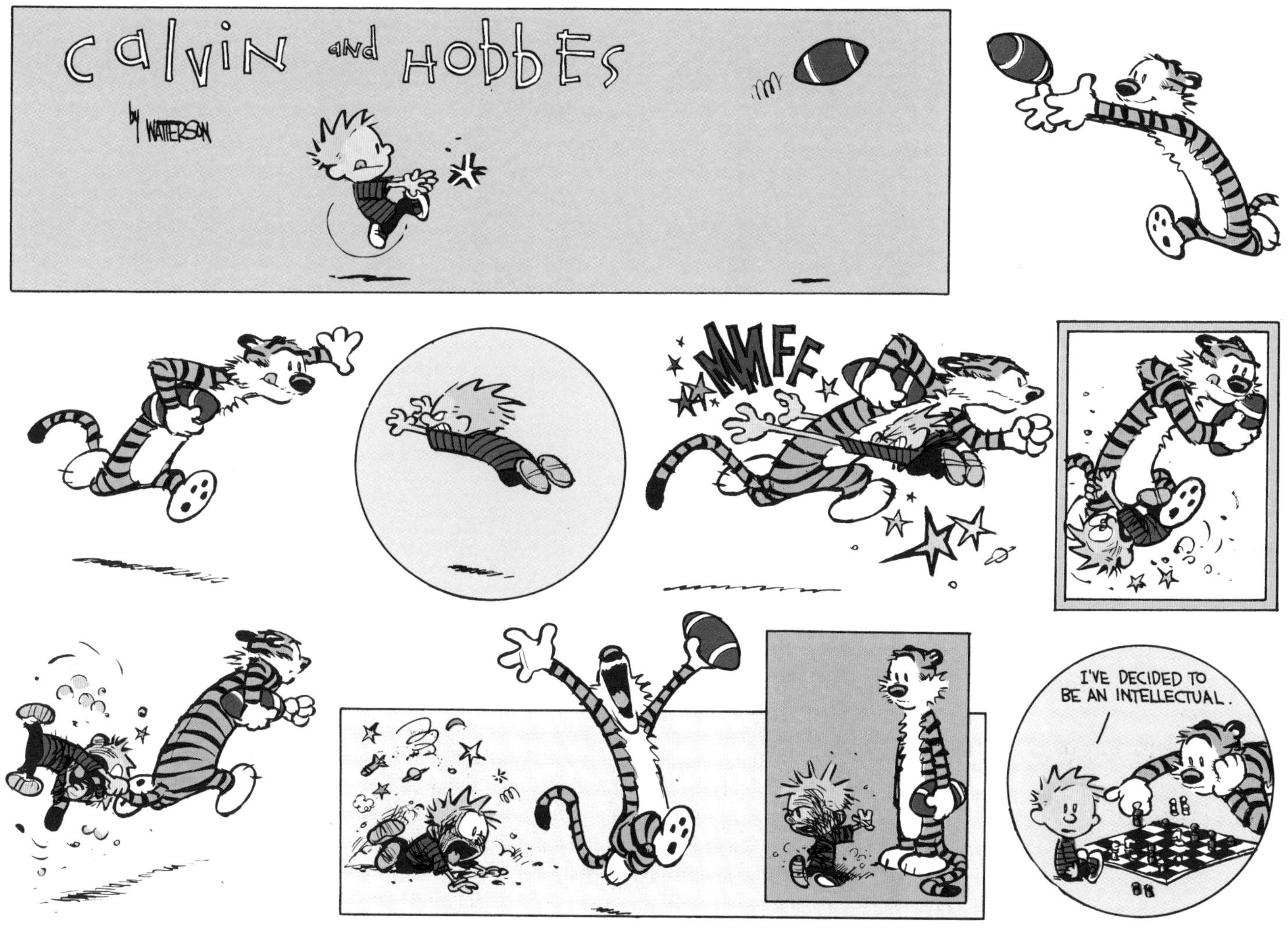
Calvin and Hobbes
by WATTERSON
MMFF
I'VE DECIDED TO BE AN INTELLECTUAL.

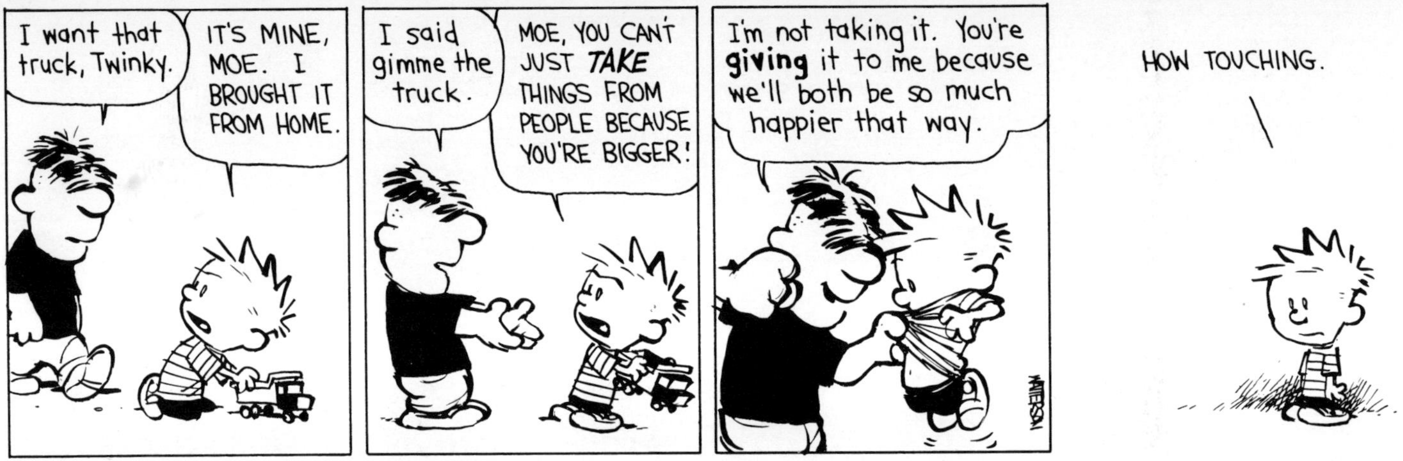
I want that truck, Twinky.
IT'S MINE, MOE. I BROUGHT IT FROM HOME.
I said gimme the truck.
MOE, YOU CAN'T JUST TAKE THINGS FROM PEOPLE BECAUSE YOU'RE BIGGER!
I'm not taking it. You're giving it to me because we'll both be so much happier that way.
HOW TOUCHING.

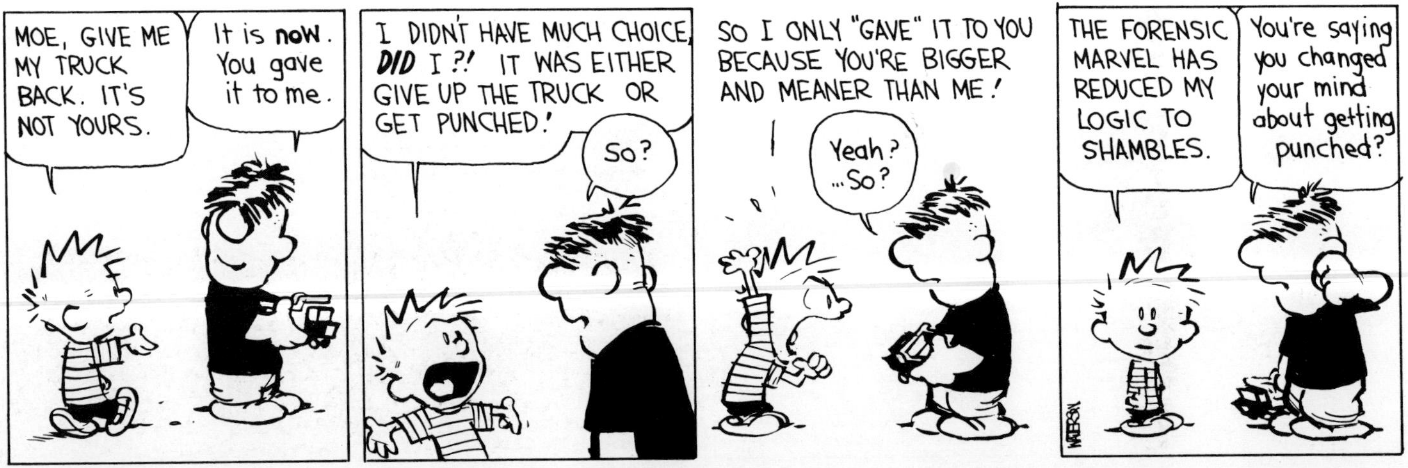
MOE, GIVE ME MY TRUCK BACK. IT'S NOT YOURS.
It is now. You gave it to me.
I DIDN'T HAVE MUCH CHOICE, DID I?! IT WAS EITHER GIVE UP THE TRUCK OR GET PUNCHED!
So?
SO I ONLY "GAVE" IT TO YOU BECAUSE YOU'RE BIGGER AND MEANER THAN ME!
Yeah? ...So?
THE FORENSIC MARVEL HAS REDUCED MY LOGIC TO SHAMBLES.
You're saying you changed your mind about getting punched?

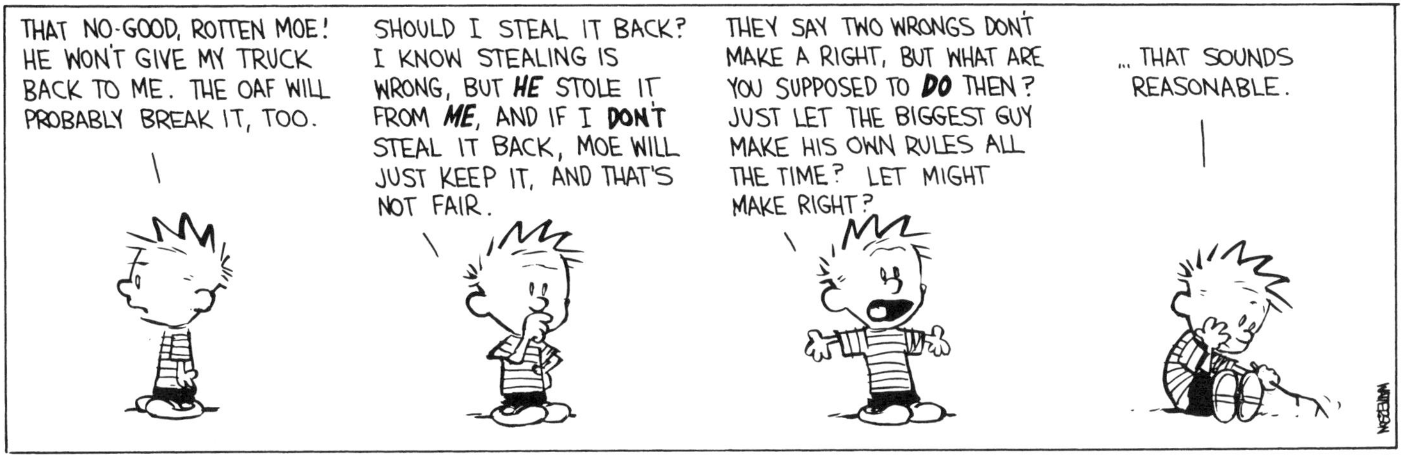
THAT NO-GOOD, ROTTEN MOE! HE WON'T GIVE MY TRUCK BACK TO ME. THE OAF WILL PROBABLY BREAK IT, TOO.
SHOULD I STEAL IT BACK? I KNOW STEALING IS WRONG, BUT **HE** STOLE IT FROM **ME**, AND IF I **DON'T** STEAL IT BACK, MOE WILL JUST KEEP IT, AND THAT'S NOT FAIR.
THEY SAY TWO WRONGS DON'T MAKE A RIGHT, BUT WHAT ARE YOU SUPPOSED TO **DO** THEN? JUST LET THE BIGGEST GUY MAKE HIS OWN RULES ALL THE TIME? LET MIGHT MAKE RIGHT?
... THAT SOUNDS REASONABLE.

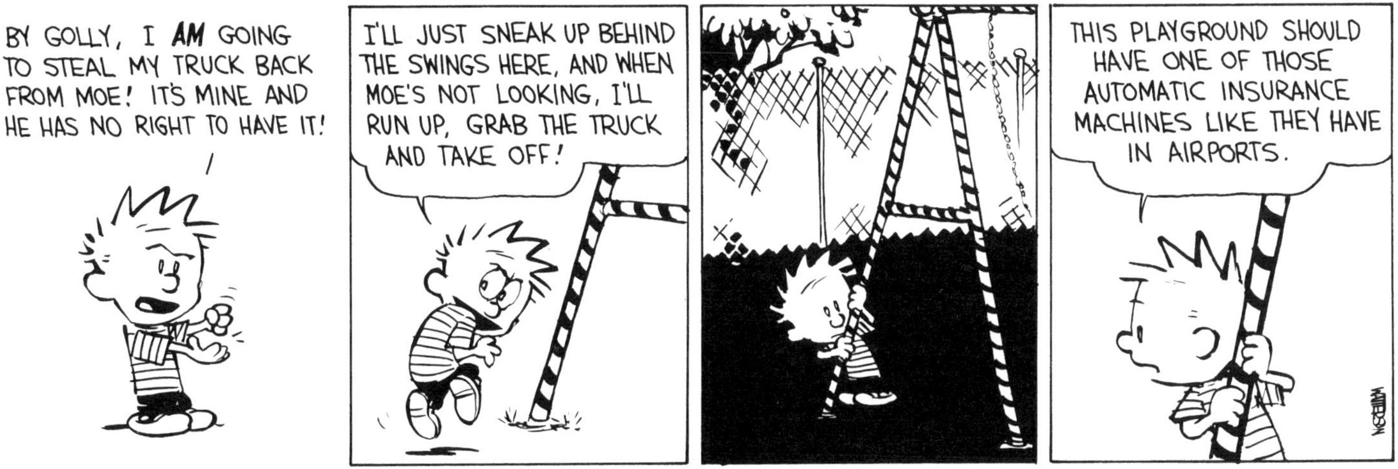
BY GOLLY, I **AM** GOING TO STEAL MY TRUCK BACK FROM MOE! IT'S MINE AND HE HAS NO RIGHT TO HAVE IT!
I'LL JUST SNEAK UP BEHIND THE SWINGS HERE, AND WHEN MOE'S NOT LOOKING, I'LL RUN UP, GRAB THE TRUCK AND TAKE OFF!
THIS PLAYGROUND SHOULD HAVE ONE OF THOSE AUTOMATIC INSURANCE MACHINES LIKE THEY HAVE IN AIRPORTS.

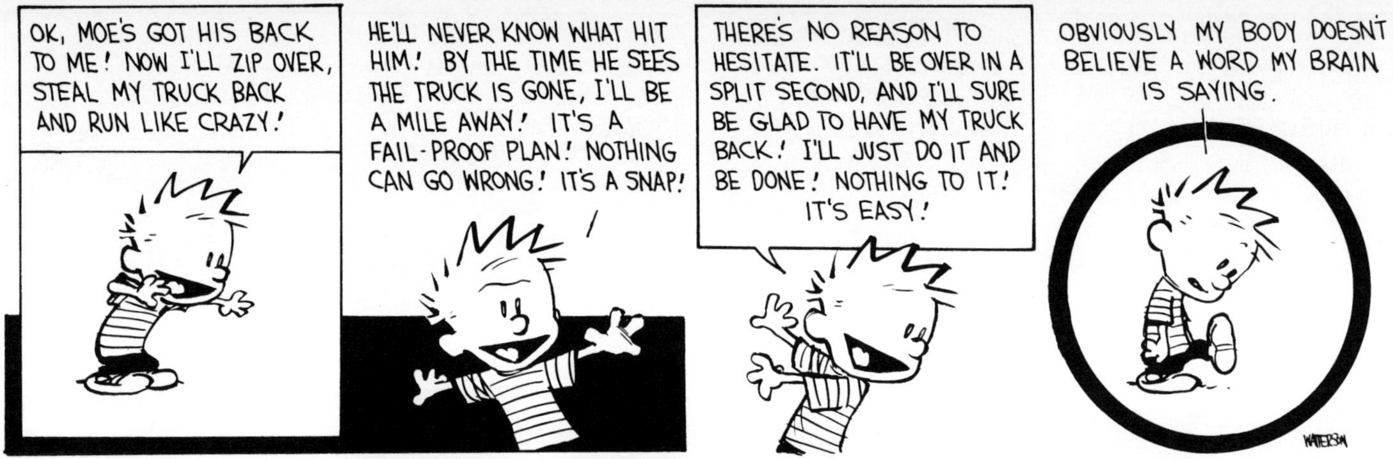
OK, MOE'S GOT HIS BACK TO ME! NOW I'LL ZIP OVER, STEAL MY TRUCK BACK AND RUN LIKE CRAZY!
HE'LL NEVER KNOW WHAT HIT HIM! BY THE TIME HE SEES THE TRUCK IS GONE, I'LL BE A MILE AWAY! IT'S A FAIL-PROOF PLAN! NOTHING CAN GO WRONG! IT'S A SNAP!
THERE'S NO REASON TO HESITATE. IT'LL BE OVER IN A SPLIT SECOND, AND I'LL SURE BE GLAD TO HAVE MY TRUCK BACK! I'LL JUST DO IT AND BE DONE! NOTHING TO IT! IT'S EASY!
OBVIOUSLY MY BODY DOESN'T BELIEVE A WORD MY BRAIN IS SAYING.
WATTERSON

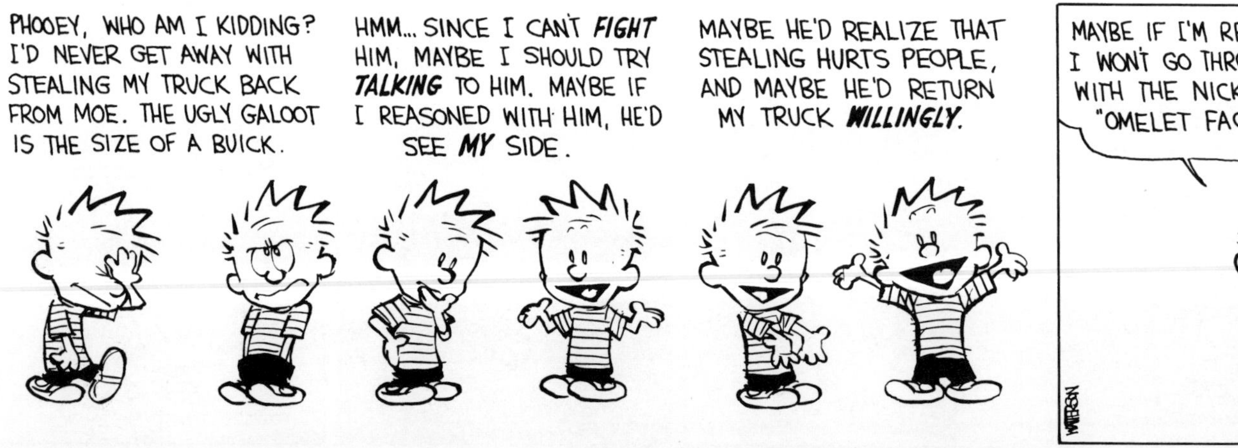
PHOOEY, WHO AM I KIDDING? I'D NEVER GET AWAY WITH STEALING MY TRUCK BACK FROM MOE. THE UGLY GALOOT IS THE SIZE OF A BUICK.
HMM... SINCE I CAN'T **FIGHT** HIM, MAYBE I SHOULD TRY **TALKING** TO HIM. MAYBE IF I REASONED WITH HIM, HE'D SEE **MY** SIDE.
MAYBE HE'D REALIZE THAT STEALING HURTS PEOPLE, AND MAYBE HE'D RETURN MY TRUCK **WILLINGLY**.
MAYBE IF I'M REALLY LUCKY I WON'T GO THROUGH LIFE WITH THE NICKNAME "OMELET FACE."
WATTERSON

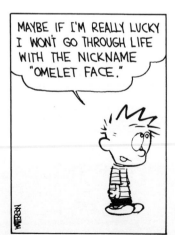

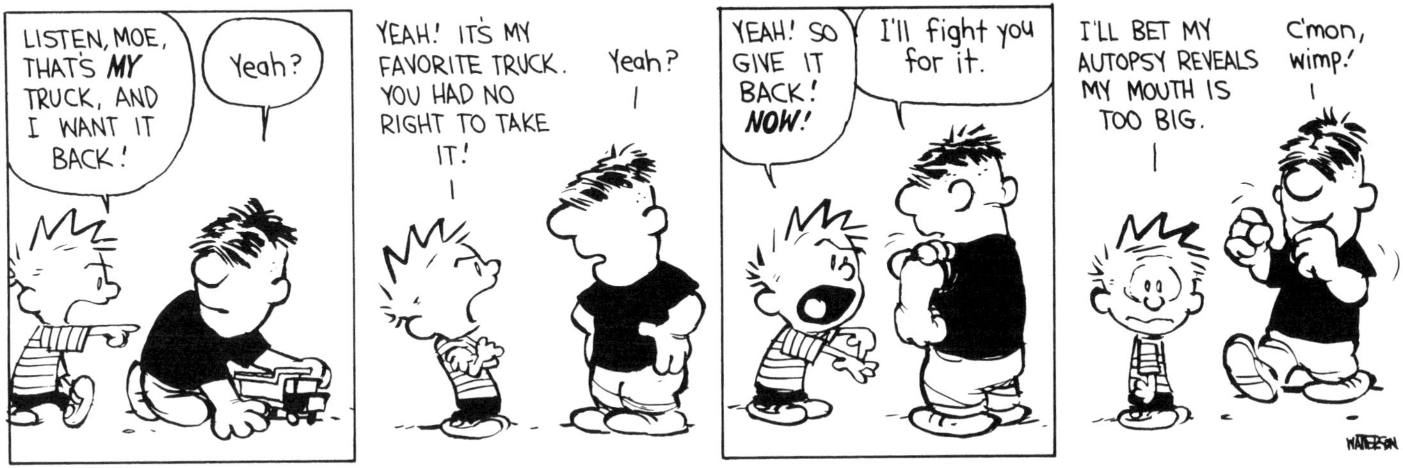
LISTEN, MOE, THAT'S **MY** TRUCK, AND I WANT IT BACK!
Yeah?
YEAH! IT'S MY FAVORITE TRUCK. YOU HAD NO RIGHT TO TAKE IT!
Yeah?
YEAH! SO GIVE IT BACK! **NOW!**
I'll fight you for it.
I'LL BET MY AUTOPSY REVEALS MY MOUTH IS TOO BIG.
C'mon, wimp!
WATTERSON

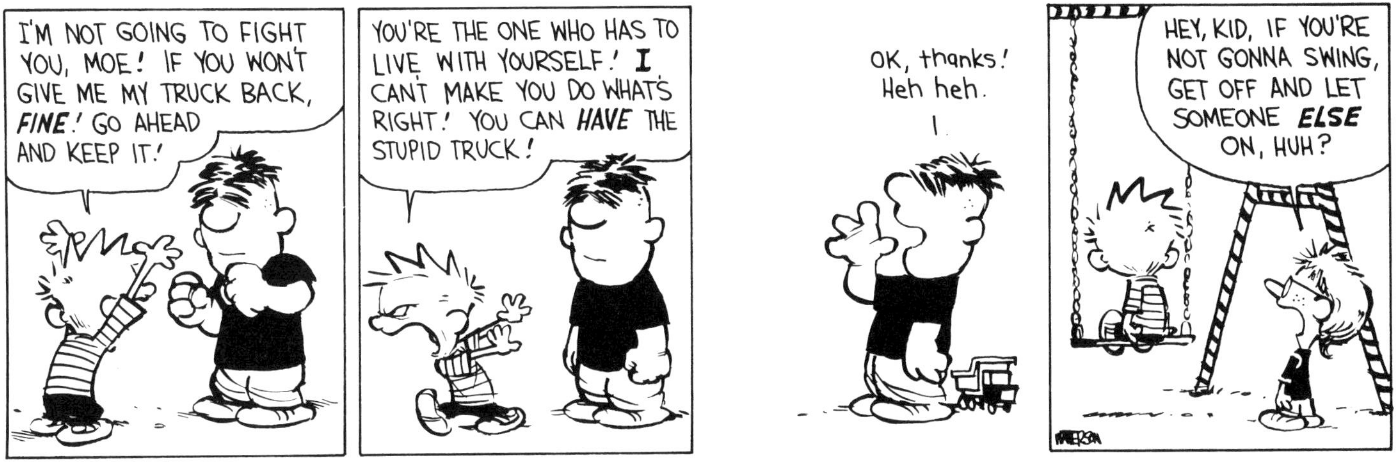
I'M NOT GOING TO FIGHT YOU, MOE! IF YOU WON'T GIVE ME MY TRUCK BACK, **FINE**! GO AHEAD AND KEEP IT!
YOU'RE THE ONE WHO HAS TO LIVE WITH YOURSELF! **I** CAN'T MAKE YOU DO WHAT'S RIGHT! YOU CAN **HAVE** THE STUPID TRUCK!
OK, thanks! Heh heh.
HEY, KID, IF YOU'RE NOT GONNA SWING, GET OFF AND LET SOMEONE **ELSE** ON, HUH?
WATTERSON

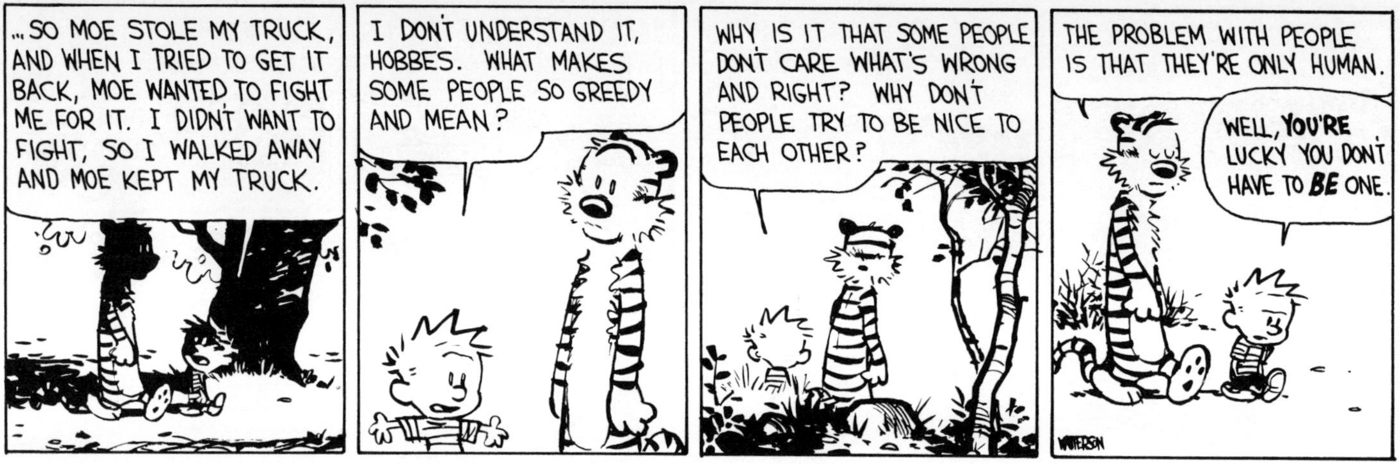
...SO MOE STOLE MY TRUCK, AND WHEN I TRIED TO GET IT BACK, MOE WANTED TO FIGHT ME FOR IT. I DIDN'T WANT TO FIGHT, SO I WALKED AWAY AND MOE KEPT MY TRUCK.
I DON'T UNDERSTAND IT, HOBBES. WHAT MAKES SOME PEOPLE SO GREEDY AND MEAN?
WHY IS IT THAT SOME PEOPLE DON'T CARE WHAT'S WRONG AND RIGHT? WHY DON'T PEOPLE TRY TO BE NICE TO EACH OTHER?
THE PROBLEM WITH PEOPLE IS THAT THEY'RE ONLY HUMAN.
WELL, **YOU'RE** LUCKY YOU DON'T HAVE TO **BE** ONE.
WATTERSON

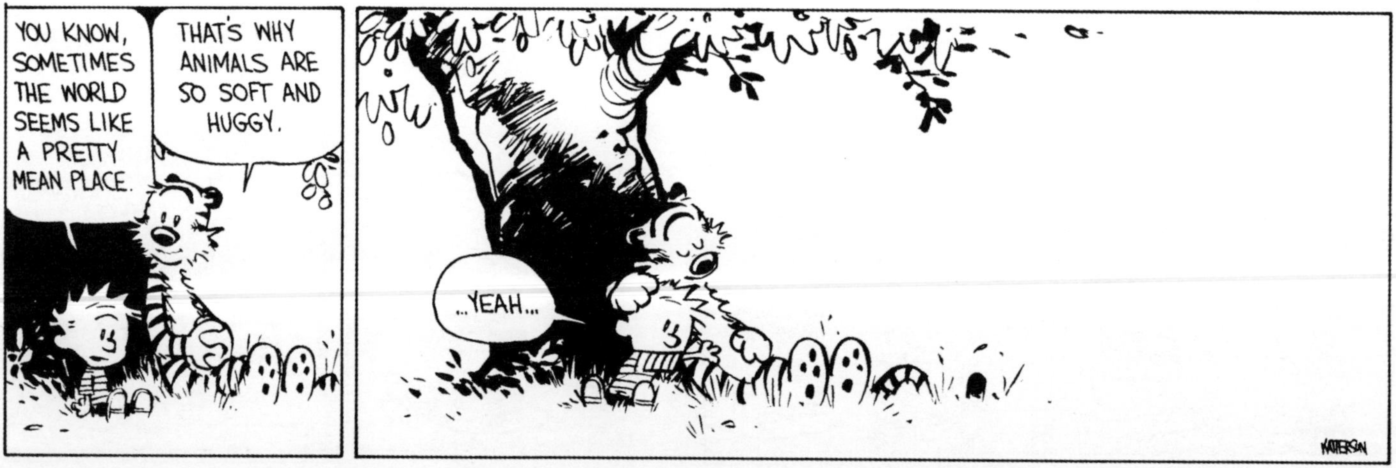
YOU KNOW, SOMETIMES THE WORLD SEEMS LIKE A PRETTY MEAN PLACE.
THAT'S WHY ANIMALS ARE SO SOFT AND HUGGY.
...YEAH...
WATTERSON

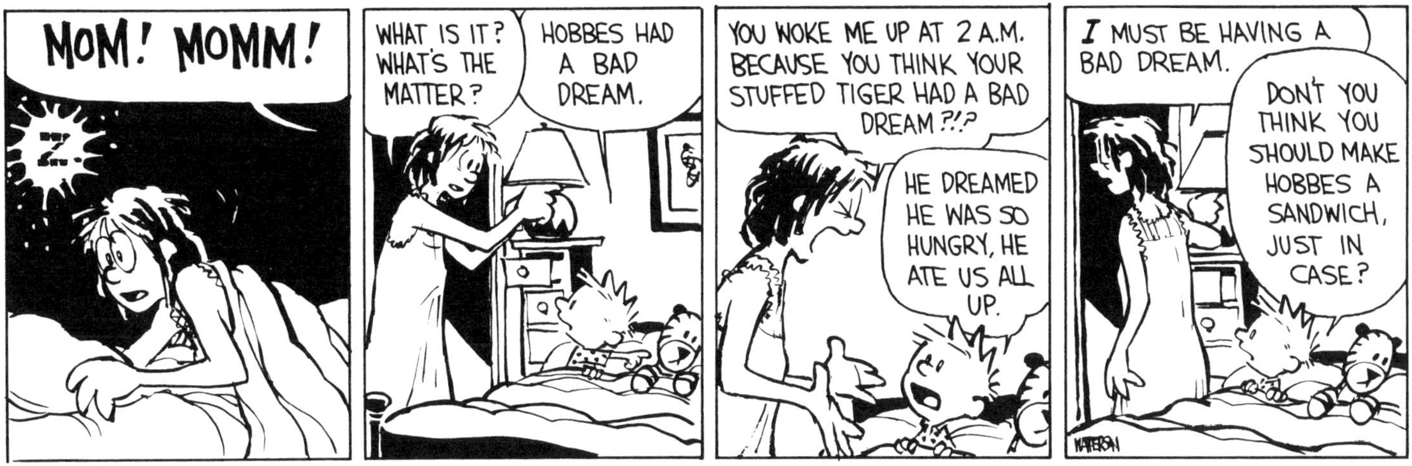
MOM! MOMM!
WHAT IS IT? WHAT'S THE MATTER?
HOBBES HAD A BAD DREAM.
YOU WOKE ME UP AT 2 A.M. BECAUSE YOU THINK YOUR STUFFED TIGER HAD A BAD DREAM?!?
HE DREAMED HE WAS SO HUNGRY, HE ATE US ALL UP.
I MUST BE HAVING A BAD DREAM.
DON'T YOU THINK YOU SHOULD MAKE HOBBES A SANDWICH, JUST IN CASE?

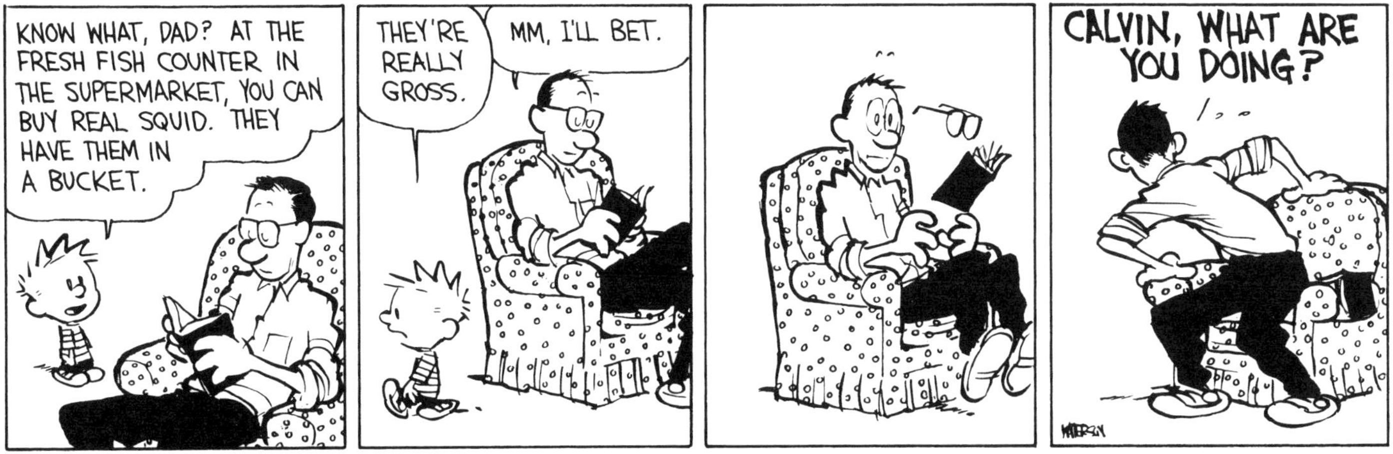
KNOW WHAT, DAD? AT THE FRESH FISH COUNTER IN THE SUPERMARKET, YOU CAN BUY REAL SQUID. THEY HAVE THEM IN A BUCKET.
THEY'RE REALLY GROSS.
MM, I'LL BET.
CALVIN, WHAT ARE YOU DOING?

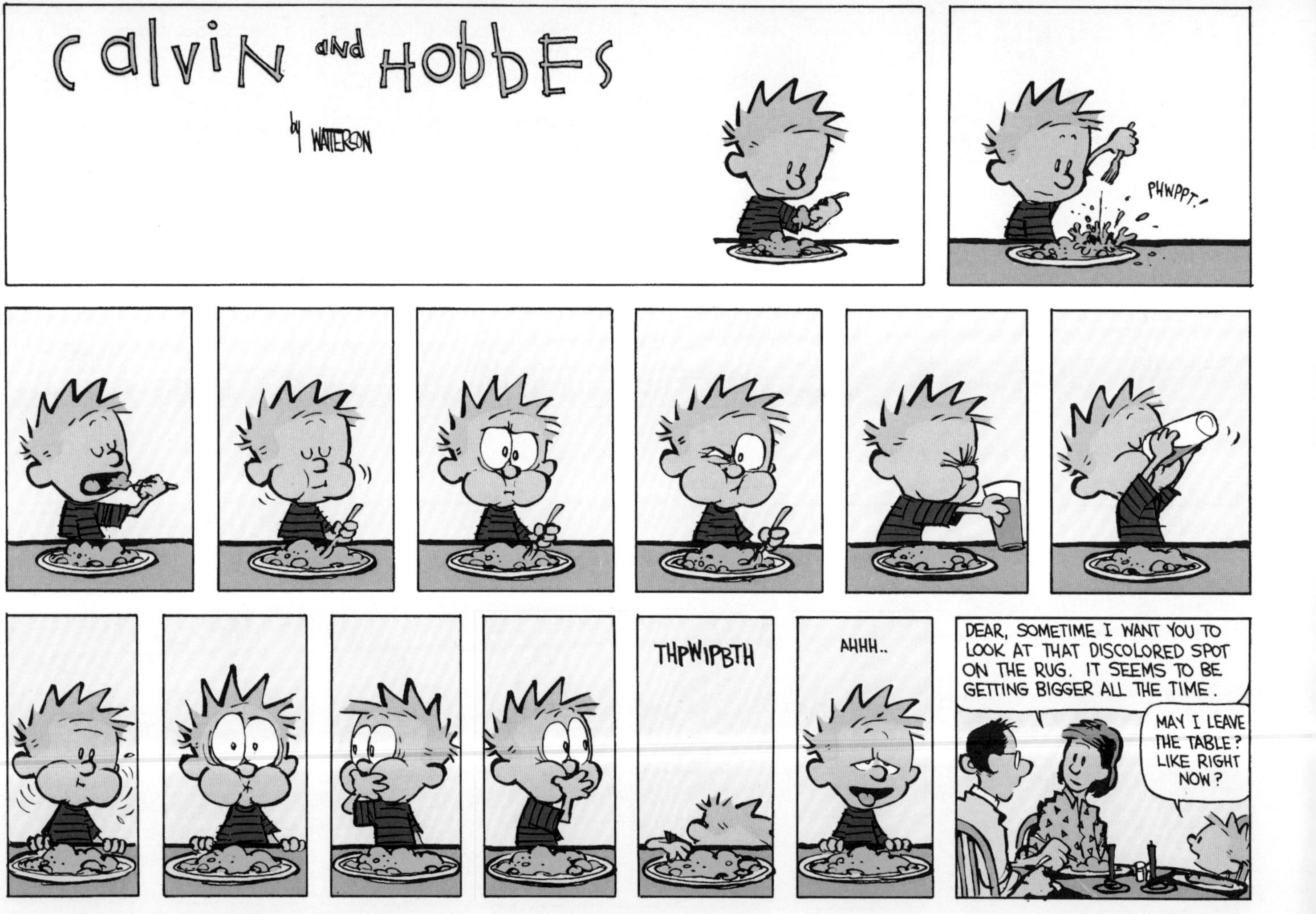
Calvin and HOBBES
by WATTERSON
PHWPPT!
THPWIPBTH
AHHH..
DEAR, SOMETIME I WANT YOU TO LOOK AT THAT DISCOLORED SPOT ON THE RUG. IT SEEMS TO BE GETTING BIGGER ALL THE TIME.
MAY I LEAVE THE TABLE? LIKE RIGHT NOW?

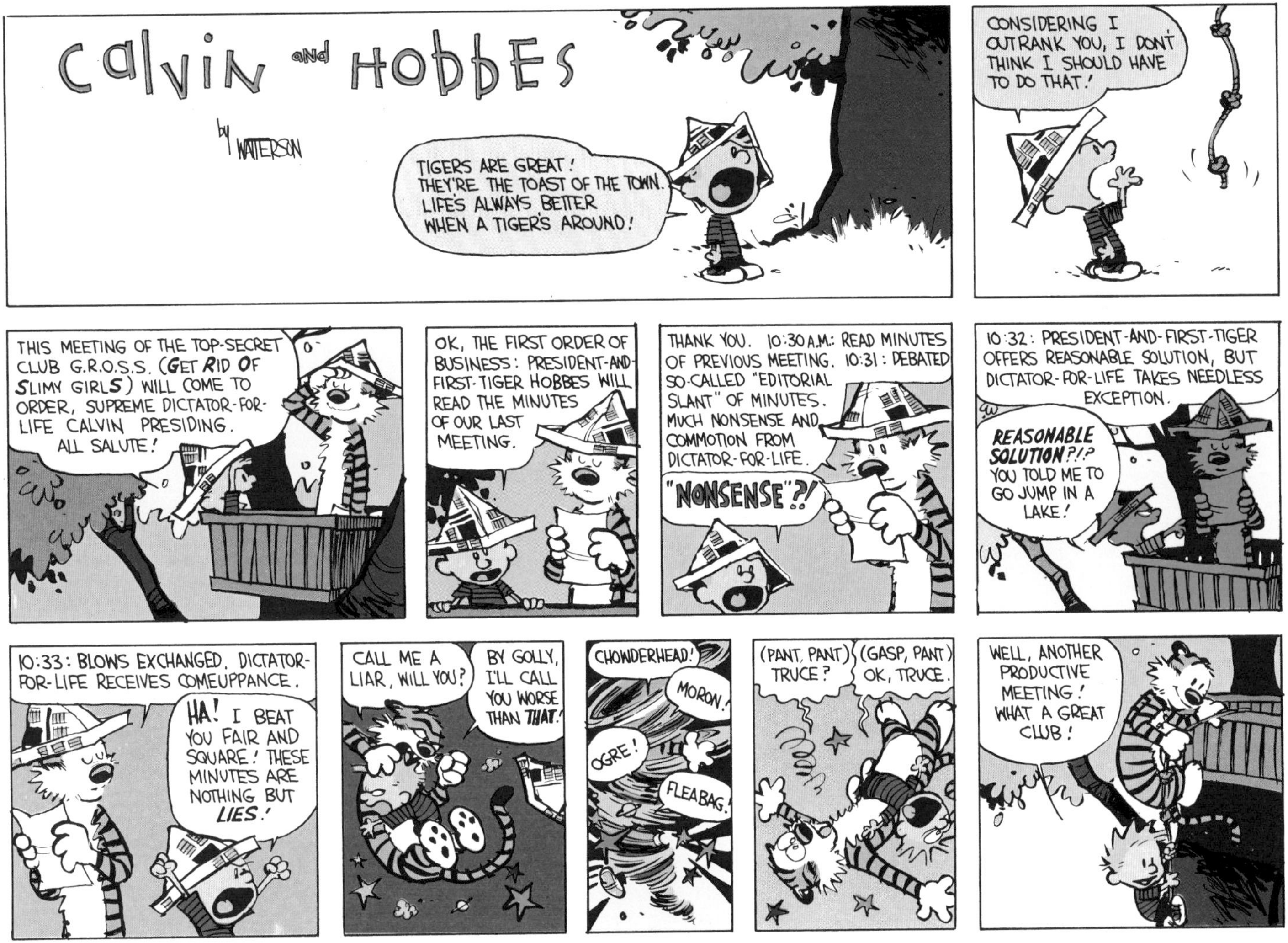
Calvin and Hobbes
by WATTERSON
TIGERS ARE GREAT! THEY'RE THE TOAST OF THE TOWN. LIFE'S ALWAYS BETTER WHEN A TIGER'S AROUND!
CONSIDERING I OUTRANK YOU, I DON'T THINK I SHOULD HAVE TO DO THAT!
THIS MEETING OF THE TOP-SECRET CLUB G.R.O.S.S. (GET RID OF SLIMY GIRLS) WILL COME TO ORDER, SUPREME DICTATOR-FOR-LIFE CALVIN PRESIDING. ALL SALUTE!
OK, THE FIRST ORDER OF BUSINESS: PRESIDENT-AND-FIRST-TIGER HOBBES WILL READ THE MINUTES OF OUR LAST MEETING.
THANK YOU. 10:30 A.M.: READ MINUTES OF PREVIOUS MEETING. 10:31: DEBATED SO-CALLED "EDITORIAL SLANT" OF MINUTES. MUCH NONSENSE AND COMMOTION FROM DICTATOR-FOR-LIFE.
"NONSENSE"?!
10:32: PRESIDENT-AND-FIRST-TIGER OFFERS REASONABLE SOLUTION, BUT DICTATOR-FOR-LIFE TAKES NEEDLESS EXCEPTION.
REASONABLE SOLUTION?!? YOU TOLD ME TO GO JUMP IN A LAKE!
10:33: BLOWS EXCHANGED. DICTATOR-FOR-LIFE RECEIVES COMEUPPANCE.
HA! I BEAT YOU FAIR AND SQUARE! THESE MINUTES ARE NOTHING BUT LIES!
CALL ME A LIAR, WILL YOU?
BY GOLLY, I'LL CALL YOU WORSE THAN THAT!
CHOWDERHEAD!
MORON!
OGRE!
FLEABAG!
(PANT, PANT) TRUCE?
(GASP, PANT) OK, TRUCE.
WELL, ANOTHER PRODUCTIVE MEETING! WHAT A GREAT CLUB!

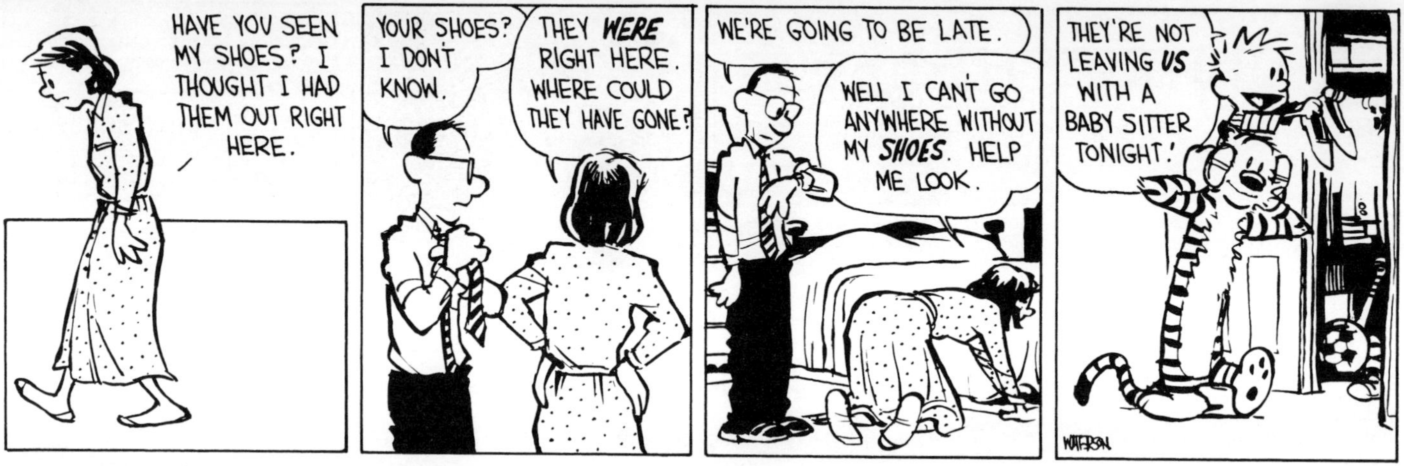
HAVE YOU SEEN MY SHOES? I THOUGHT I HAD THEM OUT RIGHT HERE.
YOUR SHOES? I DON'T KNOW.
THEY **WERE** RIGHT HERE. WHERE COULD THEY HAVE GONE?
WE'RE GOING TO BE LATE.
WELL I CAN'T GO ANYWHERE WITHOUT MY **SHOES**. HELP ME LOOK.
THEY'RE NOT LEAVING **US** WITH A BABY SITTER TONIGHT!
WATTERSON

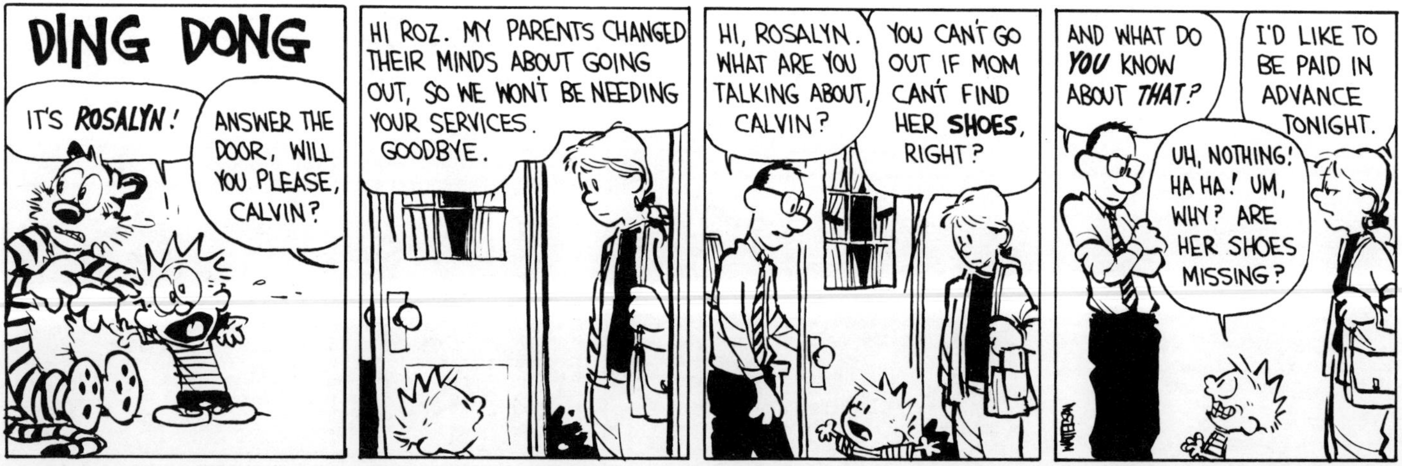
DING DONG
IT'S **ROSALYN**!
ANSWER THE DOOR, WILL YOU PLEASE, CALVIN?
HI ROZ. MY PARENTS CHANGED THEIR MINDS ABOUT GOING OUT, SO WE WON'T BE NEEDING YOUR SERVICES. GOODBYE.
HI, ROSALYN. WHAT ARE YOU TALKING ABOUT, CALVIN?
YOU CAN'T GO OUT IF MOM CAN'T FIND HER **SHOES**, RIGHT?
AND WHAT DO **YOU** KNOW ABOUT **THAT**?
I'D LIKE TO BE PAID IN ADVANCE TONIGHT.
UH, NOTHING! HA HA! UM, WHY? ARE HER SHOES MISSING?
WATTERSON

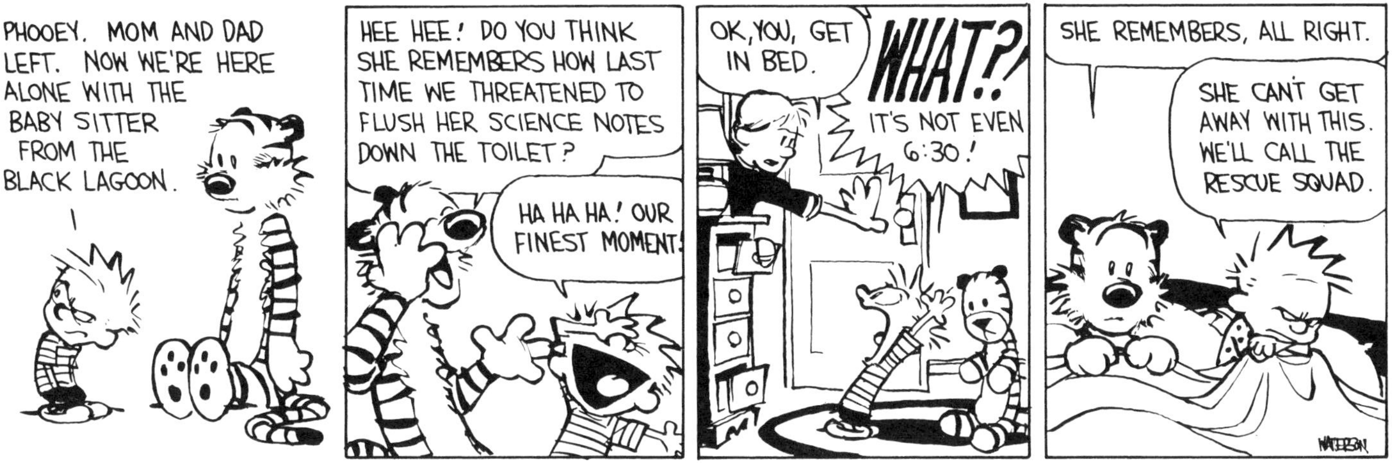
PHOOEY. MOM AND DAD LEFT. NOW WE'RE HERE ALONE WITH THE BABY SITTER FROM THE BLACK LAGOON.
HEE HEE! DO YOU THINK SHE REMEMBERS HOW LAST TIME WE THREATENED TO FLUSH HER SCIENCE NOTES DOWN THE TOILET?
HA HA HA! OUR FINEST MOMENT!
OK, YOU, GET IN BED.
WHAT?!
IT'S NOT EVEN 6:30!
SHE REMEMBERS, ALL RIGHT.
SHE CAN'T GET AWAY WITH THIS. WE'LL CALL THE RESCUE SQUAD.

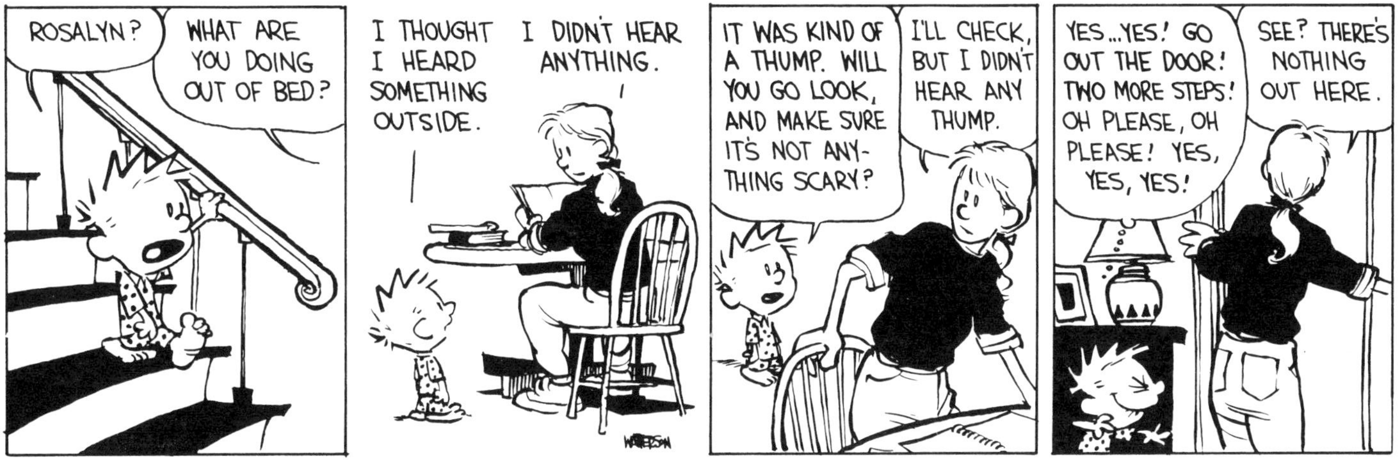
ROSALYN?
WHAT ARE YOU DOING OUT OF BED?
I THOUGHT I HEARD SOMETHING OUTSIDE.
I DIDN'T HEAR ANYTHING.
IT WAS KIND OF A THUMP. WILL YOU GO LOOK, AND MAKE SURE IT'S NOT ANYTHING SCARY?
I'LL CHECK, BUT I DIDN'T HEAR ANY THUMP.
YES...YES! GO OUT THE DOOR! TWO MORE STEPS! OH PLEASE, OH PLEASE! YES, YES, YES!
SEE? THERE'S NOTHING OUT HERE.

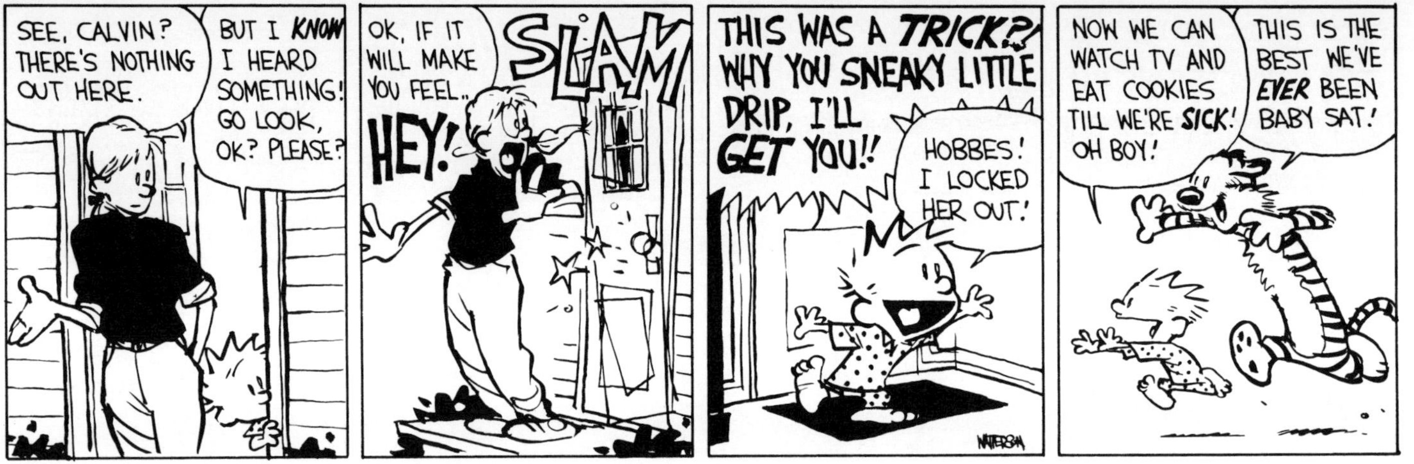
SEE, CALVIN? THERE'S NOTHING OUT HERE.
BUT I KNOW I HEARD SOMETHING! GO LOOK, OK? PLEASE?
OK, IF IT WILL MAKE YOU FEEL..
SLAM
HEY!
THIS WAS A TRICK?! WHY YOU SNEAKY LITTLE DRIP, I'LL GET YOU!!
HOBBES! I LOCKED HER OUT!
NOW WE CAN WATCH TV AND EAT COOKIES TILL WE'RE SICK! OH BOY!
THIS IS THE BEST WE'VE EVER BEEN BABY SAT!

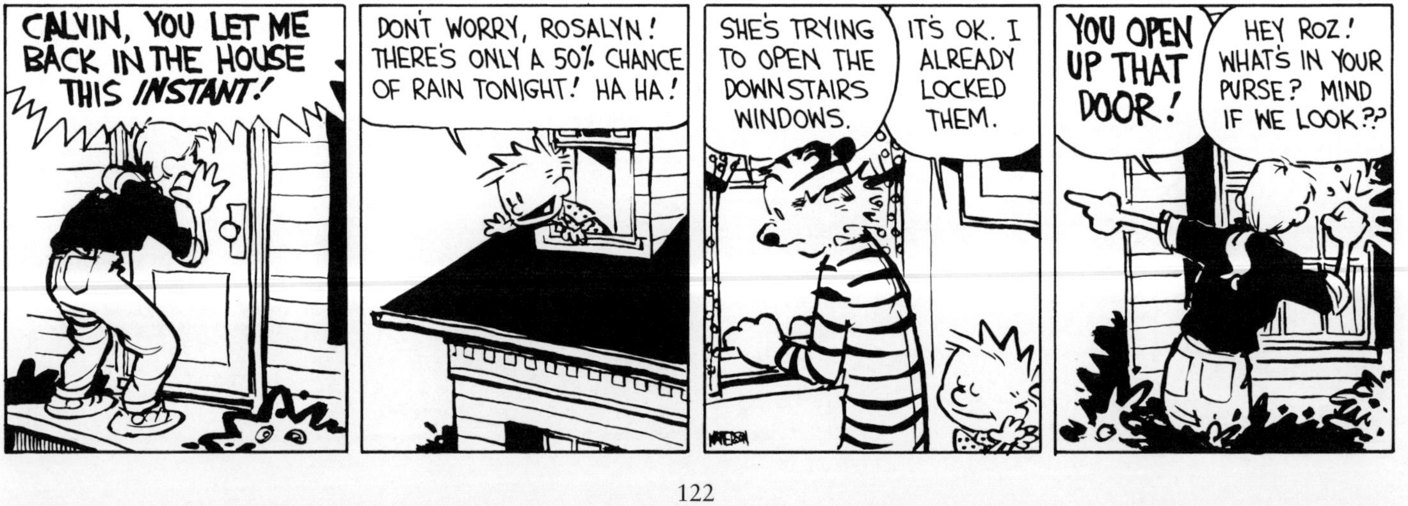
CALVIN, YOU LET ME BACK IN THE HOUSE THIS INSTANT!
DON'T WORRY, ROSALYN! THERE'S ONLY A 50% CHANCE OF RAIN TONIGHT! HA HA!
SHE'S TRYING TO OPEN THE DOWNSTAIRS WINDOWS.
IT'S OK. I ALREADY LOCKED THEM.
YOU OPEN UP THAT DOOR!
HEY ROZ! WHAT'S IN YOUR PURSE? MIND IF WE LOOK??

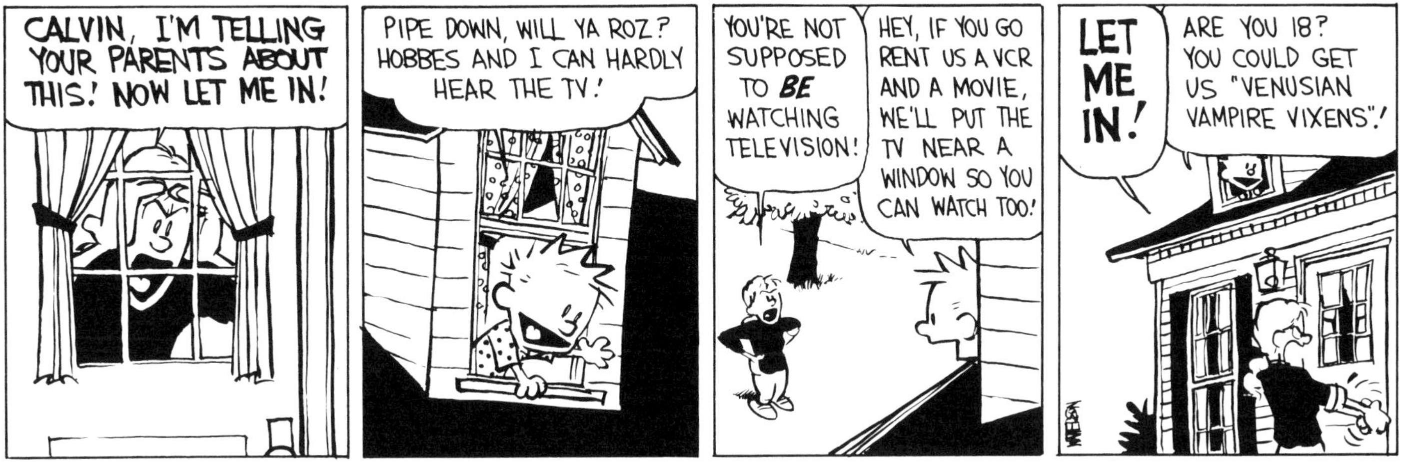
CALVIN, I'M TELLING YOUR PARENTS ABOUT THIS! NOW LET ME IN!
PIPE DOWN, WILL YA ROZ? HOBBES AND I CAN HARDLY HEAR THE TV!
YOU'RE NOT SUPPOSED TO *BE* WATCHING TELEVISION!
HEY, IF YOU GO RENT US A VCR AND A MOVIE, WE'LL PUT THE TV NEAR A WINDOW SO YOU CAN WATCH TOO!
LET ME IN!
ARE YOU 18? YOU COULD GET US "VENUSIAN VAMPIRE VIXENS"!

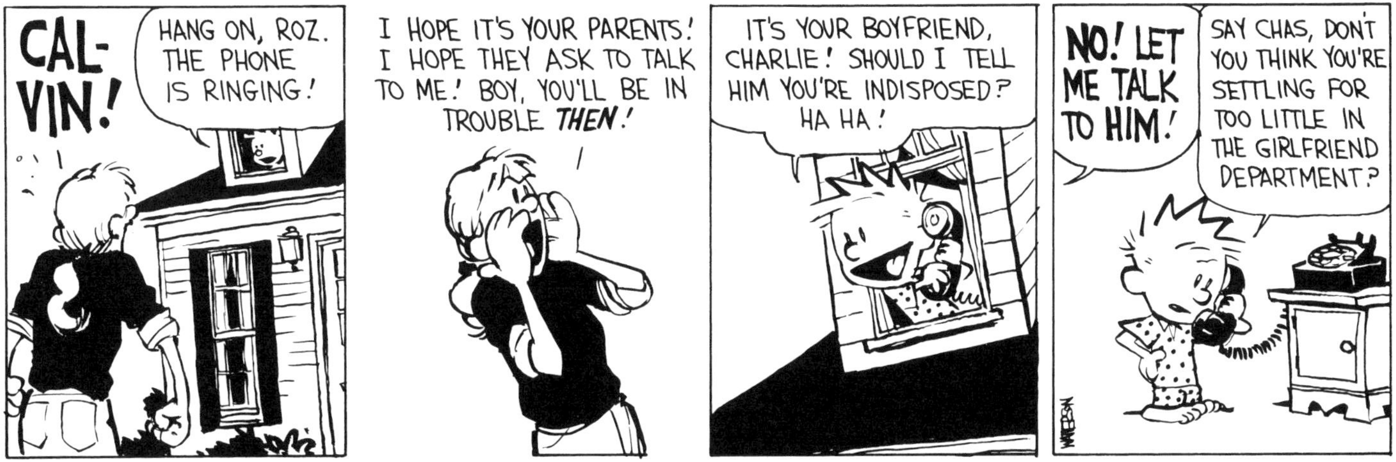
CAL-VIN!
HANG ON, ROZ. THE PHONE IS RINGING!
I HOPE IT'S YOUR PARENTS! I HOPE THEY ASK TO TALK TO ME! BOY, YOU'LL BE IN TROUBLE *THEN*!
IT'S YOUR BOYFRIEND, CHARLIE! SHOULD I TELL HIM YOU'RE INDISPOSED? HA HA!
NO! LET ME TALK TO HIM!
SAY CHAS, DON'T YOU THINK YOU'RE SETTLING FOR TOO LITTLE IN THE GIRLFRIEND DEPARTMENT?

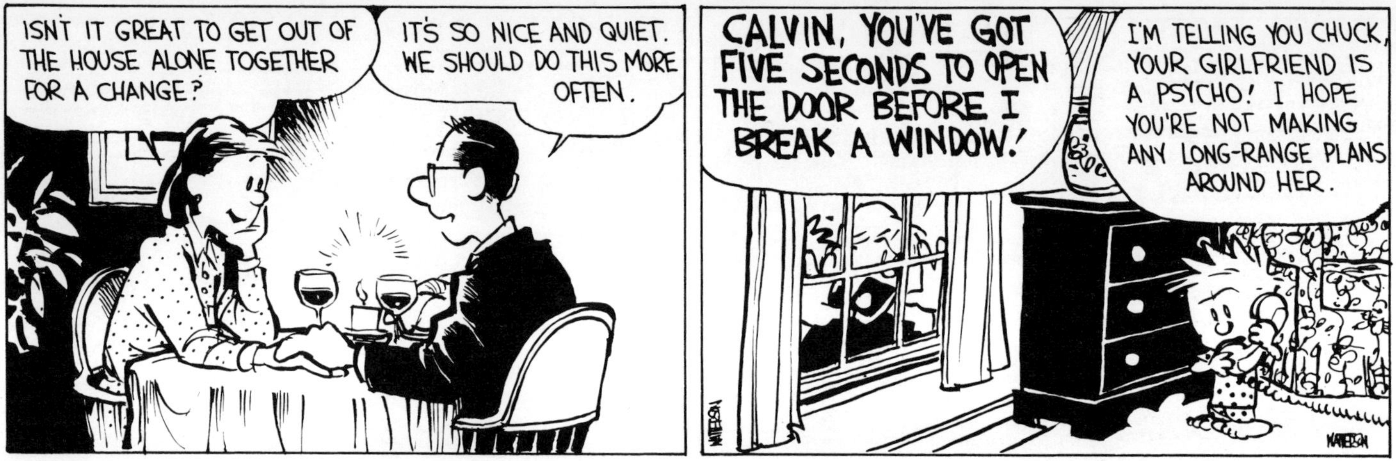
ISN'T IT GREAT TO GET OUT OF THE HOUSE ALONE TOGETHER FOR A CHANGE?
IT'S SO NICE AND QUIET. WE SHOULD DO THIS MORE OFTEN.
CALVIN, YOU'VE GOT FIVE SECONDS TO OPEN THE DOOR BEFORE I BREAK A WINDOW!
I'M TELLING YOU CHUCK, YOUR GIRLFRIEND IS A PSYCHO! I HOPE YOU'RE NOT MAKING ANY LONG-RANGE PLANS AROUND HER.

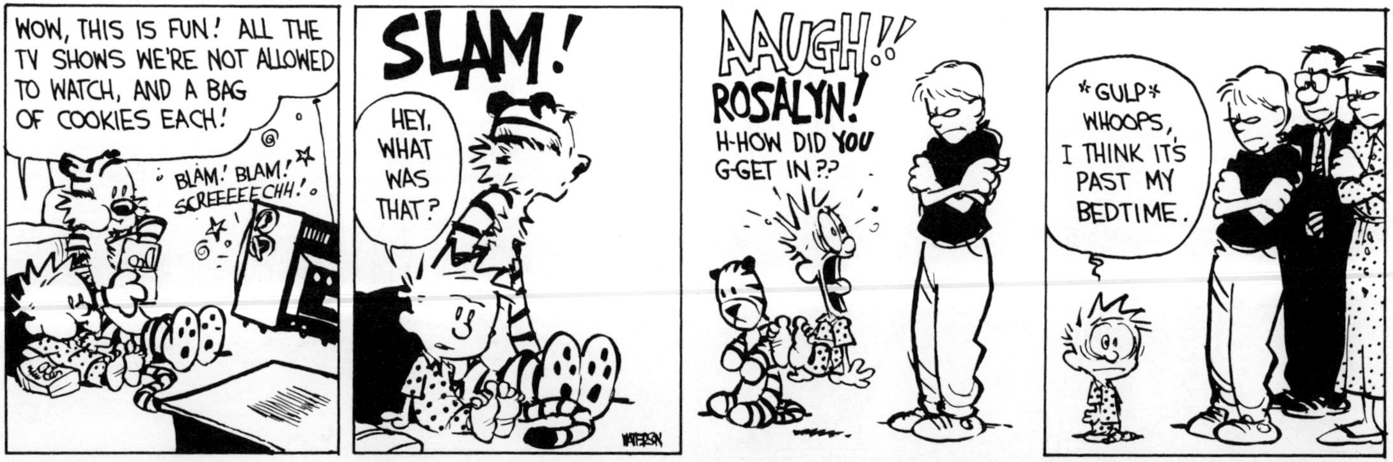
WOW, THIS IS FUN! ALL THE TV SHOWS WE'RE NOT ALLOWED TO WATCH, AND A BAG OF COOKIES EACH!
BLAM! BLAM! SCREEEEECHH!
SLAM!
HEY, WHAT WAS THAT?
AAUGH!!
ROSALYN!
H-HOW DID YOU G-GET IN??
GULP WHOOPS, I THINK IT'S PAST MY BEDTIME.

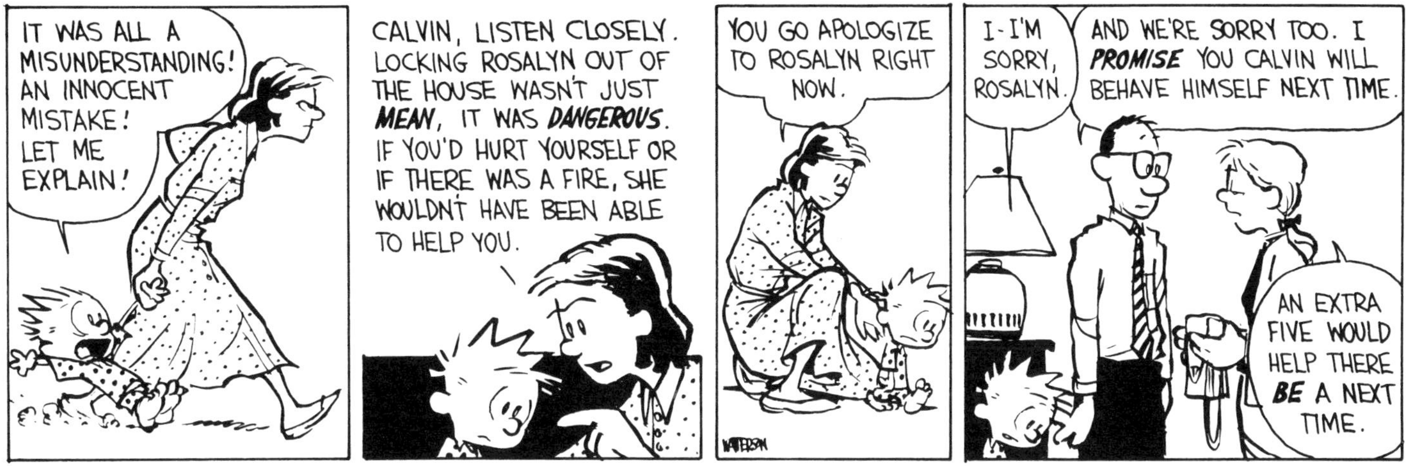
IT WAS ALL A MISUNDERSTANDING! AN INNOCENT MISTAKE! LET ME EXPLAIN!
CALVIN, LISTEN CLOSELY. LOCKING ROSALYN OUT OF THE HOUSE WASN'T JUST **MEAN**, IT WAS **DANGEROUS**. IF YOU'D HURT YOURSELF OR IF THERE WAS A FIRE, SHE WOULDN'T HAVE BEEN ABLE TO HELP YOU.
YOU GO APOLOGIZE TO ROSALYN RIGHT NOW.
I-I'M SORRY, ROSALYN.
AND WE'RE SORRY TOO. I **PROMISE** YOU CALVIN WILL BEHAVE HIMSELF NEXT TIME.
AN EXTRA FIVE WOULD HELP THERE **BE** A NEXT TIME.

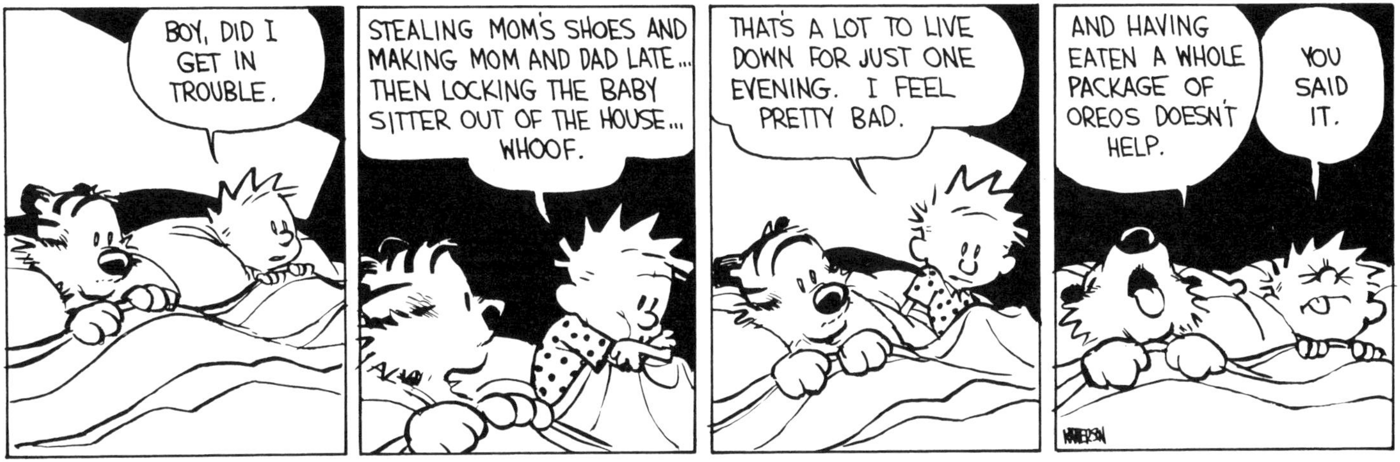
BOY, DID I GET IN TROUBLE.
STEALING MOM'S SHOES AND MAKING MOM AND DAD LATE... THEN LOCKING THE BABY SITTER OUT OF THE HOUSE... WHOOF.
THAT'S A LOT TO LIVE DOWN FOR JUST ONE EVENING. I FEEL PRETTY BAD.
AND HAVING EATEN A WHOLE PACKAGE OF OREOS DOESN'T HELP.
YOU SAID IT.

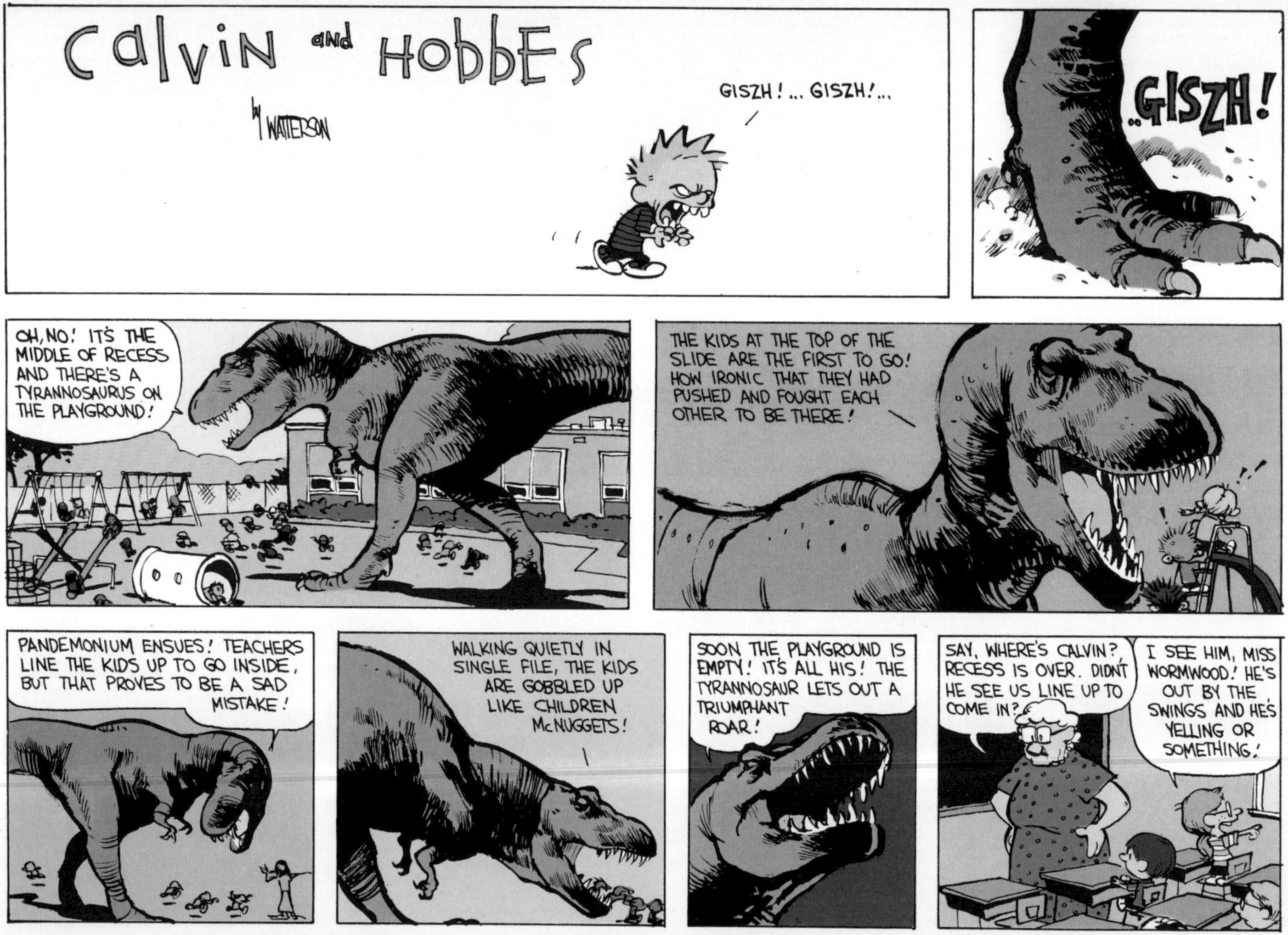
Calvin and HOBBES
by WATTERSON
GISZH! ... GISZH! ...
..GISZH!
OH, NO! IT'S THE MIDDLE OF RECESS AND THERE'S A TYRANNOSAURUS ON THE PLAYGROUND!
THE KIDS AT THE TOP OF THE SLIDE ARE THE FIRST TO GO! HOW IRONIC THAT THEY HAD PUSHED AND FOUGHT EACH OTHER TO BE THERE!
PANDEMONIUM ENSUES! TEACHERS LINE THE KIDS UP TO GO INSIDE, BUT THAT PROVES TO BE A SAD MISTAKE!
WALKING QUIETLY IN SINGLE FILE, THE KIDS ARE GOBBLED UP LIKE CHILDREN McNUGGETS!
SOON THE PLAYGROUND IS EMPTY! IT'S ALL HIS! THE TYRANNOSAUR LETS OUT A TRIUMPHANT ROAR!
SAY, WHERE'S CALVIN? RECESS IS OVER. DIDN'T HE SEE US LINE UP TO COME IN?
I SEE HIM, MISS WORMWOOD! HE'S OUT BY THE SWINGS AND HE'S YELLING OR SOMETHING!

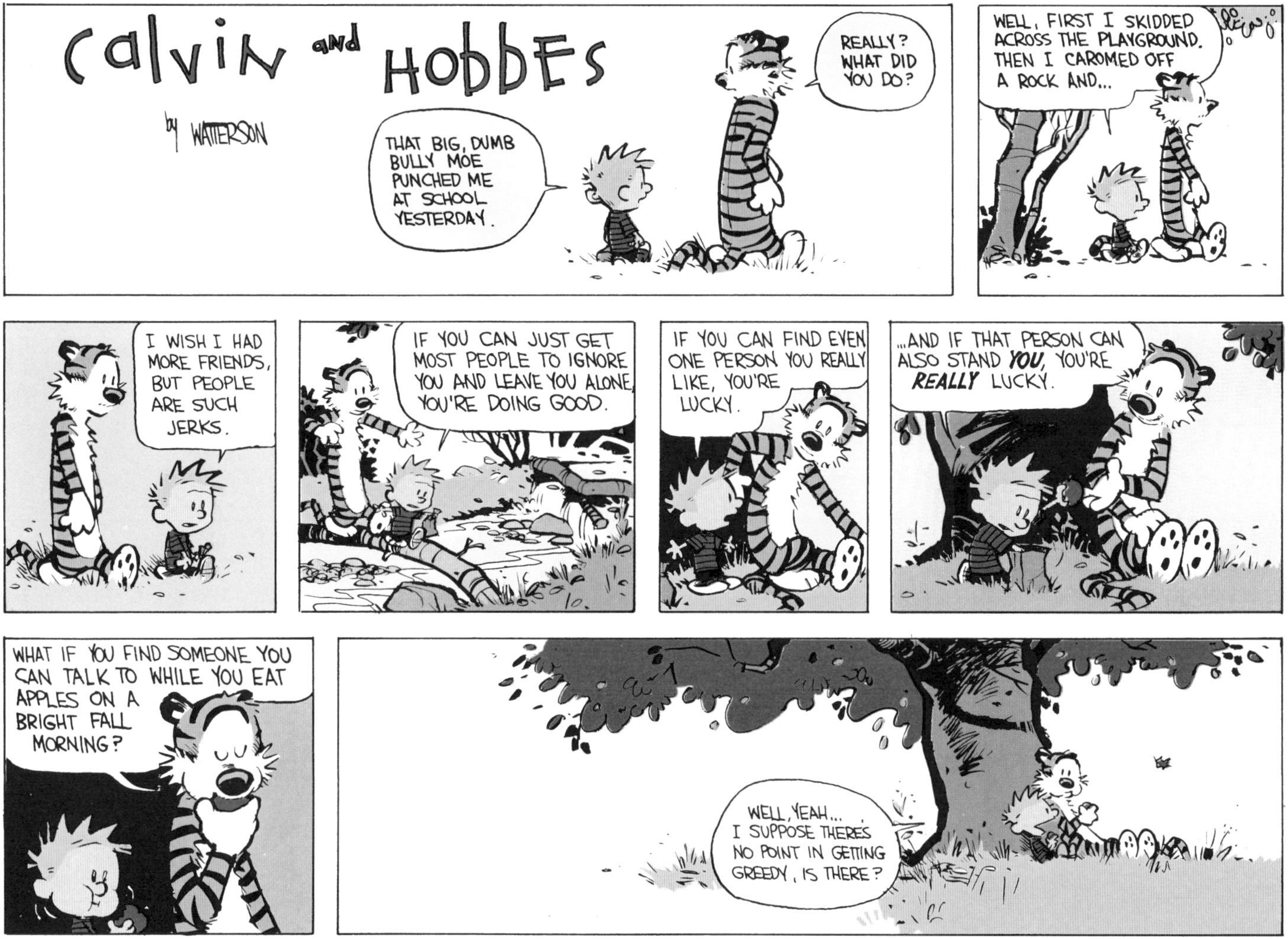
Calvin and HOBBES
by WATTERSON
THAT BIG, DUMB BULLY MOE PUNCHED ME AT SCHOOL YESTERDAY.
REALLY? WHAT DID YOU DO?
WELL, FIRST I SKIDDED ACROSS THE PLAYGROUND. THEN I CAROMED OFF A ROCK AND...
I WISH I HAD MORE FRIENDS, BUT PEOPLE ARE SUCH JERKS.
IF YOU CAN JUST GET MOST PEOPLE TO IGNORE YOU AND LEAVE YOU ALONE, YOU'RE DOING GOOD.
IF YOU CAN FIND EVEN ONE PERSON YOU REALLY LIKE, YOU'RE LUCKY.
...AND IF THAT PERSON CAN ALSO STAND YOU, YOU'RE REALLY LUCKY.
WHAT IF YOU FIND SOMEONE YOU CAN TALK TO WHILE YOU EAT APPLES ON A BRIGHT FALL MORNING?
WELL, YEAH... I SUPPOSE THERE'S NO POINT IN GETTING GREEDY, IS THERE?

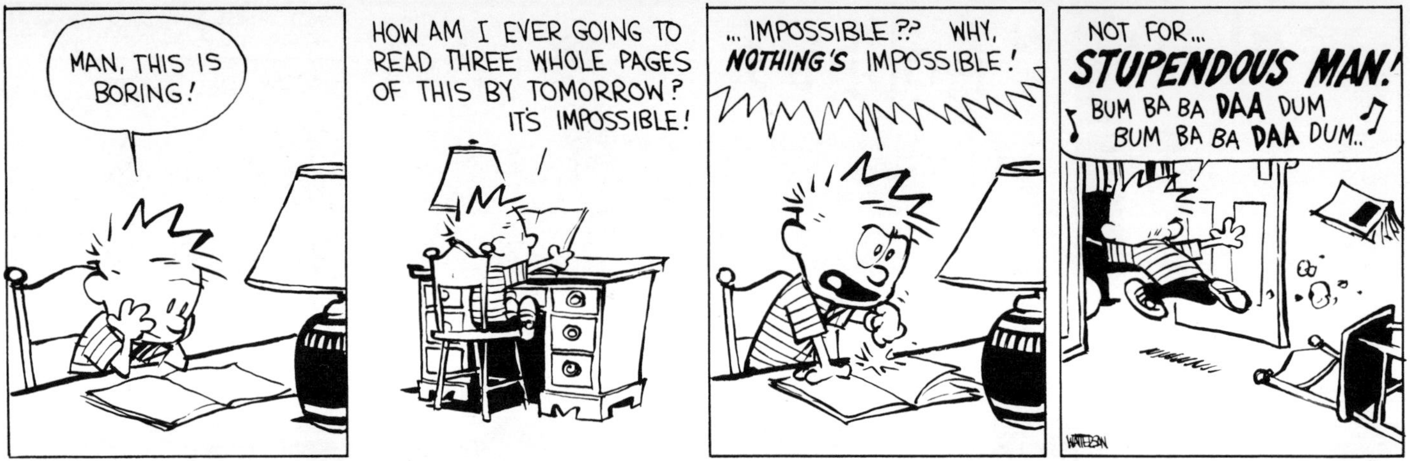
MAN, THIS IS BORING!
HOW AM I EVER GOING TO READ THREE WHOLE PAGES OF THIS BY TOMORROW? IT'S IMPOSSIBLE!
... IMPOSSIBLE?? WHY, NOTHING'S IMPOSSIBLE!
NOT FOR... STUPENDOUS MAN!
BUM BA BA DAA DUM BUM BA BA DAA DUM..
WATTERSON

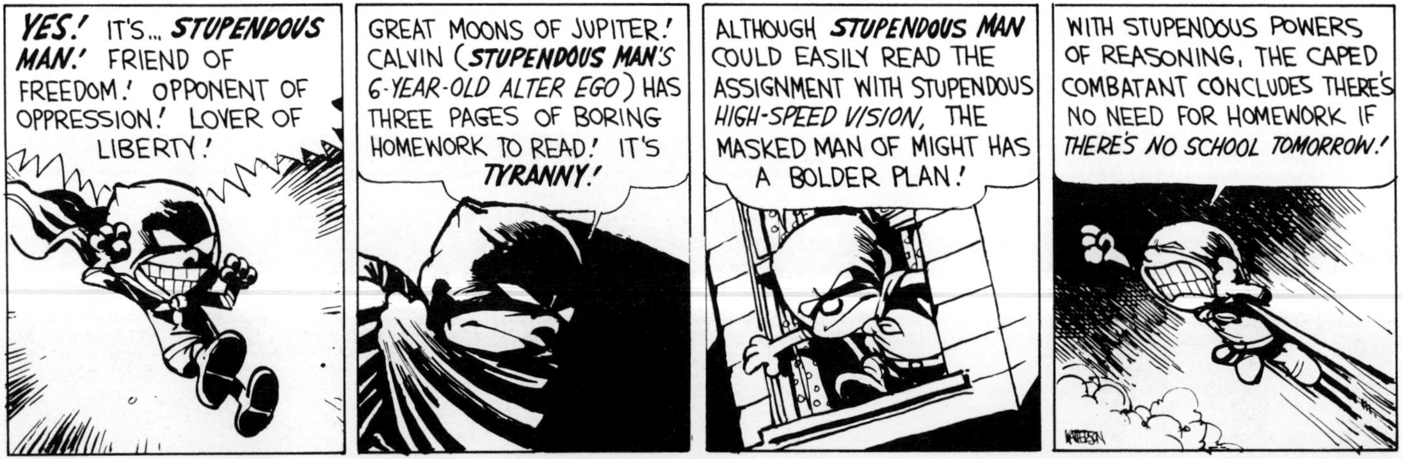
YES! IT'S... STUPENDOUS MAN! FRIEND OF FREEDOM! OPPONENT OF OPPRESSION! LOVER OF LIBERTY!
GREAT MOONS OF JUPITER! CALVIN (STUPENDOUS MAN'S 6-YEAR-OLD ALTER EGO) HAS THREE PAGES OF BORING HOMEWORK TO READ! IT'S TYRANNY!
ALTHOUGH STUPENDOUS MAN COULD EASILY READ THE ASSIGNMENT WITH STUPENDOUS HIGH-SPEED VISION, THE MASKED MAN OF MIGHT HAS A BOLDER PLAN!
WITH STUPENDOUS POWERS OF REASONING, THE CAPED COMBATANT CONCLUDES THERE'S NO NEED FOR HOMEWORK IF THERE'S NO SCHOOL TOMORROW!
WATTERSON

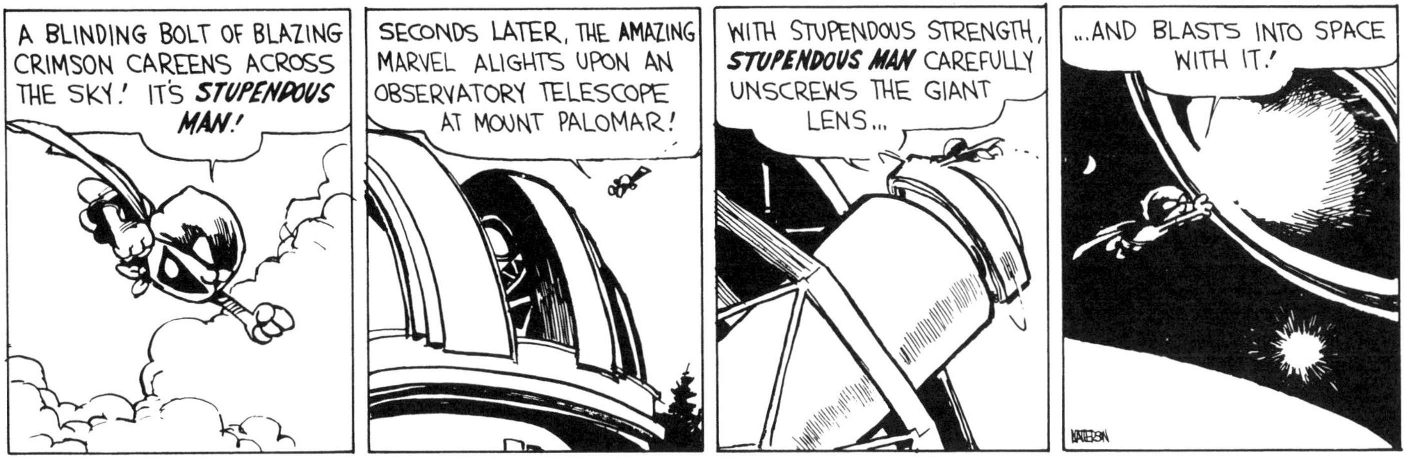
A BLINDING BOLT OF BLAZING CRIMSON CAREENS ACROSS THE SKY! IT'S STUPENDOUS MAN!
SECONDS LATER, THE AMAZING MARVEL ALIGHTS UPON AN OBSERVATORY TELESCOPE AT MOUNT PALOMAR!
WITH STUPENDOUS STRENGTH, STUPENDOUS MAN CAREFULLY UNSCREWS THE GIANT LENS...
...AND BLASTS INTO SPACE WITH IT!

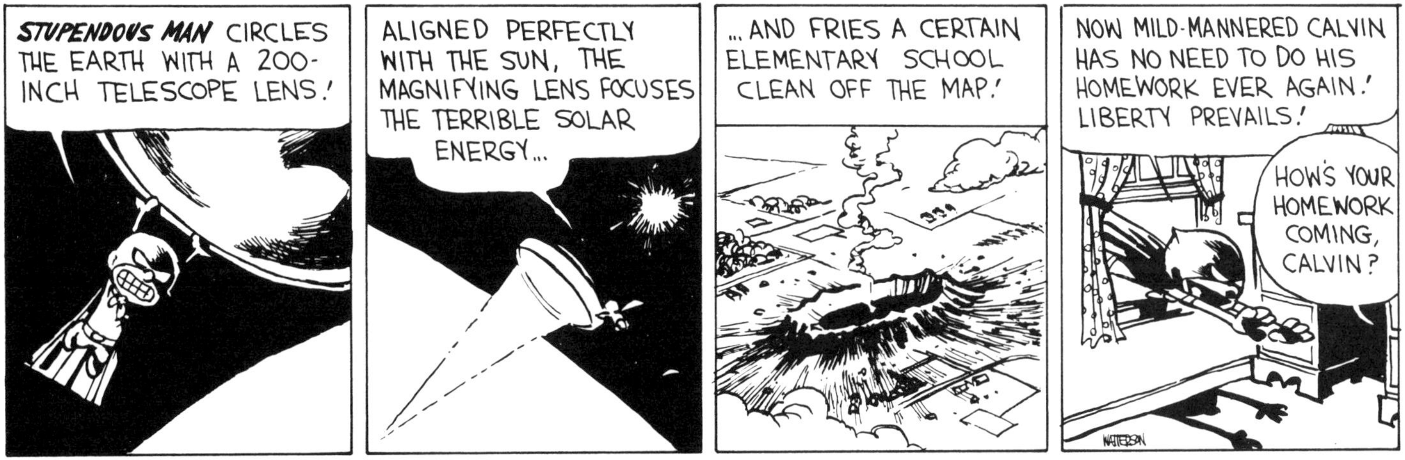
STUPENDOUS MAN CIRCLES THE EARTH WITH A 200-INCH TELESCOPE LENS!
ALIGNED PERFECTLY WITH THE SUN, THE MAGNIFYING LENS FOCUSES THE TERRIBLE SOLAR ENERGY...
...AND FRIES A CERTAIN ELEMENTARY SCHOOL CLEAN OFF THE MAP!
NOW MILD-MANNERED CALVIN HAS NO NEED TO DO HIS HOMEWORK EVER AGAIN! LIBERTY PREVAILS!
HOW'S YOUR HOMEWORK COMING, CALVIN?

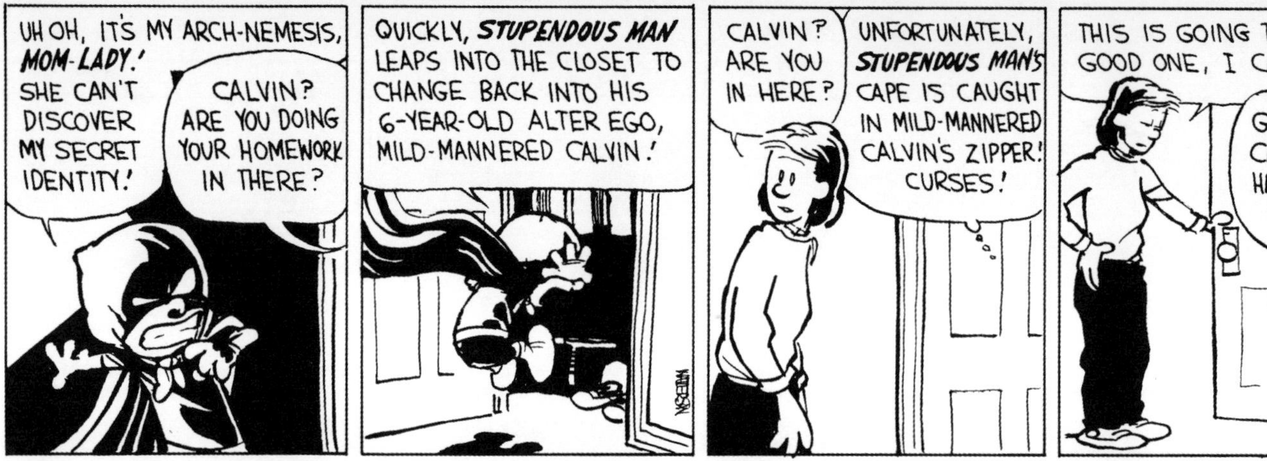
UH OH, IT'S MY ARCH-NEMESIS, **MOM-LADY!** SHE CAN'T DISCOVER MY SECRET IDENTITY!
CALVIN? ARE YOU DOING YOUR HOMEWORK IN THERE?
QUICKLY, **STUPENDOUS MAN** LEAPS INTO THE CLOSET TO CHANGE BACK INTO HIS 6-YEAR-OLD ALTER EGO, MILD-MANNERED CALVIN!
CALVIN? ARE YOU IN HERE?
UNFORTUNATELY, **STUPENDOUS MAN'S** CAPE IS CAUGHT IN MILD-MANNERED CALVIN'S ZIPPER! CURSES!
THIS IS GOING TO BE A GOOD ONE, I CAN TELL.
GEEZ, MOM! CAN'T A GUY HAVE A LITTLE PRIVACY?!

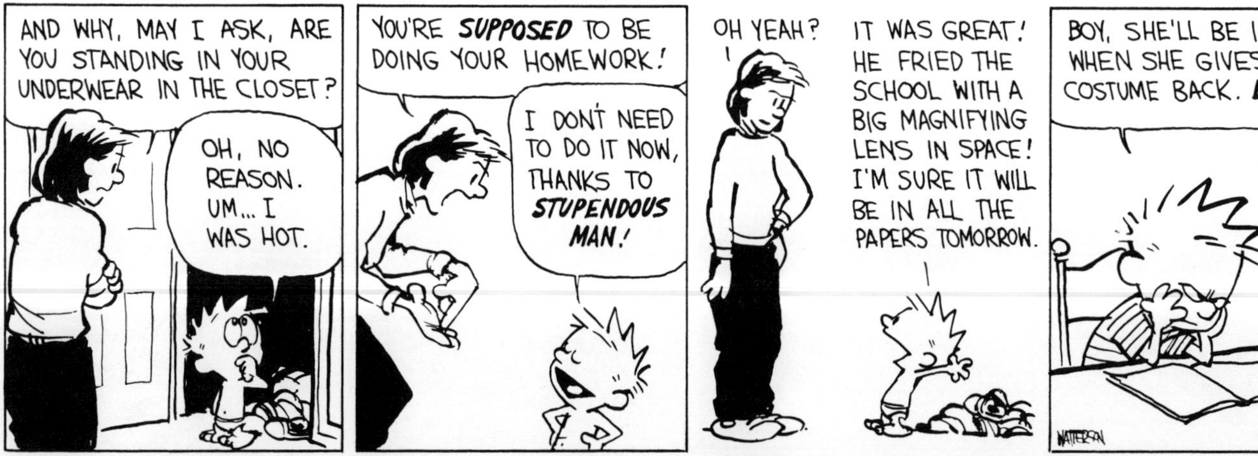
AND WHY, MAY I ASK, ARE YOU STANDING IN YOUR UNDERWEAR IN THE CLOSET?
OH, NO REASON. UM... I WAS HOT.
YOU'RE **SUPPOSED** TO BE DOING YOUR HOMEWORK!
I DON'T NEED TO DO IT NOW, THANKS TO **STUPENDOUS MAN!**
OH YEAH?
IT WAS GREAT! HE FRIED THE SCHOOL WITH A BIG MAGNIFYING LENS IN SPACE! I'M SURE IT WILL BE IN ALL THE PAPERS TOMORROW.
BOY, SHE'LL BE IN TROUBLE WHEN SHE GIVES ME MY COSTUME BACK. **BIG** TROUBLE.

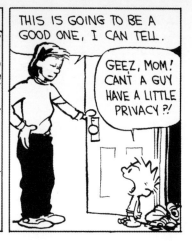

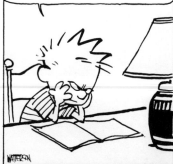

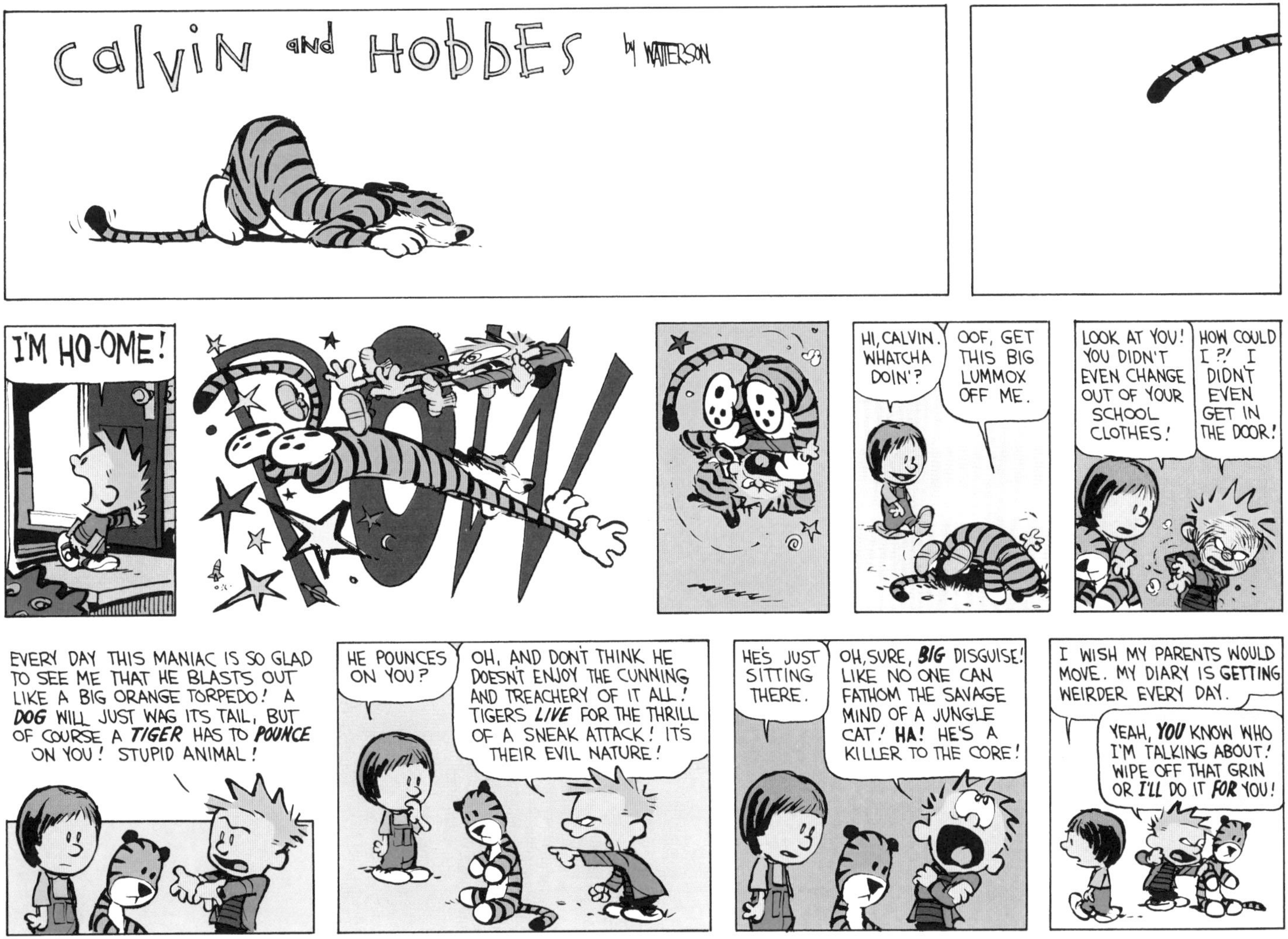
Calvin and Hobbes
by WATTERSON
I'M HO-OME!
POW
HI, CALVIN. WHATCHA DOIN'?
OOF, GET THIS BIG LUMMOX OFF ME.
LOOK AT YOU! YOU DIDN'T EVEN CHANGE OUT OF YOUR SCHOOL CLOTHES!
HOW COULD I ?! I DIDN'T EVEN GET IN THE DOOR!
EVERY DAY THIS MANIAC IS SO GLAD TO SEE ME THAT HE BLASTS OUT LIKE A BIG ORANGE TORPEDO! A DOG WILL JUST WAG ITS TAIL, BUT OF COURSE A TIGER HAS TO POUNCE ON YOU! STUPID ANIMAL!
HE POUNCES ON YOU?
OH, AND DON'T THINK HE DOESN'T ENJOY THE CUNNING AND TREACHERY OF IT ALL! TIGERS LIVE FOR THE THRILL OF A SNEAK ATTACK! IT'S THEIR EVIL NATURE!
HE'S JUST SITTING THERE.
OH, SURE, BIG DISGUISE! LIKE NO ONE CAN FATHOM THE SAVAGE MIND OF A JUNGLE CAT! HA! HE'S A KILLER TO THE CORE!
I WISH MY PARENTS WOULD MOVE. MY DIARY IS GETTING WEIRDER EVERY DAY.
YEAH, YOU KNOW WHO I'M TALKING ABOUT! WIPE OFF THAT GRIN OR I'LL DO IT FOR YOU!

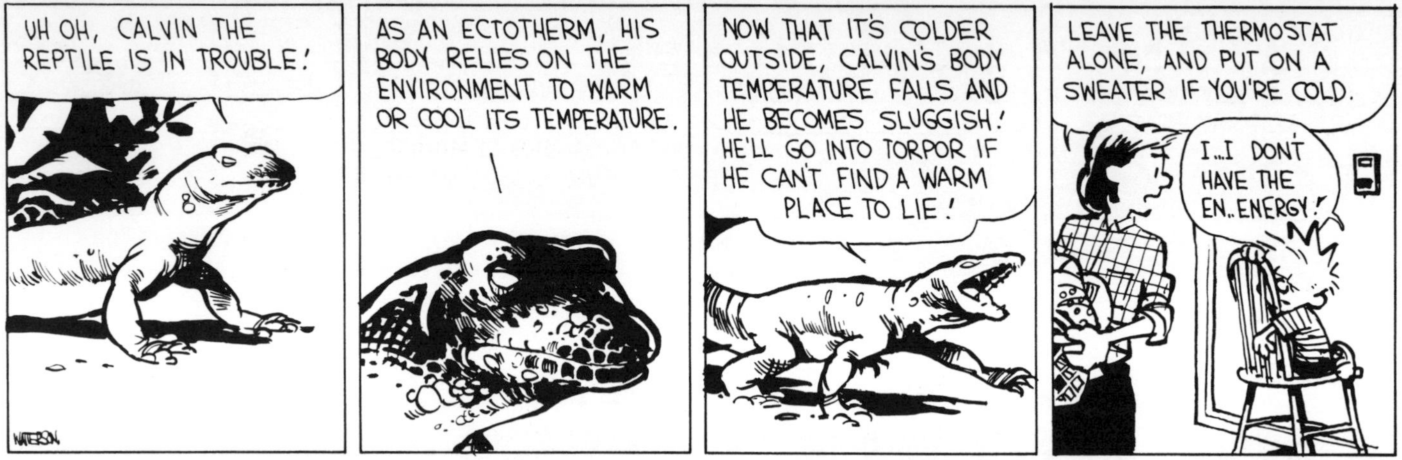

UH OH, CALVIN THE REPTILE IS IN TROUBLE!
AS AN ECTOTHERM, HIS BODY RELIES ON THE ENVIRONMENT TO WARM OR COOL ITS TEMPERATURE.
NOW THAT IT'S COLDER OUTSIDE, CALVIN'S BODY TEMPERATURE FALLS AND HE BECOMES SLUGGISH! HE'LL GO INTO TORPOR IF HE CAN'T FIND A WARM PLACE TO LIE!
LEAVE THE THERMOSTAT ALONE, AND PUT ON A SWEATER IF YOU'RE COLD.
I...I DON'T HAVE THE EN..ENERGY!
WATTERSON

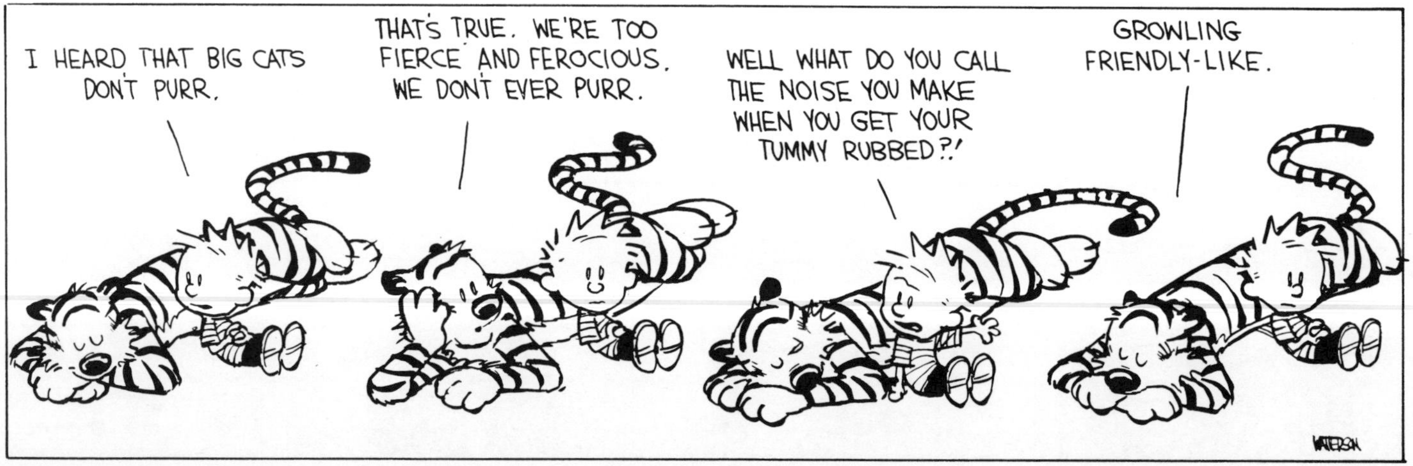

I HEARD THAT BIG CATS DON'T PURR.
THAT'S TRUE. WE'RE TOO FIERCE AND FEROCIOUS. WE DON'T EVER PURR.
WELL WHAT DO YOU CALL THE NOISE YOU MAKE WHEN YOU GET YOUR TUMMY RUBBED?!
GROWLING FRIENDLY-LIKE.
WATTERSON

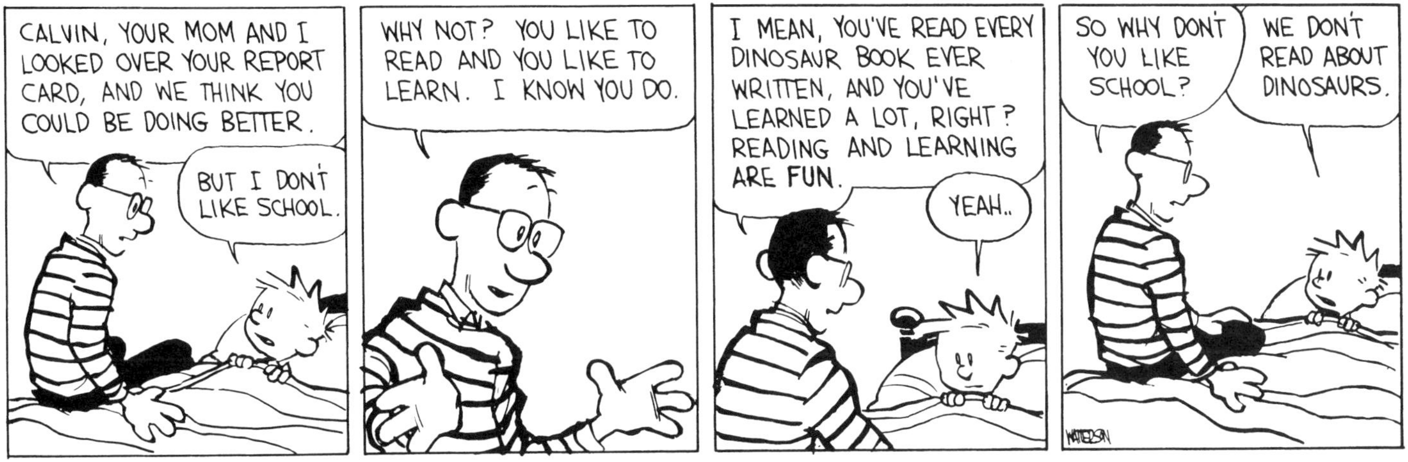
CALVIN, YOUR MOM AND I LOOKED OVER YOUR REPORT CARD, AND WE THINK YOU COULD BE DOING BETTER.
BUT I DON'T LIKE SCHOOL.
WHY NOT? YOU LIKE TO READ AND YOU LIKE TO LEARN. I KNOW YOU DO.
I MEAN, YOU'VE READ EVERY DINOSAUR BOOK EVER WRITTEN, AND YOU'VE LEARNED A LOT, RIGHT? READING AND LEARNING ARE FUN.
YEAH..
SO WHY DON'T YOU LIKE SCHOOL?
WE DON'T READ ABOUT DINOSAURS.

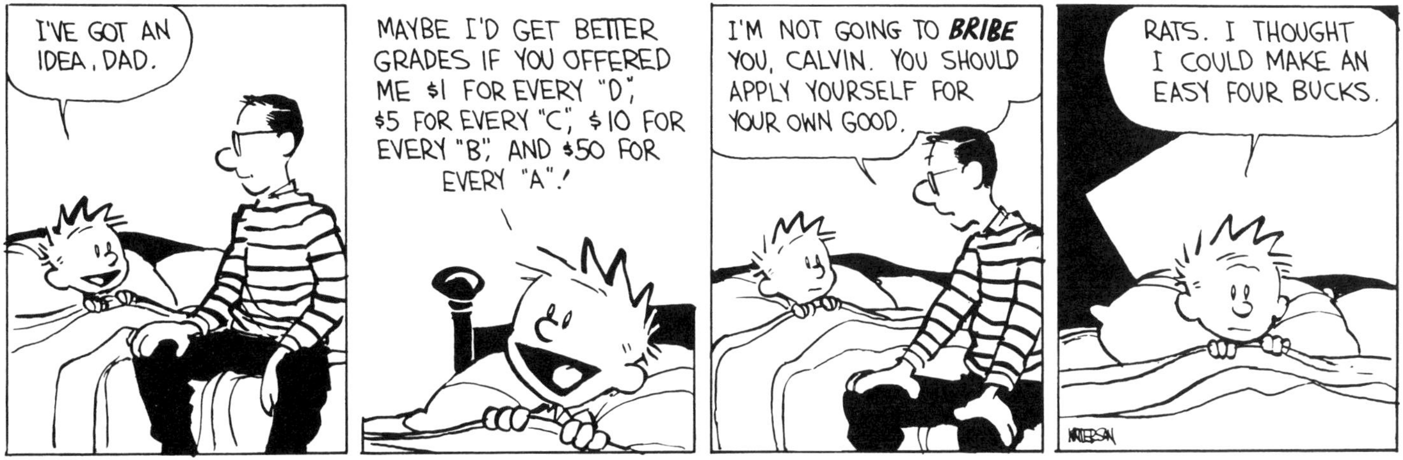
I'VE GOT AN IDEA, DAD.
MAYBE I'D GET BETTER GRADES IF YOU OFFERED ME $1 FOR EVERY "D", $5 FOR EVERY "C", $10 FOR EVERY "B", AND $50 FOR EVERY "A"!
I'M NOT GOING TO BRIBE YOU, CALVIN. YOU SHOULD APPLY YOURSELF FOR YOUR OWN GOOD.
RATS. I THOUGHT I COULD MAKE AN EASY FOUR BUCKS.

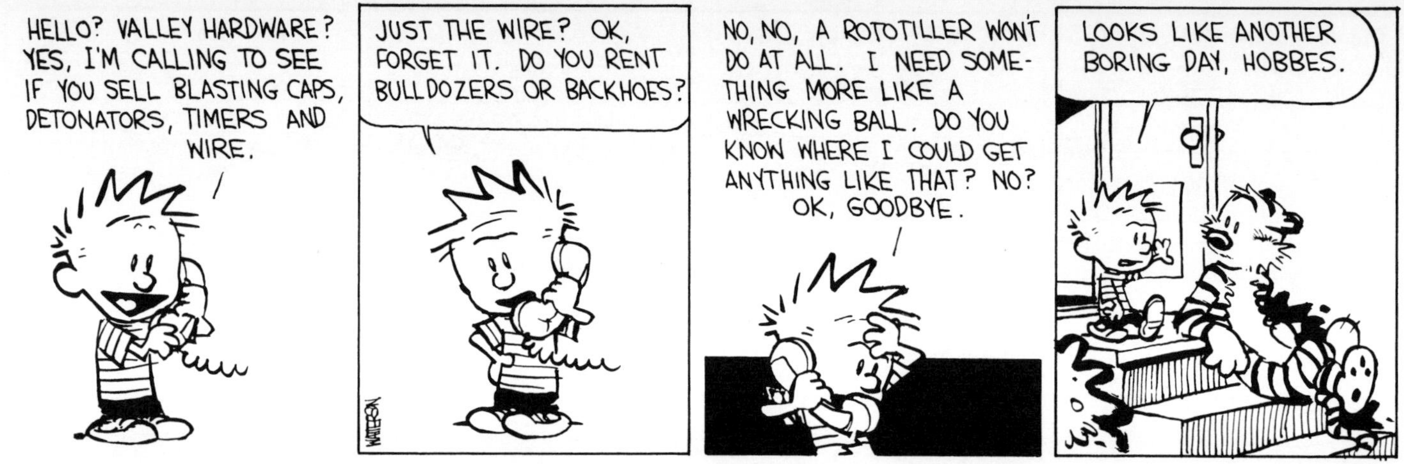
HELLO? VALLEY HARDWARE? YES, I'M CALLING TO SEE IF YOU SELL BLASTING CAPS, DETONATORS, TIMERS AND WIRE.
JUST THE WIRE? OK, FORGET IT. DO YOU RENT BULLDOZERS OR BACKHOES?
NO, NO, A ROTOTILLER WON'T DO AT ALL. I NEED SOMETHING MORE LIKE A WRECKING BALL. DO YOU KNOW WHERE I COULD GET ANYTHING LIKE THAT? NO? OK, GOODBYE.
LOOKS LIKE ANOTHER BORING DAY, HOBBES.

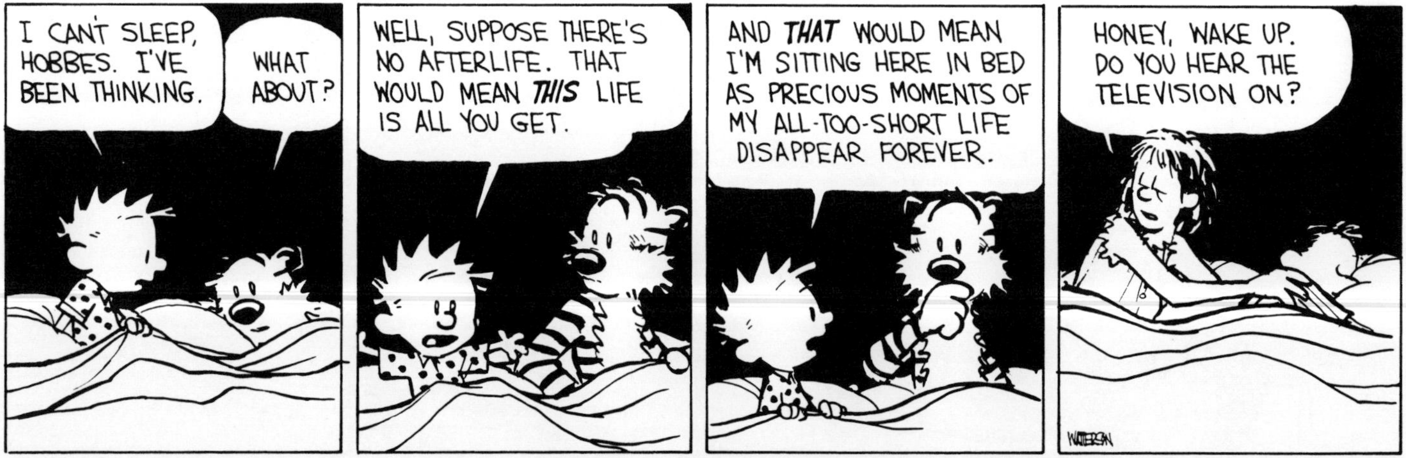
I CAN'T SLEEP, HOBBES. I'VE BEEN THINKING.
WHAT ABOUT?
WELL, SUPPOSE THERE'S NO AFTERLIFE. THAT WOULD MEAN *THIS* LIFE IS ALL YOU GET.
AND *THAT* WOULD MEAN I'M SITTING HERE IN BED AS PRECIOUS MOMENTS OF MY ALL-TOO-SHORT LIFE DISAPPEAR FOREVER.
HONEY, WAKE UP. DO YOU HEAR THE TELEVISION ON?

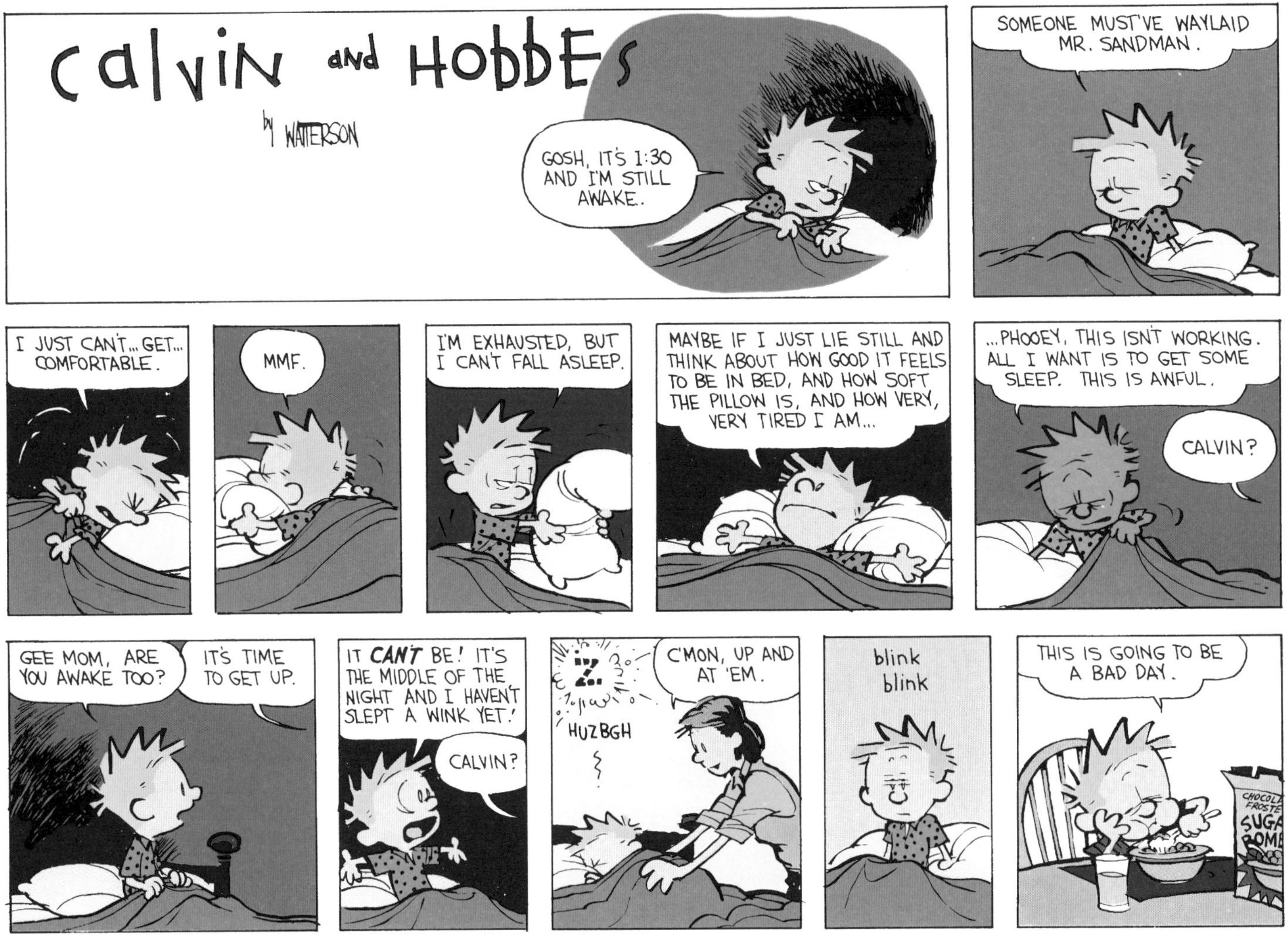
Calvin and HOBBES
by WATTERSON
GOSH, IT'S 1:30 AND I'M STILL AWAKE.
SOMEONE MUST'VE WAYLAID MR. SANDMAN.
I JUST CAN'T... GET... COMFORTABLE.
MMF.
I'M EXHAUSTED, BUT I CAN'T FALL ASLEEP.
MAYBE IF I JUST LIE STILL AND THINK ABOUT HOW GOOD IT FEELS TO BE IN BED, AND HOW SOFT THE PILLOW IS, AND HOW VERY, VERY TIRED I AM...
...PHOOEY. THIS ISN'T WORKING. ALL I WANT IS TO GET SOME SLEEP. THIS IS AWFUL.
CALVIN?
GEE MOM, ARE YOU AWAKE TOO?
IT'S TIME TO GET UP.
IT CAN'T BE! IT'S THE MIDDLE OF THE NIGHT AND I HAVEN'T SLEPT A WINK YET!
CALVIN?
HUZBGH
C'MON, UP AND AT 'EM.
blink
blink
THIS IS GOING TO BE A BAD DAY.

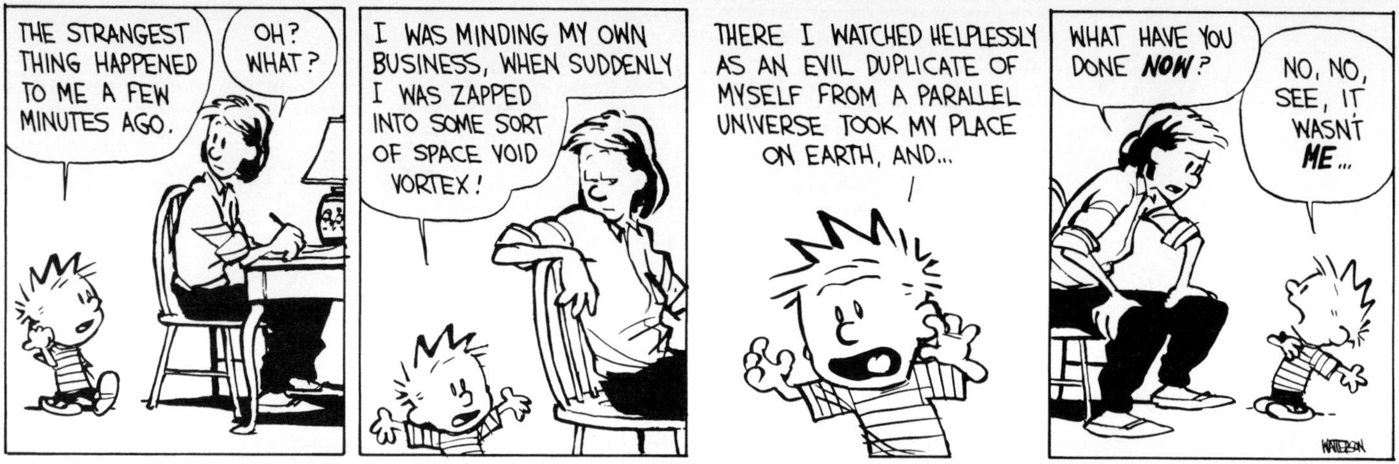
THE STRANGEST THING HAPPENED TO ME A FEW MINUTES AGO.
OH? WHAT?
I WAS MINDING MY OWN BUSINESS, WHEN SUDDENLY I WAS ZAPPED INTO SOME SORT OF SPACE VOID VORTEX!
THERE I WATCHED HELPLESSLY AS AN EVIL DUPLICATE OF MYSELF FROM A PARALLEL UNIVERSE TOOK MY PLACE ON EARTH, AND...
WHAT HAVE YOU DONE NOW?
NO, NO, SEE, IT WASN'T ME...
WATTERSON

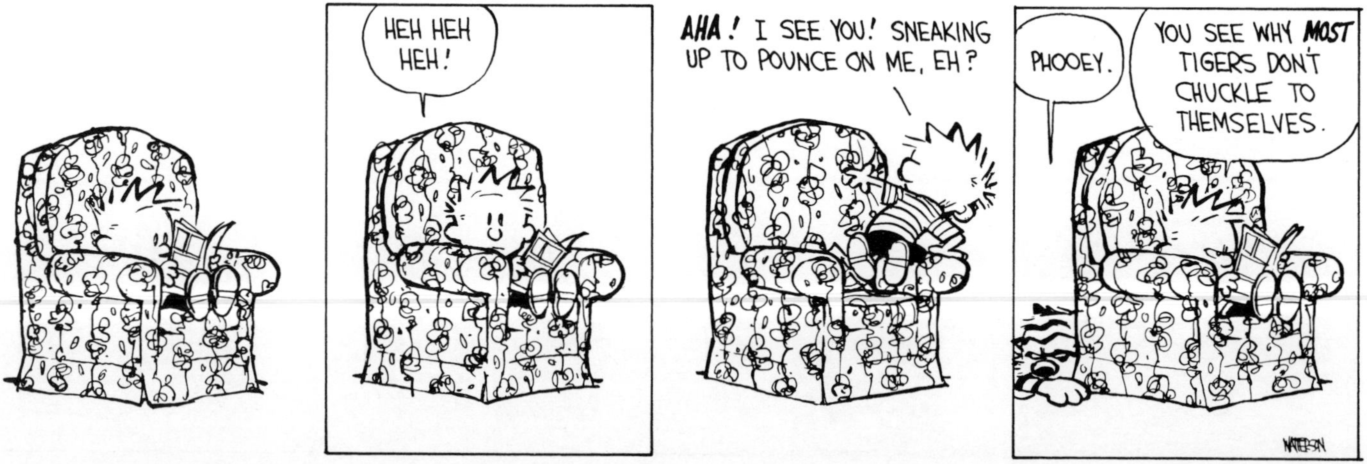
HEH HEH HEH!
AHA! I SEE YOU! SNEAKING UP TO POUNCE ON ME, EH?
PHOOEY.
YOU SEE WHY MOST TIGERS DON'T CHUCKLE TO THEMSELVES.
WATTERSON

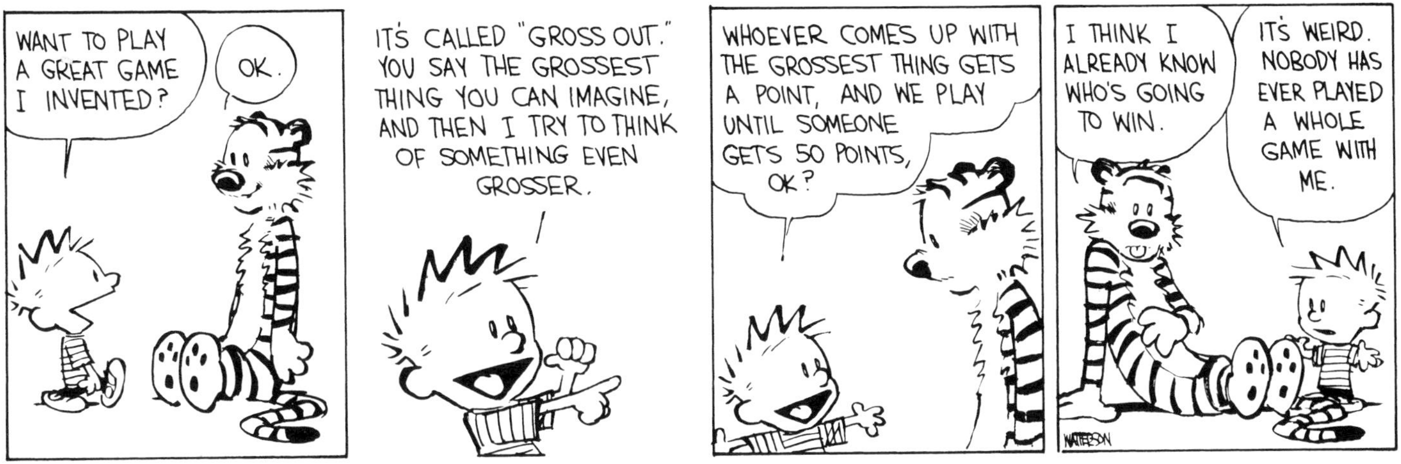
WANT TO PLAY A GREAT GAME I INVENTED?
OK.
IT'S CALLED "GROSS OUT." YOU SAY THE GROSSEST THING YOU CAN IMAGINE, AND THEN I TRY TO THINK OF SOMETHING EVEN GROSSER.
WHOEVER COMES UP WITH THE GROSSEST THING GETS A POINT, AND WE PLAY UNTIL SOMEONE GETS 50 POINTS, OK?
I THINK I ALREADY KNOW WHO'S GOING TO WIN.
IT'S WEIRD. NOBODY HAS EVER PLAYED A WHOLE GAME WITH ME.

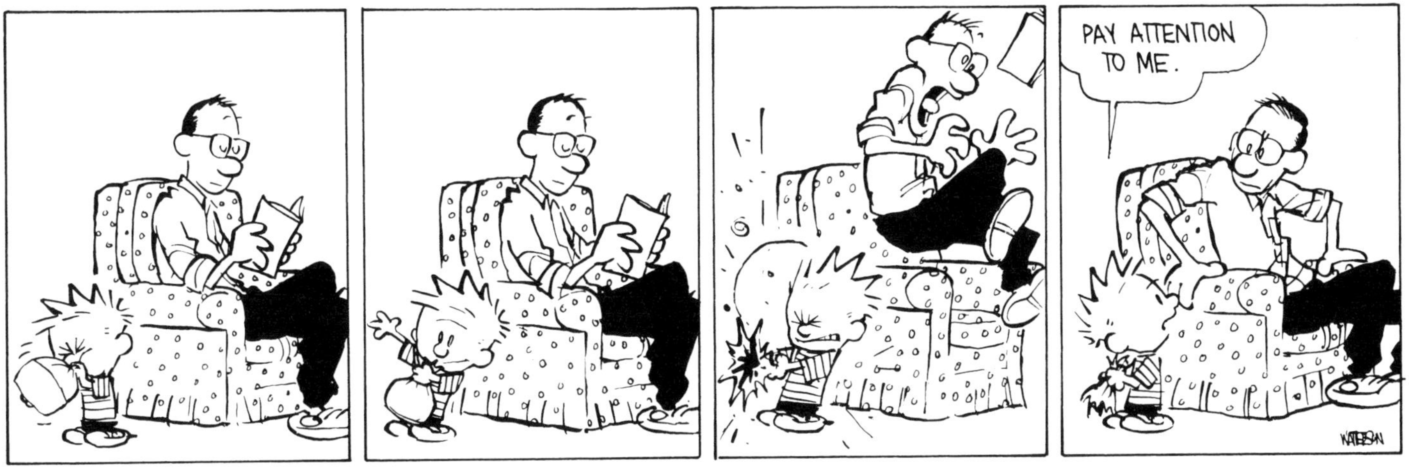
PAY ATTENTION TO ME.

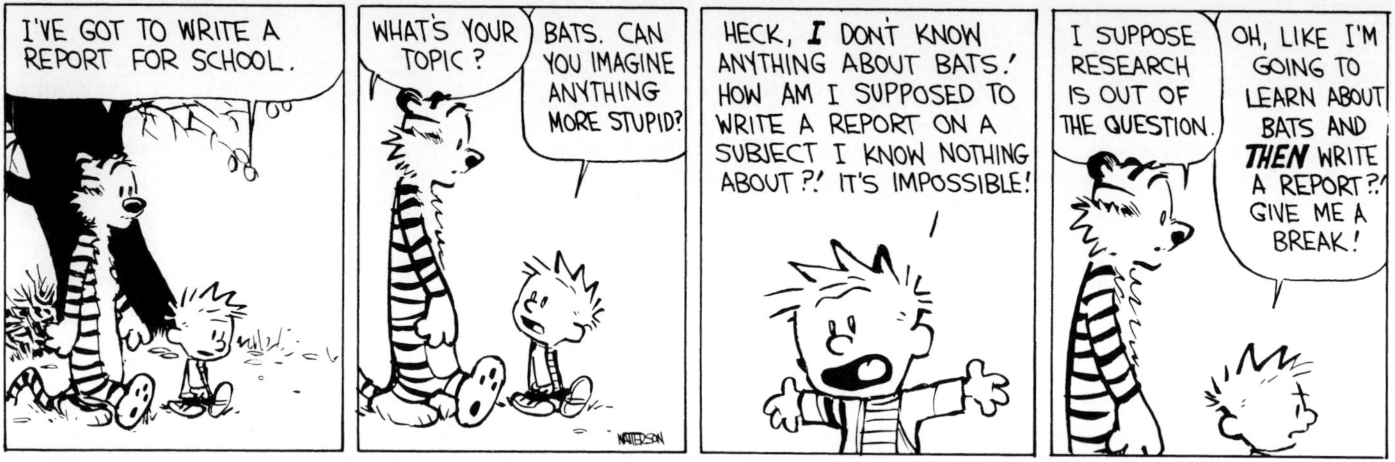
I'VE GOT TO WRITE A REPORT FOR SCHOOL.
WHAT'S YOUR TOPIC?
BATS. CAN YOU IMAGINE ANYTHING MORE STUPID?
HECK, *I* DON'T KNOW ANYTHING ABOUT BATS! HOW AM I SUPPOSED TO WRITE A REPORT ON A SUBJECT I KNOW NOTHING ABOUT?! IT'S IMPOSSIBLE!
I SUPPOSE RESEARCH IS OUT OF THE QUESTION.
OH, LIKE I'M GOING TO LEARN ABOUT BATS AND *THEN* WRITE A REPORT?! GIVE ME A BREAK!

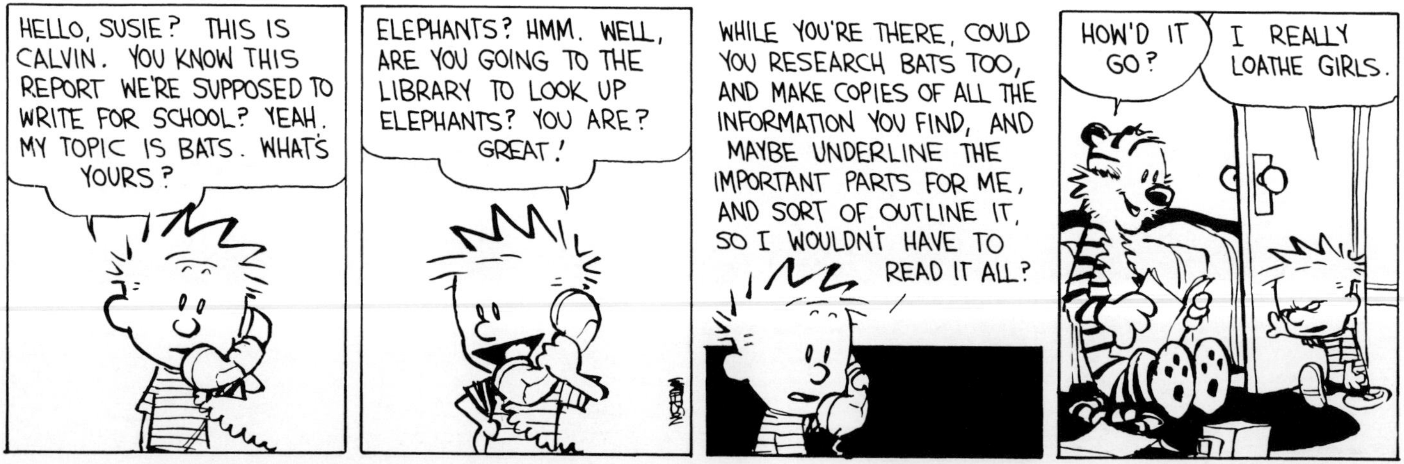
HELLO, SUSIE? THIS IS CALVIN. YOU KNOW THIS REPORT WE'RE SUPPOSED TO WRITE FOR SCHOOL? YEAH. MY TOPIC IS BATS. WHAT'S YOURS?
ELEPHANTS? HMM. WELL, ARE YOU GOING TO THE LIBRARY TO LOOK UP ELEPHANTS? YOU ARE? GREAT!
WHILE YOU'RE THERE, COULD YOU RESEARCH BATS TOO, AND MAKE COPIES OF ALL THE INFORMATION YOU FIND, AND MAYBE UNDERLINE THE IMPORTANT PARTS FOR ME, AND SORT OF OUTLINE IT, SO I WOULDN'T HAVE TO READ IT ALL?
HOW'D IT GO?
I REALLY LOATHE GIRLS.

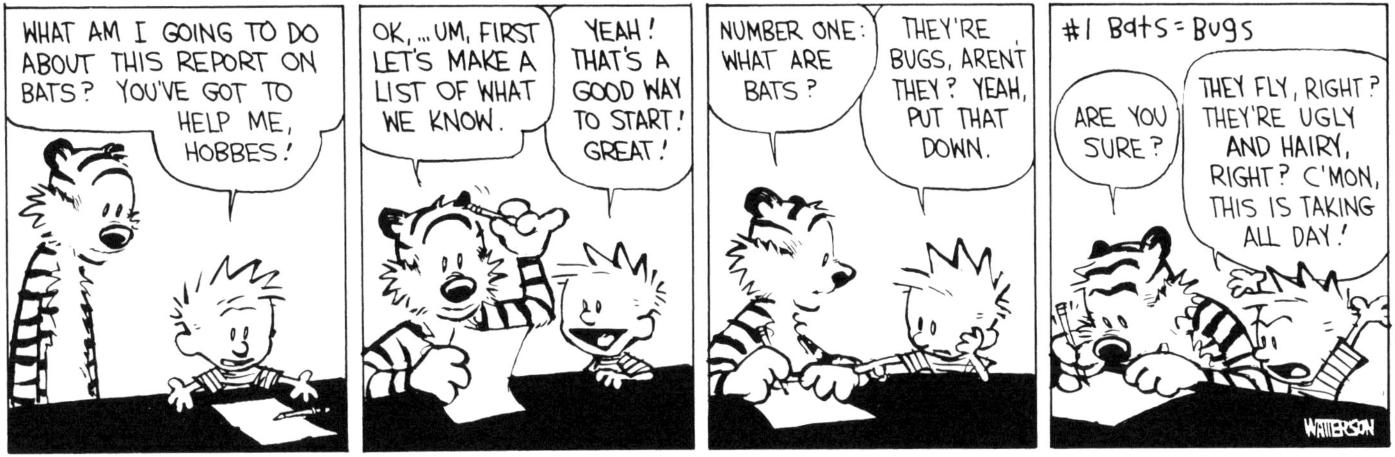
WHAT AM I GOING TO DO ABOUT THIS REPORT ON BATS? YOU'VE GOT TO HELP ME, HOBBES!
OK, ... UM, FIRST LET'S MAKE A LIST OF WHAT WE KNOW.
YEAH! THAT'S A GOOD WAY TO START! GREAT!
NUMBER ONE: WHAT ARE BATS?
THEY'RE BUGS, AREN'T THEY? YEAH, PUT THAT DOWN.
#1 Bats = Bugs
ARE YOU SURE?
THEY FLY, RIGHT? THEY'RE UGLY AND HAIRY, RIGHT? C'MON, THIS IS TAKING ALL DAY!
WATTERSON

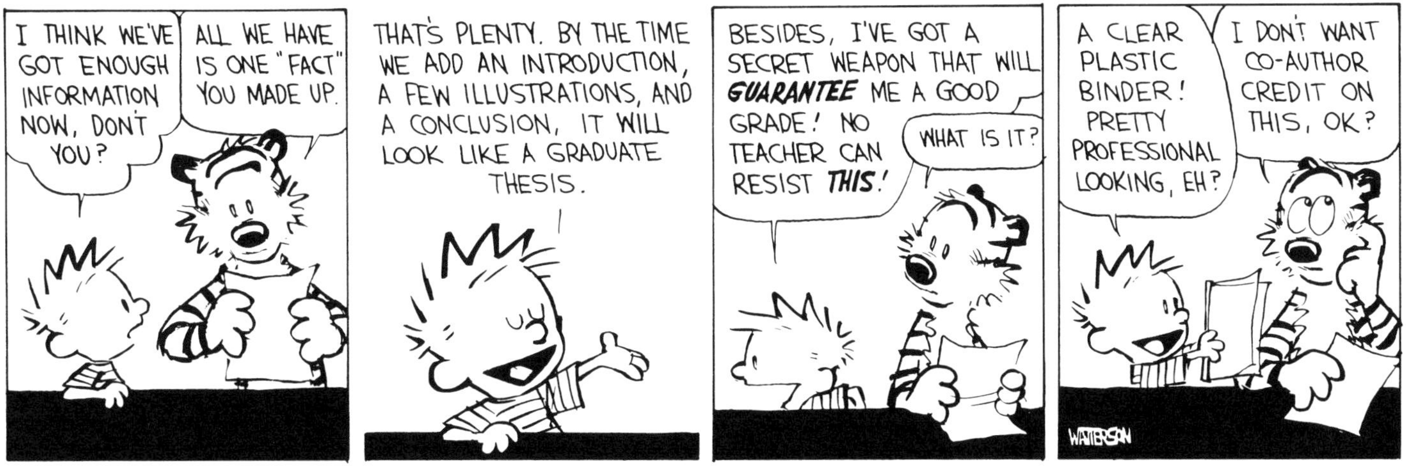
I THINK WE'VE GOT ENOUGH INFORMATION NOW, DON'T YOU?
ALL WE HAVE IS ONE "FACT" YOU MADE UP.
THAT'S PLENTY. BY THE TIME WE ADD AN INTRODUCTION, A FEW ILLUSTRATIONS, AND A CONCLUSION, IT WILL LOOK LIKE A GRADUATE THESIS.
BESIDES, I'VE GOT A SECRET WEAPON THAT WILL ***GUARANTEE*** ME A GOOD GRADE! NO TEACHER CAN RESIST ***THIS***!
WHAT IS IT?
A CLEAR PLASTIC BINDER! PRETTY PROFESSIONAL LOOKING, EH?
I DON'T WANT CO-AUTHOR CREDIT ON THIS, OK?
WATTERSON

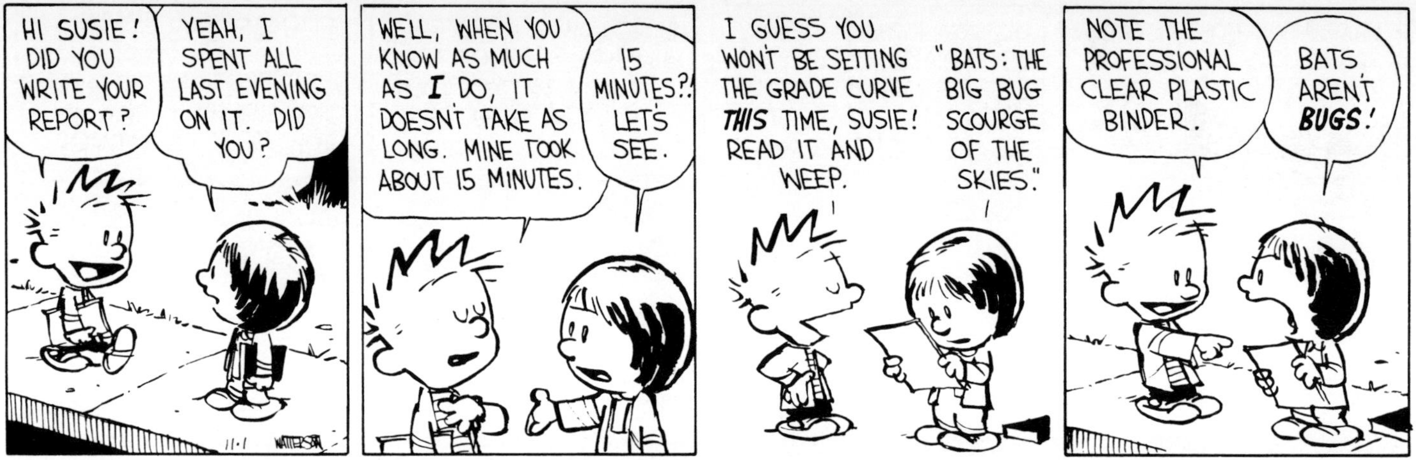
HI SUSIE! DID YOU WRITE YOUR REPORT?
YEAH, I SPENT ALL LAST EVENING ON IT. DID YOU?
WELL, WHEN YOU KNOW AS MUCH AS *I* DO, IT DOESN'T TAKE AS LONG. MINE TOOK ABOUT 15 MINUTES.
15 MINUTES?! LET'S SEE.
I GUESS YOU WON'T BE SETTING THE GRADE CURVE *THIS* TIME, SUSIE! READ IT AND WEEP.
"BATS: THE BIG BUG SCOURGE OF THE SKIES."
NOTE THE PROFESSIONAL CLEAR PLASTIC BINDER.
BATS AREN'T *BUGS*!

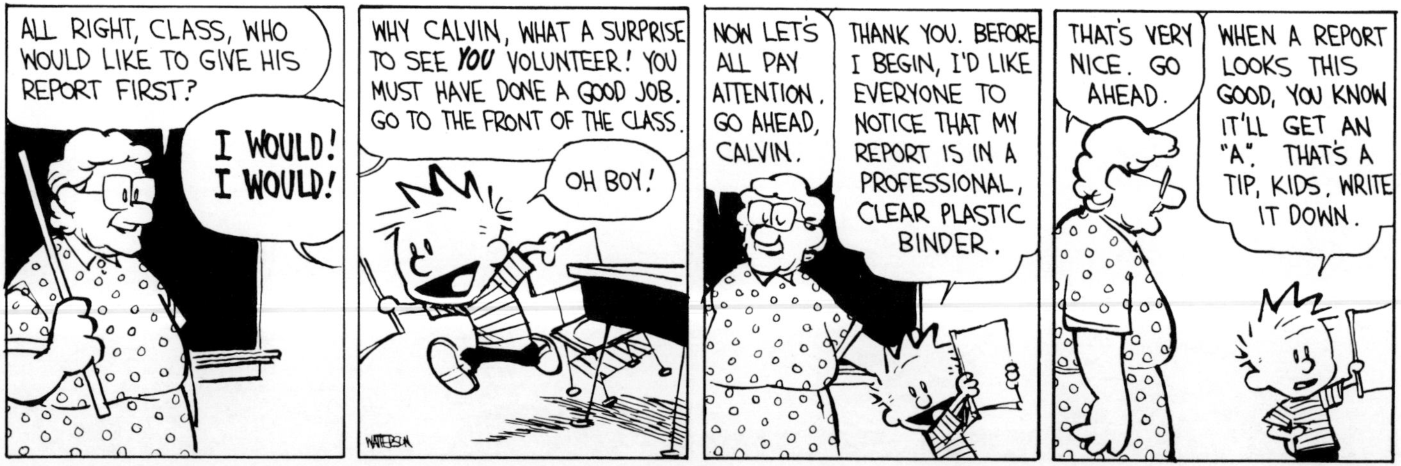
ALL RIGHT, CLASS, WHO WOULD LIKE TO GIVE HIS REPORT FIRST?
I WOULD! I WOULD!
WHY CALVIN, WHAT A SURPRISE TO SEE *YOU* VOLUNTEER! YOU MUST HAVE DONE A GOOD JOB. GO TO THE FRONT OF THE CLASS.
OH BOY!
NOW LET'S ALL PAY ATTENTION. GO AHEAD, CALVIN.
THANK YOU. BEFORE I BEGIN, I'D LIKE EVERYONE TO NOTICE THAT MY REPORT IS IN A PROFESSIONAL, CLEAR PLASTIC BINDER.
THAT'S VERY NICE. GO AHEAD.
WHEN A REPORT LOOKS THIS GOOD, YOU KNOW IT'LL GET AN "A". THAT'S A TIP, KIDS. WRITE IT DOWN.

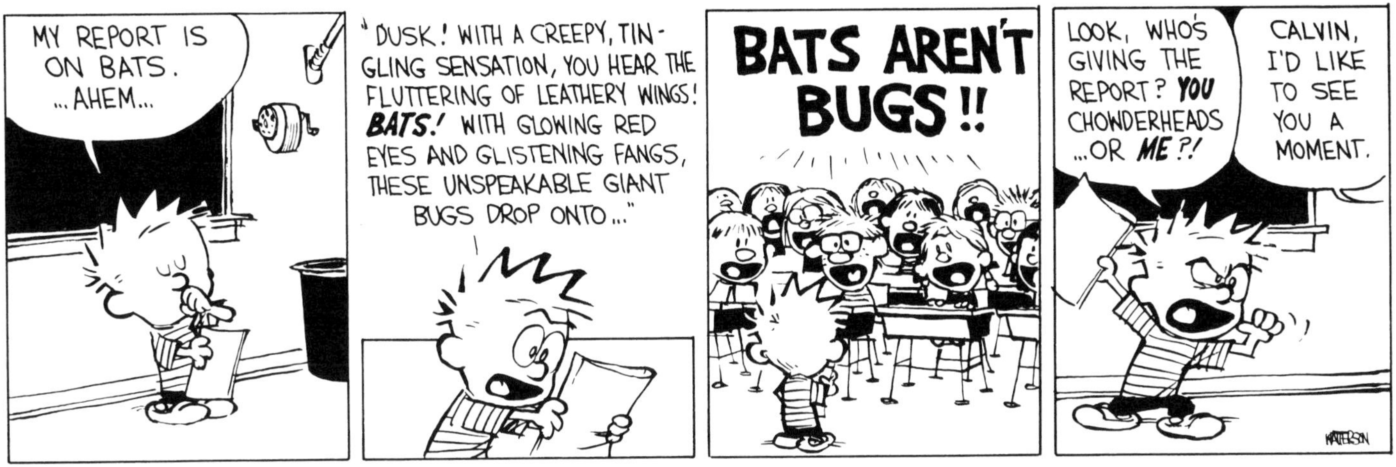
MY REPORT IS ON BATS. ...AHEM...
"DUSK! WITH A CREEPY, TINGLING SENSATION, YOU HEAR THE FLUTTERING OF LEATHERY WINGS! **BATS!** WITH GLOWING RED EYES AND GLISTENING FANGS, THESE UNSPEAKABLE GIANT BUGS DROP ONTO..."
BATS AREN'T BUGS!!
LOOK, WHO'S GIVING THE REPORT? **YOU** CHOWDERHEADS ...OR **ME**?!
CALVIN, I'D LIKE TO SEE YOU A MOMENT.

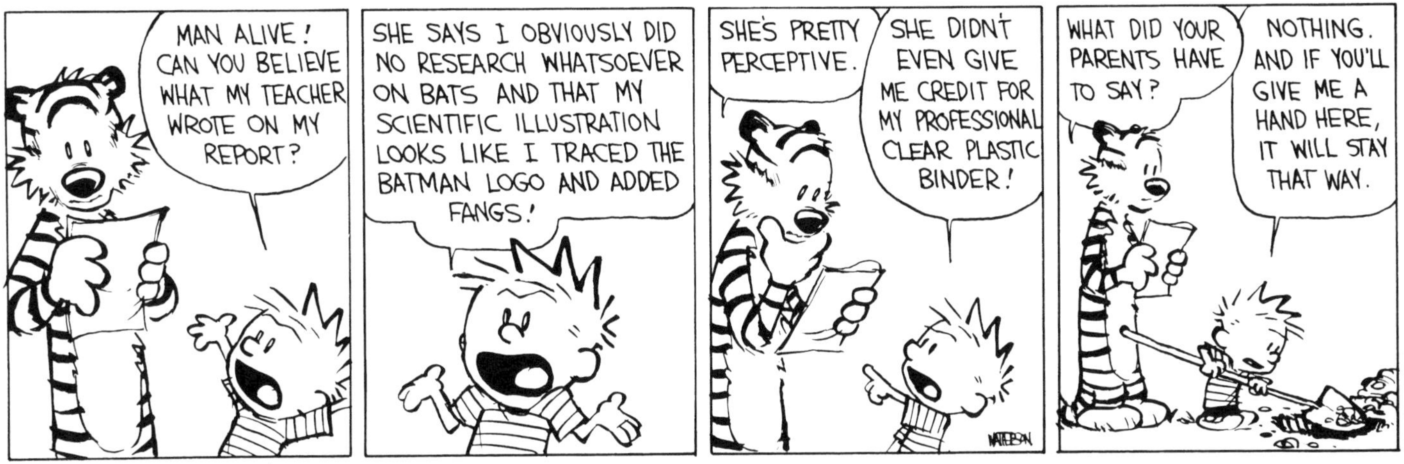
MAN ALIVE! CAN YOU BELIEVE WHAT MY TEACHER WROTE ON MY REPORT?
SHE SAYS I OBVIOUSLY DID NO RESEARCH WHATSOEVER ON BATS AND THAT MY SCIENTIFIC ILLUSTRATION LOOKS LIKE I TRACED THE BATMAN LOGO AND ADDED FANGS!
SHE'S PRETTY PERCEPTIVE.
SHE DIDN'T EVEN GIVE ME CREDIT FOR MY PROFESSIONAL CLEAR PLASTIC BINDER!
WHAT DID YOUR PARENTS HAVE TO SAY?
NOTHING. AND IF YOU'LL GIVE ME A HAND HERE, IT WILL STAY THAT WAY.

Andrews McMeel Publishing
a division of Andrews McMeel Universal
1130 Walnut Street, Kansas City, Missouri 64106

www.andrewsmcmeel.com

24 25 26 27 28 SDB 10 9 8 7 6 5 4 3 2 1

ISBN: 978-1-5248-8807-7

Library of Congress Control Number: 2024936289

ATTENTION: SCHOOLS AND BUSINESSES
Andrews McMeel books are available at quantity discounts with bulk purchase for educational, business, or sales promotional use.
For information, please e-mail the Andrews McMeel Publishing Special Sales Department: sales@amuniversal.com.